PENGUIN CLASSICS

P9-DDY-173

THE PORTABLE HANNAH ARENDT

HANNAH ARENDT was born in Hannover, Germany, in 1906. She studied at the Universities of Marburg and Frieburg and received her doctorate in philosophy at the University of Heidelberg, where she studied under Karl Jaspers. In 1933 she fled from Germany and went to France, where she worked for the immigration of Jewish refugee children into Palestine. In 1941 she came to the United States and became an American citizen ten years later.

She was research director of the Conference on Jewish Relations, chief editor of Schocken Books, executive director of Jewish Cultural Reconstruction in New York City, a visiting professor at several universities, including California, Princeton, Columbia, and Chicago, and university professor on the Graduate Faculty of the New School for Social Research. She was awarded a Guggenheim Fellowship in 1952 and won the annual Arts and Letters Grant of the National Institute of Arts and Letters in 1954.

Hannah Arendt's books include *The Origins of Totalitarianism, Crisis in the Republic, Men in Dark Times, Between Past and Future: Eight Exercises in Political Thought*, and *Eichmann in Jerusalem: A Report on the Banality of Evil*. She also edited two volumes of Karl Jaspers's *The Great Philosophers*. Hannah Arendt died in December 1975.

PETER BAEHR was born in Kuala Lumpur, Malaysia, in 1953 and came to England in 1962. Educated at Bournemouth College (Shelley Park) and the University of Leicester, he taught sociology at Coventry Polytechnic from 1979 to 1989 and at the Memorial University of Newfoundland from 1990 to 2000 before moving to Hong Kong, where he teaches in the Department of Politics and Sociology at Lingnan University. His publications include *Caesar and the Fading of the Roman World, The Protestant Ethic and the "Spirit" of Capitalism and Other Writings* (editor), and *Founders, Classics, Canons: Modern Disputes over the Origins and Appraisal of Sociology's Heritage*.

The Portable
Hannah Arendt

Edited with an Introduction by
PETER BAEHR

PENGUIN BOOKS

PENGUIN BOOKS
Published by the Penguin Group
Penguin Group (USA) Inc., 375 Hudson Street, New York, New York 10014, U.S.A.
Penguin Group (Canada), 90 Eglinton Avenue East, Suite 700, Toronto,
Ontario, Canada M4P 2Y3 (a division of Pearson Penguin Canada Inc.)
Penguin Books Ltd, 80 Strand, London WC2R 0RL, England
Penguin Ireland, 25 St Stephen's Green, Dublin 2, Ireland (a division of Penguin Books Ltd)
Penguin Group (Australia), 250 Camberwell Road, Camberwell,
Victoria 3124, Australia (a division of Pearson Australia Group Pty Ltd)
Penguin Books India Pvt Ltd, 11 Community Centre, Panchsheel Park, New Delhi – 110 017, India
Penguin Group (NZ), 67 Apollo Drive, Rosedale, Auckland 0632, New Zealand
(a division of Pearson New Zealand Ltd)
Penguin Books (South Africa) (Pty) Ltd, 24 Sturdee Avenue,
Rosebank, Johannesburg 2196, South Africa

Penguin Books Ltd, Registered Offices:
80 Strand, London WC2R 0RL, England

First published in the United States of America by Penguin Books 2000
This edition published 2003

19 20 18

Copyright © Penguin Putnam Inc., 2000
All rights reserved

Page 576 constitutes an extension of this copyright page.

LIBRARY OF CONGRESS CATALOGING IN PUBLICATION DATA
Arendt, Hannah.
The portable Hannah Arendt / edited with an introduction by Peter Baehr.
p. cm.
ISBN 978-0-14-243756-8
1. Political science. 2. Political ethics. 3. Totalitarianism.
4. Revolutions. 5. Social ethics. I. Baehr, P. (Peter) II. Title. III. Series.
JC251.A739 2000
320.5'092—dc21   99-38487

Printed in the United States of America
Set in Bembo
Designed by Sabrina Bowers

CONTENTS

IV. THE VITA ACTIVA

V. BANALITY AND CONSCIENCE: THE EICHMANN TRIAL AND ITS IMPLICATIONS

VI. REVOLUTION AND PRESERVATION

VII. OF TRUTH AND TRAPS

EDITOR'S INTRODUCTION

I

HANNAH ARENDT was a deeply paradoxical figure, and therein lies the challenge she poses to the received wisdom of modern times. She was among the greatest women political thinkers of the twentieth century, yet one strikingly at odds with academic feminism. She was an intensely private person whose unpopular public stands on such issues as the trial of the captured Nazi Adolf Eichmann, or on forced school integration in America, drew acrimony and controversy. A Jew who in the 1930s and forties campaigned tirelessly on behalf of Zionism (she was arrested by the Nazis in 1933 for Zionist activities), Arendt opposed the formation of a unitary Israeli state. And how, given commonplace modes of thought, are we to cope with a theorist who documented the twentieth century's fundamental rupture with tradition, while championing the notions of truth, facts, and common sense? Or with an author of one of the masterpieces of political "science"—*The Origins of Totalitarianism* (1951)—who expressed the strongest reservations about social science in general? Or, indeed, with an intellectual who repeatedly lamented the self-deception and opportunism to which intellectuals are perennially susceptible? Such fearless originality indicates that Hannah Arendt was "one of those writers who are well worth stealing."[1] But it is a relatively simple thing to appropriate a person's ideas, quite another to cultivate the "willed independence of judgment" and "conscious distance from all fanaticisms"[2] that animated them.

Born in Hannover on October 14, 1906,[3] Hannah Arendt was the only child of Paul and Martha (née Cohn) Arendt. Hannah Arendt's Jewish parents were well educated, leftist in their political inclinations, and tending toward religious skepticism, though this did not deter them from ensuring their daughter attend the synagogue and receive religious instruction in Judaism. Neither of Arendt's parents were Zionist; the "Jewish question" was not a major issue for them, nor was it to be for their daughter until the Nazi movement made it one. At the same time, no Jew, however bourgeois or "assimilated," could avoid recognizing the peculiar status that Jewishness conferred on them in German society, whether they lived in Hannover, or in Königsberg, to which the Arendts moved in 1909. Four years later, Paul Arendt died of paresis.

Obliged to raise the seven-year-old Hannah without her husband, Martha Arendt developed a practice that left a lasting impression on her daughter: instead of meekly tolerating the occasional anti-Semitic taunts by schoolmates, the young girl was enjoined to defend herself against them. Equally, Martha Arendt robustly took action against those of her daughter's teachers who uttered derogatory comments about Jews. From early on, Hannah Arendt learned that when attacked as a Jew, one had to defend oneself as a Jew. But in the days before, during, and immediately after the First World War, this kind of consideration lay in the background of her life. More prominent for her than even the war itself, which left Königsberg largely unscathed, or the early turbulence of the Weimar Republic, were the private matters with which to contend: the impact of her father's insanity and death, her illnesses and growing pains, the remarriage of her mother in 1920. These were also the days when the foundations of Hannah Arendt's education were being laid, and those of the brilliant scholarly "career" that followed. Headstrong and independent, she displayed a precocious aptitude for the life of the mind. And while she might risk confrontation with a teacher who offended her with an inconsiderate remark—she was briefly expelled for leading a boycott of the teacher's classes—from German *Bildung* (cultivation) there was to be no rebellion. At fifteen she was already meeting with friends to "read and translate Greek texts, a *Gymnasium* version of the *Graecae* or Greek Circles commonly established in the universities of the period."[4]

Hannah Arendt's first experience of university itself took place in Berlin, where she attended the lectures of the Christian existentialist theologian Romano Guardini. But it was as a pupil of Martin Heidegger in Marburg, and subsequently in Heidelberg as a student of the other great German *Existenz* philosopher of the day, Karl Jaspers, that she received her formative philosophical education. When Hannah Arendt first met Heidegger in 1924 she was eighteen years old. A passionate attachment to him soon followed that endured for the rest of her life, despite periods of disappointment, hostility, and exasperation. The devotion to a man who appeared the very incarnation of philosophical radicalism survived a four-year love affair that began in 1925, and found itself sufficiently sturdy, decades later, to forgive his embrace of National Socialism, to grapple with his philosophical *Kehre* ("turnabout") announced in 1949, which appeared to her unworldly in the extreme, and to play a part in rehabilitating him to a skeptical public. Punctuating these attempts at understanding and reconciliation lay her anger at his naïveté, his disloyalty to friends, his "romanticism" (generally a term of obloquy in Arendt's lexicon), his "complete lack of responsibility" and "cowardice,"[5] and his studiedly cool response to her own philosophical masterwork *The Human Condition* (1958).[6]

Conversely, Hannah Arendt found in Karl Jaspers, under whose supervision she wrote her doctoral dissertation, human qualities of integrity sadly absent in the author of *Being and Time*. The topic of Arendt's dissertation was the *Concept of Love in St. Augustine* (1929), a work that brought together personal experience and a university training in philosophy, Greek, and theology. Arendt's study of Augustine's notion of love as "craving" and its relationship to "neighborly love" and to the love of God is today the subject of vigorous reappraisal. Attention is being drawn to its ambivalent assessment of Christian doctrine, its adaptation of temporal and spatial categories derived from Heidegger and Jaspers,[7] and its treatment of ideas that, duly expanded and reshaped, would come to occupy an important position in her subsequent thought: beginning (natality), mortality, memory, and the world.[8] During the period of its composition, Jaspers offered Hannah Arendt his learning and his advice, laying the groundwork of a friendship that would blossom after the Second World War when they reestablished contact. For although Jaspers (whose wife, Gertrud, was a Jew) had not spoken out against the Nazi regime, he had at least refused to collude with it, losing his job as a result. Choosing the path of "inner emigration," Jaspers sat out the war, kept his cyanide pills in readiness, and waited for the knock at the door that never came.[9]

II

During her youth and for much of her time at university, Hannah Arendt showed little interest in practical politics. Such insouciance ended abruptly when, with her doctoral work behind her, and now married to her first husband, the writer Günther Stern, she moved to Berlin in 1929. It was in Berlin that Arendt came face-to-face with a growing Nazi movement programmatically and politically hostile to Jewry, and before which the custodians of the Republic appeared weak and vacillating. Nor, for the Jews, were the Nazis' main foes a source of great reassurance: Marxist organizations tended to downplay the propaganda and politics of anti-

Semitism (which many of its members shared) in order to ram home the
message that fascism was the last stage of capitalism. German Jews were
largely isolated. It was in this conjuncture that Hannah Arendt began to
reconsider the possibilities of Zionism, particularly as espoused by its chief
German advocate and organizer, Kurt Blumenfeld.

Arendt was attracted to Blumenfeld's version of Zionism because of
its attempts, as she saw it, to develop a politically realistic assessment of the
Jewish predicament. Because European Jews, however apparently integrated, were considered to be an alien people by their Gentile neighbors,
it was imperative for them to draw the political consequences of this fact
and work to build a Jewish homeland. Anti-Semitism was not inevitable,
nor should it be thought of as a necessary, perverse ingredient in fashion-
ing or maintaining Jewish solidarity. It was something more simple and
more complex: an historical reality demanding a political response. This
would be a difficult endeavor not least because Jews were themselves divided along axes of national culture and class, and between those who remained orthodox in their Judaism and those who had lost key elements of
their faith. Entrenched Jewish attitudes and reflexes would also have to be
confronted and erased if the worst features of adaptation in the Diaspora
were not be recapitulated in Palestine: philanthropic condescension of the
wealthy Jews toward poorer Jews; "parvenu" strategies of advancement;
the romance of being "exceptions." These were themes Arendt sought to
dramatize in the first major work to follow her doctoral dissertation, *Rahel
Varnhagen: The Life of a Jewess,* a book begun in Germany in 1929, but
first published in 1958.[10]

Hannah Arendt called *Rahel Varnhagen* a "life-story" (*Lebensgeschichte*)
but, given the book's threadbare narrative, it is best understood as something quite different: a meditation on human marginality. It focuses on a
single individual, the eponymous Rahel (née Levin, 1771–1833) and her
network of intimates, during an age when talented, middle-class "exceptional" Jews mixed with Gentile actors and nobility on terms of amiable
familiarity. The locus of this sociability was the salon, a theater of conversation within whose protective walls women of cultivation, like Rahel,
achieved a level of prominence impossible in the world outside it. What
enabled the Jewish salon, particularly in Berlin, to provide a unique arena
in which normal social conventions were suspended, was the anomalous
condition of the strata it brought together. Nobility, actors, and Jews
alike, Arendt explained, were bound by a kind of negative solidarity, for
each of them stood outside "bourgeois society." It is true that the late
eighteenth and early nineteenth centuries offered the Jews additional islands of acceptance. German Romanticism, then at its high tide, found in

the Jews' "mysterious" and exotic antiquity ample material for its musing; Enlightenment thinkers saw in the Jews an opportunity to practice the art of toleration and expand the compass of humanity itself. But these were primarily aesthetic and moral responses to the plight of the Jews, not political ones. So long as Jews were denied political equality, Arendt argued, they remained exposed and vulnerable to the fate that awaits all who stand on the periphery of citizenship: ill treatment, and the personal compromises and guilt that attend integration on unequal terms. The ease with which the articles of the German Confederation in 1815 snatched back the rights granted to Jews under the Napoleonic occupation showed how precarious was the latter's position in the absence of full citizenship. But it was before the articles were promulgated, and before Napoleon's entry into Berlin in October 1806, that Rahel's attic room on Jägerstrasse witnessed its halcyon days. Between 1790 and 1806 it played host to some of the most eminent writers and enthusiasts of the age, the Humboldt brothers, Friedrich Schlegel, Friedrich Schleiermacher, Prince Louis Ferdinand of Prussia among them. Here, background and convention counted for less than learning and wit, provided their bearers knew how best to display them. Yet shortly after Napoleon occupied Berlin, the circle collapsed, its spirit of solidarity broken by a nationalist reaction that linked the Jews to the Enlightenment and the Enlightenment to the French enemy. Where salons remained, they became highly exclusive in orientation, composed of chauvinist nobles and their hangers-on, whose by-laws prohibited the "admittance of women, Frenchmen, philistines and Jews."[11] Rahel's own salon had to wait fifteen years to be resuscitated; Hegel, Ranke, and her young friend Heinrich Heine were among its later visitors. By that time, however, she had begun a metamorphosis that transformed her from a Jew ashamed of her status, to one who unapologetically accepted it.

Arendt's study offers the reader a vivid portrait of Rahel's milieu, a rough chronology of her changing fortunes, and a sketch of her various attempts at assimilation: German patriotism (1808), baptism, and marriage to Karl August Varnhagen (1814) were foremost among them. But the book is also an examination of an internal struggle in which a woman racked with doubts gradually casts them aside. Lacking acceptance from others and acceptance from herself, Rahel is depicted as a woman who came to recognize that in a hostile society she must make a choice between two paths of Jewishness: the path of the parvenue or social climber, who through ingratiation or display as a rarefied species wins qualified acceptance by virtue of being an exception of her "race"; or, alternatively, a "pariah" who is willing to face squarely the reality of being an outsider.[12]

As Rahel experienced disappointment in love, strains in her own family, and financial insecurity; as Germany drifted into reaction and recrudescent anti-Semitism made a mockery of the "rights of man"; and as she began to realize that her own personal life was bound up with implacable political conditions, she did choose. Recognizing that the ultimate price of assimilation is self-hatred, as one assimilates anti-Semitism in the process, she acknowledged her pariah status. Such acknowledgment enabled her to realize that "Freedom and equality were not going to be conjured into existence by individuals' capturing them by fraud as privileges for themselves."[13]

Most commentators agree that *Rahel Varnhagen* is a curious work. Its claim "to narrate the story of Rahel's life as she herself might have told it" has been greeted as far-fetched and hermeneutically naïve; its willingness to pass scathing judgments on its chief protagonist has been said at times to show a lack of understanding of her plight. The author's own experiences sometimes appear to overwhelm, rather than illuminate, the book's subject. Ostensibly committed to eschewing the psychologizing mode, Arendt shows little hesitancy in deciphering Rahel's dream life to a degree that would make the hardened psychoanalyst gasp. Yet the book also contains Hannah Arendt's most astringent sketch of the inner consequences of marginality. Marginality makes a person vulnerable to suffering and alienation; as such, he or she wins the sympathy of the compassionate observer. But Arendt's objective is emphatically not to "validate" the life experiences of Rahel's marginal status, if that means according them a dignity simply in virtue of the compassion they evoke. Rahel's situation may be pitiable, but to pity her would be to add insult to injury. Instead, the book helps us understand that Rahel's follies are an explicable response to her dual position: as a woman, gifted and intelligent, but lacking wealth and beauty and thus the "weapons with which to begin the great struggle for recognition in society"; and as a Jew who is neither part of the ghetto nor an assimilated member of conventional bourgeois or aristocratic Berlin society. Part of a liminal generation where personal advancement continued to take precedence over the political struggle for equal rights, Rahel is driven *inward*. The results, trenchantly spelled out in chapter one of the "biography" (pp. 49–67 below), are activities and qualities that Arendt neither respected nor sought to champion: flights of fancy, loss of reality, introspection, self-exposure and lack of discretion, disregard for facts, capriciousness, the need to be constantly confirmed by others, and "worldlessness." Having no public responsibilities to the public world, the marginal figure is all the freer to wallow in escapism and the cult of the victim—free, in other words, to become irresponsible and vacuous. Only when Jews stopped trying to escape from their Jewishness; only when they fought for political equality rather than for the opportunity of being exceptional; only when the particularity of citizenship was valued as much as the status of humanity itself, would they stand a chance of being free.

What freedom and responsibility demanded in Berlin in the early 1930s, when *Rahel Varnhagen* was being written, had already become evident to Hannah Arendt. With no illusions that anti-Semitism had entered a new phase in Germany, though still with no inkling of how far it would go, she moved decisively toward political engagement. Nineteen thirty-three—the centenary of Rahel's death, and the year Adolf Hitler became chancellor of Germany—proved to be the critical moment. After the Reichstag fire on February 27 (a provocation blamed on the Communists, but engineered by the Nazis so as to justify emergency measures), Arendt became increasingly involved in resistance activities. Her apartment in Berlin was used as conduit for leftists and others fleeing arrest. Prompted by Kurt Blumenfeld, Arendt also agreed to work for the German Zionist Organization on one of whose assignments—collecting anti-Semitic material in the Prussian State Library—she was apprehended and taken into custody.

Luckily, Hannah Arendt's interrogator had little enthusiasm for his job. Sympathetic to the young woman, and readily bamboozled by her denials and circumlocutions, he saw to it that she was released eight days after her arrest. Shortly after her release, Arendt left Germany with her mother, heading first for Prague, and then Geneva, where she worked briefly for the Labor Department of the League of Nations. From there, while her mother returned to Germany, she went on to Paris. Reunited with Günther Stern, who had fled to the French capital immediately after the Reichstag fire, Arendt continued her Zionist activities. She found various kinds of work, notably as secretary general of Youth Aliyah, an association founded to prepare young Jewish immigrants to Palestine for the rigors of their new life; in 1935, Arendt personally accompanied one such group to its members' adoptive homeland. When, however, Youth Aliyah was constrained to move its headquarters to London, Arendt stayed on in Paris, acquiring a job with the Jewish Agency. And it was in Paris, with her marriage to Günther Stern over in all but name, that she met Heinrich Blücher—the working class, Gentile, ex-Spartacist street fighter and philosophical autodidact, who would become her second husband and companion till his death in 1970.

Many challenges lay immediately before the couple: internment as enemy aliens in 1940; immigration to the United States in 1941 and facing the necessity of earning a living from scratch; mastering English;

sharing their lives with Arendt's mother, who, separated from her second husband, had followed her daughter first to Paris, then to America, and whose relationship with Blücher was strained by disapproval and dislike;[14] coping with the news of friends who had died and with the horrors that were being revealed about the concentration camps. These were the years when Hannah Arendt learned firsthand what it meant to be a "stateless person," bereft of occupation, home, and language; to be one of those "refugees," who, as she observed in one of her most acerbic wartime essays, must constantly parade the kind of optimism that compels its greatest enthusiasts to "go home and turn on the gas or make use of a skyscraper in quite an unexpected way."[15]

Less unexpected from Arendt's standpoint was how empty the "rights of man" had proved to be for those who had become stateless. The harsh fact, Arendt argued in a 1949 essay that she reworked for *The Origins of Totalitarianism* (pp. 31–45 below), was that such rights, proclaimed since the Enlightenment, depended not on "the abstract nakedness of being nothing but human," but on political communities strong enough to enforce them. In the absence of a polity, the "inalienable" rights of man had been exposed to have no greater weight than puffs of air. Moreover, many so-called human rights—to life, liberty, and the pursuit of happiness, to equality before the law, to private property—had been misnamed, since their loss did not necessarily affect the humanity of those who had previously enjoyed them. As Arendt remarked, the "soldier during the war is deprived of his right to life, the criminal of his right to freedom, all citizens during an emergency of their right to the pursuit of happiness—yet nobody would ever claim that in any of these instances a loss of human rights has been suffered." But deprive someone of a political community, of his or her "distinct place in the world," and of government protection, and you rob the individual of something fundamental enough to be called accurately a human right: the right to have the right to life, liberty, and so on. It was no coincidence that the expulsion of millions from humanity in the concentration camps had been preceded by a loss of their worldly location. Bereft of citizenship, an artifact of civilization, not nature, the Jews' "humanity" had been no restraint on those for whom Jews were something less than human in the first place.[16]

Though redolent of some themes broached in *Rahel Varnhagen* and of some earlier journalism, Arendt's writings between 1941 and 1951 manifest a major reorientation in her work toward political theory and commentary. In particular, the position of the Jews, and the emergence of totalitarian regimes, dominate her literary output. During the war, Arendt became a columnist of *Aufbau* ("Reconstruction"), the German-language weekly, published in New York and aimed at the émigré community. Her short articles embraced a number of themes, some of which she considerably expanded upon in English-language publications.[17] Of special importance to her as the war unfolded was the urgency of forming a Jewish army to play a part in the destruction of the Nazi regime (her interesting *Aufbau* article advancing this thesis is reprinted on pp. 46–48 below). To fight the Axis forces would be valuable in its own right: it would give Jewish people a sense of being a "nation" in arms, a participant in, rather than a spectator of, their own destiny, and it would encourage a solidarity that transcended tribalism and philanthropy alike. Just as valuable, the presence of a Jewish military contingent would bolster demands for Jews to have a place at the postwar conference table, able to contribute to the new Europe.[18]

But what also becomes evident in these and related articles, particularly those following the Allied victory, was Arendt's growing disenchantment with the dominant streams of Zionist opinion. Since the days of her early friendship with Blumenfeld, Arendt's commitment to Zionism had been qualified and heterodox; now it became strained to the point of direct confrontation. What alienated her was not only the growing "ideological" tenor of Zionism, with its intolerance for dissenting views, its failure to recognize the distinctive character of Diaspora Jews, its ghetto mentality and "worldlessness," its disparagement of the *Yishuv* (the pre-Israel "homeland" in Palestine) as hopelessly outdated, and later, its apologetics for acts of terrorism perpetrated by the Irgun and the Stern Gang (Zionist paramilitary organizations) against the Arab population of Palestine. She also disagreed with the mainstream view that Israel should be a unitary state. Arendt's preference was for a federal polity in which Jews and Arabs would live as equals, possibly under the loose aegis of the British Commonwealth.[19] Without a federal solution, the new polity, having escaped British mandate vassalage, would perforce become a client of another power, dependent on it for aid and military protection. Isolated from the rest of its neighbors and virtually under a state of siege, the "sovereignty" of the Jewish polity would prove to be utterly chimerical.[20] Threatened, too, would be the great institutions of the *Yishuv,* among them the *kibbutzim* and the Hebrew University, beacons of Jewish traditions that celebrated "the universality and predominance of learning" and "the passion for justice."[21] Even after the partition of Palestine in November 1947 had all but destroyed any lingering hopes for a federal solution, Arendt enumerated the criteria for what she considered to be a sane Jewish policy in Palestine: a Jewish homeland, not the "pseudo-sovereignty of a Jewish state"; Jewish-Arab cooperation; "elimination of all terrorist

groups (and not agreements with them) and swift punishment of all terrorist deeds (and not merely protest against them)"; limited and phased
immigration to Palestine; "local self-government and mixed Jewish-Arab
municipal and rural councils. . . . It is still not too late."[22] Perhaps not, but
soon it was.

III

Hannah Arendt became an American citizen in 1951, the same year in
which *The Origins of Totalitarianism* was first published. The book quickly
established her as a thinker of truly international stature. While her essays
on Zionism had dealt with the prospects facing European Jewry in the
years ahead, *Origins* sought to examine the catastrophe that had almost entirely destroyed it as a people. It was, to that time, her most sustained "essay in understanding": an attempt, in the words of the preface, to examine
and bear "consciously the burden which our century has placed on us—
neither denying its existence nor submitting meekly to its weight."

The book's title—a suggestion of the publisher to which she reluc-
tantly agreed—was always a source of discomfort for Arendt because it did
not convey, in a concise form, what she wanted it to express.[23] For while
the term "origins" was serviceable in a broad sense, it was also open to
misunderstanding on at least three counts. To begin with, Arendt did not
attempt to trace totalitarianism back to some primal beginning or seek to
delineate the "causes" of totalitarianism, a point she sought to clarify in
her exchange with Eric Voegelin (pp. 157–164 below). She proceeded as
a political theorist, assembling and distilling the key factors whose contingent outcome was totalitarianism. Historical materials on the Jews and on
mass movements were, of course, vital sources for her analysis, but she focused on the various political and social "elements" that had transmuted
into the totalitarian phenomenon; these she identified as imperialism,
racism, anti-Semitism (the term itself was coined in 1879), the disintegration of the nation-state, and the alliance between capital and the "mob."[24]
Each reinforced the other and prepared the groundwork for the terror to
come. Anti-Semitism was both an "element" of totalitarianism, and, in
Germany, the "amalgamator" of the other elements (imperialism, racism,
etc.), "crystallizing" them into the Nazi movement and regime.

A second reason why the title *The Origins of Totalitarianism* was something of a misnomer was that it could be mistaken for a *specific kind* of historical study that Arendt assiduously sought to avoid. If totalitarianism was
not to be traced back to a beginning, or to a set of causes, neither was

it to be envisaged as the outcome of an idea—for instance, a "myth of the state," or "totalitarian democracy,"[25] or secularism, or even anti-Semitism—culminating in the Hitler and Stalin regimes. Ideas do not march forward like soldiers in procession, or as parts of a dialectical process, a perspective she equated with a simplistic "history of ideas" approach.[26] More generally, Arendt rejected any explanation that assigned responsibility for Nazism to something called "German culture," to whose language and poetry she remained deeply attached. (This point emerges clearly in the interview with Günter Gaus, pp. 3–22 below.) Totalitarian elements were present in Europe as a whole; in retrospect, France during the time of the Dreyfus Case appeared much closer to a totalitarian catastrophe than Germany under the reign of Wilhelm II ever was. In any event, the whole point about totalitarianism was that it was unprecedented,[27] "a problem of modernity itself"[28] rather than of any national history. The Third Reich could no more be extrapolated from the Second Reich—Bismarck's Realpolitik had been predicated on the existence of other states (as distinct from their annihilation) and on the limitations they imposed on German statecraft—than it could be deduced from "any part of the Western tradition, be it German or not, Catholic or Protestant, Christian, Greek, or Roman" to which it "owes nothing." Far from being the emanation of German traditions, National Socialism entailed the "radical negation" of them. For while traditions offer continuity and serve to stabilize human affairs (on whatever basis), National Socialism demanded a rupture with civilized standards and the atomization of all human relationships.[29] Characteristically, Hannah Arendt's argument on this point evinced considerable independence of mind; her attempt as early as 1945 to uncouple German culture and traditions from what came, in the 1950s, to be called the Holocaust[30] was an unlikely position for any writer to take, most of all a Jewish one.

Third and finally, only parts one (on Anti-Semitism) and two (on Imperialism) of Arendt's great work were concerned with the background and historical elements of totalitarianism (again, "origins" in the broad sense of the term). Part three, by contrast, focused on the "mass" and "mob" character of the totalitarian movement; the kind of propaganda to which the movement was susceptible; the type of "front" organization the movement generated; and the kind of totalitarian rule or domination that emerged once the movement seized power. Arendt divided such rule into two phases: the years of one-party dictatorship, albeit combined with totalitarian admixtures (Soviet Russia from around 1924 to 1928, Germany from 1933 to 1938), followed by a fully totalitarian period extant in the Soviet Union when *Origins* was first published, but that in Germany had

ended with the Allied victory of 1945. To put in context the passage on
"Total Domination" that is reprinted on pp. 119–145 below, it is worth-
while saying a little more about totalitarianism at its zenith.

A distinctive feature of totalitarian rule, Arendt argued, was its incorporation of elements of the totalitarian movement that preceded it; not
least of these was the characteristic of movement itself.[31] The result is a
series of institutional paradoxes. To survive at all, the new regime must
ceaselessly ensure that none of its political progeny stabilize into any
form—whether a system of regulations or a series of interest groups—secure enough to impede totalitarian transformation. The regime must seize
the state, but not become a state in any normal sense. Totalitarian phys-
iognomy must be so protean as to be all but shapeless. Whereas leaders of
most organizations rely on a basically stable hierarchy to undergird their
power, the totalitarian leader must continually transform his organization
the better to control it. As a result, governance by fiat replaces the solidity
of positive law; personnel are constantly replaced or reshuffled; offices are
endlessly duplicated to monitor one another. The only thing that everyone beneath the leader shares is submission to his mercurial and ultimately
inscrutable will, an obeisance symbolically cemented by rituals of idolatry
that sharply demarcate insiders from outsiders. And where symbols of devotion are insufficient to test allegiance, other means are available to be
their proxy. Chief among them is the secret police, charged with the unending task of investigating who is and who is not an insider at any particular moment, a shifting boundary demarcated by the leader's arbitrary
definition of friend and foe. And while no one is exempt from the leader's
domination, the highest echelon shares with him a distinctive kind of solidarity. This is based not on the propaganda intended for the rank and file,
for which the movement's elite displays a cynical disregard, but rather on
a sense of "human omnipotence": the "belief that everything is permitted,
rests on the solid conviction that everything is possible."[32] Such a conviction means that not a single country or region but all of them are to be
dominated; that once the committed opponents of the regime have been
liquidated, new "objective" enemies must be invented;[33] that the discovery of actual crimes be replaced by the prediction, and subsequent neu-
tralization, of imminent ones. The primary task of the secret police is "not
to discover crimes, but to be on hand when the government decides to
arrest a certain category of the population." Following detention, torture,
and murder, the victims disappear without a trace into "holes of oblivion,"[34] leaving no visible corpses behind them, no families to claim them,
no identifiable burial places to find earthly rest.

The abyss into which such bodies vanish is the death camp, the laboratory of the totalitarian experiment to prove that everything is indeed possible. In passages of great power and economy, Arendt argued that the hubristic ambition of those who run the camps in the fully totalitarian phase is nothing less than that of transforming human nature itself: to remove from it all traces of spontaneity, courage, and resistance, to reduce human "plurality" to "a primal equality"[35] in which one person is much like any other, a specimen of the species, a bundle of reactions determined by terror. In short, the objective of the camps is to make man himself superfluous, an objective that, within its own confines, had been realized to a terrifying degree. Those "inanimate men"[36] (the inmates) who survived the death factories often emerged unable to speak about their experiences—or to comprehend them. Straining for words to match her subject, Arendt compared the camps to a "hell" in which "radical evil" makes its appearance.[37] At the same time she was well aware that while theology at least provided an explanation for radical evil, and even pointed toward its redress, political science and the judicial system did not. For the camps had confounded humanity's very notions of innocence and guilt. Just as no one, whatever he or she had done, could deserve to be a camp inmate, so no punishment for those who created and operated the camp system could be commensurate with the acts they had perpetrated. Equally unsatisfactory was a cartoon of "innocence beyond virtue and guilt beyond vice," a "hell where all Jews were of necessity angelic and all Germans of necessity diabolical." "Human history," she concluded, "has known no more difficult story to tell."[38]

How, then, was one to tell it? In published essays, manuscripts, grant proposals, and lectures Arendt relentlessly sought out different answers to this question, the means to understand "the 'nightmare of reality' before which our intellectual weapons have failed so miserably."[39] The dilemma for her was clear. On the one hand, the reality of totalitarianism had decisively superseded such familiar political categories as tyranny, despotism, dictatorship, usurpation, Caesarism, Bonapartism previously employed to depict types of domination. On the other hand, totalitarianism had still to be understood, and comprehension never proceeds *de novo*. Unlike a number of her academic contemporaries, Arendt's manner of working was to make, adapt, and stretch distinctions between terms that were generally familiar (earth and world, labor and work, violence and terror, power and force), rather than produce a new conceptual casuistry. Similarly, though she opposed any attempt to define totalitarianism as a type of tyranny or dictatorship (as, for instance, Franz Neumann did),[40] she was willing to fall back on this terminology when it suited her own heuristic purposes to do so. Adapting Montesquieu,[41] Arendt claimed that it was the combination of terror and ideology that summed up what was so uniquely terrible about the totalitarian experiment.

Total terror has two major consequences for those subject to it. In the first place, it "substitutes for the boundaries and channels of communication between individual men a band of iron which holds them so tightly together that it is as though their plurality had disappeared into One Man of gigantic dimensions."[42] And second, having compressed the space in which freedom and resistance are possible, totalitarian regimes proceed continuously to mobilize their populations. Unimpeded by domestic restraints, the regimes are in a position not only to celebrate the "laws of movement," whether of Nature or of History, but actually to compel individuals to obey them. The contrast with law as it is usually understood was, for Arendt, salient and telling. Under nondespotic forms of government, laws function to stabilize human relations, lending the latter a degree of predictability, not to mention security. But under totalitarian regimes, the laws invoked are meant not to anchor interaction in something solid, but rather to throw it helter-skelter into the rapids of unceasing turbulence. Pushed or pulled ever onward by supposedly ineluctable forces, the singular event now counts for nothing, since, under the sway of laws of motion, nothing exists for itself, but only has meaning as an instrument of some higher destiny (the victory of the Aryan race), or as a stage in a process (the development of the productive forces). Hence, having frozen human intercourse through fear and violence,[43] terror now makes it fluid again but this time under its own direction. Or as Arendt puts it: "Terror is the realization of the law of movement; its chief aim is to make it possible for the force of Nature or of History to race freely through mankind, unhindered by any spontaneous human action."[44]

However, terror is never sufficient to determine human conduct in its entirety. Not everyone will fall within its orbit. Those who do may still require some signposts to guide them in a world of arbitrarily chosen victims and constantly changing pronouncements. For this reason, totalitarian regimes supplement terror by ideology, namely, an all-embracing "system of explanation" that boils down the complexity of life into one fundamental "principle." Ideologies are more than the general political credos that can be found in most modern societies. They offer those who subscribe to them a limited set of interpretive postulates with which to understand reality, and a shield against any experience that might throw these postulates into confusion or doubt. An ideology subjects the world to the coercion of an idea, to axioms and deductions that force every concrete event to comply with its logic; as such, it complements the coercion of terror that works on the senses. What had made ideology so attractive in the modern world, Arendt argued, was less any particular content than the fact that it had appeared in societies ravaged by "loneliness." To people uprooted and superfluous for whom "the fundamental unreliability of man" and "the curious inconsistency of the human world" were too much to bear,[45] ideology offered a home and a cause, "a last support in a world where nobody is reliable and nothing can be relied upon." The price of that support was incalculably high: a rupture with reality and the submission to that " 'ice-cold reasoning' and the 'mighty tentacle' of dialectics which 'seizes [the believer] as in a vise.' "[46]

When Arendt wrote these lines in the early 1950s, she appears to have envisaged totalitarianism as an almost hermetically sealed universe. True, it might be destroyed by outside intervention; Allied victory in the war against Germany had demonstrated this plainly enough. But when a totalitarian regime was not at war, as the Soviet Union was not after 1945, it appeared impregnable within its own borders. For that reason, there could be little hope of internal transformation and reform.[47] But were terror and ideology really this all-encompassing? Arendt soon had doubts, broadly prefigured in a belief, articulated whenever despair threatened to overwhelm her, that the Achilles' heel of totalitarian evil was the being it sought so completely to transform—Homo sapiens itself. This was not because human beings were inherently good, but rather because they were inherently contingent and innovative. Every birth is a new beginning; and "beginning" she would say, echoing St. Augustine, "is the supreme capacity of man." So long as people were born and inhabited the earth, their capacity to break out of totalitarian conditions, and to create a world worthy of plural human beings, could not be eliminated. One is tempted to say this was a metaphysical or religious conviction, except that for Arendt it was probably something much more down to earth: an observation on people's ability to do unpredictable and surprising things, on the often astounding lack of proportion between "cause" and effect. But though such a perspective offered Arendt some hope and solace, it was not this, but two episodes that challenged her to rethink her early diagnosis of totalitarian domination. Breaking with the emphasis on biographical chronology adopted up to now, let us examine the consequences of this revision.

IV

Following Stalin's death in 1953, unforeseen things began to happen in the Soviet Union: a period of "thaw" presaged the gradual "detotalitarianization" of Soviet society. That this was uneven, equivocal, and full of setbacks and brutalities such as the suppression of the Hungarian uprising in 1956; that the transition was not toward pluralism but to a one-party dictatorship from which totalitarianism had first emerged: all this was obvious to her. However, the Soviet transition did suggest that totalitarian regimes could be transformed from within—a possibility considered only very obliquely in *The Origins of Totalitarianism*.

The second experience was, so to speak, much closer to home and led Arendt to modify her concept of totalitarian ideology. Already in the late 1940s, Arendt had recognized that among the elite of the Nazi movement, as distinct from its rank-and-file membership, ideology had played only a limited role. What characterized the thinking of the upper echelon's members was neither a cognitive straitjacket centered on fundamental premises nor a belief that they had found the key to history. The elite mentality evinced instead a view that the very distinction between truth and falsehood was a mere construct to be fabricated as expedience dictated, and a mercurial capacity to translate "every statement of fact into a declaration of purpose." For instance, when elite members of the Nazi movement heard the statement "Jews are inferior," they understood by that expression that all Jews were to be exterminated.[48] Elite thinking promoted cynicism rather than dogmatism: for while the latter frame of mind might, in its rigidity, have impeded the movement's progress, cynicism allowed it to proceed on the assumption that "everything is possible." "These men," Arendt continued, "consider everything and everybody in terms of organization."[49] However, it was not until over a decade after she made this remark that Arendt was to get a vivid insight into the organization man par excellence and just how unideological he could be.

On May 11, 1960, Otto Adolf Eichmann, a former Nazi lieutenant-colonel who had fled Germany in 1950, was kidnapped in Buenos Aires by the Israeli Secret Service. He was kept incommunicado for nine days, and then flown to Israel on May 20 to stand trial on a total of fifteen counts including "crimes against the Jewish people, crimes against humanity, and war crimes during the whole period of the Nazi regime."[50] When Hannah Arendt read that Eichmann was to be arraigned, she contacted the editor of *The New Yorker,* William Shawn, and requested the assignment to cover the trial for the magazine. Shawn was enthusiastic. The result was a five-part essay, first published in 1963, and a book that in its English version has sold more than 260,000 copies.[51] The enduring appeal of a text that Arendt claimed too few had read properly is a posthumous vindication of the hard questions she raised and people's continued willingness to consider them. But during her own lifetime, *Eichmann in*

Jerusalem: A Report on the Banality of Evil provoked vitriolic attacks on her motives, her character, and, not least, the nature and style of the "report" itself.

Before turning to examine the nature of Arendt's analysis, let us briefly recapitulate some of the facts about Eichmann to which she drew the reader's attention.

A *"déclassé* son of a solid middle-class family" who earned his living as a traveling salesman for the Austrian-based Vacuum Oil Company, Eichmann joined the National Socialist Party in 1932 and entered the SS shortly thereafter. Noticeably absent from his decision to join the party was ideological fervor: Eichmann was later able to rattle off the usual lamentations about the Treaty of Versailles and mass unemployment, but of the Nazi Party program he was largely ignorant. Instead, he saw the opportunity to escape a humdrum existence, to become part of a movement with pretensions to greatness, and to refurbish himself with a more glamorous persona. Transferred through the labyrinthine bureaucracy of the SS, Eichmann found himself by turns in an information department concerned with collecting material on Freemasonry and a section that concentrated on Jewish affairs, an office from which he gained his experience of forced evacuation and emigration. Soon after, as the Nazi regime effectively liquidated what remained of outright internal opposition and took the path to war, Eichmann found himself a more or less willing instrument of shifts in SS policy to make Germany (and later Europe) *judenrein* (clean of Jews), a policy that evolved through plans for expulsion (the first solution) to concentration (the second solution) to extermination (the "final solution"). In these phases Eichmann played various roles, including that of negotiator with the leaders of the Jewish Councils, but it was as a logistical wizard, notably in organizing the transportation that took the Jews to the labor camps and death factories, that he acquired his niche in the SS bureaucracy. A Nazi functionary, but not a man who ever pulled a trigger, ever manned a mobile gassing van, or ever ordered others to do so; an expert on "the Jewish question," but not an individual who presided over the torture of a single Jewish body, Eichmann even claimed to have a high regard for the rigor, militancy, and self-sacrifice of the Zionists he confronted, and was contemptuous of his colleagues for their ignorance of Jewish history. In contrast, he was proud to boast that he had studied and learned from Theodor Herzl's Zionist classic *Der Judenstaat* and Adolf Böhm's *History of Zionism*. (He was more coy in admitting that he had been personally indebted earlier in life to a Jewish connection that had enabled him to get a job.) Given these attitudes, Eichmann found it unconscionable that the Jerusalem prosecutor could depict him as a Jew-hater whose blind loathing had been behind his bureaucratic work. Eichmann considered himself "not guilty in the sense of the indictment," but guilty only of "aiding and abetting" the destruction of the Jews, which he admitted was "one of the greatest crimes in the history of Humanity."

Arendt's attitude toward the trial of Eichmann was complex. Though she never doubted the right of Israel to put him on trial,[52] and though she praised as exemplary the good sense and restraint of the presiding judges, Arendt found herself troubled by a number of features the trial exposed. For the Israeli prime minister, David Ben-Gurion, and for his mouthpiece in court, the attorney general, Gideon Hausner, the presence of Eichmann was supposed to remind Jews of their persecution over four millennia, of which Nazism was the latest expression, and instruct them of the necessity of a Jewish state. Non-Jews, and not simply Germans, on the other hand, were to be told of their collective responsibility for the Holocaust. Arendt thought such a stance disastrous. Not only did she recoil from the reduction of a defendant, any defendant, to an historical instance—Arendt insisted that "on trial are his deeds, not the suffering of the Jews"[53]—she also believed that totalitarianism was so unprecedented that it was politically erroneous to collapse it into the history of Jew-hating. Moreover, if Israel were to take its place among modern states as an equal, it was important that it behave like one, and not conduct itself as morally superior to the international order it had now joined. In addition, Arendt believed that the Jerusalem court had failed to come to grips with three key issues: "the problem of impaired justice in the court of the victors; a valid definition of the 'crime against humanity'; and a clear recognition of the new criminal who commits this crime."[54] For our purposes, it will suffice to concentrate on the latter two.

Arendt argued that totalitarianism had produced a new kind of crime, one different from the horrendous catalogue of "war crimes" (like the shooting of hostages) and "inhuman acts" (like massacre) that have existed from time immemorial. A crime against humanity constituted a peculiar crime in that it referred not to an attack on particular individuals or groups of people, but on a people as a human entity; in short, it consisted of an assault upon "human diversity as such, that is, upon a characteristic of the 'human' status without which the very words 'mankind' or 'humanity' would be devoid of meaning."[55] Arendt acknowledged that genocide, the attempt to "determine who should and who should not inhabit the world,"[56] was not itself new, a concession that appeared to contradict her statement that the crime perpetrated on the Jews had no precedent.

What she meant was that the Nazi crime was unique not in its attempt at genocide, but in the grotesque institution and experiment that had accompanied this attempt: the death factory, in which all forces of calculation are coolly directed at refashioning human nature by shattering its spontaneity through a process of sustained and unmitigated terror. In this crime, "only the choice of victims, not the nature of the crime [itself], could be derived from the long history of Jew-hatred and anti-Semitism."[57] Since the Jews were the "body" upon which the crime against humanity had been committed, it made perfect sense for a Jewish *court* to put Eichmann on trial and pass judgment on his deeds. Once judgment had been handed down, however, Arendt believed the state of Israel should have waived "its right to carry out the sentence" because what was fundamentally at issue was something more than the Jews, namely, humanity itself. For that reason, Israel should have called, via the United Nations, for an international criminal tribunal to be established expressly concerned with crimes against humanity. Arendt was aware that this demand would have been a serious, and probably embarrassing, challenge to the United Nations, but it would nonetheless have put the onus on the international community to come to its juridical senses. For once the unprecedented has appeared, it is likely to repeat itself. "If genocide is an actual possibility of the future, then no people on earth . . . can feel reasonably sure of its continued existence without the help and the protection of international law." Conversely, the corollary of a Jewish state executing Eichmann, which it did on May 31, 1962, was to minimize the "monstrousness of the events" of this particular crime, because the tribunal under which it had been effected "represents one nation only."[58]

The other issue with which the Jerusalem court had failed to come to grips, Arendt argued, was the character of Eichmann himself, a man who claimed to have no animosity toward the Jewish people. While many dismissed Eichmann's remarks as pure dissimulation, Arendt took them deadly seriously. In her view, it was not a surfeit of ideology that had driven Eichmann to commit his crimes, but a deficit of thought.[59] Nor was she convinced that Eichmann was a pathologically demonic and demented figure. To paint him in these colors might simplify the relationship between Eichmann and his crimes, but then it would also put him beyond the scale of human judgment required in trial proceedings. Moreover, there was a danger that demonizing Eichmann would clothe him in a metaphysical aura of "satanic greatness" that he in no way approximated. Even the psychiatric reports showed him to be sane. What struck Arendt more about Eichmann was his banality: "his inability ever to look at anything from the other fellow's point of view," his penchant for "officialese," for stock phrases, for shallow elation, for being "genuinely incapable of uttering a single sentence that was not a cliché"; his "empty talk." "The longer one listened to him, the more obvious it became that his inability to speak was closely connected with an inability to *think*, namely, to think from the standpoint of somebody else. No communication was possible with him, not because he lied but because he was surrounded by the most reliable of all safeguards against the world and the presence of others, and hence against reality as such."[60] Behavior like this convinced Arendt that Eichmann was a man who "never realized what he was doing," meaning by this that he never realized its gravity. It was not stupidity, but vacuousness, that had enabled him to do what he did with only infrequent pangs of conscience or pity; and it was this "strange interdependence of thoughtlessness and evil," or "remoteness from reality," that had shown itself capable of wreaking "more havoc than all the evil instincts taken together."[61]

Soon after Hannah Arendt's report on the "word-and-thought-defying *banality of evil*"[62] was published in February and March 1963, it became the subject of a venomous campaign. Both the phrase "banality of evil" and Arendt's comments on the complicity of the Jewish Councils (*Judenräte*) in the deportation of their own people[63] drew angry recrimination. Initially, the bitterness was greatest in the United States; former colleagues assailed her analysis; the Anti-Defamation League of B'nai B'rith issued condemnatory memorandums; newspaper columns expanded in denunciation of this "self-hating Jewess"; lecturers were dispatched from England and Israel to trash Arendt's account; a group of scholars was commissioned to demonstrate the report's many errors; and the Eichmann trial's chief prosecutor himself arrived in New York to refute Arendt's interpretation. Controversy also quickly spread to Israel and to Germany, where Arendt's picture of the puny German wartime resistance to Hitler was met with anger and indignation. Arendt was shocked and dismayed by the maelstrom her report had provoked, particularly when its casualties included the estrangement of close friends like Kurt Blumenfeld. For their part, critics claimed that the expression "banality of evil" seemed to exonerate Eichmann and blame the victims. Others accused her of bad taste, triviality, an insultingly harsh and ironical tone, a perverse unwillingness to understand the depth of the dilemmas facing the Jewish Councils, and of failing to show love for her own kind. A "lapse into uncomprehending arrogance" was how one scholar described the report eight years after Arendt's death,[64] and compared with some of the comments she had to endure during her lifetime this was putting it mildly.

V

Eichmann in Jerusalem was not the first time, nor would it be the last, that Hannah Arendt found herself embroiled in controversy. In 1958–59 she had outraged many of her fellow American citizens, black and white alike, by opposing a Supreme Court ruling on school desegregation; some of her arguments on this matter will briefly be considered later on. But for the most part, the 1950s were years of consolidation and development for Arendt, a period when her many accomplishments for the first time found official recognition. Prestigious universities were keen to be associated with this strikingly original mind; she delivered series of lectures to Princeton, Berkeley, and Chicago in 1953, 1955, and 1956 respectively. Conference organizers and journals sought her out; granting agencies provided funds for her research. These were also the years when Heinrich Blücher, whose initial adaptation to the United States had been much more difficult than Arendt's, found his niche at Bard College as a professor of philosophy; when Arendt reestablished contact with Heidegger;[65] and when she continued to deepen her analysis of the "origins" and consequences of totalitarianism. In the early fifties Arendt had even planned to write a coda to *Origins* on the "totalitarian elements in Marxism," a work that would examine in more detail the Soviet system, and also address the aspects of Marxism that had loaned themselves so spectacularly to totalitarian interpretation. The project was soon abandoned, at least in the form Arendt had expected it to materialize, but many of its themes and arguments found themselves rehearsed in a series of individually published essays that would be collected as *Between Past and Future: Six Exercises in Political Thought* (1961; see pp. 278–310, 438–461, and 462–507). These essays are also part of a cluster of works whose jewel is *The Human Condition* (1958). It has been said with justice that most of these investigations "are like huge footnotes constructed to resolve difficulties" left in the wake of *The Origins of Totalitarianism*.[66] It follows that we should expect continuity with Arendt's earlier work rather than any obvious break with it.

The *Human Condition* contains within it two distinct, if overlapping, narrative levels. On one level, we are introduced to a quasi-historical sketch of how three fundamental activities—labor, work, and action—have been envisaged, ordered, and reordered from ancient to modern times. These activities, which in sum compose the *vita activa,* were themselves traditionally seen as inferior to the *vita contemplativa*—the life of contemplation—until the sixteenth century, when the Protestant Reformation, the scientific revolution, and the emergence of capitalism began the process that reversed this order of estimation. On a second level, however, Arendt's analysis of the human condition also contains her own map and ranking of the *vita activa,* drawn in part from ancient sources, in part from modern *Existenz* philosophy, but adding up to a uniquely Arendtian defense of the dignity of political life. It will be expedient for us to begin with this "map" and then work backward to see how she employs it for purposes of historical elucidation.

The human condition, the limitations with which humans must contend, consists of "natality and mortality, worldliness, plurality, and the earth."[67] Natality and mortality (i.e., birth and death) are the basic presuppositions and boundaries of all existence, whereas the other three conditions correspond to definite human activities (the *vita activa*) of which all able-bodied humans are capable: labor (whose condition is the "earth," the terrestrial sphere of physical and organic life), work (whose condition is "worldliness," i.e., civilization), and action (whose condition is "plurality"). In turn, each of these *vitae* can be understood, not only by its contribution to human existence, but by its proximity to human freedom and its capacity for human distinction.

Most distant from human freedom and distinction (the ability to present a unique identity in the company of others) is "labor," chained, as Arendt depicts it, to the satisfaction of repetitive, insistent needs and desires, bound to the biological, cyclical necessity of production and consumption. Like other animal species we are earthly, natural beings compelled to eat and reproduce to survive; labor is the activity, strenuous and unending, through which these exigencies are met. "Work," as opposed to labor, shows Homo sapiens as a being that, unlike other animals, is something more than an earthbound laboring creature, an *animal laborans,* forced to adapt to the demands of appetite and drive, whose products vanish almost as quickly as they appear. Work—whose paradigmatic figure is the craftsman—is oriented to utility, rather than mere survival, to production, rather than consumption, to the transformation of man's environment, rather than simple adaptation to it. Or to put it another way, it is work, the activity of man in his capacity as *homo faber,* that through tools of various kinds creates the "world": a multiplicity of cultural, technological, and political artifacts that lends human existence a degree of permanence denied to us as mortals. As human creations, the objects that compose the world throw light on those who make them, for some of these agents will be deemed particularly accomplished, just as some of the objects they create will be valued more than others. Similarly, as a product of human creativity, the world is best envisaged as an "artificial" space (rather than a "natural" datum) that houses us, affording us some stability and protection by connecting us to, and separating us from, our fellows.

Arendt argues that this spatial, in-between quality of the "world," constructed by human hand and brain, also happens to be the very condition of human freedom. For while the world brings us together through the intermediary of its material implements, artistic and cultural "works" of art, and political institutions, it also provides us with the necessary distance from one another—notably through laws and conventions—without which we would constantly be in danger of losing our distinctiveness and of being galvanized into a single, monolithic entity. The artificiality of the world, for Arendt, is thus not a hateful impediment to the realization of some primal, authentic human self (as some versions of romanticism and irrationalism believe), but actually the condition for having a self capable of political, as opposed to merely violent, concourse with other human beings. As she recalled: only when totalitarianism successfully shattered the "world" could it begin its diabolical attempt to refashion "human nature."

The third fundamental activity that Arendt considers is that of "action," for her the quintessentially political capacity. By action, Arendt understands the ability of humans to initiate a new course of events. Action realizes the human potential for freedom, albeit under conditions of "plurality," that is the existence of diverse human agents in front of whom the action takes place and whose presence confers on it some meaning. Action, in Arendt's account, is a category of politics, not of sociology; it is inherently interpersonal and public; it is closely related to, though not synonymous with, the faculty of speech (because it is through speech that the actor reveals his or her unique identity). Action is a corollary of "natality": the fact that we are born as members of a species whose character is to make unpredictable beginnings. Moreover, vital features of action are indeterminacy and irreversibility. For no person ever knows exactly what he has initiated, and the "meaning" of his action is less a force that impels the person on, and more a retrospective judgment by the spectator (this can include the actor himself) who weaves the strands of many actions into a story, which, as "history" or remembrance, preserves the actor's words and deeds.[68] What social scientists were typically writing about when they employed the concept of action, Arendt thought, was actually the largely instrumental practice of "doing-as-making" which is, of course, project-dependent, guided by rules, and pursued for a definite end. But this confusion between "acting" (*praxis*) and "making" (*poiēsis*)[69] was precisely one Arendt was keen to avoid; the failure to do so would deepen the tendency, already strongly rooted, to depict politics with the imagery of fabrication, to see it as merely a tool (as distinct from an activity in its own right), thus collapsing "action" into "work."[70]

Of all three capacities outlined by Arendt, "action" occupies the highest position in the *vita activa*. Labor and work are certainly vital activities, for without the first life would be impossible, while without the second a "world" would not exist. Nonetheless, it is action, even more than work, that reveals humanity's capacity for freedom and its capacity for distinction. And, crucially, it is through action that humans reveal their genius for politics. Unlike sociologists such as Max Weber who define politics as a mode of rulership or domination, Arendt views it as a public space where people articulate and clarify common concerns, though from different points of view, and a locus of activity where diverse individuals initiate projects of various kinds. The state is (or can be) one of these spaces, but it is not the only one; indeed, any activity can become political so long as the agents concerned join with others for some purpose, and do so in such a way as to reveal their own unique identities as individual actors. The specific means of politics is not "violence," which isolates people and compels them to be silent, but "power," rendered by Arendt as an energy that derives from collective action. What is more, the vital condition of political activity is not a mass to dominate or rule, but the (artificial) equality that citizenship confers on human beings, and the "plurality" of human beings themselves: "the fact that men, not Man, live on the earth and inhabit the world." Political and legal institutions are the frameworks that lend form, accommodation, and durability to human plurality, both giving room for human initiative and also providing a crucial degree of stability in an unpredictable world. Among the great political virtues are not only courage, which provides the strength to begin an enterprise and persist in it, but also forgiveness, and the willingness to make, and to keep, promises. Forgiveness offers a release from a past that cannot be undone, but with which we can come to terms; it allows us to begin again, to break with attitudes that condemn us to nurse old grievances and repeat endlessly the cycle of recrimination. Promising looks forward: it seeks to bind the actor to his words, thus helping to build continuity and consistency amid the flux of an uncertain universe.

So far I have attempted to describe Arendt's topography of the *vita activa,* the active life. But Arendt used this map as more than a means to estimate human activities; it was also for her a tool of historical and political interpretation. Arendt argued that in modern society "action" is often seen as analogous to "work"—politics, for example, is often considered as a mode of social engineering or "modernization" to be administered by experts. In addition, work itself, particularly over the last two centuries, has undergone a double transformation. First, the language and metaphors of work—rules, designs, means, and ends—have assumed a dominant place within conceptions of the *vita activa*. It is man as *homo faber* who is most admired today, and productivity that is elevated to the highest level of social esteem. In addition, justifications of existence are typically couched in utilitarian terms: the standards of means-ends, so appropriate for work, are illegitimately extrapolated into and colonize the moral arena with the consequence that ends themselves lose any intrinsic worth; instead, they become part of a process, a chain, to be forever converted into new means whose value consists in the contribution made to "the happiness of the greatest number." But not only does a utilitarian ethic appear to be circular—the principle of utility is to be justified by its usefulness—it also, insofar as "happiness" is its goal, seems to collapse into the "earthly" condition of the body: for happiness is a fluctuating emotion, a subjective mood, not a created object or an action.

Second, and correlatively, work increasingly assumes the properties of labor: mechanization has led to the erosion of the craftsman's skills, either stripping them down by a division of tasks in which repetition is more important than creativity, or displacing them altogether as automation takes over the worker's functions. So in both moral and economic terms, the *animal laborans* is now the dominant representative of the human condition. And, paradoxically, even the greatest critic of capitalism loaned his intellectual weight to this configuration. Marx's peculiar definition of man as *homo faber* tended not only to muddy the distinction between labor and work, Arendt claimed; it also celebrated labor as the activity that revealed man's deepest species being. Though human labor was now, under capitalist conditions, alienated, it would through the revolutionary praxis of the laboring class recover its fundamental, creative properties. In one sense, Marx's thesis involved a bold attack on the traditional philosophical view that conceived reason as man's most elevated attribute, and contemplation the royal road to Being. But in another sense Marx was caught within the very framework of thinking about the *vita activa* he appeared to overturn so radically. Above all, that framework was one that denigrated the political realm, looked down upon it suspiciously from the outside, and imposed upon it the highly disenchanted categories of the philosopher. Marx may have challenged this tradition in part and, together with Kierkegaard and Nietzsche, effectively closed it, but his thinking still bore traces of a legacy that viewed politics in instrumental terms—the terms of *homo faber,* of shaping physical material according to a design external to the object being produced—that had been bequeathed in ancient times by Plato and his school. Marx saw politics negatively in terms of rule (as exploitation, through the state, by the dominant economic class) and attempted to "escape from the frustrations and fragility of human action by construing it in the image of making."[71] Moreover, via the legacy of Hegel, Marx extrapolated the notion of fabrication to history itself. Now it was history that was to be "made," a notion antithetical to the very open-ended and contingent character of action. Similarly antithetical was the view that this historical "process" (a new idea) was one whose engine was labor.

Arendt noted at least three major problems with the Marxian formulation. First, the emphasis on "process" suggests a view of history as a series of episodes that have no inherent value; their significance lies only in their contribution to the direction in which history is moving in any case. What Arendt saw as the untidy heterogeneity of history, created by plural actions and conditions, is thus boiled down to the story of a single Subject (the proletariat) with a single destination (a liberated postcapitalist society). Second, since this process is construed in the form of "making,"[72] it appears that, as with everything a worker produces, it will have a terminus: in this case, the end of history. Third, the metaphor of fabrication tends to legitimate violence whenever it is applied to human history because fabrication is itself a violent activity: when a worker transforms nature into the object of his design, this requires the earth to be mined, trees to be cut down, animals to be killed. To view individual actors as analogous to objects of nature is to view them as pliable and dispensable.

Though Arendt considered Marx's philosophy to possess menacing implications, she held fast to the view that totalitarianism was a qualitative break with the tradition Marx had simultaneously rebelled against and been part of. Totalitarianism had not sprung from ideas. Invoking the language of "mass-society" theory, which had widespread currency during the 1950s, Arendt insisted that totalitarianism had emerged out of a "chaos of mass-perplexities on the political scene and of mass-opinions in the spiritual sphere which the totalitarian movements, through terror and ideology, crystallized into a new form of government and domination."[73] Marx's own views of history may have been dangerous and misguided, but they reflected a very real situation: the existence of a capitalist mode of production, in which labor-power is subject to coercive forms of organization, and where the dominant human type is the *animal laborans*. Still, the main tradition of philosophy with which Marx had been associated had shown itself to be fundamentally at war with the political realm. Arendt went so far as to say that the Platonic conception of rulership and obedience "became authoritative for the whole tradition of political thought, even after the roots of experience from which Plato derived his concepts had long been forgotten."[74] Yet however "authoritative," this tradition did not completely monopolize political thinking. Counterlineages existed. And it was to one of them—"classical" political republicanism—that Arendt sought to make her own distinctive contribution.

VI

Classical republicanism[75] is a political idiom that received its most potent and influential (post-Roman) expression in the Florentine Renaissance— its *locus classicus* is Machiavelli's *Discourses*—and was thereafter employed in various ways according to the culture in which it found expression. Classical republicanism was prominent, for instance, among the English "Commonwealthmen" of the seventeenth century, a group of writers that includes Henry Neville, John Milton, and James Harrington. It was adapted by Montesquieu and Rousseau in the eighteenth century, and, in a plurality of mediations, became an integral element in the discourse of the American revolutionaries and constitution-builders, and of their counterparts in France. Typically, "republicans" opposed hereditary monarchy, were anticlerical in orientation, championed political liberty for their peers (they were not democrats in the modern senses), and emphasized the collective political obligations citizens owed to their city or "commonwealth" (a translation of *res publica*: a polity that belongs to all its citizen members). Those obligations entailed responsible involvement in the affairs of public life; for instance, citizens were expected to defend their own country, not hire mercenaries to defend it for them.

Arendt[76] shared with most thinkers who subscribed to the classical variant of republicanism the conviction that politics was something irreducible to other spheres of human life. But, as always, she gave this idea her own particular twist. To say that politics is "irreducible" or sui generis does not mean that it is irrelevant to, say, religious sensibility or domestic concerns. It does mean, for Arendt, that politics has its own space and its own principles. First, politics occupies a public space: public in the senses of being visible to others and to the actor himself, and of constituting a common "world," that relates and separates us from one another. To be sure, not all that is "public" is thereby "political" in Arendt's sense: schools, churches, and all services that people require to earn their livelihood, for instance, are examples of the former but not of the latter. What makes a public space political is that in it people meet as equals, as peers, neither being ruled nor ruling over others: a principle derived not from their nature as "human beings" but from their status as citizens.

Politics as the public space of equality is to be contrasted with two other spheres—private and "social"—governed by very different principles. In the private realm, people meet not as equals but primarily as intimates, bound by ties of friendship and personal commitment. Private life is conducted in isolation—away from the brilliant light of the *polis,* it tends toward exclusivity and it is in good part a result of personal choice: within certain cultural limits, it is we who decide who our friends, lovers, and spouses will be. Moreover, whereas the political realm entails a world that belongs to all its citizen members, private life is normally only feasible if one has a place of one's own: a worldly location free from the gaze, and secure from the predations, of other people; a dwelling that is a buffer against the prying eyes of neighbors and the state. Particularly where Arendt is describing the Greek view of the private realm—the sphere of labor and of necessity, serviced by women and slaves—she tends to depict it as something less than fully human, deprived of the public light that enables action and freedom. So it is important to emphasize that Arendt's own estimation of private life is quite different. An adult existence conducted without privacy would be a meager life indeed: overly self-conscious, precarious, and shallow. And a life spent continually in the glare of the public realm would also have a seriously detrimental impact on children. Parents have the joint responsibility of protecting the world from children, from, that is, "being overrun and destroyed by the onslaught of the new that bursts upon it with each new generation,"[77] and of protecting their children from the demands of the world until they are old enough to cope with them. The family and the four walls that surround it exist ideally to provide the conditions for the child's security, nurturance, and growth. One corollary of this view is Arendt's insistence that parents have the right, within reasonable bounds, to bring up their children as they please, free of the intervention of the state; another is that they have no right to use children to fight political battles. Such politicization of children imposes burdens on them that are inappropriate not only because they are not yet mature enough to handle the conflicts and dilemmas that politics involves, but also because such politicization coexists in a confusing manner with subservience to parents: and politics is not about subservience but about equality.

Since Arendt's death the kind of distinction she drew between public and private has become a major area of contention. Feminists in particular have been keen to argue that the domains are much more porous than Arendt allowed, that domestic issues can have important political implications for women and children, and that the private domain has traditionally been a realm of patriarchal power.[78] Then again, Arendt was no academic feminist. She saw her gender, like her Jewishness, as a fact of life; she did not claim an epistemological privilege for women and "minorities" as some versions of feminism are wont to do. She had a horror of any creed that blanketly subsumed a group of people under the category of victim and hence denied its members' own responsibility for their current position.[79] She was a firm opponent of affirmative action policies in the university, believing they depressed standards of learning, invoked a principle of pseudo-equality, and would ultimately be seen as one more means to subordinate their recipients.[80] For Arendt the personal was definitely not the political, and she was convinced that the blurring of the two, as we will see below, could have adverse, and sometimes catastrophic, consequences, Moreover, to the extent that feminism is offered as a key to history, Arendt would have rejected it as an ideology just as she would have been repelled by the overweening tone of moral superiority so often accompanying it. It is true that all of these Arendtian stances can actually find supporters among feminists today. It is just as true that this does not thereby make Arendt a feminist.

Impinging on both the public and the private is what Arendt refers to as the "social," a product of the modern market economy, the concomitant transformation of fixed property into mobile, exchangeable, monetarized "wealth," and of mass culture.[81] Arendt's comments about the "social" are generally damning; they tend both to reflect and underwrite her conclusion that the *animals laborans* has today become the archetype of human existence. The "social," Arendt argues, is that realm of human relationships (and that part of us) notable for its instrumentalism and uniformity. Instead of the value placed on action and initiative, one observes the mentality of the jobholder who identifies himself above all with the function he performs in the occupational structure. Instead of the equality conferred by the public sphere, one witnesses the conformity of mass taste. Instead of the quest for distinction, one sees the predictability of imitative behavior. The social, in other words, is that sphere measured by opinion surveys, seduced by the fashion industry, orchestrated by political lobbyists, disciplined by party machines, administered by bureaucracy ("the rule of nobody")[82]—and studied by the social sciences.[83] On occasion, Arendt appears to have believed that the social had come close to eviscerating or absorbing entirely the private and public realms. In other contexts, her remarks are more restrained, her estimation of the social more measured, and the significance she imputes to it more positive. For instance, in "Reflections on Little Rock" (pp. 231–243 below), Arendt argues that the social consists of a realm that is well worth protecting—a "hybrid realm between the political and the private in which, since the beginning of the modern age, most men have spent the greater part of their lives. . . . We are driven into this sphere by the need to earn a living or attracted by the desire to follow our vocation or enticed by the pleasure of company, and once we have entered it, we become subject to the old adage of 'like attracts like' . . ."[84] If the principles governing the political and private realm are, respectively, equality and exclusivity, the principle governing the social is "discrimination": the ability to choose not who your fellow citizens are, or with whom you share your home, but what occupation you wish to pursue, what people you wish to congregate with, and so on. As Arendt says, "Without discrimination of some sort, society would simply cease to exist and very important possibilities of free association and group formation would disappear."

It transpires, then, that what Arendt objects to—at least in this particular context of argument—is not "society" as such but the emergence of "*mass* society" which "blurs lines of discrimination and levels group distinctions." And what she fears is not "discrimination" per se—described as an "indispensable . . . social right," that is "legitimate" within its borders—but its trespass onto other areas (the political and the personal) where it is dangerous and "destructive."[85] It is also quite evident that whereas in *The Human Condition* Arendt's emphasis is on deprecating the social, in "Reflections on Little Rock" she is concerned to defend its existence and the distinctive principle of discrimination it harbors. From Arendt's perspective, governments should be particularly careful not to interfere in cases of "social discrimination" lest they impose the political ideal of equality onto an arena in which they have no authority, and thereby infringe on people's civil as distinct from their political liberties. Translated to the issue of integrating black students into schools monopolized by whites, Arendt took the very unpopular position among liberals that while it was proper, indeed essential, to abolish legal enforcement of segregation and laws that made mixed marriages a criminal offense, it was wrong for the Supreme Court to enforce school integration. Arendt's formulation raised many questions, not least of which was whether schools are legitimately seen as "social" institutions governed by rights of free association and "social custom," rather than "public" institutions governed by equality. The main point is, however, that when faced with a concrete case in which the "political" threatened to overwhelm the social, it was to the latter's cause that she rallied.[86]

To make matters more complicated still, Arendt's writings distinguish between the "social" (with the various equivocal characteristics previously noted) and the "social question," a question that preceded "mass society" and that evidently had nothing specifically to do with the rights of free association canvassed in "Reflections on Little Rock." Arendt's analysis of the social question[87] (pp. 247–277 below) was most fully addressed in *On Revolution,* a belated study of the republic that had, many years before, first sheltered her from the Nazi hurricane.

On Revolution not only celebrates the founding achievement, describes some of the great political debates that had accompanied it (the writings of John Adams and Thomas Jefferson are given pride of place), and discusses what Arendt refers to as the "lost treasure of the revolutionary tradition": i.e., the eighteenth-century political ideals of "public freedom, public happiness, public spirit," and the decentralized modes of political participation with which such ideals had been conjoined. The book also contains a highly negative contrast between revolutionary America and France. While the American Revolution had produced a republic, and a founding constitutional document, strong and flexible enough to survive until our own times, the French Revolution of 1789 had soon collapsed into terror and then Bonapartism. What explained these very different trajectories? Arendt's essential line of argument was that, in France, "political" questions to do with freedom receded from the public stage to the degree that they were overtaken by utopian "social" demands to end poverty. In the process, the very meaning of "freedom" had been turned on its head.

Before the late eighteenth century, freedom had generally been conceived of as a prerogative of the leisured few who had both the time and the resources to devote themselves to politics; such persons were free of the compulsive need to labor, free from the injurious constraint of others, and free to engage with their peers in political affairs. During the French Revolution, freedom became reinterpreted to mean something far more all-encompassing. When the French revolutionaries began the process of "retrieving" their "ancient liberties," and "reforming" the monarchy they would later annihilate, they found themselves confronted by a poverty-stricken multitude who had, so far as anyone knew, always been in bondage but who now demanded liberation. "Freedom," sounded in this context, meant not the republican liberty to speak and act on the stage of the commonwealth, but freedom from want and hunger: it meant equality of social condition. Today, the assertion that no one in a civilized society should be without food and shelter is a platitude; then it was radical. And it convinced revolutionary leaders, the *sansculottes* and *les misérables* alike, that freedom was a sham and a travesty wherever it was construed as a privilege of the few.

Moreover, that the "social question" assumed paramount importance in France and not in America was itself a result of social conditions. Poverty was a much more urgent and pressing problem in Europe during the eighteenth century than it was for the white colonists of America whose relative prosperity struck all visitors to that continent. Indeed, the very existence of American abundance had shattered the time-honored perception that poverty was inherent to the human condition. America produced a successful revolution not because it had solved the social question but because it had never been compelled to confront it in its formative years; later, it would have to deal with the issue of slavery, which, when combined with the struggle to preserve the Union, almost destroyed the republic. Nonetheless Arendt contended that, in France, the drive to end destitution through political means was almost bound to recoil on its authors, bringing neither freedom nor abundance to the society for which they were intended. For one thing, the focus on poverty distracted the French revolutionaries from establishing a constitution that would enable free speech and assembly; as long as people were destitute, political freedoms assumed a lesser priority than tackling mass immiserization. For another, the very attempt to abolish scarcity through revolutionary means was a project of such immense ambition that it encouraged acts of terror and desperation to realize it. The result was that while the revolutionaries "liberated" French society through violence from the "tyranny" of the Bourbon kings, they were unable to move on to the next stage of building constitutional freedom: an achievement that required not violence but deliberation and "prudence," not extremity but balance and restraint, not force but "power." Instead, France lurched from one constitution, one government, and one coup, to another. The poor remained destitute and the polity remained unfree. In addition, the spectacle of *le peuple,* surging on to the streets, seemingly impelled by bodily necessity to stave off hunger and want, resembled an elemental force of nature against whose brute necessity "action" was helpless; the people's "unhappiness," witnesses attested, was like a tide or torrent, implacable and irrevocable, that swept away all in its path. It was a metaphor, Arendt maintained, whose plausibility under French conditions was matched only by its legacy for subsequent revolutionary thought: from then on, the French, not the American, experience became paradigmatic of a "real" revolution. The idea that revolution was the opportunity for, and consummation of, the practice of freedom gave way to the view that it was but a continuation of that force of necessity, first manifested in France during the late eighteenth century, to which societies must submit even at the price of destruction, terror, and the sacrifice of liberty itself.

Arendt recognized, as we have seen, that dire material conditions threw on to the French revolutionary agenda brutal facts that the key actors were in no position to ignore. She acknowledged, too, that henceforth a freedom for the few that coexisted with the misery of the many would be deemed intolerable by everyone with a belief in basic justice. This did not mean that modern attempts to abolish poverty through political means, as distinct from technological improvements and economic growth, would be any more successful than their predecessors had been; it meant, more bleakly, that freedom was unlikely to develop under conditions of mass destitution. But social conditions were not the only factors that interested Arendt in her investigation of the French and American Revolutions. Also pertinent were the actors themselves and the rhetoric they deployed as they wrestled to make sense of, and take control of, turbulent events.

The French and the American revolutionaries drew on many common strands of thought: classical, republican, Enlightenment. Both gained some experience in what today would be called local democracy. But in America the revolutionary actors, uninhibited by the social question, were able to embark on a path where the concern with freedom remained center stage, and where revolutionary events conduced to a defense of liberty that was more practical, more realistic, and more "worldly" than anything experienced by their French counterparts. The events of the war of liberation, of drafting the Declaration of Independence, of establishing the Articles of Confederation, of participating in conventions that formulated and then ratified the Constitution of 1787, were all highly political processes whose culmination was the American republic: a public space that both separated and combined the people within it. Such a structure encouraged the language and practice of freedom, as actors sought glory and distinction by the contributions they brought to the commonwealth; as they discovered the "public happiness" that derived from participating in the business of government, the visceral pleasure that led them to actions they had never expected from themselves; as they found in the "public spirit" an expression of solidarity fundamentally different from that found in private affairs. By contrast, in revolutionary France, faced with hunger and desperation, the key actors developed a very different vocabulary and corresponding sensibility. Arendt sought to distill this difference through analyzing the rhetoric of compassion, particularly as it emerged after the fall of the Gironde, in the speeches and writing of Robespierre and other members of the Jacobin "party."

When faced with immense suffering or misfortune, our most natural response to it is compassion. When Robespierre, Saint-Just, and others among the Jacobins were confronted by the "social question" in all its terrible reality, they went one step further, elevating compassion to the highest political virtue. Since no question seemed more in need of solving than immiserization, no virtue appeared more important than the emotional identification with those unhappy ones whom society had for so long cast into obscurity and squalor. The problem with this formulation, however humanly understandable in itself, was that it encouraged a dangerously antipolitical stance. Politics, as distinct from violence, requires spaces that separate people from one another, just as a table separates those who sit around it. Without such distance and divisibility, people are unable to act as plural persons. In contrast, compassion is an emotion that compresses the space between people the more insistently it demands that those who do not suffer join the ranks of those who do. From such a morally outraged standpoint, particular interests are considered divisive and selfish, an impediment to "unity"; similarly, differences of opinion are reckoned to be little more than perverse obstacles to the smooth operation of the general will, which as a "will" must be sovereign, not divided, if it is to act at all. Consent must simply be assumed, not built out of plural, contending, fractious views and perspectives. All efforts must be trained on solving the social question. Moreover, the reflexes that accompany this solution "will shun the drawn-out wearisome processes of persuasion, negotiation, and compromise, which are the processes of law and politics" in favor of the "swift and direct action" for which violence is the most compelling instrument.[88] If individuals have to be sacrificed in the pursuit of compassion, then this is a price worth paying for "justice" and liberation.

To make matters worse, compassion tends to generate an attitude of suspicion whose paranoia is exceeded only by the zeal that accompanies it. Whereas deeds and words have an "objective" reality (they can be seen and heard), emotions such as compassion reside in the invisible recesses of our inner life. If they are to shine in public as a beacon of policy, they must be professed, but the more a person feels bound to profess his sincerity the more it appears that his action is prompted by ulterior motives: "me thinks he doth protest too much." So begins the search to find the hypocrites, a quest that can have no intrinsic terminus because the feelings of the heart are ultimately immeasurable and constantly in flux. Furthermore, the bloodhounds of suspicion follow a scent that all too often turns out to be their own. Because compassion is a matter of changing mood and sensation rather than something stable like a physical artifact or visible like a human deed, even its exponents can never feel certain of whether they are paragons of empathy or just phonies in disguise. The result is an even greater desire to demonstrate their feelings as unfeigned and to continue a cycle of behavior that is at once bloody and self-destructive. For Arendt, the opposite of compassion is not cynical indifference to the plight of those who suffer, but rather solidarity and respect, principles that may be occasioned by an emotion, but which in their generalized concern for human dignity (of the fortunate and of the unfortunate alike), their rejection of condescension and self-righteousness, their realism and sense of perspective offer superior resources for dealing with oppression and exploitation than the passions and sentiments of the heart.[89]

Arendt also used *On Revolution* to contrast invidiously the malaise of modern representative democracy—subject to the party machine and conducive to widespread political apathy—with the independent deliberation and republican *joie de vivre* (of "being seen in action") that was so characteristic of the American founding era. More generally, Arendt reminded readers of an institution that was part of the "lost treasure" of the revolutionary tradition: the societies and local councils that had spontaneously sprung up as organs of popular rule during revolutionary conjunctures: the French Revolution of 1789, the Paris Commune of 1870, the Russian Revolutions of 1905 and 1917 and the Hungarian uprising of 1956 (see pp. 516–524 below). Free of both statist controls and the manipulation of revolutionary ideologues, all these attempts at radical participation and people's government had been unexpected, interstitial—and short-lived; either they were swept away when the old order, temporarily concussed, regained its powers, or when a new state came into existence. One important reason why these revolutionary councils, *Räte* and *soviets* functioned so effectively as political bodies, Arendt maintained, was because they were local and small-scale; they provided the opportunity for ordinary citizens not only to participate directly in public affairs but also to excel in them. In most cases, people became involved in these councils not primarily to solve the "social question" but to share power and responsibility, all the better to expand the sphere of freedom that had hitherto been so stultifyingly constricted. And it was in the inability to preserve this radical self-governance that Arendt spied the failure of the revolutionary tradition—a failure that touched even the case she admired above all others.

Before and during the American Revolution, political participation had been extensive and radically decentralized in "township" and town hall, spaces where people had experienced the pleasure of being actors and decision makers. The great flaw in the founding document of the American republic—the Constitution of 1787—lay in the barrier it erected to participation, in the displacement of power it effected from local politics to the federal government; the opportunity to divide the "counties" into "wards"—elementary republics that would keep the popular, public spirit of freedom alive—was accordingly wasted. Late in life, this came to be Thomas Jefferson's critique of the Constitution and with it Arendt was in complete agreement. According to Jefferson, the great danger of the new, centralized system that had emerged from the Revolution was that people would feel, even at the state level, remote from government and hence become increasingly indifferent to it. Coupled with accelerated economic development and the opportunities for personal advancement that this afforded, centralization would cause citizens to turn ever more readily away from a concern with public duty and ever more assiduously toward the protection of their own private—domestic and pecuniary—interests. What Jefferson now "perceived to be the mortal danger to the republic was that the Constitution had given all power to the citizens, without giving them the opportunity of being republicans and of acting as citizens. In other words, the danger was that all power had been given to the people in their private capacity and that there was no space established for them in their capacity for being citizens."[90] Jefferson's fears, Arendt continued, had been amply confirmed by subsequent events.

Arendt recognized that the appearance and reappearance of popular councils since the late eighteenth century did not constitute a tradition in the typical sense, for there was no continuity here, simply a stubborn, persistent reminder of how, when circumstances were propitious, men and women could create the spaces of freedom. Superficially, the councils appeared to vindicate the insights and proposals of anarchist thinkers, but Arendt pointed out that such writers as Proudhon and Bakunin were singularly unable to account for projects whose aim was not to abolish government and politics but instead to put them onto a radically new footing.

This is not the place to examine at length Arendt's arguments, addressed on pp. 524–534 below,[91] for the revival of the council polity; still less can we offer here a critical review of them.[92] Yet however one appraises Arendt's participatory alternative, we are still left with the intriguing question of how she reached it; how, that is, she arrived at conclusions that were both pessimistic about modern democracy but yet were simultaneously dogged in their belief that something better was, if unlikely, nonetheless possible. Arendt does not, in other words, present an "iron cage" view of modernity, nor does she resign herself to "an iron law of oligarchy" notion so popular among those for whom democracy is a fraud to begin with. But neither does she usually side with the utopians. Perhaps part of the explanation for Arendt's position lies in the tension between two tendencies that commingle in her work and which may be characterized as the republicanism of hope, leavened with an Augustinian yeast, and the republicanism of fear. The republicanism of hope found expression in Arendt's abiding conviction that the birth of every human being ushers into the world untold new possibilities. Hope found vehicles, also, in the bold attempts that had been made during the course of her own lifetime to found something new: a postwar Europe whose banner would be *liberer et federer*, the principle whose heroic bearer had been the French resistance;[93] the Hungarian and Czech uprisings of 1956 and 1968 which had shown the irrepressible hunger of people not simply to be fed but to be free; and, some major reservations notwithstanding, the student movement of the sixties and seventies whose "determination to act," whose "joy in action," and whose ability to act from "moral motives"[94] appeared to be a veritable rediscovery of the lost treasure of the eighteenth century. Coinciding with such anticipation, however, lay Arendt's ominous conclusion that totalitarian elements still composed the periodic table of modernity, and that in a mass society there would always be a majority of people whose dedication to their own social and private interests would make them easy prey for party machines and demagogues. "Corruption and perversion," she once wrote, "are more pernicious, and at the same time more likely to occur, in an egalitarian republic than in any other form of government. Schematically speaking, they come to pass when private interests invade the public domain, that is, they spring from below and not from above."[95] When the primacy of private interests coexists with a mass society, the historical prospect is even more alarming. For the really horrific discovery of totalitarian regimes had been that mass conformists—"job holders and good family men"—were much more pliant, dedicated, loyal, and abundant agents of extermination than the criminals, "fanatics, adventurers, sex maniacs, crackpots" and social failures of the mob. "The mass man whom Himmler organized for the greatest mass crimes ever committed in history bore the features of the philistine rather than of the mob man, and was the bourgeois who in the midst of the ruins of his world worried about nothing so much as his private security, was ready to sacrifice everything—belief, honor, dignity—on the slightest provocation. Nothing proved easier to destroy than the privacy and private morality of people who thought of nothing but safeguarding their private lives."[96]

VII

The last decade of Arendt's life was a time of personal loss—both Karl Jaspers and Heinrich Blücher died before her—and of continued investigation into political questions. Between 1965 and 1975 she devoted herself to understanding the "crises of the republic" that beset her adoptive country America: the struggles for civil rights, civil disobedience, the cult of violence that appeared in some sections of the students' movement, the relationship between foreign strategy and a domestic policy in which lies, half-truths, and bungled burglaries had become the very currency of government. At the same time, two previous streams of thought continued to flow in her imagination. The first concerned Eichmann, the man who could not think from the standpoint of anyone else. Could it be, then, that thought is "among the conditions that make men abstain from evil-doing or even actually 'condition' them against it"?[97] The second concerned that side of existence that in *The Human Condition* she had somewhat neglected and, seeking to rescue the life of action from the philosophers' tendentious description of it, even to some degree impugned: the *vita contemplativa*. Now she wanted to explore it more fully. "What are we 'doing' when we do nothing but think? Where are we when we, normally always surrounded by our fellow-men, are together with no one but ourselves?"[98] The result of these and related deliberations was a series of analyses that culminated in her last major treatise, posthumously published, and edited by Mary McCarthy, as *The Life of the Mind*. Arising out of the Gifford Lectures she had delivered at the University of Aberdeen in 1973 and 1974, and lecture courses at the New School of Social Research in New York City, where, since 1967, she had academically been based, *The Life of the Mind* is a formidable and, in its density, somewhat forbidding attempt to understand the qualities of the thinking, willing, and judging faculties. Each is autonomous, and thus irreducible to the other two; yet each, even as it follows its own distinctive rules, exists in a complex and a dynamic relationship with its partner faculties. At the time of the heart attack that killed her on December 4, 1975—she was sixty-nine—only the two volumes on thinking and willing were more or less complete; her ideas on judgment were pieced together from occasional comments or lecture notes on, in particular, Kant's aesthetic theory.[99] All this may seem very remote indeed from the highly political nature of her other work. And in one sense it was remote; Arendt's first love was philosophy and it was to philosophy she returned most deliberately in the last years of her life. Even so, she remained one of its most severe critics. The mainstream Western tradition of philosophy, Arendt argued, had never been able to reconcile its deductive mode of reasoning, or its search for a single Truth, or its equation of "freedom" with freedom of thought, with the inherently messy, contingent quality of action among plural persons: the domain of politics par excellence.

Judith Shklar once described the main aim of her own political theory as the strenuous attempt to "disentangle philosophy from ideology."[100] Much the same attitude can be said to have characterized her fellow émigré Hannah Arendt. "Thinking without bannisters," as Arendt put it, meant thinking boldly, yet remaining aware of the precariousness and fragility of all things human. It meant insisting over and over again that while the political theorist is committed to understanding the *Zeitgeist,* he or she is not obliged to cave in to it. It meant recognizing the limitations of our traditions to deal with new problems, while at the same time appreciating how much our "fragmented past" has still to teach us. Drawing on a favorite stanza from *The Tempest,* Hannah Arendt issued a tart warning to any dilettante who might mistake her own technique of "dismantling" traditions for dismissal of them: "If some of my listeners or readers should be tempted to try their luck at the technique of dismantling, let them be careful not to destroy the 'rich and strange,' the 'coral' and the 'pearls,' which can probably be saved only as fragments." And quoting with approval a line of W. H. Auden she continued, " 'Some books are undeservedly forgotten, none are undeservedly remembered.' "[101] Arendt's most remembered works thus far are *The Origins of Totalitarianism, The Human Condition,* and *Eichmann in Jerusalem.* My hope is that this Portable anthology will convince readers that her thoughts contain many more "pearls" than these.

Notes

1. As George Orwell once remarked about Dickens. See "Charles Dickens" (1939), reprinted in *Decline of the English Murder and Other Essays* (Harmondsworth: Penguin, 1965), pp. 80–141, at p. 80.

2. The quotations are from "Dedication to Karl Jaspers" (1948), in *Hannah Arendt: Essays in Understanding 1930–1954,* Jerome Kohn, ed. (New York: Harcourt Brace, 1994), pp. 212–16, at p. 212. The translators of the essay are Robert and Rita Kimber.

3. For information on Arendt's life and milieux, I am leaning heavily, here and in what follows, on the excellent biography by Elisabeth Young-Bruehl, *Hannah Arendt: For Love of the World* (New Haven and London: Yale University Press, 1982).

4. Young-Bruehl, p. 33.

5. "What Is Existential Philosophy?" (1946), in Arendt, *Essays in Understanding,* pp. 163–87, at p. 187, n. 2; Letter of Arendt to Heinrich Blücher, 3 January 1950, in *Hannah Arendt/Heinrich Blücher, Briefe: 1936–1968* (Munich: Piper, 1996), edited, with an introductory essay, by Lotte Kohler, p. 190. Hereafter cited as *Arendt/Blücher, Briefe.*

6. On Heidegger's hostile reception of *The Human Condition,* and on Hannah Arendt's response, see Elżbieta Ettinger, *Hannah Arendt/Martin Heidegger* (New Haven and London: Yale University Press), pp. 113–20.

7. On the significance of Heidegger and Jaspers more generally, see Seyla Benhabib, *The Reluctant Modernism of Hannah Arendt* (London: Sage, 1996), especially chapters 2 and 4; Dana R. Villa, *Arendt and Heidegger: The Fate of the Political* (Princeton: Princeton University Press, 1966); and Lewis P. Hinchman and Sandra K. Hinchman, "Existentialism Politicized: Arendt's Debt to Jaspers" (1991), reprinted in Lewis P. Hinchman and Sandra K. Hinchman, *Hannah Arendt: Critical Essays* (Albany: SUNY, 1994), pp. 143–78.

8. Hannah Arendt, *Der Liebesbegriff bei Augustin* (Berlin: J. Springer, 1929) = *Love and Saint Augustine,* edited with an interpretive essay by Joanna Vecchiarelli Scott and Judith Chelius Stark (Chicago: University of Chicago Press, 1996). Arendt returned to the systematic study of Augustine in her last posthumously published work, *The Life of the Mind,* but it is Duns Scotus, more than Augustine, for whom she reserves her greatest praise. See *The Life of the Mind, Vol. II: Willing* (New York: Harcourt Brace, 1978), pp. 84–110, 125–46.

   The English publication of *Love and Saint Augustine* is most certainly to be welcomed but, after years of neglect, the danger now is that its significance will be exaggerated. This is likely to happen whenever Arendt's mature thought is read back into her first explorations, which are then considered to be the foundation of what she later went on to write. No excerpt from the dissertation is offered in the present anthology. This is not because I wish to exclude her first book from the so-called Arendt canon, but because the density and abstract nature of Arendt's philosophical arguments make an extract, separated from the work as a whole, barely intelligible.

9. K. Jaspers, "Philosophical Autobiography," in Paul Arthur Schilpp, ed., *The Philosophy of Karl Jaspers* (La Salle, Ill.: Open Court [1957] 1981), pp. 5–94, at p. 62, transls. Paul Arthur Schilpp and Ludwig B. Lefebre.

10. Hannah Arendt, *Rahel Varnhagen: The Life of a Jewish Woman* (New York and London, Harcourt Brace [1957], 1974), transls. Richard and Clara Winston. The definitive English-language edition of this book, equipped with an illuminating introduction and notes, is *Rahel Varnhagen: The Life of a Jewess,* edited by Liliane Weissberg, transls. Richard and Clara Winston (Baltimore: Johns Hopkins University Press, 1997).

11. *Rahel Varnhagen,* p. 123.

12. The distinction, borrowed, via Kurt Blumenfeld, from Bernard Lazare, between "parvenu" and "pariah" became henceforth a salient motif of Arendt's writings on Jewishness. See, for instance, "We Refugees" (1943) and "The Jew as Pariah: A Hidden Tradition" (1944), in which Rahel is joined by other, different but representative, pariah characters: Heine, Lazare, Charlie Chaplin, and Franz Kafka. Arendt identified herself explic-

itly with the "conscious pariahdom" of Lazare. See Hannah Arendt, *The Jew as Pariah: Jewish Identity and Politics in the Modern Age,* edited with an introduction by Ron H. Feldman (New York: Grove Press, 1978), pp. 55–66, 67–90; and chapter three of *The Origins of Totalitarianism* (New York: Harcourt Brace, 1951), entitled "The Jews and Society," which is excerpted below, pp. 75–103. Unless otherwise stated, all references that follow are to the third edition (1966), with added prefaces.

13. *Rahel Varnhagen,* pp. 224, 227.

14. Arendt's mother died in 1948.

15. "We Refugees" (1943), in *The Jew as Pariah,* pp. 55–66, at p. 57.

16. The quotations come from Hannah Arendt, " 'The Rights of Man.' What Are They?," in *Modern Review* 3/1 (Summer 1949), pp. 24–37. A revised version of this article, with its professed debt to Edmund Burke, appeared in *Origins of Totalitarianism,* pp. 290–302, under the heading "The Perplexities of the Rights of Man." It is reproduced below, pp. 31–45.

17. Notably in *Jewish Social Studies, Jewish Frontier, Commentary,* and *Menorah Journal.* A number of these articles are reprinted in *The Jew as Pariah.*

18. See especially, "Die jüdische Armee—der Beginn einer jüdischen Politik?" (reprinted below: pp. 46–48), and "Papier und Wirklichkeit" in *Aufbau,* 14 November 1941, 10 April 1942, respectively. The best brief discussion is still Young-Bruehl, *Hannah Arendt,* pp. 169–81.

19. "Die Krise des Zionismus" in *Aufbau,* 20 November 1942; two earlier parts of this analysis had been published in *Aufbau* on 23 October and 6 November 1942.

Arendt's arguments for a postwar European federalism can be found in "Approaches to the 'German Problem' " (1945) in *Essays in Understanding,* pp. 106–20, at pp. 112–20. See also "Parties, Movements, and Classes," *Partisan Review* 12/4 (Fall 1945), pp. 505–13, at pp. 510–13.

20. Especially pertinent are the essays "Zionism Reconsidered" (1945), "The Jewish State: Fifty Years After" (1946), "To Save the Jewish Homeland. There Is Still Time" (1948), and "Peace or Armistice in the Near East?" (1950), all of which are reprinted in *The Jew as Pariah.* See also Dagmar Barnouw, *Visible Spaces: Hannah Arendt and the German-Jewish Experience* (Baltimore: Johns Hopkins University Press, 1990); and Richard J. Bernstein, *Hannah Arendt and the Jewish Question* (Cambridge, Mass.: MIT Press, 1996). Ron H. Feldman's introduction to *The Jew as Pariah* is also a helpful and insightful account.

21. "Peace or Armistice in the Near East?" (1950), in *The Jew as Pariah,* pp. 193–222, at p. 212. Though Arendt was proved to be wrong in this judgment, she was more prophetic in her observation that "a new category of homeless people, the Arab refugees" were in the process of being created. "These not only form a dangerous potential irredenta dispersed in all Arab countries where they could easily become the visible uniting link; much worse, no matter how their exodus came about (as a consequence of Arab

atrocity propaganda or real atrocities or a mixture of both), their flight from Palestine, prepared by Zionist plans of large-scale population transfers during the war and followed by the Israeli refusal to readmit the refugees to their old home, made the old Arab claim against Zionism finally come true: the Jews simply aimed at expelling Arabs from their homes," ibid, pp. 215–16.

22. "To Save the Jewish Homeland. There Is Still Time" (1948), in *The Jew as Pariah,* pp. 178–92, at p. 192.

23. Among the options she considered at various times were: "The Elements of Shame: Anti-Semitism—Imperialism—Racism," "Three Pillars of Hell," "A History of Totalitarianism." In Britain, the book was first published as *The Burden of Our Time,* a title she opposed. On all this see Young-Bruehl, *Hannah Arendt,* p. 200, and the illuminating analysis in Lisa Jane Disch, *Hannah Arendt and the Limits of Philosophy* (Ithaca: Cornell University Press, 1994), pp. 121–30. Arendt's book appeared in German as *Elemente und Ursprünge totaler Herrschaft* (Frankfurt: Europäische Verlaganstalt, 1955).

24. Arendt's long, multifaceted, and subtle argument can be found in parts I and II of the *Origins of Totalitarianism.* The best commentary is chapter 2 of Margaret Canovan's scrupulous and balanced *Hannah Arendt: A Reinterpretation of Her Political Thought* (Cambridge: Cambridge University Press, 1992).

25. Ernst Cassirer, *The Myth of the State* (New Haven: Yale University Press, 1946). J. L. Talmon, *The Rise of Totalitarian Democracy* (Boston: The Beacon Press, 1952).

26. It is likely that when she wrote of the "history of ideas," Arendt was thinking not of the *Ideengeschichte* typified by Friedrich Meinecke and his school, or the American "history of ideas" practiced by A. O. Lovejoy and his associates, but rather of twentieth-century versions of so-called *Geistesgeschichte.* Hegelian or neo-Kantian in form, *Geistesgeschichte* (literally, the history of Spirit) posited that each age was the product of, and was unified by, some fundamental cultural or spiritual force. The tradition was carried to the United States by writers like Ernst Cassirer and Leo Spitzer. For a helpful discussion of these different intellectual currents, see Melvin Richter, *The History of Political and Social Concepts: A Critical Introduction* (New York and Oxford: Oxford University Press, 1995), p. 22 and passim.

27. "The unprecedented is neither the murder itself nor the number of victims and not even 'the number of persons who united to perpetrate them.' It is much rather the ideological nonsense which caused them, the mechanization of their execution, and the careful and calculated establishment of a world of the dying in which nothing any longer made sense." Hannah Arendt, "Social Science Techniques and the Study of Concentration Camps" (1950), in *Essays in Understanding,* pp. 232–47, at p. 243.

28. Margaret Canovan, *Hannah Arendt: A Reinterpretation,* p. 20. Because Arendt saw "Nazism as a matter not so much of German as of *world* history [she] was able to incorporate Stalin's regime into her account. In a sense, indeed, when it turned out that Stalin had apparently reached much the same destination as Hitler by a completely different route, this confirmed her convic-

tion that what she was trying to come to terms with was a phenomenon that was not specific to any one country." See also Hannah Arendt, "On the Nature of Totalitarianism" in *Essays in Understanding*, pp. 328–60, at pp. 347–48.

29. Hannah Arendt, "Approaches to the 'German Problem'" (1945), in *Essays in Understanding*, pp. 106–20, esp. at pp. 108–9.

30. To the chagrin of Bruno Bettelheim, who objected bitterly to the use of a religious term (meaning "burnt offering") being applied to the mass murder of the Jews; the term "martyr" he found equally ridiculous and offensive. See "The Holocaust—One Generation Later" (1977), in Bruno Bettelheim, *Surviving and Other Essays* (New York: Alfred A. Knopf, 1979), pp. 84–104, esp. at pp. 91–94. The entry on "holocaust" in recent editions of *The Oxford English Dictionary* reveals that while the term gained popularity in the 1950s, as an equivalent to the Hebrew *Hurban* and *Shoah,* there were precedents for such usage as early as 1942.

31. A rare attempt to examine Arendt's many-sided understanding of movement can be found in Jonathan V. Clark, " 'Breaking the Cycle': The Concept of Movement in the Work of Hannah Arendt," M.A. thesis, Department of Sociology, Faculty of Arts, Memorial University of Newfoundland, 1997.

32. *Origins of Totalitarianism*, p. 387; cf. pp. 440–41.

33. "The chief difference between the despotic and the totalitarian secret police lies in the difference between the 'suspect' and the 'objective enemy.' The latter is defined by the policy of the government and not by his own desire to overthrow it. He is never an individual whose dangerous thoughts must be provoked or whose past justifies suspicion, but a 'carrier of tendencies' like the carrier of a disease. Practically speaking, the totalitarian ruler proceeds like a man who persistently insults another man until everybody knows that the latter is his enemy, so that he can, with some plausibility, go and kill him in self-defense." *Origins of Totalitarianism*, pp. 423–24.

34. *Origins of Totalitarianism*, pp. 434 and 452. She later came to believe that "holes of oblivion do not exist." See Hannah Arendt, *Eichmann in Jerusalem* (New York: Viking Press [1963], revised and enlarged edition, 1965), pp. 232–33; cited hereafter as *Eichmann in Jerusalem*. Also the letter to Mary McCarthy, reproduced below (pp. 389–390), dated 20 September 1963, in *Between Friends: The Correspondence of Hannah Arendt and Mary McCarthy 1949–1975* (New York: Harcourt Brace, 1995), edited with an introduction by Carol Brightman, pp. 146–48; cited hereafter as *Between Friends*.

35. Hannah Arendt, "The Image of Hell" (1946), in *Essays in Understanding*, pp. 197–205, at p. 198.

36. *Origins of Totalitarianism*, p. 441.

37. *Origins of Totalitarianism*, pp. 443–44.

38. "The Image of Hell," p. 199. Cf. Primo Levi, "The Gray Zone," in *The Drowned and the Saved* (New York: Summit Books, 1986), translated by Raymond Rosenthal, pp. 36–69.

39. Hannah Arendt, "Nightmare and Flight" (1945), in *Essays in Understanding,* pp. 133–35, at p. 133.

40. See Franz Neumann, "Notes on the Theory of Dictatorship." In F. Neumann, *The Democratic and the Authoritarian State: Essays in Political and Legal Theory,* Herbert Marcuse, ed. (Glencoe, Ill.: Free Press, 1964), pp. 233–56. Cf. F. Neumann, *Behemoth: The Structure and Practice of National Socialism, 1933–1944* (New York: Octagon Books, 1983 [1944, 1942]). On so-called totalitarian dictatorship, see also H. H. Gerth and C. Wright Mills, *Character and Social Structure: The Psychology of Social Institutions* (London: Routledge and Kegan Paul, 1954), p. 212.

41. Hannah Arendt, "On the Nature of Totalitarianism: An Essay in Understanding," in *Essays in Understanding,* pp. 328–60, at p. 348. This essay, composed in the early fifties, but not published until recently, should be compared with "Ideology and Terror: A Novel Form of Government," *The Review of Politics* 15/3 (July 1953), pp. 303–27. (Included as chapter 13 of the second [1958] edition of *Origins of Totalitarianism.*)

42. "Ideology and Terror," p. 312.

43. She would later seek to make a conceptual distinction between terror and violence: "Terror is not the same as violence; it is, rather, the form of government that comes into being when violence, having destroyed all power, does not abdicate but, on the contrary, remains in full control," "Reflections on Violence," *Journal of International Affairs* 23/1 (Winter 1969), pp. 1–35, at p. 21. For an expanded version of this essay, see "On Violence" (1970), reprinted in *Crises of the Republic* (1972), (Harmondsworth: Penguin, 1973), pp. 83–146. On pages 112–15, Arendt distinguishes between strength, force, authority, violence, and power. In *Origins of Totalitarianism* (e.g., p. 420), power is not analytically separated from violence.

44. "Ideology and Terror," p. 310.

45. "On the Nature of Totalitarianism," p. 351.

46. "Ideology and Terror," p. 326.

47. "Ideology and Terror," p. 327. Arendt did not believe, however, that totalitarianism would come to dominate the whole earth, for that presupposed "the existence of *one* authority, *one* way of life, *one* ideology in all countries and among all peoples of the world." This remark, to be found in the first edition of *Origins of Totalitarianism,* was expunged in the editions that followed. See "Concluding Comments" in *The Burden of Our Time* (= *Origins of Totalitarianism*), pp. 429–39, at p. 429.

48. *Origins of Totalitarianism,* pp. 384–85.

49. *Origins of Totalitarianism,* p. 387.

50. Hannah Arendt, *Eichmann in Jerusalem: A Report on the Banality of Evil* (Harmondsworth: Penguin, 1977), p. 21. This is the English version of the revised and enlarged edition published in 1965 by Viking. Henceforth cited as *Eichmann in Jerusalem.*

51. I take the figure from Amos Elon, "The Case of Hannah Arendt," *New York Review of Books,* November 6, 1997, pp. 25–29, at p. 25.

52. On Arendt's distinction between the legal basis of the trial and its conduct, see the letter to Jaspers of December 23, 1960, in Lotte Kohler and Hans Saner, eds., *Hannah Arendt, Karl Jaspers Correspondence: 1926–1969*, translated by Robert and Rita Kimber (New York: Harcourt Brace, 1992), pp. 414–18.

53. *Eichmann in Jerusalem*, p. 5.

54. *Eichmann in Jerusalem*, p. 274.

55. *Eichmann in Jerusalem*, pp. 268–69.

56. *Eichmann in Jerusalem*, p. 279.

57. *Eichmann in Jerusalem*, p. 269.

58. I have been quoting from *Eichmann in Jerusalem*, pp. 269–73.

59. Hannah Arendt's approach is thus very different from those historians who have sought to discover the particular ideological strain that motivated Germans, ordinary or otherwise, to commit their atrocities. For contrasting views, see for instance Daniel Jonah Goldhagen on "Eliminationist Antisemitism" in *Hitler's Willing Executioners: Ordinary Germans and the Holocaust* [1996] (London: Abacus, 1997), especially chapters 2 and 3; and Saul Friedländer on "redemptive anti-Semitism" in *Nazi Germany and the Jews Volume I: The Years of Persecution, 1933–1939* (New York: HarperCollins, 1997), especially chapter 3.

    It is also worth noting that even in the sections on ideology in *The Origins of Totalitarianism*, it is more the cognitive form of ideology, rather than its content, to which Arendt devotes the bulk of her analysis. Still, see her comments on "tribal nationalism" and on totalitarian propaganda in *Origins of Totalitarianism*, pp. 227–43 and 340–64, respectively.

60. *Eichmann in Jerusalem*, pp. 48–49.

61. *Eichmann in Jerusalem*, pp. 287–88.

62. *Eichmann in Jerusalem*, p. 252; the emphasis is in the original.

63. As Elisabeth Young-Bruehl (op. cit., p. 522, n. 56) points out, Arendt "had discussed the Jewish councils in print" as early as March 1952 "in a review of Léon Poliakov's *Bréviaire de la Haine* for *Commentary*." Arendt's criticisms of Zionist cooperation with the Nazis went back even further: see "Zionism Reconsidered" (1944), pp. 131–63, at p. 139; and "About Collaboration" (1948), pp. 237–39, at pp. 238–39, both reprinted in *The Jew as Pariah*.

64. Judith N. Shklar, "Hannah Arendt as Pariah," in *Partisan Review* 50:1 (1983), pp. 64–77, at p. 75.

65. For some of her impressions of Heidegger, see *Arendt/Blücher, Briefe*, pp. 189–90 (letter of 3 January 1950), pp. 274–77 (letter of 24 May 1952).

66. Bernard Crick, "Hannah Arendt and the Burden of Our Times," in *The Political Quarterly* 30 (1997), pp. 77–84. See also Margaret Canovan's *Hannah Arendt: A Reinterpretation*, pp. 6–7.

67. Hannah Arendt, *The Human Condition* (Chicago: University of Chicago Press, 1958), p. 11. Hereafter cited as *The Human Condition*.

68. I am greatly simplifying, and telescoping, Arendt's account. For a sophisti-

cated treatment of it, see Ronald Beiner, "Hannah Arendt on Judging," in Hannah Arendt, *Lectures on Kant's Political Philosophy,* edited with an interpretive essay by Ronald Beiner (Chicago: University of Chicago Press, 1982), pp. 89–157.

69. *The Human Condition,* pp. 189, 195; see also "Hermann Broch: 1886–1951" in *Men in Dark Times,* pp. 111–51, at pp. 147–48; and *The Life of the Mind Volume II: Willing,* pp. 123–24. A helpful clarification of this point is offered by Elisabeth Young-Bruehl (op. cit., p. 494) when she says that planning and policy-making are not, appearances to the contrary, ruled out by Arendt's concept of action. "Planning is not precluded, but action that fails to achieve its end may nevertheless be meaningful or great. . . . Action engaged in only for the sake of an end may, on the other hand, adopt any means or pervert human relations by making them into a means . . ."

70. "The only aspect of politics where Arendt did think that craftsmanship was called for was in setting up the framework for political action: drawing up a constitution to set the stage or construct the arena for free politics," Margaret Canovan, "Politics and Culture: Hannah Arendt and the Public Realm" (1985), in Lewis P. Hinchman and Sandra K. Hinchman, op. cit., pp. 179–205, at p. 184.

71. Hannah Arendt, "The Concept of History. Ancient and Modern" (1958), in *Between Past and Future,* pp. 41–90, at p. 79. Reprinted in part below: pp. 278–310.

72. Arendt argued that Marx tended to confuse "labor" and "work"; the result was an analysis in which the (biological) compulsion typical of the labor process coexists uneasily with an emphasis on Homo sapiens as a creative and dynamic species.

73. Hannah Arendt, "Tradition and the Modern Age" (1954), in *Between Past and Future,* pp. 17–40, at p. 26.

74. *The Human Condition,* p. 225.

75. I am drawing here on my *Caesar and the Fading of the Roman World: A Study in Republicanism and Caesarism* (New Brunswick: Transaction, 1998). On Arendt's republicanism, see also chapter 6 of Margaret Canovan's *Hannah Arendt: A Reinterpretation of Her Political Thought,* op. cit., a discussion to which I am considerably indebted.

76. The following discussion draws mainly on chapter 2 of *The Human Condition* (reprinted below: pp. 182–230) and on Hannah Arendt, "Reflections on Little Rock," and "A Reply to Critics," in *Dissent* 6:1 (Winter 1959), pp. 45–56; *Dissent* 6:2 (Spring 1959), pp. 179–81 (reprinted below: pp. 231–246).

77. Hannah Arendt, "The Crisis in Education" (1958), in *Between Past and Future,* pp. 173–96, at p. 186. Cf. 'Abdu'l-Bahá, "Every child is potentially the light of the world—and at the same time its darkness," in *Selections from the Writings of 'Abdu'l-Bahá* (Haifa: Bahá'í World Center), transl. Marzieh Gail, p. 130.

78. On these and other issues see the contributions to Bonnie Honig, ed., *Fem-*

inist Interpretations of Hannah Arendt (University Park: Pennsylvania State University Press, 1995).

79. See, for instance, Hannah Arendt, "The Jew as Pariah: A Hidden Tradition" (1944) in *The Jew as Pariah,* pp. 77–78.

80. See, for instance, Arendt to McCarthy, December 21, 1968, in *Between Friends,* pp. 228–32.

81. For Arendt's thoughts on the various manifestations of "society" (high, genteel, and mass), see *On Revolution* [1963] (Harmondsworth: Penguin, 1990), pp. 104ff.

82. *The Human Condition,* pp. 44–45. Also, "On Violence" (1969) in Hannah Arendt, *Crises of the Republic* (1972) (Harmondsworth: Penguin, 1973), pp. 83–163, at p. 109.

83. On the social sciences as "abominable," see the letter to McCarthy of December 21, 1968, in *Between Friends,* pp. 228–32, at p. 231.

84. "Reflections on Little Rock," p. 51.

85. "Reflections on Little Rock," p. 51.

86. Critical analyses of Arendt's concept of the "social" can be found, *inter alia,* in Seyla Benhabib, *The Reluctant Modernism of Hannah Arendt,* op. cit., pp. 22–30, 138–41; R. J. Bernstein, "Rethinking the Social and the Political," in his *Philosophical Profiles* (Philadelphia: University of Pennsylvania Press, 1986), pp. 238–60; and especially Hanna Fenichel Pitkin, *The Attack of the Blob: Hannah Arendt's Concept of the Social* (Chicago: University of Chicago Press, 1998).

87. The remarks that follow draw on "Revolution and Freedom: A Lecture," *In zwei Welten: Siegfried Moses zum fünfundsiebzigsten Geburstag* (Tel Aviv: Verlag Bitaon, 1962), pp. 578–600; and *On Revolution.*

88. *On Revolution,* pp. 86–89.

89. On compassion, see also Arendt's portrait of Bertolt Brecht, in *Men in Dark Times,* pp. 207–49, at pp. 235–42. Also, Christopher Lasch, "Communitarianism or Populism? The Ethic of Compassion and the Ethic of Respect," (1992) in C. Lasch, *The Revolt of the Elites* (New York: W. W. Norton, 1995), pp. 92–114.

90. *On Revolution,* p. 253.

91. Also see "Thoughts on Politics and Revolution. A Commentary" (1970), translated by Denver Lindley, in *Crises of the Republic,* op. cit., pp. 164–91, at p. 190.

92. For criticisms of Arendt's views see, *inter alia,* George Kateb, *Hannah Arendt. Politics, Conscience, Evil* (Totowa, N.J.: Rowman and Allanheld, 1983), chapter 4; John F. Sitton, "Hannah Arendt's Arguments for Council Democracy" (1987), in L. P. Hinchman and S. K. Hinchman, *Hannah Arendt: Critical Essays,* op. cit., pp. 307–29; and Sheldon S. Wolin, "Hannah Arendt: Democracy and the Political" (1983), in Hinchman and Hinchman, pp. 289–306. For a qualified defense of Arendt's view of council democracy, see Maurizio Passerin d'Entrèves, *The Political Philosophy of Hannah Arendt* (London: Routledge, 1994), pp. 95–99, 163–65.

93. "Approaches to the German Problem," pp. 114–20.

94. "Thoughts on Politics and Revolution," pp. 164–66.

95. *On Revolution,* p. 252. "Corruption of the people themselves—as distinguished from corruption of their representatives or a ruling class—is possible only under a government that has granted them a share in public power and has taught them how to manipulate it."

96. *Origins of Totalitarianism,* p. 338. Compare with Hannah Arendt, "Organized Guilt and Universal Responsibility" (1945), in *Essays in Understanding,* pp. 121–32, at p. 128; reprinted below: pp. 146–156.

97. *The Life of the Mind Volume 1: Thinking,* p. 5.

98. *The Life of the Mind Volume I: Thinking,* p. 8.

99. Collected as *Lectures on Kant's Political Philosophy,* edited and with an interpretive essay by Ronald Beiner (Chicago: University of Chicago Press, 1982). Beiner's own "Interpretive Essay," which focuses primarily on Arendt's notion of "judgment," is a model of clarity.

100. Judith Shklar, "A Life of Learning" (1989), in Bernard Yack, ed., *Liberalism Without Illusions: Essays on Liberal Theory and the Political Vision of Judith N. Shklar* (Chicago: University of Chicago Press, 1996), pp. 263–79, at p. 271.

101. *The Life of the Mind Volume I: Thinking,* pp. 212–13.

PRINCIPAL DATES

1941–1945	Columnist for the New York émigré paper *Aufbau;* also writes a series of articles on Zionism, statelessness, racism, and imperialism for political periodicals
1944–1946	Pursues research on behalf of the Commission on European Jewish Cultural Reconstruction
1945	In the autumn, Arendt and Karl Jaspers reestablish contact by letter, renewing a correspondence that had been interrupted by the war
1946–1948	Works as an editor of Schocken Books, New York
1948	Death of her mother
	Editor of Bernard Lazare, *Job's Dungheap: Essays on Jewish Nationalism and Social Revolution*
	Publication of *Sechs Essays*
1948–1950	In a series of articles, Arendt argues for the establishment of a federal Palestine, with Jews and Arabs as equal parties
1949–1952	Executive director of Jewish Cultural Reconstruction
1949	Begins a correspondence, and a friendship, with Mary McCarthy (they had first met in 1944)
1949–1950	Travels to Europe on behalf of Jewish Cultural Reconstruction; meets Karl and Gertrud Jaspers (December 1949); meets Heidegger (February 1950)
1951	Publication of *The Origins of Totalitarianism*
	Becomes an American citizen
1952	Begins work on *Totalitarian Elements of Marxism,* a sequel to *The Origins of Totalitarianism;* it was never completed but parts of the project appear in later essays and books
1953	Delivers a series of lectures at Princeton University on "Karl Marx and the Tradition of Political Thought"
1955	Visiting Professor at Berkeley, University of California
1956	Delivers, in the spring, the Walgreen Lectures at the University of Chicago on the *vita activa*
1958	Publication of *The Human Condition*
	Publication of *Rahel Varnhagen: The Life of a Jewess*
1959	Publication of "Reflections on Little Rock"
	Delivers lectures to Princeton University on the concept of revolution
	Receives the Lessing Prize of the Free City of Hamburg

1961	Publication of *Between Past and Future: Six Exercises in Political Thought*. (Revised edition, with two additional essays, 1968)
	Covers the Eichmann trial in Jerusalem
1963	*The New Yorker* publishes Arendt's report on Eichmann in a five-part article. A revised version is published in book form as *Eichmann in Jerusalem: A Report on the Banality of Evil*. Publication of *On Revolution*
1963–1967	Arendt teaches at the University of Chicago
1967–1975	Professor at the New School for Social Research, New York
1967	Awarded the Sigmund Freud Prize by the German Academy for Language and Literature
1968	Publication of *Men in Dark Times*
1969	Death of Karl Jaspers on 26 February. On 4 March, Arendt delivers the eulogy at the public memorial service for Jaspers at the University of Basel
	Awarded the Emerson-Thoreau Medal of the American Academy
1970	Death of Heinrich Blücher on 31 October
1972	Publication of *Crises of the Republic*
1973–1974	Delivers the Gifford Lectures in Aberdeen, Scotland
	Suffers a heart attack in May
1975	At an award ceremony in Copenhagen, Arendt receives the Danish government's Sonning Prize for Contributions to European Civilization
	Dies of a heart attack on 4 December; her funeral takes place on 8 December
1978	Posthumous publication of *The Life of the Mind* (two volumes), edited by Mary McCarthy

BIBLIOGRAPHICAL NOTES

A NOTE ON THE SELECTIONS AND
A BRIEF GUIDE TO FURTHER READING

Hannah Arendt was a rich and subtle thinker whose ideas are not easily pinned down between the covers of an anthology. Arendt engaged critically with the key intellectual traditions of the West. She conducted a dialogue with many writers and also one with herself, adapting and developing her ideas in the process. Above all, she struggled continually to understand the key events and transformations of her time so as to give them theoretical expression. Only her work read as a whole can make its versatility and interconnected character apparent. In contrast, an editor's choices must simplify, and thereby distort, the complexities of an oeuvre in the very process of making it accessible.

Other problems confront the editor of an Arendt anthology. A significant portion of her work is currently in the process of translation and subject to copyright restrictions: for instance, the correspondence with Martin Heidegger, Kurt Blumenfeld, and Heinrich Blücher. And, inevitably, I have had to skip much of value in Arendt's legacy as I wrestled with what selections to include. Arendt scholars will doubtless think of many grievous omissions. However, the point of an anthology is not to reduce the complexity of an author's work to a few extracts, or even to try and sum it up, but to give readers a palpable sense of what lies in store for those who wish to explore further. This is what *The Viking Portable Hannah Arendt* seeks to do.

Deletions from Arendt's texts are denoted by ellipses [. . .].

BOOKS BY ARENDT IN ENGLISH
PUBLISHED DURING HER LIFETIME

The Origins of Totalitarianism (New York: Harcourt Brace, 1966; 3rd edition [orig. 1951]).

Rahel Varnhagen: The Life of a Jewess (London: East-West Library, 1958). American edition, *Rahel Varnhagen: The Life of a Jewish Woman* (New York: Harcourt Brace, 1974). For a new edition, see *Rahel Varnhagen: The Life of a Jewess,* edited by Liliane Weissberg, translated by Richard and Clara Winston (Baltimore: Johns Hopkins University Press, 1997).

The Human Condition (Chicago: University of Chicago Press, 1958). A second edition, published in 1998, has an introduction by Margaret Canovan.

Between Past and Future: Eight Exercises in Political Thought (New York: Viking Press, 1968). Expanded edition of a book originally published in 1961.

Eichmann in Jerusalem: A Report on the Banality of Evil (New York: Viking Press, 1963). Revised and enlarged edition, 1965.

On Revolution (New York: Viking Press, 1965 [orig. 1963]).

Men in Dark Times (New York: Harcourt Brace, 1968).

On Violence (New York: Harcourt Brace, 1970).

Crises of the Republic (New York: Harcourt Brace, 1972).

A comprehensive chronological bibliography of works published by Hannah Arendt during her lifetime can be found in Elisabeth Young-Bruehl's biography, *Hannah Arendt: For Love of the World* (New Haven: Yale University Press, 1982), pp. 535–47.

POSTHUMOUSLY PUBLISHED BOOKS,
COLLECTIONS OF ESSAYS, AND
CORRESPONDENCE IN ENGLISH

The Life of the Mind, 2 Vols. (Thinking/Willing), Mary McCarthy, ed. (New York: Harcourt Brace, 1978).

The Jew as Pariah: Jewish Identity and Politics in the Modern Age, ed. and with an introduction by Ron H. Feldman (New York: Grove Press, 1978).

Lectures on Kant's Political Philosophy, Ronald Beiner, ed. (Chicago: University of Chicago Press, 1982).

Hannah Arendt/Karl Jaspers Correspondence 1926–1969, Lotte Kohler and Hans Saner, eds. (New York: Harcourt Brace, 1992). Translated by Robert and Rita Kimber.

Essays in Understanding 1930–1954, Jerome Kohn, ed. (New York: Harcourt Brace, 1994).

Between Friends: The Correspondence of Hannah Arendt and Mary McCarthy 1949–1975, edited with an introduction by Carol Brightman (New York: Harcourt Brace, 1995).

Love and Saint Augustine, edited and with an interpretive essay by Joanna Vecchiarelli Scott and Judith Chelius Stark; translated by E. B. Ashton (Chicago: University of Chicago Press, 1996 [orig. 1929]).

Also worth consulting is "Hannah Arendt on Hannah Arendt," Melvyn A. Hill, ed., *Hannah Arendt: The Recovery of the Public World* (New York: St. Martin's Press, 1979), pp. 301–39.

Hannah Arendt's correspondence with Martin Heidegger, Kurt Blumenfeld, and Heinrich Blücher is in the process of being translated and published by Harcourt Brace. Many more books will follow, among them *What is Politics?,* another volume of *Essays in Understanding,* and collected essays on Jewry and the state of Israel.

SELECTED SECONDARY LITERATURE

The secondary literature on Arendt has increased exponentially over the last decade, but two books in particular are outstanding: the biography by Elisabeth Young-Bruehl, *Hannah Arendt: For Love of the World* (New Haven: Yale University Press, 1982), and the analysis by Margaret Canovan, *Hannah Arendt: A Reinterpretation of Her Political Thought* (Cambridge: Cambridge University Press, 1992). Other general analyses of Arendt's political thought are Bhikhu Parekh, *Hannah Arendt and the Search for a New Political Philosophy* (London: Macmillan, 1981); George Kateb, *Hannah Arendt: Politics, Conscience, Evil* (Totowa, N.J.: Rowman and Allanheld, 1984); Maurizio Passerin D'Entrèves, *The Political Philosophy of Hannah Arendt* (London: Routledge, 1994); Michael G. Gottsegen, *The Political Thought of Hannah Arendt* (Albany: SUNY, 1994); and Seyla Benhabib, *The Reluctant Modernism of Hannah Arendt* (Thousand Oaks, Calif.: Sage, 1996).

Many texts exist on various aspects of Arendt's thought. On Zionism, the Jewish Question, and the state of Israel, see Dagmar Barnouw, *Visible Spaces: Hannah Arendt and the German-Jewish Question* (Baltimore: Johns Hopkins University Press, 1990), and Richard J. Bernstein, *Hannah Arendt and the Jewish Question.* On the relationship between feminism and Arendt, see the collection of essays in Bonnie Honig, ed., *Feminist Inter-*

pretations of Hannah Arendt (University Park: Pennsylvania State University Press, 1995), and the "Annotated Bibliography on Hannah Arendt and Feminism" by Patchen P. Markell in ibid., pp. 357–65. On "the social," see Hanna Fenichel Pitkin, *The Attack of the Blob: Hannah Arendt's Concept of the Social* (Chicago: Chicago University Press, 1998). On Arendt, Heidegger, and Jaspers, see Elżbieta Ettinger, *Hannah Arendt/Martin Heidegger* (New Haven: Yale University Press, 1995); Dana R. Villa, *Arendt and Heidegger: The Fate of the Political* (Princeton: Princeton University Press, 1996); Lewis P. Hinchman and Sandra K. Hinchman, "Existentialism Politicized: Arendt's Debt to Jaspers," in Lewis P. Hinchman and Sandra K. Hinchman, eds., *Hannah Arendt: Critical Essays* (Albany: SUNY, 1994), pp. 143–78. On Arendt's "faith," see J. W. Bernauer, S.J., ed., *Amor Mundi: Explorations in the Faith and Thought of Hannah Arendt* (Boston: Martinus Nijhoff, 1987). An interesting collection of essays dealing with many aspects of Arendt's thought can be found in Steven Aschheim, ed., *Hannah Arendt in Jerusalem* (Berkeley/Los Angeles: University of California Press, 2000).

A "Bibliography of Writings in English about Hannah Arendt" that extends up to 1995 has been compiled by Johann A. Klaassen and Angela Klaassen; it can be found in *Hannah Arendt: Twenty Years Later,* Larry May and Jerome Kohn, eds. (Cambridge, Mass.: MIT Press, 1996), pp. 347–72.

ACKNOWLEDGMENTS

Two people made this project possible: Michael Millman, of Penguin's New York office; and Lotte Kohler, executor of the Hannah Arendt Literary Trust. I am deeply grateful to both of them for their help and encouragement.

I also owe a major debt to those individuals who were kind enough to read and to comment extensively on the Introduction: Judith Adler, Bill Barker, Jeff Bursey, Margaret Canovan, Richard Matthews, Volker Meja, Stuart Pierson, Rick Johnstone, and Liliane Weissberg. My wife, Hedda Schuurman, in particular, has been an irreplaceable friend, offering insights and observations that only she can provide. My mother, Anne Baehr, is a continuing inspiration in all I do.

For over twenty years, I have benefitted from the guidance, support, and friendship of Brian Ranson, the esteemed former Head of Sociology at the Baptist University of Hong Kong. This project is dedicated to him.

PART I

OVERVIEW:
WHAT REMAINS?

"What Remains?
The Language Remains":
A Conversation with Günter Gaus

On October 28, 1964, the following conversation between Hannah Arendt and Günter Gaus, at the time a well-known journalist and later a high official in Willy Brandt's government, was broadcast on West German television. The interview was awarded the Adolf Grimme Prize and was published the following year under the title "Was bleibt? Es bleibt die Muttersprache" in Günter Gaus, Zur Person, Munich, 1965. This English translation is by Joan Stambaugh.

Gaus begins the conversation by saying that Arendt is the first woman to take part in the series of interviews he is conducting; then he immediately qualifies that statement by noting that she has a "very masculine occupation," namely, that of philosopher. This leads him to his first question: In spite of the recognition and respect she has received, does she perceive "her role in the circle of philosophers" as unusual or peculiar because she is a woman? Arendt replies:

I AM AFRAID I have to protest. I do not belong to the circle of philosophers. My profession, if one can even speak of it at all, is political theory. I neither feel like a philosopher, nor do I believe that I have been accepted in the circle of philosophers, as you so kindly suppose. But to speak of the other question that you raised in your opening remarks: you say that philosophy is generally thought to be a masculine occupation. It does not have to remain a masculine occupation! It is entirely possible that a woman will one day be a philosopher. . . .[1]

GAUS: I consider you to be a philosopher. . . .

ARENDT: Well, I can't help that, but in my opinion I am not. In my opinion I have said good-bye to philosophy once and for all. As you

From Essays in Understanding. *Headnote and endnotes by Jerome Kohn.*

know, I studied philosophy, but that does not mean that I stayed with it.

GAUS: I should like to hear from you more precisely what the difference is between political philosophy and your work as a professor of political theory.

ARENDT: The expression "political philosophy," which I avoid, is extremely burdened by tradition. When I talk about these things, academically or nonacademically, I always mention that there is a vital tension between philosophy and politics. That is, between man as a thinking being and man as an acting being, there is a tension that does not exist in natural philosophy, for example. Like everyone else, the philosopher can be objective with regard to nature, and when he says what he thinks about it he speaks in the name of all mankind. But he cannot be objective or neutral with regard to politics. Not since Plato!

GAUS: I understand what you mean.

ARENDT: There is a kind of enmity against all politics in most philosophers, with very few exceptions. Kant *is* an exception. This enmity is extremely important for the whole problem, because it is not a personal question. It lies in the nature of the subject itself.

GAUS: You want no part in this enmity against politics because you believe that it would interfere with your work?

ARENDT: "I want no part in this enmity," that's it exactly! I want to look at politics, so to speak, with eyes unclouded by philosophy.

GAUS: I understand. Now, let us turn to the question of woman's emancipation. Has this been a problem for you?

ARENDT: Yes, of course; there is always the problem as such. I have actually been rather old-fashioned. I always thought that there are certain occupations that are improper for women, that do not become them, if I may put it that way. It just doesn't look good when a woman gives orders. She should try not to get into such a situation if she wants to remain feminine. Whether I am right about this or not I do not know. I myself have always lived in accordance with this more or less unconsciously—or let us rather say, more or less consciously. The problem itself played no role for me personally. To put it very simply, I have always done what I liked to do.

GAUS: Your work—we will surely go into details later—is to a significant degree concerned with the knowledge of the conditions under which political action and behavior come about. Do you want to achieve extensive influence with these works, or do you believe that such influence is no longer possible in these times, or is it simply not important to you?

ARENDT: You know, that is not a simple question. If I am to speak very honestly I would have to say: When I am working, I am not interested in how my work might affect people.

GAUS: And when you are finished?

ARENDT: Then I am finished. What is important for me is to understand. For me, writing is a matter of seeking this understanding, part of the process of understanding. . . . Certain things get formulated. If I had a good enough memory to really retain everything that I think, I doubt very much that I would have written anything—I know my own laziness. What is important to me is the thought process itself. As long as I have succeeded in thinking something through, I am personally quite satisfied. If I then succeed in expressing my thought process adequately in writing, that satisfies me also.

You ask about the effects of my work on others. If I may wax ironical, that is a masculine question. Men always want to be terribly influential, but I see that as somewhat external. Do I imagine myself being influential? No. I want to understand. And if others understand—in the same sense that I have understood—that gives me a sense of satisfaction, like feeling at home.

GAUS: Do you write easily? Do you formulate ideas easily?

ARENDT: Sometimes I do; sometimes I don't. But in general I can tell you that I never write until I can, so to speak, take dictation from myself.

GAUS: Until you have already thought it out.

ARENDT: Yes. I know exactly what I want to write. I do not write until I do. Usually I write it all down only once. And that goes relatively quickly, since it really depends only on how fast I type.

GAUS: Your interest in political theory, in political action and behavior, is at the center of your work today. In this light, what I found in your correspondence with Professor Scholem[2] seems particularly interesting. There you wrote, if I may quote you, that you "were interested in [your] youth neither in politics nor in history." Miss Arendt, as a Jew you emigrated from Germany in 1933. You were then twenty-six years old. Is your interest in politics—the cessation of your indifference to politics and history—connected to these events?

ARENDT: Yes, of course. Indifference was no longer possible in 1933. It was no longer possible even before that.

GAUS: For you as well?

ARENDT: Yes, of course. I read the newspapers intently. I had opinions. I did not belong to a party, nor did I have need to. By 1931 I was firmly convinced that the Nazis would take the helm. I was always arguing with other people about it but I did not really concern myself systematically with these things until I emigrated.

GAUS: I have another question about what you just said. If you were convinced that the Nazis could not be stopped from taking power, didn't you feel impelled actively to do something to prevent this—for example, join a party—or did you no longer think that made sense?

ARENDT: I personally did not think it made sense. If I had thought so—it is very difficult to say all this in retrospect—perhaps I would have done something. I thought it was hopeless.

GAUS: Is there a definite event in your memory that dates your turn to the political?

ARENDT: I would say February 27, 1933, the burning of the Reichstag, and the illegal arrests that followed during the same night. The socalled protective custody. As you know, people were taken to Gestapo cellars or to concentration camps. What happened then was monstrous, but it has now been overshadowed by things that happened later. This was an immediate shock for me, and from that moment on I felt responsible. That is, I was no longer of the opinion that one can simply be a bystander. I tried to help in many ways. But what actually took me out of Germany—if I should speak of that; I've never told it because it is of no consequence—

GAUS: Please tell us.

ARENDT: I intended to emigrate anyhow. I thought immediately that Jews could not stay. I did not intend to run around Germany as a secondclass citizen, so to speak, in whatever form. In addition, I thought that things would just get worse and worse. Nevertheless, in the end I did not leave in such a peaceful way. And I must say that gives me a certain satisfaction. I was arrested, and had to leave the country illegally—I will tell you how in a minute—and that was instant gratification for me. I thought at least I had done something! At least I am not "innocent." No one could say that of me!

The Zionist organization gave me the chance. I was close friends with some of the leading people, above all with the then president, Kurt Blumenfeld. But I was not a Zionist. Nor did the Zionists try to convert me. Yet in a certain sense I was influenced by them: especially by the criticism, the self-criticism that the Zionists spread among the Jewish people. I was influenced and impressed by it, but politically I had nothing to do with Zionism. Now, in 1933 Blumenfeld and someone whom you do not know approached me and said: We want to put together a collection of all anti-Semitic statements made in ordinary circumstances. For example, statements in clubs, all kinds of professional clubs, all kinds of professional journals—in short, the sort of thing that doesn't become known in foreign countries. To organize such a collection at that time was to engage in what the Nazis called "horror propaganda." No Zionist could do this, because if he were found out, the whole organization would be exposed. . . . They asked me, "Will you do it?" I said, "Of course." I was very happy. First of all, it seemed a very intelligent idea to me, and second, it gave me the feeling that something could be done after all.

GAUS: Were you arrested in connection with this work?

ARENDT: Yes. I was found out. I was very lucky. I got out after eight days because I made friends with the official who arrested me. He was a charming fellow! He'd been promoted from the criminal police to a political division. He had no idea what to do. What was he supposed to do? He kept saying to me, "Ordinarily I have someone there in front of me, and I just check the file, and I know what's going on. But what shall I do with you?"

GAUS: That was in Berlin?

ARENDT: That was in Berlin. Unfortunately, I had to lie to him. I couldn't let the organization be exposed. I told him tall tales, and he kept saying, "I got you in here. I shall get you out again. Don't get a lawyer! Jews don't have any money now. Save your money!" Meanwhile the organization had gotten me a lawyer. Through members, of course. And I sent this lawyer away. Because this man who arrested me had such an open, decent face. I relied on him and thought that here was a much better chance than with some lawyer who himself was afraid.

GAUS: And you got out and could leave Germany?

ARENDT: I got out, but had to cross the border illegally . . . my name had not been cleared.

GAUS: In the correspondence we mentioned, Miss Arendt, you clearly rejected as superfluous Scholem's warning that you should always be mindful of your solidarity with the Jewish people. You wrote—I quote again: "To be a Jew belongs for me to the indubitable facts of my life, and I never wanted to change anything about such facts, not even in my childhood." I'd like to ask a few questions about this. You were born in 1906 in Hannover as the daughter of an engineer, and grew up in Königsberg. Do you remember what it was like for a child in prewar Germany to come from a Jewish family?

ARENDT: I couldn't answer that question truthfully for everyone. As for my personal recollection, I did not know from my family that I was Jewish. My mother was completely a-religious.

GAUS: Your father died young.

ARENDT: My father had died young. It all sounds very odd. My grandfather was the president of the liberal Jewish community and a civil official of Königsberg. I come from an old Königsberg family. Nevertheless, the word "Jew" never came up when I was a small child. I first met up with it through anti-Semitic remarks—they are not worth repeating—from children on the street. After that I was, so to speak, "enlightened."

GAUS: Was that a shock for you?

ARENDT: No.

GAUS: Did you have the feeling, now I am something special?

ARENDT: That is a different matter. It wasn't a shock for me at all. I thought to myself: That is how it is. Did I have the feeling that I was something special? Yes! But I could no longer unravel that for you today.

GAUS: In what way did you feel special?

ARENDT: Objectively, I am of the opinion that it was related to being Jewish. For example, as a child—a somewhat older child then—I knew that I looked Jewish. I looked different from other children. I was very conscious of that. But not in a way that made me feel inferior, that was just how it was. Then too, my mother, my family home, so to speak, was a bit different from the usual. There was so much that was special about it, even in comparison with the homes of other Jewish children or even of other children who were related to us, that it was hard for a child to figure out just what was special.

GAUS: I would like some elucidation as to what was special about your family home. You said that your mother never deemed it necessary to explain your solidarity with Jewishness to you until you met up with it on the street. Had your mother lost the sense of being Jewish which you claim for yourself in your letter to Scholem? Didn't it play a role for her any more at all? Was she successfully assimilated, or did she at least believe so?

ARENDT: My mother was not a very theoretical person. I do not believe that she had any special ideas about this. She herself came out of the Social Democratic movement, out of the circle of the *Sozialistische Monatshefte,*[3] as did my father. The question did not play a role for her. Of course she was a Jew. She would never have baptized me! I think she would have boxed my ears right and left if she had ever found out that I had denied being a Jew. It was unthinkable, so to speak. Out of the question! But the question was naturally much more important in the twenties, when I was young, than it was for my mother. And when I was grown up it was much more important for my mother than in her earlier life. But that was due to external circumstances.

I myself, for example, don't believe that I have ever considered myself a German—in the sense of belonging to the people as opposed to being a citizen, if I may make that distinction. I remember discussing this with Jaspers around 1930. He said, "Of course you are German!" I said, "One can see that I am not!" But that didn't bother me. I didn't feel that it was something inferior. That wasn't the case at all. And to come back once again to what was special about my family home: all Jewish children encountered anti-Semitism. And it poisoned the souls of many children. The difference with us was that my mother was always convinced that you mustn't let it get to you. You have to defend yourself! When my teachers made anti-Semitic remarks—mostly not about me, but about other Jewish girls, eastern Jewish students in particular—I was told to get up immediately, leave the classroom, come home, and report everything exactly. Then my mother wrote one of her many registered letters; and for me the matter was completely settled. I had a day off from school, and that was marvelous! But when it came from children, I was not permitted to tell about it at home. That didn't count. You defended yourself against what came from children. Thus these matters never were a problem for me. There were rules of conduct by which I retained my dignity, so to speak, and I was protected, absolutely protected, at home.

GAUS: You studied in Marburg, Heidelberg, and Freiberg with professors Heidegger, Bultmann, and Jaspers; with a major in philosophy and minors in theology and Greek. How did you come to choose these subjects?

ARENDT: You know, I have often thought about that. I can only say that I always knew I would study philosophy. Ever since I was fourteen years old.

GAUS: Why?

ARENDT: I read Kant. You can ask, Why did you read Kant? For me the question was somehow: I can either study philosophy or I can drown myself, so to speak. But not because I didn't love life! No! As I said before—I had this need to understand. . . . The need to understand was there very early. You see, all the books were in the library at home; one simply took them from the shelves.

GAUS: Besides Kant, do you remember special experiences in reading?

ARENDT: Yes. First of all, Jaspers's *Psychologie der Weltanschauungen* [Psychology of World Views], published, I believe, in 1920.[4] I was fourteen. Then I read Kierkegaard, and that fit together.

GAUS: Is this where theology came in?

ARENDT: Yes. They fit together in such a way that for me they both belonged together. I had some misgivings only as to how one deals with this if one is Jewish . . . how one proceeds. I had no idea, you know. I had difficult problems that were then resolved by themselves. Greek is another matter. I have always loved Greek poetry. And poetry has played a large role in my life. So I chose Greek in addition. It was the easiest thing to do, since I read it anyway!

GAUS: I am impressed!

ARENDT: No, you exaggerate.

GAUS: Your intellectual gifts were tested so early, Miss Arendt. Did it sometimes separate you as a schoolgirl and as a young student from the usual day-to-day relationships, painfully perhaps?

ARENDT: That would have been the case had I known about it. I thought everybody was like that.

GAUS: When did you realize you were wrong?

ARENDT: Rather late. I don't want to say how late. I am embarrassed. I was indescribably naive. That was partly due to my upbringing at home. Grades were never discussed. That was taken to be inferior. Any ambition was taken to be inferior. In any case, the situation wasn't at all clear to me. I experienced it sometimes as a sort of strangeness among people.

GAUS: A strangeness which you believed came from you?

ARENDT: Yes, exclusively. But that has nothing to do with talent. I never connected it with talent.

GAUS: Was the result sometimes disdain for others in your youth?

ARENDT: Yes, that happened. Very early. And I have often suffered because I felt such disdain, that is, knowing one really shouldn't and one really must not, and so forth.

GAUS: When you left Germany in 1933, you went to Paris, where you worked in an organization that tried to provide for Jewish youngsters in Palestine. Can you tell me something about that?

ARENDT: This organization brought Jewish youngsters between thirteen and seventeen from Germany to Palestine and housed them there in kibbutzim. For this reason, I really know these settlements pretty well.

GAUS: And from a very early period.

ARENDT: From a very early period; at that time I had a lot of respect for them. The children received vocational training and retraining. Sometimes I also smuggled in Polish children. It was regular social work, educational work. There were large camps in the country where the children were prepared for Palestine, where they also had lessons, where they learned farming, where they above all had to gain weight. We had to clothe them from head to foot. We had to cook for them. Above all, we had to get papers for them, we had to deal with the parents—and before everything else we had to get money for them. That was also largely my job. I worked together with French women. That is more or less what we did. Do you want to hear how I decided to take on this work?

GAUS: Please.

ARENDT: You see, I came out of a purely academic background. In this respect the year 1933 made a very lasting impression on me. First a positive one and then a negative one. Perhaps I had better say first a negative one and then a positive one. People often think today that German Jews were shocked in 1933 because Hitler assumed power. As far as I and people of my generation are concerned, I can say that that is a curious misunderstanding. Naturally Hitler's rise was very bad. But it was political. It wasn't personal. We didn't need Hitler's assumption of power to know that the Nazis were our enemies! That had been completely evident for at least four years to everyone who wasn't feebleminded. We also knew that a large number of the German people were behind them. That could not shock us or surprise us in 1933.

GAUS: You mean that the shock in 1933 came from the fact that events went from the generally political to the personal?

ARENDT: Not even that. Or, that too. First of all, the generally political became a personal fate when one emigrated. Second . . . friends "co-ordinated" or got in line. The problem, the personal problem, was not what our enemies did but what our friends did. In the wave of *Gleichschaltung* (co-ordination),[5] which was relatively voluntary—in any case, not yet under the pressure of terror—it was as if an empty space formed around one. I lived in an intellectual milieu, but I also knew other people. And among intellectuals *Gleichschaltung* was the rule, so to speak. But not among the others. And I never forgot that. I left Germany dominated by the idea—of course somewhat exaggerated: Never again! I shall never again get involved in any kind of intellectual business. I want nothing to do with that lot. Also I didn't believe then that Jews and German Jewish intellectuals would have acted any differently had their own circumstances been different. That was not my opinion. I thought that it had to do with this profession, with being an intellectual. I am speaking in the past tense. Today I know more about it. . . .

GAUS: I was just about to ask you if you still believe that.

ARENDT: No longer to the same degree. But I still think that it belongs to the essence of being an intellectual that one fabricates ideas about everything. No one ever blamed someone if he "co-ordinated" because he had to take care of his wife or child. The worst thing was that some people really believed in Nazism! For a short time, many for a very short time. But that means that they made up ideas about Hitler, in part terrifically interesting things! Completely fantastic and interesting and complicated things! Things far above the ordinary level! I found that grotesque. Today I would say that they were trapped by their own ideas. That is what happened. But then, at that time, I didn't see it so clearly.

GAUS: And that was the reason that it was particularly important for you to get out of intellectual circles and start to do work of a practical nature?

ARENDT: Yes. The positive side is the following. I realized what I then expressed time and again in the sentence: If one is attacked as a Jew, one must defend oneself as a Jew. Not as a German, not as a world-citizen, not as an upholder of the Rights of Man, or whatever. But: What can I specifically do as a Jew? Second, it was now my clear intention to work with an organization. For the first time. To work with the Zionists. They were the only ones who were ready. It would have been pointless to join those who had assimilated. Besides, I never really had anything to do with them. Even before this time I had concerned myself with the Jewish question. The book on Rahel Varnhagen was finished when I left Germany.[6] The problem of the Jews plays a role in it. I wrote it with the idea, "I want to understand." I wasn't discussing my personal problems as a Jew. But now, belonging to Judaism had become my own problem, and my own problem was political. Purely political! I wanted to go into practical work, exclusively and only Jewish work. With this in mind I then looked for work in France.

GAUS: Until 1940.

ARENDT: Yes.

GAUS: Then during the Second World War you went to the United States of America, where you are now a professor of political theory, not philosophy . . .

ARENDT: Thank you.

GAUS: . . . in Chicago. You live in New York. Your husband, whom you married in 1940, is also a professor, of philosophy, in America. The academic community, of which you are again a member—after the disillusionment of 1933—is international. Yet I should like to ask you whether you miss the Europe of the pre-Hitler period, which will never exist again. When you come to Europe, what, in your impression, remains and what is irretrievably lost?

ARENDT: The Europe of the pre-Hitler period? I do not long for that, I can tell you. What remains? The language remains.

GAUS: And that means a great deal to you?

ARENDT: A great deal. I have always consciously refused to lose my mother tongue. I have always maintained a certain distance from French, which I then spoke very well, as well as from English, which I write today.

GAUS: I wanted to ask you that. You write in English now?

ARENDT: I write in English, but I have never lost a feeling of distance from it. There is a tremendous difference between your mother tongue and another language. For myself I can put it extremely simply: In German I know a rather large part of German poetry by heart; the poems are always somehow in the back of my mind. I can never do that again. I do things in German that I would not permit myself to do in English. That is, sometimes I do them in English too, because I have become bold, but in general I have maintained a certain distance. The German language is the essential thing that has remained and that I have always consciously preserved.

GAUS: Even in the most bitter time?

ARENDT: Always. I thought to myself, What is one to do? It wasn't the German language that went crazy. And, second, there is no substitution for the mother tongue. People can forget their mother tongue. That's true—I have seen it. There are people who speak the new language better than I do. I still speak with a very heavy accent, and I often speak unidiomatically. They can all do these things correctly. But they do them in a language in which one cliché chases another because the productivity that one has in one's own language is cut off when one forgets that language.

GAUS: The cases in which the mother tongue was forgotten: Is it your impression that this was the result of repression?

ARENDT: Yes, very frequently. I have seen it in people as a result of shock. You know, what was decisive was not the year 1933, at least not for me. What was decisive was the day we learned about Auschwitz.

GAUS: When was that?

ARENDT: That was in 1943. And at first we didn't believe it—although my husband and I always said that we expected anything from that bunch. But we didn't believe this because militarily it was unnecessary and uncalled for. My husband is a former military historian, he understands something about these matters. He said don't be gullible, don't take these stories at face value. They can't go that far! And then a half-year later we believed it after all, because we had the proof. That was the real shock. Before that we said: Well, one has enemies. That is entirely natural. Why shouldn't a people have enemies? But this was different. It was really as if an abyss had opened. Because we had the idea that amends could somehow be made for everything else, as amends can be made for just about everything at some point in politics. But not for this. *This ought not to have happened.* And I don't mean just the number of victims. I mean the method, the fabrication of corpses and so on—I don't need to go into that. This should not have happened. Something happened there to which we cannot reconcile ourselves. None of us ever can. About everything else that happened I have to say that it was sometimes rather difficult: we were very poor, we were hunted down, we had to flee, by hook or by crook we somehow had to get through, and whatever. That's how it was. But we were young. I even had a little fun with it—I can't deny it. But not this. This was something completely different. Personally I could accept everything else.

GAUS: I should like to hear from you, Miss Arendt, how your opinions about postwar Germany, which you have often visited, and in which your most important works have been published, have changed since 1945.

ARENDT: I returned to Germany for the first time in 1949, in the service of a Jewish organization for the recovery of Jewish cultural treasures, mostly books. I came with very good will. My thoughts after 1945 were as follows: Whatever happened in 1933 is really unimportant in light of what happened after that. Certainly, the disloyalty of friends, to put it bluntly for once . . .

GAUS: . . . which you experienced personally . . .

ARENDT: Of course. But if someone really became a Nazi and wrote articles about it, he did not have to be loyal to me personally. I did not speak to him again anyhow. He didn't have to get in touch with me anymore, because as far as I was concerned he had ceased to exist. That much is clear. But they were not all murderers. There were people who fell into their own trap, as I would say today. Nor did they desire what came later. Thus it seemed to me that there should be a basis for communication precisely in the abyss of Auschwitz. And that was true in many personal relations. I argued with people; I am not particularly agreeable, nor am I very polite; I say what I think. But somehow things were set straight again with a lot of people. As I said, all these were only people who were committed to Nazism for a few months, at the worst for a few years; neither murderers nor informers. People, as I said, who "made up ideas" about Hitler. But the general, and the greatest experience when one returns to Germany—apart from the experience of recognition, which is always the crux of the action in Greek tragedy—is one of violent emotion. And then there was the experience of hearing German spoken in the streets. For me that was an indescribable joy.

GAUS: This was your reaction when you came in 1949?

ARENDT: More or less. And today, now that things are back on track, the distance I feel has become greater than it was before, when I experienced things in that highly emotional state.

GAUS: Because conditions here got back on track too quickly in your opinion?

ARENDT: Yes. And often on a track to which I do not assent. But I don't feel responsible for that. I see it from the outside now. And that means that I am far less involved than I was at that time. That could be because of the lapse of time. Listen, fifteen years are not nothing!

GAUS: You have become much more indifferent?

ARENDT: Distant . . . indifferent is too strong. But thère is distance.

GAUS: Miss Arendt, your book on the trial of Eichmann in Jerusalem was published this fall in the Federal Republic. Since its publication in America, your book has been very heatedly discussed. From the Jewish side, especially, objections have been raised which you say are partly based on misunderstandings and partly on an intentional political campaign. Above all, people were offended by the question you raised of the extent to which Jews are to blame for their passive acceptance of the German mass murders, or to what extent the collaboration of certain Jewish councils almost constitutes a kind of guilt of their own. In any case, for a portrait of Hannah Arendt, so to speak, a number of questions come out of this book. If I may begin with them: Is the criticism that your book is lacking in love for the Jewish people painful to you?

ARENDT: First of all, I must, in all friendliness, state that you yourself have become a victim of this campaign. Nowhere in my book did I reproach the Jewish people with nonresistance. Someone else did that in the Eichmann trial, namely, Mr. Haussner of the Israeli public prosecutor's office. I called such questions directed to the witnesses in Jerusalem both foolish and cruel.

GAUS: I have read the book. I know that. But some of the criticisms made of you are based on the tone in which many passages are written.

ARENDT: Well, that is another matter. What can I say? Besides, I don't want to say anything. If people think that one can only write about these things in a solemn tone of voice . . . Look, there are people who take it amiss—and I can understand that in a sense—that, for instance, I can still laugh. But I was really of the opinion that Eichmann was a buffoon. I'll tell you this: I read the transcript of his police investigation, thirty-six hundred pages, read it, and read it very carefully, and I do not know how many times I laughed—laughed out loud! People took this reaction in a bad way. I cannot do anything about that. But I know one thing: Three minutes before certain death, I probably still would laugh. And that, they say, is the tone of voice. That the tone of voice is predominantly ironic is completely true. The tone of voice in this case is really the person. When people reproach me with accusing the Jewish people, that is a malignant lie and propaganda and nothing else. The tone of voice, however, is an objection against me personally. And I cannot do anything about that.

GAUS: You are prepared to bear that?

ARENDT: Yes, willingly. What is one to do? I cannot say to people: You misunderstand me, and in truth this or that is going on in my heart. That's ridiculous.

GAUS: In this connection I should like to go back to a personal statement of yours. You said: "I have never in my life 'loved' any people or collective group, neither the German people, the French, the Americans, nor the working class or anything of that sort. I indeed love only my friends, and the only kind of love I know of and believe in is the love of persons. Moreover, this 'love of the Jews' would appear to me, since I am myself Jewish, as something rather suspect."[7] May I ask something? As a politically active being, doesn't man need commitment to a group, a commitment that can then to a certain extent be called love? Are you not afraid that your attitude could be politically sterile?

ARENDT: No. I would say it is the other attitude that is politically sterile. In the first place, belonging to a group is a natural condition. You belong to some sort of group when you are born, always. But to belong to a group in the way you mean, in a second sense, that is, to join or form an organized group, is something completely different. This kind of organization has to do with a relation to the world. People who become organized have in common what are ordinarily called interests. The directly personal relationship, where one can speak of love, exists of course foremost in real love, and it also exists in a certain sense in friendship. There a person is addressed directly, independent of his relation to the world. Thus, people of the most divergent organizations can still be personal friends. But if you confuse these things, if you bring love to the negotiating table, to put it bluntly, I find that fatal.

GAUS: You find it apolitical?

ARENDT: I find it apolitical. I find it worldless. And I really find it to be a great disaster. I admit that the Jewish people are a classic example of a worldless people maintaining themselves throughout thousands of years . . .

GAUS: "World" in the sense of your terminology as space for politics.

ARENDT: As space for politics.

GAUS: Thus the Jewish people were an apolitical people?

ARENDT: I shouldn't say that exactly, for the communities were, of course, to a certain extent, also political. The Jewish religion is a national religion. But the concept of the political was valid only with great reservations. This worldlessness which the Jewish people suffered in being dispersed, and which—as with all people who are pariahs—generated a special warmth among those who belonged, changed when the state of Israel was founded.

GAUS: Did something get lost, then, something the loss of which you regret?

ARENDT: Yes, one pays dearly for freedom. The specifically Jewish humanity signified by their worldlessness was something very beautiful. You are too young to have ever experienced that. But it was something very beautiful, this standing outside of all social connections, the complete open-mindedness and absence of prejudice that I experienced, especially with my mother, who also exercised it in relation to the whole Jewish community. Of course, a great deal was lost with the passing of all that. One pays for liberation. I once said in my Lessing speech . . .

GAUS: Hamburg in 1959 . . .[8]

ARENDT: Yes, there I said that "this humanity . . . has never yet survived the hour of liberation, of freedom, by so much as a minute." You see, that has also happened to us.

GAUS: You wouldn't like to undo it?

ARENDT: No. I know that one has to pay a price for freedom. But I cannot say that I like to pay it.

GAUS: Miss Arendt, do you feel that it is your duty to publish what you learn through political-philosophical speculation or sociological analysis? Or are there reasons to be silent about something you know?

ARENDT: Yes, that is a very difficult problem. It is at bottom the sole question that interested me in the whole controversy over the Eichmann book. But it is a question that never arose unless I broached it. It is the only serious question—everything else is pure propaganda soup. So, *fiat veritas, et pereat mundus* [let truth be told though the world may perish]?[9] But the Eichmann book did not *de facto* touch upon such things. The book really does not jeopardize anybody's legitimate interests. It was only thought to do so.

GAUS: You must leave the question of what is legitimate open to discussion.

ARENDT: Yes, that is true. You are right. The question of what is legitimate is still open to discussion. I probably mean by "legitimate" something different from what the Jewish organizations mean. But let us assume that real interests, which even I recognize, were at stake.

GAUS: Might one then be silent about the truth?

ARENDT: Might I have been? Yes! To be sure, I might have written it. . . . But look here, someone asked me, if I had anticipated one thing or another, wouldn't I have written the Eichmann book differently? I answered: No. I would have confronted the alternative: to write or not to write. Because one can also hold one's tongue.

GAUS: Yes.

ARENDT: One doesn't always have to speak. But now we come to the question of what, in the eighteenth century, were called "truths of fact." This is really a matter of truths of fact. It is not a matter of opinions. The historical sciences in the universities are the guardians of truths of fact.

GAUS: They have not always been the best ones.

ARENDT: No. They collapse. They are controlled by the state. I have been told that a historian remarked of some book about the origin of the First World War: "I won't let this spoil the memory of such an uplifting time!" That is a man who does not know who he is. But that is uninteresting. *De facto* he is the guardian of historical truth, the truth of facts. And we know how important these guardians are from Bolshevik history, for example, where history is rewritten every five years and the facts remain unknown: for instance, that there was a Mr. Trotsky. Is this what we want? Is that what governments are interested in?

GAUS: They might have that interest. But do they have that right?

ARENDT: Do they have that right? They do not appear to believe it themselves—otherwise they would not tolerate universities at all. Thus, even states are interested in the truth. I don't mean military secrets; that's something else. But these events go back approximately twenty years. Why shouldn't one speak the truth?

GAUS: Perhaps because twenty years are still too little?

ARENDT: Many people say that; others say that after twenty years one can no longer figure out the truth. In any case, there is an interest in whitewashing. That, however, is not a legitimate interest.

GAUS: In case of doubt, you would prefer the truth.

ARENDT: I would rather say that impartiality—which came into the world when Homer . . .

GAUS: For the conquered as well . . .

ARENDT: Right!

> *Wenn des Liedes Stimmen schweigen*
> *Von dem überwundnen Mann,*
> *So will ich für Hectorn zeugen. . . .*
> *[If the voices of song are silent*
> *For him who has been vanquished,*
> *I myself will testify for Hector. . . .]*[10]

Isn't that right? That's what Homer did. Then came Herodotus, who spoke of "the great deeds of the Greeks *and* the barbarians." All of science comes from this spirit, even modern science, and the science of history too. If someone is not capable of this impartiality because he pretends to love his people so much that he pays flattering homage to them all the time—well, then there's nothing to be done. I do not believe that people like that are patriots.

GAUS: In one of your most important works, *The Human Condition,* you come to the conclusion, Miss Arendt, that the modern period has dethroned the sense of what concerns everyone, that is, the sense of the prime importance of the political. You designate as modern social phenomena the uprooting and loneliness of the masses and the triumph of a type of human being who finds satisfaction in the process of mere labor and consumption. I have two questions about this. First, to what extent is this kind of philosophical knowledge dependent upon a personal experience which first gets the process of thinking going?

ARENDT: I do not believe that there is any thought process possible without personal experience. Every thought is an afterthought, that is, a reflection on some matter or event. Isn't that so? I live in the modern world, and obviously my experience is in and of the modern world. This, after all, is not controversial. But the matter of merely laboring and consuming is of crucial importance for the reason that a kind of worldlessness defines itself there too. Nobody cares any longer what the world looks like.

GAUS: "World" understood always as the space in which politics can originate.

ARENDT: I comprehend it now in a much larger sense, as the space in which things become public, as the space in which one lives and which must look presentable. In which art appears, of course. In which all kinds of things appear. You remember that Kennedy tried to expand the public space quite decisively by inviting poets and other ne'er-do-wells to the White House. So that it all could belong to this space. However, in labor and consumption man is utterly thrown back on himself.

GAUS: On the biological.

ARENDT: On the biological, and on himself. And there you have the connection with loneliness. A peculiar loneliness arises in the process of labor. I cannot go into that right now, because it would lead us too far afield. But this loneliness consists in being thrown back upon oneself a state of affairs in which, so to speak, consumption takes the place of all the truly relating activities.

GAUS: A second question in this connection: in *The Human Condition* you come to the conclusion that "truly world oriented experiences"— you mean insights and experiences of the highest political significance— "withdraw more and more from the experiential horizon of the average human life." You say that today "the ability to act is restricted to a few people." What does this mean in terms of practical politics, Miss Arendt? To what extent does a form of government based at least theoretically, on the co-operative responsibility of all citizens become a fiction under these circumstances?

ARENDT: I want to qualify that a bit. Look, this inability to be realistically oriented applies not only to the masses, but also to every other stratum of society. I would say even to the statesman. The statesman is surrounded, encircled by an army of experts. So that now the question of action lies between the statesman and the experts. The statesman has to make the final decision. He can hardly do that realistically, since he can't know everything himself. He must take the advice of experts, indeed of experts who in principle always have to contradict each other. Isn't that so? Every reasonable statesman summons experts with opposing points of view. Because he has to see the matter from all sides. That's true, isn't it? He has to judge between them. And this judging is a highly mysterious process—in which, then, common sense[11] is made manifest. As far as the masses are concerned, I would say the following: Wherever men come together, in whatever numbers, public interests come into play.

GAUS: Always.

ARENDT: And the public realm is formed. In America where there are still spontaneous associations, which then disband again—the kind of associations already described by Tocqueville—you can see this very clearly. Some public interest concerns a specific group of people, those in a neighborhood or even in just one house or in a city or in some other sort of group. Then these people will convene, and they are very capable of acting publicly in these matters—for they have an overview of them. What you were aiming at with your question applies only to the greatest decisions on the highest level. And, believe me, the difference between the statesman and the man in the street is in principle not very great.

GAUS: Miss Arendt, you have been in close contact with Karl Jaspers, your former teacher, in an ongoing dialogue. What do you think is the greatest influence that Professor Jaspers has had on you?

ARENDT: Well, where Jaspers comes forward and speaks, all becomes luminous. He has an unreservedness, a trust, an unconditionality of speech that I have never known in anyone else. This impressed me even when I was very young. Besides, he has a conception of freedom linked to reason which was completely foreign to me when I came to Heidelberg. I knew nothing about it, although I had read Kant. I saw this reason in action, so to speak. And if I may say so—I grew up without a father—I was educated by it. I don't want to make him responsible for me, for God's sake, but if anyone succeeded in instilling some sense in me, it was he. And this dialogue is, of course, quite different today. That was really my most powerful postwar experience. That there can be such conversations! That one can speak in such a way!

GAUS: Permit me a last question. In a tribute to Jaspers you said: "Humanity is never acquired in solitude, and never by giving one's work to the public. It can be achieved only by one who has thrown his life and his person into the 'venture into the public realm.' "[12] This "venture into the public realm"—which is a quotation from Jaspers—what does it mean for Hannah Arendt?

ARENDT: The venture into the public realm seems clear to me. One exposes oneself to the light of the public, as a person. Although I am of the opinion that one must not appear and act in public self-consciously, still I know that in every action the person is expressed as in no other human activity. Speaking is also a form of action. That is one venture. The other is: we start something. We weave our strand into a network of relations. What comes of it we never know. We've all been taught to say: Lord forgive them, for they know not what they do. That is true of all action. Quite simply and concretely true, because one *cannot* know. That is what is meant by a venture. And now I would say that this venture is only possible when there is trust in people. A trust—which is difficult to formulate but fundamental—in what is human in all people. Otherwise such a venture could not be made.

Notes

1. The ellipses here and elsewhere are in the original; they do not indicate omission of material.
2. Gershom Scholem (1897–1982), German-born Zionist, historian, and emi-

nent scholar of Jewish mysticism, was an old acquaintance of Hannah Arendt's. On June 23, 1963, he wrote a highly critical letter to her about her book *Eichmann in Jerusalem;* see "*Eichmann in Jerusalem:* An Exchange of Letters," *Encounter* 22, 1964. The quotation given here is from Arendt's reply, dated July 24, 1963.

3. *Sozialistische Monatshefte* (Socialist Monthly) was a well-known German journal of the time.

4. Karl Jaspers, *Psychologie der Weltanschauungen,* was first published in Berlin in 1919.

5. *Gleichschaltung,* or political co-ordination, refers to the widespread giving in, at the outset of the Nazi era, to the changed political climate in order either to secure one's position or to get employment. In addition, it describes the Nazi policy of converting traditional organizations—youth groups and all sorts of clubs and associations—into specifically Nazi organizations.

6. Except for the last two chapters, which were written sometime between 1933 and 1936 in France. Cf. *Rahel Varnhagen: The Life of a Jewish Woman,* rev. ed., New York: Harcourt Brace Jovanovich, 1974, xiii.

7. Arendt to Scholem, July 24, 1963.

8. Arendt's address on accepting the Lessing Prize of the Free City of Hamburg is reprinted as "On Humanity in Dark Times: Thoughts about Lessing," in *Men in Dark Times,* New York: Harcourt, Brace & World, 1968.

9. Arendt plays with the old Latin adage *Fiat iustitia, et periat mundus* (Let justice be done, though the world may perish). Cf. *Between Past and Future,* New York: The Viking Press, 1968, 228.

10. From Schiller's *Das Siegesfest.*

11. By common sense (*Gemeinsinn*), Arendt does not mean the unreflective prudence that every sane adult exercises continuously (*gesunder Menschenverstand*), but, rather as Kant put it, "a sense *common to all* . . . a faculty of judgment which, in its reflection, takes account . . . of the mode of representation of all other men," Immanuel Kant, *Critique of Judgment,* §40, cited in Arendt's *Lectures on Kant's Political Philosophy,* edited by R. Beiner, Chicago, 1982, 70–72.

12. "Karl Jaspers: A Laudatio," in *Men in Dark Times,* 73–74.

PART II

STATELESS PERSONS

That "Infinitely Complex
Red-tape Existence":
From a Letter to Karl Jaspers

January 29, 1946 (New York)

Dear Karl Jaspers—

Thank you so much for your warm letter. You speak of trust. Do you remember our last talks together in Berlin, in 1933? I did not find some of your arguments convincing, but on a human and personal level you were so utterly convincing that for many years I was, so to speak, more sure of you than I was of myself. I didn't write after that because I was afraid of endangering you. The Luxembourg trip didn't fall through just because of my bungling. How could I explain to you on the telephone or even in the context of a letter the infinitely complex red-tape existence of stateless persons? . . .

. . . I think about your study, which has always been that "bright room" for me—with the chair at the desk and the armchair across from it where you tied your legs in marvelous knots and then untied them again. I can well imagine how your own apartment strikes you as ghostly, but I'm very glad it is still there, and I hope someday to sit once again on that aforementioned chair.

If I were sitting on that chair, I would probably tell you more than I can here. My husband's name is Heinrich Blücher—written description impossible. During the war his knowledge of military history and affairs enabled him to do some work here for the army, some for universities, and some as a broadcaster. When the war ended, he left all these more or less official jobs, and now he is doing economic research for private companies. He comes from a working-class family in Berlin, studied history with Delbrück[1] in Berlin, then was an editor for a news service, and was involved in various political activities. I continue to use my old name.

From Hannah Arendt/Karl Jaspers Correspondence 1926–1969. *Notes by Lotte Kohler and Hans Saner.*

That's quite common here in America when a woman works, and I have gladly adopted this custom out of conservatism (and also because I wanted my name to identify me as a Jew).

By now you must be saying that I'm avoiding telling you what you really want to know. You no doubt want to know how I have fared in this life. That's hard to answer. I'm still a stateless person, and your picture of me living in furnished rooms is to some degree still accurate. We live, with my mother,[2] in a furnished apartment. I was, thank God, able to get her to France in time after the November pogroms[3] and then to bring her over here. As you see, I haven't become respectable in any way. I'm more than ever of the opinion that a decent human existence is possible today only on the fringes of society, where one then runs the risk of starving or being stoned to death. In these circumstances, a sense of humor is a great help. I'm fairly well known here, and in certain matters I have a little authority with some people; that is, they trust me. But that is partly because they know I'm not about to turn my convictions or "talents" into a career.

Perhaps some examples will clarify what I mean. If I had wanted to become respectable, I would either have had to give up my interest in Jewish affairs or not marry a non-Jewish man, either option equally inhuman and in a sense crazy. This all sounds idiotically pathetic somehow, and I don't mean it that way. For you are quite right to say "lucky America"—where, because of a basically sound political structure, so-called society has still not become so powerful that it cannot tolerate exceptions to the rules.

There is much I could say about America. There really is such a thing as freedom here and a strong feeling among many people that one cannot live without freedom. The republic is not a vapid illusion, and the fact that there is no national state and no truly national tradition creates an atmosphere of freedom or at least one not pervaded by fanaticism. (Because of the strong need the various immigrant groups feel to maintain their identity, the melting pot is in large part not even an ideal, much less a reality.) Then, too, people here feel themselves responsible for public life to an extent I have never seen in any European country. For example, when all Americans of Japanese descent were locked up willy-nilly in concentration camps at the beginning of the war, a genuine storm of protest that can still be felt today went through the country. I was visiting with an American family in New England at the time. They were thoroughly average people—what would have been called "petty bourgeoisie" in Germany—and they had, I'm sure, never laid eyes on a Japanese in their lives.

As I later learned, they and many of their friends wrote immediately and *spontaneously* to their congressmen, insisted on the constitutional rights of all Americans regardless of national background, and declared that if something like that could happen, they no longer felt safe themselves (these people were of Anglo-Saxon background, and their families had been in this country for generations), etc.

The high degree of practical political understanding, the passion to straighten things out, not to tolerate unnecessary misery, to see that in the midst of often cutthroat competition the individual is guaranteed a fair chance—all this has a flip side, however, which is that nobody worries about what cannot be changed. The attitude of this country toward death will never cease to shock us Europeans. The basic response when some-one dies or when something goes irrevocably wrong is: Forget about it. That is, of course, only another expression of this country's fundamental anti-intellectualism, which, for certain special reasons, is at its worst in the universities. (Chicago University and a few other universities are not ex-actly glowing exceptions to this rule, but they are exceptions nonetheless.) Every intellectual here is a member of the opposition simply because he is an intellectual. The reasons for that are the all-pervasive social conformity, the necessity to rebel against the god of success, etc. Among themselves, however, these intellectuals maintain a remarkable solidarity, and in their discussions and debates they are unfanatical and open-minded to an aston-ishing degree. From your acquaintance with Lasky you will have a good idea of what these people are like.

The fundamental contradiction in this country is the coexistence of political freedom and social oppression. The latter is, as I've already indi-cated, not total; but it is dangerous because the society organizes and ori-ents itself along "racial lines." And that holds true without exception at all social levels, from the bourgeoisie on down to the working class. This racial issue has to do with a person's country of origin, but it is greatly ag-gravated by the Negro question; that is, America has a real "race" prob-lem and not just a racial ideology. You doubtless know that social anti-Semitism is taken completely for granted here and that antipathy to-ward Jews is, so to speak, a consensus omnium. The Jews maintain an al-most equally radical isolation and are, of course, also protected by that isolation. A young Jewish woman, a friend of mine born in this country, had in our home what I believe to be her first social meeting with non-Jewish Americans. This doesn't mean that people would not stand up for the Jews politically, but socially both sides want to "keep to themselves."

My literary existence, as opposed to my existence as a member of society, has two major roots: First, thanks to my husband, I have learned to think politically and see historically; and, second, I have refused to abandon the Jewish question as the focal point of my historical and political thinking. And this brings me to your question about *Die Wandlung*. Need I tell you how much your request that I contribute pleased me? And how happy I would be if I could simply write something and send it.

I know you will not misunderstand me when I say that it is not an easy thing for me to contribute to a German journal. At the same time, I am unhappy about the desperate resolve of the Jews to leave Europe (you are probably aware of the mood in all the refugee camps both in and outside Germany; and that mood cannot be ignored). I am also more anxious than I care to say about the frightening possibility of further catastrophes, particularly in Palestine, given the behavior of other governments and our own suicidal tendencies in politics. Yet one thing seems clear to me: If the Jews are to be able to stay in Europe, then they cannot stay as Germans or Frenchmen, etc., as if nothing had happened. It seems to me that none of us can return (and writing is surely a form of return) merely because people again seem prepared to recognize Jews as Germans or something else. We can return only if we are welcome as Jews. That would mean that I would gladly write something if I can write as a Jew on some aspect of the Jewish question. And quite apart from other problems—objections you might raise to my text, for instance—I don't know if you would be able to print something of that nature under the present difficult circumstances.

The Thomas Mann book—the radio talks and a *Neue Rundschau* with another essay on this subject (a particularly unpleasant one, it seems to me)—is in the mail. It really is absurd to take him seriously politically, important as he is as a novelist—except that he does exert a certain vague influence. The correspondence between him and Walter von Molo[4] of all people borders almost on the comic. I've sent along a few magazines with the Mann items, and I'll send some others soon which you may find of interest. You'll find in them a few articles of mine—not that I feel you're obliged to read them and struggle with the English. I'm sending them to clear my conscience, that is, because they are things that may "put you off," and because I would feel, now that it is possible to mail things, that I was hiding something if I didn't send them.

I'm very glad that you like "Organized Guilt" (that was the original title). I wrote it when I had just learned from Tillich that you were not in Switzerland, and I thought of you often then. The astonishing thing isn't so much that something like it can be published in America but, rather, that a Jewish newspaper, after years of stupid propaganda, accepted it with glee and obvious relief and, by including it as the only statement about Germany in its anthology, put its official seal of approval on it once again. I'm sending you the original German text. Because it is really yours anyhow. If you like, you can of course use it in *Die Wandlung*.[5] (As a counterweight, as it were—ironically speaking—to the Morgenthau Plan.)[6]

I await your books with great impatience. That you were able to work like that despite the hell and loneliness you were living in is marvelous and reason to rejoice. That you are lecturing again brings a touch of order into this world out of joint. Have I ever told you how wonderful your Nietzsche book is?[7]

I've just seen here that you'd like a report on American philosophy for *Die Wandlung*. I couldn't do that because I don't know enough about it. But I know someone I could ask, an American and an editor at *Partisan Review*, William Barrett. He's an intelligent and pleasant young man. — I've just recalled, too, that Kristeller[8] asked me to send you his regards. And others have, too. (Do you remember him, a classical philologist . . . ? He's teaching Italian at Columbia University.) He'd like to know what became of his former teacher Hoffmann.[9]

I hope this letter isn't too long. If I don't stop now, there'll be no end to it.

Stay healthy (as the Jews say, with good reason), and please accept warmest greetings from

Your
Hannah Arendt

Notes

1. Hans Delbrück, 1848–1929, was a historian who taught at the University of Berlin from 1896 to 1921.
2. Martha Arendt-Cohn, 1874–1948.
3. The organized persecution of the Jews on the night of November 9, 1938 ("Crystal Night"), which resulted in the burning of the synagogues in Germany, in the demolishing of thousands of Jewish shops, in innumerable murders, and in the abduction of more than 30,000 Jews.
4. Walter von Molo, 1880–1958, was an Austrian-German novelist and playwright.
5. Hannah Arendt, "Organisierte Schuld," *Die Wandlung* 1 (1945–46): 333–44.
6. Plan of U.S. Secretary of the Treasury Henry Morgenthau, Jr., 1891–1967, the essence of which was reduction of Germany to an agrarian country. It was presented at the 1944 Quebec Conference but rejected by President Roosevelt.

7. Karl Jaspers, *Nietzsche: Einführung in das Verständnis seines Philosophierens* (Berlin/Leipzig, 1936).

8. Paul Oskar Kristeller, b. 1905, historian of philosophy and specialist in the Renaissance, went to the United States in 1939.

9. Ernst Hoffmann, 1880–1952, historian of philosophy, was, from 1922, a professor at Heidelberg and a colleague of J.'s.

The Perplexities of the Rights of Man

THE DECLARATION of the Rights of Man at the end of the eighteenth century was a turning point in history. It meant nothing more nor less than that from then on Man, and not God's command or the customs of history, should be the source of Law. Independent of the privileges which history had bestowed upon certain strata of society or certain nations, the declaration indicated man's emancipation from all tutelage and announced that he had now come of age.

Beyond this, there was another implication of which the framers of the declaration were only half aware. The proclamation of human rights was also meant to be a much-needed protection in the new era where individuals were no longer secure in the estates to which they were born or sure of their equality before God as Christians. In other words, in the new secularized and emancipated society, men were no longer sure of these social and human rights which until then had been outside the political order and guaranteed not by government and constitution, but by social, spiritual, and religious forces. Therefore throughout the nineteenth century, the consensus of opinion was that human rights had to be invoked whenever individuals needed protection against the new sovereignty of the state and the new arbitrariness of society.

Since the Rights of Man were proclaimed to be "inalienable," irreducible to and undeducible from other rights or laws, no authority was invoked for their establishment; Man himself was their source as well as their ultimate goal. No special law, moreover, was deemed necessary to protect them because all laws were supposed to rest upon them. Man appeared as the only sovereign in matters of law as the people was proclaimed the only sovereign in matters of government. The people's sovereignty (different from that of the prince) was not proclaimed by the grace of God but in the name of Man, so that it seemed only natural

---

From The Origins of Totalitarianism.

that the "inalienable" rights of man would find their guarantee and become an inalienable part of the right of the people to sovereign self-government.

In other words, man had hardly appeared as a completely emancipated, completely isolated being who carried his dignity within himself without reference to some larger encompassing order, when he disappeared again into a member of a people. From the beginning the paradox involved in the declaration of inalienable human rights was that it reckoned with an "abstract" human being who seemed to exist nowhere, for even savages lived in some kind of a social order. If a tribal or other "backward" community did not enjoy human rights, it was obviously because as a whole it had not yet reached that stage of civilization, the stage of popular and national sovereignty, but was oppressed by foreign or native despots. The whole question of human rights, therefore, was quickly and inextricably blended with the question of national emancipation; only the emancipated sovereignty of the people, of one's own people, seemed to be able to insure them. As mankind, since the French Revolution, was conceived in the image of a family of nations, it gradually became self-evident that the people, and not the individual, was the image of man.

The full implication of this identification of the rights of man with the rights of peoples in the European nation-state system came to light only when a growing number of people and peoples suddenly appeared whose elementary rights were as little safeguarded by the ordinary functioning of nation-states in the middle of Europe as they would have been in the heart of Africa. The Rights of Man, after all, had been defined as "inalienable" because they were supposed to be independent of all governments; but it turned out that the moment human beings lacked their own government and had to fall back upon their minimum rights, no authority was left to protect them and no institution was willing to guarantee them. Or when, as in the case of the minorities, an international body arrogated to itself a nongovernmental authority, its failure was apparent even before its measures were fully realized; not only were the governments more or less openly opposed to this encroachment on their sovereignty, but the concerned nationalities themselves did not recognize a nonnational guarantee, mistrusted everything which was not clear-cut support of their "national" (as opposed to their mere "linguistic, religious, and ethnic") rights, and preferred either, like the Germans or Hungarians, to turn to the protection of the "national" mother country, or, like the Jews, to some kind of interterritorial solidarity.[1]

The stateless people were as convinced as the minorities that loss of national rights was identical with loss of human rights, that the former inevitably entailed the latter. The more they were excluded from right in any form, the more they tended to look for a reintegration into a national, into their own national community. The Russian refugees were only the first to insist on their nationality and to defend themselves furiously against attempts to lump them together with other stateless people. Since them, not a single group of refugees or Displaced Persons has failed to develop a fierce, violent group consciousness and to clamor for rights as—and only as—Poles or Jews or Germans, etc.

Even worse was that all societies formed for the protection of the Rights of Man, all attempts to arrive at a new bill of human rights were sponsored by marginal figures—by a few international jurists without political experience or professional philanthropists supported by the uncertain sentiments of professional idealists. The groups they formed, the declarations they issued, showed an uncanny similarity in language and composition to that of societies for the prevention of cruelty to animals. No statesman, no political figure of any importance could possibly take them seriously; and none of the liberal or radical parties in Europe thought it necessary to incorporate into their program a new declaration of human rights. Neither before nor after the second World War have the victims themselves ever invoked these fundamental rights, which were so evidently denied them, in their many attempts to find a way out of the barbed-wire labyrinth into which events had driven them. On the contrary, the victims shared the disdain and indifference of the powers that be for any attempt of the marginal societies to enforce human rights in any elementary or general sense.

The failure of all responsible persons to meet the calamity of an ever-growing body of people forced to live outside the scope of all tangible law with the proclamation of a new bill of rights was certainly not due to ill will. Never before had the Rights of Man, solemnly proclaimed by the French and the American revolutions as the new fundament for civilized societies, been a practical political issue. During the nineteenth century, these rights had been invoked in a rather perfunctory way, to defend individuals against the increasing power of the state and to mitigate the new social insecurity caused by the industrial revolution. Then the meaning of human rights acquired a new connotation: they became the standard slogan of the protectors of the underprivileged, a kind of additional law, a right of exception necessary for those who had nothing better to fall back upon.

The reason why the concept of human rights was treated as a sort of stepchild by nineteenth-century political thought and why no liberal or radical party in the twentieth century, even when an urgent need for enforcement of human rights arose, saw fit to include them in its program seems obvious: civil rights—that is the varying rights of citizens in different countries—were supposed to embody and spell out in the form of tangible laws the eternal Rights of Man, which by themselves were supposed to be independent of citizenship and nationality. All human beings were citizens of some kind of political community; if the laws of their country did not live up to the demands of the Rights of Man, they were expected to change them, by legislation in democratic countries or through revolutionary action in despotisms.

The Rights of Man, supposedly inalienable, proved to be unenforceable—even in countries whose constitutions were based upon them—whenever people appeared who were no longer citizens of any sovereign state. To this fact, disturbing enough in itself, one must add the confusion created by the many recent attempts to frame a new bill of human rights, which have demonstrated that no one seems able to define with any assurance what these general human rights, as distinguished from the rights of citizens, really are. Although everyone seems to agree that the plight of these people consists precisely in their loss of the Rights of Man, no one seems to know which rights they lost when they lost these human rights.

The first loss which the rightless suffered was the loss of their homes, and this meant the loss of the entire social texture into which they were born and in which they established for themselves a distinct place in the world. This calamity is far from unprecedented; in the long memory of history, forced migrations of individuals or whole groups of people for political or economic reasons look like everyday occurrences. What is unprecedented is not the loss of a home but the impossibility of finding a new one. Suddenly, there was no place on earth where migrants could go without the severest restrictions, no country where they would be assimilated, no territory where they could found a new community of their own. This, moreover, had next to nothing to do with any material problem of overpopulation; it was a problem not of space but of political organization. Nobody had been aware that mankind, for so long a time considered under the image of a family of nations, had reached the stage where whoever was thrown out of one of these tightly organized closed communities found himself thrown out of the family of nations altogether.[2]

The second loss which the rightless suffered was the loss of government protection, and this did not imply just the loss of legal status in their own, but in all countries. Treaties of reciprocity and international agreements have woven a web around the earth that makes it possible for the citizen of every country to take his legal status with him no matter where he goes (so that, for instance, a German citizen under the Nazi regime might not be able to enter a mixed marriage abroad because of the Nuremberg laws). Yet, whoever is no longer caught in it finds himself out of legality altogether (thus during the last war stateless people were invariably in a worse position than enemy aliens who were still indirectly protected by their governments through international agreements).

By itself the loss of government protection is no more unprecedented than the loss of a home. Civilized countries did offer the right of asylum to those who, for political reasons, had been persecuted by their governments, and this practice, though never officially incorporated into any constitution, has functioned well enough throughout the nineteenth and even in our century. The trouble arose when it appeared that the new categories of persecuted were far too numerous to be handled by an unofficial practice destined for exceptional cases. Moreover, the majority could hardly qualify for the right of asylum, which implicitly presupposed political or religious convictions which were not outlawed in the country of refuge. The new refugees were persecuted not because of what they had done or thought, but because of what they unchangeably were—born into the wrong kind of race or the wrong kind of class or drafted by the wrong kind of government (as in the case of the Spanish Republican Army).[3]

The more the number of rightless people increased, the greater became the temptation to pay less attention to the deeds of the persecuting governments than to the status of the persecuted. And the first glaring fact was that these people, though persecuted under some political pretext, were no longer, as the persecuted had been throughout history, a liability and an image of shame for the persecutors; that they were not considered and hardly pretended to be active enemies (the few thousand Soviet citizens who voluntarily left Soviet Russia after the second World War and found asylum in democratic countries did more damage to the prestige of the Soviet Union than millions of refugees in the twenties who belonged to the wrong class), but that they were and appeared to be nothing but human beings whose very innocence—from every point of view, and especially that of the persecuting government—was their greatest misfortune. Innocence, in the sense of complete lack of responsibility, was the mark of their rightlessness as it was the seal of their loss of political status.

Only in appearance therefore do the needs for a reinforcement of human rights touch upon the fate of the authentic political refugee. Political refugees, of necessity few in number, still enjoy the right to asylum in many countries, and this right acts, in an informal way, as a genuine substitute for national law.

One of the surprising aspects of our experience with stateless people who benefit legally from committing a crime has been the fact that it seems to be easier to deprive a completely innocent person of legality than someone who has committed an offense. Anatole France's famous quip, "If I am accused of stealing the towers of Notre Dame, I can only flee the country," has assumed a horrible reality. Jurists are so used to thinking of law in terms of punishment, which indeed always deprives us of certain rights, that they may find it even more difficult than the layman to recognize that the deprivation of legality, *i.e.,* of *all* rights, no longer has a connection with specific crimes.

This situation illustrates the many perplexities inherent in the concept of human rights. No matter how they have once been defined (life, liberty, and the pursuit of happiness, according to the American formula, or as equality before the law, liberty, protection of property, and national sovereignty, according to the French); no matter how one may attempt to improve an ambiguous formulation like the pursuit of happiness, or an antiquated one like unqualified right to property; the real situation of those whom the twentieth century has driven outside the pale of the law shows that these are rights of citizens whose loss does not entail absolute rightlessness. The soldier during the war is deprived of his right to life, the criminal of his right to freedom, all citizens during an emergency of their right to the pursuit of happiness, but nobody would ever claim that in any of these instances a loss of human rights has taken place. These rights, on the other hand, can be granted (though hardly enjoyed) even under conditions of fundamental rightlessness.

The calamity of the rightless is not that they are deprived of life, liberty, and the pursuit of happiness, or of equality before the law and freedom of opinion—formulas which were designed to solve problems *within* given communities—but that they no longer belong to any community whatsoever. Their plight is not that they are not equal before the law, but that no law exists for them; not that they are oppressed but that nobody wants even to oppress them. Only in the last stage of a rather lengthy process is their right to live threatened; only if they remain perfectly "superfluous," if nobody can be found to "claim" them, may their lives be in danger. Even the Nazis started their extermination of Jews by first depriving them of all legal status (the status of second-class citizenship) and cutting them off from the world of the living by herding them into ghettos and concentration camps; and before they set the gas chambers into motion they had carefully tested the ground and found out to their satisfaction that no country would claim these people. The point is that a condition of complete rightlessness was created before the right to live was challenged.

The same is true even to an ironical extent with regard to the right of freedom which is sometimes considered to be the very essence of human rights. There is no question that those outside the pale of the law may have more freedom of movement than a lawfully imprisoned criminal or that they enjoy more freedom of opinion in the internment camps of democratic countries than they would in any ordinary despotism, not to mention in a totalitarian country.[4] But neither physical safety—being fed by some state or private welfare agency—nor freedom of opinion changes in the least their fundamental situation of rightlessness. The prolongation of their lives is due to charity and not to right, for no law exists which could force the nations to feed them; their freedom of movement, if they have it at all, gives them no right to residence which even the jailed criminal enjoys as a matter of course; and their freedom of opinion is a fool's freedom, for nothing they think matters anyhow.

These last points are crucial. The fundamental deprivation of human rights is manifested first and above all in the deprivation of a place in the world which makes opinions significant and actions effective. Something much more fundamental than freedom and justice, which are rights of citizens, is at stake when belonging to the community into which one is born is no longer a matter of course and not belonging no longer a matter of choice, or when one is placed in a situation where, unless he commits a crime, his treatment by others does not depend on what he does or does not do. This extremity, and nothing else, is the situation of people deprived of human rights. They are deprived, not of the right to freedom, but of the right to action; not of the right to think whatever they please, but of the right to opinion. Privileges in some cases, injustices in most, blessings and doom are meted out to them according to accident and without any relation whatsoever to what they do, did, or may do.

We became aware of the existence of a right to have rights (and that means to live in a framework where one is judged by one's actions and opinions) and a right to belong to some kind of organized community, only when millions of people emerged who had lost and could not regain these rights because of the new global political situation. The trouble is that this calamity arose not from any lack of civilization, backwardness, or mere tyranny, but, on the contrary, that it could not be repaired, because there was no longer any "uncivilized" spot on earth, because whether we like it or not we have really started to live in One World. Only with a completely organized humanity could the loss of home and political status become identical with expulsion from humanity altogether.

Before this, what we must call a "human right" today would have been thought of as a general characteristic of the human condition which no tyrant could take away. Its loss entails the loss of the relevance of speech (and man, since Aristotle, has been defined as a being commanding the power of speech and thought), and the loss of all human relationship (and man, again since Aristotle, has been thought of as the "political animal," that is one who by definition lives in a community), the loss, in other words, of some of the most essential characteristics of human life. This was to a certain extent the plight of slaves, whom Aristotle therefore did not count among human beings. Slavery's fundamental offense against human rights was not that it took liberty away (which can happen in many other situations), but that it excluded a certain category of people even from the possibility of fighting for freedom—a fight possible under tyranny, and even under the desperate conditions of modern terror (but not under any conditions of concentration-camp life). Slavery's crime against humanity did not begin when one people defeated and enslaved its enemies (though of course this was bad enough), but when slavery became an institution in which some men were "born" free and others slave, when it was forgotten that it was man who had deprived his fellow-men of freedom, and when the sanction for the crime was attributed to nature. Yet in the light of recent events it is possible to say that even slaves still belonged to some sort of human community; their labor was needed, used, and exploited, and this kept them within the pale of humanity. To be a slave was after all to have a distinctive character, a place in society—more than the abstract nakedness of being human and nothing but human. Not the loss of specific rights, then, but the loss of a community willing and able to guarantee any rights whatsoever, has been the calamity which has befallen ever-increasing numbers of people. Man, it turns out, can lose all so-called Rights of Man without losing his essential quality as man, his human dignity. Only the loss of a polity itself expels him from humanity.

The right that corresponds to this loss and that was never even mentioned among the human rights cannot be expressed in the categories of the eighteenth century because they presume that rights spring immediately from the "nature" of man—whereby it makes relatively little difference whether this nature is visualized in terms of the natural law or in terms of a being created in the image of God, whether it concerns "natural" rights or divine commands. The decisive factor is that these rights and the human dignity they bestow should remain valid and real even if only a single human being existed on earth; they are independent of human plurality and should remain valid even if a human being is expelled from the human community.

When the Rights of Man were proclaimed for the first time, they were regarded as being independent of history and the privileges which history had accorded certain strata of society. The new independence constituted the newly discovered dignity of man. From the beginning, this new dignity was of a rather ambiguous nature. Historical rights were replaced by natural rights, "nature" took the place of history, and it was tacitly assumed that nature was less alien than history to the essence of man. The very language of the Declaration of Independence as well as of the *Déclaration des Droits de l'Homme*—"inalienable," "given with birth," "self-evident truths"—implies the belief in a kind of human "nature" which would be subject to the same laws of growth as that of the individual and from which rights and laws could be deduced. Today we are perhaps better qualified to judge exactly what this human "nature" amounts to; in any event it has shown us potentialities that were neither recognized nor even suspected by Western philosophy and religion, which for more than three thousand years have defined and redefined this "nature." But it is not only the, as it were, human aspect of nature that has become questionable to us. Ever since man learned to master it to such an extent that the destruction of all organic life on earth with man-made instruments has become conceivable and technically possible, he has been alienated from nature. Ever since a deeper knowledge of natural processes instilled serious doubts about the existence of natural laws at all, nature itself has assumed a sinister aspect. How should one be able to deduce laws and rights from a universe which apparently knows neither the one nor the other category?

Man of the twentieth century has become just as emancipated from nature as eighteenth-century man was from history. History and nature have become equally alien to us, namely, in the sense that the essence of man can no longer be comprehended in terms of either category. On the other hand, humanity, which for the eighteenth century, in Kantian terminology, was no more than a regulative idea, has today become an inescapable fact. This new situation, in which "humanity" has in effect assumed the role formerly ascribed to nature or history, would mean in this context that the right to have rights, or the right of every individual to belong to humanity, should be guaranteed by humanity itself. It is by no means certain whether this is possible. For, contrary to the best-intentioned humanitarian attempts to obtain new declarations of human rights from international organizations, it should be understood that this idea transcends the present sphere of international law which still operates in terms of reciprocal agreements and treaties between sovereign states; and, for the time being, a sphere that is above the nations does not exist. Furthermore, this dilemma would by no means be eliminated by the establishment of a "world government." Such a world government is indeed within the realm of possibility, but one may suspect that in reality it might differ considerably from the version promoted by idealistic-minded organizations. The crimes against human rights, which have become a specialty of totalitarian regimes, can always be justified by the pretext that right is equivalent to being good or useful for the whole in distinction to its parts. (Hitler's motto that "Right is what is good for the German people" is only the vulgarized form of a conception of law which can be found everywhere and which in practice will remain ineffectual only so long as older traditions that are still effective in the constitutions prevent this.) A conception of law which identifies what is right with the notion of what is good for—for the individual, or the family, or the people, or the largest number—becomes inevitable once the absolute and transcendent measurements of religion or the law of nature have lost their authority. And this predicament is by no means solved if the unit to which the "good for" applies is as large as mankind itself. For it is quite conceivable, and even within the realm of practical political possibilities, that one fine day a highly organized and mechanized humanity will conclude quite democratically—namely by majority decision—that for humanity as a whole it would be better to liquidate certain parts thereof. Here, in the problems of factual reality, we are confronted with one of the oldest perplexities of political philosophy, which could remain undetected only so long as a stable Christian theology provided the framework for all political and philosophical problems, but which long ago caused Plato to say: "Not man, but a god, must be the measure of all things."

These facts and reflections offer what seems an ironical, bitter, and belated confirmation of the famous arguments with which Edmund Burke opposed the French Revolution's Declaration of the Rights of Man. They appear to buttress his assertion that human rights were an "abstraction," that it was much wiser to rely on an "entailed inheritance" of rights which one transmits to one's children like life itself, and to claim one's rights to be the "rights of an Englishman" rather than the inalienable rights of man.[5] According to Burke, the rights which we enjoy spring "from within the nation," so that neither natural law, nor divine command, nor any concept of mankind such as Robespierre's "human race," "the sovereign of the earth," are needed as a source of law.[6]

The pragmatic soundness of Burke's concept seems to be beyond doubt in the light of our manifold experiences. Not only did loss of national rights in all instances entail the loss of human rights; the restoration of human rights, as the recent example of the State of Israel proves, has been achieved so far only through the restoration or the establishment of national rights. The conception of human rights, based upon the assumed existence of a human being as such, broke down at the very moment when those who professed to believe in it were for the first time confronted with people who had indeed lost all other qualities and specific relationships—except that they were still human. The world found nothing sacred in the abstract nakedness of being human. And in view of objective political conditions, it is hard to say how the concepts of man upon which human rights are based—that he is created in the image of God (in the American formula), or that he is the representative of mankind, or that he harbors within himself the sacred demands of natural law (in the French formula)—could have helped to find a solution to the problem.

The survivors of the extermination camps, the inmates of concentration and internment camps, and even the comparatively happy stateless people could see without Burke's arguments that the abstract nakedness of being nothing but human was their greatest danger. Because of it they were regarded as savages and, afraid that they might end by being considered beasts, they insisted on their nationality, the last sign of their former citizenship, as their only remaining and recognized tie with humanity. Their distrust of natural, their preference for national, rights comes precisely from their realization that natural rights are granted even to savages. Burke had already feared that natural "inalienable" rights would confirm only the "right of the naked savage,"[7] and therefore reduce civilized nations to the status of savagery. Because only savages have nothing more to fall back upon than the minimum fact of their human origin, people cling to their nationality all the more desperately when they have lost the rights and protection that such nationality once gave them. Only their past with its "entailed inheritance" seems to attest to the fact that they still belong to the civilized world.

If a human being loses his political status, he should, according to the implications of the inborn and inalienable rights of man, come under exactly the situation for which the declarations of such general rights provided. Actually the opposite is the case. It seems that a man who is nothing but a man has lost the very qualities which make it possible for other people to treat him as a fellow-man. This is one of the reasons why it is far more difficult to destroy the legal personality of a criminal, that is of a man who has taken upon himself the responsibility for an act whose consequences now determine his fate, than of a man who has been disallowed all common human responsibilities.

Burke's arguments therefore gain an added significance if we look only at the general human condition of those who have been forced out of all political communities. Regardless of treatment, independent of liberties or oppression, justice or injustice, they have lost all those parts of the world and all those aspects of human existence which are the result of our common labor, the outcome of the human artifice. If the tragedy of savage tribes is that they inhabit an unchanged nature which they cannot master, yet upon whose abundance or frugality they depend for their livelihood, that they live and die without leaving any trace, without having contributed anything to a common world, then these rightless people are indeed thrown back into a peculiar state of nature. Certainly they are not barbarians; some of them, indeed, belong to the most educated strata of their respective countries; nevertheless, in a world that has almost liquidated savagery, they appear as the first signs of a possible regression from civilization.

The more highly developed a civilization, the more accomplished the world it has produced, the more at home men feel within the human artifice—the more they will resent everything they have not produced, everything that is merely and mysteriously given them. The human being who has lost his place in a community, his political status in the struggle of his time, and the legal personality which makes his actions and part of his destiny a consistent whole, is left with those qualities which usually can become articulate only in the sphere of private life and must remain unqualified, mere existence in all matters of public concern. This mere existence, that is, all that which is mysteriously given us by birth and which includes the shape of our bodies and the talents of our minds, can be adequately dealt with only by the unpredictable hazards of friendship and sympathy, or by the great and incalculable grace of love, which says with Augustine, "*Volo ut sis* (I want you to be)," without being able to give any particular reason for such supreme and unsurpassable affirmation.

Since the Greeks, we have known that highly developed political life breeds a deep-rooted suspicion of this private sphere, a deep resentment against the disturbing miracle contained in the fact that each of us is made as he is—single, unique, unchangeable. This whole sphere of the merely given, relegated to private life in civilized society, is a permanent threat to the public sphere, because the public sphere is as consistently based on the law of equality as the private sphere is based on the law of universal difference and differentiation. Equality, in contrast to all that is involved in mere existence, is not given us, but is the result of human organization insofar as it is guided by the principle of justice. We are not born equal; we become equal as members of a group on the strength of our decision to guarantee ourselves mutually equal rights.

Our political life rests on the assumption that we can produce equality through organization, because man can act in and change and build a common world, together with his equals and only with his equals. The dark background of mere givenness, the background formed by our unchangeable and unique nature, breaks into the political scene as the alien which in its all too obvious difference reminds us of the limitations of human activity—which are identical with the limitations of human equality. The reason why highly developed political communities, such as the ancient city-states or modern nation-states, so often insist on ethnic homogeneity is that they hope to eliminate as far as possible those natural and always present differences and differentiations which by themselves arouse dumb hatred, mistrust, and discrimination because they indicate all too clearly those spheres where men cannot act and change at will, *i.e.,* the limitations of the human artifice. The "alien" is a frightening symbol of the fact of difference as such, of individuality as such, and indicates those realms in which man cannot change and cannot act and in which, therefore, he has a distinct tendency to destroy. If a Negro in a white community is considered a Negro and nothing else, he loses along with his right to equality that freedom of action which is specifically human; all his deeds are now explained as "necessary" consequences of some "Negro" qualities; he has become some specimen of an animal species, called man. Much the same thing happens to those who have lost all distinctive political qualities and have become human beings and nothing else. No doubt, wherever public life and its law of equality are completely victorious, wherever a civilization succeeds in eliminating or reducing to a minimum the dark background of difference, it will end in complete petrifaction and be punished, so to speak, for having forgotten that man is only the master, not the creator of the world.

The great danger arising from the existence of people forced to live outside the common world is that they are thrown back, in the midst of civilization, on their natural givenness, on their mere differentiation. They lack that tremendous equalizing of differences which comes from being citizens of some commonwealth and yet, since they are no longer allowed to partake in the human artifice, they begin to belong to the human race in much the same way as animals belong to a specific animal species. The paradox involved in the loss of human rights is that such loss coincides with the instant when a person becomes a human being in general—without a profession, without a citizenship, without an opinion, without a deed by which to identify and specify himself—*and* different in general, representing nothing but his own absolutely unique individuality which, deprived of expression within and action upon a common world, loses all significance.

The danger in the existence of such people is twofold: first and more obviously, their ever-increasing numbers threaten our political life, our human artifice, the world which is the result of our common and co-ordinated effort in much the same, perhaps even more terrifying, way as the wild elements of nature once threatened the existence of man-made cities and countrysides. Deadly danger to any civilization is no longer likely to come from without. Nature has been mastered and no barbarians threaten to destroy what they cannot understand, as the Mongolians threatened Europe for centuries. Even the emergence of totalitarian governments is a phenomenon within, not outside, our civilization. The danger is that a global, universally interrelated civilization may produce barbarians from its own midst by forcing millions of people into conditions which, despite all appearances, are the conditions of savages.[8]

Notes

1. Pathetic instances of this exclusive confidence in national rights were the consent, before the second World War, of nearly 75 per cent of the German minority in the Italian Tyrol to leave their homes and resettle in Germany, the voluntary repatriation of a German island in Slovenia which had been there since the fourteenth century or, immediately after the close of the war, the unanimous rejection by Jewish refugees in an Italian DP [Displaced Persons—ed.] camp of an offer of mass naturalization by the Italian government. In the face of the experience of European peoples between the two wars, it would be a serious mistake to interpret this behavior simply as another example of fanatic nationalist sentiment; these people no longer felt sure of their elementary rights if these were not protected by a government to which they belonged by birth. See Eugene M. Kulisher, *The Displacement of Population in Europe.* Montreal, 1943.

2. The few chances for reintegration open to the new migrants were mostly based on their nationality: Spanish refugees, for instance, were welcomed to a certain extent in Mexico. The United States, in the early twenties, adopted a quota system according to which each nationality already represented in the country received, so to speak, the right to receive a number of former countrymen proportionate to its numerical part in the total population.

3. How dangerous it can be to be innocent from the point of view of the persecuting government, became very clear when, during the last war, the American government offered asylum to all those German refugees who were threatened by the extradition paragraph in the German-French Armistice. The

condition was, of course, that the applicant could prove that he had done something against the Nazi regime. The proportion of refugees from Germany who were able to fulfill this condition was very small, and they, strangely enough, were not the people who were most in danger.

4. Even under the conditions of totalitarian terror, concentration camps sometimes have been the only place where certain remnants of freedom of thought and discussion still existed. See David Rousset, *Les Jours de Notre Mort,* Paris, 1947, *passim,* for freedom of discussion in Buchenwald, and Anton Ciliga, *The Russian Enigma,* London, 1940, p. 200, about "isles of liberty," "the freedom of mind" that reigned in some of the Soviet places of detention.

5. Edmund Burke, *Reflections on the Revolution in France,* 1790, edited by E. J. Payne, Everyman's Library.

6. Robespierre, *Speeches,* 1927. Speech of April 24, 1793.

7. Introduction by Payne to Burke, *op. cit.*

8. This modern expulsion from humanity has much more radical consequences than the ancient and medieval custom of outlawry. Outlawry, certainly the "most fearful fate which primitive law could inflict," placing the life of the outlawed person at the mercy of anyone he met, disappeared with the establishment of an effective system of law enforcement and was finally replaced by extradition treaties between the nations. It had been primarily a substitute for a police force, designed to compel criminals to surrender.

The early Middle Ages seem to have been quite conscious of the danger involved in "civil death." Excommunication in the late Roman Empire meant ecclesiastical death but left a person who had lost his membership in the church full freedom in all other respects. Ecclesiastical and civil death became identical only in the Merovingian era, and there excommunication "in general practice [was] limited to temporary withdrawal or suspension of the rights of membership which might be regained." See the articles "Outlawry" and "Excommunication" in the *Encyclopedia of Social Sciences.* Also the article "Friedlosigkeit" in the *Schweizer Lexikon.*

The Jewish Army—the Beginning of
a Jewish Politics?

ON THE OCCASION of the anniversary of the Balfour Declaration,[1] America's Zionist organisations have publicly called for a Jewish army for the defence of Palestine. Demands and resolutions by a political avant-garde which does not directly express the will of the whole community can only become creative policy if they succeed in mobilizing wide sections of the nation. If they do not succeed in this, then the finest programmes and the most correct resolutions will simply go down in history as lost opportunities. What is today still the isolated demand of Palestinian Jewry and of its representatives abroad must tomorrow become the living will of large sections of the nation to take up the struggle against Hitler as Jews, in Jewish units, under the Jewish flag. *The defence of Palestine is a part of the struggle for the freedom of the Jewish people.* Only when the Jewish people is ready to commit itself fully to this struggle will it be able to defend Palestine.

The Jewish will to live is both famous and notorious. Famous, because it occupies a relatively long period of time in the history of European peoples. Notorious, because in the last 200 years it has threatened to degenerate into something quite negative: the will to survive at all costs. Our national decline began with the collapse of the Sabbatai-Zwi [sic] movement.[2] Since then we have proclaimed existence as such, without national content and usually without even religious content, as a value in itself. The Jewish people began to resemble an old man, who at the age of 80 makes a wager with himself that he will make it to 120, and who now, with the aid of an ingenious diet, and by avoiding any movement turns his back on life in order to devote himself to survival; thus he lives from one birthday to the next and looks forward to this one day in the year, so

From Aufbau (Reconstruction), *November 14, 1941. A translation of "Die jüdische Armee–der Beginn einer jüdischen Politik?" by Gordon C. Wells. Notes by Peter Baehr.*

that he can call out to the astonished and no longer entirely well-wishing relations: Look, I've done it again. At the moment, Hitler is busy snuffing out this old man's life. It is the hope of all of us that he is making a mistake: that he will have to deal not with old men but with the men and women of a nation.

A Jewish army need not be a utopia if Jews from every country demand it and are prepared to join it as volunteers. It is, however, utopian to believe that we could profit in any way from the defeat of Hitler if this defeat is not in part our doing. Only a real war of the Jewish people against Hitler will put an end—a well-deserved end—to the fantastic talk of the Jewish war. "Freedom is not a gift" as the old and yet very relevant Zionist saying has it. *Neither is freedom a reward for suffering endured.*

A truth hitherto unknown to the Jewish people, which it is only just beginning to learn, is *that you can only defend yourself as that for which you are being attacked.* A man attacked as a Jew cannot defend himself as an Englishman or a Frenchman. The world can only conclude from this that he is simply not defending himself at all. This principle of the political struggle will perhaps now have been learned by those tens of thousands of French Jews who also feared the "Jewish war" and believed they had to defend themselves as Frenchmen, only to end up being held in special Jewish prison camps in Germany by their French fellow combatants. One group of people who have certainly learned it are the throngs of Jewish volunteers who thought they could combine their fight against Hitler with the fight for naturalisation, and who now find themselves in French internment camps, or building the Sahara Railway. They can count themselves lucky if they are not compelled to take part in the war against England and Russia.

Just as in human life being fixated on a person can lead to a distorted image and the ruination of the friendship, so also in politics unconditional identification of one's own cause with the cause of another can lead to a distorted image and the ruination of the alliance. The Jews of Palestine know this, as they struggle to prevent their own cause becoming swallowed up by the cause of the English—and yet desire nothing more than really to help the English. They know that they can help neither themselves nor the English people if they do not, in a way that is clearly visible to all, fight for themselves as Jews, in Jewish units, under the Jewish flag, as well (plainly for all to see) as allies of England.

Today Jews seem to be obsessed with their own insignificance. In part they hope this will enable them to leave the political stage once again; in part they are honestly in despair at belonging to a powerless and apparently completely depoliticized group. We too are not immune to the disease which has affected the European nations: despair, the cynicism that comes from disappointment, and feeling of helplessness.

The storm of indignation that the formation of a Jewish army of volunteers from all over the world will cause in our own ranks will make it clear to honest doubters that we too are only human; that we do engage in political action, even if it usually has to be labouriously pieced together from obscure petitions organised by notables and charities, and even if this kind of politics has proved particularly adept at alienating the people from politics. However, we are by no means the only ones to have been led to the brink of an abyss of corruption by a plutocratic regime. As Clemenceau put it, war is too serious a matter to leave to the generals. Now, *the existence of a nation is definitely too serious a matter to leave to wealthy men.*

The formation of a Jewish army will not be decided upon in secret talks with statesmen, nor by means of petitions from influential Jews. We shall never get this army unless the Jewish nation demands it and unless hundreds of thousands are prepared to arm themselves to fight for their freedom and for the nation's right to life. Only the nation itself, young and old, rich and poor, men and women, can turn public opinion, which today is against us, in our favour; *only the nation itself is strong enough for a real alliance.*

Notes

1. Named after the British Foreign Secretary, A. J. Balfour, the Declaration of 2 November 1917 affirmed British support for a Jewish national homeland in Palestine. The Declaration, which became a component of the League of Nations' mandate for Palestine (1920), also contained the proviso that Arab and other communities in Palestine were to have their rights protected.

2. Sabbatai (or Shabbetai) Zevi (1626–1676) was a mystic, who, proclaiming himself the Messiah, was the figurehead of a movement to unite the Jewish communities of the Diaspora. Arendt saw the Sabbatai Zevi movement as one of the great attempts by Jews "to change their condition by direct political action." Hannah Arendt, "The Jewish State: Fifty Years After. Where Have Herzl's Politics Led?" [1946], in Ron H. Feldman, ed., *Hannah Arendt, The Jew as Pariah: Jewish Identity and Politics in the Modern Age* (New York: Grove Press, 1978), pp. 164–77, at p. 166.

Jewess and Shlemihl

(1771–1795)

"WHAT A HISTORY!—A fugitive from Egypt and Palestine, here I am and find help, love, fostering in you people. With real rapture I think of these origins of mine and this whole nexus of destiny, through which the oldest memories of the human race stand side by side with the latest developments. The greatest distances in time and space are bridged. The thing which all my life seemed to me the greatest shame, which was the misery and misfortune of my life—having been born a Jewess—this I should on no account now wish to have missed." These are the words Karl August Varnhagen von Ense reports Rahel to have said on her deathbed. It had taken her sixty-three years to come to terms with a problem which had its beginnings seventeen hundred years before her birth, which underwent a crucial upheaval during her life, and which one hundred years after her death—she died on March 7, 1833—was slated to come to an end.

It may well be difficult for us to understand our own history when we are born in 1771 in Berlin and that history has already begun seventeen hundred years earlier in Jerusalem. But if we do not understand it, and if we are not outright opportunists who always accept the here-and-now, who circumvent unpleasantness by lies and forget the good, our history will take its revenge, will exert its superiority and become our personal destiny. And that is never any pleasure for the person affected. Rahel's history would not be curtailed because she had forgotten it, nor would it turn out to be any more original because she, in utter innocence, experienced the whole of it as if it were happening for the first time. But history becomes more definitive when (and how rarely this happens) it concentrates its whole force upon an individual's destiny; when it encounters a person who has no way of barricading herself behind character traits and talents, who cannot hide under moralities and conventions as if

From Rahel Varnhagen. *Translated by Richard and Clara Winston. For the context of this extract, see Editor's Introduction, pp. x–xiii.*

these were an umbrella for rainy weather; when it can impress something
of its significance upon the hapless human being, the *shlemihl,* who has anticipated nothing.

"What is man without his history? Product of nature—not personality." The history of any given personality is far older than the individual as
product of nature, begins long before the individual's life, and can foster
or destroy the elements of nature in his heritage. Whoever wants aid and
protection from History, in which our insignificant birth is almost lost,
must be able to know and understand it. History bashes the "product of
nature" on the head, stifles its most useful qualities, makes it degenerate—
"like a plant that grows downward into the earth: the finest characteristics
become the most repulsive."

If we feel at home in this world, we can see our lives as the development of the "product of nature," as the unfolding and realization of what
we already were. The world in that case becomes a school in the broadest
sense, and other people are cast in the roles of either educators or mis-
leaders. The great trouble is that human nature, which might otherwise
develop smoothly, is as dependent upon luck as seed is upon good
weather. For should anyone's life fail in the few most important things
that are naturally expected of him, his development is stopped—development which is the sole continuity in time that nature recognizes. Then
the pain, the grief, is overwhelming. And the person who has no recourse
but nature is destroyed by his own inexperience, by his inability to comprehend more than himself.

German literature offers only a single example of real identity between nature and history. "When I was eighteen years old, Germany had
also just turned eighteen" (Goethe). In case of such an identity, indeed,
the purity of a person's beginnings may immediately be transformed, materialized as it were, and "stand for" something impersonal, not to be sure
for some definite notion or concept, but for a world and history in general. It is his singularity not to need experience to know a world and a history which he contains in himself. Confronted with this kind of identity,
with so great, well-known and deeply loved an exemplar, persons wiser
and more gifted than Rahel could find themselves losing their hold on
standards; those even more sensible and cultivated than she could be de-
luded into excessive demands upon life, excessive susceptibility to disappointment. In such a fortunate case, to be sure, the person's initial purity
is transformed; his function becomes to "stand for"—not for anything
particular, anything different, but for himself. And then the person in
whom history is embodied can know the world even without experience.

In those days Jews in Berlin could grow up like the children of savage tribes. Rahel was one of these. She learned nothing, neither her own history nor that of the country in which her family dwelt. The earning of money and the study of the Law—these were the vital concerns of the ghetto. Wealth and culture helped to throw open the gates of the ghetto—court Jews on the one hand and Moses Mendelssohn on the other. Nineteenth-century Jews mastered the trick of obtaining both wealth and culture. Rich Jewish parents sought an extra measure of security by having their sons attend the university. In the brief and highly tempestuous interval between ghetto and assimilation, however, this practice had not yet developed. The rich were not cultured and the cultured not rich. Rahel's father was a dealer in precious stones who had made a fortune. That fact alone decided the complexion of her education. All her life she remained "the greatest ignoramus."

Unfortunately, she did not remain rich. When the father died, the sons took over his business, settled a lifetime allowance upon the mother, and determined to marry off the two sisters as quickly as possible. With the younger sister they succeeded; with Rahel they failed. Left without any portion of her own, she was dependent upon her mother's allowance, and after her mother's death upon the dubious generosity of her brothers. Poverty, it seemed, would condemn her to remain a Jew, stranded within a society that was rapidly disintegrating, that scarcely existed any longer as an environment with a specific self-awareness, with its own customs and judgments. The only ties among German Jews of the period seemed to be that questionable solidarity which survives among people who all want the same thing: to save themselves as individuals. Only failures and "shlemihls," it would seem, were left behind within this German-Jewish society.

Beauty in a woman can mean power, and Jewish girls were frequently not married for their dowries alone. With Rahel, however, nature went to no great trouble. She had about her something "unpleasantly unprepossessing, without there being immediately apparent any striking deformities." Small in body, with hands and feet too small, a disproportion between the upper and lower parts of her face, she had, below a clear brow and fine, translucent eyes, a chin too long and too limp, as though it were only appended to the face. In this chin, she thought, her "worst trait" was expressed, an "excessive gratitude and excess of consideration for others." These same qualities struck others as a lack of standards or taste. This, too, she was aware of. "I have no grace, not even the grace to see what the cause of that is; in addition to not being pretty, I also have no inner grace. . . . I am unprepossessing rather than ugly. . . . Some people have not a single good-looking feature, not a single praiseworthy proportion, and yet they make a pleasing impression. . . . With me it is just the opposite." So she wrote in her diary when she had occasion to think back upon a succession of unhappy love affairs. Although this was written fairly late in life, she adds in explanation: "I have thought this for a long time."

In a woman beauty creates a perspective from which she can judge and choose. Neither intelligence nor experience can make up for the lack of that natural perspective. Not rich, not cultivated and not beautiful— that meant that she was entirely without weapons with which to begin the great struggle for recognition in society, for social existence, for a morsel of happiness, for security and an established position in the bourgeois world.

A political struggle for equal rights might have taken the place of the personal struggle. But that was wholly unknown to this generation of Jews whose representatives even offered to accept mass baptism (David Friedländer). Jews did not even want to be emancipated as a whole; all they wanted was to escape from Jewishness, as individuals if possible. Their urge was secretly and silently to settle what seemed to them a personal problem, a personal misfortune. In Frederick the Second's Berlin a personal solution of the Jewish problem, an individual escape into society, was difficult but not flatly impossible. Anyone who did not convert his personal gifts into weapons to achieve that end, who failed to concentrate these gifts toward this single goal, might as well give up all hope of happiness in this world. Thus Rahel wrote to David Veit, the friend of her youth: "I have a strange fancy: it is as if some supramundane being, just as I was thrust into this world, plunged these words with a dagger into my heart: 'Yes, have sensibility, see the world as few see it, be great and noble, nor can I take from you the faculty of eternally thinking. But I add one thing more: be a Jewess!' And now my life is a slow bleeding to death. By keeping still I can delay it. Every movement in an attempt to staunch it—new death; and immobility is possible for me only in death itself. . . . I can, if you will, derive every evil, every misfortune, every vexation from *that*."

Under the influence of the Enlightenment the demand for "civil betterment of the Jews" began to advance toward realization in Prussia. It was spelled out in detail by the Prussian official Christian Wilhelm Dohm. Excluded for centuries from the culture and history of the lands they lived in, the Jews had in the eyes of their host peoples remained on a lower stage of civilization. Their social and political situation had been unchanged during those same centuries: everywhere they were in the rarest and best case only tolerated but usually oppressed and persecuted. Dohm was appealing to the conscience of humanity to take up the cause of the oppressed; he was not appealing for fellow citizens, nor even for a people with whom anyone felt any ties. To the keener consciences of men of the Enlightenment, it had become intolerable to know that there were among them people without rights. The cause of humanity thus became the cause of the Jews. "It is fortunate for us that no one can insist on the rights of man without at the same time espousing our own rights" (Moses Mendelssohn). The Jews, an accidental and embarrassing hangover of the Middle Ages, no longer thought of themselves as the chosen people of God; equally, the others no longer viewed them as suffering condign punishment for resisting Christianity. The Old Testament, their ancient possession, had in part become so remote, in part entered so completely into the body of European culture, that the Jews, the contemporary Jews, were no longer recognized as the people who had been its authors. The Old Testament was an element of culture, perhaps "one of the oldest documents of the human race" (Herder), but the Jews were merely members of an oppressed, uncultured, backward people who must be brought into the fold of humanity. What was wanted was to make human beings out of the Jews. Of course it was unfortunate that Jews existed at all; but since they did, there was nothing for it but to make people of them, that is to say, people of the Enlightenment.

The Jews concurred in this and similar emancipation theories of the Enlightenment. Fervently, they confessed their own inferiority; after all, were not the others to blame for it? Wicked Christianity and its sinister history had corrupted them; their own dark history was completely forgotten. It was as if they saw the whole of European history as nothing but one long era of Inquisition in which the poor good Jews had had no part, thank God, and for which they must now be recompensed. Naturally one was not going to cling to Judaism—why should one, since the whole of Jewish history and tradition was now revealed as a sordid product of the ghetto—for which, moreover, one was not to blame at all? Aside from the question of guilt, the fact of inferiority secretly hung on.

Rahel's life was bound by this inferiority, by her "infamous birth," from youth on up. Everything that followed was only confirmation, "bleeding to death." Therefore she must avoid everything that might give rise to further confirmation, must not act, not love, not become involved with the world. Given such absolute renunciation, all that seemed left was *thought*. The handicaps imposed upon her by nature and society would be neutralized by the mania "for examining everything and asking questions with inhuman persistence." Objective and impersonal thought was able to minimize the purely human, purely accidental quality of unhappiness.

Drawing up the balance sheet of life, one needed only to think "in order to know how one must feel and what is or is not left to one." Thinking amounted to an enlightened kind of magic which could substitute for, evoke and predict experience, the world, people and society. The power of Reason lent posited possibilities a tinge of reality, breathed a kind of illusory life into rational desires, fended off ungraspable actuality and refused to recognize it. The twenty-year-old Rahel wrote: "I shall never be convinced that I am a Schlemihl and a Jewess; since in all these years and after so much thinking about it, it has not dawned upon me, I shall never really grasp it. That is why 'the clang of the murderous axe does not nibble at my root'; that is why I am still living."

The Enlightenment raised Reason to the status of an authority. It declared thought and what Lessing called "self-thinking," which anyone can engage in alone and of his own accord, the supreme capacities of man. "Everything depends on self-thinking," Rahel remarked to Gustav von Brinckmann in conversation. She promptly added a thought that would hardly have occurred to the men of the Enlightenment: "The objects often matter very little, just as the beloved often matters far less than loving." Self-thinking brings liberation from objects and their reality, creates a sphere of pure ideas and a world which is accessible to any rational being without benefit of knowledge or experience. It brings liberation from the object just as romantic love liberates the lover from the reality of his beloved. Romantic love produces the "great lovers" whose love cannot be disturbed by the specific qualities of their sweethearts, whose feelings can no longer be rubbed raw by any contact with actuality. Similarly, self-thinking in this sense provides a foundation for cultivated ignoramuses. Being by birth exempt from obligation to any object in their alien cultural environment, they need merely, in order to become contemporaries, peel off old prejudices and free themselves for the business of thinking.

Reason can liberate from the prejudices of the past and it can guide the future. Unfortunately, however, it appears that it can free isolated individuals only, can direct the future only of Crusoes. The individual who has been liberated by reason is always running head-on into a world, a society, whose past in the shape of "prejudices" has a great deal of power; he is forced to learn that past reality is also a reality. Although being born a Jewess might seem to Rahel a mere reference to something out of the remote past, and although she may have entirely eradicated the fact from her thinking, it remained a nasty present reality as a prejudice in the minds of others.

How can the present be rendered ineffective? How can human freedom be so enormously extended that it no longer collides with limits;

how can introspection be so isolated that the thinking individual no longer need smash his head against the wall of "irrational" reality? How can you peel off the disgrace of unhappiness, the infamy of birth? How can you—a second creator of the world—transform reality back into its potentialities and so escape the "murderous axe"?

If thinking rebounds back upon itself and finds its solitary object within the soul—if, that is, it becomes introspection—it distinctly produces (so long as it remains rational) a semblance of unlimited power by the very act of isolation from the world; by ceasing to be interested in the world it also sets up a bastion in front of the one "interesting" object: the inner self. In the isolation achieved by introspection thinking becomes limitless because it is no longer molested by anything exterior; because there is no longer any demand for action, the consequences of which necessarily impose limits even upon the freest spirit. Man's autonomy becomes hegemony over all possibilities; reality merely impinges and rebounds. Reality can offer nothing new; introspection has already anticipated everything. Even the blows of fate can be escaped by flight into the self if every single misfortune has already been generalized beforehand as an inevitable concomitant of the bad outside world, so that there is no reason to feel shock at having been struck this one particular time. The one unpleasant feature is that memory itself perpetuates the present, which otherwise would only touch the soul fleetingly. As a consequence of memory, therefore, one subsequently discovers that outer events have a degree of reality that is highly disturbing.

Rousseau is the greatest example of the mania for introspection because he succeeded even in getting the best of memory; in fact, he converted it in a truly ingenious fashion into the most dependable guard against the outside world. By sentimentalizing memory he obliterated the contours of the remembered event. What remained were the feelings experienced in the course of those events—in other words, once more nothing but reflections within the psyche. Sentimental remembering is the best method for completely forgetting one's own destiny. It presupposes that the present itself is instantly converted into a "sentimental" past. For Rousseau (*Confessions*) the present always first rises up out of memory, and it is immediately drawn into the inner self, where everything is eternally present and converted back into potentiality. Thus the power and autonomy of the soul are secured. Secured at the price of truth, it must be recognized, for without reality shared with other human beings, truth loses all meaning. Introspection and its hybrids engender *mendacity*.

"Facts mean nothing at all to me," she writes to Veit, and signs this letter: "Confessions de J. J. Rahel"—"for whether true or not, facts can be denied; if I have done something, I did it because I wanted to; and if someone wants to blame me or lie to me, there's nothing for me to do but say 'No,' and I do." Every fact can be undone, can be wiped out by a lie. Lying can obliterate the outside event which introspection has already converted into a purely psychic factor. Lying takes up the heritage of introspection, sums it up, and makes a reality of the freedom that introspection has won. "Lying is lovely if we choose it, and is an important component of our freedom." How can a fact mean anything if the person himself refuses to corroborate it? For example: Jews may not go driving on the Sabbath; Rahel went driving with the actress Marchetti "in broad daylight on the Sabbath; nobody saw me; I would have and would and shall deny it to anyone's face." If she denies it, nothing remains of the fact except one opinion against other opinions. Facts can be disintegrated into opinions as soon as one refuses to consent to them and withdraws from their context. They have their own peculiar way of being true: their truth must always be recognized, testified to. Perhaps reality consists only in the agreement of everybody, is perhaps only a social phenomenon, would perhaps collapse as soon as someone had the courage forthrightly and consistently to deny its existence. Every event passes—who may claim to know tomorrow whether it really took place? Whatever is not proved by thinking is not provable—therefore, make your denials, falsify by lies, make use of your freedom to change and render reality ineffective at will. Only truths discovered by reason are irrefutable; only these can always be made plain to everyone. Poor reality, dependent upon human beings who believe in it and confirm it. For it as well as their confirmation are transitory and not even always presentable.

That facts (or history) are not acceptable to reason, no matter how well confirmed they are, because both their factuality and their confirmation are accidental; that only "rational truths" (Lessing), the products of pure thought, can lay claim to validity, truth, cogency—this was (for the sophistries of the Assimilation) the most important element of the German Enlightenment that Mendelssohn adopted from Lessing. Adopted and falsified. For to Lessing history is the teacher of mankind and the mature individual recognizes "historical truths" by virtue of his reason. The freedom of reason, too, is a product of history, a higher stage of historical development. It is only in Mendelssohn's version that "historical and rational truths" are separated so finally and completely that the truth-seeking man himself withdraws from history. Mendelssohn expressly opposes Lessing's philosophy of history, referring slightingly to "the Education of the Human Race, of which my late friend Lessing allowed himself to be persuaded by I do not know what historian." Mendelssohn held that all realities such as environment, history and society could not—thank God—be warranted by Reason.

Rahel's struggle against the facts, above all against the fact of having been born a Jew, very rapidly became a struggle against herself. She herself refused to consent to herself; she, born to so many disadvantages, had to deny, change, reshape by lies this self of hers, since she could not very well deny her existence out of hand.

As long as Don Quixote continues to ride forth to conjure a possible, imagined, illusory world out of the real one, he is only a fool, and perhaps a happy fool, perhaps even a noble fool when he undertakes to conjure up within the real world a definite ideal. But if without a definite ideal, without aiming at a definite imaginary revision of the world, he attempts only to transform himself into some sort of empty possibility which he *might* be, he becomes merely a "foolish dreamer," and an opportunist one in addition, who is seeking to destroy his existence for the sake of certain advantages.

For the possibilities of being different from what one is are infinite. Once one has negated oneself, however, there are no longer any particular choices. There is only one aim: always, at any given moment, to be different from what one is; never to assert oneself, but with infinite pliancy to become anything else, so long as it is not oneself. It requires an inhuman alertness not to betray oneself, to conceal everything and yet have no definite secret to cling to. Thus, at the age of twenty-one, Rahel wrote to Veit: "For do what I will, I shall be ill, out of *gêne,* as long as I live; I live against my inclinations. I dissemble, I am courteous . . . but I am too *small* to stand it, too *small.* . . . My eternal dissembling, my being reasonable, my yielding which I myself no longer notice, swallowing my own insights—I can no longer stand it; and nothing, no one, can help me."

Omnipotent as opinion and mendacity are, they have, however, a limit beyond which alteration cannot go; one cannot change one's face; neither thought nor liberty, neither lies nor nausea nor disgust can lift one out of one's own skin. That same winter she wrote: "I wish nothing more ardently now than to change myself, outwardly and inwardly. I . . . am sick of myself; but I can do nothing about it and will remain the way I am, just as my face will; we can both grow older, but nothing more. . . ." At best, then, there remains time which makes everyone older and carries every human being along, from the moment of birth on, into constant change. The only drawback is that this change is useless because it leads to no dream paradise, to no New World of unlimited possibilities. No human being can isolate himself completely; he will always be thrown back upon the world again if he has any hopes at all for the things that only the world can give: "ordinary things, but things one must have." In the end the world always has the last word because one can introspect only into one's own self, but not out of it again. "Ah yes, if I could live out of the world, without conventions, without relationships, live an honest, hard-working life in a village." But that, too, is only possible if the world has so arranged matters, whereas: "But I have nothing to live on."

Relationships and conventions, in their general aspects, are as irrevocable as nature. A person probably can defy a single fact by denying it, but not that totality of facts which we call the world. In the world one can live if one has a station, a place on which one stands, a position to which one belongs. If one has been so little provided for by the world as Rahel, one is nothing because one is not defined from outside. Details, customs, relationships, conventions, cannot be surveyed and grasped; they become a part of the indefinite world in general which in its totality is only a hindrance. "Also, I fear *every* change!" Here insight no longer helps; insight can only foresee and predict, can only "consume" the hope. "Nothing, no one can help me."

Nothing foreseeable, and no one whom she knows can help her, at any rate. Therefore, perhaps the absolutely unforeseeable, chance, luck, will do it. It is senseless to attempt to *do* anything in this disordered, indefinite world. Therefore, perhaps the answer is simply to wait, to wait for life itself. "And yet, wherever I can get the opportunity to meet her, I shall kiss the dust from the feet of Fortune, out of gratitude and wonder." Chance is a glorious cause for hope, which so resembles despair that the two can easily be confounded. Hope seduces one into peering about in the world for a tiny, infinitesimally tiny crack which circumstances may have overlooked, for a crack, be it ever so narrow, which nevertheless would help to define, to organize, to provide a center for the indefinite world—because the longed-for unexpected something might ultimately emerge through it in the form of a definite happiness. Hope leads to despair when all one's searching discovers no such crack, no chance for happiness: "It seems to me I am so glad not to be unhappy that a blind man could not fail to see that I cannot really be happy at all."

Such was the inner landscape of this twenty-four-year-old girl who as yet had not actually experienced anything, whose life was still without any personal content. "I am unhappy; I won't let anyone reason me out of it; and that always has a disturbing effect." This insight rapidly became a final one, unaffected by the fact that Rahel went on hoping for happiness almost all her life; secretly, no matter what happened to her, Rahel always knew that the insight of her youth was only waiting to be confirmed. Suffering disadvantages from birth on, unhappy without having been struck down by destiny, without being compelled to endure any specific misfortune, her sorrow was "greater than its cause . . . more ripely prepared," as Wilhelm von Burgsdorff, the close friend of Caroline von Humboldt, wrote to her during those years. By renouncing—without having had anything definite to renounce—she had already anticipated all experiences, seemed to know suffering without having suffered. "A long sorrow has 'educated' you; . . . it is true that a trace of suffered destiny is visible in you, that one sees in you silence and reticence early learned."

In waiting for the concrete confirmation, which for the present did not come, she converted her vagueness about the world and life into a generalization. She saw herself as blocked not by individual and therefore removable obstacles, but by everything, by *the* world. Out of her hopeless struggle with indefiniteness arose her "inclination to generalize." Reason grasped conceptually what could not be specifically defined, thereby saving her a second time. By abstraction reason diverted attention from the concrete; it transformed the yearning to be happy into a "passion for truth"; it taught "pleasures" which had no connection with the personal self. Rahel loved no other human being, but she loved encounters with others in the realm of truth. Reason met its counterpart in all people, and these encounters remained "pleasurable" so long as she kept her distance and sold her soul to no one. "How happy is the man who loves his friends and can live without them without restiveness." Generalities cannot be lost; they can be found again or reproduced at any time. She was not happy, could not be happy, but she was also not unhappy. She could love no one, but in many people she could love a variety of qualities.

She made the acquaintance of many people. The "garret" on Jägerstrasse became a meeting place for her friends. The oldest of these, and for many years the closest, was David Veit, a young Jewish student of Berlin. In the mid-nineties he was studying medicine at Göttingen University. They wrote frequently to one another, their letters constituting journals, diary entries. He knew her and her milieu because he came from a similar one himself. He knew the conditions in her household; she told him everything without reticence, showed him, giving a thousand details as proof, the incompatibility between herself and her domestic environment; she demonstrated it, provided circumstantial evidence for it, adduced petty incidents. Veit did not understand the strength of her despair. The solution, as he saw it, was to get out of Judaism, to be baptized (this he did a few years later); it was possible to escape these surroundings and these experiences, and later they could be forgotten. She became aware that her complaint lacked content. Single obstacles could be removed;

how well she knew that specific things or events could be denied. But she could not yet express the essence to which she was referring; only experience could explain that, only experiences serve as examples of it.

More important for her than his comprehension of these matters was the fact that Veit became her first correspondent from the contemporary world. She prized his accurate, reliable reports, always remembered him for having suppressed not a word, not a detail, in describing his visit with Goethe. Her letters were equally precise, equally reliable answers. Never did he write a word into a void; she unfailingly took up, commented on, answered everything. Letters served as a substitute for conversations; she used them to talk about people and things. Excluded from society, deprived of any normal social intercourse, she had a tremendous hunger for people, was greedy for every smallest event, tensely awaited every utterance. The world was unknown and hostile to her; she had no education, tradition or convention with which to make order out of it; and hence orientation was impossible to her. Therefore she devoured mere details with indiscriminate curiosity. No aristocratic elegance, no exclusiveness, no innate taste restrained her craving for the new and the unknown; no knowledge of people, no social instinct and no tact limited her indiscriminateness or prescribed for her any particular, well-founded, proper conduct toward acquaintances. "You are," wrote Veit, "*candid* toward acquaintances who understand not a syllable of what you say and who misinterpret this candor. These acquaintances ask candor of you where you are reticent, and do not thank you for the truth." Instead of saying little to a few, Rahel talked with everybody about everything. She was maligned as malicious—and was made a confidant. Her curiosity operated like a hidden magnet; her passionate tension drew people's secrets out of them. In her absence, however, she struck people as equivocal. You never knew what she thought of you, what your relationship to her was; when you went away, you knew nothing about her. Not that she had anything specific to conceal or to confess; it was her general condition that she hid. And precisely that engendered the atmosphere of equivocation and uncertainty.

This faulty relationship to people pursued her all her life. Not until twenty years later did she realize what her reputation, good and bad, her equivocation despite her innocent intent, was based on. "Although in one penetrating look I form an undeviating opinion of people, I can find myself involved in crude errors without being mistaken in those whom I have, so to speak, right before me. Because I do not decide on the madly arbitrary assumption that any one particular individual would be capable of carrying out any one crude, ugly action. I won't say I cannot decide; I do not like to decide. If I did, I would be shaming, sullying myself." Essentially, she expected the same thing from everybody, could deal with people only in generalizations, could not recognize the accidental character of individuals' physiognomies, the "crude and common" chanciness of a particular person, a particular juxtaposition of traits. Details were so important to her because she immediately saw them as typical; they communicated much more, contributed far more information to her hungry curiosity, revealed far more to her mind, which depended on deduction in its attempts at orientation, than anyone could guess or possibly understand. "Since, for me, very small traits . . . decide the whole inner value of a person for all eternity, it obviously becomes impossible for me to show him what I think of him, what are my ideas about the particular circumstances in which we happen to be. They must think me mad. . . . Therefore there remains for me only keeping silent, withholding myself, annoying, avoiding, observing, distracting and using people, being clumsily angry, and on top of all suffering criticism all the time from stupid vulgarians!" She could not admit that a person may be no more than his qualities, since she herself started out with none but the most formal qualities, such as intelligence, alertness, passionateness. To make any such assertion would be, for her, an offense against the dignity of man. But at the same time she could not be consistent in treating people as though they were different from themselves, as though they were more than the accidental sum of their qualities. For "what a person is capable of, no one knows *better* than I; *no one* grasps more quickly." Her equivocation resulted from this attitude and this knowledge of people which she owed to an extreme sensitivity. Moreover, her sensitivity was constantly sharpened by repression. "This penetration, then, and that lack of decisiveness produce a dichotomy in my treatment of people: full of consideration and respect outwardly; and inwardly a stern, judging, contemptuous or worshipful attitude. Anyone can easily find me inconsistent, cowardly, pliable and timid . . . and believe that my better judgment operates only before or after the event, while in the course of it passion throws my good sense to the winds." The discrepancy between treatment and judgment, "before and after," the decision taken behind the back of the person concerned, was naïve and not malicious. If she was to associate with people, she could only treat them as if they were as independent of their good and bad qualities as she herself; but when she wished to judge them, she could not blind her keen insight. After all, no one was too likely to ask her opinion of himself to her face. And even if someone did, she had the defense that, after all, she did not judge on the basis of particular actions; she passed no moral condemnations upon this person or that; and she had no standard of value and no prejudices, no matter how useful these might be; she availed herself only of "very small traits," nothing tangible; her judgment was, so to speak, based upon the very substance of which a person was made, upon the consistency of his soul, the level he attained or did not attain.

She acquired insight into these matters quite late, and paid disproportionately dear for them. No one, she rightly commented in her youth, was more candid than she; no one wanted more to be known. She repeatedly told Veit he was free to show all of her letters to others; she had no secrets, she wrote. On the contrary, she believed people would know her better from her letters, would be more just toward her. The world and people were so boundless, and whatever happened to her seemed so little directed toward her in particular, that discretion was incomprehensible to her. "Why won't you show anyone a whole letter of mine? It would not matter to me; nothing I have written need be hidden. If only I could throw myself open to people as a cupboard is opened, and with one gesture show the things arranged in order in their compartments. They would certainly be content, and as soon as they saw, would understand."

The true joy of conversation consisted in being understood. The more imaginary a life is, the more imaginary its sufferings, the greater is the craving for an audience, for confirmation. Precisely because Rahel's despair was visible, but its cause unknown and incomprehensible to herself, it would become pure hypochondria unless it were talked about, exposed. A morsel of reality lay hidden in other people's intelligent replies. She needed the experience of others to supplement her own. For that purpose, the particular qualifications of the individuals were a matter of indifference. The more people there were who understood her, the more real she would become. Silence was only a shield against being misunderstood, a shutting oneself off in order not to be touched. But silence out of fear of being understood was unknown to her. She was indiscreet toward herself.

Indiscretion and shamelessness were phenomena of the age, of Romanticism. But the first great model of indiscretion toward oneself had been provided by Rousseau's confessions, in which the self was exposed to its farthermost corners before the anonymous future reader, posterity. Posterity would no longer have any power over the life of the strange confessor; it could neither judge nor forgive; posterity was only the fantasied *foil* of the perceiving inner self. With the loss of the priest and his judgment, the solitude of the would-be confessor had become boundless. The singularity of the person, the uniqueness of the individual character, stood out against a background of indefinite anonymity. Everything was equally important and nothing forbidden. In complete isolation, shame was extinguished. The importance of emotions existed independently of possible consequences, independently of actions or motives. Rousseau related neither his life story nor his experiences. He merely confessed what he had felt, desired, wished, sensed in the course of his life. In the course of such a ruthless confessional the individual is isolated not only from the events of public life, but also from the events of his private life. His own life acquires reality only in the course of confessing it, only in recollections of emotions which he had at some time. Not the emotions, but *narrated* emotions alone can convince and overwhelm the hypochondriac. The utter absence of inhibition, so that no residue of silence is left, formed—according to Rousseau's own judgment—the uniqueness of his confessions. Such absence of inhibition is possible only within an absolute solitude which no human being and no objective force is capable of piercing.

Uninhibited utterance becomes open indiscretion if it is not addressed to posterity, but to a real listener who is merely treated as if he were anonymous, as if he could not reply, as if he existed simply and solely to listen. We find only too ample evidence of such indiscretion among Rahel's closest associates; its "classic" representation may be found in Friedrich Schlegel's *Lucinde,* which will serve for an example.

Lucinde is no more the story of a life than Rousseau's *Confessions.* All that we learn about the hero's life in the novel is couched in terms so general that only a mood, no real events, can be represented. Every situation is wrenched out of its context, introspected, and dressed up as a specially interesting chance occurrence. Life is without any continuity, a "mass of fragments without connection" (Schlegel). Since each of these fragments is enormously intensified by the endless introspection, life itself is shown as a fragment in the Romantic sense, "a small work of art entirely separated from the surrounding world and as complete in itself as a hedgehog" (Schlegel).

Introspection accomplishes two feats: it annihilates the actual existing situation by dissolving it in mood, and at the same time it lends everything subjective an aura of objectivity, publicity, extreme interest. In mood the boundaries between what is intimate and what is public become blurred; intimacies are made public, and public matters can be experienced and expressed only in the realm of the intimate—ultimately, in gossip. The shamelessness of *Lucinde,* which aroused a storm of indignation when it was published, is supposed to be justified by the magic of its mood. This mood supposedly possesses the power to convert reality back into potentiality and to confer, for the moment, the appearance of reality upon mere potentialities. The mood thus embodies the "fearful omnipotence of the imagination" (Schlegel). The imagination need hold no limit sacred, since it is limitless in itself. In the enchantment of mood, which expands a detail to infinity, the infinite appears as the most precious aspect of intimacy. In the flimsiness of a society which, as it were, exists only in a twilight state, communication is interesting only at the cost of unmasking; no limits may be placed upon revelation if it is to do justice to the claim that mood has no limits. But the less anything definite and objective may be communicated, the more it becomes necessary to relate intimate, unknown, curiosity-arousing details. It is precisely the ultimate intimacy which is intended to denote, in its uniqueness and un-generality, the breakthrough of the infinite which has withdrawn from everything real, tangible, understandable. If the infinite was revealed to earlier centuries, if its mystery was beginning to unfold to the Reason of a generation not yet dead, this generation now insisted that it betray its secrets privately. That alone is what Schlegel was really concerned with in all the shamelessness of his confessions—namely, with the "objectivity of his love" (Schlegel).

What the novel fails to do because mood, fascination, cannot survive when divorced from the personality, can be done in conversation. Young Schlegel must have possessed the magic of personality just as strongly as Rahel, of whom Gentz once said that she had been Romantic before the word was invented. In the limitlessness of conversation, in personal fascination, reality could be excluded just as effectively as in introspection or pure self-thinking. Rahel's friendships during this period were all, so to speak, tête-à-têtes. "You are never really with a person unless you are alone with him." Every chance additional person could disturb the intimacy. Even the interlocutor in the mood-drenched conversation was almost superfluous. "I will go still further—you are never more actually with a person than when you think of him in his absence and imagine what you will say to him," and—it might be added—when he is cheated of any chance to reply and you yourself are free of any risk of being rejected.

In such converse Rahel withdrew from the society which had excluded her; in it she could confirm her own situation and neutralize the bitterness of being involuntarily at a disadvantage. Confirmation must always be renewed, just as the sense of being wronged must repeatedly be revived. All praise was an inspiration: "Blame has little power over me, but I can be caught with praise." Only in an atmosphere of praise could she prove her uniqueness; she consumed more and more flatterers. Even listening to reproof would be tantamount to admitting that she was "nothing." But by never attempting to defend herself against blame, she rendered it powerless. Toward Wilhelm von Humboldt, who could not endure her and her indiscriminateness, she was curiously hard of hearing—and yet she attempted to captivate him anyway. Indiscriminately, she tried to win everyone over. If in spite of this she was rejected, she saw the rejection only as an insult that frightened her and thought she could prevent such insults by intriguing. Thus she wrote "the most *servile* letters to wholly unimportant people, in the vain hope of changing the only relationship really possible between us: bad feeling."

This misunderstanding seemed to be inescapable. Other people were never the "mirror images which reflected her inner self"—a specific, unalterable inner self—whose existence could help make her "inner self more distinct" (Goethe). For she did not possess herself; the purpose of her introspection was merely to know what could happen to her, in order to be armed against it; in introspection she must never let herself know who she was, for that might possibly be a "shlemihl or a Jew." She was so little mistress of her inner self that even her consciousness of reality was dependent upon confirmation by others. Only because she was in no sense sure of herself did condemnation have little power over her; and her words are remote indeed from the proud serenity with which Goethe could say: "Antagonists are out of the question . . . ; they reject the purposes toward which my actions are directed. . . . Therefore I wave them away and refuse to know them. . . ."

Among the "praisers" the most important, for a time, were Gustav von Brinckmann and Wilhelm von Burgsdorff. Brinckmann, the Swedish ambassador in Berlin, is known for his letters to Schleiermacher and Gentz, letters full of pen portraits of acquaintances, of gossip and affairs with women. This extremely commonplace and highly typical child of his time was never heavily committed to anything; he was pliant and had the gift of politeness; he moved from one person to another, was a cultivated man without any center to his personality. Prince Louis Ferdinand, writing to Pauline Wiesel, commented: "Brinckmann is really so sweet. Lovers write letters for the sake of love, but he loves for the sake of letters." He also indulged in philosophical speculations—leaning heavily on Schleiermacher, whose disciple he called himself; his *point d'appui* was always in the realm of psychology, and his ponderings were without consistency. Women as the most important because least explored psychological territory were by no means his discovery. Interest in man, during this period, degenerated on the whole to psychological interest in a newly discovered type of man. Brinckmann was merely one "brooder on humanity" among many "for whom women are the principal study" (Brinckmann). Rahel was splendidly suited to be a "friend without adjectives or connotations" (Brinckmann); psychologically she was the hardest of women to understand, while for her part she affected to be able to understand everything. She was a brilliant interlocutor: "She came, *talked* and *conquered*" (Brinckmann).

Burgsdorff met Rahel at Bad Teplitz in the summer of 1795, through Brinckmann's introduction. She was spending the summer with Countess Pachta and was happy to have a companion who was an indefatigable talker and a cultivated person; she delighted in the extraordinary "receptivity of his mind" (Varnhagen). In spite of his pretended rejection of the world, Brinckmann nevertheless possessed ambition; her friend Veit was endeavoring with every means at his disposal to force his way into society, precisely because he had been originally excluded from it; in Burgsdorff, on the other hand, Rahel saw a nobleman's unstrained repudiation of offices, dignities and effectiveness in the world.

These few names are intended only as examples of the nature of her friendships: neither Brinckmann nor Burgsdorff nor Veit loved her. With all these men it is difficult to imagine how they could possibly become involved in a love situation. Brinckmann was driven by restless curiosity from one woman to another; Burgsdorff's love for Caroline von Humboldt is a familiar tale. The decay of that love was no less fearful for being peculiarly unmotivated: Caroline's love became burdensome to him; he fled from Paris to escape it when it began to involve more than "grasping the most individual character traits, the faintest nuances."

Veit, as Rahel's first friend and her ally in the struggle with the alien world, occupied a special position. He was the first to whom Rahel said: "Only galley slaves know one another." He was the first to discover everything praiseworthy in her: her understanding, her precision, her intelligence. He was the first person who knew how "to use" her, who knew that she was good for more than "helping to consume the sugar." But in this relationship, too, there was never any talk of love.

Alongside this life with her friends she lived another, unofficial life whose details she concealed from these friends; she candidly admitted the wretchedness of it only to her brothers. In this other life she kept alive the reality of her first setbacks. In fact she noted carefully, with a "cruel joy," every confirmation of her being a shlemihl: not rich, not beautiful and Jewish. She told her friends about this only in generalities. Thus she wrote to Brinckmann from Teplitz, where she had by chance encountered Goethe, and briefly became acquainted with him: "I don't know—it is as though many years ago something was shattered inside me and I take a cruel pleasure in knowing that henceforth it can no longer be broken, pulled at and beaten—although now it has become a place to which I myself can no longer reach. (And if there is *such* a place inside one, all possibility of happiness is ruled out.) I can no longer remember what it was; and if I do not succeed in minor things, I must at once provide so many rationalizations for my bunglings, that no one else will believe me and I myself become frightened. . . . For it is frightful to be forced to consider oneself the only creature that makes *everything* come to grief . . . for that, as far as I know, is my only accomplishment."

Writing *Rahel Varnhagen*.
From a Letter to Karl Jaspers

September 7, 1952 (Palenville)

Arendt had sent Karl Jaspers a draft of Rahel Varnhagen: The Life of a Jewess *to which he had responded critically; his letter can be found on pp. 192–96 of the Arendt/Jaspers correspondence. The letter printed below is Arendt's rejoinder to Jaspers's comments and objections. The notes following the letter are by Lotte Kohler and Hans Saner.*

It was written from the perspective of a Zionist critique of assimilation, which I had adopted as my own and which I still consider basically justified today. But that critique was as politically naïve as what it was criticizing. Personally, the book is alien to me in many ways, and perhaps that's why I feel it as particularly alien to me now, especially in its tone, in its mode of reflection, but not in the Jewish experience, which I made my own with no little difficulty. By virtue of my background I was simply naïve. I found the so-called Jewish question boring. The person who opened my eyes in this area was Kurt Blumenfeld, who then became a close friend and still is. He was able to do that because he was one of those few Jews I've met who was as naïvely assimilated and as unprejudiced by his background as I was myself. He is also one of my few Jewish friends who knew about Heinrich and then, completely free of prejudice, became very friendly with him. It's a pity that you don't know him. He is a prematurely old man now and very ill. He used to say: I'm a Zionist by the grace of Goethe. Or: Zionism is Germany's gift to the Jews.

You're absolutely right when you say this book "can make one feel that if a person is a Jew he cannot really live his life to the full." And that is of course a central point. I still believe today that under the conditions

---

From Hannah Arendt/Karl Jaspers: Correspondence 1926–1969.

of social assimilation and political emancipation the Jews could not "live." Rahel's life seems to me a proof of that precisely because she tried out everything on herself without attempting to spare herself anything and without a trace of dishonesty. What always intrigued me about her was the phenomenon of life striking her like "rain pouring down on someone without an umbrella." That's why, it seems to me, her life illustrates everything with such clarity. And that's also what made her so insufferable.

The picture of Rahel that you put up against mine is in all its essential features the one drawn by Varnhagen. You know what I think of Varnhagen. But aside from that, one could have demonstrated, as long as the Varnhagen archive still existed (it has disappeared; I searched for it all over Germany,[1]) that this picture is totally false. He falsified it doubly—he eliminated the altogether insufferable side of Rahel and at the same time the altogether lovable side. Both can still be seen in six volumes of letters[2] between Rahel and Varnhagen, which came out without emendations after Varnhagen's death. The bad thing about this falsification is that it is basically done in a way in which Rahel herself would have liked to falsify. But of course never would have falsified. As far as the falsifications are concerned, they consist of the following, as far as I can recall without having the material at hand: Three volumes of Rahel's letters (*Ein Buch des Andenkens*[3]) 1. always change the name of the recipient—Rebekka Friedländer[4] is called Frau v. V. etc., 2. always omit passages that refer to the Jewish question, which creates the impression that Rahel was surrounded by a large circle of close non-Jewish friends and that the Jewish question played a relatively minor role in her life, 3. certain people who either do not belong to "good society" (like Pauline Wiesel) or whose relationship with Rahel does not conform to the standards of good society (like Gentz) are either completely left out, or everything of real importance relating to them is eliminated, 4. relationships with other people that reflect prestigiously on Rahel are presented as more important than they in fact were (e.g., the relationship with Caroline v. Humboldt[5]).

As far as the Enlightenment is concerned, I probably didn't express myself clearly. My focus was only the Enlightenment as it was relevant to Rahel, and by that I mean to her as a Jewish girl who had to bring about her own assimilation (that is, had to do consciously what others at a later time would have simply handed to them). Under those special conditions the Enlightenment played a highly questionable role. I illustrate it with "negative" examples because in this historical context there aren't any positive ones. Mendelssohn and Friedländer were the key figures, not Lessing. And unlike you, I see Mendelssohn as nothing but flat and opportunistic. Spinoza is as absent in him, it seems to me, as he is in Rahel herself. Spinoza was a great philosopher and as such *sui generis*. He was indifferent—or at least in every essential respect indifferent—to the fact that he was a Jew. It was his background, the thing that he left behind. He was not yet confronted with a Jewish problem in his time either. Everything was personal history. That he was a Jew and as such stood outside society was just one opportunity more for him. Mendelssohn's and Rahel's primary objective was to enter society, which one can hardly hold against them. The first who would be able to find his place outside it again was Heine, because he was a poet the way Spinoza was a philosopher, and he was a revolutionary as well.

That brings me to the really central question. You assume something like a more or less unbroken tradition of Judaism in which Rahel would have her place the way Spinoza and Mendelssohn do. But Mendelssohn is the only one of the three who has a place in Judaism, and that for reasons that are quite unimportant here. He translated the Bible into German with Hebrew letters, that is, he taught the Jews German. He also played a role as a representative of Judaism in the "learned circles of Germany" and even became in Mirabeau's[6] eyes the example to show that Jews are not necessarily barbarians. As a philosopher (?) Mendelssohn is completely without significance in Judaism. And if we were thinking only in terms of Jewish tradition, Spinoza would be completely forgotten today, not remembered even as a heretic. (I couldn't talk Schocken into publishing a Spinoza volume because "Spinoza wasn't a Jew.")

Judaism doesn't exist outside orthodoxy on the one hand or outside the Yiddish-speaking, folklore-producing Jewish people on the other. There are also people of Jewish background who are unaware of any Jewish substance in their lives in the sense of a tradition and who for certain social reasons and because they found themselves constituting a clique within society produced something like a "Jewish type." This type has nothing to do with what we understand under Judaism historically or with its genuine content. Here there is much that is positive, namely, all those things that I classify as pariah qualities and what Rahel called the "true realities of life"—"love, trees, children, music." In this type there is an extraordinary awareness of injustices; there is great generosity and a lack of prejudice; and there is—more questionably but nonetheless demonstrably present—respect for the "life of the mind." Of all these things only the last one can still be shown to have a link with originally and specifically Jewish substance. The element of Judaism that has persisted longest simply in the way people live is family loyalty. That is not an intellectual quality, however, but, rather, a sociological and political phenomenon. The negative "Jewish" qualities have nothing to do with Judaism in this sense and all derive from parvenu stories. Rahel is "interesting" because, with utter naïveté and utterly unprejudiced, she stands right in the middle between pariah and parvenu. Jewish history, to the extent that it is an independent history of the Jewish people in the Diaspora, ends with the Sabbatai Zwi movement.[7] Zionism marks the beginning of a new chapter; perhaps, too, the great migration to America since the end of the last century. Perhaps there will be still another renaissance of Judaism (I hardly think so).

You reproach me for "moralizing" about Rahel. I may well have slipped into moralizing, and I shouldn't have. What I meant to do was argue further with her, the way she argued with herself, and always within the categories that were available to her and that she somehow accepted as valid. In other words, I tried to measure and correct the parvenu by constantly applying the standards of the pariah because I felt that was her own method of proceeding, even though she was perhaps often not aware of it.

On the externals: The lack of a title page is no doubt an oversight. Heinrich sent the copy that was bound and easy to put his hand on. The title was to be simply *Rahel Varnhagen: Eine Biographie*. There must be a chronological table in one of the copies. But perhaps it, too, has been lost with many other notes. Repetitions—absolutely. I never went through the book again to prepare it for print, hardly ever even checked it for typos. Despite the unseemly length of this self-protective (I hope not!) epistle, this whole project has not been very important to me for a long time, actually not since 1933. My reason is not so much, as I first recognized with the help of your letter, because I see the entire subject itself differently now (I might see some points differently if I read the book again, but not the essentials) but, rather, because I feel this whole so-called problem isn't so very important or at least is no longer important to me. Whatever of the straightforward historical insights I still consider relevant are contained in shorter form and devoid of all "psychology" in the first part of my totalitarianism book. And there I'm content to let the matter rest. . . .

With warmest and fondest greetings

Your

Hannah

Notes

1. The Varnhagen Archives, almost fully intact and catalogued, are in the Jagiellonian Library in Cracow, Poland. See Deborah Hertz, "The Varnhagen Collection Is in Krakau," *The American Archivist* 44, no. 3 (Summer 1981).

2. *Correspondence between Varnhagen and Rahel,* ed. Ludmilla Assing-Grimelli, 6 vols. (Leipzig, 1874–75).
3. *Rahel: Ein Buch des Andenkens für ihre Freunde,* 3 vols. (Berlin, 1834).
4. Rebekka Friedländer, b. 1782, wife of Moses Friedländer, was a successful novelist under the name Regina Frohberg.
5. Caroline von Humboldt, 1766–1829, was the wife of Wilhelm von Humboldt.
6. Comte de Mirabeau, 1749–1791, French revolutionary leader and orator, was a member of the States-General, 1789, and president of the National Assembly, 1791.
7. Shabbatai Zevi, 1626–1676, was a messianic Jewish heretic who later converted to Islam. He proclaimed himself the Messiah and had many followers among Eastern European Jews. His influence was felt into the eighteenth century.

PART III

TOTALITARIANISM

The Jews and Society

THE JEWS' POLITICAL IGNORANCE, which fitted them so well for their special role and for taking roots in the state's sphere of business, and their prejudices against the people and in favor of authority, which blinded them to the political dangers of antisemitism, caused them to be oversensitive toward all forms of social discrimination. It was difficult to see the decisive difference between political argument and mere antipathy when the two developed side by side. The point, however, is that they grew out of exactly opposite aspects of emancipation: political antisemitism developed because the Jews were a separate body, while social discrimination arose because of the growing equality of Jews with all other groups.

Equality of condition, though it is certainly a basic requirement for justice, is nevertheless among the greatest and most uncertain ventures of modern mankind. The more equal conditions are, the less explanation there is for the differences that actually exist between people; and thus all the more unequal do individuals and groups become. This perplexing consequence came fully to light as soon as equality was no longer seen in terms of an omnipotent being like God or an unavoidable common destiny like death. Whenever equality becomes a mundane fact in itself, without any gauge by which it may be measured or explained, then there is one chance in a hundred that it will be recognized simply as a working principle of a political organization in which otherwise unequal people have equal rights; there are ninety-nine chances that it will be mistaken for an innate quality of every individual, who is "normal" if he is like everybody else and "abnormal" if he happens to be different. This perversion of equality from a political into a social concept is all the more dangerous when a society leaves but little space for special groups and individuals, for then their differences become all the more conspicuous.

From The Origins of Totalitarianism.

The great challenge to the modern period, and its peculiar danger, has been that in it man for the first time confronted man without the protection of differing circumstances and conditions. And it has been precisely this new concept of equality that has made modern race relations so difficult, for there we deal with natural differences which by no possible and conceivable change of conditions can become less conspicuous. It is because equality demands that I recognize each and every individual as my equal, that the conflicts between different groups, which for reasons of their own are reluctant to grant each other this basic equality, take on such terribly cruel forms.

Hence the more equal the Jewish condition, the more surprising were Jewish differences. This new awareness led to social resentment against the Jews and at the same time to a peculiar attraction toward them; the combined reactions determined the social history of Western Jewry. Discrimination, however, as well as attraction, were politically sterile. They neither produced a political movement against the Jews nor served in any way to protect them against their enemies. They did succeed, though, in poisoning the social atmosphere, in perverting all social intercourse between Jews and Gentiles, and had a definite effect on Jewish behavior. The formation of a Jewish type was due to both—to special discrimination and to special favor.

Social antipathy for Jews, with its varying forms of discrimination, did no great political harm in European countries, for genuine social and economic equality was never achieved. To all appearances new classes developed as groups to which one belonged by birth. There is no doubt that it was only in such a framework that society could suffer the Jews to establish themselves as a special clique.

The situation would have been entirely different if, as in the United States, equality of condition had been taken for granted; if every member of society—from whatever stratum—had been firmly convinced that by ability and luck he might become the hero of a success story. In such a society, discrimination becomes the only means of distinction, a kind of universal law according to which groups may find themselves outside the sphere of civic, political, and economic equality. Where discrimination is not tied up with the Jewish issue only, it can become a crystallization point for a political movement that wants to solve all the natural difficulties and conflicts of a multinational country by violence, mob rule, and the sheer vulgarity of race concepts. It is one of the most promising and dangerous paradoxes of the American Republic that it dared to realize equality on the basis of the most unequal population in the world, physically and historically. In the United States, social antisemitism may one day become the very dangerous nucleus for a political movement.[1] In Europe, however, it had little influence on the rise of political antisemitism.

I : BETWEEN PARIAH AND PARVENU

The precarious balance between society and state, upon which the nation-state rested socially and politically, brought about a peculiar law governing Jewish admission to society. During the 150 years when Jews truly lived amidst, and not just in the neighborhood of, Western European peoples, they always had to pay with political misery for social glory and with social insult for political success. Assimilation, in the sense of acceptance by non-Jewish society, was granted them only as long as they were clearly distinguished exceptions from the Jewish masses even though they still shared the same restricted and humiliating political conditions, or later only when, after an accomplished emancipation and resulting social isolation, their political status was already challenged by antisemitic movements. Society, confronted with political, economic, and legal equality for Jews, made it quite clear that none of its classes was prepared to grant them social equality, and that only exceptions from the Jewish people would be received. Jews who heard the strange compliment that they were exceptions, exceptional Jews, knew quite well that it was this very ambiguity—that they were Jews and yet presumably not *like* Jews—which opened the doors of society to them. If they desired this kind of intercourse, they tried, therefore, "to be and yet not to be Jews."[2]

The seeming paradox had a solid basis in fact. What non-Jewish society demanded was that the newcomer be as "educated" as itself, and that, although he not behave like an "ordinary Jew," he be and produce something out of the ordinary, since, after all, he was a Jew. All advocates of emancipation called for assimilation, that is, adjustment to and reception by, society, which they considered either a preliminary condition to Jewish emancipation or its automatic consequence. In other words, whenever those who actually tried to improve Jewish conditions attempted to think of the Jewish question from the point of view of the Jews themselves, they immediately approached it merely in its social aspect. It has been one of the most unfortunate facts in the history of the Jewish people that only its enemies, and almost never its friends, understood that the Jewish question was a political one.

The defenders of emancipation tended to present the problem as one of "education," a concept which originally applied to Jews as well as non-

Jews.[3] It was taken for granted that the vanguard in both camps would consist of specially "educated," tolerant, cultured persons. It followed, of course, that the particularly tolerant, educated and cultured non-Jews could be bothered socially only with exceptionally educated Jews. As a matter of course, the demand, among the educated, for the abolition of prejudice was very quickly to become a rather one-sided affair, until only the Jews, finally, were urged to educate themselves.

This, however, is only one side of the matter. Jews were exhorted to become educated enough not to behave like ordinary Jews, but they were, on the other hand, accepted only because they were Jews, because of their foreign, exotic appeal. In the eighteenth century, this had its source in the new humanism which expressly wanted "new specimens of humanity" (Herder), intercourse with whom would serve as an example of possible intimacy with all types of mankind. To the enlightened Berlin of Mendelssohn's time, the Jews served as living proof that all men are human. For this generation, friendship with Mendelssohn or Markus Herz was an ever-renewed demonstration of the dignity of man. And because Jews were a despised and oppressed people, they were for it an even purer and more exemplary model of mankind. It was Herder, an outspoken friend of the Jews, who first used the later misused and misquoted phrase, "strange people of Asia driven into our regions."[4] With these words, he and his fellow-humanists greeted the "new specimens of humanity" for whom the eighteenth century had "searched the earth,"[5] only to find them in their age-old neighbors. Eager to stress the basic unity of mankind, they wanted to show the origins of the Jewish people as more alien, and hence more exotic, than they actually were, so that the demonstration of humanity as a universal principle might be more effective.

For a few decades at the turn of the eighteenth century, when French Jewry already enjoyed emancipation and German Jewry had almost no hope or desire for it, Prussia's enlightened intelligentsia made "Jews all over the world turn their eyes to the Jewish community in Berlin"[6] (and not in Paris!). Much of this was due to the success of Lessing's *Nathan the Wise,* or to its misinterpretation, which held that the "new specimens of humanity," because they had become examples of mankind, must also be more intensely human individuals.[7] Mirabeau was strongly influenced by this idea and used to cite Mendelssohn as his example.[8] Herder hoped that educated Jews would show a greater freedom from prejudice because "the Jew is free of certain political judgments which it is very hard or impossible for us to abandon." Protesting against the habit of the time of granting "concessions of new mercantile advantages," he proposed education as the true road to emancipation of Jews from Judaism, from "the old and proud

national prejudices, . . . customs that do not belong to our age and constitutions," so that Jews could become "purely humanized," and of service
to "the development of the sciences and the entire culture of mankind."[9]
At about the same time, Goethe wrote in a review of a book of poems
that their author, a Polish Jew, did "not achieve more than a Christian
étudiant en belles lettres," and complained that where he had expected
something genuinely new, some force beyond shallow convention, he
had found ordinary mediocrity.[10]

One can hardly overestimate the disastrous effect of this exaggerated
good will on the newly Westernized, educated Jews and the impact it had
on their social and psychological position. Not only were they faced with
the demoralizing demand that they be exceptions to their own people,
recognize "the sharp difference between them and the others," and ask
that such "separation . . . be also legalized" by the governments;[11] they
were expected even to become exceptional specimens of humanity. And
since this, and not Heine's conversion, constituted the true "ticket of admission" into cultured European society, what else could these and future
generations of Jews do but try desperately not to disappoint anybody?[12]

In the early decades of this entry into society, when assimilation had
not yet become a tradition to follow, but something achieved by few and
exceptionally gifted individuals, it worked very well indeed. While France
was the land of political glory for the Jews, the first to recognize them as
citizens, Prussia seemed on the way to becoming the country of social
splendor. Enlightened Berlin, where Mendelssohn had established close
connections with many famous men of his time, was only a beginning.
His connections with non-Jewish society still had much in common with
the scholarly ties that had bound Jewish and Christian learned men together in nearly all periods of European history. The new and surprising
element was that Mendelssohn's friends used these relationships for non-
personal, ideological, or even political purposes. He himself explicitly
disavowed all such ulterior motives and expressed time and again his
complete satisfaction with the conditions under which he had to live, as
though he had foreseen that his exceptional social status and freedom had
something to do with the fact that he still belonged to "the lowliest inhabitants of the (Prussian king's) domain."[13]

This indifference to political and civil rights survived Mendelssohn's
innocent relationships with the learned and enlightened men of his time;
it was carried later into the salons of those Jewish women who gathered
together the most brilliant society Berlin was ever to see. Not until after
the Prussian defeat of 1806, when the introduction of Napoleonic legislation into large regions of Germany put the question of Jewish emancipa-

tion on the agenda of public discussion, did this indifference change into outright fear. Emancipation would liberate the educated Jews, together with the "backward" Jewish people, and their equality would wipe out that precious distinction, upon which, as they were very well aware, their social status was based. When the emancipation finally came to pass, most assimilated Jews escaped into conversion to Christianity, characteristically finding it bearable and not dangerous to be Jews before emancipation, but not after.

Most representative of these salons, and the genuinely mixed society they brought together in Germany, was that of Rahel Varnhagen. Her original, unspoiled, and unconventional intelligence, combined with an absorbing interest in people and a truly passionate nature, made her the most brilliant and the most interesting of these Jewish women. The modest but famous soirées in Rahel's "garret" brought together "enlightened" aristocrats, middle-class intellectuals, and actors—that is, all those who, like the Jews, did not belong to respectable society. Thus Rahel's salon, by definition and intentionally, was established on the fringe of society, and did not share any of its conventions or prejudices.

It is amusing to note how closely the assimilation of Jews into society followed the precepts Goethe had proposed for the education of his *Wilhelm Meister,* a novel which was to become the great model of middle-class education. In this book the young burgher is educated by noblemen and actors, so that he may learn how to present and represent his individuality, and thereby advance from the modest status of a burgher's son into a nobleman. For the middle classes and for the Jews, that is, for those who were actually outside of high aristocratic society, everything depended upon "personality" and the ability to express it. To know how to play the role of what one actually was, seemed the most important thing. The peculiar fact that in Germany the Jewish question was held to be a question of education was closely connected with this early start and had its consequence in the educational philistinism of both the Jewish and non-Jewish middle classes, and also in the crowding of Jews into the liberal professions.

The charm of the early Berlin salons was that nothing really mattered but personality and the uniqueness of character, talent, and expression. Such uniqueness, which alone made possible an almost unbounded communication and unrestricted intimacy, could be replaced neither by rank, money, success, nor literary fame. The brief encounter of true personalities, which joined a Hohenzollern prince, Louis Ferdinand, to the banker Abraham Mendelssohn; or a political publicist and diplomat, Friedrich Gentz, to Friedrich Schlegel, a writer of the then ultramodern romantic school—these were a few of the more famous visitors at Rahel's "garret"—came to an end in 1806 when, according to their hostess, this unique meeting place "foundered like a ship containing the highest enjoyment of life." Along with the aristocrats, the romantic intellectuals became antisemitic, and although this by no means meant that either group gave up all its Jewish friends, the innocence and splendor were gone.

The real turning point in the social history of German Jews came not in the year of the Prussian defeat, but two years later, when, in 1808, the government passed the municipal law giving full civic, though not political, rights to the Jews. In the peace treaty of 1807, Prussia had lost with her eastern provinces the majority of her Jewish population; the Jews left within her territory were "protected Jews" in any event, that is, they already enjoyed civic rights in the form of individual privileges. The municipal emancipation only legalized these privileges, and outlived the general emancipation decree of 1812; Prussia, having regained Posen and its Jewish masses after the defeat of Napoleon, practically rescinded the decree of 1812, which now would have meant political rights even for poor Jews, but left the municipal law intact.

Though of little political importance so far as the actual improvement of the Jews' status is concerned, these final emancipation decrees together with the loss of the provinces in which the majority of Prussian Jews lived, had tremendous social consequences. Before 1807, the protected Jews of Prussia had numbered only about 20 per cent of the total Jewish population. By the time the emancipation decree was issued, protected Jews formed the majority in Prussia, with only 10 per cent of "foreign Jews" left for contrast. Now the dark poverty and backwardness against which "exception Jews" of wealth and education had stood out so advantageously was no longer there. And this background, so essential as a basis of comparison for social success and psychological self-respect, never again became what it had been before Napoleon. When the Polish provinces were regained in 1816, the formerly "protected Jews" (now registered as Prussian citizens of Jewish faith) still numbered above 60 per cent.[14]

Socially speaking, this meant that the remaining Jews in Prussia had lost the native background against which they had been measured as exceptions. Now they themselves composed such a background, but a contracted one, against which the individual had to strain doubly in order to stand out at all. "Exception Jews" were once again simply Jews, not exceptions from but representatives of a despised people. Equally bad was the social influence of governmental interference. Not only the classes antagonistic to the government and therefore openly hostile to the Jews, but all strata of society, became more or less aware that Jews of their acquaintance were not so much individual exceptions as members of a group in whose favor the state was ready to take exceptional measures. And this was precisely what the "exception Jews" had always feared.

Berlin society left the Jewish salons with unmatched rapidity, and by 1808 these meeting-places had already been supplanted by the houses of the titled bureaucracy and the upper middle class. One can see, from any of the numerous correspondences of the time, that the intellectuals as well as the aristocrats now began to direct their contempt for the Eastern European Jews, whom they hardly knew, against the educated Jews of Berlin, whom they knew very well. The latter would never again achieve the self-respect that springs from a collective consciousness of being exceptional; henceforth, each one of them had to prove that although he was a Jew, yet he was not a Jew. No longer would it suffice to distinguish oneself from a more or less unknown mass of "backward brethren"; one had to stand out—as an individual who could be congratulated on being an exception—from "*the* Jew," and thus from the people as a whole.

Social discrimination, and not political antisemitism, discovered the phantom of "*the* Jew." The first author to make the distinction between the Jewish individual and "the Jew in general, the Jew everywhere and nowhere" was an obscure publicist who had, in 1802, written a biting satire on Jewish society and its hunger for education, the magic wand for general social acceptance. Jews were depicted as a "principle" of philistine and upstart society.[15] This rather vulgar piece of literature not only was read with delight by quite a few prominent members of Rahel's salon, but even indirectly inspired a great romantic poet, Clemens von Brentano, to write a very witty paper in which again the philistine was identified with the Jew.[16]

With the early idyll of a mixed society something disappeared which was never, in any other country and at any other time, to return. Never again did any social group accept Jews with a free mind and heart. It would be friendly with Jews either because it was excited by its own daring and "wickedness" or as a protest against making pariahs of fellow-citizens. But social pariahs the Jews did become wherever they had ceased to be political and civil outcasts.

It is important to bear in mind that assimilation as a group phenomenon really existed only among Jewish intellectuals. It is no accident that the first educated Jew, Moses Mendelssohn, was also the first who, despite his low civic status, was admitted to non-Jewish society. The court Jews and their successors, the Jewish bankers and businessmen in the West, were never socially acceptable, nor did they care to leave the very narrow limits of their invisible ghetto. In the beginning they were proud, like all un-spoiled upstarts, of the dark background of misery and poverty from which they had risen; later, when they were attacked from all sides, they had a vested interest in the poverty and even backwardness of the masses because it became an argument, a token of their own security. Slowly, and with misgivings, they were forced away from the more rigorous demands of Jewish law—they never left religious traditions altogether—yet demanded all the more orthodoxy from the Jewish masses.[17] The dissolution of Jewish communal autonomy made them that much more eager not only to protect Jewish communities against the authorities, but also to rule over them with the help of the state, so that the phrase denoting the "double dependence" of poor Jews on "both the government and their wealthy brethren" only reflected reality.[18]

The Jewish notables (as they were called in the nineteenth century) ruled the Jewish communities, but they did not belong to them socially or even geographically. They stood, in a sense, as far outside Jewish society as they did outside Gentile society. Having made brilliant individual careers and been granted considerable privileges by their masters, they formed a kind of community of exceptions with extremely limited social opportunities. Naturally despised by court society, lacking business connections with the non-Jewish middle class, their social contacts were as much outside the laws of society as their economic rise had been independent of contemporary economic conditions. This isolation and independence frequently gave them a feeling of power and pride, illustrated by the following anecdote told in the beginning eighteenth century: "A certain Jew . . . , when gently reproached by a noble and cultured physician with (the Jewish) pride although they had no princes among them and no part in government . . . replied with insolence: We are not princes, but we govern them."[19]

Such pride is almost the opposite of class arrogance, which developed but slowly among the privileged Jews. Ruling as absolute princes among their own people, they still felt themselves to be *primi inter pares*. They were prouder of being a "privileged Rabbi of all Jewry" or a "Prince of the Holy Land" than of any titles their masters might offer them.[20] Until the middle of the eighteenth century, they would all have agreed with the Dutch Jew who said: *"Neque in toto orbi alicui nationi inservimus,"* and neither then nor later would they have understood fully the answer of the "learned Christian" who replied: "But this means happiness only for a few. The people considered as a *corpo* (*sic*) is hunted everywhere, has no self-government, is subject to foreign rule, has no power and no dignity, and wanders all over the world, a stranger everywhere."[21]

Class arrogance came only when business connections were established among state bankers of different countries; intermarriage between
leading families soon followed, and culminated in a real international caste
system, unknown thus far in Jewish society. This was all the more glaring
to non-Jewish observers, since it took place when the old feudal estates
and castes were rapidly disappearing into new classes. One concluded,
very wrongly, that the Jewish people were a remnant of the Middle Ages
and did not see that this new caste was of quite recent birth. It was completed only in the nineteenth century and comprised numerically no more
than perhaps a hundred families. But since these were in the limelight, the
Jewish people as a whole came to be regarded as a caste.[22]

Great, therefore, as the role of the court Jews had been in political
history and for the birth of antisemitism, social history might easily neglect
them were it not for the fact that they had certain psychological traits and
behavior patterns in common with Jewish intellectuals who were, after all,
usually the sons of businessmen. The Jewish notables wanted to dominate
the Jewish people and therefore had no desire to leave it, while it was
characteristic of Jewish intellectuals that they wanted to leave their people
and be admitted to society; they both shared the feeling that they were
exceptions, a feeling perfectly in harmony with the judgment of their environment. The "exception Jews" of wealth felt like exceptions from the
common destiny of the Jewish people and were recognized by the governments as exceptionally useful; the "exception Jews" of education felt
themselves exceptions from the Jewish people and also exceptional human
beings, and were recognized as such by society.

Assimilation, whether carried to the extreme of conversion or not,
never was a real menace to the survival of the Jews.[23] Whether they were
welcomed or rejected, it was because they were Jews, and they were well
aware of it. The first generations of educated Jews still wanted sincerely to
lose their identity as Jews, and Boerne wrote with a great deal of bitterness, "Some reproach me with being a Jew, some praise me because
of it, some pardon me for it, but all think of it."[24] Still brought up on
eighteenth-century ideas, they longed for a country without either Christians or Jews; they had devoted themselves to science and the arts, and
were greatly hurt when they found out that governments which would
give every privilege and honor to a Jewish banker, condemned Jewish intellectuals to starvation.[25] The conversions which, in the early nineteenth
century, had been prompted by fear of being lumped together with the
Jewish masses, now became a necessity for daily bread. Such a premium
on lack of character forced a whole generation of Jews into bitter opposition against state and society. The "new specimens of humanity," if they

were worth their salt, all became rebels, and since the most reactionary governments of the period were supported and financed by Jewish bankers, their rebellion was especially violent against the official representatives of their own people. The anti-Jewish denunciations of Marx and Boerne cannot be properly understood except in the light of this conflict between rich Jews and Jewish intellectuals.

This conflict, however, existed in full vigor only in Germany and did not survive the antisemitic movement of the century. In Austria, there was no Jewish intelligentsia to speak of before the end of the nineteenth century, when it felt immediately the whole impact of antisemitic pressure. These Jews, like their wealthy brethren, preferred to trust themselves to the Hapsburg monarchy's protection, and became socialist only after the first World War, when the Social Democratic party came to power. The most significant, though not the only, exception to this rule was Karl Kraus, the last representative of the tradition of Heine, Boerne, and Marx. Kraus's denunciations of Jewish businessmen on one hand, and Jewish journalism as the organized cult of fame on the other, were perhaps even more bitter than those of his predecessors because he was so much more isolated in a country where no Jewish revolutionary tradition existed. In France, where the emancipation decree had survived all changes of governments and regimes, the small number of Jewish intellectuals were neither the forerunners of a new class nor especially important in intellectual life. Culture as such, education as a program, did not form Jewish behavior patterns as it did in Germany.

In no other country had there been anything like the short period of true assimilation so decisive for the history of German Jews, when the real vanguard of a people not only accepted Jews, but was even strangely eager to associate with them. Nor did this attitude ever completely disappear from German society. To the very end, traces of it could easily be discerned, which showed, of course, that relations with Jews never came to be taken for granted. At best it remained a program, at worst a strange and exciting experience. Bismarck's well-known remark about "German stallions to be paired off with Jewish mares," is but the most vulgar expression of a prevalent point of view.

It is only natural that this social situation, though it made rebels out of the first educated Jews, would in the long run produce a specific kind of conformism rather than an effective tradition of rebellion.[26] Conforming to a society which discriminated against "ordinary" Jews and in which, at the same time, it was generally easier for an educated Jew to be admitted to fashionable circles than for a non-Jew of similar condition, Jews had to differentiate themselves clearly from the "Jew in general," and just as clearly to indicate that they were Jews; under no circumstances were they allowed simply to disappear among their neighbors. In order to rationalize an ambiguity which they themselves did not fully understand, they might pretend to "be a man in the street and a Jew at home."[27] This actually amounted to a feeling of being different from other men in the street because they were Jews, and different from other Jews at home because they were not like "ordinary Jews."

The behavior patterns of assimilated Jews, determined by this continuous concentrated effort to distinguish themselves, created a Jewish type that is recognizable everywhere. Instead of being defined by nationality or religion, Jews were being transformed into a social group whose members shared certain psychological attributes and reactions, the sum total of which was supposed to constitute "Jewishness." In other words, Judaism became a psychological quality and the Jewish question became an involved personal problem for every individual Jew.

In his tragic endeavor to conform through differentiation and distinction, the new Jewish type had as little in common with the feared "Jew in general" as with that abstraction, the "heir of the prophets and eternal promoter of justice on earth," which Jewish apologetics conjured up whenever a Jewish journalist was being attacked. The Jew of the apologists was endowed with attributes that are indeed the privileges of pariahs, and which certain Jewish rebels living on the fringe of society did possess—humanity, kindness, freedom from prejudice, sensitiveness to injustice. The trouble was that these qualities had nothing to do with the prophets and that, worse still, these Jews usually belonged neither to Jewish society nor to fashionable circles of non-Jewish society. In the history of assimilated Jewry, they played but an insignificant role. The "Jew in general," on the other hand, as described by professional Jew-haters, showed those qualities which the parvenu must acquire if he wants to arrive—inhumanity, greed, insolence, cringing servility, and determination to push ahead. The trouble in this case was that these qualities have also nothing to do with national attributes and that, moreover, these Jewish business-class types showed little inclination for non-Jewish society and played almost as small a part in Jewish social history. As long as defamed peoples and classes exist, parvenu- and pariah-qualities will be produced anew by each generation with incomparable monotony, in Jewish society and everywhere else.

For the formation of a social history of the Jews within nineteenth-century European society, it was, however, decisive that to a certain extent every Jew in every generation had somehow at some time to decide whether he would remain a pariah and stay out of society altogether, or become a parvenu, or conform to society on the demoralizing condition that he not so much hide his origin as "betray with the secret of his origin the secret of his people as well."[28] The latter road was difficult, indeed, as such secrets did not exist and had to be made up. Since Rahel Varnhagen's unique attempt to establish a social life outside of official society had failed, the way of the pariah and the parvenu were equally ways of extreme solitude, and the way of conformism one of constant regret. The so-called complex psychology of the average Jew, which in a few favored cases developed into a very modern sensitiveness, was based on an ambiguous situation. Jews felt simultaneously the pariah's regret at not having become a parvenu and the parvenu's bad conscience at having betrayed his people and exchanged equal rights for personal privileges. One thing was certain: if one wanted to avoid all ambiguities of social existence, one had to resign oneself to the fact that to be a Jew meant to belong either to an overprivileged upper class or to an underprivileged mass which, in Western and Central Europe, one could belong to only through an intellectual and somewhat artificial solidarity.

The social destinies of average Jews were determined by their eternal lack of decision. And society certainly did not compel them to make up their minds, for it was precisely this ambiguity of situation and character that made the relationship with Jews attractive. The majority of assimilated Jews thus lived in a twilight of favor and misfortune and knew with certainty only that both success and failure were inextricably connected with the fact that they were Jews. For them the Jewish question had lost, once and for all, all political significance; but it haunted their private lives and influenced their personal decisions all the more tyrannically. The adage, "a man in the street and a Jew at home," was bitterly realized: political problems were distorted to the point of pure perversion when Jews tried to solve them by means of inner experience and private emotions; private life was poisoned to the point of inhumanity—for example in the question of mixed marriages—when the heavy burden of unsolved problems of public significance was crammed into that private existence which is much better ruled by the unpredictable laws of passion than by considered policies.

It was by no means easy not to resemble the "Jew in general" and yet remain a Jew; to pretend not to be like Jews and still show with sufficient clarity that one was Jewish. The average Jew, neither a parvenu nor a "conscious pariah" (Bernard Lazare), could only stress an empty sense of difference which continued to be interpreted, in all its possible psychological aspects and variations from innate strangeness to social alienation. As long as the world was somewhat peaceful, this attitude did not work out badly and for generations even became a *modus vivendi*. Concentration on an artificially complicated inner life helped Jews to respond to the unreasonable demands of society, to be strange and exciting, to develop a certain immediacy of self-expression and presentation which were originally the attributes of the actor and the virtuoso, people whom society has always half denied and half admired. Assimilated Jews, half proud and half ashamed of their Jewishness, clearly were in this category.

The process by which bourgeois society developed out of the ruins of its revolutionary traditions and memories added the black ghost of boredom to economic saturation and general indifference to political questions. Jews became people with whom one hoped to while away some time. The less one thought of them as equals, the more attractive and entertaining they became. Bourgeois society, in its search for entertainment and its passionate interest in the individual, insofar as he differed from the norm that is man, discovered the attraction of everything that could be supposed to be mysteriously wicked or secretly vicious. And precisely this feverish preference opened the doors of society to Jews; for within the framework of this society, Jewishness, after having been distorted into a psychological quality, could easily be perverted into a vice. The Enlightenment's genuine tolerance and curiosity for everything human was being replaced by a morbid lust for the exotic, abnormal, and different as such. Several types in society, one after the other, represented the exotic, the anomalous, the different, but none of them was in the least connected with political questions. Thus only the role of Jews in this decaying society could assume a stature that transcended the narrow limits of a society affair.

Before we follow the strange ways which led the "exception Jews," famous and notorious strangers, into the salons of the Faubourg St. Germain in *fin-de-siècle* France, we must recall the only great man whom the elaborate self-deception of the "exception Jews" ever produced. It seems that every commonplace idea gets one chance in at least one individual to attain what used to be called historical greatness. The great man of the "exception Jews" was Benjamin Disraeli.

I I :   T H E   P O T E N T   W I Z A R D [29]

Benjamin Disraeli, whose chief interest in life was the career of Lord Beaconsfield, was distinguished by two things: first, the gift of the gods which we moderns banally call luck, and which other periods revered as a goddess named Fortune, and second, more intimately and more wondrously connected with Fortune than one may be able to explain, the great care-free innocence of mind and imagination which makes it impossible to classify the man as a careerist, though he never thought seriously of anything except his career. His innocence made him recognize how foolish it would be to feel *déclassé* and how much more exciting it would be for himself and for others, how much more useful for his career, to accentuate the fact that he was a Jew "by dressing differently, combing his hair oddly, and by queer manners of expression and verbiage."[30] He cared for admission to high and highest society more passionately and shamelessly than any other Jewish intellectual did; but he was the only one of them who discovered the secret of how to preserve luck, that natural miracle of pariahdom, and who knew from the beginning that one never should bow down in order to "move up from high to higher."

He played the game of politics like an actor in a theatrical performance, except that he played his part so well that he was convinced by his own make-believe. His life and his career read like a fairy-tale, in which he appeared as the prince—offering the blue flower of the romantics, now the primrose of imperialist England, to his princess, the Queen of England. The British colonial enterprise was the fairyland upon which the sun never sets and its capital the mysterious Asiatic Delhi whence the prince wanted to escape with his princess from foggy prosaic London. This may have been foolish and childish; but when a wife writes to her husband as Lady Beaconsfield wrote to hers: "You know you married me for money, and I know that if you had to do it again you would do it for love,"[31] one is silenced before a happiness that seemed to be against all the rules. Here was one who started out to sell his soul to the devil, but the devil did not want the soul and the gods gave him all the happiness of this earth.

Disraeli came from an entirely assimilated family; his father, an enlightened gentleman, baptized the son because he wanted him to have the opportunities of ordinary mortals. He had few connections with Jewish society and knew nothing of Jewish religion or customs. Jewishness, from the beginning, was a fact of origin which he was at liberty to embellish, unhindered by actual knowledge. The result was that somehow he looked at this fact much in the same way as a Gentile would have looked at it. He realized much more clearly than other Jews that being a Jew could be as much an opportunity as a handicap. And since, unlike his simple and modest father, he wanted nothing less than to become an ordinary mortal and nothing more than "to distinguish himself above all his contemporaries,"[32] he began to shape his "olive complexion and coal-black eyes" until he with "the mighty dome of his forehead—no Christian temple, to be sure—(was) unlike any living creature one has met."[33] He knew instinctively that everything depended upon the "division between him and mere mortals," upon an accentuation of his lucky "strangeness."

All this demonstrates a unique understanding of society and its rules. Significantly, it was Disraeli who said, "What is a crime among the multitude is only a vice among the few"[34]—perhaps the most profound insight into the very principle by which the slow and insidious decline of nineteenth-century society into the depth of mob and underworld morality took place. Since he knew this rule, he knew also that Jews would have no better chances anywhere than in circles which pretended to be exclusive and to discriminate against them; for inasmuch as these circles of the few, together with the multitude, thought of Jewishness as a crime, this "crime" could be transformed at any moment into an attractive "vice." Disraeli's display of exoticism, strangeness, mysteriousness, magic, and power drawn from secret sources, was aimed correctly at this disposition in society. And it was his virtuosity at the social game which made him choose the Conservative Party, won him a seat in Parliament, the post of Prime Minister, and, last but not least, the lasting admiration of society and the friendship of a Queen.

One of the reasons for his success was the sincerity of his play. The impression he made on his more unbiased contemporaries was a curious mixture of acting and "absolute sincerity and unreserve."[35] This could only be achieved by a genuine innocence that was partly due to an upbringing from which all specific Jewish influence had been excluded.[36] But Disraeli's good conscience was also due to his having been born an Englishman. England did not know Jewish masses and Jewish poverty, as she had admitted them centuries after their expulsion in the Middle Ages; the Portuguese Jews who settled in England in the eighteenth century were wealthy and educated. Not until the end of the nineteenth century, when the pogroms in Russia initiated the modern Jewish emigrations, did Jewish poverty enter London, and along with it the difference between the Jewish masses and their well-to-do brethren. In Disraeli's time the Jewish question, in its Continental form, was quite unknown, because only Jews welcome to the state lived in England. In other words, the English "exception Jews" were not so aware of being exceptions as their Continental brothers were. When Disraeli scorned the "pernicious doctrine of modern times, the natural equality of men,"[37] he consciously followed in the footsteps of Burke who had "preferred the rights of an Englishman to the Rights of Man," but ignored the actual situation in which privileges for the few had been substituted for rights for all. He was so ignorant of the real conditions among the Jewish people, and so convinced of "the influence of the Jewish race upon modern communities," that he frankly demanded that the Jews "receive all that honour and favour from the northern and western races, which, in civilized and refined nations, should be the lot of those who charm the public taste and elevate the public feeling."[38] Since political influence of Jews in England centered around the English branch of the Rothschilds, he felt very proud about the Rothschilds' help in defeating Napoleon and did not see any reason why he should not be outspoken in his political opinions as a Jew.[39] As a baptized Jew, he was of course never an official spokesman for any Jewish community, but it remains true that he was the only Jew of his kind and his century who tried as well as he knew to represent the Jewish people politically.

Disraeli, who never denied that "the fundamental fact about (him) was that he was a Jew,"[40] had an admiration for all things Jewish that was matched only by his ignorance of them. The mixture of pride and ignorance in these matters, however, was characteristic of all the newly assimilated Jews. The great difference is that Disraeli knew even a little less of Jewish past and present and therefore dared to speak out openly what others betrayed in the half-conscious twilight of behavior patterns dictated by fear and arrogance.

The political result of Disraeli's ability to gauge Jewish possibilities by the political aspirations of a normal people was more serious; he almost automatically produced the entire set of theories about Jewish influence and organization that we usually find in the more vicious forms of antisemitism. First of all, he actually thought of himself as the "chosen man of the chosen race."[41] What better proof was there than his own career: a Jew without name and riches, helped only by a few Jewish bankers, was carried to the position of the first man in England; one of the less liked men of Parliament became Prime Minister and earned genuine popularity among those who for a long time had "regarded him as a charlatan and treated him as a pariah."[42] Political success never satisfied him. It was more difficult and more important to be admitted to London's society than to conquer the House of Commons, and it was certainly a greater triumph to be elected a member of Grillion's dining club—"a select coterie of which it has been customary to make rising politicians of both parties, but from which the socially objectionable are rigorously excluded"[43]—than to be Her Majesty's Minister. The delightfully unexpected climax of all these sweet triumphs was the sincere friendship of the Queen, for if the monarchy in England had lost most of its political prerogatives in a strictly controlled, constitutional nation-state, it had won and retained undisputed primacy in English society. In measuring the greatness of Disraeli's triumph, one should remember that Lord Robert Cecil, one of his eminent colleagues in the Conservative Party, could still, around 1850, justify a particularly bitter attack by stating that he was only "plainly speaking out what every one is saying of Disraeli in private and no one will say in public."[44] Disraeli's greatest victory was that finally nobody said in private what would not have flattered and pleased him if it had been said in public. It was precisely this unique rise to genuine popularity which Disraeli had achieved through a policy of seeing only the advantages, and preaching only the privileges, of being born a Jew.

Part of Disraeli's good fortune is the fact that he always fitted his time, and that consequently his numerous biographers understood him more completely than is the case with most great men. He was a living embodiment of ambition, that powerful passion which had developed in a century seemingly not allowing for any distinctions and differences. Carlyle, at any rate, who interpreted the whole world's history according to a nineteenth-century ideal of the hero, was clearly in the wrong when he refused a title from Disraeli's hands.[45] No other man among his contemporaries corresponded to Carlyle's heroes as well as Disraeli, with his concept of greatness as such, emptied of all specific achievements; no other man fulfilled so exactly the demands of the late nineteenth century for genius in the flesh as this charlatan who took his role seriously and acted the great part of the Great Man with genuine naïveté and an overwhelming display of fantastic tricks and entertaining artistry. Politicians fell in love with the charlatan who transformed boring business transactions into dreams with an oriental flavor; and when society sensed an aroma of black magic in Disraeli's shrewd dealings, the "potent wizard" had actually won the heart of his time.

Disraeli's ambition to distinguish himself from other mortals and his longing for aristocratic society were typical of the middle classes of his time and country. Neither political reasons nor economic motives, but the impetus of his social ambition, made him join the Conservative Party and follow a policy that would always "select the Whigs for hostility and the Radicals for alliance."[46] In no European country did the middle classes ever achieve enough self-respect to reconcile their intelligentsia with their social status, so that aristocracy could continue to determine the social scale when it had already lost all political significance. The unhappy German philistine discovered his "innate personality" in his desperate struggle against caste arrogance, which had grown out of the decline of nobility and the necessity to protect aristocratic titles against bourgeois money.

Vague blood theories and strict control of marriages are rather recent phenomena in the history of European aristocracy. Disraeli knew much better than the German philistines what was required to meet the demands of aristocracy. All attempts of the bourgeoisie to attain social status failed to convince aristocratic arrogance because they reckoned with individuals and lacked the most important element of caste conceit, the pride in privilege without individual effort and merit, simply by virtue of birth. The "innate personality" could never deny that its development demanded education and special effort of the individual. When Disraeli "summoned up a pride of race to confront a pride of caste,"[47] he knew that the social status of the Jews, whatever else might be said of it, at least depended solely on the fact of birth and not on achievement.

Disraeli went even a step further. He knew that the aristocracy, which year after year had to see quite a number of rich middle-class men buy titles, was haunted by very serious doubts of its own value. He therefore defeated them at their game by using his rather trite and popular imagination to describe fearlessly how the Englishmen "came from a parvenu and hybrid race, while he himself was sprung from the purest blood in Europe," how "the life of a British peer (was) mainly regulated by Arabian laws and Syrian customs," how "a Jewess is the queen of heaven" or that "the flower of the Jewish race is even now sitting on the right hand of the Lord God of Sabaoth."[48] And when he finally wrote that "there is no longer in fact an aristocracy in England, for the superiority of the animal man is an essential quality of aristocracy,"[49] he had in fact touched the weakest point of modern aristocratic race theories, which were later to be the point of departure for bourgeois and upstart race opinions.

Judaism, and belonging to the Jewish people, degenerated into a simple fact of birth only among assimilated Jewry. Originally it had meant a specific religion, a specific nationality, the sharing of specific memories and specific hopes, and, even among the privileged Jews, it meant at least still sharing specific economic advantages. Secularization and assimilation of the Jewish intelligentsia had changed self-consciousness and self-interpretation in such a way that nothing was left of the old memories and hopes but the awareness of belonging to a chosen people. Disraeli, though certainly not the only "exception Jew" to believe in his own chosenness without believing in Him who chooses and rejects, was the only one who produced a full-blown race doctrine out of this empty concept of a historic mission. He was ready to assert that the Semitic principle "represents all that is spiritual in our nature," that "the vicissitudes of history find their main solution—all is race," which is "the key to history" regardless of "language and religion," for "there is only one thing which makes a race and that is blood" and there is only one aristocracy, the "aristocracy of nature" which consists of "an unmixed race of a first-rate organization."[50]

The close relationship of this to more modern race ideologies need not be stressed, and Disraeli's discovery is one more proof of how well they serve to combat feelings of social inferiority. For if race doctrines finally served much more sinister and immediately political purposes, it is still true that much of their plausibility and persuasiveness lay in the fact that they helped anybody feel himself an aristocrat who had been selected by birth on the strength of "racial" qualification. That these new selected ones did not belong to an elite, to a selected few—which, after all, had been inherent in the pride of a nobleman—but had to share chosenness with an ever-growing mob, did no essential harm to the doctrine, for those who did not belong to the chosen race grew numerically in the same proportion.

Disraeli's race doctrines, however, were as much the result of his extraordinary insight into the rules of society as the outgrowth of the specific secularization of assimilated Jewry. Not only was the Jewish intelligentsia caught up in the general secularization process, which in the nineteenth century had already lost the revolutionary appeal of the Enlightenment along with the confidence in an independent, self-reliant humanity and therefore remained without any protection against transformation of formerly genuine religious beliefs into superstitions. The Jewish intelligentsia was exposed also to the influences of the Jewish reformers who wanted to change a national religion into a religious denomination. To do so, they had to transform the two basic elements of Jewish piety— the Messianic hope and the faith in Israel's chosenness, and they deleted from Jewish prayerbooks the visions of an ultimate restoration of Zion, along with the pious anticipation of the day at the end of days when the segregation of the Jewish people from the nations of the earth would come to an end. Without the Messianic hope, the idea of chosenness meant eternal segregation; without faith in chosenness, which charged one specific people with the redemption of the world, Messianic hope evaporated into the dim cloud of general philanthropy and universalism which became so characteristic of specifically Jewish political enthusiasm.

The most fateful element in Jewish secularization was that the concept of chosenness was being separated from the Messianic hope, whereas in Jewish religion these two elements were two aspects of God's redemptory plan for mankind. Out of Messianic hope grew that inclination toward final solutions of political problems which aimed at nothing less than establishing a paradise on earth. Out of the belief in chosenness by God grew that fantastic delusion, shared by unbelieving Jews and non-Jews alike, that Jews are by nature more intelligent, better, healthier, more fit for survival—the motor of history and the salt of the earth. The enthusiastic Jewish intellectual dreaming of the paradise on earth, so certain of freedom from all national ties and prejudices, was in fact farther removed from political reality than his fathers, who had prayed for the coming of Messiah and the return of the people to Palestine. The assimilationists, on the other hand, who without any enthusiastic hope had persuaded themselves that they were the salt of the earth, were more effectively separated from the nations by this unholy conceit than their fathers had been by the fence of the Law, which, as it was faithfully believed, separated Israel from the Gentiles but would be destroyed in the days of the Messiah. It was this conceit of the "exception Jews," who were too "enlightened" to believe in God and, on the grounds of their exceptional position everywhere, superstitious enough to believe in themselves, that actually tore down the strong bonds of pious hope which had tied Israel to the rest of mankind.

Secularization, therefore, finally produced that paradox, so decisive for the psychology of modern Jews, by which Jewish assimilation—in its liquidation of national consciousness, its transformation of a national religion into a confessional denomination, and its meeting of the half-hearted and ambiguous demands of state and society by equally ambiguous devices and psychological tricks—engendered a very real Jewish chauvinism, if by chauvinism we understand the perverted nationalism in which (in the words of Chesterton) "the individual is himself the thing to be worshipped; the individual is his own ideal and even his own idol." From now on, the old religious concept of chosenness was no longer the essence of Judaism; it became instead the essence of Jewishness.

This paradox has found its most powerful and charming embodiment in Disraeli. He was an English imperialist and a Jewish chauvinist; but it is not difficult to pardon a chauvinism which was rather a play of imagination because, after all, "England was the Israel of his imagination";[51] and it is not difficult, either, to pardon his English imperialism, which had so little in common with the single-minded resoluteness of expansion for expansion's sake, since he was, after all, "never a thorough Englishman and was proud of the fact."[52] All those curious contradictions which indicate so clearly that the potent wizard never took himself quite seriously and always played a role to win society and to find popularity, add up to a unique charm, they introduce into all his utterances an element of charlatan enthusiasm and day-dreaming which makes him utterly different from his imperialist followers. He was lucky enough to do his dreaming and acting in a time when Manchester and the businessmen had not yet taken over the imperial dream and were even in sharp and furious opposition to "colonial adventures." His superstitious belief in blood and race—into which he mixed old romantic folk credulities about a powerful supranational connection between gold and blood—carried no suspicion of possible massacres, whether in Africa, Asia, or Europe proper. He began as a not too gifted writer and remained an intellectual whom chance made a member of Parliament, leader of his party, Prime Minister, and a friend of the Queen of England.

Disraeli's notion of the Jews' role in politics dates back to the time when he was still simply a writer and had not yet begun his political career. His ideas on the subject were therefore not the result of actual experience, but he clung to them with remarkable tenacity throughout his later life.

In his first novel, *Alroy* (1833), Disraeli evolved a plan for a Jewish Empire in which Jews would rule as a strictly separated class. The novel shows the influence of current illusions about Jewish power-possibilities as well as the young author's ignorance of the actual power conditions of his time. Eleven years later, political experience in Parliament and intimate intercourse with prominent men taught Disraeli that "the aims of the Jews, whatever they may have been before and since, were, in his day, largely divorced from the assertion of political nationality in any form."[53] In a new novel, *Coningsby,* he abandoned the dream of a Jewish Empire and unfolded a fantastic scheme according to which Jewish money dominates the rise and fall of courts and empires and rules supreme in diplomacy. Never in his life did he give up this second notion of a secret and mysterious influence of the chosen men of the chosen race, with which he replaced his earlier dream of an openly constituted, mysterious ruler caste. It became the pivot of his political philosophy. In contrast to his much-admired Jewish bankers who granted loans to governments and earned commissions, Disraeli looked at the whole affair with the outsider's incomprehension that such power-possibilities could be handled day after day by people who were not ambitious for power. What he could not understand was that a Jewish banker was even less interested in politics than his non-Jewish colleagues; to Disraeli, at any rate, it was a matter of course that Jewish wealth was only a means for Jewish politics. The more he learned about the Jewish bankers' well-functioning organization in business matters and their international exchange of news and information, the more convinced he became that he was dealing with something like a secret society which, without anybody knowing it, had the world's destinies in its hands.

It is well known that the belief in a Jewish conspiracy that was kept together by a secret society had the greatest propaganda value for antise-mitic publicity, and by far outran all traditional European superstitions about ritual murder and well-poisoning. It is of great significance that Dis-raeli, for exactly opposite purposes and at a time when nobody thought seriously of secret societies, came to identical conclusions, for it shows clearly to what extent such fabrications were due to social motives and re-sentments and how much more plausibly they explained events or politi-cal and economic activities than the more trivial truth did. In Disraeli's eyes, as in the eyes of many less well-known and reputable charlatans after him, the whole game of politics was played between secret societies. Not only the Jews, but every other group whose influence was not politically organized or which was in opposition to the whole social and political system, became for him powers behind the scenes. In 1863, he thought he witnessed "a struggle between the secret societies and the European mil-lionaires; Rothschild hitherto has won."[54] But also "the natural equality of men and the abrogation of property are proclaimed by secret societies";[55] as late as 1870, he could still talk seriously of forces "beneath the surface" and believe sincerely that "secret societies and their international energies, the Church of Rome and her claims and methods, the eternal conflict be-tween science and faith" were at work to determine the course of human history.[56]

Disraeli's unbelievable naïveté made him connect all these "secret" forces with the Jews. "The first Jesuits were Jews; that mysterious Russian diplomacy which so alarms Western Europe is organized and principally carried on by Jews; that mighty revolution which is at this moment preparing in Germany and which will be in fact a second and greater Re-formation . . . is entirely developing under the auspices of Jews," "men of Jewish race are found at the head of every one of (communist and social-ist groups). The people of God co-operates with atheists; the most skilful accumulators of property ally themselves with communists, the peculiar and chosen race touch the hands of the scum and low castes of Europe! And all this because they wish to destroy that ungrateful Christendom which owes them even its name and whose tyranny they can no longer endure."[57] In Disraeli's imagination, the world had become Jewish.

In this singular delusion, even that most ingenious of Hitler's public-ity stunts, the cry of a secret alliance between the Jewish capitalist and the Jewish socialist, was already anticipated. Nor can it be denied that the whole scheme, imaginary and fantastic as it was, had a logic of its own. If one started, as Disraeli did, from the assumption that Jewish millionaires were makers of Jewish politics, if one took into account the insults Jews had suffered for centuries (which were real enough, but still stupidly exaggerated by Jewish apologetic propaganda), if one had seen the not infrequent instances when the son of a Jewish millionaire became a leader of the workers' movement and knew from experience how closely knit Jewish family ties were as a rule, Disraeli's image of a calculated revenge upon the Christian peoples was not so far-fetched. The truth was, of course, that the sons of Jewish millionaires inclined toward leftist movements precisely because their banker fathers had never come into an open class conflict with workers. They therefore completely lacked that class consciousness that the son of any ordinary bourgeois family would have had as a matter of course, while, on the other side, and for exactly the same reasons, the workers did not harbor those open or hidden antisemitic sentiments which every other class showed the Jews as a matter of course. Obviously leftist movements in most countries offered the only true possibilities for assimilation.

Disraeli's persistent fondness for explaining politics in terms of secret societies was based on experiences which later convinced many lesser European intellectuals. His basic experience had been that a place in English society was much more difficult to win than a seat in Parliament. English society of his time gathered in fashionable clubs which were independent of party distinctions. The clubs, although they were extremely important in the formation of a political elite, escaped public control. To an outsider they must have looked very mysterious indeed. They were secret insofar as not everybody was admitted to them. They became mysterious only when members of other classes asked admittance and were either refused or admitted after a plethora of incalculable, unpredictable, apparently irrational difficulties. There is no doubt that no political honor could replace the triumphs that intimate association with the privileged could give. Disraeli's ambitions, significantly enough, did not suffer even at the end of his life when he experienced severe political defeats, for he remained "the most commanding figure of London society."[58]

In his naïve certainty of the paramount importance of secret societies, Disraeli was a forerunner of those new social strata who, born outside the framework of society, could never understand its rules properly. They found themselves in a state of affairs where the distinctions between society and politics were constantly blurred and where, despite seemingly chaotic conditions, the same narrow class interest always won. The outsider could not but conclude that a consciously established institution with definite goals achieved such remarkable results. And it is true that this whole society game needed only a resolute political will to transform its half-conscious play of interests and essentially purposeless machinations into a definite policy. This is what occurred briefly in France during the Dreyfus Affair, and again in Germany during the decade preceding Hitler's rise to power.

Disraeli, however, was not only outside of English, he was outside of Jewish, society as well. He knew little of the mentality of the Jewish bankers whom he so deeply admired, and he would have been disappointed indeed had he realized that these "exception Jews," despite exclusion from bourgeois society (they never really tried to be admitted), shared its foremost political principle that political activity centers around protection of property and profits. Disraeli saw, and was impressed by, only a group with no outward political organization, whose members were still connected by a seeming infinity of family and business connections. His imagination went to work whenever he had to deal with them and found everything "proved"—when, for instance, the shares of the Suez Canal were offered the English government through the information of Henry Oppenheim (who had learned that the Khedive of Egypt was anxious to sell) and the sale was carried through with the help of a four million sterling loan from Lionel Rothschild.

Disraeli's racial convictions and theories about secret societies sprang, in the last analysis, from his desire to explain something apparently mysterious and in fact chimerical. He could not make a political reality out of the chimerical power of "exception Jews"; but he could, and did, help transform chimeras into public fears and to entertain a bored society with highly dangerous fairy-tales.

With the consistency of most race fanatics, Disraeli spoke only with contempt of the "modern newfangled sentimental principle of nationality."[59] He hated the political equality at the basis of the nation-state and he feared for the survival of the Jews under its conditions. He fancied that race might give a social as well as political refuge against equalization. Since he knew the nobility of his time far better than he ever came to know the Jewish people, it is not surprising that he modeled the race concept after aristocratic caste concepts.

No doubt these concepts of the socially underprivileged could have gone far, but they would have had little significance in European politics had they not met with real political necessities when, after the scramble for Africa, they could be adapted to political purposes. This willingness to believe on the part of bourgeois society gave Disraeli, the only Jew of the nineteenth century, his share of genuine popularity. In the end, it was not his fault that the same trend that accounted for his singular great good fortune finally led to the great catastrophe of his people. . . .

Notes

1. Although Jews stood out more than other groups in the homogeneous populations of European countries, it does not follow that they are more threatened by discrimination than other groups in America. In fact, up to now, not the Jews but the Negroes—by nature and history the most unequal among the peoples of America—have borne the burden of social and economic discrimination.

   This could change, however, if a political movement ever grew out of this merely social discrimination. Then Jews might very suddenly become the principal objects of hatred for the simple reason that they, alone among all other groups, have themselves, within their history and their religion, expressed a well-known principle of separation. This is not true of the Negroes or Chinese, who are therefore less endangered politically, even though they may differ more from the majority than the Jews.

2. This surprisingly apt observation was made by the liberal Protestant theologian H. E. G. Paulus in a valuable little pamphlet, *Die jüdische Nationalabsonderung nach Ursprung, Folgen und Besserungsmitteln*, 1831. Paulus, much attacked by Jewish writers of the time, advocated a gradual individual emancipation on the basis of assimilation.

3. This attitude is expressed in Wilhelm v. Humboldt's "Expert Opinion" of 1809: "The state should not exactly teach respect for the Jews, but should abolish an inhuman and prejudiced way of thinking etc. . . ." In Ismar Freund, *Die Emancipation der Juden in Preussen*, Berlin, 1912, II, 270.

4. J. G. Herder, "Über die politische Bekehrung der Juden" in *Adrastea und das 18. Jahrhundert*, 1801–3.

5. Herder, *Briefe zur Beförderung der Humanität* (1793–97), 40. Brief.

6. Felix Priebatsch, "Die Judenpolitik des fürstlichen Absolutismus im 17. und 18. Jahrhundert," in *Forschungen und Versuche zur Geschichte des Mittelalters und der Neuzeit*, 1915, 646.

7. Lessing himself had no such illusions. His last letter to Moses Mendelssohn expressed most clearly what he wanted: "the shortest and safest way to that European country without either Christians or Jews." For Lessing's attitude toward Jews, see Franz Mehring, *Die Lessinglegende*, 1906.

8. See Honoré Q. R. de Mirabeau, *Sur Moses Mendelssohn*, London, 1788.

9. J. G. Herder, "Ueber die politische Bekehrung der Juden," *op. cit.*

10. Johann Wolfgang v. Goethe's review of Isachar Falkensohn Behr, *Gedichte eines polnischen Juden*, Mietau and Leipzig, 1772, in *Frankfurter Gelehrte Anzeigen*.

11. Friedrich Schleiermacher, *Briefe bei Gelegenheit der politisch theologischen Aufgabe und des Sendschreibens jüdischer Hausväter*, 1799, in *Werke*, 1846, Abt. I, Band V, 34.

12. This does not, however, apply to Moses Mendelssohn, who hardly knew the thoughts of Herder, Goethe, Schleiermacher, and other members of the younger generation. Mendelssohn was revered for his uniqueness. His firm adherence to his Jewish religion made it impossible for him to break ulti-

mately with the Jewish people, which his successors did as a matter of course. He felt he was "a member of an oppressed people who must beg for the good will and protection of the governing nation" (see his "Letter to Lavater," 1770, in *Gesammelte Schriften,* Vol. VII, Berlin, 1930); that is, he always knew that the extraordinary esteem for his person paralleled an extraordinary contempt for his people. Since he, unlike Jews of following generations, did not share this contempt, he did not consider himself an exception.

13. The Prussia which Lessing had described as "Europe's most enslaved country" was to Mendelssohn "a state in which one of the wisest princes who ever ruled men has made the arts and sciences flourish, has made national freedom of thought so general that its beneficent effects reach even the lowliest inhabitants of his domain." Such humble contentment is touching and surprising if one realizes that the "wisest prince" had made it very hard for the Jewish philosopher to get permission to sojourn in Berlin and, at a time when his *Münzjuden* enjoyed all privileges, did not even grant him the regular status of a "protected Jew." Mendelssohn was even aware that he, the friend of all educated Germany, would be subject to the same tax levied upon an ox led to the market if ever he decided to visit his friend Lavater in Leipzig, but no political conclusion regarding the improvement of such conditions ever occurred to him. (See the "Letter to Lavater," *op. cit.,* and his preface to his translation of Menasseh Ben Israel in *Gesammelte Schriften,* Vol. III, Leipzig, 1843–45.)

14. See Heinrich Silbergleit, *Die Bevölkerungs- und Berufsverhältnisse der Juden im Deutschen Reich,* Vol. I, Berlin, 1930.

15. C.W.F. Grattenauer's widely read pamphlet *Wider die Juden* of 1802 had been preceded as far back as 1791 by another, *Ueber die physische und moralische Verfassung der heutigen Juden* in which the growing influence of the Jews in Berlin was already pointed out. Although the early pamphlet was reviewed in the *Allgemeine Deutsche Bibliothek,* 1792, Vol. CXII, almost nobody ever read it.

16. Clemens Brentano's *Der Philister vor, in und nach der Geschichte* was written for and read to the so-called *Christlich-Deutsche Tischgesellschaft,* a famous club of writers and patriots, founded in 1808 for the struggle against Napoleon.

17. Thus the Rothschilds in the 1820's withdrew a large donation from their native community of Frankfurt, in order to counteract the influence of reformers who wanted Jewish children to receive a general education. See Isaak Markus Jost, *Neuere Geschichte der Israeliten,* 1846, X, 102.

18. *Op. cit.,* IX, 38.—The court Jews and the rich Jewish bankers who followed in their footsteps never wanted to leave the Jewish community. They acted as its representatives and protectors against public authorities; they were frequently granted official power over communities which they ruled from afar so that the old autonomy of Jewish communities was undermined and destroyed from within long before it was abolished by the nation-state. The first court Jew with monarchical aspirations in his own "nation" was a Jew of Prague, a purveyor of supplies to the Elector Maurice of Saxony in the sixteenth century. He demanded that all rabbis and community heads be se-

lected from members of his family. (See Bondy-Dworsky, *Geschichte der Juden in Boehmen, Maehren und Schlesien,* Prague, 1906, II, 727.) The practice of installing court Jews as dictators in their communities became general in the eighteenth century and was followed by the rule of "notables" in the nineteenth century.

19. Johann Jacob Schudt, *Jüdische Merkwürdigkeiten,* Frankfurt a.M., 1715–1717, IV, Annex, 48.

20. Selma Stern, *Jud Suess,* Berlin, 1929, 18 f.

21. Schudt, *op. cit.,* I, 19.

22. Christian Friedrich Ruehs defines the whole Jewish people as a "caste of merchants." "Ueber die Ansprüche der Juden an das deutsche Bürgerrecht," in *Zeitschrift für die neueste Geschichte,* 1815.

23. A remarkable, though little-known, fact is that assimilation as a program led much more frequently to conversion than to mixed marriage. Unfortunately statistics cover up rather than reveal this fact because they consider all unions between converted and nonconverted Jewish partners to be mixed marriages. We know, however, that there were quite a number of families in Germany who had been baptized for generations and yet remained purely Jewish. That the converted Jew only rarely left his family and even more rarely left his Jewish surroundings altogether, accounts for this. The Jewish family, at any rate, proved to be a more conserving force than Jewish religion.

24. *Briefe aus Paris.* 74th Letter, February 1832.

25. *Ibid.,* 72nd Letter.

26. The "conscious pariah" (Bernard Lazare) was the only tradition of rebellion which established itself, although those who belonged to it were hardly aware of its existence. See the author's "The Jew as Pariah. A Hidden Tradition," in *Jewish Social Studies,* Vol. VI, No. 2 (1944).

27. It is not without irony that this excellent formula, which may serve as a motto for Western European assimilation, was propounded by a Russian Jew and first published in Hebrew. It comes from Judah Leib Gordon's Hebrew poem, *Hakitzah ami,* 1863. See S. M. Dubnow, *History of the Jews in Russia and Poland,* 1918, II, 228 f.

28. This formulation was made by Karl Kraus around 1912. See *Untergang der Welt durch schwarze Magie,* 1925.

29. The title phrase is taken from a sketch of Disraeli by Sir John Skleton in 1867. See W. F. Monypenny and G. E. Buckle, *The Life of Benjamin Disraeli, Earl of Beaconsfield,* New York, 1929, II, 292–93.

30. Morris S. Lazaron, *Seed of Abraham,* New York, 1930, "Benjamin Disraeli," 260 ff.

31. Horace B. Samuel, "The Psychology of Disraeli," in *Modernities,* London, 1914.

32. J. A. Froude thus closes his biography of *Lord Beaconsfield,* 1890: "The aim with which he started in life was to distinguish himself above all his contemporaries, and wild as such an ambition must have appeared, he at last won the stake for which he played so bravely."

33. Sir John Skleton, *op. cit.*

34. In his novel *Tancred*, 1847.

35. Sir John Skleton, *op. cit.*

36. Disraeli himself reported: "I was not bred among my race and was nourished in great prejudice against them." For his family background, see especially Joseph Caro, "Benjamin Disraeli, Juden und Judentum," in *Monatsschrift für Geschichte und Wissenschaft des Judentums*, 1932, Jahrgang 76.

37. *Lord George Bentinck. A Political Biography*, London, 1852, 496.

38. *Ibid.*, 491.

39. *Ibid.*, pp. 497 ff.

40. Monypenny and Buckle, *op. cit.*, 1507.

41. Horace S. Samuel, *op. cit.*

42. Monypenny and Buckle, *op. cit.*, 147.

43. *Ibid.*

44. Robert Cecil's article appeared in the most authoritative organ of the Tories, the *Quarterly Review*. See Monypenny and Buckle, *op. cit.*, 19–22.

45. This happened as late as 1874. Carlyle is reported to have called Disraeli "a cursed Jew," "the worst man who ever lived." See Caro, *op. cit.*

46. Lord Salisbury in an article in the *Quarterly Review*, 1869.

47. E. T. Raymond, *Disraeli, The Alien Patriot*, London, 1925, 1.

48. H. B. Samuel, *op. cit.*, Disraeli, *Tancred*, and *Lord George Bentinck*, respectively.

49. In his novel *Coningsby*, 1844.

50. See *Lord George Bentinck* and the novels *Endymion*, 1881, and *Coningsby*.

51. Sir John Skleton, *op. cit.*

52. Horace B. Samuel, *op. cit.*

53. Monypenny and Buckle, *op. cit.*, 882.

54. *Ibid.*, p. 73. In a letter to Mrs. Brydges Williams of July 21, 1863.

55. *Lord George Bentinck*, 497.

56. In his novel *Lothair*, 1870.

57. *Lord George Bentinck*.

58. Monypenny and Buckle, *op. cit.*, 1470. This excellent biography gives a correct evaluation of Disraeli's triumph. After having quoted Tennyson's *In Memoriam*, canto 64, it continues as follows: "In one respect Disraeli's success was more striking and complete than that suggested in Tennyson's lines; he not only scaled the political ladder to the topmost rung and 'shaped the whisper of the throne'; he also conquered Society. He dominated the dinner-tables and what we would call the salons of Mayfair . . . and his social triumph, whatever may be thought by philosophers of its intrinsic value, was certainly not less difficult of achievement for a despised outsider than his political, and was perhaps sweeter to his palate" (1506).

59. *Ibid.*, Vol. I, Book 3.

Expansion

THE THREE DECADES from 1884 to 1914 separate the nineteenth century, which ended with the scramble for Africa and the birth of the pan-movements, from the twentieth, which began with the first World War. This is the period of Imperialism, with its stagnant quiet in Europe and breath-taking developments in Asia and Africa.[1] Some of the fundamental aspects of this time appear so close to totalitarian phenomena of the twentieth century that it may be justifiable to consider the whole period a preparatory stage for coming catastrophes. Its quiet, on the other hand, makes it appear still very much a part of the nineteenth century. We can hardly avoid looking at this close and yet distant past with the too-wise eyes of those who know the end of the story in advance, who know it led to an almost complete break in the continuous flow of Western history as we had known it for more than two thousand years. But we must also admit a certain nostalgia for what can still be called a "golden age of security," for an age, that is, when even horrors were still marked by a certain moderation and controlled by respectability, and therefore could be related to the general appearance of sanity. In other words, no matter how close to us this past is, we are perfectly aware that our experience of concentration camps and death factories is as remote from its general atmosphere as it is from any other period in Western history.

The central inner-European event of the imperialist period was the political emancipation of the bourgeoisie, which up to then had been the first class in history to achieve economic pre-eminence without aspiring to political rule. The bourgeoisie had developed within, and together with, the nation-state, which almost by definition ruled over and beyond a class-divided society. Even when the bourgeoisie had already established itself as the ruling class, it had left all political decisions to the state. Only when the nation-state proved unfit to be the framework for the further

---

From The Origins of Totalitarianism.

growth of capitalist economy did the latent fight between state and society become openly a struggle for power. During the imperialist period neither the state nor the bourgeoisie won a decisive victory. National institutions resisted throughout the brutality and megalomania of imperialist aspirations, and bourgeois attempts to use the state and its instruments of violence for its own economic purposes were always only half successful. This changed when the German bourgeoisie staked everything on the Hitler movement and aspired to rule with the help of the mob, but then it turned out to be too late. The bourgeoisie succeeded in destroying the nation-state but won a Pyrrhic victory; the mob proved quite capable of taking care of politics by itself and liquidated the bourgeoisie along with all other classes and institutions.

"Expansion is everything," said Cecil Rhodes, and fell into despair, for every night he saw overhead "these stars . . . these vast worlds which we can never reach. I would annex the planets if I could."[2] He had discovered the moving principle of the new, the imperialist era (within less than two decades, British colonial possessions increased by 4½ million square miles and 66 million inhabitants, the French nation gained 3½ million square miles and 26 million people, the Germans won a new empire of a million square miles and 13 million natives, and Belgium through her king acquired 900,000 square miles with 8½ million population[3]); and yet in a flash of wisdom Rhodes recognized at the same moment its inherent insanity and its contradiction to the human condition. Naturally, neither insight nor sadness changed his policies. He had no use for the flashes of wisdom that led him so far beyond the normal capacities of an ambitious businessman with a marked tendency toward megalomania.

"World politics is for a nation what megalomania is for an individual,"[4] said Eugen Richter (leader of the German progressive party) at about the same historical moment. But his opposition in the Reichstag to Bismarck's proposal to support private companies in the foundation of trading and maritime stations, showed clearly that he understood the economic needs of a nation in his time even less than Bismarck himself. It looked as though those who opposed or ignored imperialism—like Eugen Richter in Germany, or Gladstone in England, or Clemenceau in France—had lost touch with reality and did not realize that trade and economics had already involved every nation in world politics. The national principle was leading into provincial ignorance and the battle fought by sanity was lost.

Moderation and confusion were the only rewards of any statesman's consistent opposition to imperialist expansion. Thus Bismarck, in 1871, rejected the offer of French possessions in Africa in exchange for Alsace-Lorraine, and twenty years later acquired Heligoland from Great Britain in return for Uganda, Zanzibar, and Vitu—two kingdoms for a bathtub, as the German imperialists told him, not without justice. Thus in the eighties Clemenceau opposed the imperialist party in France when they wanted to send an expeditionary force to Egypt against the British, and thirty years later he surrendered the Mosul oil fields to England for the sake of a French-British alliance. Thus Gladstone was being denounced by Cromer in Egypt as "not a man to whom the destinies of the British Empire could safely be entrusted."

That statesmen, who thought primarily in terms of the established national territory, were suspicious of imperialism was justified enough, except that more was involved than what they called "overseas adventures." They knew by instinct rather than by insight that this new expansion movement, in which "patriotism . . . is best expressed in money-making" (Huebbe-Schleiden) and the national flag is a "commercial asset" (Rhodes), could only destroy the political body of the nation-state. Conquest as well as empire building had fallen into disrepute for very good reasons. They had been carried out successfully only by governments which, like the Roman Republic, were based primarily on law, so that conquest could be followed by integration of the most heterogeneous peoples by imposing upon them a common law. The nation-state, however, based upon a homogeneous population's active consent to its government ("*le plébiscite de tous les jours*"[5]), lacked such a unifying principle and would, in the case of conquest, have to assimilate rather than to integrate, to enforce consent rather than justice, that is, to degenerate into tyranny. Robespierre was already well aware of this when he exclaimed: "*Périssent les colonies si elles nous en coûtent l'honneur, la liberté.*"

Expansion as a permanent and supreme aim of politics is the central political idea of imperialism. Since it implies neither temporary looting nor the more lasting assimilation of conquest, it is an entirely new concept in the long history of political thought and action. The reason for this surprising originality—surprising because entirely new concepts are very rare in politics—is simply that this concept is not really political at all, but has its origin in the realm of business speculation, where expansion meant the permanent broadening of industrial production and economic transactions characteristic of the nineteenth century.

In the economic sphere, expansion was an adequate concept because industrial growth was a working reality. Expansion meant increase in actual production of goods to be used and consumed. The processes of production are as unlimited as the capacity of man to produce for, establish, furnish, and improve on the human world. When production and economic growth slowed down, their limits were not so much economic as political, insofar as production depended on, and products were shared by, many different peoples who were organized in widely differing political bodies.

Imperialism was born when the ruling class in capitalist production came up against national limitations to its economic expansion. The bourgeoisie turned to politics out of economic necessity; for if it did not want to give up the capitalist system whose inherent law is constant economic growth, it had to impose this law upon its home governments and to proclaim expansion to be an ultimate political goal of foreign policy.

With the slogan "expansion for expansion's sake," the bourgeoisie tried and partly succeeded in persuading their national governments to enter upon the path of world politics. The new policy they proposed seemed for a moment to find its natural limitations and balances in the very fact that several nations started their expansions simultaneously and competitively. Imperialism in its initial stages could indeed still be described as a struggle of "competing empires" and distinguished from the "idea of empire in the ancient and medieval world (which) was that of a federation of States, under a hegemony, covering . . . the entire recognized world."[6] Yet such a competition was only one of the many remnants of a past era, a concession to that still prevailing national principle according to which mankind is a family of nations vying for excellence, or to the liberal belief that competition will automatically set up its own stabilizing predetermined limits before one competitor has liquidated all the others. This happy balance, however, had hardly been the inevitable outcome of mysterious economic laws, but had relied heavily on political, and even more on police institutions that prevented competitors from using revolvers. How a competition between fully armed business concerns—"empires"—could end in anything but victory for one and death for the others is difficult to understand. In other words, competition is no more a principle of politics than expansion, and needs political power just as badly for control and restraint.

In contrast to the economic structure, the political structure cannot be expanded indefinitely, because it is not based upon the productivity of man, which is, indeed, unlimited. Of all forms of government and organizations of people, the nation-state is least suited for unlimited growth because the genuine consent at its base cannot be stretched indefinitely, and is only rarely, and with difficulty, won from conquered peoples. No nation-state could with a clear conscience ever try to conquer foreign peoples, since such a conscience comes only from the conviction of the conquering nation that it is imposing a superior law upon barbarians.[7] The nation, however, conceived of its law as an outgrowth of a unique national substance which was not valid beyond its own people and the boundaries of its own territory.

Wherever the nation–state appeared as conqueror, it aroused national consciousness and desire for sovereignty among the conquered people, thereby defeating all genuine attempts at empire building. Thus the French incorporated Algeria as a province of the mother country, but could not bring themselves to impose their own laws upon an Arab people. They continued rather to respect Islamic law and granted their Arab citizens "personal status," producing the nonsensical hybrid of a nominally French territory, legally as much a part of France as the Département de la Seine, whose inhabitants are not French citizens.

The early British "empire builders," putting their trust in conquest as a permanent method of rule, were never able to incorporate their nearest neighbors, the Irish, into the far-flung structure either of the British Empire or the British Commonwealth of Nations; but when, after the last war, Ireland was granted dominion status and welcomed as a full-fledged member of the British Commonwealth, the failure was just as real, if less palpable. The oldest "possession" and newest dominion unilaterally denounced its dominion status (in 1937) and severed all ties with the English nation when it refused to participate in the war. England's rule by permanent conquest, since it "simply failed to destroy" Ireland (Chesterton), had not so much aroused her own "slumbering genius of imperialism"[8] as it had awakened the spirit of national resistance in the Irish.

The national structure of the United Kingdom had made quick assimilation and incorporation of the conquered peoples impossible; the British Commonwealth was never a "Commonwealth of Nations" but the heir of the United Kingdom, *one* nation dispersed throughout the world. Dispersion and colonization did not expand, but transplanted, the political structure, with the result that the members of the new federated body remained closely tied to their common mother country for sound reasons of common past and common law. The Irish example proves how ill fitted the United Kingdom was to build an imperial structure in which many different peoples could live contentedly together.[9] The British nation proved to be adept not at the Roman art of empire building but at following the Greek model of colonization. Instead of conquering and imposing their own law upon foreign peoples, the English colonists settled on newly won territory in the four corners of the world and remained members of the same British nation.[10] Whether the federated structure of the Commonwealth, admirably built on the reality of one nation dispersed over the earth, will be sufficiently elastic to balance the nation's inherent difficulties in empire building and to admit permanently non-British peoples as full-fledged "partners in the concern" of the Commonwealth, remains to be seen. The present dominion status of India—a status, by the way, flatly refused by Indian nationalists during the war—has frequently been considered to be a temporary and transitory solution.[11]

The inner contradiction between the nation's body politic and conquest as a political device has been obvious since the failure of the Napoleonic dream. It is due to this experience and not to humanitarian considerations that conquest has since been officially condemned and has played a minor role in the adjustment of borderline conflicts. The Napoleonic failure to unite Europe under the French flag was a clear indication that conquest by a nation led either to the full awakening of the conquered people's national consciousness and to consequent rebellion against the conqueror, or to tyranny. And though tyranny, because it needs no consent, may successfully rule over foreign peoples, it can stay in power only if it destroys first of all the national institutions of its own people.

The French, in contrast to the British and all other nations in Europe, actually tried in recent times to combine *ius* with *imperium* and to build an empire in the old Roman sense. They alone at least attempted to develop the body politic of the nation into an imperial political structure, believed that "the French nation (was) marching . . . to spread the benefits of French civilization"; they wanted to incorporate overseas possessions into the national body by treating the conquered peoples as "both . . . brothers and . . . subjects—brothers in the fraternity of a common French civilization, and subjects in that they are disciples of French light and followers of French leading."[12] This was partly carried out when colored delegates took their seats in the French Parliament and when Algeria was declared to be a department of France.

The result of this daring enterprise was a particularly brutal exploitation of overseas possessions for the sake of the nation. All theories to the contrary, the French Empire actually was evaluated from the point of view of national defense,[13] and the colonies were considered lands of soldiers which could produce a *force noire* to protect the inhabitants of France against their national enemies. Poincaré's famous phrase in 1923, "France is not a country of forty millions; she is a country of one hundred millions," pointed simply to the discovery of an "economical form of gunfodder, turned out by mass-production methods."[14] When Clemenceau insisted at the peace table in 1918 that he cared about nothing but "an un-

limited right of levying black troops to assist in the defense of French territory in Europe if France were attacked in the future by Germany,"[15] he
did not save the French nation from German aggression, as we are now
unfortunately in a position to know, although his plan was carried out by
the General Staff; but he dealt a death-blow to the still dubious possibility
of a French Empire.[16] Compared with this blind desperate nationalism,
British imperialists compromising on the mandate system looked like
guardians of the self-determination of peoples. And this despite the fact
that they started at once to misuse the mandate system by "indirect rule,"
a method which permits the administrator to govern a people "not directly but through the medium of their own tribal and local authorities."[17]

The British tried to escape the dangerous inconsistency inherent in
the nation's attempt at empire building by leaving the conquered peoples
to their own devices as far as culture, religion, and law were concerned,
by staying aloof and refraining from spreading British law and culture.
This did not prevent the natives from developing national consciousness
and from clamoring for sovereignty and independence—though it may
have retarded the process somewhat. But it has strengthened tremendously the new imperialist consciousness of a fundamental, and not just a
temporary, superiority of man over man, of the "higher" over the "lower
breeds." This in turn exacerbated the subject peoples' fight for freedom
and blinded them to the unquestionable benefits of British rule. From the
very aloofness of their administrators who, "despite their genuine respect
for the natives as a people, and in some cases even their love for them . . .
almost to a man, do not believe that they are or ever will be capable of
governing themselves without supervision,"[18] the "natives" could not but
conclude that they were being excluded and separated from the rest of
mankind forever.

Imperialism is not empire building and expansion is not conquest.
The British conquerors, the old "breakers of law in India" (Burke), had
little in common with the exporters of British money or the administrators of the Indian peoples. If the latter had changed from applying decrees
to the making of laws, they might have become empire builders. The
point, however, is that the English nation was not interested in this and
would hardly have supported them. As it was, the imperialist-minded
businessmen were followed by civil servants who wanted "the African to
be left an African," while quite a few, who had not yet outgrown what
Harold Nicolson once called their "boyhood-ideals,"[19] wanted to help
them to "become a better African"[20]—whatever that may mean. In no
case were they "disposed to apply the administrative and political system

of their own country to the government of backward populations,"[21] and to tie the far-flung possessions of the British Crown to the English nation.

In contrast to true imperial structures, where the institutions of the mother country are in various ways integrated into the empire, it is characteristic of imperialism that national institutions remain separate from the colonial administration although they are allowed to exercise control. The actual motivation for this separation was a curious mixture of arrogance and respect: the new arrogance of the administrators abroad who faced "backward populations" or "lower breeds" found its correlative in the respect of old-fashioned statesmen at home who felt that no nation had the right to impose its law upon a foreign people. It was in the very nature of things that the arrogance turned out to be a device for rule, while the respect, which remained entirely negative, did not produce a new way for peoples to live together, but managed only to keep the ruthless imperialist rule by decree within bounds. To the salutary restraint of national institutions and politicians we owe whatever benefits the non-European peoples have been able, after all and despite everything, to derive from Western domination. But the colonial services never ceased to protest against the interference of the "inexperienced majority"—the nation—that tried to press the "experienced minority"—the imperialist administrators—"in the direction of imitation,"[22] namely, of government in accordance with the general standards of justice and liberty at home.

That a movement of expansion for expansion's sake grew up in nation-states which more than any other political bodies were defined by boundaries and the limitations of possible conquest, is one example of the seemingly absurd disparities between cause and effect which have become the hallmark of modern history. The wild confusion of modern historical terminology is only a by-product of these disparities. By comparisons with ancient Empires, by mistaking expansion for conquest, by neglecting the difference between Commonwealth and Empire (which pre-imperialist historians called the difference between plantations and possessions, or colonies and dependencies, or, somewhat later, colonialism and imperialism[23]), by neglecting, in other words, the difference between export of (British) people and export of (British) money,[24] historians tried to dismiss the disturbing fact that so many of the important events in modern history look as though molehills had labored and had brought forth mountains.

Contemporary historians, confronted with the spectacle of a few capitalists conducting their predatory searches round the globe for new investment possibilities and appealing to the profit motives of the much-too-rich and the gambling instincts of the much-too-poor, want to clothe imperialism with the old grandeur of Rome and Alexander the Great, a grandeur which would make all following events more humanly tolerable. The disparity between cause and effect was betrayed in the famous, and unfortunately true, remark that the British Empire was acquired in a fit of absent-mindedness; it became cruelly obvious in our own time when a World War was needed to get rid of Hitler, which was shameful precisely because it was also comic. Something similar was already apparent during the Dreyfus Affair when the best elements in the nation were needed to conclude a struggle which had started as a grotesque conspiracy and ended as a farce.

The only grandeur of imperialism lies in the nation's losing battle against it. The tragedy of this half-hearted opposition was not that many national representatives could be bought by the new imperialist business-men; worse than corruption was the fact that the incorruptible were con-vinced that imperialism was the only way to conduct world politics. Since maritime stations and access to raw materials were really necessary for all nations, they came to believe that annexation and expansion worked for the salvation of the nation. They were the first to fail to understand the fundamental difference between the old foundation of trade and maritime stations for the sake of trade and the new policy of expansion. They be-lieved Cecil Rhodes when he told them to "wake up to the fact that you cannot live unless you have the trade of the world," "that your trade is the world, and your life is the world, and not England," and that therefore they "must deal with these questions of expansion and retention of the world."[25] Without wanting to, sometimes even without knowing it, they not only became accomplices in imperialist politics, but were the first to be blamed and exposed for their "imperialism." Such was the case of Clemenceau who, because he was so desperately worried about the future of the French nation, turned "imperialist" in the hope that colonial man-power would protect French citizens against aggressors.

The conscience of the nation, represented by Parliament and a free press, functioned, and was resented by colonial administrators, in all Euro-pean countries with colonial possessions—whether England, France, Bel-gium, Germany, or Holland. In England, in order to distinguish between the imperial government seated in London and controlled by Parliament and colonial administrators, this influence was called the "imperial factor," thereby crediting imperialism with the merits and remnants of justice it so eagerly tried to eliminate.[26] The "imperial factor" was expressed politi-cally in the concept that the natives were not only protected but in a way represented by the British, the "Imperial Parliament."[27] Here the English came very close to the French experiment in empire building, although they never went so far as to give actual representation to subject peoples. Nevertheless, they obviously hoped that the nation as a whole could act as a kind of trustee for its conquered peoples, and it is true that it invariably tried its best to prevent the worst.

The conflict between the representatives of the "imperial factor" (which should rather be called the national factor) and the colonial administrators runs like a red thread through the history of British imperialism. The "prayer" which Cromer addressed to Lord Salisbury during his administration of Egypt in 1896, "save me from the English Departments,"[28] was repeated over and over again, until in the twenties of this century the nation and everything it stood for were openly blamed by the extreme imperialist party for the threatened loss of India. The imperialists had always been deeply resentful that the government of India should have "to justify its existence and its policy before public opinion in England"; this control now made it impossible to proceed to those measures of "administrative massacres"[29] which, immediately after the close of the first World War, had been tried occasionally elsewhere as a radical means of pacification,[30] and which indeed might have prevented India's independence.

A similar hostility prevailed in Germany between national representatives and colonial administrators in Africa. In 1897, Carl Peters was removed from his post in German Southeast Africa and had to resign from the government service because of atrocities against the natives. The same thing happened to Governor Zimmerer. And in 1905, the tribal chiefs for the first time addressed their complaints to the Reichstag, with the result that when the colonial administrators threw them into jail, the German Government intervened.[31]

The same was true of French rule. The governors general appointed by the government in Paris were either subject to powerful pressure from French colonials as in Algeria, or simply refused to carry out reforms in the treatment of natives, which were allegedly inspired by "the weak democratic principles of (their) government."[32] Everywhere imperialist administrators felt that the control of the nation was an unbearable burden and threat to domination.

And the imperialists were perfectly right. They knew the conditions of modern rule over subject peoples better than those who on the one hand protested against government by decree and arbitrary bureaucracy and on the other hoped to retain their possessions forever for the greater glory of the nation. The imperialists knew better than nationalists that the body politic of the nation is not capable of empire building. They were perfectly aware that the march of the nation and its conquest of peoples, if allowed to follow its own inherent law, ends with the peoples' rise to nationhood and the defeat of the conqueror. French methods, therefore, which always tried to combine national aspirations with empire building, were much less successful than British methods, which, after the eighties of the last century, were openly imperialistic, although restrained by a mother country that retained its national democratic institutions.

Notes

1. J. A. Hobson, *Imperialism,* London, 1905, 1938, p. 19: "Though, for convenience, the year 1870 has been taken as indicative of the beginning of a conscious policy of Imperialism, it will be evident that the movement did not attain its full impetus until the middle of the eighties . . . from about 1884."

2. S. Gertrude Millin, *Rhodes,* London, 1933, p. 138.

3. These figures are quoted by Carlton J. H. Hayes, *A Generation of Materialism,* New York, 1941, p. 237, and cover the period from 1871–1900.—See also Hobson, *op. cit.,* p. 19: "Within 15 years some 3¾ millions of square miles were added to the British Empire, 1 million square miles with 14 millions inhabitants to the German, 3½ millions square miles with 37 millions inhabitants to the French."

4. See Ernst Hasse, *Deutsche Weltpolitik,* Flugschriften des Alldeutschen Verbandes, No. 5, 1897, p. 1.

5. Ernest Renan in his classical essay *Qu'est-ce qu'une nation?,* Paris, 1882, stressed "the actual consent, the desire to live together, the will to preserve worthily the undivided inheritance which has been handed down" as the chief elements which keep the members of a people together in such a way that they form a nation. (Translation quoted from *The Poetry of the Celtic Races, and other Studies,* London, 1896.)

6. Hobson, *op. cit.*

7. This bad conscience springing from the belief in consent as the basis of all political organization is very well described by Harold Nicolson, *Curzon: The Last Phase 1919–1925,* Boston–New York, 1934, in the discussion of British policy in Egypt: "The justification of our presence in Egypt remains based, not upon the defensible right of conquest, or on force, but upon our own belief in the element of consent. That element, in 1919, did not in any articulate form exist. It was dramatically challenged by the Egyptian outburst of March 1919."

8. As Lord Salisbury put it, rejoicing over the defeat of Gladstone's first Home Rule Bill. During the following twenty years of Conservative—and that was at that time imperialist—rule (1885–1905), the English-Irish conflict was not only not solved but became much more acute. (See also Gilbert K. Chesterton, *The Crimes of England,* 1915, pp. 57 ff.)

9. Why in the initial stages of national development the Tudors did not succeed in incorporating Ireland into Great Britain as the Valois had succeeded in incorporating Brittany and Burgundy into France, is still a riddle. It may be, however, that a similar process was brutally interrupted by the Cromwell regime, which treated Ireland as one great piece of booty to be divided among its servants. After the Cromwell revolution, at any rate, which was as crucial for the formation of the British nation as the French Revolution became for the French, the United Kingdom had already reached that stage of maturity that is always accompanied by a loss of the power of assimilation and integration which the body politic of the nation possesses only in its initial stages. What then followed was, indeed, one long sad story of "coercion [that] was not imposed that the people might live quietly but that people might die quietly" (Chesterton, *op. cit.,* p. 60).

   For a historical survey of the Irish question that includes the latest developments, compare the excellent unbiased study of Nicholas Mansergh, *Britain and Ireland* (in *Longman's Pamphlets on the British Commonwealth,* London, 1942).

10. Very characteristic is the following statement of J. A. Froude made shortly before the beginning of the imperialist era: "Let it be once established that an Englishman emigrating to Canada or the Cape, or Australia, or New Zealand did not forfeit his nationality, that he was still on English soil as much as if he was in Devonshire or Yorkshire, and would remain an Englishman while the English Empire lasted; and if we spent a quarter of the sums which were sunk in the morasses at Balaclava in sending out and establishing two millions of our people in those colonies, it would contribute more to the essential strength of the country than all the wars in which we have been entangled from Agincourt to Waterloo." (Quoted from Robert Livingston Schuyler, *The Fall of the Old Colonial System,* New York, 1945, pp. 280–81.)

11. The eminent South African writer, Jan Disselboom, expressed very bluntly the attitude of the Commonwealth peoples on this question: "Great Britain is merely a partner in the concern . . . all descended from the same closely allied stock. . . . Those parts of the Empire which are not inhabited by races of which this is true, were never partners in the concern. They were the private property of the predominant partner. . . . You can have the white dominion, or you can have the Dominion of India, but you cannot have both." (Quoted from A. Carthill, *The Lost Dominion,* 1924.)

12. Ernest Barker, *Ideas and Ideals of the British Empire,* Cambridge, 1941, p. 4. See also the very good introductory remarks on the foundations of the French Empire in *The French Colonial Empire* (in *Information Department Papers* No. 25, published by The Royal Institute of International Affairs, London, 1941), pp. 9 ff. "The aim is to assimilate colonial peoples to the French people, or, where this is not possible in more primitive communities, to 'associate' them, so that more and more the difference between *la France métropole* and *la France d'outremer* shall be a geographical difference and not a fundamental one."

13. See Gabriel Hanotaux, "Le Général Mangin" in *Revue des Deux Mondes* (1925), Tome 27.

14. W. P. Crozier, "France and her 'Black Empire' " in *New Republic,* January 23, 1924.

15. David Lloyd George, *Memoirs of the Peace Conference,* New Haven, 1939, I, pp. 362 ff.

16. A similar attempt at brutal exploitation of overseas possessions for the sake of the nation was made by the Netherlands in the Dutch East Indies after the defeat of Napoleon had restored the Dutch colonies to the much impoverished mother country. By means of compulsory cultivation the natives were reduced to slavery for the benefit of the government in Holland. Multatuli's *Max Havelaar,* first published in the sixties of the last century, was aimed at the government at home and not at the services abroad. (See de Kat Angelino, *Colonial Policy,* Vol. II, *The Dutch East Indies,* Chicago, 1931, p. 45.)

    This system was quickly abandoned and the Netherlands Indies, for a while, became "the admiration of all colonizing nations." (Sir Hesketh Bell, former Governor of Uganda, Northern Nigeria, etc., *Foreign Colonial Administration in the Far East,* 1928, Part I). The Dutch methods have many similarities with the French: the granting of European status to deserving natives, introduction of a European school system, and other devices of gradual assimilation. The Dutch thereby achieved the same result: a strong national independence movement among the subject people.

    In the present study Dutch and Belgian imperialism are being neglected. The first is a curious and changing mixture of French and English methods; the second is the story not of the expansion of the Belgian nation or even the Belgian bourgeoisie, but of the expansion of the Belgian king personally, unchecked by any government, unconnected with any other institution. Both the Dutch and the Belgian forms of imperialism are atypical. The Netherlands did not expand during the eighties, but only consolidated and modernized their old possessions. The unequalled atrocities committed in the Belgian Congo, on the other hand, would offer too unfair an example for what was generally happening in overseas possessions.

17. Ernest Barker, *op. cit.,* p. 69.

18. Selwyn James, *South of the Congo,* New York, 1943, p. 326.

19. About these boyhood ideals and their role in British imperialism, see chapter vii. How they were developed and cultivated is described in Rudyard Kipling's *Stalky and Company*.

20. Ernest Barker, *op. cit.,* p. 150.

21. Lord Cromer, "The Government of Subject Races," in *Edinburgh Review,* January, 1908.

22. *Ibid*.

23. The first scholar to use the term imperialism to differentiate clearly between the "Empire" and the "Commonwealth" was J. A. Hobson. But the essential difference was always well known. The principle of "colonial freedom" for instance, cherished by all liberal British statesmen after the American Revo-

lution, was held valid only insofar as the colony was "formed of the British people or . . . such admixture of the British population as to make it safe to introduce representative institutions." See Robert Livingston Schuyler, *op. cit.,* pp. 236 ff.

In the nineteenth century, we must distinguish three types of overseas possessions within the British Empire: the settlements or plantations or colonies, like Australia and other dominions; the trade stations and possessions like India; and the maritime and military stations like the Cape of Good Hope, which were held for the sake of the former. All these possessions underwent a change in government and political significance in the era of imperialism.

24. Ernest Barker, *op. cit.*

25. Millin, *op. cit.,* p. 175.

26. The origin of this misnomer probably lies in the history of British rule in South Africa, and goes back to the times when the local governors, Cecil Rhodes and Jameson, involved the "Imperial Government" in London, much against its intentions, in the war against the Boers. "In fact Rhodes, or rather Jameson, was absolute ruler of a territory three times the size of England, which could be administered 'without waiting for the grudging assent or polite censure of the High Commissioner' " who was the representative of an Imperial Government that retained only "nominal control." (Reginald Ivan Lovell, *The Struggle for South Africa, 1875–1899,* New York, 1934, p. 194.) And what happens in territories in which the British government has resigned its jurisdiction to the local European population that lacks all traditional and constitutional restraint of nation-states, can best be seen in the tragic story of the South African Union since its independence, that is, since the time when the "Imperial Government" no longer had any right to interfere.

27. The discussion in the House of Commons in May, 1908, between Charles Dilke and the Colonial Secretary is interesting in this respect. Dilke warned against giving self-government to the Crown colonies because this would result in rule of the white planters over their colored workers. He was told that the natives too had a representation in the English House of Commons. (See G. Zoepfi, "Kolonien und Kolonialpolitik" in *Handwörterbuch der Staatswissenschaften.*)

28. Lawrence J. Zetland, *Lord Cromer,* 1923, p. 224.

29. A. Carthill, *The Lost Dominion,* 1924, pp. 41–42, 93.

30. An instance of "pacification" in the Near East was described at great length by T. E. Lawrence in an article "France, Britain and the Arabs" written for *The Observer* (1920): "There is a preliminary Arab success, the British reinforcements go out as a punitive force. They fight their way . . . to their objective, which is meanwhile bombarded by artillery, aeroplanes, or gunboats. Finally perhaps a village is burnt and the district pacified. It is odd that we don't use poison gas on these occasions. Bombing the houses is a patchy way of getting the women and children. . . . By gas attacks the whole population

of offending districts could be wiped out neatly; and as a method of government it would be no more immoral than the present system." (See his *Letters*, edited by David Garnett, New York, 1939, pp. 311 ff.)

31. In 1910, on the other hand, the Colonial Secretary B. Dernburg had to resign because he had antagonized the colonial planters by protecting the natives. (See Mary E. Townsend, *Rise and Fall of Germany's Colonial Empire*, New York, 1930, and P. Leutwein, *Kämpfe um Afrika*, Luebeck, 1936.)

32. In the words of Léon Cayla, former Governor General of Madagascar and friend of Pétain.

Total Domination

THE CONCENTRATION and extermination camps of totalitarian regimes serve as the laboratories in which the fundamental belief of totalitarianism that everything is possible is being verified. Compared with this, all other experiments are secondary in importance—including those in the field of medicine whose horrors are recorded in detail in the trials against the physicians of the Third Reich—although it is characteristic that these laboratories were used for experiments of every kind.

Total domination, which strives to organize the infinite plurality and differentiation of human beings as if all of humanity were just one individual, is possible only if each and every person can be reduced to a never-changing identity of reactions, so that each of these bundles of reactions can be exchanged at random for any other. The problem is to fabricate something that does not exist, namely, a kind of human species resembling other animal species whose only "freedom" would consist in "preserving the species."[1] Totalitarian domination attempts to achieve this goal both through ideological indoctrination of the elite formations and through absolute terror in the camps; and the atrocities for which the elite formations are ruthlessly used become, as it were, the practical application of the ideological indoctrination—the testing ground in which the latter must prove itself—while the appalling spectacle of the camps themselves is supposed to furnish the "theoretical" verification of the ideology.

The camps are meant not only to exterminate people and degrade human beings, but also serve the ghastly experiment of eliminating, under scientifically controlled conditions, spontaneity itself as an expression of human behavior and of transforming the human personality into a mere thing, into something that even animals are not; for Pavlov's dog, which, as we know, was trained to eat not when it was hungry but when a bell rang, was a perverted animal.

From The Origins of Totalitarianism.

Under normal circumstances this can never be accomplished, because spontaneity can never be entirely eliminated insofar as it is connected not only with human freedom but with life itself, in the sense of simply keeping alive. It is only in the concentration camps that such an experiment is at all possible, and therefore they are not only *"la société la plus totalitaire encore réalisée"* (David Rousset) but the guiding social ideal of total domination in general. Just as the stability of the totalitarian regime depends on the isolation of the fictitious world of the movement from the outside world, so the experiment of total domination in the concentration camps depends on sealing off the latter against the world of all others, the world of the living in general, even against the outside world of a country under totalitarian rule. This isolation explains the peculiar unreality and lack of credibility that characterize all reports from the concentration camps and constitute one of the main difficulties for the true understanding of totalitarian domination, which stands or falls with the existence of these concentration and extermination camps; for, unlikely as it may sound, these camps are the true central institution of totalitarian organizational power.

There are numerous reports by survivors.[2] The more authentic they are, the less they attempt to communicate things that evade human understanding and human experience—sufferings, that is, that transform men into "uncomplaining animals."[3] None of these reports inspires those passions of outrage and sympathy through which men have always been mobilized for justice. On the contrary, anyone speaking or writing about concentration camps is still regarded as suspect; and if the speaker has resolutely returned to the world of the living, he himself is often assailed by doubts with regard to his own truthfulness, as though he had mistaken a nightmare for reality.[4]

This doubt of people concerning themselves and the reality of their own experience only reveals what the Nazis have always known: that men determined to commit crimes will find it expedient to organize them on the vastest, most improbable scale. Not only because this renders all punishments provided by the legal system inadequate and absurd; but because the very immensity of the crimes guarantees that the murderers who proclaim their innocence with all manner of lies will be more readily believed than the victims who tell the truth. The Nazis did not even consider it necessary to keep this discovery to themselves. Hitler circulated millions of copies of his book in which he stated that to be successful, a lie must be enormous—which did not prevent people from believing him as, similarly, the Nazis' proclamations, repeated *ad nauseam,* that the Jews would be exterminated like bedbugs (*i.e.,* with poison gas), prevented anybody from *not* believing them.

There is a great temptation to explain away the intrinsically incredible by means of liberal rationalizations. In each one of us, there lurks such a liberal, wheedling us with the voice of common sense. The road to totalitarian domination leads through many intermediate stages for which we can find numerous analogies and precedents. The extraordinarily bloody terror during the initial stage of totalitarian rule serves indeed the exclusive purpose of defeating the opponent and rendering all further opposition impossible; but total terror is launched only after this initial stage has been overcome and the regime no longer has anything to fear from the opposition. In this context it has been frequently remarked that in such a case the means have become the end, but this is after all only an admission, in paradoxical disguise, that the category "the end justifies the means" no longer applies, that terror has lost its "purpose," that it is no longer the means to frighten people. Nor does the explanation suffice that the revolution, as in the case of the French Revolution, was devouring its own children, for the terror continues even after everybody who might be described as a child of the revolution in one capacity or another—the Russian factions, the power centers of party, the army, the bureaucracy—has long since been devoured. Many things that nowadays have become the specialty of totalitarian government are only too well known from the study of history. There have almost always been wars of aggression; the massacre of hostile populations after a victory went unchecked until the Romans mitigated it by introducing the *parcere subjectis;* through centuries the extermination of native peoples went hand in hand with the colonization of the Americas, Australia and Africa; slavery is one of the oldest institutions of mankind and all empires of antiquity were based on the labor of state-owned slaves who erected their public buildings. Not even concentration camps are an invention of totalitarian movements. They emerge for the first time during the Boer War, at the beginning of the century, and continued to be used in South Africa as well as India for "undesirable elements"; here, too, we first find the term "protective custody" which was later adopted by the Third Reich. These camps correspond in many respects to the concentration camps at the beginning of totalitarian rule; they were used for "suspects" whose offenses could not be proved and who could not be sentenced by ordinary process of law. All this clearly points to totalitarian methods of domination; all these are elements they utilize, develop and crystallize on the basis of the nihilistic principle that "everything is permitted," which they inherited and already take for granted. But wherever these new forms of domination assume their authentically totalitarian structure they transcend this principle, which is still tied to the utilitarian motives and self-interest of the rulers,

and try their hand in a realm that up to now has been completely unknown to us: the realm where "everything is possible." And, characteristically enough, this is precisely the realm that cannot be limited by either
utilitarian motives or self-interest, regardless of the latter's content.

What runs counter to common sense is not the nihilistic principle
that "everything is permitted," which was already contained in the nineteenth-century utilitarian conception of common sense. What common
sense and "normal people" refuse to believe is that everything is possible.[5]
We attempt to understand elements in present or recollected experience
that simply surpass our powers of understanding. We attempt to classify as
criminal a thing which, as we all feel, no such category was ever intended
to cover. What meaning has the concept of murder when we are confronted with the mass production of corpses? We attempt to understand
the behavior of concentration-camp inmates and SS-men psychologically,
when the very thing that must be realized is that the psyche *can* be destroyed even without the destruction of the physical man; that, indeed,
psyche, character, and individuality seem under certain circumstances to
express themselves only through the rapidity or slowness with which they
disintegrate.[6] The end result in any case is inanimate men, *i.e.,* men who
can no longer be psychologically understood, whose return to the psychologically or otherwise intelligibly human world closely resembles the resurrection of Lazarus. All statements of common sense, whether of a
psychological or sociological nature, serve only to encourage those who
think it "superficial" to "dwell on horrors."[7]

If it is true that the concentration camps are the most consequential
institution of totalitarian rule, "dwelling on horrors" would seem to be
indispensable for the understanding of totalitarianism. But recollection can
no more do this than can the uncommunicative eyewitness report. In
both these genres there is an inherent tendency to run away from the experience; instinctively or rationally, both types of writer are so much
aware of the terrible abyss that separates the world of the living from that
of the living dead, that they cannot supply anything more than a series of
remembered occurrences that must seem just as incredible to those who
relate them as to their audience. Only the fearful imagination of those
who have been aroused by such reports but have not actually been smit-
ten in their own flesh, of those who are consequently free from the bes-
tial, desperate terror which, when confronted by real, present horror,
inexorably paralyzes everything that is not mere reaction, can afford to
keep thinking about horrors. Such thoughts are useful only for the perception of political contexts and the mobilization of political passions. A
change of personality of any sort whatever can no more be induced by

thinking about horrors than by the real experience of horror. The reduction of a man to a bundle of reactions separates him as radically as mental disease from everything within him that is personality or character. When, like Lazarus, he rises from the dead, he finds his personality or character unchanged, just as he had left it.

Just as the horror, or the dwelling on it, cannot affect a change of character in him, cannot make men better or worse, thus it cannot become the basis of a political community or party in a narrower sense. The attempts to build up a European elite with a program of intra-European understanding based on the common European experience of the concentration camps have foundered in much the same manner as the attempts following the first World War to draw political conclusions from the international experience of the front generation. In both cases it turned out that the experiences themselves can communicate no more than nihilistic banalities.[8] Political consequences such as postwar pacifism, for example, derived from the general fear of war, not from the experiences in war. Instead of producing a pacifism devoid of reality, the insight into the structure of modern wars, guided and mobilized by fear, might have led to the realization that the only standard for a necessary war is the fight against conditions under which people no longer wish to live—and our experiences with the tormenting hell of the totalitarian camps have enlightened us only too well about the possibility of such conditions.[9] Thus the fear of concentration camps and the resulting insight into the nature of total domination might serve to invalidate all obsolete political differentiations from right to left and to introduce beside and above them the politically most important yardstick for judging events in our time, namely: whether they serve totalitarian domination or not.

In any event, the fearful imagination has the great advantage to dissolve the sophistic-dialectical interpretations of politics which are all based on the superstition that something good might result from evil. Such dialectical acrobatics had at least a semblance of justification so long as the worst that man could inflict upon man was murder. But, as we know today, murder is only a limited evil. The murderer who kills a man—a man who has to die anyway—still moves within the realm of life and death familiar to us; both have indeed a necessary connection on which the dialectic is founded, even if it is not always conscious of it. The murderer leaves a corpse behind and does not pretend that his victim has never existed; if he wipes out any traces, they are those of his own identity, and not the memory and grief of the persons who loved his victim; he destroys a life, but he does not destroy the fact of existence itself.

The Nazis, with the precision peculiar to them, used to register their operations in the concentration camps under the heading "under cover of the night (*Nacht und Nebel*)." The radicalism of measures to treat people as if they had never existed and to make them disappear in the literal sense of the word is frequently not apparent at first glance, because both the German and the Russian system are not uniform but consist of a series of categories in which people are treated very differently. In the case of Germany, these different categories used to exist in the same camp, but without coming into contact with each other; frequently, the isolation between the categories was even stricter than the isolation from the outside world. Thus, out of racial considerations, Scandinavian nationals during the war were quite differently treated by the Germans than the members of other peoples, although the former were outspoken enemies of the Nazis. The latter in turn were divided into those whose "extermination" was immediately on the agenda, as in the case of the Jews, or could be expected in the predictable future, as in the case of the Poles, Russians and Ukrainians, and into those who were not yet covered by instructions about such an over-all "final solution," as in the case of the French and Belgians. In Russia, on the other hand, we must distinguish three more or less independent systems. First, there are the authentic forced-labor groups that live in relative freedom and are sentenced for limited periods. Secondly, there are the concentration camps in which the human material is ruthlessly exploited and the mortality rate is extremely high, but which are essentially organized for labor purposes. And, thirdly, there are the annihilation camps in which the inmates are systematically wiped out through starvation and neglect.

The real horror of the concentration and extermination camps lies in the fact that the inmates, even if they happen to keep alive, are more effectively cut off from the world of the living than if they had died, because terror enforces oblivion. Here, murder is as impersonal as the squashing of a gnat. Someone may die as the result of systematic torture or starvation, or because the camp is overcrowded and superfluous human material must be liquidated. Conversely, it may happen that due to a shortage of new human shipments the danger arises that the camps become depopulated and that the order is now given to reduce the death rate at any price.[10] David Rousset called his report on the period in a German concentration camp *"Les Jours de Notre Mort,"* and it is indeed as if there were a possibility to give permanence to the process of dying itself and to enforce a condition in which both death and life are obstructed equally effectively.

It is the appearance of some radical evil, previously unknown to us, that puts an end to the notion of developments and transformations of qualities. Here, there are neither political nor historical nor simply moral standards but, at the most, the realization that something seems to be involved in modern politics that actually should never be involved in politics as we used to understand it, namely all or nothing—all, and that is an undetermined infinity of forms of human living-together, or nothing, for a victory of the concentration-camp system would mean the same inexorable doom for human beings as the use of the hydrogen bomb would mean the doom of the human race.

There are no parallels to the life in the concentration camps. Its horror can never be fully embraced by the imagination for the very reason that it stands outside of life and death. It can never be fully reported for the very reason that the survivor returns to the world of the living, which makes it impossible for him to believe fully in his own past experiences. It is as though he had a story to tell of another planet, for the status of the inmates in the world of the living, where nobody is supposed to know if they are alive or dead, is such that it is as though they had never been born. Therefore all parallels create confusion and distract attention from what is essential. Forced labor in prisons and penal colonies, banishment, slavery, all seem for a moment to offer helpful comparisons, but on closer examination lead nowhere.

Forced labor as a punishment is limited as to time and intensity. The convict retains his rights over his body; he is not absolutely tortured and he is not absolutely dominated. Banishment banishes only from one part of the world to another part of the world, also inhabited by human beings; it does not exclude from the human world altogether. Throughout history slavery has been an institution within a social order; slaves were not, like concentration-camp inmates, withdrawn from the sight and hence the protection of their fellow-men; as instruments of labor they had a definite price and as property a definite value. The concentration-camp inmate has no price, because he can always be replaced; nobody knows to whom he belongs, because he is never seen. From the point of view of normal society he is absolutely superfluous, although in times of acute labor shortage, as in Russia and in Germany during the war, he is used for work.

The concentration camp as an institution was not established for the sake of any possible labor yield; the only permanent economic function of the camps has been the financing of their own supervisory apparatus; thus from the economic point of view the concentration camps exist mostly for their own sake. Any work that has been performed could have been done much better and more cheaply under different conditions.[11] Especially Russia, whose concentration camps are mostly described as forced-labor camps because Soviet bureaucracy has chosen to dignify them with this name, reveals most clearly that forced labor is not the primary issue; forced labor is the normal condition of all Russian workers, who have no freedom of movement and can be arbitrarily drafted for work to any place at any time. The incredibility of the horrors is closely bound up with their economic uselessness. The Nazis carried this uselessness to the point of open anti-utility when in the midst of the war, despite the shortage of building material and rolling stock, they set up enormous, costly extermination factories and transported millions of people back and forth.[12] In the eyes of a strictly utilitarian world the obvious contradiction between these acts and military expediency gave the whole enterprise an air of mad unreality.

This atmosphere of madness and unreality, created by an apparent lack of purpose, is the real iron curtain which hides all forms of concentration camps from the eyes of the world. Seen from outside, they and the things that happen in them can be described only in images drawn from a life after death, that is, a life removed from earthly purposes. Concentration camps can very aptly be divided into three types corresponding to three basic Western conceptions of a life after death: Hades, Purgatory, and Hell. To Hades correspond those relatively mild forms, once popular even in nontotalitarian countries, for getting undesirable elements of all sorts—refugees, stateless persons, the asocial and the unemployed—out of the way; as DP camps, which are nothing other than camps for persons who have become superfluous and bothersome, they have survived the war. Purgatory is represented by the Soviet Union's labor camps, where neglect is combined with chaotic forced labor. Hell in the most literal sense was embodied by those types of camp perfected by the Nazis, in which the whole of life was thoroughly and systematically organized with a view to the greatest possible torment.

All three types have one thing in common: the human masses sealed off in them are treated as if they no longer existed, as if what happened to them were no longer of any interest to anybody, as if they were already dead and some evil spirit gone mad were amusing himself by stopping them for a while between life and death before admitting them to eternal peace.

It is not so much the barbed wire as the skillfully manufactured unreality of those whom it fences in that provokes such enormous cruelties and ultimately makes extermination look like a perfectly normal measure. Everything that was done in the camps is known to us from the world of perverse, malignant fantasies. The difficult thing to understand is that, like such fantasies, these gruesome crimes took place in a phantom world, which, however, has materialized, as it were, into a world which is complete with all sensual data of reality but lacks that structure of consequence and responsibility without which reality remains for us a mass of incomprehensible data. The result is that a place has been established where men can be tortured and slaughtered, and yet neither the tormentors nor the tormented, and least of all the outsider, can be aware that what is happening is anything more than a cruel game or an absurd dream.[13]

The films which the Allies circulated in Germany and elsewhere after the war showed clearly that this atmosphere of insanity and unreality is not dispelled by pure reportage. To the unprejudiced observer these pictures are just about as convincing as snapshots of mysterious substances taken at spiritualist séances.[14] Common sense reacted to the horrors of Buchenwald and Auschwitz with the plausible argument: "What crime must these people have committed that such things were done to them!"; or, in Germany and Austria, in the midst of starvation, overpopulation, and general hatred: "Too bad that they've stopped gassing the Jews"; and everywhere with the skeptical shrug that greets ineffectual propaganda.

If the propaganda of truth fails to convince the average person because it is too monstrous, it is positively dangerous to those who know from their own imaginings what they themselves are capable of doing and who are therefore perfectly willing to believe in the reality of what they have seen. Suddenly it becomes evident that things which for thousands of years the human imagination had banished to a realm beyond human competence can be manufactured right here on earth, that Hell and Purgatory, and even a shadow of their perpetual duration, can be established by the most modern methods of destruction and therapy. To these people (and they are more numerous in any large city than we like to admit) the totalitarian hell proves only that the power of man is greater than they ever dared to think, and that man can realize hellish fantasies without making the sky fall or the earth open.

These analogies, repeated in many reports from the world of the dying,[15] seem to express more than a desperate attempt at saying what is outside the realm of human speech. Nothing perhaps distinguishes modern masses as radically from those of previous centuries as the loss of faith in a Last Judgment: the worst have lost their fear and the best have lost their hope. Unable as yet to live without fear and hope, these masses are attracted by every effort which seems to promise a man-made fabrication of the Paradise they had longed for and of the Hell they had feared. Just as the popularized features of Marx's classless society have a queer resemblance to the Messianic Age, so the reality of concentration camps resembles nothing so much as medieval pictures of Hell.

The one thing that cannot be reproduced is what made the traditional conceptions of Hell tolerable to man: the Last Judgment, the idea of an absolute standard of justice combined with the infinite possibility of grace. For in the human estimation there is no crime and no sin commensurable with the everlasting torments of Hell. Hence the discomfiture of common sense, which asks: What crime must these people have committed in order to suffer so inhumanly? Hence also the absolute innocence of the victims: no man ever deserved this. Hence finally the grotesque haphazardness with which concentration-camp victims were chosen in the perfected terror state: such "punishment" can, with equal justice and injustice, be inflicted on anyone.

In comparison with the insane end-result—concentration-camp society—the process by which men are prepared for this end, and the methods by which individuals are adapted to these conditions, are transparent and logical. The insane mass manufacture of corpses is preceded by the historically and politically intelligible preparation of living corpses. The impetus and what is more important, the silent consent to such unprecedented conditions are the products of those events which in a period of political disintegration suddenly and unexpectedly made hundreds of thousands of human beings homeless, stateless, outlawed and unwanted, while millions of human beings were made economically superfluous and socially burdensome by unemployment. This in turn could only happen because the Rights of Man, which had never been philosophically established but merely formulated, which had never been politically secured but merely proclaimed, have, in their traditional form, lost all validity.

The first essential step on the road to total domination is to kill the juridical person in man. This was done, on the one hand, by putting certain categories of people outside the protection of the law and forcing at the same time, through the instrument of denationalization, the nontotalitarian world into recognition of lawlessness; it was done, on the other, by placing the concentration camp outside the normal penal system, and by selecting its inmates outside the normal judicial procedure in which a definite crime entails a predictable penalty. Thus criminals, who for other reasons are an essential element in concentration-camp society, are ordinarily sent to a camp only on completion of their prison sentence. Under all circumstances totalitarian domination sees to it that the categories gathered in the camps—Jews, carriers of diseases, representatives of dying classes—have already lost their capacity for both normal or criminal action. Propagandistically this means that the "protective custody" is handled as a "preventive police measure,"[16] that is, a measure that deprives people of the ability to act. Deviations from this rule in Russia must be attributed to the catastrophic shortage of prisons and to a desire, so far unrealized, to transform the whole penal system into a system of concentration camps.[17]

The inclusion of criminals is necessary in order to make plausible the propagandistic claim of the movement that the institution exists for asocial elements.[18] Criminals do not properly belong in the concentration camps, if only because it is harder to kill the juridical person in a man who is guilty of some crime than in a totally innocent person. If they constitute a permanent category among the inmates, it is a concession of the totalitarian state to the prejudices of society, which can in this way most readily be accustomed to the existence of the camps. In order, on the other hand, to keep the camp system itself intact, it is essential as long as there is a penal system in the country that criminals should be sent to the camps only on completion of their sentence, that is when they are actually entitled to their freedom. Under no circumstances must the concentration camp become a calculable punishment for definite offenses.

The amalgamation of criminals with all other categories has moreover the advantage of making it shockingly evident to all other arrivals that they have landed on the lowest level of society. It soon turns out, to be sure, that they have every reason to envy the lowest thief and murderer; but meanwhile the lowest level is a good beginning. Moreover it is an effective means of camouflage: this happens only to criminals and nothing worse is happening than that what deservedly happens to criminals.

The criminals everywhere constitute the aristocracy of the camps. (In Germany, during the war, they were replaced in the leadership by the Communists, because not even a minimum of rational work could be performed under the chaotic conditions created by a criminal administration. This was merely a temporary transformation of concentration camps into forced-labor camps, a thoroughly atypical phenomenon of limited duration.)[19] What places the criminals in the leadership is not so much the affinity between supervisory personnel and criminal elements—in the Soviet Union apparently the supervisors are not, like the SS, a special elite trained to commit crimes[20]—as the fact that only criminals have been sent to the camp in connection with some definite activity. They at least know why they are in a concentration camp and therefore have kept a remnant of their juridical person. For the politicals this is only subjectively true; their actions, insofar as they were actions and not mere opinions or someone else's vague suspicions, or accidental membership in a politically disapproved group, are as a rule not covered by the normal legal system of the country and not juridically defined.[21]

To the amalgam of politicals and criminals with which concentration camps in Russia and Germany started out, was added at an early date a third element which was soon to constitute the majority of all concentration-camp inmates. This largest group has consisted ever since of people who had done nothing whatsoever that, either in their own consciousness or the consciousness of their tormenters, had any rational connection with their arrest. In Germany, after 1938, this element was represented by masses of Jews, in Russia by any groups which, for any reason having nothing to do with their actions, had incurred the disfavor of the authorities. These groups, innocent in every sense, are the most suitable for thorough experimentation in disfranchisement and destruction of the juridical person, and therefore they are both qualitatively and quantitatively the most essential category of the camp population. This principle was most fully realized in the gas chambers which, if only because of their enormous capacity, could not be intended for individual cases but only for people in general. In this connection, the following dialogue sums up the situation of the individual: "For what purpose, may I ask, do the gas chambers exist?"—"For what purpose were you born?"[22] It is this third group of the totally innocent who in every case fare the worst in the camps. Criminals and politicals are assimilated to this category; thus deprived of the protective distinction that comes of their having done something, they are utterly exposed to the arbitrary. The ultimate goal, partly achieved in the Soviet Union and clearly indicated in the last phases of Nazi terror, is to have the whole camp population composed of this category of innocent people.

Contrasting with the complete haphazardness with which the inmates are selected are the categories, meaningless in themselves but useful from the standpoint of organization, into which they are usually divided on their arrival. In the German camps there were criminals, politicals, asocial elements, religious offenders, and Jews, all distinguished by insignia. When the French set up concentration camps after the Spanish Civil War, they immediately introduced the typical totalitarian amalgam of politicals with criminals and the innocent (in this case the stateless), and despite their inexperience proved remarkably inventive in creating meaningless categories of inmates.[23] Originally devised in order to prevent any growth of solidarity among the inmates, this technique proved particularly valuable because no one could know whether his own category was better or worse than someone else's. In Germany this eternally shifting though pedantically organized edifice was given an appearance of solidity by the fact that under any and all circumstances the Jews were the lowest category. The gruesome and grotesque part of it was that the inmates identified themselves with these categories, as though they represented a last authentic remnant of their juridical person. Even if we disregard all other circumstances, it is no wonder that a Communist of 1933 should have come out of the camps more Communistic than he went in, a Jew more Jewish, and, in France, the wife of a Foreign Legionary more convinced of the value of the Foreign Legion; it would seem as though these categories promised some last shred of predictable treatment, as though they embodied some last and hence most fundamental juridical identity.

While the classification of inmates by categories is only a tactical, organizational measure, the arbitrary selection of victims indicates the essential principle of the institution. If the concentration camps had been dependent on the existence of political adversaries, they would scarcely have survived the first years of the totalitarian regimes. One only has to take a look at the number of inmates at Buchenwald in the years after 1936 in order to understand how absolutely necessary the element of the innocent was for the continued existence of the camps. "The camps would have died out if in making its arrests the Gestapo had considered only the principle of opposition,"[24] and toward the end of 1937 Buchenwald, with less than 1,000 inmates, was close to dying out until the November pogroms brought more than 20,000 new arrivals.[25] In Germany, this element of the innocent was furnished in vast numbers by the Jews since 1938; in Russia, it consisted of random groups of the population which for some reason entirely unconnected with their actions had fallen into disgrace.[26] But if in Germany the really totalitarian type of concentration camp with its enormous majority of completely "innocent" inmates was not established until 1938, in Russia it goes back to the early thirties, since up to 1930 the majority of the concentration-camp population still consisted of criminals, counterrevolutionaries and "politicals" (meaning, in this case, members of deviationist factions). Since then there have been so many innocent people in the camps that it is difficult to classify them— persons who had some sort of contact with a foreign country, Russians of Polish origin (particularly in the years 1936 to 1938), peasants whose villages for some economic reason were liquidated, deported nationalities, demobilized soldiers of the Red Army who happened to belong to regiments that stayed too long abroad as occupation forces or had become prisoners of war in Germany, etc. But the existence of a political opposition is for a concentration-camp system only a pretext, and the purpose of the system is not achieved even when, under the most monstrous terror, the population becomes more or less voluntarily co-ordinated, *i.e.,* relinquishes its political rights. The aim of an arbitrary system is to destroy the civil rights of the whole population, who ultimately become just as outlawed in their own country as the stateless and homeless. The destruction of a man's rights, the killing of the juridical person in him, is a prerequisite for dominating him entirely. And this applies not only to special categories such as criminals, political opponents, Jews, homosexuals, on whom the early experiments were made, but to every inhabitant of a totalitarian state. Free consent is as much an obstacle to total domination as free opposition.[27] The arbitrary arrest which chooses among innocent people destroys the validity of free consent, just as torture—as distinguished from death—destroys the possibility of opposition.

Any, even the most tyrannical, restriction of this arbitrary persecution to certain opinions of a religious or political nature, to certain modes of intellectual or erotic social behavior, to certain freshly invented "crimes," would render the camps superfluous, because in the long run no attitude and no opinion can withstand the threat of so much horror; and above all it would make for a new system of justice, which, given any stability at all, could not fail to produce a new juridical person in man, that would elude the totalitarian domination. The so-called *"Volksnutzen"* of the Nazis, constantly fluctuating (because what is useful today can be injurious tomorrow) and the eternally shifting party line of the Soviet Union which, being retroactive, almost daily makes new groups of people available for the concentration camps, are the only guaranty for the continued existence of the concentration camps, and hence for the continued total disfranchisement of man.

The next decisive step in the preparation of living corpses is the murder of the moral person in man. This is done in the main by making martyrdom, for the first time in history, impossible: "How many people here still believe that a protest has even historic importance? This skepticism is the real masterpiece of the SS. Their great accomplishment. They have corrupted all human solidarity. Here the night has fallen on the future. When no witnesses are left, there can be no testimony. To demonstrate when death can no longer be postponed is an attempt to give death a meaning, to act beyond one's own death. In order to be successful, a gesture must have social meaning. There are hundreds of thousands of us here, all living in absolute solitude. That is why we are subdued no matter what happens."[28]

The camps and the murder of political adversaries are only part of organized oblivion that not only embraces carriers of public opinion such as the spoken and the written word, but extends even to the families and friends of the victim. Grief and remembrance are forbidden. In the Soviet Union a woman will sue for divorce immediately after her husband's arrest in order to save the lives of her children; if her husband chances to come back, she will indignantly turn him out of the house.[29] The Western world has hitherto, even in its darkest periods, granted the slain enemy the right to be remembered as a self-evident acknowledgment of the fact that we are all men (and *only* men). It is only because even Achilles set out for Hector's funeral, only because the most despotic governments honored the slain enemy, only because the Romans allowed the Christians to write their martyrologies, only because the Church kept its heretics alive in the memory of men, that all was not lost and never could be lost. The concentration camps, by making death itself anonymous (making it impossible to find out whether a prisoner is dead or alive) robbed death of its meaning as the end of a fulfilled life. In a sense they took away the individual's own death, proving that henceforth nothing belonged to him and he belonged to no one. His death merely set a seal on the fact that he had never really existed.

This attack on the moral person might still have been opposed by man's conscience which tells him that it is better to die a victim than to live as a bureaucrat of murder. Totalitarian terror achieved its most terrible triumph when it succeeded in cutting the moral person off from the individualist escape and in making the decisions of conscience absolutely questionable and equivocal. When a man is faced with the alternative of betraying and thus murdering his friends or of sending his wife and children, for whom he is in every sense responsible, to their death; when even suicide would mean the immediate murder of his own family—how is he to decide? The alternative is no longer between good and evil, but between murder and murder. Who could solve the moral dilemma of the Greek mother, who was allowed by the Nazis to choose which of her three children should be killed?[30]

Through the creation of conditions under which conscience ceases to be adequate and to do good becomes utterly impossible, the consciously organized complicity of all men in the crimes of totalitarian regimes is extended to the victims and thus made really total. The SS implicated concentration-camp inmates—criminals, politicals, Jews—in their crimes by making them responsible for a large part of the administration, thus confronting them with the hopeless dilemma whether to send their friends to their death, or to help murder other men who happened to be strangers, and forcing them, in any event, to behave like murderers.[31] The point is not only that hatred is diverted from those who are guilty (the *capos* were more hated than the SS), but that the distinguishing line between persecutor and persecuted, between the murderer and his victim, is constantly blurred.[32]

Once the moral person has been killed, the one thing that still prevents men from being made into living corpses is the differentiation of the individual, his unique identity. In a sterile form such individuality can be preserved through a persistent stoicism, and it is certain that many men under totalitarian rule have taken and are each day still taking refuge in this absolute isolation of a personality without rights or conscience. There is no doubt that this part of the human person, precisely because it depends so essentially on nature and on forces that cannot be controlled by the will, is the hardest to destroy (and when destroyed is most easily repaired).[33]

The methods of dealing with this uniqueness of the human person are numerous and we shall not attempt to list them. They begin with the monstrous conditions in the transports to the camps, when hundreds of human beings are packed into a cattle-car stark naked, glued to each other, and shunted back and forth over the countryside for days on end; they continue upon arrival at the camp, the well-organized shock of the first hours, the shaving of the head, the grotesque camp clothing; and they end in the utterly unimaginable tortures so gauged as not to kill the body, at any event not quickly. The aim of all these methods, in any case, is to manipulate the human body—with its infinite possibilities of suffering—in such a way as to make it destroy the human person as inexorably as do certain mental diseases of organic origin.

It is here that the utter lunacy of the entire process becomes most apparent. Torture, to be sure, is an essential feature of the whole totalitarian police and judiciary apparatus; it is used every day to make people talk. This type of torture, since it pursues a definite, rational aim, has certain limitations: either the prisoner talks within a certain time, or he is killed. To this rationally conducted torture another, irrational, sadistic type was added in the first Nazi concentration camps and in the cellars of the Gestapo. Carried on for the most part by the SA, it pursued no aims and was not systematic, but depended on the initiative of largely abnormal elements. The mortality was so high that only a few concentration-camp inmates of 1933 survived these first years. This type of torture seemed to be not so much a calculated political institution as a concession of the regime to its criminal and abnormal elements, who were thus rewarded for services rendered. Behind the blind bestiality of the SA, there often lay a deep hatred and resentment against all those who were socially, intellectually, or physically better off than themselves, and who now, as if in fulfillment of their wildest dreams, were in their power. This resentment, which never died out entirely in the camps, strikes us as a last remnant of humanly understandable feeling.[34]

The real horror began, however, when the SS took over the administration of the camps. The old spontaneous bestiality gave way to an absolutely cold and systematic destruction of human bodies, calculated to destroy human dignity; death was avoided or postponed indefinitely. The camps were no longer amusement parks for beasts in human form, that is, for men who really belonged in mental institutions and prisons; the reverse became true: they were turned into "drill grounds," on which perfectly normal men were trained to be full-fledged members of the SS.[35]

The killing of man's individuality, of the uniqueness shaped in equal parts by nature, will, and destiny, which has become so self-evident a premise for all human relations that even identical twins inspire a certain uneasiness, creates a horror that vastly overshadows the outrage of the juridical-political person and the despair of the moral person. It is this horror that gives rise to the nihilistic generalizations which maintain plausibly enough that essentially all men alike are beasts.[36] Actually the experience of the concentration camps does show that human beings can be transformed into specimens of the human animal, and that man's "nature" is only "human" insofar as it opens up to man the possibility of becoming something highly unnatural, that is, a man.

After murder of the moral person and annihilation of the juridical person, the destruction of the individuality is almost always successful. Conceivably some laws of mass psychology may be found to explain why millions of human beings allowed themselves to be marched unresistingly into the gas chambers, although these laws would explain nothing else but the destruction of individuality. It is more significant that those individually condemned to death very seldom attempted to take one of their executioners with them, that there were scarcely any serious revolts, and that even in the moment of liberation there were very few spontaneous massacres of SS men. For to destroy individuality is to destroy spontaneity, man's power to begin something new out of his own resources, something that cannot be explained on the basis of reactions to environment and events.[37] Nothing then remains but ghastly marionettes with human faces, which all behave like the dog in Pavlov's experiments, which all react with perfect reliability even when going to their own death, and which do nothing but react. This is the real triumph of the system: "The triumph of the SS demands that the tortured victim allow himself to be led to the noose without protesting, that he renounce and abandon himself to the point of ceasing to affirm his identity. And it is not for nothing. It is not gratuitously, out of sheer sadism, that the SS men desire his defeat. They know that the system which succeeds in destroying its victim before he mounts the scaffold . . . is incomparably the best for keeping a whole people in slavery. In submission. Nothing is more terrible than these processions of human beings going like dummies to their death. The man who sees this says to himself: 'For them to be thus reduced, what power must be concealed in the hands of the masters,' and he turns away, full of bitterness but defeated."[38]

If we take totalitarian aspirations seriously and refuse to be misled by the common-sense assertion that they are utopian and unrealizable, it develops that the society of the dying established in the camps is the only form of society in which it is possible to dominate man entirely. Those who aspire to total domination must liquidate all spontaneity, such as the mere existence of individuality will always engender, and track it down in its most private forms, regardless of how unpolitical and harmless these may seem. Pavlov's dog, the human specimen reduced to the most elementary reactions, the bundle of reactions that can always be liquidated and replaced by other bundles of reactions that behave in exactly the same way, is the model "citizen" of a totalitarian state; and such a citizen can be produced only imperfectly outside of the camps.

The uselessness of the camps, their cynically admitted anti-utility, is only apparent. In reality they are most essential to the preservation of the regime's power than any of its other institutions. Without concentration camps, without the undefined fear they inspire and the very well-defined training they offer in totalitarian domination, which can nowhere else be fully tested with all of its most radical possibilities, a totalitarian state can neither inspire its nuclear troops with fanaticism nor maintain a whole people in complete apathy. The dominating and the dominated would only too quickly sink back into the "old bourgeois routine"; after early "excesses," they would succumb to everyday life with its human laws; in short, they would develop in the direction which all observers counseled by common sense were so prone to predict. The tragic fallacy of all these prophecies, originating in a world that was still safe, was to suppose that there was such a thing as one human nature established for all time, to identify this human nature with history, and thus to declare that the idea of total domination was not only inhuman but also unrealistic. Meanwhile we have learned that the power of man is so great that he really can be what he wishes to be.

It is in the very nature of totalitarian regimes to demand unlimited power. Such power can only be secured if literally all men, without a single exception, are reliably dominated in every aspect of their life. In the realm of foreign affairs new neutral territories must constantly be subjugated, while at home ever-new human groups must be mastered in expanding concentration camps, or, when circumstances require liquidated to make room for others. The question of opposition is unimportant both in foreign and domestic affairs. Any neutrality, indeed any spontaneously given friendship, is from the standpoint of totalitarian domination just as dangerous as open hostility, precisely because spontaneity as such, with its incalculability, is the greatest of all obstacles to total domination over man. The Communists of non-Communist countries, who fled or were called to Moscow, learned by bitter experience that they constituted a menace to the Soviet Union. Convinced Communists are in this sense, which alone has any reality today, just as ridiculous and just as menacing to the regime in Russia, as, for example, the convinced Nazis of the Röhm faction were to the Nazis.

What makes conviction and opinion of any sort so ridiculous and dangerous under totalitarian conditions is that totalitarian regimes take the greatest pride in having no need of them, or of any human help of any kind. Men insofar as they are more than animal reaction and fulfillment of functions are entirely superfluous to totalitarian regimes. Totalitarianism strives not toward despotic rule over men, but toward a system in which men are superfluous. Total power can be achieved and safeguarded only in a world of conditioned reflexes, of marionettes without the slightest trace of spontaneity. Precisely because man's resources are so great, he can be fully dominated only when he becomes a specimen of the animal-species man.

Therefore character is a threat and even the most unjust legal rules are an obstacle; but individuality, anything indeed that distinguishes one man from another, is intolerable. As long as all men have not been made equally superfluous—and this has been accomplished only in concentration camps—the ideal of totalitarian domination has not been achieved. Totalitarian states strive constantly, though never with complete success, to establish the superfluity of man—by the arbitrary selection of various groups for concentration camps, by constant purges of the ruling apparatus, by mass liquidations. Common sense protests desperately that the masses are submissive and that all this gigantic apparatus of terror is therefore superfluous; if they were capable of telling the truth, the totalitarian rulers would reply: The apparatus seems superfluous to you only because it serves to make men superfluous.

The totalitarian attempt to make men superfluous reflects the experience of modern masses of their superfluity on an overcrowded earth. The world of the dying, in which men are taught they are superfluous through a way of life in which punishment is meted out without connection with crime, in which exploitation is practiced without profit, and where work is performed without product, is a place where senselessness is daily produced anew. Yet, within the framework of the totalitarian ideology, nothing could be more sensible and logical; if the inmates are vermin, it is logical that they should be killed by poison gas; if they are degenerate, they should not be allowed to contaminate the population; if they have "slave-like souls" (Himmler), no one should waste his time trying to re-educate them. Seen through the eyes of the ideology, the trouble with the camps is almost that they make too much sense, that the execution of the doctrine is too consistent.

While the totalitarian regimes are thus resolutely and cynically emptying the world of the only thing that makes sense to the utilitarian expectations of common sense, they impose upon it at the same time a kind of supersense which the ideologies actually always meant when they pretended to have found the key to history or the solution to the riddles of the universe. Over and above the senselessness of totalitarian society is enthroned the ridiculous supersense of its ideological superstition. Ideologies are harmless, uncritical, and arbitrary opinions only as long as they are not believed in seriously. Once their claim to total validity is taken literally they become the nuclei of logical systems in which, as in the systems of paranoiacs, everything follows comprehensibly and even compulsorily once the first premise is accepted. The insanity of such systems lies not only in their first premise but in the very logicality with which they are constructed. The curious logicality of all isms, their simple-minded trust in the salvation value of stubborn devotion without regard for specific, varying factors, already harbors the first germs of totalitarian contempt for reality and factuality.

Common sense trained in utilitarian thinking is helpless against this ideological supersense, since totalitarian regimes establish a functioning world of no-sense. The ideological contempt for factuality still contained the proud assumption of human mastery over the world; it is, after all, contempt for reality which makes possible changing the world, the erection of the human artifice. What destroys the element of pride in the totalitarian contempt for reality (and thereby distinguishes it radically from revolutionary theories and attitudes) is the supersense which gives the contempt for reality its cogency, logicality, and consistency. What makes a truly totalitarian device out of the Bolshevik claim that the present Russian system is superior to all others is the fact that the totalitarian ruler draws from this claim the logically impeccable conclusion that without this system people never could have built such a wonderful thing as, let us say, a subway; from this, he again draws the logical conclusion that anyone who knows of the existence of the Paris subway is a suspect because he may cause people to doubt that one can do things only in the Bolshevik way. This leads to the final conclusion that in order to remain a loyal Bolshevik, you have to destroy the Paris subway. Nothing matters but consistency.

With these new structures, built on the strength of supersense and driven by the motor of logicality, we are indeed at the end of the bourgeois era of profits and power, as well as at the end of imperialism and expansion. The aggressiveness of totalitarianism springs not from lust for power, and if it feverishly seeks to expand, it does so neither for expansion's sake nor for profit, but only for ideological reasons: to make the world consistent, to prove that its respective supersense has been right.

It is chiefly for the sake of this supersense, for the sake of complete consistency, that it is necessary for totalitarianism to destroy every trace of what we commonly call human dignity. For respect for human dignity implies the recognition of my fellow-men or our fellow-nations as subjects, as builders of worlds or cobuilders of a common world. No ideology which aims at the explanation of all historical events of the past and at mapping out the course of all events of the future can bear the unpredictability which springs from the fact that men are creative, that they can bring forward something so new that nobody ever foresaw it.

What totalitarian ideologies therefore aim at is not the transformation of the outside world or the revolutionizing transmutation of society, but the transformation of human nature itself. The concentration camps are the laboratories where changes in human nature are tested, and their shamefulness therefore is not just the business of their inmates and those who run them according to strictly "scientific" standards; it is the concern of all men. Suffering, of which there has been always too much on earth, is not the issue, nor is the number of victims. Human nature as such is at stake, and even though it seems that these experiments succeed not in changing man but only in destroying him, by creating a society in which the nihilistic banality of *homo homini lupus* is consistently realized, one should bear in mind the necessary limitations to an experiment which requires global control in order to show conclusive results.

Until now the totalitarian belief that everything is possible seems to have proved only that everything can be destroyed. Yet, in their effort to prove that everything is possible, totalitarian regimes have discovered without knowing it that there are crimes which men can neither punish nor forgive. When the impossible was made possible it became the unpunishable, unforgivable absolute evil which could no longer be understood and explained by the evil motives of self-interest, greed, covetousness, resentment, lust for power, and cowardice; and which therefore anger could not revenge, love could not endure, friendship could not forgive. Just as the victims in the death factories or the holes of oblivion are no longer "human" in the eyes of their executioners, so this newest species of criminals is beyond the pale even of solidarity in human sinfulness.

It is inherent in our entire philosophical tradition that we cannot conceive of a "radical evil," and this is true both for Christian theology, which conceded even to the Devil himself a celestial origin, as well as for Kant, the only philosopher who, in the word he coined for it, at least must have suspected the existence of this evil even though he immediately rationalized it in the concept of a "perverted ill will" that could be explained by comprehensible motives. Therefore, we actually have nothing to fall back on in order to understand a phenomenon that nevertheless confronts us with its overpowering reality and breaks down all standards we know. There is only one thing that seems to be discernible: we may say that radical evil has emerged in connection with a system in which all men have become equally superfluous. The manipulators of this system believe in their own superfluousness as much as in that of all others, and the totalitarian murderers are all the more dangerous because they do not care if they themselves are alive or dead, if they ever lived or never were born. The danger of the corpse factories and holes of oblivion is that today, with populations and homelessness everywhere on the increase, masses of people are continuously rendered superfluous if we continue to think of our world in utilitarian terms. Political, social, and economic events everywhere are in a silent conspiracy with totalitarian instruments devised for making men superfluous. The implied temptation is well understood by the utilitarian common sense of the masses, who in most countries are too desperate to retain much fear of death. The Nazis and the Bolsheviks can be sure that their factories of annihilation which demonstrate the swiftest solution to the problem of over-population, of economically superfluous and socially rootless human masses, are as much of an attraction as a warning. Totalitarian solutions may well survive the fall of totalitarian regimes in the form of strong temptations which will come up whenever it seems impossible to alleviate political, social, or economic misery in a manner worthy of man.

Notes

1. In the *Tischgespräche,* Hitler mentions several times that he "[strives] for a condition in which each individual knows that he lives and dies for the preservation of his species" (p. 349). See also p. 347: "A fly lays millions of eggs, all of which perish. But the flies remain."

2. The best reports on Nazi concentration camps are David Rousset, *Les Jours de Notre Mort,* Paris, 1947; Eugen Kogon, *Der SS–Staat,* Munich, 1946; Bruno Bettelheim, "On Dachau and Buchenwald" (from May 1938, to April 1939), in *Nazi Conspiracy and Aggression,* Washington, 1946, VII, 824 ff. For Soviet concentration camps, see the excellent collection of reports by Polish survivors published under the title *The Dark Side of the Moon;* also David J. Dallin, *The New Leader,* January 8, 1949, though his reports are sometimes less convincing because they come from "prominent" personalities who are intent on drawing up manifestos and indictments.

3. *The Dark Side of the Moon;* the introduction also stresses this peculiar lack of communication: "They record but do not communicate."

4. See especially Bruno Bettelheim, *op. cit.* "It seemed as if I had become convinced that these horrible and degrading experiences somehow did not happen to 'me' as subject but to 'me' as an object. This experience was corroborated by the statements of other prisoners. . . . It was as if I watched things happening in which I only vaguely participated. . . . 'This cannot be true, such things just do not happen.' . . . The prisoners had to convince themselves that this was real, was really happening and not just a nightmare. They were never wholly successful."

   See also Rousset, *op. cit.,* p. 213. ". . . Those who haven't seen it with their own eyes can't believe it. Did you yourself, before you came here, take the rumors about the gas chambers seriously?"

   "No," I said.

   ". . . You see? Well, they're all like you. The lot of them in Paris, London, New York, even at Birkenau, right outside the crematoriums . . . still incredulous, five minutes before they were sent down into the cellar of the crematorium. . . ."

5. The first to understand this was Rousset in his *Univers Concentrationnaire,* 1947.

6. Rousset, *op. cit.,* p. 587.

7. See Georges Bataille in *Critique,* January 1948, p. 72.

8. Rousset's book contains many such "insights" into human "nature," based chiefly on the observation that after a while the mentality of the inmates is scarcely distinguishable from that of the camp guards.

9. In order to avoid misunderstandings it may be appropriate to add that with the invention of the hydrogen bomb the whole war question has undergone another decisive change. A discussion of this question is of course beyond the theme of this book.

10. This happened in Germany toward the end of 1942, whereupon Himmler served notice to all camp commandants "to reduce the death rate at all costs." For it had turned out that of the 136,000 new arrivals, 70,000 were already dead on reaching the camp or died immediately thereafter. See *Nazi Conspiracy,* IV, Annex II.—Later reports from Soviet Russian camps unanimously confirm that after 1949—that is, when Stalin was still alive—the death rate in the concentration camps, which previously had reached up to 60 per cent of

the inmates, was systematically lowered, presumably due to a general and acute labor shortage in the Soviet Union. This improvement in living conditions should not be confused with the crisis of the regime after Stalin's death which, characteristically enough, first made itself felt in the concentration camps. Cf. Wilhelm Starlinger, *Grenzen der Sowjetmacht,* Würzburg, 1955.

11. See Eugen Kogon, *Der SS-Staat,* Munich, 1946, p. 58: "A large part of the work exacted in the concentration camps was useless, either it was superfluous or it was so miserably planned that it had to be done over two or three times." Also Bettelheim, *op. cit.,* pp. 831–32: "New prisoners particularly were forced to perform nonsensical tasks. . . . They felt debased . . . and preferred even harder work when it produced something useful. . . ." Even Dallin, who has built his whole book on the thesis that the purpose of Russian camps is to provide cheap labor, is forced to admit the inefficiency of camp labor, *op. cit.,* p. 105.—The current theories about the Russian camp system as an economic measure for providing a cheap labor supply would stand clearly refuted if recent reports on mass amnesties and the abolition of concentration camps should prove to be true. For if the camps had served an important economic purpose, the regime certainly could not have afforded their rapid liquidation without grave consequences for the whole economic system.

12. Apart from the millions of people whom the Nazis transported to the extermination camps, they constantly attempted new colonization plans—transported Germans from Germany or the occupied territories to the East for colonization purposes. This was of course a serious handicap for military actions and economic exploitation. For the numerous discussions on these subjects and the constant conflict between the Nazi civilian hierarchy in the Eastern occupied territories and the SS hierarchy see especially Vol. XXIX of *Trial of the Major War Criminals,* Nuremberg, 1947.

13. Bettelheim, *op. cit.,* notes that the guards in the camps embraced an attitude toward the atmosphere of unreality similar to that of the prisoners themselves.

14. It is of some importance to realize that all pictures of concentration camps are misleading insofar as they show the camps in their last stages, at the moment the Allied troops marched in. There were no death camps in Germany proper, and at that point all extermination equipment had already been dismantled. On the other hand, what provoked the outrage of the Allies most and what gives the films their special horror—namely, the sight of the human skeletons—was not at all typical for the German concentration camps; extermination was handled systematically by gas, not by starvation. The condition of the camps was a result of the war events during the final months: Himmler had ordered the evacuation of all extermination camps in the East, the German camps were consequently vastly overcrowded, and he was no longer in a position to assure the food supply in Germany.

15. That life in a concentration camp was simply a dragged-out process of dying is stressed by Rousset, *op. cit., passim.*

16. Theodor Maunz, *Gestalt und Recht der Polizei* (Hamburg, 1943), p. 50, insists that criminals should never be sent to the camps for the time of their regular sentences.

17. The shortage of prison space in Russia has been such that in the year 1925–26, only 36 per cent of all court sentences could be carried out. See Dallin, *op. cit.,* pp. 158 ff.

18. "Gestapo and SS have always attached great importance to mixing the categories of inmates in the camps. In no camp have the inmates belonged exclusively to one category" (Kogon, *op. cit.,* p. 19).

    In Russia, it has also been customary from the beginning to mix political prisoners and criminals. During the first ten years of Soviet power, the Left political groups enjoyed certain privileges; only with the full development of the totalitarian character of the regime "after the end of the twenties, the politicals were even officially treated as inferior to the common criminals" (Dallin, *op. cit.,* p. 177 ff.).

19. Rousset's book suffers from his overestimation of the influence of the German Communists, who dominated the internal administration of Buchenwald during the war.

20. See for instance the testimony of Mrs. Buber-Neumann (former wife of the German Communist Heinz Neumann), who survived Soviet and German concentration camps: "The Russians never . . . evinced the sadistic streak of the Nazis. . . . Our Russian guards were decent men and not sadists, but they faithfully fulfilled the requirements of the inhuman system" (*Under Two Dictators*).

21. Bruno Bettelheim, "Behavior in Extreme Situations," in *Journal of Abnormal and Social Psychology,* Vol. XXXVIII, No. 4, 1943, describes the self-esteem of the criminals and the political prisoners as compared with those who have not done anything. The latter "were least able to withstand the initial shock," the first to disintegrate. Bettelheim blames this on their middle-class origin.

22. Rousset, *op. cit.,* p. 71.

23. For conditions in French concentration camps, see Arthur Koestler, *Scum of the Earth,* 1941.

24. Kogon, *op. cit.,* p. 6.

25. See *Nazi Conspiracy,* IV, pp. 800 ff.

26. Beck and Godin state explicitly that "opponents constituted only a relatively small proportion of the [Russian] prison population" (p. 87), and that there was no connection whatever between "a man's imprisonment and any offense" (p. 95). F. Beck and W. Godin, *Russian Purge and the Extraction of Confession,* London and New York, 1951.

27. Bruno Bettelheim, "On Dachau and Buchenwald," when discussing the fact that most prisoners "made their peace with the values of the Gestapo," emphasizes that "this was not the result of propaganda . . . the Gestapo insisted that it would prevent them from expressing their feelings anyway" (pp. 834–35).

    Himmler explicitly prohibited propaganda of any kind in the camps.

"Education consists of discipline, never of any kind of instruction on an ideological basis." "On Organization and Obligation of the SS and the Police,"
in *National-politischer Lehrgang der Wehrmacht,* 1937. Quoted from *Nazi Conspiracy,* IV, pp. 616 ff.

28. Rousset, *op. cit.,* p. 464.

29. See the report of Sergei Malakhov in Dallin, *op. cit.,* pp. 20 ff.

30. See Albert Camus in *Twice A Year,* 1947.

31. Rousset's book, *op. cit.,* consists largely of discussions of this dilemma by prisoners.

32. Bettelheim, *op. cit.,* describes the process by which the guards as well as the
prisoners became "conditioned" to the life in the camp and were afraid of re-
turning to the outer world.

Rousset, therefore, is right when he insists that the truth is that "victim
and executioner are alike ignoble; the lesson of the camps is the brotherhood
of abjection" (p. 588).

33. Bettelheim, *op. cit.,* describes how "the main concern of the new prisoners
seemed to be to remain intact as a personality" while the problem of the old
prisoners was "how to live as well as possible within the camp."

34. Rousset, *op. cit.,* p. 390, reports an SS-man haranguing a professor as follows:
"You used to be a professor. Well, you're no professor now. You're no big
shot any more. You're nothing but a little runt now. Just as little as you can
be. I'm the big fellow now."

35. Kogon, *op. cit.,* p. 6, speaks of the possibility that the camps will be maintained as training and experimental grounds for the SS. He also gives a good
report on the difference between the early camps administered by the SA and
the later ones under the SS. "None of these first camps had more than a
thousand inmates. . . . Life in them beggared all description. The accounts of
the few old prisoners who survived those years agree that there was scarcely
any form of sadistic perversion that was not practiced by the SA men. But
they were all acts of individual bestiality, there was still no fully organized
cold system, embracing masses of men. This was the accomplishment of the
SS" (p. 7).

This new mechanized system eased the feeling of responsibility as much
as was humanly possible. When, for instance, the order came to kill every day
several hundred Russian prisoners, the slaughter was performed by shooting
through a hole without seeing the victim. (See Ernest Feder, "Essai sur la
Psychologie de la Terreur," in *Synthèses,* Brussels, 1946.) On the other hand,
perversion was artificially produced in otherwise normal men. Rousset reports the following from a SS guard: "Usually I keep on hitting until I ejac-
ulate. I have a wife and three children in Breslau. I used to be perfectly
normal. That's what they've made of me. Now when they give me a pass out
of here, I don't go home. I don't dare look my wife in the face" (p. 273).—
The documents from the Hitler era contain numerous testimonials for the
average normality of those entrusted with carrying out Hitler's program of
extermination. A good collection is found in Léon Poliakov's "The Weapon

of Antisemitism," published by UNESCO in *The Third Reich,* London, 1955. Most of the men in the units used for these purposes were not volunteers but had been drafted from the ordinary police for these special assignments. But even trained SS-men found this kind of duty worse than front-line fighting. In his report of a mass execution by the SS, an eyewitness gives high praise to this troop which had been so "idealistic" that it was able to bear "the entire extermination without the help of liquor."

That one wanted to eliminate all personal motives and passions during the "exterminations" and hence keep the cruelties to a minimum is revealed by the fact that a group of doctors and engineers entrusted with handling the gas installations were making constant improvements that were not only designed to raise the productive capacity of the corpse factories but also to accelerate and ease the agony of death.

36. This is very prominent in Rousset's work. "The social conditions of life in the camps have transformed the great mass of inmates, both the Germans and the deportees, regardless of their previous social position and education . . . into a degenerate rabble, entirely submissive to the primitive reflexes of the animal instinct" (p. 183).

37. In this context also belongs the astonishing rarity of suicides in the camps. Suicide occurred far more often before arrest and deportation than in the camp itself, which is of course partly explained by the fact that every attempt was made to prevent suicides which are, after all, spontaneous acts. From the statistical material for Buchenwald (*Nazi Conspiracy,* IV, 800 ff.) it is evident that scarcely more than one-half per cent of the deaths could be traced to suicide, that frequently there were only two suicides per year, although in the same year the total number of deaths reached 3,516. The reports from Russian camps mention the same phenomenon. Cf., for instance, Starlinger, *op. cit.,* p. 57.

38. Rousset, *op. cit.,* p. 525.

Organized Guilt
and Universal Responsibility

I

THE GREATER the military defeats of the Wehrmacht in the field, the greater becomes that victory of Nazi political warfare which is so often incorrectly described as mere propaganda. It is the central thesis of this Nazi political strategy that there is no difference between Nazis and Germans, that the people stand united behind the government, that all Allied hopes of finding part of the people uninfected ideologically and all appeals to a democratic Germany of the future are pure illusion. The implication of this thesis is, of course, that there is no distinction as to responsibility, that German anti-Fascists will suffer from defeat equally with German Fascists, and that the Allies had made such distinctions at the beginning of the war only for propaganda purposes. A further implication is that Allied provisions for punishment of war criminals will turn out to be empty threats because they will find no one to whom the title of war criminal could not be applied.

That such claims are not mere propaganda but are supported by very real and fearful facts, we have all learned in the past seven years. The terror organizations which were at first strictly separated from the mass of the people, admitting only persons who could show a criminal past or prove their preparedness to become criminals, have since been continually expanded. The ban on party membership for members of the army has been dissolved by the general order which subordinates all soldiers to the party. Whereas those crimes which have always been a part of the daily routine of concentration camps since the beginning of the Nazi regime were at first a jealously guarded monopoly of the SS and Gestapo, today members of the Wehrmacht are assigned at will to duties of mass murder. These

From Essays in Understanding. *Originally published in* Jewish Frontier, *no. 12, January 1945, as "German Guilt." Notes 1, 3, and 4 by Jerome Kohn.*

crimes were at first kept secret by every possible means and any publication of such reports was made punishable as atrocity propaganda. Later, however, such reports were spread by Nazi-organized whispering campaigns and today these crimes are openly proclaimed under the title of "measures of liquidation" in order to force "Volksgenossen"—whom difficulties of organization made it impossible to induct into the "Volksgemeinschaft" of crime—at least to bear the onus of complicity and awareness of what was going on. These tactics, as the Allies abandoned the distinction between Germans and Nazis, resulted in a victory for the Nazis. In order to appreciate the decisive change of political conditions in Germany since the lost battle of Britain, one must note that until the war, even until the first military defeats, only relatively small groups of active Nazis, among whom not even the Nazi sympathizers were included, and equally small numbers of active anti-Fascists really knew what was going on. All others, whether German or non-German, had the natural inclination to believe the statements of an official, universally recognized government rather than the charges of refugees, which, coming from Jews or Socialists, were suspect in any case. Even of those refugees, only a relatively small proportion knew the full truth and even a smaller fraction was prepared to bear the odium of unpopularity involved in telling the truth.

As long as the Nazis expected victory, their terror organizations were strictly isolated from the people and, in time of war, from the army. The army was not used to commit atrocities and SS troops were increasingly recruited from "qualified" circles of whatever nationality. If the planned New Order of Europe had succeeded, we would have been witnesses of an inter-European organization of terror under German leadership. The terror would have been exercised by members of all European nationalities, with the exception of Jews, in an organization graded according to the racial classification of the various countries. The German people, of course, would not have been spared by it. Himmler was always of the opinion that authority in Europe should be in the hands of a racial élite, organized in SS troops without national ties.

It was only their defeats which forced the Nazis to abandon this concept and pretend to return to old nationalist slogans. The active identification of the whole German people with the Nazis was part of this turning. National Socialism's chances of organizing an underground movement in the future depend on no one's being able to know any longer who is a Nazi and who is not, on there being no visible signs of distinction any longer, and above all on the victorious powers' being convinced that there really are no differences between Germans. To bring this about, an intensified terror in Germany, which proposed to leave no person alive whose past or reputation proclaimed him an anti-Fascist, was necessary. In the first years of the war the regime was remarkably "magnanimous" to its opponents, provided they remained peaceful. Of late, however, countless persons have been executed even though, for the reason that for years there has been no freedom of movement, they could not constitute any immediate danger to the regime. On the other hand, prudently foreseeing that in spite of all precautionary measures the Allies might still find a few hundred persons in each city with an irreproachable anti-Fascist record—testified to by former war prisoners or foreign laborers, and supported by records of imprisonment or concentration-camp internment—the Nazis have already provided their own trusted cohorts with similar documentation and testimony, making these criteria worthless. Thus in the case of inmates of concentration camps (whose number nobody knows precisely, but which is estimated at several million), the Nazis can safely either liquidate them or let them escape: in the improbable event of their survival (a massacre of the type which occurred in Buchenwald is not even punishable under the war-crimes provisions), it will not be possible to identify them unmistakably.

Whether any person in Germany is a Nazi or an anti-Nazi can be determined only by the One who knows the secrets of the human heart, which no human eye can penetrate. At any rate, those who actively organize an anti-Nazi underground movement in Germany today would meet a speedy death if they failed to act and talk precisely like Nazis. In a country where a person attracts immediate attention by failing either to murder upon command or to be a ready accomplice of murderers, this is no light task. The most extreme slogan which this war has evoked among the Allies, that the only "good German" is a "dead German," has this much basis in fact: the only way in which we can identify an anti-Nazi is when the Nazis have hanged him. There is no other reliable token.

I I

These are the real political conditions which underlie the charge of the collective guilt of the German people. They are the consequences of a policy which, in the deepest sense, is a- and anti-national; which is utterly determined that there shall be a German people only if it is in the power of its present rulers; and which will rejoice as at its greatest victory if the defeat of the Nazis involves with it the physical destruction of the German people. The totalitarian policy, which has completely destroyed the neutral zone in which the daily life of human beings is ordinarily lived, has achieved the result of making the existence of each individual in Germany depend either upon committing crimes or on complicity in crimes. The success of Nazi propaganda in Allied countries, as expressed in the attitude commonly called Vansittartism, is a secondary matter in comparison. It is a product of general war propaganda, and something quite apart from the specific modern political phenomenon described above. All the documents and pseudo-historical demonstrations of this tendency sound like relatively innocent plagiarism of the French literature of the last war—and it makes no essential difference that a few of those writers who twenty-five years ago kept the presses rolling with their attacks on "perfidious Albion" have now placed their experience at the Allies' disposal.

Yet even the best-intended discussions between the defenders of the "good" Germans and the accusers of the "bad" not only miss the essence of the question, but also plainly fail to apprehend the magnitude of the catastrophe. Either they are betrayed into trivial general comments on good and bad people, and into a fantastic over-estimation of the power of education, or they simply adopt an inverted version of Nazi racial theory. There is a certain danger in all this only because, since Churchill's famous declaration,[1] the Allies have refrained from fighting an ideological war and have thus unconsciously given an advantage to the Nazis (who, without regard to Churchill, are organizing their defeat ideologically) and a chance of survival to all racial theories.

The true problem however is not to prove what is self-evident, namely, that Germans have not been potential Nazis ever since Tacitus' times, nor what is impossible, that all Germans harbor Nazi views. It is, rather, to consider how to conduct ourselves and how to bear the trial of confronting a people among whom the boundaries dividing criminals from normal persons, the guilty from the innocent, have been so completely effaced that nobody will be able to tell in Germany whether in any case he is dealing with a secret hero or with a former mass murderer. In this situation we will not be aided either by a definition of those responsible, or by the punishment of "war criminals." Such definitions by their very nature can apply only to those who not only took responsibility upon themselves, but also produced this whole inferno—and yet strangely enough are still not to be found on the lists of war criminals. The number of those who are responsible *and* guilty will be relatively small. There are many who share responsibility without any visible proof of guilt. There are many more who have become guilty without being in the least responsible. Among the responsible in a broader sense must be included all those who continued to be sympathetic to Hitler as long as it was possible, who aided his rise to power, and who applauded him in Germany and in other European countries. Who would dare to brand all these ladies and gentlemen of high society as war criminals? And as a matter of fact they really do not deserve such a title. Unquestionably they have proved their inability to judge modern political organizations, some of them because they regarded all principles in politics as moralistic nonsense, others because they were affected by a romantic predilection for gangsters whom they confused with "pirates" of an older time. Yet these people, who were co-responsible for Hitler's crimes in a broader sense, did not incur any guilt in a stricter sense. They, who were the Nazis' first accomplices and their best aides, truly did not know what they were doing nor with whom they were dealing.

The extreme horror with which persons of good will react whenever the case of Germany is discussed is not evoked by those irresponsible co-responsibles, nor even by the particular crimes of the Nazis themselves. It is, rather, the product of that vast machine of administrative mass murder, in whose service not only thousands of persons, not even scores of thousands of selected murderers, but a whole people could be and was employed: In that organization which Himmler has prepared against the defeat, everyone is either an executioner, a victim, or an automaton, marching onward over the corpses of his comrades—chosen at first out of the various Storm Troop formations and later from any army unit or other mass organization. That everyone, whether or not he is directly active in a murder camp, is forced to take part in one way or another in the workings of this machine of mass murder—that is the horrible thing. For systematic mass murder—the true consequence of all race theories and other modern ideologies which preach that might is right—strains not only the imagination of human beings, but also the framework and categories of our political thought and action. Whatever the future of Germany, it will not be determined by anything more than the inevitable consequences of a lost war—consequences which in the nature of the case are temporary. There is no political method for dealing with German mass crimes, and the destruction of seventy or eighty million Germans, or even their gradual death through starvation (of which, of course, nobody except a few psychotic fanatics dream), would simply mean that the ideology of the Nazis had won, even if power and the rights of might had fallen to other peoples.

Just as there is no political solution within human capacity for the crime of administrative mass murder, so the human need for justice can find no satisfactory reply to the total mobilization of a people for that purpose. Where all are guilty, nobody in the last analysis can be judged.[2] For that guilt is not accompanied by even the mere appearance, the mere pretense of responsibility. So long as punishment is the right of the criminal—and this paradigm has for more than two thousand years been the basis of the sense of justice and right of Occidental man—guilt implies the consciousness of guilt, and punishment evidence that the criminal is a responsible person. How it is in this matter has been well described by an American correspondent,[3] in a story whose dialogue is worthy of the imagination and creative power of a great poet.

> Q. Did you kill people in the camp? A. Yes.
> Q. Did you poison them with gas? A. Yes.
> Q. Did you bury them alive? A. It sometimes happened.
> Q. Were the victims picked from all over Europe? A. I suppose so.
> Q. Did you personally help kill people? A. Absolutely not. I was only paymaster in the camp.
> Q. What did you think of what was going on? A. It was bad at first but we got used to it.
> Q. Do you know the Russians will hang you? A. (Bursting into tears) Why should they? *What have I done?* [Italics mine. *PM,* Sunday, Nov. 12, 1944.]

Really he had done nothing. He had only carried out orders and since when has it been a crime to carry out orders? Since when has it been a virtue to rebel? Since when could one only be decent by welcoming death? What then had he done?

In his play *The Last Days of Mankind,* about the last war, Karl Kraus rang down the curtain after Wilhelm II had cried, "I did not want this." And the horribly comic part of it was that this was the fact. When the curtain falls this time, we will have to listen to a whole chorus calling out, "We did not do this." And even though we shall no longer be able to appreciate the comic element, the horrible part of it will still be that this is the fact.

I I I

In trying to understand what were the real motives which caused people to act as cogs in the mass-murder machine, we shall not be aided by speculations about German history and the so-called German national character, of whose potentialities those who knew Germany most intimately had not the slightest idea fifteen years ago. There is more to be learned from the characteristic personality of the man who can boast that he was the organizing spirit of the murder. Heinrich Himmler is not one of those intellectuals stemming from the dim No Man's Land between the Bohemian and the Pimp, whose significance in the composition of the Nazi élite has been repeatedly stressed of late. He is neither a Bohemian like Goebbels, nor a sex criminal like Streicher, nor a perverted fanatic like Hitler, nor an adventurer like Goering. He is a "bourgeois" with all the outer aspect of respectability, all the habits of a good *paterfamilias* who does not betray his wife and anxiously seeks to secure 'a decent future for his children; and he has consciously built up his newest terror organization, covering the whole country, on the assumption that most people are not Bohemians nor fanatics, nor adventurers, nor sex maniacs, nor sadists, but first and foremost jobholders, and good family men.

It was Péguy, I believe, who called the family man the "grand aventurier du 20e siècle." He died too soon to learn that he was also the great criminal of the century. We had been so accustomed to admire or gently ridicule the family man's kind concern and earnest concentration on the welfare of his family, his solemn determination to make life easy for his wife and children, that we hardly noticed how the devoted *paterfamilias,* worried about nothing so much as his security, was transformed under the pressure of the chaotic economic conditions of our time into an involuntary adventurer, who for all his industry and care could never be certain what the next day would bring. The docility of this type was already manifest in the very early period of Nazi "Gleichschaltung." It became clear that for the sake of his pension, his life insurance, the security of his wife and children, such a man was ready to sacrifice his beliefs, his honor, and his human dignity. It needed only the Satanic genius of Himmler to discover that after such degradation he was entirely prepared to do literally anything when the ante was raised and the bare existence of his family was threatened. The only condition he put was that he should be fully exempted from responsibility for his acts. Thus that very person, the average German, whom the Nazis notwithstanding years of the most furious propaganda could not induce to kill a Jew on his own account (not even when they made it quite clear that such a murder would go unpunished) now serves the machine of destruction without opposition. In contrast to the earlier units of the SS men and Gestapo, Himmler's over-all organization relies not on fanatics, nor on congenital murderers, nor on sadists; it relies entirely upon the normality of jobholders and family men.

We need not specially mention the sorry reports about Latvians, Lithuanians, or even Jews who have participated in Himmler's murder organization in order to show that it requires no particular national character in order to supply this new type of functionary. They are not even all natural murderers or traitors out of perversity. It is not even certain that they would do the work if it were only their own lives and future that were at stake. They felt (after they no longer needed to fear God, their conscience cleared through the bureaucratic organization of their acts) only the responsibility toward their own families. The transformation of the family man from a responsible member of society, interested in all public affairs, to a "bourgeois" concerned only with his private existence and knowing no civic virtue, is an international modern phenomenon. The exigencies of our time—"Bedenkt den Hunger und die grosse Kälte in diesem Tale, das von Jammer schallt" (Brecht)[4]—can at any moment transform him into the mob man and make him the instrument of whatsoever madness and horror. Each time society, through unemployment, frustrates the small man in his normal functioning and normal self-respect, it trains him for that last stage in which he will willingly undertake any function, even that of hangman. A Jew released from Buchenwald once discovered among the SS men who gave him the certificates of release a former schoolmate, whom he did not address but yet stared at. Spontaneously the man stared at remarked: You must understand, I have five years of unemployment behind me. They can do anything they want with me.

It is true that the development of this modern type of man, who is the exact opposite of the "citoyen" and whom for lack of a better name we have called the "bourgeois," enjoyed particularly favorable conditions in Germany. Hardly another country of Occidental culture was so little imbued with the classic virtues of civic behavior. In no other country did private life and private calculations play so great a role. This is a fact which the Germans in time of national emergency disguised with great success, but never altered. Behind the façade of proclaimed and propagandized national virtues, such as "love of the Fatherland," "German courage," "German loyalty," etc., there lurked corresponding real national vices. There is hardly another country where on the average there is so little patriotism as Germany; and behind the chauvinistic claims of loyalty and courage, a fatal tendency to disloyalty and betrayal for opportunistic reasons is hidden.

The mob man, however, the end-result of the "bourgeois," is an international phenomenon; and we would do well not to submit him to too many temptations in the blind faith that only the German mob man is capable of such frightful deeds. What we have called the "bourgeois" is the modern man of the masses, not in his exalted moments of collective excitement, but in the security (today one should say the insecurity) of his own private domain. He has driven the dichotomy of private and public functions, of family and occupation, so far that he can no longer find in his own person any connection between the two. When his occupation forces him to murder people he does not regard himself as a murderer because he has not done it out of inclination but in his professional capacity. Out of sheer passion he would never do harm to a fly.

If we tell a member of this new occupational class which our time has produced that he is being held to account for what he did, he will feel nothing except that he has been betrayed. But if in the shock of the catastrophe he really becomes conscious that in fact he was not only a functionary but also a murderer, then his way out will not be that of rebellion, but suicide—just as so many have already chosen the way of suicide in Germany, where it is plain that there has been one wave of self-destruction after another. And that too would be of little use to us.

I V

For many years now we have met Germans who declare that they are ashamed of being Germans. I have often felt tempted to answer that I am ashamed of being human. This elemental shame, which many people of the most various nationalities share with one another today, is what finally is left of our sense of international solidarity; and it has not yet found an adequate political expression. Our fathers' enchantment with humanity was of a sort which not only light-mindedly ignored the national question; what is far worse, it did not even conceive of the terror of the idea of humanity and of the Judeo-Christian faith in the unitary origin of the human race. It was not very pleasant even when we had to bury our false illusions about "the noble savage," having discovered that men were capable of being cannibals. Since then peoples have learned to know one another better and learned more and more about the evil potentialities in men. The result has been that they have recoiled more and more from the idea of humanity and become more susceptible to the doctrine of race, which denies the very possibility of a common humanity. They instinctively felt that the idea of humanity, whether it appears in a religious or humanistic form, implies the obligation of a general responsibility which they do not wish to assume. For the idea of humanity, when purged of all sentimentality, has the very serious consequence that in one form or another men must assume responsibility for all crimes committed by men and that all nations share the onus of evil committed by all others. Shame at being a human being is the purely individual and still non-political expression of this insight.

In political terms, the idea of humanity, excluding no people and assigning a monopoly of guilt to no one, is the only guarantee that one "superior race" after another may not feel obligated to follow the "natural law" of the right of the powerful, and exterminate "inferior races unworthy of survival"; so that at the end of an "imperialistic age" we should find ourselves in a stage which would make the Nazis look like crude precursors of future political methods. To follow a non-imperialistic policy and maintain a non-racist faith becomes daily more difficult because it becomes daily clearer how great a burden mankind is for man.

Perhaps those Jews, to whose forefathers we owe the first conception of the idea of humanity, knew something about that burden when each year they used to say "Our Father and King, we have sinned before you," taking not only the sins of their own community but all human offenses upon themselves. Those who today are ready to follow this road in a modern version do not content themselves with the hypocritical confession "God be thanked, I am not like that," in horror at the undreamed-of potentialities of the German national character. Rather, in fear and trembling, have they finally realized of what man is capable—and this is indeed the precondition of any modern political thinking. Such persons will not serve very well as functionaries of vengeance. This, however, is certain: Upon them and only upon them, who are filled with a genuine fear of the inescapable guilt of the human race, can there be any reliance when it comes to fighting fearlessly, uncompromisingly, everywhere against the incalculable evil that men are capable of bringing about.

Notes

1. Speaking to the House of Commons on May 24, 1944, Churchill said: "As this war has progressed, it has become less ideological in its character in my opinion." On August 2 of that year he noted the "confusion" this statement had caused, and went on to defend it. He was becoming increasingly convinced not only that the defeat of Germany must be total and her surrender "unconditional," but also that after the war the German state should be restructured in such a way as to prevent its re-emergence as a continental power for at least fifty years. *The War Speeches of Winston S. Churchill,* compiled by Charles Eade, vol. III, Boston: Houghton Mifflin, 1953, 149–50, 196.

2. That German refugees, who had the good fortune either to be Jews or to have been persecuted by the Gestapo early enough, have been saved from this guilt is of course not their merit. Because they know this and because their horror at what might have been still haunts them, they often introduce into discus-

sions of this kind that insufferable tone of self-righteousness which frequently, and particularly among Jews, can turn into the vulgar obverse of Nazi doctrines—and in fact already has. —Hannah Arendt.

3. Raymond A. Davies, a correspondent for the Jewish Telegraph Agency and broadcaster for the Canadian Broadcasting Corporation, gave the first eyewitness account of the death camp at Maidanek.

4. "Think of the hunger and the great cold in this valley that rings with lamentations." Arendt apparently quoted from memory the final verses of the *Dreigroschenoper*, substituting "hunger" for "darkness": *"Bedenkt das Dunkel und die grosse Kälte/In diesem Tale, das von Jammer schallt."*

A Reply to Eric Voegelin

Arendt is responding to Eric Voegelin's review of The Origins of
Totalitarianism *that appeared in the same issue of* Review of Politics, *pp. 68–76. Arendt's rejoinder is notable for its attempt to clarify
the methodological procedures and assumptions that underpinned* The
Origins of Totalitarianism.

MUCH AS I appreciate the unusual kindness of the editors of *The Review of
Politics* who asked me to answer Professor Eric Voegelin's criticism of my
book, I am not quite sure that I decided wisely when I accepted their offer. I certainly would not, and should not, have accepted if his review
were of the usual friendly or unfriendly kind. Such replies, by their very
nature, all too easily tempt the author either to review his own book or to
write a review of the review. In order to avoid such temptations, I have
refrained as much as I could, even on the level of personal conversation,
to take issue with any reviewer of my book, no matter how much I
agreed or disagreed with him.

Professor Voegelin's criticism, however, is of a kind that can be
answered in all propriety. He raises certain very general questions of
method, on one side, and of general philosophical implications on the
other. Both of course belong together; but while I feel that within the
necessary limitations of a historical study and political analysis I made myself sufficiently clear on certain general perplexities which have come to
light through the full development of totalitarianism, I also know that I
failed to explain the particular method which I came to use, and to account for a rather unusual approach—not to the different historical and

---

From Essays in Understanding. *Originally published in* Review of Politics *15 (January
1953), as "Rejoinder to Eric Voegelin's Review of* The Origins of Totalitarianism."

political issues where account or justification would only distract—to the whole field of political and historical sciences as such. One of the difficulties of the book is that it does not belong to any school and hardly uses any of the officially recognized or officially controversial instruments.

The problem originally confronting me was simple and baffling at the same time: all historiography is necessarily salvation and frequently justification; it is due to man's fear that he may forget and to his striving for something which is even more than remembrance. These impulses are already implicit in the mere observation of chronological order and they are not likely to be overcome through the interference of value-judgments which usually interrupt the narrative and make the account appear biased and "unscientific." I think the history of anti-Semitism is a good example of this kind of history-writing. The reason why this whole literature is so extraordinarily poor in terms of scholarship is that the historians—if they were not conscious anti-Semites, which of course they never were—had to write the history of a subject which they did not want to conserve; they had to write in a destructive way and to write history for purposes of destruction is somehow a contradiction in terms. The way out has been to hold on, so to speak, to the Jews, to make them the subject of conservation. But this was no solution, for to look at the events only from the side of the victim resulted in apologetics—which of course is no history at all.

Thus my first problem was how to write historically about something—totalitarianism—which I did not want to conserve but, on the contrary, felt engaged to destroy. My way of solving this problem has given rise to the reproach that the book was lacking in unity. What I did—and what I might have done anyway because of my previous training and the way of my thinking—was to discover the chief elements of totalitarianism and to analyze them in historical terms, tracing these elements back in history as far as I deemed proper and necessary. That is, I did not write a history of totalitarianism but an analysis in terms of history; I did not write a history of anti-Semitism or of imperialism, but analyzed the element of Jew-hatred and the element of expansion insofar as these elements were still clearly visible and played a decisive role in the totalitarian phenomenon itself. The book, therefore, does not really deal with the "origins" of totalitarianism—as its title unfortunately claims—but gives a historical account of the elements which crystallized into totalitarianism; this account is followed by an analysis of the elemental structure of totalitarian movements and domination itself. The elementary structure of totalitarianism is the hidden structure of the book, while its more apparent unity is provided by certain fundamental concepts which run like red threads through the whole.

The same problem of method can be approached from another side and then presents itself as a problem of "style." This has been praised as passionate and criticized as sentimental. Both judgments seem to me a little beside the point. I parted quite consciously with the tradition of *sine ira et studio* of whose greatness I was fully aware, and to me this was a methodological necessity closely connected with my particular subject matter.

Let us suppose—to take one among many possible examples—that the historian is confronted with excessive poverty in a society of great wealth, such as the poverty of the British working classes during the early stages of the Industrial Revolution. The natural human reaction to such conditions is one of anger and indignation because these conditions are against the dignity of man. If I describe these conditions without permitting my indignation to interfere, I have lifted this particular phenomenon out of its context in human society and have thereby robbed it of part of its nature, deprived it of one of its important inherent qualities. For to arouse indignation is one of the qualities of excessive poverty insofar as poverty occurs among human beings. I therefore cannot agree with Professor Voegelin that the "morally abhorrent and the emotionally existing will overshadow the essential," because I believe them to form an integral part of it. This has nothing to do with sentimentality or moralizing, although, of course, either can become a pitfall for the author. If I moralized or became sentimental, I simply did not do well what I was supposed to do, namely, to describe the totalitarian phenomenon as occurring, not on the moon, but in the midst of human society. To describe the concentration camps *sine ira* is not to be "objective," but to condone them; and such condoning cannot be changed by a condemnation which the author may feel duty bound to add but which remains unrelated to the description itself. When I used the image of Hell, I did not mean this allegorically but literally: it seems rather obvious that men who have lost their faith in Paradise will not be able to establish it on earth; but it is not so certain that those who have lost their belief in Hell as a place of the hereafter may not be willing and able to establish on earth exact imitations of what people used to believe about Hell. In this sense I think that a description of the camps as Hell on earth is more "objective," that is, more adequate to their essence than statements of a purely sociological or psychological nature.

The problem of style is a problem of adequacy and of response. If I write in the same "objective" manner about the Elizabethan age and the twentieth century, it may well be that my dealing with both periods is inadequate because I have renounced the human faculty to respond to either. Thus the question of style is bound up with the problem of under-standing, which has plagued the historical sciences almost from their be-ginnings. I do not wish to go into this matter here, but I may add that I am convinced that understanding is closely related to that faculty of imag-ination which Kant called *Einbildungskraft* and which has nothing in com-mon with fictional ability. The *Spiritual Exercises* are exercises of imagination and they may be more relevant to method in the historical sciences than academic training realizes.

Reflections of this kind, originally caused by the special nature of my subject, and the personal experience which is necessarily involved in a his-torical investigation that employs imagination consciously as an important tool of cognition resulted in a critical approach toward almost all interpre-tation of contemporary history. I hinted at this in two short paragraphs of the Preface, where I warned the reader against the concepts of Progress and of Doom as "two sides of the same medal" as well as against any at-tempt at "deducing the unprecedented from precedents." These two ap-proaches are closely interconnected. The reason why Professor Voegelin can speak of "the putrefaction of Western civilization" and the "earthwide expansion of Western foulness" is that he treats "phenomenal differ-ences"—which to me as differences of factuality are all-important—as minor outgrowths of some "essential sameness" of a doctrinal nature. Numerous affinities between totalitarianism and some other trends in Oc-cidental political or intellectual history have been described with this re-sult, in my opinion: they all failed to point out the distinct quality of what was actually happening. The "phenomenal differences," far from "obscur-ing" some essential sameness, are those phenomena which make totalitar-ianism "totalitarian," which distinguish this one form of government and movement from all others and therefore can alone help us in finding its essence. What is unprecedented in totalitarianism is not primarily its ideo-logical content, but the *event* of totalitarian domination itself. This can be seen clearly if we have to admit that the deeds of its considered policies have exploded our traditional categories of political thought (totalitarian domination is unlike all forms of tyranny and despotism we know of) and the standards of our moral judgment (totalitarian crimes are very inade-quately described as "murder" and totalitarian criminals can hardly be punished as "murderers").

Professor Voegelin seems to think that totalitarianism is only the other side of liberalism, positivism, and pragmatism. But whether one agrees with liberalism or not (and I may say here that I am rather certain that I am neither a liberal nor a positivist nor a pragmatist), the point is that liberals are clearly not totalitarians. This, of course, does not exclude the fact that liberal or positivistic elements also lend themselves to totalitarian thinking; but such affinities would only mean that one has to draw even sharper distinctions because of the *fact* that liberals are not totalitarians.

I hope that I do not belabor this point unduly. It is important to me because I think that what separates my approach from Professor Voegelin's is that I proceed from facts and events instead of intellectual affinities and influences. This is perhaps a bit difficult to perceive because I am of course much concerned with philosophical implications and changes in spiritual self-interpretation. But this certainly does not mean that I described "a gradual revelation of the essence of totalitarianism from its inchoate forms in the eighteenth century to the fully developed," because this essence, in my opinion, did not exist before it had come into being. I therefore talk only of "elements," which eventually crystallize into totalitarianism, some of which are traceable to the eighteenth century, some perhaps even farther back (although I would doubt Voegelin's own theory that the "rise of immanentist sectarianism" since the late Middle Ages eventually ended in totalitarianism). Under no circumstances would I call any of them totalitarian.

For similar reasons and for the sake of distinguishing between ideas and actual events in history, I cannot agree with Professor Voegelin's remark that "the spiritual disease is the decisive feature that distinguishes modern masses from those of earlier centuries." To me, modern masses are distinguished by the fact that they are "masses" in a strict sense of the word. They are distinguished from the multitudes of former centuries in that they do not have common interests to bind them together or any kind of common "consent" which, according to Cicero, constitutes *interest,* that which is between men, ranging all the way from material to spiritual and other matters. This "between" can be a common ground and it can be a common purpose; it always fulfills the double function of binding men together *and* separating them in an articulate way. The lack of common interest so characteristic of modern masses is therefore only another sign of their homelessness and rootlessness. But it alone accounts for the curious fact that these modern masses are formed by the atomization of society, that the mass-men who lack all communal relationships nevertheless offer the best possible "material" for movements in which peoples are so closely pressed together that they seem to have become one. The loss of interests is identical with the loss of "self," and modern masses are distinguished in my view by their selflessness, that is, their lack of "selfish interests."

I know that problems of this sort can be avoided if one interprets to-

talitarian movements as a new—and perverted—religion, a substitute for
the lost creed of traditional beliefs. From this, it would follow that some
"need for religion" is a cause of the rise of totalitarianism. I feel unable to
follow even the very qualified form in which Professor Voegelin uses the
concept of a secular religion. There is no substitute for God in the totalitarian ideologies—Hitler's use of the "Almighty" was a concession to
what he himself believed to be a superstition. More than that, the metaphysical place for God has remained empty. The introduction of these
semi-theological arguments in the discussion of totalitarianism, on the
other hand, is only too likely to further the wide-spread and strictly blasphemous modern "ideas" about a God who is "good for you"—for your
mental or other health, for the integration of your personality, and God
knows what—that is, "ideas" which make of God a function of man or
society. This functionalization seems to me in many respects the last and
perhaps the most dangerous stage of atheism.

By this, I do not mean to say that Professor Voegelin could ever become guilty of such functionalization. Nor do I deny that there is some
connection between atheism and totalitarianism. But this connection
seems to me purely negative and not at all peculiar to the rise of totalitarianism. It is true that a Christian cannot become a follower of either
Hitler or Stalin; and it is true that morality as such is in jeopardy whenever the faith in God who gave the Ten Commandments is no longer secure. But this is at most a condition *sine qua non,* nothing which could
positively explain whatever happened afterward. Those who conclude
from the frightening events of our times that we have got to go back to
religion and faith for political reasons seem to me to show just as much
lack of faith in God as their opponents.

Professor Voegelin deplores, as I do, the "insufficiency of theoretical
instruments" in the political sciences (and with what to me appeared as inconsistency accuses me a few pages later of not having availed myself
more readily of them). Apart from the present trends of psychologism and
sociologism, about which I think Professor Voegelin and I are in agreement, my chief quarrel with the present state of the historical and political
sciences is their growing incapacity for making distinctions. Terms like
nationalism, imperialism, totalitarianism, etc., are used indiscriminately for
all kinds of political phenomena (usually just as "high-brow" words for
aggression), and none of them is any longer understood with its particular
historical background. The result is a generalization in which the words
themselves lose all meaning. Imperialism does not mean a thing if it is
used indiscriminately for Assyrian and Roman and British and Bolshevik

history; nationalism is discussed in times and countries which never experienced the nation-state; totalitarianism is discovered in all kinds of tyrannies or forms of collective communities, etc. This kind of confusion —where everything distinct disappears and everything that is new and shocking is (not explained but) explained away either through drawing some analogies or reducing it to a previously known chain of causes and influences—seems to me to be the hallmark of the modern historical and political sciences.

In conclusion, I may be permitted to clarify my statement that in our modern predicament "human nature as such is at stake," a statement which provoked Professor Voegelin's sharpest criticism because he sees in the very idea of "changing the nature of man or of anything" and in the very fact that I took this claim of totalitarianism at all seriously a "symptom of the intellectual breakdown of Western civilization." The problem of the relationship between essence and existence in Occidental thought seems to me to be a bit more complicated and controversial than Voegelin's statement on "nature" (identifying "a thing as a thing" and therefore incapable of change by definition) implies, but this I can hardly discuss here. It may be enough to say that, terminological differences apart, I hardly proposed more change of nature than Professor Voegelin himself in his book on *The New Science of Politics;* discussing the Platonic-Aristotelian theory of soul, he states: "one might almost say that before the discovery of psyche man had no soul" (p. 67). In Voegelin's terms, I could have said that after the discoveries of totalitarian domination and its experiments we have reason to fear that man may lose his soul.

In other words, the success of totalitarianism is identical with a much more radical liquidation of freedom as a political and as a human reality than anything we have ever witnessed before. Under these conditions, it will be hardly consoling to cling to an unchangeable nature of man and conclude that either man himself is being destroyed or that freedom does not belong to man's essential capabilities. Historically we know of man's nature only insofar as it has existence, and no realm of eternal essences will ever console us if man loses his essential capabilities.

My fear, when I wrote the concluding chapter of my book, was not unlike the fear which Montesquieu already expressed when he saw that Western civilization was no longer guaranteed by laws, although its peoples were still ruled by customs which he did not deem sufficient to resist an onslaught of despotism. He says in the Preface to *L'Esprit des Lois,* "L'homme, cet être flexible, se pliant dans la société aux pensées et aux impressions des autres, est également capable de connaître sa propre nature lorsqu'on la lui montre, et d'en perdre jusqu'au sentiment lorsqu'on la lui dérobe." (Man, this flexible being, who submits himself in society to the thoughts and impressions of his fellow-men, is equally capable of knowing his own nature when it is shown to him and of losing it to the point where he has no realization that he is robbed of it.)

PART IV

THE VITA ACTIVA

Labor, Work, Action

FOR THIS SHORT HOUR, I should like to raise an apparently odd question. My question is: What does an active life consist of? What do we do when we are active? In asking this question, I shall assume that the age-old distinction between two ways of life, between a *vita contemplativa* and a *vita activa*, which we encounter in our tradition of philosophical and religious thought up to the threshold of the modern age, is valid, and that when we speak of contemplation and action we speak not only of certain human faculties but of two distinct ways of life. Surely, the question is of some relevance. For even if we don't contest the traditional assumption that contemplation is of a higher order than action, or that all action actually is but a means whose true end is contemplation, we can't doubt—and no one ever doubted—that it is quite possible for human beings to go through life without ever indulging in contemplation, while, on the other hand, no man can remain in the contemplative state throughout his life. Active life, in other words, is not only what most men are engaged in but even what no man can escape altogether. For it is in the nature of the human condition that contemplation remains dependent upon all sorts of activities—it depends upon labor to produce whatever is necessary to keep the human organism alive, it depends upon work to create whatever is needed to house the human body, and it needs action in order to organize the living together of many human beings in such a way that peace, the condition for the quiet of contemplation is assured.

Since I started with our tradition, I just described the three chief articulations of active life in a traditional way, that is, as serving the ends of contemplation. It is only natural that active life has always been described

From Amor Mundi: Explorations in the Faith and Thought of Hannah Arendt. *Edited by J.W. Bernauer. S.J. "Labor, Work, Action" was originally a lecture that Hannah Arendt delivered, on November 10, 1964, to a conference devoted to "Christianity and Economic Man: Moral Decisions in an Affluent Society." The conference was held at the Divinity School of the University of Chicago.*

by those who themselves followed the contemplative way of life. Hence, the *vita activa* was always defined from the viewpoint of contemplation; compared with the absolute quiet of contemplation, all sorts of human activity appeared to be similar insofar as they were characterized by unquiet, by something negative: by *a-skholia* or by *nec-octium,* non-leisure or absence of the conditions which make contemplation possible. Compared with this attitude of quiet, all distinctions and articulations within the *vita activa* disappear. Seen from the viewpoint of contemplation, it does not matter what disturbs the necessary quiet so long as it is disturbed.

Traditionally therefore the *vita activa* received its meaning from the *vita contemplativa;* a very restricted dignity was bestowed upon it because it served the needs and wants of contemplation in a living body. Christianity with its belief in a hereafter, whose joys announce themselves in the delights of contemplation, conferred a religious sanction upon the abasement of the *vita activa* while, on the other hand, the command to love your neighbor acted as a counterweight against this estimation unknown to antiquity. But the determination of the order itself, according to which contemplation was the highest of the human faculties, was Greek, and not Christian in origin; it coincided with the discovery of contemplation as the philosopher's way of life which as such was found superior to the political way of life of the citizen in the polis. The point of the matter, which I can only mention here in passing, is that Christianity, contrary to what has frequently been assumed, did not elevate active life to a higher position, did not save it from its being derivative, and did not, at least not theoretically, look upon it as something which has its meaning and end within itself. And a change in this hierarchical order was indeed impossible so long as truth was the one comprehensive principle to establish an order among the human faculties, a truth moreover, which was understood as revelation, as something essentially given to man, as distinguished from truth being either the result of some mental activity—thought or reasoning—or as that knowledge which I acquire through making.

Hence, the question arises: Why was the *vita activa,* with all its distinction and articulations, not discovered after the modern break with tradition and the eventual reversal of its hierarchical order, the "reevaluation of all values" through Marx and Nietzsche? And the answer, though in actual analysis quite complicated, may be summed up briefly here: It lies in the very nature of the famous turning upside-down of philosophic systems or hierarchies of values that the conceptual framework itself is left intact. This is especially true for Marx who was convinced that turning Hegel upside down was enough to find the truth—i.e., the truth of the Hegelian system, which is the discovery of the dialectical nature of history.

Let me shortly explain how this identity shows itself in our context. When I enumerated the chief human activities: Labor-Work-Action, it was obvious that action occupied the highest position. Insofar as action relates to the political sphere of human life, this estimation agrees with the pre-philosophic, pre-Platonic current opinion of Greek polis life. The introduction of contemplation as the highest point of the hierarchy had the result that this order was in fact rearranged, though not always in explicit theory. (Lip service to the old hierarchy was frequently paid when it had already been reversed in the actual teaching of the philosophers.) Seen from the viewpoint of contemplation, the highest activity was not action but work; the rise of the activity of the craftsman in the scale of estimations makes its first dramatic appearance in the Platonic dialogues. Labor, to be sure, remained at the bottom but political activity as something necessary for the life of contemplation was now recognized only to the extent that it could be pursued in the same way as the activity of the craftsman. Only if seen in the image of a working activity, could political action be trusted to produce lasting results. And such lasting results meant peace, the peace needed for contemplation: No change.

If you now look upon the reversal in the modern age, you are immediately aware that its most important feature in this respect is its glorification of labor, surely the last thing any member of one of the classical communities, be it Rome or Greece, would have thought of as worthy of this position. However, the moment you go deeper into this matter you will see that not labor as such occupied this position (Adam Smith, Locke; Marx are unanimous in their contempt for menial tasks, unskilled labor which helps only to consume), but *productive* labor. Again the standard of lasting results is the actual yardstick. Thus Marx, surely the greatest of the labor philosophers, was constantly trying to re-interpret labor in the image of the working activity—again at the expense of political activity. To be sure, things had changed. Political activity was no longer seen as the laying down of immutable laws which would *make* a commonwealth, have as its end-result a reliable product, looking exactly as it had been blueprinted by the maker—as though laws or constitutions were things of the same nature as the table fabricated by the carpenter according to the blueprint he had in mind before he started to make it. Political activity was now supposed to "make history"—a phrase that occurred for the first time in Vico—and not a commonwealth, and this history had, as we all know, its end-product, the classless society which would be the end of the historical process just as the table is indeed the end of the fabrication process. In other words, since on the theoretical level, no more was done by the great re-evaluators of the old values than to turn things upside-down, the old hierarchy within the *vita activa* was hardly disturbed; the old modes of thinking prevailed, and the only relevant distinction between the new and the old was that this order, whose origin and meaningfulness lay in the actual experience of contemplation, became highly questionable. For the actual event which characterizes the modern age in this respect was that contemplation itself had become meaningless.

With this event we shall not deal here. Instead, accepting the oldest, pre-philosophical hierarchy, I propose to look into these activities themselves. And the first thing of which you might have become aware by now is my distinction between labor and work which probably sounded somewhat unusual to you. I draw it from a rather casual remark in Locke who speaks of "the labor of our body and the work of our hands." (Laborers, in Aristotelic language, are those who "with their bodies administer to the needs of life.") The phenomenal evidence in favor of this distinction is too striking to be ignored, and yet it is a fact that, apart from a few scattered remarks and important testimony of social and institutional history, there is hardly anything to support it.

Against this scarcity of evidence stands the simple obstinate fact that every European language, ancient or modern, contains two etymologically unrelated words for what we have come to think of as the same activity: Thus, the Greek distinguished between *ponein* and *ergazesthai,* the Latin between *laborare* and *facere* or *fabricari,* the French between *travailler* and *ouvrer,* the German between *arbeiten* and *werken.* In all these cases, the equivalents for labor have an unequivocal connotation of bodily experiences, of toil and trouble, and in most cases they are significantly also used for the pangs of birth. The last to use this original connection was Marx, who defined labor as the "reproduction of individual life" and begetting, the production of "foreign life," as the production of the species.

If we leave aside all theories, especially the modern labor theories after Marx, and follow solely the etymological and historical evidence, it is obvious that labor is an activity which corresponds to the biological processes of the body, that it is, as the young Marx said, the metabolism between man and nature or the human mode of this metabolism which we share with all living organisms. By laboring, men produce the vital necessities that must be fed into the life process of the human body. And since this life process, though it leads us from birth to death in a rectilinear progress of decay, is in itself circular, the laboring activity itself must follow the cycle of life, the circular movement of our bodily functions, which means that the laboring activity never comes to an end as long as life lasts; it is endlessly repetitive. Unlike working, whose end has come when the object is finished, ready to be added to the common world of things and objects, laboring always moves in the same circle prescribed by the living organism, and the end of its toil and trouble comes only with the end, i.e., the death of the individual organism.

Labor, in other words, produces consumer goods, and laboring and consuming are but two stages of the ever-recurring cycle of biological life. These two stages of the life process follow each other so closely that they almost constitute one and the same movement, which is hardly ended when it must be started all over again. Labor, unlike all other human activities, stands under the sign of necessity, the "necessity of subsisting" as Locke used to say, or the "eternal necessity imposed by nature" in the words of Marx. Hence, the actual goal of the revolution in Marx is not merely the emancipation of the laboring or working classes, but the emancipation of man from labor. For "the realm of freedom begins only where labor determined through want" and the immediacy of "physical needs" ends. And this emancipation, as we know now, to the extent that it is possible at all, occurs not by political emancipation—the equality of all classes of the citizenry—but through technology. I said: To the extent that it is possible, and I meant by this qualification that consumption, as a stage of the cyclical movement of the living organism is in a way also laborious.

Goods for consumption, the immediate result of the laboring process, are the least durable of tangible things. They are, as Locke pointed out, "of short duration, such as—if they are not consumed—will decay and perish by themselves." After a brief stay in the world, they return into the natural process that yielded them either through absorption into the life process of the human animal or through decay; in their man-made shape they disappear more quickly than any other part of the world. They are the least worldly and, at the same time, the most natural and the most necessary of all things. Although they are man-made, they come and go, are produced and consumed, in accordance with the ever-recurrent cyclical movement of nature. Hence, they cannot be "heaped up" and "stored away", as would have been necessary if they were to serve Locke's main purpose, to establish the validity of private property on the rights men have to own their own body.

But while labor in the sense of producing anything lasting—something outlasting the activity itself and even the life-span of the producer—is quite "unproductive" and futile, it is highly productive in another sense. Man's labor power is such that he produces more consumer goods than is necessary for the survival of himself and his family. This, as it were, natural abundance of the laboring process has enabled men to enslave or exploit their fellowmen, thus liberating themselves from life's burden; and while this liberation of the few has always been achieved through the use of force by a ruling class, it would never have been possible without this inherent fertility of human labor itself. Yet even this specifically human "productivity" is part and parcel of nature, it partakes of the superabundance we see everywhere in nature's household. It is but another mode of "Be ye fruitful and multiply" in which it is as though the voice of nature herself speaks to us.

Since labor corresponds to the condition of life itself, it partakes not only in life's toil and trouble but also in the sheer bliss with which we can experience our being alive. The "blessing or the joy of labor," which plays so great a part in modern labor theories, is no empty notion. Man, the author of the human artifice, which we call world in distinction to nature, and men, who are always involved with each other through action and speech, are by no means merely natural beings. But insofar as we too are just living creatures, laboring is the only way we can also remain and swing contentedly in nature's prescribed cycle, toiling and resting, laboring and consuming, with the same happy and purposeless regularity with which day and night, life and death follow each other. The reward of toil and trouble, though it does not leave anything behind itself, is even more real, less futile than any other form of happiness. It lies in nature's fertility, in the quiet confidence that he who in "toil and trouble" had done his part, remains a part of nature in the future of his children and his children's children. The Old Testament, which, unlike classical antiquity, held life to be sacred and therefore neither death nor labor to be an evil (certainly not an argument against life), shows in the stories of the patriarchs how unconcerned about death they were and how death came to them in the familiar shape of night and quiet and eternal rest "in a good old age and full of years."

The blessing of life as a whole, inherent in labor, can never be found in work and should not be mistaken for the inevitably brief spell of joy that follows accomplishment and attends achievement. The blessing of labor is that effort and gratification follow each other as closely as producing and consuming, so that happiness is a concomitant of the process itself. There is no lasting happiness and contentment for human beings outside the prescribed cycle of painful exhaustion and pleasurable regeneration. Whatever throws this cycle out of balance—misery where exhaustion is followed by wretchedness or an entirely effortless life where boredom takes the place of exhaustion and where the mills of necessity, or consumption and digestion grind an impotent human body mercilessly to death—ruins the elemental happiness that comes from being alive. An element of laboring is present in all human activities, even the highest, insofar as they are undertaken as "routine" jobs by which we make our living and keep ourselves alive. Their very repetitiveness, which more often than not we feel to be a burden that exhausts us, is what provides that minimum of animal contentment for which the great and meaningful spells of joy that are rare and never last, can never be a substitute, and without which the longer lasting though equally rare spells of real grief and sorrow could hardly be borne.

The work of our hands, as distinguished from the labor of our bodies, fabricates the sheer unending variety of things whose sum total constitutes the human artifice, the world we live in. They are not consumer goods but use-objects, and their proper use does not cause them to disappear. They give the world the stability and solidity without which it could not be relied upon to house the unstable and mortal creature that is man.

To be sure, the durability of the world of things is not absolute; we do not consume things but use them up, and if we don't, they will simply decay, return into the overall natural process from which they were drawn and against which they were erected by us. If left to itself or expelled from the human world, the chair will again become wood, and the wood will decay and return to the soil from which the tree sprang before it was cut down to become the material upon which to work and with which to build. However, while usage is bound to use up these objects, this end is not planned before, it was not the goal for which it was made, as the "destruction" or immediate consumption of the bread is its inherent end; what usage wears out is durability. In other words, destruction, though unavoidable, is incidental to use but inherent in consumption. What distinguishes the most flimsy pair of shoes from mere consumer goods is that they do not spoil if I don't wear them, they are objects and therefore possess a certain "objective" independence of their own, however modest. Used or unused they will remain in the world for a certain while unless they are wantonly destroyed.

It is this durability that gives the things of the world their relative independence from men who produced and use them, their "objectivity" that makes them withstand, "stand against" and endure at least for a time the voracious needs and wants of their living users. From this viewpoint, the things of the world have the function of stabilizing human life, and their objectivity lies in the fact that men, their ever-changing nature notwithstanding, can retrieve their identity by being related to the enduring sameness of objects, the same chair today and tomorrow, the same house formerly from birth to death. Against the subjectivity of men stands the objectivity of the man-made artifice, not the indifference of nature. Only because we have erected a world of objects from what nature gives us and have built this artificial environment into nature, thus protecting us from her, can we look upon nature as something "objective". Without a world between men and nature, there would be eternal movement, but no objectivity.

Durability and objectivity are the result of fabrication, the work of *homo faber*. It consists of reification. Solidity, inherent in even the most fragile things, comes ultimately from matter which is transformed into material. Material is already a product of human hands that have removed it from its natural location, either killing a life process, as in the case of the tree which provides wood, or interrupting one of nature's slower processes, as in the case of iron, stone, or marble torn out of the womb of the earth. This element of violation and violence is present in all fabrication, and man as the creator of the human artifice has always been a destroyer of nature. The experience of this violence is the most elemental experience of human strength, and by the same token the very opposite of the painful, exhausting effort experienced in sheer labor. This is no longer the earning of one's bread "in the sweat of his brow," in which man may indeed be the lord and master of all living creatures but still remains the servant of nature, his own natural needs, and of the earth. *Homo faber* becomes lord and master of nature herself insofar as he violates and partly destroys what was given to him.

The process of making is itself entirely determined by the categories of means and end. The fabricated thing is an end product in the twofold sense that the production process comes to an end in it and that it is only a means to produce this end. Unlike the laboring activity, where labor and consumption are only two stages of an identical process—the life process of the individual or of society—fabrication and usage are two altogether different processes. The end of the fabrication process has come when the thing is finished, and this process need not be repeated. The impulse toward repetition comes from the craftsman's need to earn his means of subsistence, that is, from the element of labor inherent in his work. It also may come from the demand for multiplication on the market. In either case, the process is repeated for reasons outside itself, unlike the compulsory repetition inherent in laboring, where one must eat in order to labor and must labor in order to eat. Multiplication should not be confused with repetition, although it may be felt by the individual craftsman as mere repetition which a machine can better and more productively achieve. Multiplication actually multiplies things, whereas repetition merely follows the recurrent cycle of life in which its products disappear almost as fast as they have appeared.

To have a definite beginning and a definite predictable end is the mark of fabrication, which through this characteristic alone distinguishes itself from all other human activities. Labor, caught in the cyclical movement of the biological process, has neither a beginning nor an end properly speaking—only pauses, intervals between exhaustion and regeneration. Action, though it may have a definite beginning, never, as we shall see, has a predictable end. This great reliability of work is reflected in that the fabrication process, unlike action, is not irreversible: every thing produced by human hands can be destroyed by them, and no use object is so urgently needed in the life process that its maker cannot survive and afford its destruction. Man, the fabricator of the human artifice, his own world, is indeed a lord and master, not only because he has set himself up as the master of all nature, but because he is master of himself and his doings. This is true neither of laboring, where men remain subject to the necessity of their life, nor of acting, where they remain in dependence upon their fellow men. Alone with his image of the future product, *homo faber* is free to produce, and again facing alone the work of his hands, he is free to destroy.

I said before that all fabrication processes are determined by the category of means and end. This shows itself most clearly in the enormous role which tools and instruments play in it. From the standpoint of *homo faber,* man is indeed, as Benjamin Franklin said, a "tool-maker". To be sure, tools and implements are also used in the laboring process, as every housewife proudly owning all the gadgets of a modern kitchen knows; but these implements have a different character and function when used for laboring; they serve to lighten the burden and mechanize the labor of the laborer, they are, as it were, anthropocentric, whereas the tools of fabrication are designed and invented for the fabrication of things, their fitness and precision are dictated by "objective" aims rather than subjective needs and wants. Moreover, every fabrication process produces things that last considerably longer than the process which brought them into existence, whereas in a laboring process, bringing forth these goods of "short duration," the tools and instruments it uses are the only things which survive the laboring process itself. They are the use-things for laboring, and as such not the result of the laboring activity itself. What dominates the laboring with one's body, and incidentally all work processes performed in the mode of laboring, is neither the purposeful effort nor the product itself, but the motion of the process and the rhythm it imposes upon the laborers. Labor implements are drawn into this rhythm where body and

tool swing in the same repetitive movement—until in the use of machines, which are best suited to the performance of laboring because of
their movement, it is no longer the body's movement that determines the
movement of the implement, but the machine's movement that enforces
the movements of the body, while, in a more advanced state, it replaces it
altogether. It seems to me highly characteristic that the much discussed
question of whether man should be "adjusted" to the machine or the machines should be adjusted to the nature of man never arose with respect to
mere tools or instruments. And the reason is that all tools of workmanship
remain the servants of the hand, whereas machines indeed demand that
the laborer should serve them, adjust the natural rhythm of his body to
their mechanical movement. In other words, even the most refined tool
remains a servant unable to guide or to replace the hand; even the most
primitive machine guides and ideally replaces the body's labor.

The most fundamental experience we have with instrumentality arises
out of the fabrication process. Here it is indeed true that the end justifies
the means; it does more, it produces and organizes them. The end justifies the violence done to nature to win the material, as the wood justifies
killing the tree, and the table justifies destroying the wood. In the same
way, the end product organizes the work process itself, decides about the
needed specialists, the measure of co-operation, the number of assistants or
cooperators. Hence, everything and everybody is judged here in terms of
suitability and usefulness for the desired end product, and nothing else.

Strangely enough, the validity of the means-end category is not exhausted with the finished product for which everything and everybody
becomes a means. Though the object is an end with respect to the means
by which it was produced and the actual end of the making process, it
never becomes, so to speak, an end in itself, at least not as long as it remains an object for use. It immediately takes its place in another means-
end chain by virtue of its very usefulness; as a mere use-object it becomes
a means for, let us say, comfortable living, or as an exchange object, that
is, insofar [as] a definite value has been bestowed upon the material used
for fabrication, it becomes a means for obtaining other objects. In other
words, in a strictly utilitarian world, all ends are bound to be of short duration; they are transformed into means for some further ends. Once the
end is attained, it ceases to be an end, it becomes an object among objects
which at any moment can be transformed into means to pursue further
ends. The perplexity of utilitarianism, the philosophy, as it were, of *homo
faber,* is that it gets caught in the unending chain of means and ends without ever arriving at some principle which could justify the category, that
is, utility itself.

The usual way out of this dilemma is to make the user, man himself, the ultimate end to stop the unending chain of ends and means. That man is an end in himself and should never be used as a means to pursue other ends, no matter how elevated these might be, is well-known to us from the moral philosophy of Kant, and there is no doubt that Kant wanted first of all to relegate the means-end category and its philosophy of utilitarianism to its proper place and prevent it from ruling the relations between man and man instead of the relationship between men and things. However, even Kant's intrinsically paradoxical formula fails to solve the perplexities of *homo faber*. By elevating man the user into the position of an ultimate end, he degrades even more forcefully all other "ends" to mere means. If man the user is the highest end, "the measure of all things," then not only nature, treated by fabrication as the almost "worthless material" upon which to work and to bestow "value" (as Locke said), but the "valuable" things themselves have become mere means, losing thereby their own intrinsic worth. Or to put it another way, the most worldly of all activities loses its original objective meaning, it becomes a means to fulfill subjective needs; in and by itself, it is no longer meaningful, no matter how useful it may be.

From the viewpoint of fabrication the finished product is as much an end in itself, an independent durable entity with an existence of its own, as man is an end in himself in Kant's moral philosophy. Of course, the issue at stake here is not instrumentality as such, the use of means to achieve an end, but rather the generalization of the fabrication experience in which usefulness and utility are established as the ultimate standards for the world as well as for the life of acting men moving in it. *Homo faber,* we can say, has transgressed the limits of his activity when, under the disguise of utilitarianism, he proposes that instrumentality rule the realm of the finished world as exclusively as it rules the activity through which all things contained in it come into being. This generalization will always be the specific temptation of *homo faber* although, in the final analysis, it will be his own undoing: he will be left with meaninglessness in the midst of usefulness; utilitarianism never can find the answer to the question Lessing once put to the utilitarian philosophers of his time: "And what, if you please, is the use of use?"

In the sphere of fabrication itself, there is only one kind of objects to which the unending chain of means and ends does not apply, and this is the work of art, the most useless and, at the same time, the most durable thing human hands can produce. Its very characteristic is its remoteness from the whole context of ordinary usage, so that in case a former use object, say a piece of furniture of a by-gone age, is considered by a later generation to be a "masterpiece," it is put into a museum and thus carefully removed from any possible usage. Just as the purpose of a chair is actualized when it is sat upon, the inherent purpose of a work of art—whether the artist knows it or not, whether the purpose is achieved or not—is to attain permanence throughout the ages. Nowhere else does the sheer durability of the man-made world appear in such purity and clarity, nowhere else therefore does this thing-world reveal itself so spectacularly as the non-mortal home for mortal beings. And though the actual source of inspiration of these permanent things is thought, this does not prevent their being things. The thought process no more produces anything tangible than the sheer ability to use objects produces them. It is the reification that occurs in writing something down, painting an image, composing a piece of music, etc., which actually *makes* the thought a reality; and in order to produce these thought things, which we usually call art works, the same workmanship is required that through the primordial instrument of human hands builds the other, less durable and more useful things of the human artifice.

The man-made world of things becomes a home for mortal men, whose stability will endure and outlast the ever-changing movement of their lives and deeds, only insomuch as it transcends both the sheer functionalism of consumer-goods and the sheer utility of use objects. Life in its non-biological sense, the span of time each man is given between birth and death, manifests itself in action and speech, to which we now must turn our attention. With word and deed we insert ourselves into the human world, and this insertion is like a second birth, in which we confirm and take upon ourselves the naked fact of our original physical appearance. Since through birth we entered Being, we share with all other entities the quality of Otherness, an important aspect of plurality that makes [sic] that we can define only by distinction, that we are unable to say what anything *is* without distinguishing it from something else. In addition to this we share with all living organisms that kind of distinguishing trait which makes it an individual entity. However, only man can *express* otherness and individuality, only he can distinguish himself and communicate *himself,* and not merely something—thirst or hunger, affection or hostility or fear. In man, otherness and distinctness become uniqueness, and what man inserts with word and deed into the company of his own kind is uniqueness. This insertion is not forced upon us through necessity like labor and it is not prompted by wants and desires like work. It is unconditioned; its impulse springs from the beginning that came into the world when we were born and to which we respond by beginning something new on our own initiative. To act, in its most general sense, means to take an initiative, to begin, as the Greek word: *arkhein* indicates, or to set something into motion, which is the original meaning of the Latin *agere*.

All human activities are conditioned by the fact of human plurality, that not One man, but men in the plural inhabit the earth and in one way or another live together. But only action and speech relate specifically to this fact that to live always means to live among men, among those who are my equals. Hence, when I insert myself into the world, it is a world where others are already present. Action and speech are so closely related because the primordial and specifically human act must always also answer the question asked of every newcomer: "Who are you?" The disclosure of "who somebody is" is implicit in the fact that speechless action somehow does not exist, or if it exists [it] is irrelevant; without speech, action loses the actor, and the doer of deeds is possible only to the extent that he is at the same time the speaker of words, who identifies himself as the actor and announces what he is doing, what he has done, or what he intends to do. It is exactly as Dante once said—and more succinctly than I could (*De Monarchia,* I, 13)—: "For in every action what is primarily intended by the doer . . . is the disclosure of his own image. Hence it comes about that every doer, in so far as he does, takes delight in doing; since everything that is desires its own being, and since in action the being of the doer is somehow intensified, delight necessarily follows . . . Thus nothing acts unless by acting it makes patent its latent self." To be sure, this disclosure of "who" always remains hidden from the person himself—like the *daimon* in Greek religion who accompanies man throughout his life, always looking over his shoulder from behind and thus visible only to those he encounters. Still, though unknown to the person, action is intensely personal. Action without a name, a "who" attached to it, is meaningless whereas an art work retains its relevance whether or not we know the master's name. Let me remind you of the monuments to the Unknown Soldier after World War I. They bear testimony to the need for finding a "who", an indentifiable somebody, whom four years of mass slaughter should have revealed. The unwillingness to resign oneself to the brutal fact that the agent of the war was actually Nobody inspired the erection of the monuments to the unknown ones—that is to all those whom the war had failed to make known, robbing them thereby, not of their achievement, but of their human dignity.

Wherever men live together, there exists a web of human relationships which is, as it were, woven by the deeds and words of innumerable persons, by the living as well as by the dead. Every deed and every new beginning falls into an already existing web, where it nevertheless somehow starts a new process that will affect many others even beyond those with whom the agent comes into direct contact. It is because of this already existing web of human relationships with its conflicting wills and intentions, that action almost never achieves its purpose. And it is also because of this medium and the attending quality of unpredictability that action always produces stories, with or without intention, as naturally as fabrication produces tangible things. These stories may then be recorded in documents and monuments, they may be told in poetry and historiography, and worked into all kinds of material. They themselves, however, are of an entirely different nature than these reifications. They tell us more about their subjects, the "hero" in each story, than any product of human hands ever tells us about the master who produced it, and yet they are not products properly speaking. Although everybody starts his own story, at least his own life-story, nobody is the author or producer of it. And yet, it is precisely in these stories that the actual meaning of a human life finally reveals itself. That every individual life between birth and death can eventually be told as a story with beginning and end is the prepolitical and prehistorical condition of history, the great story without beginning and end. But the reason why each human life tells its story and why history ultimately becomes the storybook of mankind, with many actors and speakers and yet without any recognizable author, is that both are the outcome of action. The real story in which we are engaged as long as we live has no visible or invisible maker because it is not *made*.

The absence of a maker in this realm accounts for the extraordinary frailty and unreliability of strictly human affairs. Since we always act into a web of relationships, the consequences of each deed are boundless, every action touches off not only a reaction but a chain reaction, every process is the cause of unpredictable new processes. This boundlessness is inescapable; it could not be cured by restricting one's acting to a limited graspable framework or circumstances or by feeding all pertinent material into giant computers. The smallest act in the most limited circumstances bears the seed of the same boundlessness and unpredictability; one deed, one gesture, one word may suffice to change every constellation. In acting, in contradistinction to working, it is indeed true that we can really never know what we are doing.

There stands however in stark contrast to this frailty and unreliability of human affairs another character of human action which seems to make it even more dangerous than we are entitled to assume anyhow. And this is the simple fact that, though we don't know what we are doing when we are acting, we have no possibility ever to undo what we have done. Action processes are not only unpredictable, they are also irreversible; there is no author or maker who can undo, destroy, what he has done if he does not like it or when the consequences prove to be disastrous. This peculiar resiliency of action, apparently in opposition to the frailty of its results, would be altogether unbearable if this capability had not some remedy within its own range.

The possible redemption from the predicament of irreversibility is the faculty of forgiving, and the remedy for unpredictability is contained in the faculty to make and keep promises. The two remedies belong together: forgiving relates to the past and serves to undo its deeds, while binding oneself through promises serves to set up in the ocean of future uncertainty islands of security without which not even continuity, let alone durability of any kind, would ever be possible in the relationships between men. Without being forgiven, released from the consequences of what we have done, our capacity to act would, as it were, be confined to one single deed from which we could never recover; we would remain the victims of its consequences forever, not unlike the sorcerer's apprentice who lacked the magic formula to break the spell. Without being bound to the fulfilment of promises, we would never be able to achieve that amount of identity and continuity which together produce the "person" about whom a story can be told; each of us would be condemned to wander helplessly and without direction in the darkness of his own lonely heart, caught in its ever changing moods, contradictions, and equivocalities. (This subjective identity, achieved through binding oneself in promises, must be distinguished from the "objective", i.e., object-related, identity that arises out of being confronted with the sameness of the world which I mentioned in the discussion of work.) In this respect, forgiving and making promises are like control mechanisms built into the very faculty to start new and unending processes.

Without action, without the capacity to start something new and thus articulate the new beginning that comes into the world with the birth of each human being, the life of man, spent between birth and death, would indeed be doomed beyond salvation. The life span itself, running toward death would inevitably carry everything human to ruin and destruction. Action, with all its uncertainties, is like an ever-present reminder that men, though they must die, are not born in order to die but in order to begin something new. *Initium ut esset homo creatus est*—"that there be a beginning man was created," said Augustine. With the creation of man, the principle of beginning came into the world—which, of course, is only another way of saying that with the creation of man, the principle of freedom appeared on earth.

The Public
and the Private Realm

4
MAN: A SOCIAL OR A
POLITICAL ANIMAL

THE *VITA ACTIVA,* human life in so far as it is actively engaged in doing something, is always rooted in a world of men and of man-made things which it never leaves or altogether transcends. Things and men form the environment for each of man's activities, which would be pointless without such location; yet this environment, the world into which we are born, would not exist without the human activity which produced it, as in the case of fabricated things; which takes care of it, as in the case of cultivated land; or which established it through organization, as in the case of the body politic. No human life, not even the life of the hermit in nature's wilderness, is possible without a world which directly or indirectly testifies to the presence of other human beings.

All human activities are conditioned by the fact that men live together, but it is only action that cannot even be imagined outside the society of men. The activity of labor does not need the presence of others, though a being laboring in complete solitude would not be human but an *animal laborans* in the word's most literal significance. Man working and fabricating and building a world inhabited only by himself would still be a fabricator, though not *homo faber:* he would have lost his specifically human quality and, rather, be a god—not, to be sure, the Creator, but a divine-demiurge as Plato described him in one of his myths. Action alone is the exclusive prerogative of man; neither a beast nor a god is capable of it,[1] and only action is entirely dependent upon the constant presence of others.

This special relationship between action and being together seems fully to justify the early translation of Aristotle's *zōon politikon* by *animal*

From The Human Condition.

socialis, already found in Seneca, which then became the standard translation through Thomas Aquinas: *homo est naturaliter politicus, id est, socialis* ("man is by nature political, that is, social").[2] More than any elaborate theory, this unconscious substitution of the social for the political betrays the extent to which the original Greek understanding of politics had been lost. For this, it is significant but not decisive that the word "social" is Roman in origin and has no equivalent in Greek language or thought. Yet the Latin usage of the word *societas* also originally had a clear, though limited, political meaning; it indicated an alliance between people for a specific purpose, as when men organize in order to rule others or to commit a crime.[3] It is only with the later concept of a *societas generis humani,* a "society of man-kind,"[4] that the term "social" begins to acquire the general meaning of a fundamental human condition. It is not that Plato or Aristotle was ignorant of, or unconcerned with, the fact that man cannot live outside the company of men, but they did not count this condition among the specifically human characteristics; on the contrary, it was something human life had in common with animal life, and for this reason alone it could not be fundamentally human. The natural, merely social companionship of the human species was considered to be a limitation imposed upon us by the needs of biological life, which are the same for the human animal as for other forms of animal life.

According to Greek thought, the human capacity for political organization is not only different from but stands in direct opposition to that natural association whose center is the home (*oikia*) and the family. The rise of the city-state meant that man received "besides his private life a sort of second life, his *bios politikos.* Now every citizen belongs to two orders of existence; and there is a sharp distinction in his life between what is his own (*idion*) and what is communal (*koinon*)."[5] It was not just an opinion or theory of Aristotle but a simple historical fact that the foundation of the *polis* was preceded by the destruction of all organized units resting on kinship, such as the *phratria* and the *phylē.*[6] Of all the activities necessary and present in human communities, only two were deemed to be political and to constitute what Aristotle called the *bios politikos,* namely action (*praxis*) and speech (*lexis*), out of which rises the realm of human affairs (*ta tōn anthrōpōn pragmata,* as Plato used to call it) from which everything merely necessary or useful is strictly excluded.

However, while certainly only the foundation of the city-state enabled men to spend their whole lives in the political realm, in action and speech, the conviction that these two human capacities belonged together and are the highest of all seems to have preceded the *polis* and was already present in pre-Socratic thought. The stature of the Homeric Achilles can be understood only if one sees him as "the doer of great deeds and the speaker of great words."[7] In distinction from modern understanding, such words were not considered to be great because they expressed great thoughts; on the contrary, as we know from the last lines of *Antigone*, it may be the capacity for "great words" (*megaloi logoi*) with which reply to striking blows that will eventually teach thought in old age.[8] Thought was secondary to speech, but speech and action were considered to be coeval and coequal, of the same rank and the same kind; and this originally meant not only that most political action, in so far as it remains outside the sphere of violence, is indeed transacted in words, but more fundamentally that finding the right words at the right moment, quite apart from the information or communication they may convey, is action. Only sheer violence is mute, and for this reason violence alone can never be great. Even when, relatively late in antiquity, the arts of war and speech (*rhetoric*) emerged as the two principal political subjects of education, the development was still inspired by this older pre-*polis* experience and tradition and remained subject to it.

In the experience of the *polis,* which not without justification has been called the most talkative of all bodies politic, and even more in the political philosophy which sprang from it, action and speech separated and became more and more independent activities. The emphasis shifted from action to speech, and to speech as a means of persuasion rather than the specifically human way of answering, talking back and measuring up to whatever happened or was done.[9] To be political, to live in a *polis,* meant that everything was decided through words and persuasion and not through force and violence. In Greek self-understanding, to force people by violence, to command rather than persuade, were prepolitical ways to deal with people characteristic of life outside the *polis,* of home and family life, where the household head ruled with uncontested, despotic powers, or of life in the barbarian empires of Asia, whose despotism was frequently likened to the organization of the household.

Aristotle's definition of man as *zōon politikon* was not only unrelated and even opposed to the natural association experienced in household life; it can be fully understood only if one adds his second famous definition of man as a *zōon logon ekhon* ("a living being capable of speech"). The Latin translation of this term into *animal rationale* rests on no less fundamental a misunderstanding than the term "social animal." Aristotle meant neither to define man in general nor to indicate man's highest capacity, which to him was not *logos,* that is, not speech or reason, but *nous,* the capacity of contemplation, whose chief characteristic is that its content cannot be rendered in speech.[10] In his two most famous definitions, Aristotle only formulated the current opinion of the *polis* about man and the political way of life, and according to this opinion, everybody outside the *polis*—slaves and barbarians—was *aneu logou,* deprived, of course, not of the faculty of speech, but of a way of life in which speech and only speech made sense and where the central concern of all citizens was to talk with each other.

The profound misunderstanding expressed in the Latin translation of "political" as "social" is perhaps nowhere clearer than in a discussion in which Thomas Aquinas compares the nature of household rule with political rule: the head of the household, he finds, has some similarity to the head of the kingdom, but, he adds, his power is not so "perfect" as that of the king.[11] Not only in Greece and the *polis* but throughout the whole of occidental antiquity, it would indeed have been self-evident that even the power of the tyrant was less great, less "perfect" than the power with which the *paterfamilias,* the *dominus,* ruled over his household of slaves and family. And this was not because the power of the city's ruler was matched and checked by the combined powers of household heads, but because absolute, uncontested rule and a political realm properly speaking were mutually exclusive.[12]

5

THE *POLIS* AND THE HOUSEHOLD

Although misunderstanding and equating the political and social realms is as old as the translation of Greek terms into Latin and their adaption to Roman-Christian thought, it has become even more confusing in modern usage and modern understanding of society. The distinction between a private and a public sphere of life corresponds to the household and the political realms, which have existed as distinct, separate entities at least since the rise of the ancient city-state; but the emergence of the social realm, which is neither private nor public, strictly speaking, is a relatively new phenomenon whose origin coincided with the emergence of the modern age and which found its political form in the nation-state.

What concerns us in this context is the extraordinary difficulty with which we, because of this development, understand the decisive division between the public and private realms, between the sphere of the *polis* and the sphere of household and family, and, finally, between activities related to a common world and those related to the maintenance of life, a division upon which all ancient political thought rested as self-evident and axiomatic. In our understanding, the dividing line is entirely blurred, because we see the body of peoples and political communities in the image of a family whose everyday affairs have to be taken care of by a gigantic, nation-wide administration of housekeeping. The scientific thought that corresponds to this development is no longer political science but "national economy" or "social economy" or *Volkswirtschaft,* all of which indicate a kind of "collective house-keeping";[13] the collective of families economically organized into the facsimile of one super-human family is what we call "society," and its political form of organization is called "nation."[14] We therefore find it difficult to realize that according to ancient thought on these matters, the very term "political economy" would have been a contradiction in terms: whatever was "economic," related to the life of the individual and the survival of the species, was a non-political, household affair by definition.[15]

Historically, it is very likely that the rise of the city-state and the public realm occurred at the expense of the private realm of family and household.[16] Yet the old sanctity of the hearth, though much less pronounced in classical Greece than in ancient Rome, was never entirely lost. What prevented the *polis* from violating the private lives of its citizens and made it hold sacred the boundaries surrounding each property was not respect for private property as we understand it, but the fact that without owning a house a man could not participate in the affairs of the world because he had no location in it which was properly his own.[17] Even Plato, whose political plans foresaw the abolition of private property and an extension of the public sphere to the point of annihilating private life altogether, still speaks with great reverence of Zeus Herkeios, the protector of border lines, and calls the *horoi,* the boundaries between one estate and another, divine, without seeing any contradiction.[18]

The distinctive trait of the household sphere was that in it men lived together because they were driven by their wants and needs. The driving force was life itself—the penates, the household gods, were, according to Plutarch, "the gods who make us live and nourish our body"[19]—which, for its individual maintenance and its survival as the life of the species needs the company of others. That individual maintenance should be the task of the man and species survival the task of the woman was obvious, and both of these natural functions, the labor of man to provide nourishment and the labor of the woman in giving birth, were subject to the same urgency of life. Natural community in the household therefore was born of necessity, and necessity ruled over all activities performed in it.

The realm of the *polis,* on the contrary, was the sphere of freedom, and if there was a relationship between these two spheres, it was a matter of course that the mastering of the necessities of life in the household was the condition for freedom of the *polis*. Under no circumstances could politics be only a means to protect society—a society of the faithful, as in the Middle Ages, or a society of property-owners, as in Locke, or a society relentlessly engaged in a process of acquisition, as in Hobbes, or a society of producers, as in Marx, or a society of jobholders, as in our own society, or a society of laborers, as in socialist and communist countries. In all these cases, it is the freedom (and in some instances so-called freedom) of society which requires and justifies the restraint of political authority. Freedom is located in the realm of the social, and force or violence becomes the monopoly of government.

What all Greek philosophers, no matter how opposed to *polis* life, took for granted is that freedom is exclusively located in the political realm, that necessity is primarily a prepolitical phenomenon, characteristic of the private household organization, and that force and violence are justified in this sphere because they are the only means to master necessity—for instance, by ruling over slaves—and to become free. Because all human beings are subject to necessity, they are entitled to violence toward others; violence is the prepolitical act of liberating oneself from the necessity of life for the freedom of world. This freedom is the essential condition of what the Greeks called felicity, *eudaimonia,* which was an objective status depending first of all upon wealth and health. To be poor or to be in ill health meant to be subject to physical necessity, and to be a slave meant to be subject, in addition, to man-made violence. This twofold and doubled "unhappiness" of slavery is quite independent of the actual subjective well-being of the slave. Thus, a poor free man preferred the insecurity of a daily-changing labor market to regular assured work, which, because it restricted his freedom to do as he pleased every day, was already felt to be servitude (*douleia*), and even harsh, painful labor was preferred to the easy life of many household slaves.[20]

The prepolitical force, however, with which the head of the household ruled over the family and its slaves and which was felt to be necessary because man is a "social" before he is a "political animal," has nothing in common with the chaotic "state of nature" from whose violence, according to seventeenth-century political thought, men could escape only by establishing a government that, through a monopoly of power and of violence, would abolish the "war of all against all" by "keeping them all in awe."[21] On the contrary, the whole concept of rule and being ruled, of government and power in the sense in which we understand them as well as the regulated order attending them, was felt to be prepolitical and to belong in the private rather than the public sphere.

The *polis* was distinguished from the household in that it knew only "equals," whereas the household was the center of the strictest inequality. To be free meant both not to be subject to the necessity of life or to the command of another *and* not to be in command oneself. It meant neither to rule nor to be ruled.[22] Thus within the realm of the household, freedom did not exist, for the household head, its ruler, was considered to be free only in so far as he had the power to leave the household and enter the political realm, where all were equals. To be sure, this equality of the political realm has very little in common with our concept of equality: it meant to live among and to have to deal only with one's peers, and it presupposed the existence of "unequals" who, as a matter of fact, were always the majority of the population in a city-state.[23] Equality, therefore, far from being connected with justice, as in modern times, was the very essence of freedom: to be free meant to be free from the inequality present in rulership and to move in a sphere where neither rule nor being ruled existed.

However, the possibility of describing the profound difference between the modern and the ancient understanding of politics in terms of a clear-cut opposition ends here. In the modern world, the social and the political realms are much less distinct. That politics is nothing but a function of society, that action, speech, and thought are primarily superstructures upon social interest, is not a discovery of Karl Marx but on the contrary is among the axiomatic assumptions Marx accepted uncritically from the political economists of the modern age. This functionalization makes it impossible to perceive any serious gulf between the two realms; and this is not a matter of a theory or an ideology, since with the rise of society, that is, the rise of the "household" (*oikia*) or of economic activities to the public realm, housekeeping and all matters pertaining formerly to the private sphere of the family have become a "collective" concern.[24] In the modern world, the two realms indeed constantly flow into each other like waves in the never-resting stream of the life process itself.

The disappearance of the gulf that the ancients had to cross daily to transcend the narrow realm of the household and "rise" into the realm of politics is an essentially modern phenomenon. Such a gulf between the private and the public still existed somehow in the Middle Ages, though it had lost much of its significance and changed its location entirely. It has been rightly remarked that after the downfall of the Roman Empire, it was the Catholic Church that offered men a substitute for the citizenship which had formerly been the prerogative of municipal government.[25] The medieval tension between the darkness of everyday life and the grandiose splendor attending everything sacred, with the concomitant rise from the secular to the religious, corresponds in many respects to the rise from the private to the public in antiquity. The difference is of course very marked, for no matter how "worldly" the Church became, it was always essentially an other-worldly concern which kept the community of believers together. While one can equate the public with the religious only with some difficulty, the secular realm under the rule of feudalism was indeed in its entirety what the private realm had been in antiquity. Its hallmark was the absorption of all activities into the household sphere, where they had only private significance, and consequently the very absence of a public realm.[26]

It is characteristic of this growth of the private realm, and incidentally of the difference between the ancient household head and the feudal lord, that the feudal lord could render justice within the limits of his rule, whereas the ancient household head, while he might exert a milder or harsher rule, knew neither of laws nor justice outside the political realm.[27] The bringing of all human activities into the private realm and the modeling of all human relationships upon the example of the household reached far into the specifically medieval professional organizations in the cities themselves, the guilds, *confréries,* and *compagnons,* and even into the early business companies, where "the original joint household would seem to be indicated by the very word 'company' (*companis*) . . . [and] such phrases as 'men who eat one bread,' 'men who have one bread and one wine.' "[28] The medieval concept of the "common good," far from indicating the existence of a political realm, recognizes only that private individuals have interests in common, material and spiritual, and that they can retain their privacy and attend to their own business only if one of them takes it upon himself to look out for this common interest. What distinguishes this essentially Christian attitude toward politics from the modern reality is not so much the recognition of a "common good" as the exclusivity of the private sphere and the absence of that curiously hybrid realm where private interests assume public significance that we call "society."

It is therefore not surprising that medieval political thought, concerned exclusively with the secular realm, remained unaware of the gulf between the sheltered life in the household and the merciless exposure of the *polis* and, consequently, of the virtue of courage as one of the most elemental political attitudes. What remains surprising is that the only postclassical political theorist who, in an extraordinary effort to restore its old dignity to politics, perceived the gulf and understood something of the courage needed to cross it was Machiavelli, who described it in the rise "of the Condottiere from low condition to high rank," from privacy to princedom, that is, from circumstances common to all men to the shining glory of great deeds.[29]

To leave the household, originally in order to embark upon some adventure and glorious enterprise and later simply to devote one's life to the affairs of the city, demanded courage because only in the household was one primarily concerned with one's own life and survival. Whoever entered the political realm had first to be ready to risk his life, and too great a love for life obstructed freedom, was a sure sign of slavishness.[30] Courage therefore became the political virtue par excellence, and only those men who possessed it could be admitted to a fellowship that was political in content and purpose and thereby transcended the mere togetherness imposed on all—slaves, barbarians, and Greeks alike—through the urgencies of life.[31] The "good life," as Aristotle called the life of the citizen, therefore was not merely better, more carefree or nobler than ordinary life, but of an altogether different quality. It was "good" to the extent that by having mastered the necessities of sheer life, by being freed from labor and work, and by overcoming the innate urge of all living creatures for their own survival, it was no longer bound to the biological life process.

At the root of Greek political consciousness we find an unequaled clarity and articulateness in drawing this distinction. No activity that served only the purpose of making a living, of sustaining only the life process, was permitted to enter the political realm, and this at the grave risk of abandoning trade and manufacture to the industriousness of slaves and foreigners, so that Athens indeed became the "pensionopolis" with a "proletariat of consumers" which Max Weber so vividly described.[32] The true character of this *polis* is still quite manifest in Plato's and Aristotle's political philosophies, even if the borderline between household and *polis* is occasionally blurred, especially in Plato who, probably following Socrates, began to draw his examples and illustrations for the *polis* from everyday experiences in private life, but also in Aristotle when he, following Plato, tentatively assumed that at least the historical origin of the *polis* must be connected with the necessities of life and that only its content or inherent aim (*telos*) transcends life in the "good life."

These aspects of the teachings of the Socratic school, which soon were to become axiomatic to the point of banality, were then the newest and most revolutionary of all and sprang not from actual experience in political life but from the desire to be freed from its burden, a desire which in their own understanding the philosophers could justify only by demonstrating that even this freest of all ways of life was still connected with and subject to necessity. But the background of actual political experience, at least in Plato and Aristotle, remained so strong that the distinction between the spheres of household and political life was never doubted. Without mastering the necessities of life in the household, neither life nor the "good life" is possible, but politics is never for the sake of life. As far as the members of the *polis* are concerned, household life exists for the sake of the "good life" in the *polis*.

6
THE RISE OF THE SOCIAL

The emergence of society—the rise of housekeeping, its activities, problems, and organizational devices—from the shadowy interior of the household into the light of the public sphere, has not only blurred the old borderline between private and political, it has also changed almost beyond recognition the meaning of the two terms and their significance for the life of the individual and the citizen. Not only would we not agree with the Greeks that a life spent in the privacy of "one's own" (*idion*), outside the world of the common, is "idiotic" by definition, or with the Romans to whom privacy offered but a temporary refuge from the business of the *res publica;* we call private today a sphere of intimacy whose beginnings we may be able to trace back to late Roman, though hardly to any period of Greek antiquity, but whose peculiar manifoldness and variety were certainly unknown to any period prior to the modern age.

This is not merely a matter of shifted emphasis. In ancient feeling the privative trait of privacy, indicated in the word itself, was all-important; it meant literally a state of being deprived of something, and even of the highest and most human of man's capacities. A man who lived only a private life, who like the slave was not permitted to enter the public realm, or like the barbarian had chosen not to establish such a realm, was not fully human. We no longer think primarily of deprivation when we use the word "privacy," and this is partly due to the enormous enrichment of the private sphere through modern individualism. However, it seems even more important that modern privacy is at least as sharply opposed to the social realm—unknown to the ancients who considered its content a private matter—as it is to the political, properly speaking. The decisive historical fact is that modern privacy in its most relevant function, to shelter the intimate, was discovered as the opposite not of the political sphere but of the social, to which it is therefore more closely and authentically related.

The first articulate explorer and to an extent even theorist of intimacy was Jean-Jacques Rousseau who, characteristically enough, is the only great author still frequently cited by his first name alone. He arrived at his discovery through a rebellion not against the oppression of the state but against society's unbearable perversion of the human heart, its intrusion upon an innermost region in man which until then had needed no special protection. The intimacy of the heart, unlike the private household, has no objective tangible place in the world, nor can the society against which it protests and asserts itself be localized with the same certainty as the public space. To Rousseau, both the intimate and the social were, rather, subjective modes of human existence, and in his case, it was as though Jean-Jacques rebelled against a man called Rousseau. The modern individual and his endless conflicts, his inability either to be at home in society or to live outside it altogether, his ever-changing moods and the radical subjectivism of his emotional life, was born in this rebellion of the heart. The authenticity of Rousseau's discovery is beyond doubt, no matter how doubtful the authenticity of the individual who was Rousseau. The astonishing flowering of poetry and music from the middle of the eighteenth century until almost the last third of the nineteenth, accompanied by the rise of the novel, the only entirely social art form, coinciding with a no less striking decline of all the more public arts, especially architecture, is sufficient testimony to a close relationship between the social and the intimate.

The rebellious reaction against society during which Rousseau and the Romanticists discovered intimacy was directed first of all against the leveling demands of the social, against what we would call today the conformism inherent in every society. It is important to remember that this rebellion took place before the principle of equality, upon which we have blamed conformism since Tocqueville, had had the time to assert itself in either the social or the political realm. Whether a nation consists of equals or non-equals is of no great importance in this respect, for society always demands that its members act as though they were members of one enormous family which has only one opinion and one interest. Before the modern disintegration of the family, this common interest and single opinion was represented by the household head who ruled in accordance with it and prevented possible disunity among the family members.[33] The striking coincidence of the rise of society with the decline of the family indicates clearly that what actually took place was the absorption of the family unit into corresponding social groups. The equality of the members of these groups, far from being an equality among peers, resembles nothing so much as the equality of household members before the despotic power of the household head, except that in society, where the natural strength of one common interest and one unanimous opinion is tremendously enforced by sheer number, actual rule exerted by one man, representing the common interest and the right opinion, could eventually be dispensed with. The phenomenon of conformism is characteristic of the last stage of this modern development.

It is true that one-man, monarchical rule, which the ancients stated to be the organizational device of the household, is transformed in society—as we know it today, when the peak of the social order is no longer formed by the royal household of an absolute ruler—into a kind of no-man rule. But this nobody, the assumed one interest of society as a whole in economics as well as the assumed one opinion of polite society in the salon, does not cease to rule for having lost its personality. As we know from the most social form of government, that is, from bureaucracy (the last stage of government in the nation-state just as one-man rule in benevolent despotism and absolutism was its first), the rule by nobody is not necessarily no-rule; it may indeed, under certain circumstances, even turn out to be one of its cruelest and most tyrannical versions.

It is decisive that society, on all its levels, excludes the possibility of action, which formerly was excluded from the household. Instead, society expects from each of its members a certain kind of behavior, imposing innumerable and various rules, all of which tend to "normalize" its members, to make them behave, to exclude spontaneous action or outstanding achievement. With Rousseau, we find these demands in the salons of high society, whose conventions always equate the individual with his rank within the social framework. What matters is this equation with social status, and it is immaterial whether the framework happens to be actual rank in the half-feudal society of the eighteenth century, title in the class society of the nineteenth, or mere function in the mass society of today. The rise of mass society, on the contrary, only indicates that the various social groups have suffered the same absorption into one society that the family units had suffered earlier; with the emergence of mass society, the realm of the social has finally, after several centuries of development, reached the point where it embraces and controls all members of a given community equally and with equal strength. But society equalizes under all circumstances, and the victory of equality in the modern world is only the political and legal recognition of the fact that society has conquered the public realm, and that distinction and difference have become private matters of the individual.

This modern equality, based on the conformism inherent in society and possible only because behavior has replaced action as the foremost mode of human relationship, is in every respect different from equality in antiquity, and notably in the Greek city-states. To belong to the few "equals" (*homoioi*) meant to be permitted to live among one's peers; but the public realm itself, the *polis*, was permeated by a fiercely agonal spirit, where everybody had constantly to distinguish himself from all others, to show through unique deeds or achievements that he was the best of all (*aien aristeuein*).[34] The public realm, in other words, was reserved for individuality; it was the only place where men could show who they really and inexchangeably were. It was for the sake of this chance, and out of love for a body politic that made it possible to them all, that each was more or less willing to share in the burden of jurisdiction, defense, and administration of public affairs.

It is the same conformism, the assumption that men behave and do not act with respect to each other, that lies at the root of the modern science of economics, whose birth coincided with the rise of society and which, together with its chief technical tool, statistics, became the social science par excellence. Economics—until the modern age a not too important part of ethics and politics and based on the assumption that men act with respect to their economic activities as they act in every other respect[35]—could achieve a scientific character only when men had become social beings and unanimously followed certain patterns of behavior, so that those who did not keep the rules could be considered to be asocial or abnormal.

The laws of statistics are valid only where large numbers or long periods are involved, and acts or events can statistically appear only as deviations or fluctuations. The justification of statistics is that deeds and events are rare occurrences in everyday life and in history. Yet the meaningfulness of everyday relationships is disclosed not in everyday life but in rare deeds, just as the significance of a historical period shows itself only in the few events that illuminate it. The application of the law of large numbers and long periods to politics or history signifies nothing less than the wilful obliteration of their very subject matter, and it is a hopeless enterprise to search for meaning in politics or significance in history when everything that is not everyday behavior or automatic trends has been ruled out as immaterial.

However, since the laws of statistics are perfectly valid where we deal with large numbers, it is obvious that every increase in population means an increased validity and a marked decrease of "deviation." Politically, this means that the larger the population in any given body politic, the more likely it will be the social rather than the political that constitutes the public realm. The Greeks, whose city-state was the most individualistic and least conformable body politic known to us, were quite aware of the fact that the *polis,* with its emphasis on action and speech, could survive only if the number of citizens remained restricted. Large numbers of people, crowded together, develop an almost irresistible inclination toward despotism, be this the despotism of a person of a majority rule; and although statistics, that is, the mathematical treatment of reality, was unknown prior to the modern age, the social phenomena which make such treatment possible—great numbers, accounting for conformism, behaviorism, and automatism in human affairs—were precisely those traits which, in Greek self-understanding, distinguished the Persian civilization from their own.

The unfortunate truth about behaviorism and the validity of its "laws" is that the more people there are, the more likely they are to behave and the less likely to tolerate non-behavior. Statistically, this will be shown in the leveling out of fluctuation. In reality, deeds will have less and less chance to stem the tide of behavior, and events will more and more lose their significance, that is, their capacity to illuminate historical time. Statistical uniformity is by no means a harmless scientific ideal; it is the no longer secret political ideal of a society which, entirely submerged in the routine of everyday living, is at peace with the scientific outlook inherent in its very existence.

The uniform behavior that lends itself to statistical determination, and therefore to scientifically correct prediction, can hardly be explained by the liberal hypothesis of a natural "harmony of interests," the foundation of "classical" economics; it was not Karl Marx but the liberal economists themselves who had to introduce the "communistic fiction," that is, to assume that there is one interest of society as a whole which with "an invisible hand" guides the behavior of men and produces the harmony of their conflicting interests.[36] The difference between Marx and his forerunners was only that he took the reality of conflict, as it presented itself in the society of his time, as seriously as the hypothetical fiction of harmony; he was right in concluding that the "socialization of man" would produce automatically a harmony of all interests, and was only more courageous than his liberal teachers when he proposed to establish in reality the "communistic fiction" underlying all economic theories. What Marx did not—and, at his time, could not—understand was that the germs of communistic society were present in the reality of a national household, and that their full development was not hindered by any class-interest as such, but only by the already obsolete monarchical structure of the nation-state. Obviously, what prevented society from smooth functioning was only certain traditional remnants that interfered and still influenced the behavior of "backward" classes. From the viewpoint of society, these were merely disturbing factors in the way of a full development of "social forces"; they no longer corresponded to reality and were therefore, in a sense, much more "fictitious" than the scientific "fiction" of one interest.

A complete victory of society will always produce some sort of "communistic fiction," whose outstanding political characteristic is that it is indeed ruled by an "invisible hand," namely, by nobody. What we traditionally call state and government gives place here to pure administration—a state of affairs which Marx rightly predicted as the "withering away of the state," though he was wrong in assuming that only a revolution could bring it about, and even more wrong when he believed that this complete victory of society would mean the eventual emergence of the "realm of freedom."[37]

To gauge the extent of society's victory in the modern age, its early substitution of behavior for action and its eventual substitution of bureaucracy, the rule of nobody, for personal rulership, it may be well to recall that its initial science of economics, which substitutes patterns of behavior only in this rather limited field of human activity, was finally followed by the all-comprehensive pretension of the social sciences which, as "behavioral sciences," aim to reduce man as a whole, in all his activities, to the level of a conditioned and behaving animal. If economics is the science of society in its early stages, when it could impose its rules of behavior only on sections of the population and on parts of their activities, the rise of the "behavioral sciences" indicates clearly the final stage of this development, when mass society has devoured all strata of the nation and "social behavior" has become the standard for all regions of life.

Since the rise of society, since the admission of household and housekeeping activities to the public realm, an irresistible tendency to grow, to devour the older realms of the political and private as well as the more recently established sphere of intimacy, has been one of the outstanding characteristics of the new realm. This constant growth, whose no less constant acceleration we can observe over at least three centuries, derives its strength from the fact that through society it is the life process itself which in one form or another has been channeled into the public realm. The private realm of the household was the sphere where the necessities of life, of individual survival as well as of continuity of the species, were taken care of and guaranteed. One of the characteristics of privacy, prior to the discovery of the intimate, was that man existed in this sphere not as a truly human being but only as a specimen of the animal species man-kind. This, precisely, was the ultimate reason for the tremendous contempt held for it by antiquity. The emergence of society has changed the estimate of this whole sphere but has hardly transformed its nature. The monolithic character of every type of society, its conformism which allows for only one interest and one opinion, is ultimately rooted in the one-ness of man-kind. It is because this one-ness of man-kind is not fantasy and not even merely a scientific hypothesis, as in the "communistic fiction" of classical economics, that mass society, where man as a social animal rules supreme and where apparently the survival of the species could be guaranteed on a world-wide scale, can at the same time threaten humanity with extinction.

Perhaps the clearest indication that society constitutes the public organization of the life process itself may be found in the fact that in a relatively short time the new social realm transformed all modern communities into societies of laborers and jobholders; in other words, they became at once centered around the one activity necessary to sustain life. (To have a society of laborers, it is of course not necessary that every member actually be a laborer or worker—not even the emancipation of the working class and the enormous potential power which majority rule accords to it are decisive here—but only that all members consider whatever they do primarily as a way to sustain their own lives and those of their families.) Society is the form in which the fact of mutual dependence for the sake of life and nothing else assumes public significance and where the activities connected with sheer survival are permitted to appear in public.

Whether an activity is performed in private or in public is by no means a matter of indifference. Obviously, the character of the public realm must change in accordance with the activities admitted into it, but to a large extent the activity itself changes its own nature too. The laboring activity, though under all circumstances connected with the life process in its most elementary, biological sense, remained stationary for thousands of years, imprisoned in the eternal recurrence of the life process to which it was tied. The admission of labor to public stature, far from eliminating its character as a process—which one might have expected, remembering that bodies politic have always been designed for permanence and their laws always understood as limitations imposed upon movement—has, on the contrary, liberated this process from its circular, monotonous recurrence and transformed it into a swiftly progressing development whose results have in a few centuries totally changed the whole inhabited world.

The moment laboring was liberated from the restrictions imposed by its banishment into the private realm—and this emancipation of labor was not a consequence of the emancipation of the working class, but preceded it—it was as though the growth element inherent in all organic life had completely overcome and overgrown the processes of decay by which organic life is checked and balanced in nature's household. The social realm, where the life process has established its own public domain, has let loose an unnatural growth, so to speak, of the natural; and it is against this growth, not merely against society but against a constantly growing social realm, that the private and intimate, on the one hand, and the political (in the narrower sense of the word), on the other, have proved incapable of defending themselves.

What we described as the unnatural growth of the natural is usually considered to be the constantly accelerated increase in the productivity of labor. The greatest single factor in this constant increase since its inception has been the organization of laboring, visible in the so-called division of labor, which preceded the industrial revolution; even the mechanization of labor processes, the second greatest factor in labor's productivity, is based upon it. Inasmuch as the organizational principle itself clearly derives from the public rather than the private realm, division of labor is precisely what happens to the laboring activity under conditions of the public realm and what could never have happened in the privacy of the household.[38] In no other sphere of life do we appear to have attained such excellence as in the revolutionary transformation of laboring, and this to the point where the verbal significance of the word itself (which always had been connected with hardly bearable "toil and trouble," with effort and pain and, consequently, with a deformation of the human body, so that only extreme misery and poverty could be its source), has begun to lose its meaning for us.[39] While dire necessity made labor indispensable to sustain life, excellence would have been the last thing to expect from it.

Excellence itself, *aretē* as the Greeks, *virtus* as the Romans would have called it, has always been assigned to the public realm where one could excel, could distinguish oneself from all others. Every activity performed in public can attain an excellence never matched in privacy; for excellence, by definition, the presence of others is always required, and this presence needs the formality of the public, constituted by one's peers, it cannot be the casual, familiar presence of one's equals or inferiors.[40] Not even the social realm—though it made excellence anonymous, emphasized the progress of mankind rather than the achievements of men, and changed the content of the public realm beyond recognition—has been able altogether to annihilate the connection between public performance and excellence. While we have become excellent in the laboring we perform in public, our capacity for action and speech has lost much of its former quality since the rise of the social realm banished these into the sphere of the intimate and the private. This curious discrepancy has not escaped public notice, where it is usually blamed upon an assumed time lag between our technical capacities and our general humanistic development or between the physical sciences, which change and control nature, and the social sciences, which do not yet know how to change and control society. Quite apart from other fallacies of the argument which have been pointed out so frequently that we need not repeat them, this criticism concerns only a possible change in the psychology of human beings—their so-called behavior patterns—not a change of the world they move in. And this psychological interpretation, for which the absence or presence of a public realm is as irrelevant as any tangible, worldly reality, seems rather doubtful in view of the fact that no activity can become excellent if the world does not provide a proper space for its exercise. Neither education nor ingenuity nor talent can replace the constituent elements of the public realm, which make it the proper place for human excellence.

7

THE PUBLIC REALM: THE COMMON

The term "public" signifies two closely interrelated but not altogether identical phenomena:

It means, first, that everything that appears in public can be seen and heard by everybody and has the widest possible publicity. For us, appearance—something that is being seen and heard by others as well as by ourselves—constitutes reality. Compared with the reality which comes from being seen and heard, even the greatest forces of intimate life—the passions of the heart, the thoughts of the mind, the delights of the senses—lead an uncertain, shadowy kind of existence unless and until they are transformed, deprivatized and deindividualized, as it were, into a shape to fit them for public appearance.[41] The most current of such transformations occurs in storytelling and generally in artistic transposition of individual experiences. But we do not need the form of the artist to witness this transfiguration. Each time we talk about things that can be experienced only in privacy or intimacy, we bring them out into a sphere where they will assume a kind of reality which, their intensity notwithstanding, they never could have had before. The presence of others who see what we see and hear what we hear assures us of the reality of the world and ourselves, and while the intimacy of a fully developed private life, such as had never been known before the rise of the modern age and the concomitant decline of the public realm, will always greatly intensify and enrich the whole scale of subjective emotions and private feelings, this intensification will always come to pass at the expense of the assurance of the reality of the world and men.

Indeed, the most intense feeling we know of, intense to the point of blotting out all other experiences, namely, the experience of great bodily pain, is at the same time the most private and least communicable of all. Not only is it perhaps the only experience which we are unable to transform into a shape fit for public appearance, it actually deprives us of our feeling for reality to such an extent that we can forget it more quickly and easily than anything else. There seems to be no bridge from the most radical subjectivity, in which I am no longer "recognizable," to the outer world of life.[42] Pain, in other words, truly a borderline experience between life as "being among men" (*inter homines esse*) and death, is so subjective and removed from the world of things and men that it cannot assume an appearance at all.[43]

Since our feeling for reality depends utterly upon appearance and therefore upon the existence of a public realm into which things can appear out of the darkness of sheltered existence, even the twilight which illuminates our private and intimate lives is ultimately derived from the much harsher light of the public realm. Yet there are a great many things which cannot withstand the implacable, bright light of the constant presence of others on the public scene; there, only what is considered to be relevant, worthy of being seen or heard, can be tolerated, so that the irrelevant becomes automatically a private matter. This, to be sure, does not mean that private concerns are generally irrelevant; on the contrary, we shall see that there are very relevant matters which can survive only in the realm of the private. For instance, love, in distinction from friendship, is killed, or rather extinguished, the moment it is displayed in public. ("Never seek to tell thy love/Love that never told can be.") Because of its inherent worldlessness, love can only become false and perverted when it is used for political purposes such as the change or salvation of the world.

What the public realm considers irrelevant can have such an extraordinary and infectious charm that a whole people may adopt it as their way of life, without for that reason changing its essentially private character. Modern enchantment with "small things," though preached by early twentieth-century poetry in almost all European tongues, has found its classical presentation in the *petit bonheur* of the French people. Since the decay of their once great and glorious public realm, the French have become masters in the art of being happy among "small things," within the space of their own four walls, between chest and bed, table and chair, dog and cat and flowerpot, extending to these things a care and tenderness which, in a world where rapid industrialization constantly kills off the things of yesterday to produce today's objects, may even appear to be the world's last, purely humane corner. This enlargement of the private, the enchantment, as it were, of a whole people, does not make it public, does not constitute a public realm, but, on the contrary, means only that the public realm has almost completely receded, so that greatness has given way to charm everywhere; for while the public realm may be great, it cannot be charming precisely because it is unable to harbor the irrelevant.

Second, the term "public" signifies the world itself, in so far as it is common to all of us and distinguished from our privately owned place in it. This world, however, is not identical with the earth or with nature, as the limited space for the movement of men and the general condition of organic life. It is related, rather, to the human artifact, the fabrication of human hands, as well as to affairs which go on among those who inhabit the man-made world together. To live together in the world means essentially that a world of things is between those who have it in common, as a table is located between those who sit around it; the world like every in-between, relates and separates men at the same time.

The public realm, as the common world, gathers us together and yet prevents our falling over each other, so to speak. What makes mass society so difficult to bear is not the number of people involved, or at least not primarily, but the fact that the world between them has lost its power to gather them together, to relate and to separate them. The weirdness of this situation resembles a spiritualistic séance where a number of people gathered around a table might suddenly, through some magic trick, see the table vanish from their midst, so that two persons sitting opposite each other were no longer separated but also would be entirely unrelated to each other by anything tangible.

Historically, we know of only one principle that was ever devised to keep a community of people together who had lost their interest in the common world and felt themselves no longer related and separated by it. To find a bond between people strong enough to replace the world was the main political task of early Christian philosophy, and it was Augustine who proposed to found not only the Christian "brotherhood" but all human relationships on charity. But this charity, though its worldlessness clearly corresponds to the general human experience of love, is at the same time clearly distinguished from it in being something which, like the world, is between men: "Even robbers have between them [*inter se*] what they call charity."[44] This surprising illustration of the Christian political principle is in fact very well chosen, because the bond of charity between people, while it is incapable of founding a public realm of its own, is quite adequate to the main Christian principle of worldlessness and is admirably fit to carry a group of essentially worldless people through the world, a group of saints or a group of criminals, provided only it is understood that the world itself is doomed and that every activity in it is undertaken with the proviso *quamdiu mundus durat* ("as long as the world lasts").[45] The unpolitical, non-public character of the Christian community was early defined in the demand that it should form a *corpus,* a "body," whose members were to be related to each other like brothers of the same family.[46] The structure of communal life was modeled on the relationships between the members of a family because these were known to be nonpolitical and even antipolitical. A public realm had never come into being between the members of a family, and it was therefore not likely to develop from Christian community life if this life was ruled by the principle of charity and nothing else. Even then, as we know from the history and the rules of the monastic orders—the only communities in which the principle of charity as a political device was ever tried—the danger that the activities undertaken under "the necessity of present life" (*necessitas vitae praesentis*)[47] would lead by themselves, because they were performed in the presence of others, to the establishment of a kind of counterworld, a public realm within the orders themselves, was great enough to require additional rules and regulations, the most relevant one in our context being the prohibition of excellence and its subsequent pride.[48]

Worldlessness as a political phenomenon is possible only on the assumption that the world will not last; on this assumption, however, it is almost inevitable that worldlessness, in one form or another, will begin to dominate the political scene. This happened after the downfall of the Roman Empire and, albeit for quite other reasons and in very different, perhaps even more disconsolate forms, it seems to happen again in our own days. The Christian abstention from worldly things is by no means the only conclusion one can draw from the conviction that the human artifice, a product of mortal hands, is as mortal as its makers. This, on the contrary, may also intensify the enjoyment and consumption of the things of the world, all manners of intercourse in which the world is not primarily understood to be the *koinon,* that which is common to all. Only the existence of a public realm and the world's subsequent transformation into a community of things which gathers men together and relates them to each other depends entirely on permanence. If the world is to contain a public space, it cannot be erected for one generation and planned for the living only; it must transcend the life-span of mortal men.

Without this transcendence into a potential earthly immortality, no politics, strictly speaking, no common world and no public realm, is possible. For unlike the common good as Christianity understood it—the salvation of one's soul as a concern common to all—the common world is what we enter when we are born and what we leave behind when we die. It transcends our life-span into past and future alike; it was there before we came and will outlast our brief sojourn in it. It is what we have in common not only with those who live with us, but also with those who were here before and with those who will come after us. But such a common world can survive the coming and going of the generations only to the extent that it appears in public. It is the publicity of the public realm which can absorb and make shine through the centuries whatever men may want to save from the natural ruin of time. Through many ages before us—but now not any more—men entered the public realm because they wanted something of their own or something they had in common with others to be more permanent than their earthly lives. (Thus, the curse of slavery consisted not only in being deprived of freedom and of visibility, but also in the fear of these obscure people themselves "that from being obscure they should pass away leaving no trace that they have existed.")[49] There is perhaps no clearer testimony to the loss of the public realm in the modern age than the almost complete loss of authentic concern with immortality, a loss somewhat overshadowed by the simultaneous loss of the metaphysical concern with eternity. The latter, being the concern of the philosophers and the *vita contemplativa,* must remain outside our present considerations. But the former is testified to by the current classification of striving for immortality with the private vice of vanity. Under modern conditions, it is indeed so unlikely that anybody should earnestly aspire to an earthly immortality that we probably are justified in thinking it is nothing but vanity.

The famous passage in Aristotle, "Considering human affairs, one must not . . . consider man as he is and not consider what is mortal in mortal things, but think about them [only] to the extent that they have the possibility of immortalizing," occurs very properly in his political writings.[50] For the *polis* was for the Greeks, as the *res publica* was for the Romans, first of all their guarantee against the futility of individual life, the space protected against this futility and reserved for the relative permanence, if not immortality, of mortals.

What the modern age thought of the public realm, after the spectacular rise of society to public prominence, was expressed by Adam Smith when, with disarming sincerity, he mentions "that unprosperous race of men commonly called men of letters" for whom "public admiration . . . makes always a part of their reward . . . , a considerable part . . . in the profession of physic; a still greater perhaps in that of law; in poetry and philosophy it makes almost the whole."[51] Here it is self-evident that public admiration and monetary reward are of the same nature and can become substitutes for each other. Public admiration, too, is something to be used and consumed, and status, as we would say today, fulfils one need as food fulfils another: public admiration is consumed by individual vanity as food is consumed by hunger. Obviously, from this viewpoint the test of reality does not lie in the public presence of others, but rather in the greater or lesser urgency of needs to whose existence or non-existence nobody can ever testify except the one who happens to suffer them. And since the need for food has its demonstrable basis of reality in the life process itself, it is also obvious that the entirely subjective pangs of hunger are more real than "vainglory," as Hobbes used to call the need for public admiration. Yet, even if these needs, through some miracle of sympathy, were shared by others, their very futility would prevent their ever establishing anything so solid and durable as a common world. The point then is not that there is a lack of public admiration for poetry and philosophy in the modern world, but that such admiration does not constitute a space in which things are saved from destruction by time. The futility of public admiration, which daily is consumed in ever greater quantities, on the contrary, is such that monetary reward, one of the most futile things there is, can become more "objective" and more real.

As distinguished from this "objectivity," whose only basis is money as a common denominator for the fulfilment of all needs, the reality of the public realm relies on the simultaneous presence of innumerable perspectives and aspects in which the common world presents itself and for which no common measurement or denominator can ever be devised. For though the common world is the common meeting ground of all, those who are present have different locations in it, and the location of one can no more coincide with the location of another than the location of two objects. Being seen and being heard by others derive their significance from the fact that everybody sees and hears from a different position. This is the meaning of public life, compared to which even the richest and most satisfying family life can offer only the prolongation or multiplication of one's own position with its attending aspects and perspectives. The subjectivity of privacy can be prolonged and multiplied in a family, it can even become so strong that its weight is felt in the public realm; but this family "world" can never replace the reality rising out of the sum total of aspects presented by one object to a multitude of spectators. Only where things can be seen by many in a variety of aspects without changing their identity, so that those who are gathered around them know they see sameness in utter diversity, can worldly reality truly and reliably appear.

Under the conditions of a common world, reality is not guaranteed primarily by the "common nature" of all men who constitute it, but rather by the fact that, differences of position and the resulting variety of perspectives notwithstanding, everybody is always concerned with the same object. If the sameness of the object can no longer be discerned, no common nature of men, least of all the unnatural conformism of a mass society, can prevent the destruction of the common world, which is usually preceded by the destruction of the many aspects in which it presents itself to human plurality. This can happen under conditions of radical isolation, where nobody can any longer agree with anybody else, as is usually the case in tyrannies. But it may also happen under conditions of mass society or mass hysteria, where we see all people suddenly behave as though they were members of one family, each multiplying and prolonging the perspective of his neighbor. In both instances, men have become entirely private, that is, they have been deprived of seeing and hearing others, of being seen and being heard by them. They are all imprisoned in the subjectivity of their own singular experience, which does not cease to be singular if the same experience is multiplied innumerable times. The end of the common world has come when it is seen only under one aspect and is permitted to present itself in only one perspective.

8
THE PRIVATE REALM: PROPERTY

It is with respect to this multiple significance of the public realm that the term "private," in its original privative sense, has meaning. To live an entirely private life means above all to be deprived of things essential to a truly human life: to be deprived of the reality that comes from being seen and heard by others, to be deprived of an "objective" relationship with them that comes from being related to and separated from them through the intermediary of a common world of things, to be deprived of the possibility of achieving something more permanent than life itself. The privation of privacy lies in the absence of others; as far as they are concerned, private man does not appear, and therefore it is as though he did not exist. Whatever he does remains without significance and consequence to others, and what matters to him is without interest to other people.

Under modern circumstances, this deprivation of "objective" relationships to others and of a reality guaranteed through them has become the mass phenomenon of loneliness, where it has assumed its most extreme and most antihuman form.[52] The reason for this extremity is that mass society not only destroys the public realm but the private as well, deprives men not only of their place in the world but of their private home, where they once felt sheltered against the world and where, at any rate, even those excluded from the world could find a substitute in the warmth of the hearth and the limited reality of family life. The full development of the life of hearth and family into an inner and private space we owe to the extraordinary political sense of the Roman people who, unlike the Greeks, never sacrificed the private to the public, but on the contrary understood that these two realms could exist only in the form of coexistence. And although the conditions of slaves probably were hardly better in Rome than in Athens, it is quite characteristic that a Roman writer should have believed that to slaves the household of the master was what the *res publica* was to citizens.[53] Yet no matter how bearable private life in the family might have been, it could obviously never be more than a substitute, even though the private realm in Rome as in Athens offered plenty of room for activities which we today class higher than political activity, such as the accumulation of wealth in Greece or the devotion to art and science in Rome. This "liberal" attitude, which could under certain circumstances result in very prosperous and highly educated slaves, meant only that to be prosperous had no reality in the Greek *polis* and to be a philosopher was without much consequence in the Roman republic.[54]

It is a matter of course that the privative trait of privacy, the consciousness of being deprived of something essential in a life spent exclusively in the restricted sphere of the household, should have been weakened almost to the point of extinction by the rise of Christianity. Christian morality, as distinguished from its fundamental religious precepts, has always insisted that everybody should mind his own business and that political responsibility constituted first of all a burden, undertaken exclusively for the sake of the well-being and salvation of those it freed from worry about public affairs.[55] It is surprising that this attitude should have survived into the secular modern age to such an extent that Karl Marx, who in this as in other respects only summed up, conceptualized, and transformed into a program the underlying assumptions of two hundred years of modernity, could eventually predict and hope for the "withering away" of the whole public realm. The difference between the Christian and socialist viewpoints in this respect, the one viewing government as a necessary evil because of man's sinfulness and the other hoping to abolish it eventually, is not a difference in estimate of the public sphere itself, but of human nature. What is impossible to perceive from either point of view is that Marx's "withering away of the state" had been preceded by a withering away of the public realm, or rather by its transformation into a very restricted sphere of government; in Marx's day, this government had already begun to wither further, that is, to be transformed into a nation-wide "housekeeping," until in our own day it has begun to disappear altogether into the even more restricted, impersonal sphere of administration.

It seems to be in the nature of the relationship between the public and private realms that the final stage of the disappearance of the public realm should be accompanied by the threatened liquidation of the private realm as well. Nor is it an accident that the whole discussion has eventually turned into an argument about the desirability or undesirability of privately owned property. For the word "private" in connection with property, even in terms of ancient political thought, immediately loses its privative character and much of its opposition to the public realm in general; property apparently possesses certain qualifications which, though lying in the private realm, were always thought to be of utmost importance to the political body.

The profound connection between private and public, manifest on its most elementary level in the question of private property, is likely to be misunderstood today because of the modern equation of property and wealth on one side and propertylessness and poverty on the other. This misunderstanding is all the more annoying as both, property as well as wealth, are historically of greater relevance to the public realm than any other private matter or concern and have played, at least formally, more or less the same role as the chief condition for admission to the public realm and full-fledged citizenship. It is therefore easy to forget that wealth and property, far from being the same, are of an entirely different nature. The present emergence everywhere of actually or potentially very wealthy societies which at the same time are essentially propertyless, because the wealth of any single individual consists of his share in the annual income of society as a whole, clearly shows how little these two things are connected.

Prior to the modern age, which began with the expropriation of the poor and then proceeded to emancipate the new propertyless classes, all civilizations have rested upon the sacredness of private property. Wealth, on the contrary, whether privately owned or publicly distributed, had never been sacred before. Originally, property meant no more or less than to have one's location in a particular part of the world and therefore to belong to the body politic, that is, to be the head of one of the families which together constituted the public realm. This piece of privately owned world was so completely identical with the family who owned it[56] that the expulsion of a citizen could mean not merely the confiscation of his estate but the actual destruction of the building itself.[57] The wealth of a foreigner or a slave was under no circumstances a substitute for this

property,[58] and poverty did not deprive the head of a family of this location in the world and the citizenship resulting from it. In early times, if he
happened to lose his location, he almost automatically lost his citizenship
and the protection of the law as well.[59] The sacredness of this privacy was
like the sacredness of the hidden, namely, of birth and death, the beginning and end of the mortals who, like all living creatures, grow out of and
return to the darkness of an underworld.[60] The non-privative trait of the
household realm originally lay in its being the realm of birth and death
which must be hidden from the public realm because it harbors the things
hidden from human eyes and impenetrable to human knowledge.[61] It is
hidden because man does not know where he comes from when he is
born and where he goes when he dies.

Not the interior of this realm, which remains hidden and of no public significance, but its exterior appearance is important for the city as
well, and it appears in the realm of the city through the boundaries between one household and the other. The law originally was identified
with this boundary line,[62] which in ancient times was still actually a space,
a kind of no man's land[63] between the private and the public, sheltering
and protecting both realms while, at the same time, separating them from
each other. The law of the *polis,* to be sure, transcended this ancient understanding from which, however, it retained its original spatial significance. The law of the city-state was neither the content of political action
(the idea that political activity is primarily legislating, though Roman in
origin, is essentially modern and found its greatest expression in Kant's
political philosophy) nor was it a catalogue of prohibitions, resting, as all
modern laws still do, upon the Thou Shalt Nots of the Decalogue. It was
quite literally a wall, without which there might have been an agglomer-
ation of houses, a town (*asty*), but not a city; a political community. This
wall-like law was sacred, but only the inclosure was political.[64] Without it
a public realm could no more exist than a piece of property without a
fence to hedge it in; the one harbored and inclosed political life as the
other sheltered and protected the biological life process of the family.[65]

It is therefore not really accurate to say that private property, prior to
the modern age, was thought to be a self-evident condition for admission
to the public realm; it is much more than that. Privacy was like the other,
the dark and hidden side of the public realm, and while to be political
meant to attain the highest possibility of human existence, to have no private place of one's own (like a slave) meant to be no longer human.

Of an altogether different and historically later origin is the political
significance of private wealth from which one draws the means of one's
livelihood. We mentioned earlier the ancient identification of necessity

with the private realm of the household, where each had to master the necessities of life for himself. The free man, who disposed of his own privacy and was not, like a slave, at the disposition of a master, could still be "forced" by poverty. Poverty forces the free man to act like a slave.[66] Private wealth, therefore, became a condition for admission to public life not because its owner was engaged in accumulating it but, on the contrary, because it assured with reasonable certainty that its owner would not have to engage in providing for himself the means of use and consumption and was free for public activity.[67] Public life, obviously, was possible only after the much more urgent needs of life itself had been taken care of. The means to take care of them was labor, and the wealth of a person therefore was frequently counted in terms of the number of laborers, that is, slaves, he owned.[68] To own property meant here to be master over one's own necessities of life and therefore potentially to be a free person, free to transcend his own life and enter the world all have in common.

Only with the emergence of such a common world in concrete tangibility, that is, with the rise of the city-state, could this kind of private ownership acquire its eminent political significance, and it is therefore almost a matter of course that the famous "disdain for menial occupations" is not yet to be found in the Homeric world. If the property-owner chose to enlarge his property instead of using it up in leading a political life, it was as though he willingly sacrificed his freedom and became voluntarily what the slave was against his own will, a servant of necessity.[69]

Up to the beginning of the modern age, this kind of property had never been held to be sacred, and only where wealth as the source of income coincided with the piece of land on which a family was located, that is, in an essentially agricultural society, could these two types of property coincide to such an extent that all property assumed the character of sacredness. Modern advocates of private property, at any rate, who unanimously understand it as privately owned wealth and nothing else, have little cause to appeal to a tradition according to which there could be no free public realm without a proper establishment and protection of privacy. For the enormous and still proceeding accumulation of wealth in modern society, which was started by expropriation—the expropriation of the peasant classes which in turn was the almost accidental consequence of the expropriation of Church and monastic property after the Reformation[70]—has never shown much consideration for private property but has sacrificed it whenever it came into conflict with the accumulation of wealth. Proudhon's dictum that property is theft has a solid basis of truth in the origins of modern capitalism; it is all the more significant that even Proudhon hesitated to accept the doubtful remedy of general expropriation, because he knew quite well that the abolition of private property, while it might cure the evil of poverty, was only too likely to invite the greater evil of tyranny.[71] Since he did not distinguish between property and wealth, his two insights appear in his work like contradictions, which in fact they are not. Individual appropriation of wealth will in the long run respect private property no more than socialization of the accumulation process. It is not an invention of Karl Marx but actually in the very nature of this society itself that privacy in every sense can only hinder the development of social "productivity" and that considerations of private ownership therefore should be overruled in favor of the ever-increasing process of social wealth.[72]

9

THE SOCIAL AND THE PRIVATE

What we called earlier the rise of the social coincided historically with the transformation of the private care for private property into a public concern. Society, when it first entered the public realm, assumed the disguise of an organization of property-owners who, instead of claiming access to the public realm because of their wealth, demanded protection from it for the accumulation of more wealth. In the words of Bodin, government belonged to kings and property to subjects, so that it was the duty of the kings to rule in the interest of their subjects' property. "The commonwealth," as has recently been pointed out, "largely existed for the common *wealth*."[73]

When this common wealth, the result of activities formerly banished to the privacy of the households, was permitted to take over the public realm, private possessions—which are essentially much less permanent and much more vulnerable to the mortality of their owners than the common world, which always grows out of the past and is intended to last for future generations—began to undermine the durability of the world. It is true that wealth can be accumulated to a point where no individual lifespan can use it up, so that the family rather than the individual becomes its owner. Yet wealth remains something to be used and consumed no matter how many individual life-spans it may sustain. Only when wealth became capital, whose chief function was to generate more capital, did private property equal or come close to the permanence inherent in the commonly shared world.[74] However, this permanence is of a different nature; it is the permanence of a process rather than the permanence of a stable structure. Without the process of accumulation, wealth would at once fall back into the opposite process of disintegration through use and consumption.

Common wealth, therefore, can never become common in the sense we speak of a common world; it remained, or rather was intended to remain, strictly private. Only the government, appointed to shield the private owners from each other in the competitive struggle for more wealth, was common. The obvious contradiction in this modern concept of government, where the only thing people have in common is their private interests, need no longer bother us as it still bothered Marx, since we know that the contradiction between private and public, typical of the initial stages of the modern age, has been a temporary phenomenon which introduced the utter extinction of the very difference between the private and public realms, the submersion of both in the sphere of the social. By the same token, we are in a far better position to realize the consequences for human existence when both the public and private spheres of life are gone, the public because it has become a function of the private and the private because it has become the only common concern left.

Seen from this viewpoint, the modern discovery of intimacy seems a flight from the whole outer world into the inner subjectivity of the individual, which formerly had been sheltered and protected by the private realm. The dissolution of this realm into the social may most conveniently be watched in the progressing transformation of immobile into mobile property until eventually the distinction between property and wealth, between the *fungibiles* and the *consumptibiles* of Roman law, loses all significance because every tangible, "fungible" thing has become an object of "consumption"; it lost its private use value which was determined by its location and acquired an exclusively social value determined through its ever-changing exchangeability whose fluctuation could itself be fixed only temporarily by relating it to the common denominator of money.[75] Closely connected with this social evaporation of the tangible was the most revolutionary modern contribution to the concept of property, according to which property was not a fixed and firmly located part of the world acquired by its owner in one way or another but, on the contrary, had its source in man himself, in his possession of a body and his indisputable ownership of the strength of this body, which Marx called "labor-power."

Thus modern property lost its worldly character and was located in the person himself, that is, in what an individual could lose only along with his life. Historically, Locke's assumption that the labor of one's body is the origin of property is more than doubtful; but in view of the fact that we already live under conditions where our only reliable property is our skill and our labor power, it is more than likely that it will become true. For wealth, after it became a public concern, has grown to such proportions that it is almost unmanageable by private ownership. It is as though the public realm had taken its revenge against those who tried to use it for their private interests. The greatest threat here, however, is not the abolition of private ownership of wealth but the abolition of private property in the sense of a tangible, worldly place of one's own.

In order to understand the danger to human existence from the elimination of the private realm, for which the intimate is not a very reliable substitute, it may be best to consider those nonprivate traits of privacy which are older than, and independent of, the discovery of intimacy. The difference between what we have in common and what we own privately is first that our private possessions, which we use and consume daily, are much more urgently needed than any part of the common world; without property, as Locke pointed out, "the common is of no use."[76] The same necessity that, from the standpoint of the public realm, shows only its negative aspect as a deprivation of freedom possesses a driving force whose urgency is unmatched by the so-called higher desires and aspirations of man; not only will it always be the first among man's needs and worries, it will also prevent the apathy and disappearance of initiative which so obviously threatens all overly wealthy communities.[77] Necessity and life are so intimately related and connected that life itself is threatened where necessity is altogether eliminated. For the elimination of necessity, far from resulting automatically in the establishment of freedom, only blurs the distinguishing line between freedom and necessity. (Modern discussions of freedom, where freedom is never understood as an objective state of human existence but either presents an unsolvable problem of subjectivity, of an entirely undetermined or determined will, or develops out of necessity, all point to the fact that the objective, tangible difference between being free and being forced by necessity is no longer perceived.)

The second outstanding non-privative characteristic of privacy is that the four walls of one's private property offer the only reliable hiding place from the common public world, not only from everything that goes on in it but also from its very publicity, from being seen and being heard. A life spent entirely in public, in the presence of others, becomes, as we would say, shallow. While it retains its visibility, it loses the quality of rising into sight from some darker ground which must remain hidden if it is not to lose its depth in a very real, non-subjective sense. The only efficient way to guarantee the darkness of what needs to be hidden against the light of publicity is private property, a privately owned place to hide in.[78]

While it is only natural that the non-privative traits of privacy should appear most clearly when men are threatened with deprivation of it, the practical treatment of private property by premodern political bodies indicates clearly that men have always been conscious of their existence and importance. This, however, did not make them protect the activities in the private realm directly, but rather the boundaries separating the privately owned from other parts of the world, most of all from the common world itself. The distinguishing mark of modern political and economic theory, on the other hand, in so far as it regards private property as a crucial issue, has been its stress upon the private activities of property-owners and their need of government protection for the sake of accumulation of wealth at the expense of the tangible property itself. What is important to the public realm, however, is not the more or less enterprising spirit of private businessmen but the fences around the houses and gardens of citizens. The invasion of privacy by society, the "socialization of man" (Marx), is most efficiently carried through by means of expropriation, but this is not the only way. Here, as in other respects, the revolutionary measures of socialism or communism can very well be replaced by a slower and no less certain "withering away" of the private realm in general and of private property in particular.

The distinction between the private and public realms, seen from the viewpoint of privacy rather than of the body politic, equals the distinction between things that should be shown and things that should be hidden. Only the modern age, in its rebellion against society, has discovered how rich and manifold the realm of the hidden can be under the conditions of intimacy; but it is striking that from the beginning of history to our own time it has always been the bodily part of human existence that needed to be hidden in privacy, all things connected with the necessity of the life process itself, which prior to the modern age comprehended all activities serving the subsistence of the individual and the survival of the species. Hidden away were the laborers who "with their bodies minister to the [bodily] needs of life,"[79] and the women who with their bodies guarantee the physical survival of the species. Women and slaves belonged to the same category and were hidden away not only because they were somebody else's property but because their life was "laborious," devoted to bodily functions.[80] In the beginning of the modern age, when "free" labor had lost its hiding place in the privacy of the household, the laborers were hidden away and segregated from the community like criminals behind high walls and under constant supervision.[81] The fact that the modern age emancipated the working classes and the women at nearly the same historical moment must certainly be counted among the characteristics of an age which no longer believes that bodily functions and material concerns should be hidden. It is all the more symptomatic of the nature of these phenomena that the few remnants of strict privacy even in our own civilization relate to "necessities" in the original sense of being necessitated by having a body.

1 0
THE LOCATION OF HUMAN ACTIVITIES

Although the distinction between private and public coincides with the opposition of necessity and freedom, of futility and permanence, and, finally, of shame and honor, it is by no means true that only the necessary, the futile, and the shameful have their proper place in the private realm. The most elementary meaning of the two realms indicates that there are things that need to be hidden and others that need to be displayed publicly if they are to exist at all. If we look at these things, regardless of where we find them in any given civilization, we shall see that each human activity points to its proper location in the world. This is true for the chief activities of the *vita activa,* labor, work, and action; but there is one, admittedly extreme, example of this phenomenon, whose advantage for illustration is that it played a considerable role in political theory.

Goodness in an absolute sense, as distinguished from the "good-for" or the "excellent" in Greek and Roman antiquity, became known in our civilization only with the rise of Christianity. Since then, we know of good works as one important variety of possible human action. The well-known antagonism between early Christianity and the *res publica,* so admirably summed up in Tertullian's formula: *nec ulla magis res aliena quam publica* ("no matter is more alien to us than what matters publicly"),[82] is usually and rightly understood as a consequence of early eschatological expectations that lost their immediate significance only after experience had taught that even the downfall of the Roman Empire did not mean the end of the world.[83] Yet the otherworldliness of Christianity has still another root, perhaps even more intimately related to the teachings of Jesus of Nazareth, and at any rate so independent of the belief in the perishability of the world that one is tempted to see in it the true inner reason why Christian alienation from the world could so easily survive the obvious non-fulfilment of its eschatological hopes.

The one activity taught by Jesus in word and deed is the activity of goodness, and goodness obviously harbors a tendency to hide from being seen or heard. Christian hostility toward the public realm, the tendency at

least of early Christians to lead a life as far removed from the public realm
as possible, can also be understood as a self-evident consequence of devotion to good works, independent of all beliefs and expectations. For it is
manifest that the moment a good work becomes known and public, it
loses its specific character of goodness, of being done for nothing but
goodness' sake. When goodness appears openly, it is no longer goodness,
though it may still be useful as organized charity or an act of solidarity.
Therefore: "Take heed that ye do not your alms before men, to be seen
of them." Goodness can exist only when it is not perceived, not even by
its author; whoever sees himself performing a good work is no longer
good, but at best a useful member of society or a dutiful member of a
church. Therefore: "Let not thy left hand know what thy right hand
doeth."

It may be this curious negative quality of goodness, the lack of outward phenomenal manifestation, that makes Jesus of Nazareth's appearance in history such a profoundly paradoxical event; it certainly seems to
be the reason why he thought and taught that no man can be good:
"Why callest thou me good? none is good, save one, that is, God."[84] The
same conviction finds its expression in the talmudic story of the thirty-six
righteous men, for the sake of whom God saves the world and who also
are known to nobody, least of all to themselves. We are reminded of
Socrates' great insight that no man can be wise, out of which love for wisdom, or philo-sophy, was born; the whole life story of Jesus seems to testify how love for goodness arises out of the insight that no man can be
good.

Love of wisdom and love of goodness, if they resolve themselves into
the activities of philosophizing and doing good works, have in common
that they come to an immediate end, cancel themselves, so to speak,
whenever it is assumed that man can *be* wise or *be* good. Attempts to bring
into being that which can never survive the fleeting moment of the deed
itself have never been lacking and have always led into absurdity. The
philosophers of late antiquity who demanded of themselves to *be* wise
were absurd when they claimed to be happy when roasted alive in the famous Phaleric Bull. And no less absurd is the Christian demand to *be* good
and to turn the other cheek, when not taken metaphorically but tried as a
real way of life.

But the similarity between the activities springing from love of goodness and love of wisdom ends here. Both, it is true, stand in a certain opposition to the public realm, but the case of goodness is much more
extreme in this respect and therefore of greater relevance in our context.
Only goodness must go into absolute hiding and flee all appearance if it is

not to be destroyed. The philosopher, even if he decides with Plato to leave the "cave" of human affairs, does not have to hide from himself; on the contrary, under the sky of ideas he not only finds the true essences of everything that is, but also himself, in the dialogue between "me and myself" (*eme emautō*) in which Plato apparently saw the essence of thought.[85] To be in solitude means to be with one's self, and thinking, therefore, though it may be the most solitary of all activities, is never altogether without a partner and without company.

The man, however, who is in love with goodness can never afford to lead a solitary life, and yet his living with others and for others must remain essentially without testimony and lacks first of all the company of himself. He is not solitary, but lonely; when living with others he must hide from them and cannot even trust himself to witness what he is doing. The philosopher can always rely upon his thoughts to keep him company, whereas good deeds can never keep anybody company; they must be forgotten the moment they are done, because even memory will destroy their quality of being "good." Moreover, thinking, because it can be remembered, can crystallize into thought, and thoughts, like all things that owe their existence to remembrance, can be transformed into tangible objects which, like the written page or the printed book, become part of the human artifice. Good works, because they must be forgotten instantly, can never become part of the world; they come and go, leaving no trace. They truly are not of this world.

It is this worldlessness inherent in good works that makes the lover of goodness an essentially religious figure and that makes goodness, like wisdom in antiquity, an essentially non-human, superhuman quality. And yet love of goodness, unlike love of wisdom, is not restricted to the experience of the few, just as loneliness, unlike solitude, is within the range of every man's experience. In a sense, therefore, goodness and loneliness are of much greater relevance to politics than wisdom and solitude, yet only solitude can become an authentic way of life in the figure of the philosopher, whereas the much more general experience of loneliness is so contradictory to the human condition of plurality that it is simply unbearable for any length of time and needs the company of God, the only imaginable witness of good works, if it is not to annihilate human existence altogether. The otherworldliness of religious experience, in so far as it is truly the experience of love in the sense of an activity, and not the much more frequent one of beholding passively a revealed truth, manifests itself within the world itself; this, like all other activities, does not leave the world, but must be performed within it. But this manifestation, though it appears in the space where other activities are performed and depends upon it, is of an actively negative nature; fleeing the world and hiding from its inhabitants, it negates the space the world offers to men, and most of all that public part of it where everything and everybody are seen and heard by others.

Goodness, therefore, as a consistent way of life, is not only impossible within the confines of the public realm, it is even destructive of it. Nobody perhaps has been more sharply aware of this ruinous quality of doing good than Machiavelli, who, in a famous passage, dared to teach men "how not to be good."[86] Needless to add, he did not say and did not mean that men must be taught how to be bad; the criminal act, though for other reasons, must also flee being seen and heard by others. Machiavelli's criterion for political action was glory, the same as in classical antiquity, and badness can no more shine in glory than goodness. Therefore all methods by which "one may indeed gain power, but not glory" are bad.[87] Badness that comes out of hiding is impudent and directly destroys the common world; goodness that comes out of hiding and assumes a public role is no longer good, but corrupt in its own terms and will carry its own corruption wherever it goes. Thus, for Machiavelli, the reason for the Church's becoming a corrupting influence in Italian politics was her participation in secular affairs as such and not the individual corruptness of bishops and prelates. To him, the alternative posed by the problem of religious rule over the secular realm was inescapably this: either the public realm corrupted the religious body and thereby became itself corrupt, or the religious body remained uncorrupt and destroyed the public realm altogether. A reformed Church therefore was even more dangerous in Machiavelli's eyes, and he looked with great respect but greater apprehension upon the religious revival of his time, the "new orders" which, by "saving religion from being destroyed by the licentiousness of the prelates and heads of the Church," teach people to be good and not "to resist evil"—with the result that "wicked rulers do as much evil as they please."[88]

We chose the admittedly extreme example of doing good works, extreme because this activity is not even at home in the realm of privacy, in order to indicate that the historical judgments of political communities, by which each determined which of the activities of the *vita activa* should be shown in public and which be hidden in privacy, may have their correspondence in the nature of these activities themselves. By raising this question, I do not intend to attempt an exhaustive analysis of the activities of the *vita activa*, whose articulations have been curiously neglected by a tradition which considered it chiefly from the standpoint of the *vita con-templativa,* but to try to determine with some measure of assurance their political significance.

Notes

1. It seems quite striking that the Homeric gods act only with respect to men, ruling them from afar or interfering in their affairs. Conflicts and strife be-tween the gods also seem to arise chiefly from their part in human affairs or their conflicting partiality with respect to mortals. What then appears is a story in which men and gods act together, but the scene is set by the mortals, even when the decision is arrived at in the assembly of gods on Olympus. I think such a "co-operation" is indicated in the Homeric *erg' andrōn te theōn te* (*Odyssey* i. 338): the bard sings the deeds of gods and men, not stories of the gods and stories of men. Similarly, Hesiod's *Theogony* deals not with the deeds of gods but with the genesis of the world (116); it therefore tells how things came into being through begetting and giving birth (constantly recur-ring). The singer, servant of the Muses, sings "the glorious deeds of men of old and the blessed gods" (97 ff.), but nowhere, as far as I can see, the glori-ous deeds of the gods.

2. The quotation is from the Index Rerum to the Taurinian edition of Aquinas (1922). The word "politicus" does not occur in the text, but the Index sum-marizes Thomas' meaning correctly, as can be seen from *Summa theologica* i. 96. 4; ii. 2. 109. 3.

3. *Societas regni* in Livius, *societas sceleris* in Cornelius Nepos. Such an alliance could also be concluded for business purposes, and Aquinas still holds that a "true *societas*" between businessmen exists only "where the investor himself shares in the risk," that is, where the partnership is truly an alliance (see W. J. Ashley, *An Introduction to English Economic History and Theory* [1931], p. 419).

4. I use here and in the following the word "man-kind" to designate the human species, as distinguished from "mankind," which indicates the sum total of human beings.

5. Werner Jaeger, *Paideia* (1945), III, 111.

6. Although Fustel de Coulanges' chief thesis, according to the Introduction to *The Ancient City* (Anchor ed.; 1956), consists of demonstrating that "the same religion" formed the ancient family organization and the ancient city-state, he brings numerous references to the fact that the regime of the *gens* based on the religion of the family and the regime of the city "were in reality two an-tagonistic forms of government. . . . Either the city could not last, or it must in the course of time break up the family" (p. 252). The reason for the con-tradiction in this great book seems to me to be in Coulanges' attempt to treat Rome and the Greek city-states together; for his evidence and categories he relies chiefly on Roman institutional and political sentiment, although he recognizes that the Vesta cult "became weakened in Greece at a very early

date . . . but it never became enfeebled at Rome" (p. 146). Not only was the gulf between household and city much deeper in Greece than in Rome, but only in Greece was the Olympian religion, the religion of Homer and the city-state, separate, from and superior to the older religion of family and household. While Vesta, the goddess of the hearth, became the protectress of a "city hearth" and part of the official, political cult after the unification and second foundation of Rome, her Greek colleague, Hestia, is mentioned for the first time by Hesiod, the only Greek poet who, in conscious opposition to Homer, praises the life of the hearth and the household; in the official religion of the *polis,* she had to cede her place in the assembly of the twelve Olympian gods to Dionysos (see Mommsen, *Römische Geschichte* [5th ed.], Book I, ch. 12, and Robert Graves, *The Greek Myths* [1955], 27. k).

7. The passage occurs in Phoenix' speech, *Iliad* ix. 443. It clearly refers to education for war and *agora,* the public meeting, in which men can distinguish themselves. The literal translation is: "[your father] charged me to teach you all this, to be a speaker of words and a doer of deeds" (*mythōn te rhētēr' emenai prēktēra te ergōn*).

8. The literal translation of the last lines of *Antigone* (1350–54) is as follows: "But great words, counteracting [or paying back] the great blows of the overproud, teach understanding in old age." The content of these lines is so puzzling to modern understanding that one rarely finds a translator who dares to give the bare sense. An exception is Hölderlin's translation: "Grosse Blicke aber, / Grosse Streiche der hohen Schultern / Vergeltend, / Sie haben im Alter gelehrt, zu denken." An anecdote, reported by Plutarch, may illustrate the connection between acting and speaking on a much lower level. A man once approached Demosthenes and related how terribly he had been beaten. "But you," said Demosthenes, "suffered nothing of what you tell me." Whereupon the other raised his voice and cried out: "I suffered nothing?" "Now," said Demosthenes, "I hear the voice of somebody who was injured and who suffered" (*Lives,* "Demosthenes"). A last remnant of this ancient connection of speech and thought, from which our notion of expressing thought through words is absent, may be found in the current Ciceronian phrase of *ratio et oratio.*

9. It is characteristic for this development that every politician was called a "rhetor" and that rhetoric, the art of public speaking, as distinguished from dialectic, the art of philosophic speech, is defined by Aristotle as the art of persuasion (see *Rhetoric* 1354a12 ff., 1355b26 ff.). (The distinction itself is derived from Plato, *Gorgias* 448.) It is in this sense that we must understand the Greek opinion of the decline of Thebes, which was ascribed to Theban neglect of rhetoric in favor of military exercise (see Jacob Burckhardt, *Griechische Kulturgeschichte,* ed. Kroener, III, 190).

10. *Nicomachean Ethics* 1142a25 and 1178a6 ff.

11. Aquinas *op. cit.* ii. 2. 50. 3.

12. The terms *dominus* and *paterfamilias* therefore were synonymous, like the terms *servus* and *familiaris: Dominum patrem familiae appellaverunt; servos . . . fa-*

miliares (Seneca *Epistolae* 47. 12). The old Roman liberty of the citizen disappeared when the Roman emperors adopted the title *dominus,* "ce nom, qu'Auguste et que Tibère encore, repoussaient comme une malédiction et une injure" (H. Wallon, *Histoire de l'esclavage dans l'antiquité* [1847], III, 21).

13. According to Gunnar Myrdal (*The Political Element in the Development of Economic Theory* [1953], p. xl), the "idea of Social Economy or collective housekeeping (*Volkswirtschaft*)" is one of the "three main foci" around which "the political speculation which has permeated economics from the very beginning is found to be crystallized."

14. This is not to deny that the nation-state and its society grew out of the medieval kingdom and feudalism, in whose framework the family and household unit have an importance unequalled in classical antiquity. The difference, however, is marked. Within the feudal framework, families and households were mutually almost independent, so that the royal household, representing a given territorial region and ruling the feudal lords as *primus inter pares,* did not pretend, like an absolute ruler, to be the head of one family. The medieval "nation" was a conglomeration of families; its members did not think of themselves as members of one family comprehending the whole nation.

15. The distinction is very clear in the first paragraphs of the Ps. Aristotelian *Economics,* because it opposes the despotic one-man rule (*mon-archia*) of the household organization to the altogether different organization of the *polis.*

16. In Athens, one may see the turning point in Solon's legislation. Coulanges rightly sees in the Athenian law that made it a filial duty to support parents the proof of the loss of paternal power (*op.cit.,* pp. 315–16). However, paternal power was limited only if it conflicted with the interest of the city and never for the sake of the individual family member. Thus the sale of children and the exposure of infants lasted throughout antiquity (see R. H. Barrow, *Slavery in the Roman Empire* [1928], p. 8: "Other rights in the *patria potestas* had become obsolete; but the right of exposure remained unforbidden till A.D. 374").

17. It is interesting for this distinction that there were Greek cities where citizens were obliged by law to share their harvest and consume it in common, whereas each of them had the absolute uncontested property of his soil. See Coulanges (*op. cit.,* p. 61), who calls this law "a singular contradiction"; it is no contradiction, because these two types of property had nothing in common in ancient understanding.

18. See *Laws* 842.

19. Quoted from Coulanges, *op. cit.,* p. 96; the reference to Plutarch is *Quaestiones Romanae* 51. It seems strange that Coulanges' one-sided emphasis on the underworld deities in Greek and Roman religion should have overlooked that these gods were not mere gods of the dead and the cult not merely a "death cult," but that this early earth-bound religion served life and death as two aspects of the same process. Life rises out of the earth and returns to it; birth and death are but two different stages of the same biological life over which the subterranean gods hold sway.

20. The discussion between Socrates and Eutherus in Xenophon's *Memorabilia* (ii. 8) is quite interesting: Eutherus is forced by necessity to labor with his body and is sure that his body will not be able to stand this kind of life for very long and also that in his old age he will be destitute. Still, he thinks that to labor is better than to beg. Whereupon Socrates proposes that he look for somebody "who is better off and needs an assistant." Eutherus replies that he could not bear servitude (*douleia*).

21. The reference is to Hobbes, *Leviathan,* Part I, ch. 13.

22. The most famous and the most beautiful reference is the discussion of the different forms of government in Herodotus (iii. 80–83), where Otanes, the defender of Greek equality (*isonomiē*), states that he "wishes neither to rule nor to be ruled." But it is the same spirit in which Aristotle states that the life of a free man is better than that of a despot, denying freedom to the despot as a matter of course (*Politics* 1325a24). According to Coulanges, all Greek and Latin words which express some rulership over others, such as *rex, pater, anax, basileus,* refer originally to household relationships and were names the slaves gave to their master (*op. cit.,* pp. 89 ff., 228).

23. The proportion varied and is certainly exaggerated in Xenophon's report from Sparta, where among four thousand people in the market place, a foreigner counted no more than sixty citizens (*Hellenica* iii. 35).

24. See Myrdal, *op. cit.:* "The notion that society, like the head of a family, keeps house for its members, is deeply rooted in economic terminology. . . . In German *Volkswirtschaftslehre* suggests . . . that there is a collective subject of economic activity . . . with a common purpose and common values. In English, . . . 'theory of wealth' or 'theory of welfare' express similar ideas" (p. 140). "What is meant by a social economy whose function is social housekeeping? In the first place, it implies or suggests an analogy between the individual who runs his own or his family household and society. Adam Smith and James Mill elaborated this analogy explicitly. After J. S. Mill's criticism, and with the wider recognition of the distinction between practical and theoretical political economy, the analogy was generally less emphasized" (p. 143). The fact that the analogy was no longer used may also be due to a development in which society devoured the family unit until it became a full-fledged substitute for it.

25. R. H. Barrow, *The Romans* (1953), p. 194.

26. The characteristics which E. Levasseur (*Histoire des classes ouvrières et le de l'industrie en France avant 1789* [1900]) finds for the feudal organization of labor are true for the whole of feudal communities: "Chacun vivait chez soi et vivait de soi-même, le noble sur sa seigneurie, le vilain sur sa culture, le citadin dans sa ville" (p. 229).

27. The fair treatment of slaves which Plato recommends in the *Laws* (777) has little to do with justice and is not recommended "out of regard for the [slaves], but more out of respect to ourselves." For the coexistence of two laws, the political law of justice and the household law of rule, see Wallon, *op. cit.,* II, 200: "La loi, pendant bien longtemps, donc . . . s'abstenait de

pénétrer dans la famille, où elle reconnaissait l'empire d'une autre loi." Ancient, especially Roman, jurisdiction with respect to household matters, treatment of slaves, family relationships, etc., was essentially designed to restrain the otherwise unrestricted power of the household head; that there could be a rule of justice within the entirely "private" society of the slaves themselves was unthinkable—they were by definition outside the realm of the law and subject to the rule of their master. Only the master himself, in so far as he was also a citizen, was subject to the rules of laws, which for the sake of the city eventually even curtailed his powers in the household.

28. W. J. Ashley, *op. cit.*, p. 415.

29. This "rise" from one realm or rank to a higher is a recurrent theme in Machiavelli (see esp. *Prince,* ch. 6 about Hiero of Syracuse and ch. 7; and *Discourses,* Book II, ch. 13).

30. "By Solon's time slavery had come to be looked on as worse than death" (Robert Schlaifer, "Greek Theories of Slavery from Homer to Aristotle," *Harvard Studies in Classical Philology* [1936], XLVII). Since then, *philopsychia* ("love of life") and cowardice became identified with slavishness. Thus, Plato could believe he had demonstrated the natural slavishness of slaves by the fact that they had not preferred death to enslavement (*Republic* 386A). A late echo of this might still be found in Seneca's answer to the complaints of slaves: "Is freedom so close at hand, yet is there any one a slave?" (*Ep.* 77. 14) or in his *vita si moriendi virtus abest, servitus est*—"life is slavery without the virtue which knows how to die" (77. 13). To understand the ancient attitude toward slavery, it is not immaterial to remember that the majority of slaves were defeated enemies and that generally only a small percentage were born slaves. And while under the Roman Republic slaves were, on the whole, drawn from outside the limits of Roman rule, Greek slaves usually were of the same nationality as their masters; they had proved their slavish nature by not committing suicide, and since courage was the political virtue par excellence, they had thereby shown their "natural" unworthiness, their unfitness to be citizens. The attitude toward slaves changed in the Roman Empire, not only because of the influence of Stoicism but because a much greater portion of the slave population were slaves by birth. But even in Rome, *labos* is considered to be closely connected with unglorious death by Vergil (*Aeneis* vi).

31. That the free man distinguishes himself from the slave through courage seems to have been the theme of a poem by the Cretan poet Hybrias: "My riches are spear and sword and the beautiful shield. . . . But those who do not dare to bear spear and sword and the beautiful shield that protects the body fall all down unto their knees with awe and address me as Lord and great King" (quoted from Eduard Meyer, *Die Sklaverei im Altertum* [1898], p. 22).

32. Max Weber, "Agrarverhältnisse im Altertum," *Gesammelte Aufsätze zur Sozial-und Wirtschaftsgeschichte* (1924), p. 147.

33. This is well illustrated by a remark of Seneca, who, discussing the usefulness of highly educated slaves (who know all the classics by heart) to an assumedly rather ignorant master, comments: "What the household knows the master

knows" (*Ep.* 27. 6, quoted from Barrow, *Slavery in the Roman Empire*, p. 61).

34. *Aien aristeuein kai hypeirochon emmenai allōn* ("always to be the best and to rise above others") is the central concern of Homer's heroes (*Iliad* vi. 208), and Homer was "the educator of Hellas."

35. "The conception of political economy as primarily a 'science' dates only from Adam Smith" and was unknown not only to antiquity and the Middle Ages, but also to canonist doctrine, the first "complete and economic doctrine" which "differed from modern economics in being an 'art' rather than a 'science' " (W. J. Ashley, *op. cit.,* pp. 379 ff.). Classical economics assumed that man, in so far as he is an active being, acts exclusively from self-interest and is driven by only one desire, the desire for acquisition. Adam Smith's introduction of an "invisible hand to promote an end which was no part of [anybody's] intention" proves that even this minimum of action with its uniform motivation still contains too much unpredictable initiative for the establishment of a science. Marx developed classical economics further by substituting group or class interests for individual and personal interests and by reducing these class interests to two major classes, capitalists and workers, so that he was left with one conflict, where classical economics had seen a multitude of contradictory conflicts. The reason why the Marxian economic system is more consistent and coherent, and therefore apparently so much more "scientific" than those of his predecessors, lies primarily in the construction of "socialized man," who is even less an acting being than the "economic man" of liberal economics.

36. That liberal utilitarianism, and not socialism, is "forced into an untenable 'communistic fiction' about the unity of society" and that "the communist fiction [is] implicit in most writings on economics" constitutes one of the chief theses of Myrdal's brilliant work (*op. cit.,* pp. 54 and 150). He shows conclusively that economics can be a science only if one assumes that one interest pervades society as a whole. Behind the "harmony of interests" stands always the "communistic fiction" of one interest, which may then be called welfare or commonwealth. Liberal economists consequently were always guided by a "communistic" ideal, namely, by "interest of society as a whole" (pp. 194–95). The crux of the argument is that this "amounts to the assertion that society must be conceived as a single subject. This, however, is precisely what cannot be conceived. If we tried, we would be attempting to abstract from the essential fact that social activity is the result of the intentions of several individuals" (p. 154).

37. For a brilliant exposition of this usually neglected aspect of Marx's relevance for modern society, see Siegfried Landshut, "Die Gegenwart im Lichte der Marxschen Lehre," *Hamburger Jahrbuch für Wirtschafts- und Gesellschaftspolitik,* Vol. I (1956).

38. Here and later I apply the term "division of labor" only to modern labor conditions where one activity is divided and atomized into innumerable minute manipulations, and not to the "division of labor" given in professional specialization. The latter can be so classified only under the assumption

that society must be conceived as one single subject, the fulfilment of whose needs are then subdivided by "an invisible hand" among its members. The same holds true, *mutatis mutandis,* for the odd notion of a division of labor between the sexes, which is even considered by some writers to be the most original one. It presumes as its single subject man-kind, the human species, which has divided its labors among men and women. Where the same argument is used in antiquity (see, for instance, Xenophon *Oeconomicus* vii. 22), emphasis and meaning are quite different. The main division is between a life spent indoors, in the household, and a life spent outside, in the world. Only the latter is a life fully worthy of man, and the notion of equality between man and woman, which is a necessary assumption for the idea of division of labor, is of course entirely absent (cf. n. 81). Antiquity seems to have known only professional specialization, which assumedly was predetermined by natural qualities and gifts. Thus work in the gold mines, which occupied several thousand workers, was distributed according to strength and skill. See J.-P. Vernant, "Travail et nature dans la Grèce ancienne," *Journal de psychologie normale et pathologique,* Vol. LII, No. 1 (January–March, 1955).

39. All the European words for "labor," the Latin and English *labor,* the Greek *ponos,* the French *travail,* the German *Arbeit,* signify pain and effort and are also used for the pangs of birth. *Labor* has the same etymological root as *labare* ("to stumble under a burden"); *ponos* and *Arbeit* have the same etymological roots as "poverty" (*penia* in Greek and *Armut* in German). Even Hesiod, currently counted among the few defenders of labor in antiquity, put *ponon alginoenta* ("painful labor") as first of the evils plaguing man (*Theogony* 226). For the Greek usage, see G. Herzog-Hauser, *"Ponos,"* in Pauly-Wissowa. The German *Arbeit* and *arm* are both derived from the Germanic *arbma-,* meaning lonely and neglected, abandoned. See Kluge/Götze, *Etymologisches Wörterbuch* (1951). In medieval German, the word is used to translate *labor, tribulatio, persecutio, adversitas, malum* (see Klara Vontobel, *Das Arbeitsethos des deutschen Protestantismus* [Dissertation, Bern, 1946]).

40. Homer's much quoted thought that Zeus takes away half of a man's excellence (*aretē*) when the day of slavery catches him (*Odyssey* xvii. 320 ff.) is put into the mouth of Eumaios, a slave himself, and meant as an objective statement, not a criticism or a moral judgment. The slave lost excellence because he lost admission to the public realm, where excellence can show.

41. This is also the reason why it is impossible "to write a character sketch of any slave who lived. . . . Until they emerge into freedom and notoriety, they remain shadowy types rather than persons" (Barrow, *Slavery in the Roman Empire,* p. 156).

42. I use here a little-known poem on pain from Rilke's deathbed: The first lines of the untitled poem are: "Komm du, du letzter, den ich anerkenne, / heilloser Schmerz im leiblichen Geweb"; and it concludes as follows: "Bin ich es noch, der da unkenntlich brennt? / Erinnerungen reiss ich nicht herein. / O Leben, Leben: Draussensein. / Und ich in Lohe. Niemand, der mich kennt."

43. On the subjectivity of pain and its relevance for all variations of hedonism

and sensualism, see §§ 15 and 43. For the living, death is primarily disappearance. But unlike pain, there is one aspect of death in which it is as though death appeared among the living, and that is in old age. Goethe once remarked that growing old is "gradually receding from appearance" (*stufenweises Zurücktreten aus der Erscheinung*); the truth of this remark as well as the actual appearance of this process of disappearing becomes quite tangible in the old-age self-portraits of the great masters—Rembrandt, Leonardo, etc.—in which the intensity of the eyes seems to illuminate and preside over the receding flesh.

44. *Contra Faustum Manichaeum* v. 5.

45. This is of course still the presupposition even of Aquinas' political philosophy (see *op. cit.* ii. 2. 181. 4).

46. The term *corpus rei publicae* is current in pre-Christian Latin, but has the connotation of the population inhabiting a *res publica,* a given political realm. The corresponding Greek term *sōma* is never used in pre-Christian Greek in a political sense. The metaphor seems to occur for the first time in Paul (I Cor. 12: 12–27) and is current in all early Christian writers (see, for instance, Tertullian *Apologeticus* 39, or Ambrosius *De officiis ministrorum* iii. 3. 17). It became of the greatest importance for medieval political theory, which unanimously assumed that all men were *quasi unum corpus* (Aquinas *op. cit.* ii. 1. 81. 1). But while the early writers stressed the equality of the members, which are all equally necessary for the well-being of the body as a whole, the emphasis later shifted to the difference between the head and the members, to the duty of the head to rule and of the members to obey. (For the Middle Ages, see Anton-Hermann Chroust, "The Corporate Idea in the Middle Ages," *Review of Politics,* Vol. VIII [1947].)

47. Aquinas *op. cit.* ii. 2. 179. 2.

48. See Article 57 of the Benedictine rule, in Levasseur, *op. cit.,* p. 187: If one of the monks became proud of his work, he had to give it up.

49. Barrow (*Slavery in the Roman Empire,* p. 168), in an illuminating discussion of the membership of slaves in the Roman colleges, which provided, besides "good fellowship in life and the certainty of a decent burial . . . the crowning glory of an epitaph; and in this last the slave found a melancholy pleasure."

50. *Nicomachean Ethics* 1177b31.

51. *Wealth of Nations,* Book I, ch. 10 (pp. 120 and 95 of Vol. I of Everyman's ed.).

52. For modern loneliness as a mass phenomenon see David Riesman, *The Lonely Crowd* (1950).

53. So Plinius Junior, quoted in W. L. Westermann, "Sklaverei," in Pauly-Wissowa, Suppl. VI, p. 1045.

54. There is plenty of evidence for this different estimation of wealth and culture in Rome and Greece. But it is interesting to note how consistently this estimate coincided with the position of slaves. Roman slaves played a much greater role in Roman culture than in Greece, where, on the other hand, their role in economic life was much more important (see Westermann, in Pauly-Wissowa, p. 984).

55. Augustine (*De civitate Dei* xix. 19) sees in the duty of *caritas* toward the *utilitas proximi* ("the interest of one's neighbor") the limitation of *otium* and contemplation. But "in active life, it is not the honors or power of this life we should covet, . . . but the welfare of those who are under us [*salutem subditorum*]." Obviously, this kind of responsibility resembles the responsibility of the household head for his family more than political responsibility, properly speaking. The Christian precept to mind one's own business is derived from I Thess. 4: 11: "that ye study to be quiet and to do your own business" (*prattein ta idia*, whereby *ta idia* is understood as opposed to *ta koina* ["public common affairs"]).

56. Coulanges (*op. cit.*) holds: "The true signification of *familia* is property; it designates the field, the house, money, and slaves" (p. 107). Yet, this "property" is not seen as attached to the family; on the contrary, "the family is attached to the hearth, the hearth is attached to the soil" (p. 62). The point is: "The fortune is immovable like the hearth and the tomb to which it is attached. It is the man who passes away" (p. 74).

57. Levasseur (*op. cit.*) relates the medieval foundation of a community and the conditions of admission to it: "Il ne suffisait pas d'habiter la ville pour avoir droit à cette admission. Il fallait . . . posséder une maison. . . ." Furthermore: "Toute injure proférée en public contre la commune entraînait la démolition de la maison et le bannissement du coupable" (p. 240, including n. 3).

58. The distinction is most obvious in the case of slaves who, though without property in the ancient understanding (that is, without a place of their own), were by no means propertyless in the modern sense. The *peculium* (the "private possession of a slave") could amount to considerable sums and even contain slaves of his own (*vicarii*). Barrow speaks of "the property which the humblest of his class possessed" (*Slavery in the Roman Empire*, p. 122; this work is the best report on the role of the *peculium*).

59. Coulanges reports a remark of Aristotle that in ancient times the son could not be a citizen during the lifetime of his father; upon his death, only the eldest son enjoyed political rights (*op. cit.*, p. 228). Coulanges holds that the Roman *plebs* originally consisted of people without home and hearth, that it therefore was clearly distinct from the *populus Romanus* (pp. 229 ff.).

60. "The whole of this religion was inclosed within the walls of each house. . . . All these gods, the Hearth, the Lares, and the Manes, were called the hidden gods, or gods of the interior. To all the acts of this religion secrecy was necessary, *sacrificia occulta*, as Cicero said (De arusp. respl. 17)" (Coulanges, *op. cit.*, p. 37).

61. It seems as though the Eleusinian Mysteries provided for a common and quasi-public experience of this whole realm, which, because of its very nature and even though it was common to all, needed to be hidden, kept secret from the public realm: Everybody could participate in them, but nobody was permitted to talk about them. The mysteries concerned the unspeakable, and experiences beyond speech were non-political and perhaps antipolitical by definition (see Karl Kerenyi, *Die Geburt der Helena* [1943–45], pp. 48 ff.).

That they concerned the secret of birth and death seems proved by a fragment of Pindar: *oide men biou teleutan, oiden de diosdoton archan* (frag. 137*a*), where the initiated is said to know "the end of life and the Zeus-given beginning."

62. The Greek word for law, *nomos*, derives from *nemein*, which means to distribute, to possess (what has been distributed), and to dwell. The combination of law and hedge in the word *nomos* is quite manifest in a fragment of Heraclitus: *machesthai chrē ton dēmon hyper tou nomou hokōsper teicheos* ("the people should fight for the law as for a wall"). The Roman word for law, *lex*, has an entirely different meaning; it indicates a formal relationship between people rather than the wall that separates them from others. But the boundary and its god, Terminus, who separated the *agrum publicum a privato* (Livius) was more highly revered than the corresponding *theoi horoi* in Greece.

63. Coulanges reports an ancient Greek law according to which two buildings never were permitted to touch (*op. cit.,* p. 63).

64. The word *polis* originally connoted something like a "ring-wall," and it seems the Latin *urbs* also expressed the notion of a "circle" and was derived from the same root as *orbis*. We find the same connection in our word "town," which originally, like the German *Zaun*, meant a surrounding fence (see R. B. Onians, *The Origins of European Thought* [1954], p. 444, n. 1).

65. The legislator therefore did not need to be a citizen and frequently was called in from the outside. His work was not political; political life, however, could begin only after he had finished his legislation.

66. Demosthenes *Orationes 57. 45:* "Poverty forces the free to do many slavish and base things" (*polla doulika kai tapeina pragmata tous eleutherous hē penia biazetai poiein*).

67. This condition for admission to the public realm was still in existence in the earlier Middle Ages. The English "Books of Customs" still drew "a sharp distinction between the craftsman and the freeman, *franke homme,* of the town. . . . If a craftsman became so rich that he wished to become a freeman, he must first foreswear his craft and get rid of all his tools from his house" (W. J. Ashley, *op. cit.,* p. 83). It was only under the rule of Edward III that the craftsmen became so rich that "instead of the craftsmen being incapable of citizenship, citizenship came to be bound up with membership of one of the companies" (p. 89).

68. Coulanges, in distinction from other authors, stresses the time- and strength-consuming activities demanded from an ancient citizen, rather than his "leisure," and sees rightly that Aristotle's statement that no man who had to work for his livelihood could be a citizen is a simple statement of fact rather than the expression of a prejudice (*op. cit.,* pp. 335 ff.). It is characteristic of the modern development that riches as such, regardless of the occupation of their owner, became a qualification for citizenship: only now was it a mere privilege to be a citizen, unconnected with any specifically political activities.

69. This seems to me to be the solution of the "well-known puzzle in the study of the economic history of the ancient world that industry developed up to a

certain point, but stopped short of making progress which might have been expected . . . [in view of the fact that] thoroughness and capacity for organization on a large scale is shown by the Romans in other departments, in the public services and the army" (Barrow, *Slavery in the Roman Empire,* pp. 109–10). It seems a prejudice due to modern conditions to expect the same capacity for organization in private as in "public services." Max Weber, in his remarkable essay (*op. cit.*) had already insisted on the fact that ancient cities were rather "centers of consumption than of production" and that the ancient slave owner was a "*rentier* and not a capitalist [*Unternehmer*]" (pp. 13, 22 ff., and 144). The very indifference of ancient writers to economic questions, and the lack of documents in this respect, give additional weight to Weber's argument.

70. All histories of the working class, that is, a class of people who are without any property and live only from the work of their hands, suffer from the naïve assumption that there has always been such a class. Yet, as we saw, even slaves were not without property in antiquity, and the so-called free labor in antiquity usually turns out to consist of "free shopkeepers, traders and craftsmen" (Barrow, *Slavery in the Roman Empire,* p. 126). M. E. Park (*The Plebs Urbana in Cicero's Day* [1921]), therefore, comes to the conclusion that there was no free labor, since the free man always appears to be an owner of some sort. W. J. Ashley sums up the situation in the Middle Ages up to the fifteenth century: "There was as yet no large class of wage laborers, no 'working class' in the modern sense of the term. By 'working men,' we mean a number of men, from among whom individuals may indeed rise to become masters, but the majority of whom cannot hope ever to rise to a higher position. But in the fourteenth century a few year's work as a journeyman was but a stage through which the poorer men had to pass, while the majority probably set up for themselves as master craftsmen as soon as apprenticeship was over" (*op. cit.,* pp. 93–94).

Thus, the working class in antiquity was neither free nor without property; if, through manumission, the slave was given (in Rome) or had bought (in Athens) his freedom, he did not become a free laborer but instantly became an independent businessman or craftsman. ("Most slaves seem to have taken into freedom some capital of their own" to set up in trade and industry [Barrow, *Slavery in the Roman Empire,* p. 103]). And in the Middle Ages, to be a worker in the modern sense of the term was a temporary stage in one's life, a preparation for mastership and manhood. Hired labor in the Middle Ages was an exception, and the German day laborers (the *Tagelöhner* in Luther's Bible translation) or the French *manœuvres* lived outside the settled communities and were identical with the poor, the "labouring poor" in England (see Pierre Brizon, *Histoire du travail et des travailleurs* [1926], p. 40). Moreover, the fact that no code of law before the *Code Napoléon* offers any treatment of free labor (see W. Endemann, *Die Behandlung der Arbeit im Privatrecht* [1896], pp. 49, 53) shows conclusively how recent the existence of a working class is.

71. See the ingenious comment on "property is theft" which occurs in Proudhon's posthumously published *Théorie de la propriété*, pp. 209–10, where he presents property in its "egoist, satanic nature" as the "most efficient means to resist despotism without overthrowing the state."

72. I must confess that I fail to see on what grounds in present-day society liberal economists (who today call themselves conservatives) can justify their optimism that the private appropriation of wealth will suffice to guard individual liberties—that is, will fulfil the same role as private property. In a jobholding society, these liberties are safe only as long as they are guaranteed by the state, and even now they are constantly threatened, not by the state, but by society, which distributes the jobs and determines the share of individual appropriation.

73. R. W. K. Hinton, "Was Charles I a Tyrant?" *Review of Politics,* Vol. XVIII (January, 1956).

74. For the history of the word "capital" deriving from the Latin *caput,* which in Roman law was employed for the principal of a debt, see W. J. Ashley, *op. cit.,* pp. 429 and 433, n. 183. Only eighteenth-century writers began to use the word in the modern sense as "wealth invested in such a way as to bring gain."

75. Medieval economic theory did not yet conceive of money as a common denominator and yardstick but counted it among the *consumptibiles.*

76. *Second Treatise of Civil Government,* sec. 27.

77. The relatively few instances of ancient authors praising labor and poverty are inspired by this danger (for references see G. Herzog-Hauser, *op. cit.*).

78. The Greek and Latin words for the interior of the house, *megaron* and *atrium,* have a strong connotation of darkness and blackness (see Mommsen, *op. cit.,* pp. 22 and 236).

79. Aristotle *Politics* 1254b25.

80. The life of a woman is called *ponē tikos* by Aristotle, *On the Generation of Animals* 775a33. That women and slaves belonged and lived together, that no woman, not even the wife of the household head, lived among her equals—other free women—so that rank depended much less on birth than on "occupation" or function, is very well presented by Wallon (*op. cit.,* I, 77 ff.), who speaks of a "confusion des rangs, ce partage de toutes les fonctions domestiques": "Les femmes . . . se confondaient avec leurs esclaves dans les soins habituels de la vie intérieure. De quelque rang qu'elles fussent, le travail était leur apanage, comme aux hommes la guerre."

81. See Pierre Brizon, *Histoire du travail et des travailleurs* (4th ed.; 1926), p. 184, concerning the conditions of factory work in the seventeenth century.

82. Tertullian *op. cit.* 38.

83. This difference of experience may partly explain the difference between the great sanity of Augustine and the horrible concreteness of Tertullian's views on politics. Both were Romans and profoundly shaped by Roman political life.

84. Luke 8:19. The same thought occurs in Matt. 6:1–18, where Jesus warns

against hypocrisy, against the open display of piety. Piety cannot "appear unto men" but only unto God, who "seeth in secret." God, it is true, "shall reward" man, but not, as the standard translation claims, "openly." The German word *Scheinheiligkeit* expresses this religious phenomenon, where mere appearance is already hypocrisy, quite adequately.

85. One finds this idiom *passim* in Plato (see esp. *Gorgias* 482).
86. *Prince,* ch. 15.
87. *Ibid.,* ch. 8.
88. *Discourses,* Book III, ch. 1.

Reflections on Little Rock

PRELIMINARY REMARKS

This article was written more than a year ago upon the suggestion of one of the editors of Commentary. *It was a topical article whose publication was delayed for months because of the controversial nature of my reflections which, obviously, were at variance with the magazine's stand on matters of discrimination and segregation. Meanwhile, things had quieted down temporarily; I had hopes that my fears concerning the seriousness of the situation might prove exaggerated and no longer wished to publish this article. Recent developments have convinced me that such hopes are futile and that the routine repetition of liberal clichés may be even more dangerous than I thought a year ago. I therefore agreed to let* Dissent *publish the article as it was written—not because I thought that a year-old topical essay could possibly exhaust the subject or even do justice to the many difficult problems involved, but in the hope that even an inadequate attempt might help to break the dangerous routine in which the discussion of these issues is being held from both sides.*

There are, however, two points which were brought to my attention after I wrote the article which I would like to mention at least. The first concerns my contention that the marriage laws in 29 of the 49 states constitute a much more flagrant breach of letter and spirit of the Constitution than segregation of schools. To this, Sidney Hook (New Leader, April 13), replied that Negroes were "profoundly uninterested" in these laws; in their eyes, "the discriminatory ban against intermarriages and miscegenation is last in the order of priorities." I have my doubts about this, especially with respect to the educated strata in the Negro population, but it is of course perfectly true that Negro public opinion and the policies of the NAACP are almost exclusively concerned

From Dissent *6/1 (Winter 1959). For the theoretical context of this article, see Editor's Introduction, pp. xxxiii–xxxvi.*

with discrimination in employment, housing and education. This is un-
derstandable; oppressed minorities were never the best judges on the order
of priorities in such matters and there are many instances when they pre-
ferred to fight for social opportunity rather than for basic human or polit-
ical rights. But this does not make the marriage laws any more
constitutional or any less shameful; the order of priorities in the question
of rights is to be determined by the Constitution, and not by public
opinion or by majorities.

The second point was mentioned by a friend who rightly observed
that my criticism of the Supreme Court's decision did not take into ac-
count the role education plays, and has always played, in the political
framework of this country. This criticism is entirely just and I would
have tried to insert a discussion of this role into the article if I had not
meanwhile published a few remarks on the wide-spread, uncritical accep-
tance of a Rousseauian ideal in education in another context, i.e. in an
article in the Fall 1958 issue of Partisan Review, *entitled "The Cri-*
sis in Education." In order not to repeat myself, I left the article un-
changed.

Finally, I should like to remind the reader that I am writing as an
outsider. I have never lived in the South and have even avoided occa-
sional trips to Southern states because they would have brought me into
a situation that I personally would find unbearable. Like most people of
European origin I have difficulty in understanding, let alone sharing, the
common prejudices of Americans in this area. Since what I wrote may
shock good people and be misused by bad ones, I should like to make it
clear that as a Jew I take my sympathy for the cause of the Negroes as
for all oppressed or under-privileged peoples for granted and should ap-
preciate it if the reader did likewise.

IT IS UNFORTUNATE and even unjust (though hardly unjustified) that the
events at Little Rock should have had such an enormous echo in public
opinion throughout the world and have become a major stumbling block
to American foreign policy. For unlike other domestic problems which
have beset this country since the end of World War II (a security hysteria,
a runaway prosperity, and the concomitant transformation of an economy
of abundance into a market where sheer superfluity and nonsense almost
wash out the essential and the productive), and unlike such long-range
difficulties as the problem of mass culture and mass education—both of
which are typical of modern society in general and not only of America—
the country's attitude to its Negro population is rooted in American tradi-

tion and nothing else. The color question was created by the one great crime in America's history and is soluble only within the political and historical framework of the Republic. The fact that this question has also become a major issue in world affairs is sheer coincidence as far as American history and politics are concerned; for the color problem in world politics grew out of the colonialism and imperialism of European nations—that is, the one great crime in which America was never involved. The tragedy is that the unsolved color problem within the United States may cost her the advantages she otherwise would rightly enjoy as a world power.

For historical and other reasons, we are in the habit of identifying the Negro question with the South, but the unsolved problems connected with Negroes living in our midst concern of course the whole country, not the South alone. Like other race questions, it has a special attraction for the mob and is particularly well fitted to serve as the point around which a mob ideology and a mob organization can crystallize. This aspect may one day even prove more explosive in the big Northern urban centers than in the more tradition-bound South, especially if the number of Negroes in Southern cities continues to decline while the Negro population of non-Southern cities increases at the same rate as in recent years. The United States is not a nation-state in the European sense and never was. The principle of its political structure is, and always has been, independent of a homogeneous population and of a common past. This is somewhat less true of the South whose population is more homogeneous and more rooted in the past than that of any other part of the country. When William Faulkner recently declared that in a conflict between the South and Washington he would utimately have to act as a citizen of Mississippi, he sounded more like a member of a European nation-state than a citizen of this Republic. But this difference between North and South, though still marked, is bound to disappear with the growing industrialization of Southern states and plays no role in some of them even today. In all parts of the country, in the East and North with its host of nationalities no less than in the more homogeneous South, the Negroes stand out because of their "visibility." They are not the only "visible minority," but they are the most visible one. In this respect, they somewhat resemble new immigrants, who invariably constitute the most "audible" of all minorities and therefore are always the most likely to arouse xenophobic sentiments. But while audibility is a temporary phenomenon, rarely persisting beyond one generation, the Negroes' visibility is unalterable and permanent. This is not a trivial matter. In the public realm, where nothing counts that cannot make itself seen and heard, visibility and audibility are of prime importance. To argue that they are merely exterior appearances is to beg the question. For it is precisely appearances that "appear" in public, and inner qualities, gifts of heart or mind, are political only to the extent that their owner wishes to expose them in public, to place them in the limelight of the market place.

The American Republic is based on the equality of all citizens, and while equality before the law has become an inalienable principle of all modern constitutional government, equality as such is of greater importance in the political life of a republic than in any other form of government. The point at stake, therefore, is not the well-being of the Negro population alone, but, at least in the long run, the survival of the Republic. Tocqueville saw over a century ago that equality of opportunity and condition, as well as equality of rights, constituted the basic "law" of American democracy, and he predicted that the dilemmas and perplexities inherent in the principle of equality might one day become the most dangerous challenge to the American way of life. In its all-comprehensive, typically American form, equality possesses an enormous power to equalize what by nature and origin is different—and it is only due to this power that the country has been able to retain its fundamental identity against the waves of immigrants who have always flooded its shores. But the principle of equality, even in its American form, is not omnipotent; it cannot equalize natural, physical characteristics. This limit is reached only when inequalities of economic and educational condition have been ironed out, but at that juncture a danger point, well known to students of history, invariably emerges: the more equal people have become in every respect, and the more equality permeates the whole texture of society, the more will differences be resented, the more conspicuous will those become who are visibly and by nature unlike the others.

It is therefore quite possible that the achievement of social, economic, and educational equality for the Negro may sharpen the color problem in this country instead of assuaging it. This, of course, does not have to happen, but it would be only natural if it did, and it would be very surprising if it did not. We have not yet reached the danger point, but we shall reach it in the foreseeable future, and a number of developments have already taken place which clearly point toward it. Awareness of future trouble does not commit one to advocating a reversal of the trend which happily for more than fifteen years now has been greatly in favor of the Negroes. But it does commit one to advocating that government intervention be guided by caution and moderation rather than by impatience and ill-advised measures. Since the Supreme Court decision to enforce desegregation in public schools, the general situation in the South has deteriorated. And while recent events indicate that it will not be pos-

sible to avoid Federal enforcement of Negro civil rights in the South altogether, conditions demand that such intervention be restricted to the few
instances in which the law of the land and the principle of the Republic
are at stake. The question therefore is whether this is the case in general,
and whether it is the case in public education in particular.

The administration's Civil Rights program covers two altogether different
points. It reaffirms the franchise of the Negro population, a matter of
course in the North, but not at all in the South. And it also takes up the
issue of segregation, which is a matter of fact in the whole country and a
matter of discriminatory legislation only in Southern states. The present
massive resistance throughout the South is an outcome of enforced desegregation, and not of legal enforcement of the Negroes' right to vote. The
results of a public opinion poll in Virginia showing that 92% of the citizens were totally opposed to school integration, that 65% were willing to
forgo public education under these conditions, and that 79% denied any
obligation to accept the Supreme Court decision as binding, illustrates
how serious the situation is. What is frightening here is not the 92% opposed to integration, for the dividing line in the South was never between
those who favored and those who opposed segregation—practically
speaking, no such opponents existed—but the proportion of people who
prefer mob rule to law-abiding citizenship. The so-called liberals and
moderates of the South are simply those who are law-abiding, and they
have dwindled to a minority of 21%.

No public opinion poll was necessary to reveal this information. The
events in Little Rock were quite sufficiently enlightening; and those who
wish to blame the disturbances solely on the extraordinary misbehavior of
Governor Faubus can set themselves right by listening to the eloquent silence of Arkansas' two liberal Senators. The sorry fact was that the town's
law-abiding citizens left the streets to the mob, that neither white nor
black citizens felt it their duty to see the Negro children safely to school.
That is, even prior to the arrival of Federal troops, law-abiding Southerners had decided that enforcement of the law against mob rule and protection of children against adult mobsters were none of their business. In
other words, the arrival of troops did little more than change passive into
massive resistance.

It has been said, I think again by Mr. Faulkner, that enforced integration is no better than enforced segregation, and this is perfectly true. The
only reason that the Supreme Court was able to address itself to the matter of desegregation in the first place was that segregation has been a legal,
and not just a social, issue in the South for many generations. For the cru-

cial point to remember is that it is not the social custom of segregation that is unconstitutional, but its *legal enforcement*. To abolish this legislation is of great and obvious importance and in the case of that part of the Civil Rights bill regarding the right to vote, no Southern state in fact dared to offer strong opposition. Indeed, with respect to unconstitutional legislation, the Civil Rights bill did not go far enough, for it left untouched the most outrageous law of Southern states—the law which makes mixed marriage a criminal offense. The right to marry whoever one wishes is an elementary human right compared to which "the right to attend an integrated school, the right to sit where one pleases on a bus, the right to go into any hotel or recreation area or place of amusement, regardless of one's skin or color or race" are minor indeed. Even political rights, like the right to vote, and nearly all other rights enumerated in the Constitution, are secondary to the inalienable human rights to "life, liberty and the pursuit of happiness" proclaimed in the Declaration of Independence; and to this category the right to home and marriage unquestionably belongs. It would have been much more important if this violation had been brought to the attention of the Supreme Court; yet had the Court ruled the anti-miscegenation laws unconstitutional, it would hardly have felt compelled to encourage, let alone enforce, mixed marriages.

However, the most startling part of the whole business was the Federal decision to start integration in, of all places, the public schools. It certainly did not require too much imagination to see that this was to burden children, black and white, with the working out of a problem which adults for generations have confessed themselves unable to solve. I think no one will find it easy to forget the photograph reproduced in newspapers and magazines throughout the country, showing a Negro girl, accompanied by a white friend of her father, walking away from school, persecuted and followed into bodily proximity by a jeering and grimacing mob of youngsters. The girl, obviously, was asked to be a hero—that is, something neither her absent father nor the equally absent representatives of the NAACP felt called upon to be. It will be hard for the white youngsters, or at least those among them who outgrow their present brutality, to live down this photograph which exposes so mercilessly their juvenile delinquency. The picture looked to me like a fantastic caricature of progressive education which, by abolishing the authority of adults, implicitly denies their responsibility for the world into which they have borne their children and refuses the duty of guiding them into it. Have we now come to the point where it is the children who are being asked to change or improve the world? And do we intend to have our political battles fought out in the school yards?

Segregation is discrimination enforced by law, and desegregation can do no more than abolish the laws enforcing discrimination; it cannot abolish discrimination and force equality upon society but it can, and indeed must, enforce equality within the body politic. For equality not only has its origin in the body politic; its validity is clearly restricted to the political realm. Only there are we all equals. Under modern conditions, this equality has its most important embodiment in the right to vote, according to which the judgment and opinion of the most exalted citizen are on a par with the judgment and opinion of the hardly literate. Eligibility, the right to be voted into office, is also an inalienable right of every citizen; but here equality is already restricted, and though the necessity for personal distinction in an election arises out of the numerical equality, in which everybody is literally reduced to being one, it is distinction and qualities which count in the winning of votes and not sheer equality.

Yet unlike other differences (for example, professional specialization, occupational qualification, or social and intellectual distinction) the political qualities needed for winning office are so closely connected with being an equal among equals, that one may say that, far from being specialties, they are precisely those distinctions to which all voters equally aspire—not necessarily as human beings, but as citizens and political beings. Thus the qualities of officials in a democracy always depend upon the qualities of the electorate. Eligibility, therefore, is a necessary corollary of the right to vote; it means that everyone is given the opportunity to distinguish himself in those things in which all are equals to begin with. Strictly speaking, the franchise and eligibility for office are the only political rights, and they constitute in a modern democracy the very quintessence of citizenship. In contrast to all other rights, civil or human, they cannot be granted to resident aliens.

What equality is to the body politic—its innermost principle—discrimination is to society. Society is that curious, somewhat hybrid realm between the political and the private in which, since the beginning of the modern age, most men have spent the greater part of their lives. For each time we leave the protective four walls of our private homes and cross over the threshold into the public world, we enter first, not the political realm of equality, but the social sphere. We are driven into this sphere by the need to earn a living or attracted by the desire to follow our vocation or enticed by the pleasure of company, and once we have entered it, we become subject to the old adage of "like attracts like" which controls the whole realm of society in the innumerable variety of its groups and associations. What matters here is not personal distinction but the differences by which people belong to certain groups whose very identifiability demands that they discriminate against other groups in the same domain. In American society, people group together, and therefore discriminate against each other, along lines of profession, income, and ethnic origin, while in Europe the lines run along class origin, education, and manners. From the viewpoint of the human person, none of these discriminatory practices makes sense; but then it is doubtful whether the human person as such ever appears in the social realm. At any rate, without discrimination of some sort, society would simply cease to exist and very important possibilities of free association and group formation would disappear.

Mass society—which blurs lines of discrimination and levels group distinctions—is a danger to society as such, rather than to the integrity of the person, for personal identity has its source beyond the social realm. Conformism, however, is not a characteristic of mass society alone, but of every society insofar as only those are admitted to a given social group who conform to the general traits of difference which keep the group together. The danger of conformism in this country—a danger almost as old as the Republic—is that, because of the extraordinary heterogeneity of its population, social conformism tends to become an absolute and a substitute for national homogeneity. In any event, discrimination is as indispensable a social right as equality is a political right. The question is not how to abolish discrimination, but how to keep it confined within the social sphere, where it is legitimate, and prevent its trespassing on the political and the personal sphere, where it is destructive.

In order to illustrate this distinction between the political and the social, I shall give two examples of discrimination, one in my opinion entirely justified and outside the scope of government intervention, the other scandalously unjustified and positively harmful to the political realm.

It is common knowledge that vacation resorts in this country are frequently "restricted" according to ethnic origin. There are many people who object to this practice; nevertheless it is only an extension of the right to free association. If as a Jew I wish to spend my vacations only in the company of Jews, I cannot see how anyone can reasonably prevent my doing so; just as I see no reason why other resorts should not cater to a clientele that wishes not to see Jews while on a holiday. There cannot be a "right to go into any hotel or recreation area or place of amusement," because many of these are in the realm of the purely social where the right to free association, and therefore to discrimination, has greater validity than the principle of equality. (This does not apply to theaters and museums, where people obviously do not congregate for the purpose of associating with each other.) The fact that the "right" to enter social places is silently granted in most countries and has become highly controversial only in American democracy is due not to the greater tolerance of other countries but in part to the homogeneity of their population and in part to their class system, which operates socially even when its economic foundations have disappeared. Homogeneity and class working together assure a "likeness" of clientele in any given place that even restriction and discrimination cannot achieve in America.

It is, however, another matter altogether when we come to "the right to sit where one pleases in a bus" or a railroad car or station, as well as the right to enter hotels and restaurants in business districts—in short, when we are dealing with services which, whether privately or publicly owned, are in fact public services that everyone needs in order to pursue his business and lead his life. Though not strictly in the political realm, such services are clearly in the public domain where all men are equal; and discrimination in Southern railroads and buses is as scandalous as discrimination in hotels and restaurants throughout the country. Obviously the situation is far worse in the South because segregation in public services is enforced by law and plainly visible to all. It is unfortunate indeed that the first steps toward clearing up the segregation situation in the South after so many decades of complete neglect did not begin with its most inhuman and its most conspicuous aspects.

The third realm, finally, in which we move and live together with other people—the realm of privacy—is ruled neither by equality nor by discrimination, but by exclusiveness. Here we choose those with whom we wish to spend our lives, personal friends and those we love; and our choice is guided not by likeness or qualities shared by a group of people— it is not guided, indeed, by any objective standards or rules—but strikes, inexplicably and unerringly, at one person in his uniqueness, his unlikeness to all other people we know. The rules of uniqueness and exclusiveness are, and always will be, in conflict with the standards of society precisely because social discrimination violates the principle, and lacks validity for the conduct, of private life. Thus every mixed marriage constitutes a challenge to society and means that the partners to such a marriage have so far preferred personal happiness to social adjustment that they are willing to bear the burden of discrimination. This is and must remain their private business. The scandal begins only when their challenge to society and prevailing customs, to which every citizen has a right, is interpreted as a criminal offense so that by stepping outside the social realm they find themselves in conflict with the law as well. Social standards are not legal standards and if legislature follows social prejudice, society has become tyrannical.

For reasons too complicated to discuss here, the power of society in our time is greater than it ever was before, and not many people are left who know the rules of and live a private life. But this provides the body politic with no excuse for forgetting the rights of privacy, for failing to understand that the rights of privacy are grossly violated whenever legislation begins to enforce social discrimination. While the government has no right to interfere with the prejudices and discriminatory practices of society, it has not only the right but the duty to make sure that these practices are not legally enforced.

Just as the government has to ensure that social discrimination never curtails political equality, it must also safeguard the rights of every person to do as he pleases within the four walls of his own home. The moment social discrimination is legally enforced it becomes persecution, and of this crime many Southern states have been guilty. The moment social discrimination is legally abolished, the freedom of society is violated, and the danger is that thoughtless handling of the civil rights issue by the Federal government will result in such a violation. The government can legitimately take no steps against social discrimination because government can act only in the name of equality—a principle which does not obtain in the social sphere. The only public force that can fight social prejudice is the churches, and they can do so in the name of the uniqueness of the person, for it is on the principle of the uniqueness of souls that religion (and especially the Christian faith) is based. The churches are indeed the only communal and public place where appearances do not count, and if discrimination creeps into the houses of worship, this is an infallible sign of their religious failing. They then have become social and are no longer religious institutions.

Another issue involved in the present conflict between Washington and the South is the matter of states' rights. For some time it has been customary among liberals to maintain that no such issue exists at all but is only a ready-made subterfuge of Southern reactionaries who have nothing in their hands except "abstruse arguments and constitutional history." In my opinion, this is a dangerous error. In contradistinction to the classical principle of the European nation-state that power, like sovereignty, is indivisible, the power structure of this country rests on the principle of division of power and on the conviction that the body politic as a whole is strengthened by the division of power. To be sure, this principle is embodied in the system of checks and balances between the three branches of government; but it is no less rooted in the government's Federal structure which demands that there also be a balance and a mutual check between Federal power and the powers of the forty-eight states. If it is true (and I am convinced it is) that unlike force, power generates more power when it is divided, then it follows that every attempt of the Federal government to deprive the states of some of their legislative sovereignty can be justified only on grounds of legal argument and constitutional history. Such arguments are not abstruse; they are based on a principle which indeed was uppermost in the minds of the founders of the Republic.

All this has nothing to do with being a liberal or a conservative, although it may be that where the nature of power is at stake, liberal judgment with its long and honorable history of deep distrust of power in any form can be less trusted than on other questions. Liberals fail to understand that the nature of power is such that the power potential of the Union as a whole will suffer if the regional foundations on which this power rests are undermined. The point is that force can, indeed must, be centralized in order to be effective, but power cannot and must not. If the various sources from which it springs are dried up, the whole structure becomes impotent. And states' rights in this country are among the most authentic sources of power, not only for the promotion of regional interests and diversity, but for the Republic as a whole.

The trouble with the decision to force the issue of desegregation in the field of public education rather than in some other field in the campaign for Negro rights has been that this decision unwittingly touched upon an area in which every one of the different rights and principles we have discussed is involved. It is perfectly true, as Southerners have repeatedly pointed out, that the Constitution is silent on education and that legally as well as traditionally, public education lies in the domain of state legislation. The counter-argument that all public schools today are Federally supported is weak, for Federal subvention is intended in these instances to match and supplement local contributions and does not transform the schools into Federal institutions, like the Federal District courts. It would be very unwise indeed if the Federal government—which now must come to the assistance of more and more enterprises that once were the sole responsibility of the states—were to use its financial support as a means of whipping the states into agreement with positions they would otherwise be slow or altogether unwilling to adopt.

The same overlapping of rights and interests becomes apparent when we examine the issue of education in the light of the three realms of human life—the political, the social, and the private. Children are first of all part of family and home, and this means that they are, or should be, brought up in that atmosphere of idiosyncratic exclusiveness which alone makes a home a home, strong and secure enough to shield its young against the demands of the social and the responsibilities of the political realm. The right of parents to bring up their children as they see fit is a right of privacy, belonging to home and family. Ever since the introduction of compulsory education, this right has been challenged and restricted, but not abolished, by the right of the body politic to prepare children to fulfill their future duties as citizens. The stake of the government in the matter is undeniable—as is the right of the parents. The possibility of private education provides no way out of the dilemma, because it would make the safe-guarding of certain private rights dependent upon economic status and consequently underprivilege those who are forced to send their children to public schools.

Parents' rights over their children are legally restricted by compulsory education and nothing else. The state has the unchallengeable right to prescribe minimum requirements for future citizenship and beyond that to further and support the teaching of subjects and professions which are felt to be desirable and necessary to the nation as a whole. All this involves, however, only the content of the child's education, not the context of association and social life which invariably develops out of his attendance at school; otherwise one would have to challenge the right of private schools to exist. For the child himself, school is the first place away from home where he establishes contact with the public world that surrounds him and his family. This public world is not political but social, and the school is to the child what a job is to an adult. The only difference is that the element of free choice which, in a free society, exists at least in principle in the choosing of jobs and the associations connected with them, is not yet at the disposal of the child but rests with his parents.

To force parents to send their children to an integrated school against their will means to deprive them of rights which clearly belong to them in all free societies—the private right over their children and the social right to free association. As for the children, forced integration means a very serious conflict between home and school, between their private and their social life, and while such conflicts are common in adult life, children cannot be expected to handle them and therefore should not be exposed to them. It has often been remarked that man is never so much of a conformer—that is, a purely social being—as in childhood. The reason is that every child instinctively seeks authorities to guide it into the world in which he is still a stranger, in which he cannot orient himself by his own judgment. To the extent that parents and teachers fail him as authorities, the child will conform more strongly to his own group, and under certain conditions the peer group will become his supreme authority. The result can only be a rise of mob and gang rule, as the news photograph we mentioned above so eloquently demonstrates. The conflict between a segregated home and a desegregated school, between family prejudice and school demands, abolishes at one stroke both the teachers' and the parents' authority, replacing it with the rule of public opinion among children who have neither the ability nor the right to establish a public opinion of their own.

Because the many different factors involved in public education can quickly be set to work at cross purposes, government intervention, even at its best, will always be rather controversial. Hence it seems highly questionable whether it was wise to begin enforcement of civil rights in a domain where no basic human and no basic political right is at stake, and where other rights—social and private—whose protection is no less vital, can so easily be hurt.

A REPLY TO CRITICS

Arendt is responding to David Spitz and Melvin Tumin, who had criticized her article in the Winter 1959 number of Dissent.

OF MY TWO OPPONENTS, Mr. Tumin has put himself outside the scope of discussion and discourse through the tone he adopted in his rebuttal. Mr. Spitz's argument, on the contrary, would deserve a point-by-point analysis if it constituted a refutation of my position. Unfortunately, despite his fairness and the consistency of his own position, Mr. Spitz has misunderstood and misconstrued my argument to such an extent that I would have to quote and requote from our articles sentence after sentence, not to answer his rebuttal, but only in order to correct the misunderstandings upon which this rebuttal was based. This would be tedious and space-consuming, and still could not result in anything better than a restatement of my original argument. I therefore prefer to take my cue from the simple fact that my article was not understood in the terms I wrote it, and I shall try to repeat its essential points on a different, less theoretical level.

The point of departure of my reflections was a picture in the newspapers, showing a Negro girl on her way home from a newly integrated school; she was persecuted by a mob of white children, protected by a white friend of her father, and her face bore eloquent witness to the obvious fact that she was not precisely happy. The picture showed the situation in a nutshell because those who appeared in it were directly affected by the Federal Court order, the children themselves. My first question was: what would I do if I were a Negro mother? The answer: under no circumstances would I expose my child to conditions which made it appear as though it wanted to push its way into a group where it was not wanted. Psychologically, the situation of being unwanted (a typically social predicament) is more difficult to bear than outright persecution (a political predicament) because personal pride is involved. By pride, I do not mean anything like being "proud of being a Negro," or a Jew, or a white Anglo-Saxon Protestant, etc., but that untaught and natural feeling of identity with whatever we happen to be by the accident of birth. Pride, which does not compare and knows neither inferiority nor superiority complexes, is indispensable for personal integrity, and it is lost not so much by persecution as by pushing, or rather being pushed into pushing, one's way out of one group and into another. If I were a Negro mother in the South, I would feel that the Supreme Court ruling, unwillingly but unavoidably, has put my child into a more humiliating position than it had been in before.

Moreover, if I were a Negro I would feel that the very attempt to start desegregation in education and in schools had not only, and very unfairly, shifted the burden of responsibility from the shoulders of adults to those of children. I would in addition be convinced that there is an implication in the whole enterprise of trying to avoid the real issue. The real issue is equality before the law of the country, and equality is violated by segregation laws, that is, by laws enforcing segregation, not by social customs and the manners of educating children. If it were only a matter of equally good education for my children, an effort to grant them equality of opportunity, why was I not asked to fight for an improvement of schools for Negro children and for the immediate establishment of special classes for those children whose scholastic record now makes them acceptable to white schools? Instead of being called upon to fight a clear-cut battle for my indisputable rights—my right to vote and be protected in it, to marry whom I please and be protected in my marriage (though, of course, not in attempts to become anybody's brother-in-law), or my right to equal opportunity—I would feel I had become involved in an affair of social climbing; and if I chose this way of bettering myself, I certainly would prefer to do it by myself, unaided by any government agencies. To be sure, even pushing and using my elbows might not entirely depend upon my own inclinations. I might be forced into it in order to make a decent living or raise the standard of life for my family. Life can be very unpleasant, but whatever it may force me to do—and it certainly does not force me to buy my way into restricted neighborhoods—I can retain my personal integrity precisely to the extent that I act under compulsion and out of some vital necessity, and not merely for social reasons.

My second question was: what would I do if I were a white mother in the South? Again I would try to prevent my child's being dragged into a political battle in the schoolyard. In addition, I would feel that my consent was necessary for any such drastic changes no matter what my opinion of them happened to be. I would agree that the government has a stake in the education of my child insofar as this child is supposed to grow up into a citizen, but I would deny that the government had any right to tell me in whose company my child received its instruction. The rights of parents to decide such matters for their children until they are grown-ups are challenged only by dictatorships.

If, however, I were strongly convinced that the situation in the South could be materially helped by integrated education, I would try— perhaps with the help of the Quakers or some other body of like-minded citizens—to organize a new school for white and colored children and to run it like a pilot project, as a means to persuade other white parents to change their attitudes. To be sure, there, too, I would use the children in what is essentially a political battle, but at least I would have made sure that the children in school are all there with the consent and the help of their parents; there would be no conflict between home and school, though there might arise a conflict between home and school, on one side, and the street on the other. Let us now assume that in the course of such an enterprise, southern citizens who object to integrated education also organized themselves and even succeeded in persuading the state authorities to prevent the opening and functioning of the school. This would be the precise moment when, in my opinion, the federal government should be called upon to intervene. For here we would have again a clear case of segregation enforced by governmental authority.

This now brings us to my third question. I asked myself: what exactly distinguishes the so-called Southern way of life from the American way of life with respect to the color question? And the answer, of course, is simply that while discrimination and segregation are the rule in the whole country, they are enforced by legislation only in the southern states. Hence, whoever wishes to change the situation in the South can hardly

avoid abolishing the marriage laws and intervening to effect free exercise
of the franchise. This is by no means an academic question. It is partly a
matter of constitutional principle which by definition is beyond majority
decisions and practicality; and it also involves, of course, the rights of citizens, as, for instance, the rights of those twenty-five or so Negro boys
from Texas who, while in the Army, had married European girls and
therefore could not go home because in the eyes of Texas legislation they
were guilty of a crime.

The reluctance of American liberals to touch the issue of the marriage laws, their readiness to invoke practicality and shift the ground of the
argument by insisting that the Negroes themselves have no interest in this
matter, their embarrassment when they are reminded of what the whole
world knows to be the most outrageous piece of legislation in the whole
western hemisphere, all this recalls to mind the earlier reluctance of the
founders of the Republic to follow Jefferson's advice and abolish the
crime of slavery. Jefferson, too, yielded for practical reasons, but he, at
least, still had enough political sense to say after the fight was lost: "I
tremble when I think that God is just." He trembled not for the Negroes,
not even for the whites, but for the destiny of the Republic because he
knew that one of its vital principles had been violated right at the beginning. Not discrimination and social segregation, in whatever forms, but
racial legislation constitutes the perpetuation of the original crime in this
country's history.

One last word about education and politics. The idea that one can
change the world by educating the children in the spirit of the future has
been one of the hallmarks of political utopias since antiquity. The trouble
with this idea has always been the same: it can succeed only if the children
are really separated from their parents and brought up in state institutions,
or are indoctrinated in school so that they will turn against their own parents. This is what happens in tyrannies. If, on the other hand, public
authorities are unwilling to draw the consequences of their own vague
hopes and premises, the whole educational experiment remains at best
without result, while, at worst, it irritates and antagonizes both parents
and children who feel that they are deprived of some essential rights. The
series of events in the South that followed the Supreme Court ruling, after which this administration committed itself to fight its battle for civil
rights on the grounds of education and public schools, impresses one with
a sense of futility and needless embitterment as though all parties concerned knew very well that nothing was being achieved under the pretext
that something was being done.

The Social Question

Les malheureux sont la puissance de la terre.
—Saint Just

1

THE PROFESSIONAL REVOLUTIONARIES of the early twentieth century may have been the fools of history, but they certainly were themselves no fools. As a category of revolutionary thought, the notion of historical necessity had more to recommend itself than the mere spectacle of the French Revolution, more even than the thoughtful remembrance of its course of events and the subsequent condensation of happenings into concepts. Behind the appearances was a reality, and this reality was biological and not historical, though it appeared now perhaps for the first time in the full light of history. The most powerful necessity of which we are aware in self-introspection is the life process which permeates our bodies and keeps them in a constant state of a change whose movements are automatic, independent of our own activities, and irresistible—i.e., of an overwhelming urgency. The less we are doing ourselves, the less active we are, the more forcefully will this biological process assert itself, impose its inherent necessity upon us, and overawe us with the fateful automatism of sheer happening that underlies all human history. The necessity of historical processes, originally seen in the image of the revolving, lawful, and necessary motion of the heavenly bodies, found its powerful counterpart in the recurring necessity to which all human life is subject. When this had happened, and it happened when the poor, driven by the needs of their bodies, burst on to the scene of the French Revolution, the astronomic metaphor so plausibly apposite to the sempiternal change, the ups and downs of human destiny, lost its old connotations and acquired the biological imagery which underlies and pervades the organic and social theories of history, which all have in common that they see a multitude—the factual plurality of a nation or a people or society—in the image of one supernatural body driven by one superhuman, irresistible 'general will'.

From On Revolution.

247

The reality which corresponds to this modern imagery is what, since the eighteenth century, we have come to call the social question and what we may better and more simply call the existence of poverty. Poverty is more than deprivation, it is a state of constant want and acute misery whose ignominy consists in its dehumanizing force; poverty is abject because it puts men under the absolute dictate of their bodies, that is, under the absolute dictate of necessity as all men know it from their most intimate experience and outside all speculations. It was under the rule of this necessity that the multitude rushed to the assistance of the French Revolution, inspired it, drove it onward, and eventually sent it to its doom, for this was the multitude of the poor. When they appeared on the scene of politics, necessity appeared with them, and the result was that the power of the old regime became impotent and the new republic was stillborn; freedom had to be surrendered to necessity, to the urgency of the life process itself. When Robespierre declared that 'everything which is necessary to maintain life must be common good and only the surplus can be recognized as private property', he was not only reversing premodern political theory, which held that it was precisely the citizens' surplus in time and goods that must be given and shared in common; he was, again in his own words, finally subjecting revolutionary government to 'the most sacred of all laws, the welfare of the people, the most irrefragable of all titles, necessity'.[1] In other words, he had abandoned his own 'despotism of liberty', his dictatorship for the sake of the foundation of freedom, to the 'rights of the Sans-Culottes', which were 'dress, food and the reproduction of their species'.[2] It was necessity, the urgent needs of the people, that unleashed the terror and sent the Revolution to its doom. Robespierre, finally, knew well enough what had happened though he formulated it (in his last speech) in the form of prophecy: 'We shall perish because, in the history of mankind, we missed the moment to found freedom.' Not the conspiracy of kings and tyrants but the much more powerful conspiracy of necessity and poverty distracted them long enough to miss the 'historical moment'. Meanwhile, the revolution had changed its direction; it aimed no longer at freedom, the goal of the revolution had become the happiness of the people.[3]

The transformation of the Rights of Man into the rights of Sans-Culottes was the turning point not only of the French Revolution but of all revolutions that were to follow. This is due in no small measure to the fact that Karl Marx, the greatest theorist the revolutions ever had, was so much more interested in history than in politics and therefore neglected, almost entirely, the original intentions of the men of the revolutions, the foundation of freedom, and concentrated his attention, almost exclusively, on the seemingly objective course of revolutionary events. In other words, it took more than half a century before the transformation of the Rights of Man into the rights of Sans-Culottes, the abdication of freedom before the dictate of necessity, had found its theorist. When this happened in the work of Karl Marx, the history of modern revolutions seemed to have reached a point of no return: since nothing even remotely comparable in quality on the level of thought resulted from the course of the American Revolution, revolutions had definitely come under the sway of the French Revolution in general and under the predominance of the social question in particular. (This is even true for Tocqueville, whose main concern was to study in America the consequences of that long and inevitable revolution of which the events of 1789 were only the first stage. In the American Revolution itself and the theories of the founders, he remained curiously uninterested.) The enormous impact of Marx's articulations and concepts upon the course of revolution is undeniable, and while it may be tempting, in view of the absurd scholasticism of twentieth-century Marxism, to ascribe this influence to the ideological elements in Marx's work, it may be more accurate to argue the other way round and to ascribe the pernicious influence of Marxism to the many authentic and original discoveries made by Marx. Be that as it may, there is no doubt that the young Marx became convinced that the reason why the French Revolution had failed to found freedom was that it had failed to solve the social question. From this he concluded that freedom and poverty were incompatible. His most explosive and indeed most original contribution to the cause of revolution was that he interpreted the compelling needs of mass poverty in political terms as an uprising, not for the sake of bread or wealth, but for the sake of freedom as well. What he learned from the French Revolution was that poverty can be a political force of the first order. The ideological elements in his teachings, his belief in 'scientific' socialism, in historical necessity, in superstructures, in 'materialism', et cetera, are secondary and derivative in comparison; he shared them with the entire modern age and we find them today not only in the various brands of socialism and communism but in the whole body of the social sciences. . . .

2

. . . The idea that poverty should help men to break the shackles of oppression, because the poor have nothing to lose but their chains, has become so familiar through Marx's teachings that we are tempted to forget that it was unheard of prior to the actual course of the French Revolution. True, a common prejudice, dear to the hearts of those who loved freedom, told men of the eighteenth century that 'Europe for more than twelve centuries past, has presented to view . . . a constant effort, on the part of the people to extricate themselves from the oppression of their rulers.'[4] But by people these men did not mean the poor, and the prejudice of the nineteenth century that all revolutions are social in origin was still quite absent from eighteenth-century theory or experience. As a matter of fact, when the men of the American Revolution came to France and were actually confronted with the social conditions on the continent, with those of the poor as well as of the rich, they no longer believed with Washington that 'the American Revolution . . . seems to have opened the eyes of almost every nation in Europe, and [that] a spirit of equal liberty appears fast to be gaining ground everywhere.' Some of them, even before, had warned the French officers, who had fought with them in the War of Independence, lest their 'hopes be influenced by our triumphs on this virgin soil. You will carry our sentiments with you, but if you try to plant them in a country that has been corrupt for centuries, you will encounter obstacles more formidable than ours. Our liberty has been won with blood; yours will have to be shed in torrents before liberty can take root in the old world.'[5] But their chief reason was much more concrete. It was (as Jefferson wrote two years before the outbreak of the French Revolution) that 'of twenty millions of people . . . there are nineteen millions more wretched, more accursed in every circumstance of human existence than the most conspicuously wretched individual of the whole United States.' (Thus Franklin before him had found himself in Paris thinking 'often of the happiness of New England, where every man is a Freeholder, has a vote in publick Affairs, lives in a tidy warm House, has plenty of good Food and Fewel . . .') Nor did Jefferson expect any great deeds from the rest of society, from those who lived in comfort and luxury; their conduct in his view was ruled by 'manners', the adoption of which would be 'a step to perfect misery' everywhere.[6] Not for a moment did it occur to him that people so 'loaded with misery'—the twofold misery of poverty and corruption—would be able to achieve what had been achieved in America. On the contrary, he warned that these were 'by no means the free-minded people we suppose them in America', and John Adams was convinced that a free republican government 'was as unnatural, irrational, and impracticable as it would be over elephants, lions, tigers, panthers, wolves, and bears, in the royal menagerie at Versailles'.[7] And when, some twenty-five years later, events to an extent had proved him right, and Jefferson thought back to 'the canaille of the cities of Europe' in whose hands any degree of freedom 'would be instantly perverted to the demolition and destruction of everything private and public',[8] he had in mind both the rich and the poor, corruption and misery.

Nothing could be less fair than to take the success of the American Revolution for granted and to sit in judgement over the failure of the men of the French Revolution. The success was not due merely to the wisdom of the founders of the republic, although this wisdom was of a very high calibre indeed. The point to remember is that the American Revolution succeeded, and still did not usher in the *novus ordo saeclorum*, that the Constitution could be established 'in fact', as 'a real existence . . . , in a visible form', and still did not become 'to Liberty what grammar is to language'.[9] The reason for success and failure was that the predicament of poverty was absent from the American scene but present everywhere else in the world. This is a sweeping statement and stands in need of a twofold qualification.

What were absent from the American scene were misery and want rather than poverty, for 'the controversy between the rich and the poor, the laborious and the idle, the learned and the ignorant' was still very much present on the American scene and preoccupied the minds of the founders, who, despite the prosperity of their country, were convinced that these distinctions—'as old as the creation and as extensive as the globe'—were eternal.[10] Yet, since the laborious in America were poor but not miserable—the observations of English and Continental travellers are unanimous and unanimously amazed: 'In a course of 1,200 miles I did not see a single object that solicited charity' (Andrew Burnaby)—they were not driven by want, and the revolution was not overwhelmed by them. The problem they posed was not social but political, it concerned not the order of society but the form of government. The point was that the 'continual toil' and want of leisure of the majority of the population would automatically exclude them from active participation in government—though, of course, not from being represented and from choosing their representatives. But representation is no more than a matter of 'self-preservation' or self-interest, necessary to protect the lives of the labourers and to shield them against the encroachment of government; these essentially negative safeguards by no means open the political realm to the many, nor can they arouse in them that 'passion for distinction'—the 'desire not only to equal or resemble, but to excel'—which, according to John Adams, 'next to self-preservation will forever be the great spring of human actions'.[11] Hence the predicament of the poor after their self-preservation has been assured is that their lives are without consequence, and that they remain excluded from the light of the public realm where excellence can shine; they stand in darkness wherever they go. As John Adams saw it: 'The poor man's conscience is clear; yet he is ashamed . . . He feels himself out of the sight of others, groping in the dark. Mankind takes no notice of him. He rambles and wanders unheeded. In the midst of a crowd, at church, in the market . . . he is in as much obscurity as he would be in a garret or a cellar. He is not disapproved, censured, or reproached; *he is only not seen* . . . To be wholly overlooked, and to know it, are intolerable. If Crusoe on his island had the library of Alexandria, and a certainty that he should never again see the face of man, would he ever open a volume?'[12]

I have quoted these words at some length because the feeling of injustice they express, the conviction that darkness rather than want is the curse of poverty, is extremely rare in the literature of the modern age, although one may suspect that Marx's effort to rewrite history in terms of class struggle was partially at least inspired by the desire to rehabilitate posthumously those to whose injured lives history had added the insult of oblivion. Obviously, it was the absence of misery which enabled John Adams to discover the political predicament of the poor, but his insight into the crippling consequences of obscurity, in contrast to the more obvious ruin which want brought to human life, could hardly be shared by the poor themselves; and since it remained a privileged knowledge it had hardly any influence upon the history of revolutions or the revolutionary tradition. When, in America and elsewhere, the poor became wealthy, they did not become men of leisure whose actions were prompted by a desire to excel, but succumbed to the boredom of vacant time, and while they too developed a taste for 'consideration and congratulation', they were content to get these 'goods' as cheaply as possible, that is, they eliminated the passion for distinction and excellence that can exert itself only in the broad daylight of the public. The end of government remained for them self-preservation, and John Adams' conviction that 'it is a principal end of government to regulate [the passion for distinction]'[13] has not even become a matter of controversy, it is simply forgotten. Instead of entering the market-place, where excellence can shine, they preferred, as it were, to throw open their private houses in 'conspicuous consumption', to display their wealth and to show what, by its very nature, is not fit to be seen by all.

However, these present-day worries of how to prevent the poor of yesterday from developing their own code of behaviour and from imposing it on the body politic, once they have become rich, were still quite absent from the eighteenth century, and even today these American cares, though real enough under the conditions of affluence, may appear sheer luxury in comparison with the cares and worries of the rest of the world. Moreover, modern sensibility is not touched by obscurity, not even by the frustration of 'natural talent' and of the 'desire of superiority' which goes with it. And the fact that John Adams was so deeply moved by it, more deeply than he or anyone else of the Founding Fathers was ever moved by sheer misery, must strike us as very strange indeed when we remind ourselves that the absence of the social question from the American scene was, after all, quite deceptive, and that abject and degrading misery was present everywhere in the form of slavery and Negro labour.

History tells us that it is by no means a matter of course for the spectacle of misery to move men to pity; even during the long centuries when the Christian religion of mercy determined moral standards of Western civilization, compassion operated outside the political realm and frequently outside the established hierarchy of the Church. Yet we deal here with men of the eighteenth century, when this age-old indifference was about to disappear, and when, in the words of Rousseau, an 'innate repugnance at seeing a fellow creature suffer' had become common in certain strata of European society and precisely among those who made the French Revolution. Since then, the passion of compassion has haunted and driven the best men of all revolutions, and the only revolution in which compassion played no role in the motivation of the actors was the American Revolution. If it were not for the presence of Negro slavery on the American scene, one would be tempted to explain this striking aspect exclusively by American prosperity, by Jefferson's 'lovely equality', or by the fact that America was indeed, in William Penn's words, 'a good poor Man's country'. As it is, we are tempted to ask ourselves if the goodness of the poor white man's country did not depend to a considerable degree upon black labour and black misery—there lived roughly 400,000 Negroes along with approximately 1,850,000 white men in America in the middle of the eighteenth century, and even in the absence of reliable statistical data we may be sure that the percentage of complete destitution and misery was considerably lower in the countries of the Old World. From this, we can only conclude that the institution of slavery carries an obscurity even blacker than the obscurity of poverty; the slave, not the poor man, was 'wholly overlooked'. For if Jefferson, and others to a lesser degree, were aware of the primordial crime upon which the fabric of American society rested, if they 'trembled when [they] thought that God is just' (Jefferson), they did so because they were convinced of the incompatibility of the institution of slavery with the foundation of freedom, not because they were moved by pity or by a feeling of solidarity with their fellow men. And this indifference, difficult for us to understand, was not peculiar to Americans and hence must be blamed on slavery rather than on any perversion of the heart or upon the dominance of self-interest. For European witnesses in the eighteenth century, who were moved to compassion by the spectacle of European social conditions, did not react differently. They too thought the specific difference between America and Europe lay 'in the absence of that abject state which condemns [a part of the human race] to ignorance and poverty'.[14] Slavery was no more part of the social question for Europeans than it was for Americans, so that the social question, whether genuinely absent or only hidden in darkness, was non-existent for all practical purposes, and with it, the most powerful and perhaps the most devastating passion motivating revolutionaries, the passion of compassion.

In order to avoid misunderstandings: the social question with which we are concerned here because of its role in revolution must not be equated with the lack of equality of opportunity or the problem of social status which in the last few decades has become a major topic of the social sciences. The game of status-seeking is common enough in certain strata of our society, but it was entirely absent from the society of the eighteenth and nineteenth centuries, and no revolutionary ever thought it his task to introduce mankind to it or to teach the underprivileged the rules of the game. How alien these present-day categories would have been to the minds of the founders of the republic can perhaps best be seen in their attitude to the question of education, which was of great importance to them, not, however, in order to enable every citizen to rise on the social ladder, but because the welfare of the country and the functioning of its political institutions hinged upon education of all citizens. They demanded 'that every citizen should receive an education proportioned to the condition and pursuits of his life', whereby it was understood that for the purpose of education the citizens would 'be divided into two classes—the labouring and the learned' since it would be 'expedient for promoting the public happiness that those persons, whom nature hath endowed with genius and virtue, should be rendered . . . able to guard the sacred deposit of the rights and liberties of their fellow citizens . . . without regard to wealth, birth, or other accidental condition and circumstance'.[15] Even the nineteenth-century liberals' concern with the individual's right to full development of all his gifts was clearly absent from these considerations, as was their special sensitivity to the injustice inherent in the frustration of talent, closely connected with their worship of genius, let alone the present-day notion that everybody has a right to social advancement and hence to education, not because he is gifted but because society owes him the development of skills with which to improve his status.

The realistic views of the Founding Fathers with regard to the shortcomings of human nature are notorious, but the new assumptions of social scientists that those who belong to the lower classes of society have, as it were, a right to burst with resentment, greed, and envy would have astounded them, not only because they would have held that envy and greed are vices no matter where we find them, but perhaps also because their very realism might have told them that such vices are much more frequent in the upper than in the lower social strata.[16] Social mobility was of course relatively high even in eighteenth-century America, but it was not promoted by the Revolution; and if the French Revolution opened careers to talent, and very forcefully indeed, this did not occur until after the Directory and Napoleon Bonaparte, when it was no longer freedom and the foundation of a republic which were at stake but the liquidation of the Revolution and the rise of the bourgeoisie. In our context, the point of the matter is that only the predicament of poverty, and not either individual frustration or social ambitions, can arouse compassion. And with the role of compassion in revolutions, that is, in all except the American Revolution, we must now concern ourselves.

3

To avert one's eyes from the misery and unhappiness of the mass of humankind was no more possible in eighteenth-century Paris, or in nineteenth-century London, where Marx and Engels were to ponder the lessons of the French Revolution, than it is today in some European, most Latin American, and nearly all Asian and African countries. To be sure, the men of the French Revolution had been inspired by hatred of tyranny, and they had no less risen in rebellion against oppression than the men who, in the admiring words of Daniel Webster, 'went to war for a preamble', and 'fought seven years for a declaration'. Against tyranny and oppression, not against exploitation and poverty, they had asserted the rights of the people from whose consent—according to Roman antiquity, in whose school the revolutionary spirit was taught and educated—all power must derive its legitimacy. Since they themselves were clearly politically powerless and hence among the oppressed, they felt they belonged to the people, and they did not need to summon up any solidarity with them. If they became their spokesmen, it was not in the sense that they did something for the people, be it for the sake of power over them or out of love for them; they spoke and acted as their representatives in a common cause. However, what turned out to remain true through the thirteen years of the American Revolution was quickly revealed to be mere fiction in the course of the French Revolution.

In France the downfall of the monarchy did not change the relationship between rulers and ruled, between government and the nation, and no change of government seemed able to heal the rift between them. The revolutionary governments, in this respect not unlike their predecessors, were neither of the people nor by the people, but at best for the people, and at worst a 'usurpation of sovereign power' by self-styled representatives who had put themselves 'in absolute independence with respect to the nation'.[17] The trouble was that the chief difference between the nation and its representatives in all factions had very little to do with 'virtue and genius', as Robespierre and others had hoped, but lay exclusively in the conspicuous difference of social condition which came to light only after the revolution had been achieved. The inescapable fact was that liberation from tyranny spelled freedom only for the few and was hardly felt by the many who remained loaded down by their misery. These had to be liberated once more, and compared to this liberation from the yoke of necessity, the original liberation from tyranny must have looked like child's play. Moreover, in this liberation, the men of the Revolution and the people whom they represented were no longer united by objective bonds in a common cause; a special effort was required of the representatives, an effort of solidarization which Robespierre called virtue, and this virtue was not Roman, it did not aim at the *res publica* and had nothing to do with freedom. Virtue meant to have the welfare of the people in mind, to identify one's own will with the will of the people—*il faut une volonté UNE*—and this effort was directed primarily toward the happiness of the many. After the downfall of the Gironde, it was no longer freedom but happiness that became the 'new idea in Europe' (Saint-Just).

The words *le peuple* are the key words for every understanding of the French Revolution, and their connotations were determined by those who were exposed to the spectacle of the people's sufferings, which they themselves did not share. For the first time, the word covered more than those who did not participate in government, not the citizens but the low people.[18] The very definition of the word was born out of compassion, and the term became the equivalent for misfortune and unhappiness—*le peuple, les malheureux m'applaudissent,* as Robespierre was wont to say; *le peuple toujours malheureux,* as even Sieyès, one of the least sentimental and most sober figures of the Revolution, would put it. By the same token, the personal legitimacy of those who represented the people and were convinced that all legitimate power must derive from them, could reside only in *ce zèle compatissant*, in 'that imperious impulse which attracts us towards *les hommes faibles'*,[19] in short, in the capacity to suffer with the 'immense class of the poor', accompanied by the will to raise compassion to the rank of the supreme political passion and of the highest political virtue.

Historically speaking, compassion became the driving force of the revolutionaries only after the Girondins had failed to produce a constitution and to establish a republican government. The Revolution had come to its turning point when the Jacobins, under the leadership of Robespierre, seized power, not because they were more radical but because they did not share the Girondins' concern with forms of government, because they believed in the people rather than in the republic, and 'pinned their faith on the natural goodness of a class' rather than on institutions and constitutions: 'Under the new Constitution', Robespierre insisted, 'laws should be promulgated "in the name of the French people" instead of the "French Republic".'[20]

This shift of emphasis was caused not by any theory but by the course of the Revolution. However, it is obvious that under these circumstances ancient theory, with its emphasis on popular consent as a prerequisite of lawful government, could no longer be adequate, and to the wisdom of hindsight it appears almost as a matter of course that Rousseau's *volonté générale* should have replaced the ancient notion of consent which, in Rousseau's theory, may be found as the *volonté de tous*.[21] The latter, the will of all, or consent, was not only not dynamic or revolutionary enough for the constitution of a new body politic, or the establishment of government, it obviously presupposed the very existence of government and hence could be deemed sufficient only for particular decisions and the settling of problems as they arose within a given body politic. These formalistic considerations, however, are of secondary importance. It was of greater relevance that the very word 'consent', with its overtones of deliberate choice and considered opinion, was replaced by the word 'will', which essentially excludes all processes of exchange of opinions and an eventual agreement between them. The will, if it is to function at all, must indeed be one and indivisible, 'a divided will would be inconceivable'; there is no possible mediation between wills as there is between opinions. The shift from the republic to the people meant that the enduring unity of the future political body was guaranteed not in the worldly institutions which this people had in common, but in the will of the people themselves. The outstanding quality of this popular will as *volonté générale* was its unanimity, and when Robespierre constantly referred to 'public opinion', he meant by it the unanimity of the general will; he did not think of an opinion upon which many publicly were in agreement.

This enduring unity of a people inspired by one will must not be mistaken for stability. Rousseau took his metaphor of a general will seriously and literally enough to conceive of the nation as a body driven by one will, like an individual, which also can change direction at any time without losing its identity. It was precisely in this sense that Robespierre demanded: 'Il faut une volonté *UNE* . . . Il faut qu'elle soit républicaine ou royaliste.' Rousseau therefore insisted that it would be absurd for the will to bind itself for the future',[22] thus anticipating the fateful instability and faithlessness of revolutionary governments as well as justifying the old fateful conviction of the nation-state that treaties are binding only so long as they serve the so-called national interest. This notion of *raison d'état* is older than the French Revolution for the simple reason that the concept of one will, presiding over the destinies and representing the interests of the nation as a whole, was the current interpretation of the national role to be played by an enlightened monarch whom the revolution had abolished. The problem was indeed how 'to bring twenty-five millions of Frenchmen who had never known or thought of any law but the King's will to rally round any free constitution at all', as John Adams once remarked. Hence, the very attraction of Rousseau's theory for the men of the French Revolution was that he apparently had found a highly ingenious means to put a multitude into the place of a single person; for the general will was nothing more or less than what bound the many into one.

For his construction of such a many-headed one, Rousseau relied on a deceptively simple and plausible example. He took his cue from the common experience that two conflicting interests will bind themselves together when they are confronted by a third that equally opposes them both. Politically speaking, he presupposed the existence and relied upon the unifying power of the common national enemy. Only in the presence of the enemy can such a thing as *la nation une et indivisible,* the ideal of French and of all other nationalism, come to pass. Hence, national unity can assert itself only in foreign affairs, under circumstances of, at least, potential hostility. This conclusion has been the seldom-admitted stock-in-trade of national politics in the nineteenth and twentieth centuries; it is so obviously a consequence of the general-will theory that Saint-Just was already quite familiar with it: only foreign affairs, he insisted, can properly be called 'political', while human relations as such constitute 'the social'.

('Scules les affaires étrangères relevaient de la "politique", tandis que les rapports humains formaient "le social".')[23]

Rousseau himself, however, went one step further. He wished to discover a unifying principle within the nation itself that would be valid for domestic politics as well. Thus, his problem was where to detect a common enemy outside the range of foreign affairs, and his solution was that such an enemy existed within the breast of each citizen, namely, in his particular will and interest; the point of the matter was that this hidden, particular enemy could rise to the rank of a common enemy—unifying the nation from within—if one only added up all particular wills and interests. The common enemy within the nation is the sum total of the particular interests of all citizens. ' "The agreement of two particular interests" ', says Rousseau, quoting the Marquis d'Argenson, ' "is formed by opposition to a third." [Argenson] might have added that *the agreement of all interests is formed by opposition to that of each.* If there were no different interests, the common interest would be barely felt, as it would encounter no obstacle; all would go on of its own accord, and politics would cease to be an art'[24] (my italics).

The reader may have noted the curious equation of will and interest on which the whole body of Rousseau's political theory rests. He uses the terms synonymously throughout the *Social Contract,* and his silent assumption is that the will is some sort of automatic articulation of interest. Hence, the general will is the articulation of a general interest, the interest of the people or the nation as a whole, and because this interest or will is general, its very existence hinges on its being opposed to each interest or will in particular. In Rousseau's construction, the nation need not wait for an enemy to threaten its borders in order to rise 'like one man' and to bring about the *union sacrée;* the oneness of the nation is guaranteed in so far as each citizen carries within himself the common enemy as well as the general interest which the common enemy brings into existence; for the common enemy is the particular interest or the particular will of each man. If only each particular man rises against himself in his particularity, he will be able to arouse in himself his own antagonist, the general will, and thus he will become a true citizen of the national body politic. For 'if one takes away from [all particular] wills the plusses and minuses that cancel one another, the general will remains the sum of the differences.' To partake in the body politic of the nation, each national must rise and remain in constant rebellion against himself.

To be sure, no national statesman has followed Rousseau to this logical extreme, and while the current nationalist concepts of citizenship depend to a very large extent upon the presence of the common enemy from abroad, we find nowhere the assumption that the common enemy resides in everybody's heart. It is different, however, with the revolutionists and the tradition of revolution. It was not only in the French Revolution but in all revolutions which its example inspired that the common interest appeared in the guise of the common enemy, and the theory of terror from Robespierre to Lenin and Stalin presupposes that the interest of the whole must automatically, and indeed permanently, be hostile to the particular interest of the citizen.[25] One has often been struck by the peculiar selflessness of the revolutionists, which should not be confused with 'idealism' or heroism. Virtue has indeed been equated with selflessness ever since Robespierre preached a virtue that was borrowed from Rousseau, and it is the equation which has put, as it were, its indelible stamp upon the revolutionary man and his innermost conviction that the value of a policy may be gauged by the extent to which it will contradict all particular interests, and that the value of a man may be judged by the extent to which he acts against his own interest and against his own will.

Whatever theoretically the explanations and consequences of Rousseau's teachings might be, the point of the matter is that the actual experiences underlying Rousseau's selflessness and Robespierre's 'terror of virtue' cannot be understood without taking into account the crucial role compassion had come to play in the minds and hearts of those who prepared and of those who acted in the course of the French Revolution. To Robespierre, it was obvious that the one force which could and must unite the different classes of society into one nation was the compassion of those who did not suffer with those who were *malheureux,* of the higher classes with the low people. The goodness of man in a state of nature had become axiomatic for Rousseau because he found compassion to be the most natural human reaction to the suffering of others, and therefore the very foundation of all authentic 'natural' human intercourse. Not that Rousseau, or Robespierre for that matter, had ever experienced the innate goodness of natural man outside society; they deduced his existence from the corruption of society, much as one who has intimate knowledge of rotten apples may account for their rottenness by assuming the original existence of healthy ones. What they knew from inner experience was the eternal play between reason and the passions, on one side, the inner dialogue of thought in which man converses with himself, on the other. And since they identified thought with reason, they concluded that reason interfered with passion and compassion alike, that it 'turns man's mind back upon itself, and divides him from everything that could disturb or afflict him'. Reason makes man selfish; it prevents nature 'from identifying itself with the unfortunate sufferer'; or, in the words of Saint-Just: 'Il faut ramener toutes les définitions à la conscience; l'esprit est un sophiste qui conduit toutes les vertus à l'échafaud.'[26]

We are so used to ascribing the rebellion against reason to the early romanticism of the nineteenth century and to understanding, in contrast, the eighteenth century in terms of an 'enlightened' rationalism, with the Temple of Reason as its somewhat grotesque symbol, that we are likely to overlook or to underestimate the strength of these early pleas for passion, for the heart, for the soul, and especially for the soul torn into two, for Rousseau's *âme déchirée*. It is as though Rousseau, in his rebellion against reason, had put a soul, torn into two, into the place of the two-in-one that manifests itself in the silent dialogue of the mind with itself which we call thinking. And since the two-in-one of the soul is a conflict and not a dialogue, it engenders passion in its twofold sense of intense suffering and of intense passionateness. It was this capacity for suffering that Rousseau had pitted against the selfishness of society on one side, against the undisturbed solitude of the mind, engaged in a dialogue with itself, on the other. And it was to this emphasis on suffering, more than to any other part of his teachings, that he owed the enormous, predominant influence over the minds of the men who were to make the Revolution and who found themselves confronted with the overwhelming sufferings of the poor to whom they had opened the doors to the public realm and its light for the first time in history. What counted here, in this great effort of a general human solidarization, was selflessness, the capacity to lose oneself in the sufferings of others, rather than active goodness, and what appeared most odious and even most dangerous was selfishness rather than wickedness. These men, moreover, were much better acquainted with vice than they were with evil; they had seen the vices of the rich and their incredible selfishness, and they concluded that virtue must be 'the appanage of misfortune and the patrimony' of the poor. They had watched how 'the charms of pleasure were escorted by crime', and they argued that the torments of misery must engender goodness.[27] The magic of compassion was that it opened the heart of the sufferer to the sufferings of others, whereby it established and confirmed the 'natural' bond between men which only the rich had lost. Where passion, the capacity for suffering, and compassion, the capacity for suffering with others, ended, vice began. Selfishness was a kind of 'natural' depravity. If Rousseau had introduced compassion into political theory, it was Robespierre who brought it on to the marketplace with the vehemence of his great revolutionary oratory.

It was perhaps unavoidable that the problem of good and evil, of

their impact upon the course of human destinies, in its stark, unsophisti-
cated simplicity should have haunted the minds of men at the very moment when they were asserting or reasserting human dignity without any
resort to institutionalized religion. But the depth of this problem could
hardly be sounded by those who mistook for goodness the natural, 'innate
repugnance of man to see his fellow creatures suffer' (Rousseau), and who
thought that selfishness and hypocrisy were the epitome of wickedness.
More importantly even, the terrifying question of good and evil could not
even be posed, at least not in the framework of Western traditions, without taking into account the only completely valid, completely convincing
experience Western mankind had ever had with active love of goodness as
the inspiring principle of all actions, that is, without consideration of the
person of Jesus of Nazareth. This consideration came to pass in the aftermath of the Revolution, and while it is true that neither Rousseau nor
Robespierre had been able to measure up to the questions which the
teachings of the one and the acts of the other had brought onto the
agenda of the following generations, it may also be true that without them
and without the French Revolution neither Melville nor Dostoevski
would have dared to undo the haloed transformation of Jesus of Nazareth
into Christ, to make him return to the world of men—the one in *Billy
Budd,* and the other in 'The Grand Inquisitor'—and to show openly and
concretely, though of course poetically and metaphorically, upon what
tragic and self-defeating enterprise the men of the French Revolution had
embarked almost without knowing it. If we want to know what absolute
goodness would signify for the course of human affairs (as distinguished
from the course of divine matters), we had better turn to the poets, and
we can do it safely enough as long as we remember that 'the poet but embodies in verse those exaltations of sentiment that a nature like Nelson's,
the opportunity being given, vitalizes into acts' (Melville). At least we can
learn from them that absolute goodness is hardly any less dangerous than
absolute evil, that it does not consist in selflessness, for surely the Grand
Inquisitor is selfless enough, and that it is beyond virtue, even the virtue of Captain Vere. Neither Rousseau nor Robespierre was capable of
dreaming of a goodness beyond virtue, just as they were unable to imagine that radical evil would 'partake nothing of the sordid or sensual'
(Melville), that there could be wickedness beyond vice.

    That the men of the French Revolution should have been unable to
think in these terms, and therefore never really touched the heart of the
matter which their own actions had brought to the fore, is actually almost
a matter of course. Obviously, they knew at most the principles that inspired their acts, but hardly the meaning of the story which eventually was

to result from them. Melville and Dostoevski, at any rate, even if they had not been the great writers and thinkers they actually both were, certainly were in a better position to know what it all had been about. Melville especially, since he could draw from a much richer range of political experience than Dostoevski, knew how to talk back directly to the men of the French Revolution and to their proposition that man is good in a state of nature and becomes wicked in society. This he did in *Billy Budd,* where it is as though he said: Let us assume you are right and your 'natural man', born outside the ranks of society, a 'foundling' endowed with nothing but a barbarian's innocence and goodness, were to walk the earth again—for surely it would be a return, a second coming; you certainly remember that this happened before; you can't have forgotten the story which became the foundation legend of Christian civilization. But in case you have forgotten, let me retell you the story in the context of your own circumstances and even in your own terminology.

Compassion and goodness may be related phenomena, but they are not the same. Compassion plays a role, even an important one, in *Billy Budd,* but its topic is goodness beyond virtue and evil beyond vice, and the plot of the story consists in confronting these two. Goodness beyond virtue is natural goodness and wickedness beyond vice is 'a depravity according to nature' which 'partakes nothing of the sordid or sensual'. Both are outside society, and the two men who embody them come, socially speaking, from nowhere. Not only is Billy Budd a foundling; Claggart, his antagonist, is likewise a man whose origin is unknown. In the confrontation itself there is nothing tragic; natural goodness, though it 'stammers' and cannot make itself heard and understood, is stronger than wickedness because wickedness is nature's depravity, and 'natural' nature is stronger than depraved and perverted nature. The greatness of this part of the story lies in that goodness, because it is part of 'nature', does not act meekly but asserts itself forcefully and, indeed, violently so that we are convinced: only the violent act with which Billy Budd strikes dead the man who bore false witness against him is adequate, it eliminates nature's 'depravity'. This, however, is not the end but the beginning of the story. The story unfolds after 'nature' has run its course, with the result that the wicked man is dead and the good man has prevailed. The trouble now is that the good man, because he encountered evil, has become a wrong-doer too, and this even if we assume that Billy Budd did not lose his innocence, that he remained 'an angel of God'. It is at this point that 'virtue' in the person of Captain Vere is introduced into the conflict between absolute good and absolute evil, and here the tragedy begins. Virtue—which perhaps is less than goodness but still alone is capable 'of embodiment in lasting institutions'—must prevail at the expense of the good man as well; absolute, natural innocence, because it can only act violently, is 'at war with the peace of the world and the true welfare of mankind', so that virtue finally interferes not to prevent the crime of evil but to punish the violence of absolute innocence. Claggart was 'struck by an angel of God! Yet the angel must hang!' The tragedy is that the law is made for men, and neither for angels nor for devils. Laws and all 'lasting institutions' break down not only under the onslaught of elemental evil but under the impact of absolute innocence as well. The law, moving between crime and virtue, cannot recognize what is beyond it, and while it has no punishment to mete out to elemental evil, it cannot but punish elemental goodness even if the virtuous man, Captain Vere, recognizes that only the violence of this goodness is adequate to the depraved power of evil. The absolute— and to Melville an absolute was incorporated in the Rights of Man—spells doom to everyone when it is introduced into the political realm.

We noted before that the passion of compassion was singularly absent from the minds and hearts of the men who made the American Revolution. Who would doubt that John Adams was right when he wrote: 'The envy and rancor of the multitude against the rich is universal and restrained only by fear or necessity. A beggar can never comprehend the reason why another should ride in a coach while he has no bread',[28] and still no one familiar with misery can fail to be shocked by the peculiar coldness and indifferent 'objectivity' of his judgement. Because he was an American, Melville knew better how to talk back to the theoretical proposition of the men of the French Revolution—that man is good by nature—than how to take into account the crucial passionate concern which lay behind their theories, the concern with the suffering multitude. Envy in *Billy Budd,* characteristically, is not envy of the poor for the rich but of 'depraved nature' for natural integrity—it is Claggart who is envious of Billy Budd—and compassion is not the suffering of the one who is spared with the man who is stricken in the flesh; on the contrary, it is Billy Budd, the victim, who feels compassion for Captain Vere, for the man who sends him to his doom.

The classical story of the other, non-theoretical side of the French Revolution, the story of the motivation behind the words and deeds of its main actors, is 'The Grand Inquisitor', in which Dostoevski contrasts the mute compassion of Jesus with the eloquent pity of the Inquisitor. For compassion, to be stricken with the suffering of someone else as though it were contagious, and pity, to be sorry without being touched in the flesh, are not only not the same, they may not even be related. Compassion, by its very nature, cannot be touched off by the sufferings of a whole class or a people, or, least of all, mankind as a whole. It cannot reach out farther than what is suffered by one person and still remain what it is supposed to be, co-suffering. Its strength hinges on the strength of passion itself, which, in contrast to reason, can comprehend only the particular, but has no notion of the general and no capacity for generalization. The sin of the Grand Inquisitor was that he, like Robespierre, was 'attracted toward *les hommes faibles*', not only because such attraction was indistinguishable from lust for power, but also because he had depersonalized the sufferers, lumped them together into an aggregate—the people *toujours malheureux,* the suffering masses, et cetera. To Dostoevski, the sign of Jesus's divinity clearly was his ability to have compassion with all men in their singularity, that is, without lumping them together into some such entity as one suffering mankind. The greatness of the story, apart from its theological implications, lies in that we are made to feel how false the idealistic, high-flown phrases of the most exquisite pity sound the moment they are confronted with compassion.

Closely connected with this inability to generalize is the curious muteness or, at least, awkwardness with words that, in contrast to the eloquence of virtue, is the sign of goodness, as it is the sign of compassion in contrast to the loquacity of pity. Passion and compassion are not speechless, but their language consists in gestures and expressions of countenance rather than in words. It is because he listens to the Grand Inquisitor's speech with compassion, and not for lack of arguments, that Jesus remains silent, struck, as it were, by the suffering which lay behind the easy flow of his opponent's great monologue. The intensity of this listening transforms the monologue into a dialogue, but it can be ended only by a gesture, the gesture of the kiss, not by words. It is upon the same note of compassion—this time the compassion of the doomed man with the compassionate suffering felt for him by the man who doomed him—that Billy Budd ends his life, and, by the same token, the argument over the Captain's sentence, and his 'God bless Captain Vere!' is certainly closer to a gesture than to a speech. Compassion, in this respect not unlike love, abolishes the distance, the in-between which always exists in human intercourse, and if virtue will always be ready to assert that it is better to suffer wrong than to do wrong, compassion will transcend this by stating in complete and even naïve sincerity that it is easier to suffer than to see others suffer.

Because compassion abolishes the distance, the worldly space between men where political matters, the whole realm of human affairs, are located, it remains, politically speaking irrelevant and without consequence. In the words of Melville, it is incapable of establishing 'lasting institutions'. Jesus's silence in 'The Grand Inquisitor' and Billy Budd's stammer indicate the same, namely their incapacity (or unwillingness) for all kinds of predicative or argumentative speech, in which someone talks *to* somebody *about* something that is of interest to both because it *inter-est,* it is between them. Such talkative and argumentative interest in the world is entirely alien to compassion, which is directed solely, and with passionate intensity, towards suffering man himself; compassion speaks only to the extent that it has to reply directly to the sheer expressionist sound and gestures through which suffering becomes audible and visible in the world. As a rule, it is not compassion which sets out to change worldly conditions in order to ease human suffering, but if it does, it will shun the drawn-out wearisome processes of persuasion, negotiation, and compromise, which are the processes of law and politics, and lend its voice to the suffering itself, which must claim for swift and direct action, that is, for action with the means of violence.

Here again, the relatedness of the phenomena of goodness and compassion is manifest. For goodness that is beyond virtue, and hence beyond temptation, ignorant of the argumentative reasoning by which man fends off temptations and, by this very process, comes to know the ways of wickedness, is also incapable of learning the arts of persuading and arguing. The great maxim of all civilized legal systems, that the burden of proof must always rest with the accuser, sprang from the insight that only guilt can be irrefutably proved. Innocence, on the contrary, to the extent that it is more than 'not guilty', cannot be proved but must be accepted on faith, whereby the trouble is that this faith cannot be supported by the given word, which can be a lie. Billy Budd could have spoken with the tongues of angels, and yet would not have been able to refute the accusations of the 'elemental evil' that confronted him; he could only raise his hand and strike the accuser dead.

Clearly, Melville reversed the primordial legendary crime, Cain slew Abel, which has played such an enormous role in our tradition of political thought, but this reversal was not arbitrary; it followed from the reversal the men of the French Revolution had made of the proposition of original sin, which they had replaced by the proposition of original goodness. Melville states the guiding question of his story himself in the Preface: How was it possible that after 'the rectification of the Old World's hereditary wrongs . . . straightway the Revolution itself became a wrongdoer, one more oppressive than the Kings?' He found the answer—surprisingly enough if one considers the common equations of goodness with meekness and weakness—in that goodness is strong, stronger perhaps even than wickedness, but that it shares with 'elemental evil' the elementary violence inherent in all strength and detrimental to all forms of political organization. It is as though he said: Let us suppose that from now on the foundation stone of our political life will be that Abel slew Cain. Don't you see that from this deed of violence the same chain of wrongdoing will follow, only that now mankind will not even have the consolation that the violence it must call crime is indeed characteristic of evil men only?

4

It is more than doubtful that Rousseau discovered compassion out of suffering with others, and it is more than probable that in this, as in nearly all other respects, he was guided by his rebellion against high society, especially against its glaring indifference towards the suffering of those who surrounded it. He had summoned up the resources of the heart against the indifference of the salon and against the 'heartlessness' of reason, both of which will say 'at the sight of the misfortunes of others: Perish if you wish, I am secure'.[29] Yet while the plight of others aroused his heart, he became involved in his heart rather than in the sufferings of others, and he was enchanted with its moods and caprices as they disclosed themselves in the sweet delight of intimacy which Rousseau was one of the first to discover and which from then on began playing its important role in the formation of modern sensibility. In this sphere of intimacy, compassion became talkative, as it were, since it came to serve, together with the passions and with suffering, as stimulus for the vitality of the newly discovered range of emotions. Compassion, in other words, was discovered and understood as an emotion or a sentiment, and the sentiment which corresponds to the passion of compassion is, of course, pity.

Pity may be the perversion of compassion, but its alternative is solidarity. It is out of pity that men are 'attracted toward *les hommes faibles*', but it is out of solidarity that they establish deliberately and, as it were, dispassionately a community of interest with the oppressed and exploited. The common interest would then be 'the grandeur of man', or 'the honour of the human race', or the dignity of man. For solidarity, because it partakes of reason, and hence of generality, is able to comprehend a multitude conceptually, not only the multitude of a class or a nation or a people, but eventually all mankind. But this solidarity, though it may be aroused by suffering, is not guided by it, and it comprehends the strong and the rich no less than the weak and the poor; compared with the sentiment of pity, it may appear cold and abstract, for it remains committed to 'ideas'—to greatness, or honour, or dignity—rather than to any 'love' of men. Pity, because it is not stricken in the flesh and keeps its sentimental distance, can succeed where compassion always will fail; it can reach out to the multitude and therefore, like solidarity, enter the market-place. But pity, in contrast to solidarity, does not look upon both fortune and misfortune, the strong and the weak, with an equal eye; without the presence of misfortune, pity could not exist, and it therefore has just as much vested interest in the existence of the unhappy as thirst for power has a vested interest in the existence of the weak. Moreover, by virtue of being a sentiment, pity can be enjoyed for its own sake, and this will almost automatically lead to a glorification of its cause, which is the suffering of others. Terminologically speaking, solidarity is a principle that can inspire and guide action, compassion is one of the passions, and pity is a sentiment. Robespierre's glorification of the poor, at any rate, his praise of suffering as the spring of virtue were sentimental in the strict sense of the word, and as such dangerous enough, even if they were not, as we are inclined to suspect, a mere pretext for lust for power.

Pity, taken as the spring of virtue, has proved to possess a greater capacity for cruelty than cruelty itself. 'Par pitié, par amour pour l'humanité, soyez inhumains!'—these words, taken almost at random from a petition of one of the sections of the Parisian Commune to the National Convention, are neither accidental nor extreme; they are the authentic language of pity. They are followed by a crude but nevertheless precise and very common rationalization of pity's cruelty: 'Thus, the clever and helpful surgeon with his cruel and benevolent knife cuts off the gangrened limb in order to save the body of the sick man.'[30] Moreover, sentiments, as distinguished from passion and principle, are boundless, and even if Robespierre had been motivated by the passion of compassion, his compassion would have become pity when he brought it out into the open where he could no longer direct it towards specific suffering and focus it on particular persons. What had perhaps been genuine passions turned into the boundlessness of an emotion that seemed to respond only too well to the boundless suffering of the multitude in their sheer overwhelming numbers. By the same token, he lost the capacity to establish and hold fast to rapports with persons in their singularity; the ocean of suffering around him and the turbulent sea of emotion within him, the latter geared to receive and respond to the former, drowned all specific considerations, the considerations of friendship no less than considerations of statecraft and principle. It is in these matters, rather than in any particular fault of character, that we must look for the roots of Robespierre's surprising faithlessness that foreshadowed the greater perfidy which was to play such a monstrous role in the revolutionary tradition. Since the days of the French

Revolution, it has been the boundlessness of their sentiments that made revolutionaries so curiously insensitive to reality in general and to the reality of persons in particular, whom they felt no compunctions in sacrificing to their 'principles', or to the course of history, or to the cause of revolution as such. While this emotion-laden insensitivity to reality was quite conspicuous already in Rousseau's own behaviour, his fantastic irresponsibility and unreliability, it became a political factor of importance only with Robespierre, who introduced it into the factional strife of the Revolution.[31]

Politically speaking, one may say that the evil of Robespierre's virtue was that it did not accept any limitations. In Montesquieu's great insight that even virtue must have its limits, he would have seen no more than the dictum of a cold heart. Thanks to the doubtful wisdom of hindsight, we can be aware of Montesquieu's greater wisdom of foresight and recall how Robespierre's pity-inspired virtue, from the beginning of his rule, played havoc with justice and made light of laws.[32] Measured against the immense sufferings of the immense majority of the people, the impartiality of justice and law, the application of the same rules to those who sleep in palaces and those who sleep under the bridges of Paris, was like a mockery. Since the revolution had opened the gates of the political realm to the poor, this realm had indeed become 'social'. It was overwhelmed by the cares and worries which actually belonged in the sphere of the household and which, even if they were permitted to enter the public realm, could not be solved by political means, since they were matters of administration, to be put into the hands of experts, rather than issues which could be settled by the twofold process of decision and persuasion. It is true that social and economic matters had intruded into the public realm before the revolutions of the late eighteenth century, and the transformation of government into administration, the replacement of personal rule by bureaucratic measures, even the attending transmutation of laws into decrees, had been one of the outstanding characteristics of absolutism. But with the downfall of political and legal authority and the rise of revolution, it was people rather than general economic and financial problems that were at stake, and they did not merely intrude into but burst upon the political domain. Their need was violent, and, as it were, prepolitical; it seemed that only violence could be strong and swift enough to help them.

By the same token, the whole question of politics, including the then gravest problem, the problem of form of government, became a matter of foreign affairs. Just as Louis XVI had been beheaded as a traitor rather than as a tyrant, so the whole issue of monarchy versus republic turned into an affair of armed foreign aggression against the French nation. This is the same decisive shift, occurring at the turning point of the Revolution, which we identified earlier as the shift from forms of government to 'the natural goodness of a class', or from the republic to the people. Historically it was at this point that the Revolution disintegrated into war, into civil war within and foreign wars without, and with it the newly won but never duly constituted power of the people disintegrated into a chaos of violence. If the question of the new form of government was to be decided on the battlefield, then it was violence, and not power, that was to turn the scale. If liberation from poverty and the happiness of the people were the true and exclusive aims of the Revolution, then Saint Just's youthfully blasphemous witticism, 'Nothing resembles virtue so much as a great crime', was no more than an everyday observation, for then it followed indeed that all must be 'permitted to those who act in the revolutionary direction.'[33]

It would be difficult to find, in the whole body of revolutionary oratory, a sentence that pointed with greater precision to the issues about which the founders and the liberators, the men of the American Revolution and the men in France, parted company. The direction of the American Revolution remained committed to the foundation of freedom and the establishment of lasting institutions, and to those who acted in this direction nothing was permitted that would have been outside the range of civil law. The direction of the French Revolution was deflected almost from its beginning from this course of foundation through the immediacy of suffering; it was determined by the exigencies of liberation not from tyranny but from necessity, and it was actuated by the limitless immensity of both the people's misery and the pity this misery inspired. The lawlessness of the 'all is permitted' sprang here still from the sentiments of the heart whose very boundlessness helped in the unleashing of a stream of boundless violence.

Not that the men of the American Revolution could have been ignorant of the great force which violence, the purposeful violation of all laws of civil society, could release. On the contrary, the fact that the horror and repulsion at the news of the reign of terror in France were clearly greater and more unanimous in the United States than in Europe can best be explained by the greater familiarity with violence and lawlessness in a colonial country. The first paths through the 'unstoried wilderness' of the continent had been opened then, as they were to be opened for a hundred more years, 'in general by the most vicious elements', as though 'the first steps [could not be] trod, . . . [the] first trees [not be] felled' without 'shocking violations' and 'sudden devastations'.[34] But although those who, for whatever reasons, rushed out of society into the wilderness acted as if all was permitted to them who had left the range of enforceable law, neither they themselves nor those who watched them, and not even those who admired them, ever thought that a new law and a new world could spring from such conduct. However criminal and even beastly the deeds might have been that helped colonize the American continent, they remained acts of single men, and if they gave cause for generalization and reflection, these reflections were perhaps upon some beastly potentialities inherent in man's nature, but hardly upon the political behaviour of organized groups, and certainly not upon a historical necessity that could progress only via crimes and criminals.

To be sure, the men living on the American frontier also belonged to the people for whom the new body politic was devised and constituted, but neither they nor those who were populating the settled regions ever became a singular to the founders. The word 'people' retained for them the meaning of manyness, of the endless variety of a multitude whose majesty resided in its very plurality. Opposition to public opinion, namely to the potential unanimity of all, was therefore one of the many things upon which the men of the American Revolution were in complete agreement; they knew that the public realm in a republic was constituted by an exchange of opinion between equals, and that this realm would simply disappear the very moment an exchange became superfluous because all equals happened to be of the same opinion. They never referred to public opinion in their argument, as Robespierre and the men of the French Revolution invariably did to add force to their own opinions; in their eyes, the rule of public opinion was a form of tyranny. To such an extent indeed was the American concept of people identified with a multitude of voices and interests that Jefferson could establish it as a principle 'to make us one nation as to foreign concerns, and keep us distinct in domestic ones',[35] just as Madison could assert that their regulation 'forms the principal task of . . . legislation, and involves the spirit of party and faction in the operations of the government'. The positive accent here on faction is noteworthy, since it stands in flagrant contradiction to classical tradition, to which the Founding Fathers otherwise paid the closest attention. Madison must have been conscious of his deviation on so important a point, and he was explicit in stating its cause, which was his insight into the nature of human reason rather than any reflection upon the diversity of conflicting interests in society. According to him, party and faction in government correspond to the many voices and differences in opinion which must continue 'as long as the reason of man continues fallible, and he is at liberty to exercise it'.[36]

The fact of the matter was, of course, that the kind of multitude which the founders of the American republic first represented and then constituted politically, if it existed at all in Europe, certainly ceased to exist as soon as one approached the lower strata of the population. The *malheureux* whom the French Revolution had brought out of the darkness of their misery were a multitude only in the mere numerical sense. Rousseau's image of a 'multitude . . . united in one body' and driven by one will was an exact description of what they actually were, for what urged them on was the quest for bread, and the cry for bread will always be uttered with one voice. In so far as we all need bread, we are indeed all the same, and may as well unite into one body. It is by no means merely a matter of misguided theory that the French concept of *le peuple* has carried, from its beginning, the connotation of a multiheaded monster, a mass that moves as one body and acts as though possessed by one will; and if this notion has spread to the four corners of the earth, it is not because of any influence of abstract ideas but because of its obvious plausibility under conditions of abject poverty. The political trouble which misery of the people holds in store is that manyness can in fact assume the guise of oneness, that suffering indeed breeds moods and emotions and attitudes that resemble solidarity to the point of confusion, and that—last, not least—pity for the many is easily confounded with compassion for one person when the 'compassionate zeal' (*le zèle compatissant*) can fasten upon an object whose oneness seems to fulfil the prerequisites of compassion, while its immensity, at the same time, corresponds to the boundlessness of sheer emotion. Robespierre once compared the nation to the ocean; it was indeed the ocean of misery and the ocean-like sentiments it aroused that combined to drown the foundations of freedom.

The superior wisdom of the American founders in theory and practice is conspicuous and impressive enough, and yet has never carried with it sufficient persuasiveness and plausibility to prevail in the tradition of revolution. It is as though the American Revolution was achieved in a kind of ivory tower into which the fearful spectacle of human misery, the haunting voices of abject poverty, never penetrated. And this was, and remained for a long time, the spectacle and the voice not of humanity but of humankind. Since there were no sufferings around them that could have aroused their passions, no overwhelmingly urgent needs that would have tempted them to submit to necessity, no pity to lead them astray from reason, the men of the American Revolution remained men of action from beginning to end, from the Declaration of Independence to the framing of the Constitution. Their sound realism was never put to the test of compassion, their common sense was never exposed to the absurd hope that man, whom Christianity had held to be sinful and corrupt in his nature, might still be revealed to be an angel. Since passion had never tempted them in its noblest form as compassion, they found it easy to think of passion in terms of desire and to banish from it any connotation of its original meaning, which is παθετν, to suffer *and* to endure. This lack of experience gives their theories, even if they are sound, an air of lightheartedness, a certain weightlessness, which may well put into jeopardy their durability. For, humanly speaking, it is endurance which enables man to create durability and continuity. Their thought did not carry them any further than to the point of understanding government in the image of individual reason and construing the rule of government over the governed according to the age-old model of the rule of reason over the passions. To bring the 'irrationality' of desires and emotions under the control of rationality was, of course, a thought dear to the Enlightenment, and as such was quickly found wanting in many respects, especially in its facile and superficial equation of thought with reason and of reason with rationality.

There is, however, another side to this matter. Whatever the passions and the emotions may be, and whatever their true connection with thought and reason, they certainly are located in the human heart. And not only is the human heart a place of darkness which, with certainty, no human eye can penetrate; the qualities of the heart need darkness and protection against the light of the public to grow and to remain what they are meant to be, innermost motives which are not for public display. However deeply heartfelt a motive may be, once it is brought out and exposed for public inspection it becomes an object of suspicion rather than insight; when the light of the public falls upon it, it appears and even shines, but, unlike deeds and words which are meant to appear, whose very existence hinges on appearance, the motives behind such deeds and words are destroyed in their essence through appearance; when they appear they become 'mere appearances' behind which again other, ulterior motives may luck, such as hypocrisy and deceit. The same sad logic of the human heart, which has almost automatically caused modern 'motivational research' to develop into an eerie sort of filing cabinet for human vices, into a veritable science of misanthropy, made Robespierre and his followers, once they had equated virtue with the qualities of the heart, see intrigue and calumny, treachery and hypocrisy everywhere. The fateful mood of suspicion, so glaringly omnipresent through the French Revolution even before a Law of Suspects spelled out its frightful implications, and so conspicuously absent from even the most bitter disagreements between the men of the American Revolution, arose directly out of this misplaced emphasis on the heart as the source of political virtue, on *le cœur, une âme droite, un caractère moral.*

The heart, moreover—as the great French moralists from Montaigne to Pascal knew well enough even before the great psychologists of the nineteenth century, Kierkegaard, Dostoevski, Nietzsche—keeps its resources alive through a constant struggle that goes on in its darkness and because of its darkness. When we say that nobody but God can see (and, perhaps, can bear to see) the nakedness of a human heart, 'nobody' includes one's own self—if only because our sense of unequivocal reality is so bound up with the presence of others that we can never be sure of anything that only we ourselves know and no one else. The consequence of this hiddenness is that our entire psychological life, the process of moods in our souls, is cursed with a suspicion we constantly feel we must raise against ourselves, against our innermost motives. Robespierre's insane lack of trust in others, even in his close friends, sprang ultimately from his not so insane but quite normal suspicion of himself. Since his very credo forced him to play the 'incorruptible' in public every day and to display his virtue, to open his heart as he understood it, at least once a week, how could he be sure that he was not the one thing he probably feared most in his life, a hypocrite? The heart knows many such intimate struggles, and it knows too that what was straight when it was hidden must appear crooked when it is displayed. It knows how to deal with these problems of darkness according to its own 'logic', although it has no solution for them, since a solution demands light, and it is precisely the light of the world that distorts the life of the heart. The truth of Rousseau's *âme déchirée,* apart from its function in the formation of the *volonté générale,* is that the heart begins to beat properly only when it has been broken or is being torn in conflict, but this is a truth which cannot prevail outside the life of the soul and within the realm of human affairs.

Robespierre carried the conflicts of the soul, Rousseau's *âme déchirée,* into politics, where they became murderous because they were insoluble. 'The hunt for hypocrites is boundless and can produce nothing but demoralization.'[37] If, in the words of Robespierre, 'patriotism was a thing of the heart', then the reign of virtue was bound to be at worst the rule of hypocrisy, and at best the never-ending fight to ferret out the hypocrites, a fight which could only end in defeat because of the simple fact that it was impossible to distinguish between true and false patriots. When his heartfelt patriotism or his ever-suspicious virtue were displayed in public, they were no longer principles upon which to act or motives by which to be inspired; they had degenerated into mere appearances and had become part of a show in which Tartuffe was bound to play the principal part. It was as though the Cartesian doubt—*je doute donc je suis*—had become the principle of the political realm, and the reason was that Robespierre had performed the same introversion upon the deeds of action that Descartes had performed upon the articulations of thought. To be sure, every deed has its motives as it has its goal and its principle; but the act itself, though it proclaims its goal and makes manifest its principle, does not reveal the innermost motivation of the agent. His motives remain dark, they do not shine but are hidden not only from others but, most of the time, from himself, from his self-inspection, as well. Hence, the search for motives, the demand that everybody display in public his innermost motivation, since it actually demands the impossible, transforms all actors into hypocrites; the moment the display of motives begins, hypocrisy begins to poison all human relations. The effort, moreover, to drag the dark and the hidden into the light of day can only result in an open and blatant manifestation of those acts whose very nature makes them seek the protection of darkness; it is, unfortunately, in the essence of these things that every effort to make goodness manifest in public ends with the appearance of crime and criminality on the political scene. In politics, more than anywhere else, we have no possibility of distinguishing between being and appearance. In the realm of human affairs, being and appearance are indeed one and the same. . . .

Notes

1. *Œuvres,* ed. Laponneraye, 1840, vol. 3, p. 514.
2. A 'Declaration of the Rights of Sans-Culottes' was proposed by Boisset, a friend of Robespierre. See J. M. Thompson, *Robespierre,* Oxford, 1939, p. 365.
3. *Le But de la Révolution est le bonheur du peuple,* as the manifest of Sans-Culottism proclaimed it in November 1793. See no. 52 in *Die Sanskulotten von Paris. Dokumente zur Geschichte der Volksbewegung 1793–1794,* ed. Walter Markov and Albert Soboul, Berlin (East), 1957.
4. James Monroe in J. Elliot, *Debates in the Several State Conventions on the Adoption of the Federal Constitution . . . ,* vol. 3, 1861.
5. Both quotations are drawn from Lord Acton, *Lectures on the French Revolution* (1910), Noonday paperback edition, 1959.
6. In a letter from Paris to Mrs Trist, 18 August 1785.
7. Jefferson in a letter from Paris to Mr Wythe, 13 August 1786; John Adams in a letter to Jefferson, 13 July 1813.
8. In a letter to John Adams, 28 October 1813.
9. Thomas Paine, *The Rights of Man* (1791), Everyman's Library edition, pp. 48, 77.

10. John Adams, *Discourses on Davila, Works,* Boston, 1851, vol. VI, p. 280.

11. ibid., pp. 267 and 279.

12. ibid., pp. 239–40.

13. ibid., p. 234.

14. Quoted from D. Echeverria, *Mirage in the West: A History of the French Image of American Society to 1815,* Princeton, 1957, p. 152.

15. See Jefferson, 'A Bill for the More General Diffusion of Knowledge' of 1779 and his 'Plan for an Educational System' of 1814, in *The Complete Jefferson,* edited by Saul K. Padover, 1943, pp. 1048 and 1065.

16. A recent study of the opinions of working-class men on the subject of equality by Robert E. Lane—'The Fear of Equality' in *American Political Science Review,* vol. 53, March 1959—for instance, evaluates the lack of resentment on the part of the working man as 'fear of equality', their conviction that the rich are not happier than other people as an attempt 'to take care of a gnawing and illegitimate envy', their refusal to disregard their friends if they came into money as lack of 'security', et cetera. The short essay manages to turn every virtue into a hidden vice—a *tour de force* in the art of hunting for non-existent ulterior motives.

17. Robespierre, *Œuvres complètes,* ed. G. Laurent, 1939, vol. IV; *Le Défenseur de la constitution* (1792), no. 11, p. 328.

18. *Le peuple* was identical with *menu* or *petit peuple,* and it consisted of 'small businessmen, grocers, artisans, workers, employees, salesmen, servants, day labourers, *lumpenproletariem,* but also of poor artists, play-actors, penniless writers'. See Walter Markov, 'Uber das Ende der Pariser Sansculottenbewegung', in *Beiträge zum neuen Geschichtsbild, zum 60. Geburstag von Alfred Meusel,* Berlin, 1956.

19. Robespierre in 'Adresse aux Français' of July 1791, quoted from J. M. Thompson, op. cit., 1939, p. 176.

20. ibid., p. 365, and speech before the National Convention of February 1794.

21. See *Du contrat social* (1762), translated by G. D. H. Cole, New York, 1950, Book II, chapter 3.

22. ibid., Book II, chapter 1.

23. Albert Ollivier, *Saint-Just et la force des choses,* Paris, 1954, p. 203.

24. This sentence contains the key to Rousseau's concept of the general will. The fact that it appears merely in a footnote (op. cit., II, 3) shows only that the concrete experience from which Rousseau derived his theory had become so natural to him that he hardly thought it worth mentioning. For this rather common difficulty in the interpretation of theoretical works, the empirical and very simple background to the complicated general-will concept is quite instructive, since very few concepts in political theory have been surrounded with a mystifying aura of so much plain nonsense.

25. The classical expression of this revolutionary version of republican virtue can be found in Robespierre's theory of magistracy and popular representation, which he himself summed up as follows: 'Pour aimer la justice et l'égalité le peuple n'a pas besoin d'une grande vertue; il lui suffit de s'aimer lui-même.

Mais le magistrat est obligé d'immoler son intérêt à l'intérêt du peuple, et l'orgueil du pouvoir à l'égalité. . . . Il faut donc que le corps représentatif commence par soumettre dans son sein toutes les passions privées à la passion générale du bien public. . . .' Speech to the National Convention, 5 February 1794; see *Œuvres,* ed. Laponneraye, 1840, vol. III, p. 548.,

26. For Rousseau, see *Discours sur l'origine de l'inégalité parmi les hommes* (1755), translated by G. D. H. Cole, New York, 1950, p. 226. Saint-Just is quoted from Albert Ollivier, op. cit., p. 19.

27. R. R. Palmer, *Twelve Who Ruled: The Year of the Terror in the French Revolution,* Princeton, 1941, from which the words of Robespierre are quoted (p. 265), is, together with Thompson's biography, mentioned earlier, the fairest and most painstakingly objective study of Robespierre and the men around him in recent literature. Palmer's book especially is an outstanding contribution to the controversy over the nature of the Terror.

28. Quoted from Zoltán Haraszti, *John Adams and the Prophets of Progress,* Harvard, 1952, p. 205.

29. Rousseau, *A Discourse on the Origin of Inequality,* p. 226.

30. The documents of the Parisian sections, now first published in a bilingual edition (French-German) in the work quoted in note 3, are full of such and similar formulations. I have quoted from no. 57. Generally speaking, one may say that the more bloodthirsty the speaker the more likely that he will insist on *ces tendres affections de l'âme*—on the tenderness of his soul.

31. Thompson (op. cit., p. 108) recalls that Desmoulins told Robespierre as early as 1790, 'You are faithful to your principles, however it may be with your friends.'

32. To give an instance, Robespierre, speaking on the subject of revolutionary government, insisted: 'Il ne s'agit point d'entraver la justice du peuple par des formes nouvelles; la loi pénale doit nécessairement avoir quelque chose de vague, parce que le caractère actuel des conspirateurs étant la dissimulation et l'hypocrisie, il faut que la justice puisse les saisir sous toutes les formes.' Speech in the National Convention, 26 July 1794; *Œuvres,* ed. Laponneraye, vol. III, p. 723. About the problem of hypocrisy with which Robespierre justified the lawlessness of popular justice, see below.

33. The phrase occurs as a principle in the 'Instruction to the Constituted Authorities' drawn up by the temporary commission charged with the administration of revolutionary law in Lyons. Characteristically enough, the Revolution here was exclusively made for 'the immense class of the poor'. See Markov and Soboul, op. cit., No. 52.

34. Crèvecœur, *Letters from an American Farmer* (1782), Dutton paperback edition, 1957, Letter 3.

35. In a letter to Madison from Paris of 16 December 1786.

36. *The Federalist* (1787), ed. Jacob E. Cooke, Meridian, 1961, no. 10.

37. R. R. Palmer, op. cit., p. 163.

The Concept of History

Ancient and Modern

I : HISTORY AND NATURE

LET US BEGIN with Herodotus, whom Cicero called *pater historiae* and who has remained father of Western history.[1] He tells us in the first sentence of the Persian Wars that the purpose of his enterprise is to preserve that which owes its existence to men, τὰ γενόμενα ἐξ ἀνθρώπων, lest it be obliterated by time, and to bestow upon the glorious, wondrous deeds of Greeks and barbarians sufficient praise to assure their posterity and thus make their glory shine through the centuries.

This tells us a great deal and yet does not tell us enough. For us, concern with immortality is not a matter of course, and Herodotus, since this was a matter of course to him, does not tell us much about it. His understanding of the task of history—to save human deeds from the futility that comes from oblivion—was rooted in the Greek concept and experience of nature, which comprehended all things that come into being by themselves without assistance from men or gods—the Olympian gods did not claim to have created the world[2]—and therefore are immortal. Since the things of nature are ever-present, they are not likely to be overlooked or forgotten; and since they are forever, they do not need human remembrance for their further existence. All living creatures, man not excepted, are contained in this realm of being-forever, and Aristotle explicitly assures us that man, insofar as he is a natural being and belongs to the species of mankind, possesses immortality; through the recurrent cycle of life, nature assures the same kind of being-forever to things that are born and die as to things that are and do not change. "Being for living creatures is Life," and being-forever (ἀεὶ εἶναι) corresponds to ἀειγενές, procreation.[3]

No doubt this eternal recurrence "is the closest possible approxima-

---

From Between Past and Future. *Originally published as "The Modern Concept of History" in* Review of Politics *20/4 (October 1958).*

tion of a world of becoming to that of being,"[4] but it does not, of course, make individual men immortal; on the contrary, embedded in a cosmos in which everything was immortal, it was mortality which became the hallmark of human existence. Men are "the mortals," the only mortal things there are, for animals exist only as members of their species and not as individuals. The mortality of man lies in the fact that individual life, a βίος with a recognizable life-story from birth to death, rises out of biological life, ζωή. This individual life is distinguished from all other things by the rectilinear course of its movement, which, so to speak, cuts through the circular movements of biological life. This is mortality: to move along a rectilinear line in a universe where everything, if it moves at all, moves in a cyclical order. Whenever men pursue their purposes, tilling the effortless earth, forcing the free-flowing wind into their sails, crossing the ever-rolling waves, they cut across a movement which is purposeless and turning within itself. When Sophocles (in the famous chorus of *Antigone*) says that there is nothing more awe-inspiring than man, he goes on to exemplify this by evoking purposeful human activities which do violence to nature because they disturb what, in the absence of mortals, would be the eternal quiet of being-forever that rests or swings within itself.

What is difficult for us to realize is that the great deeds and works of which mortals are capable, and which become the topic of historical narrative, are not seen as parts of either an encompassing whole or a process; on the contrary, the stress is always on single instances and single gestures. These single instances, deeds or events, interrupt the circular movement of daily life in the same sense that the rectilinear βίος of the mortals interrupts the circular movement of biological life. The subject matter of history is these interruptions—the extraordinary, in other words.

When in late antiquity speculations began about the nature of history in the sense of a historical process and about the historical fate of nations, their rise and fall, where the particular actions and events were engulfed in a whole, it was at once assumed that these processes must be circular. The historical movement began to be construed in the image of biological life. In terms of ancient philosophy, this could mean that the world of history had been reintegrated into the world of nature, the world of the mortals into the universe that is forever. But in terms of ancient poetry and historiography it meant that the earlier sense of the greatness of mortals, as distinguished from the undoubtedly higher greatness of the gods and nature, had been lost.

In the beginning of Western history the distinction between the mortality of men and the immortality of nature, between man-made things and things which come into being by themselves, was the tacit assumption of historiography. All things that owe their existence to men, such as works, deeds, and words, are perishable, infected, as it were, by the mortality of their authors. However, if mortals succeeded in endowing their works, deeds, and words with some permanence and in arresting their perishability, then these things would, to a degree at least, enter and be at home in the world of everlastingness, and the mortals themselves would find their place in the cosmos, where everything is immortal except men. The human capacity to achieve this was remembrance. Mnemosyne, who therefore was regarded as the mother of all the other muses.

In order to understand quickly and with some measure of clarity how far we today are removed from this Greek understanding of the relationship between nature and history, between the cosmos and men, we may be permitted to quote four lines from Rilke and leave them in their original language; their perfection seems to defy translation.

> *Berge ruhn, von Sternen überprächtigt;*
> *aber auch in ihnen flimmert Zeit.*
> *Ach, in meinem wilden Herzen nächtigt*
> *obdachlos die Unvergänglichkeit.*[5]

Here even the mountains only seem to rest under the light of the stars; they are slowly, secretly devoured by time; nothing is forever, immortality has fled the world to find an uncertain abode in the darkness of the human heart that still has the capacity to remember and to say: forever. Immortality or imperishability, if and when it occurs at all, is homeless. If one looks upon these lines through Greek eyes it is almost as though the poet had tried consciously to reverse the Greek relationships: everything has become perishable, except perhaps the human heart; immortality is no longer the medium in which mortals move, but has taken its homeless refuge in the very heart of mortality; immortal things, works and deeds, events and even words, though men might still be able to externalize, reify as it were, the remembrance of their hearts, have lost their home in the world; since the world, since nature is perishable and since man-made things, once they have come into being, share the fate of all being—they begin to perish the moment they have come into existence.

With Herodotus words and deeds and events—that is, those things that owe their existence exclusively to men—became the subject matter of history. Of all man-made things, these are the most futile. The works of human hands owe part of their existence to the material nature provides and therefore carry within themselves some measure of permanence, borrowed, as it were, from the being-forever of nature. But what goes on between mortals directly, the spoken word and all the actions and deeds which the Greeks called πράξεις or πράγματα, as distinguished from ποίησις, fabrication, can never outlast the moment of their realization, would never leave any trace without the help of remembrance. The task of the poet and historiographer (both of whom Aristotle still puts in the same category because their subject is πρᾶξις)[6] consists in making something lasting out of remembrance. They do this by translating πρᾶξις and λέξις, action and speech, into that kind of ποίησις or fabrication which eventually becomes the written word.

History as a category of human existence is of course older than the written word, older than Herodotus, older even than Homer. Not historically but poetically speaking, its beginning lies rather in the moment when Ulysses, at the court of the king of the Phaeacians, listened to the story of his own deeds and sufferings, to the story of his life, now a thing outside himself, an "object" for all to see and to hear. What had been sheer occurrence now became "history." But the transformation of single events and occurrences into history was essentially the same "imitation of action" in words which was later employed in Greek tragedy,[7] where, as Burckhardt once remarked, "external action is hidden from the eye" through the reports of messengers, even though there was no objection at all to showing the horrible.[8] The scene where Ulysses listens to the story of his own life is paradigmatic for both history and poetry; the "reconciliation with reality," the catharsis, which, according to Aristotle, was the essence of tragedy, and, according to Hegel, was the ultimate purpose of history, came about through the tears of remembrance. The deepest human motive for history and poetry appears here in unparalleled purity: since listener, actor, and sufferer are the same person, all motives of sheer curiosity and lust for new information, which, of course, have always played a large role in both historical inquiry and aesthetic pleasure, are naturally absent in Ulysses himself, who would have been bored rather than moved if history were only news and poetry only entertainment.

Such distinctions and reflections may seem commonplace to modern ears. Implied in them, however, is one great and painful paradox which contributed (perhaps more than any other single factor) to the tragic aspect of Greek culture in its greatest manifestations. The paradox is that, on the one hand, everything was seen and measured against the background of the things that are forever, while, on the other, true human greatness was understood, at least by the pro-Platonic Greeks, to reside in deeds and words, and was rather represented by Achilles, "the doer of great deeds and the speaker of great words," than by the maker and fabricator, even the poet and writer. This paradox, that greatness was understood in terms of permanence while human greatness was seen in precisely the most futile and least lasting activities of men, has haunted Greek poetry and historiography as it has perturbed the quiet of the philosophers.

The early Greek solution of the paradox was poetic and nonphilosophical. It consisted in the immortal fame which the poets could bestow upon word and deed to make them outlast not only the futile moment of speech and action but even the mortal life of their agent. Prior to the Socratic school—with the possible exception of Hesiod—we encounter no real criticism of immortal fame; even Heraclitus thought that it was the greatest of all human aspirations, and while he denounced with violent bitterness the political conditions in his native Ephesus, it never would have occurred to him to condemn the realm of human affairs as such or doubt its potential greatness.

The change, prepared by Parmenides, came about with Socrates and reached its culmination in Plato's philosophy, whose teaching regarding a potential immortality of mortal men become authoritative for all philosophy schools in antiquity. To be sure, Plato was still confronted with the same paradox and he seems to have been the first who considered "the desire to become famous and not to lie in the end without a name" on the same level as the natural desire for children through which nature secures the immortality of the species, though not the αθαυασία of the individual person. In his political philosophy, therefore, he proposed to substitute the latter for the former, as though the desire for immortality through fame could as well be fulfilled when men "are immortal because they leave children's children behind them, and partake of immortality through the unity of a sempiternal becoming"; when he declared the begetting of children to be a law he obviously hoped this would be sufficient for the "common man's" natural yearning for deathlessness. For neither Plato nor Aristotle any longer believed that mortal men could "immortalize" (αθαυατίζειν, in the Aristotelian terminology, an activity whose object is by no means necessarily one's own self, the immortal fame of the name, but includes a variety of occupations with immortal things in general) through great deeds and words.[9] They had discovered, in the activity of thought itself, a hidden human capacity for turning away from the whole realm of human affairs which should not be taken too seriously by men (Plato) because it was patently absurd to think that man is the highest being there is (Aristotle). While begetting might be enough for the many, to "immortalize" meant for the philosopher to dwell in the neighborhood of those things which are forever, to be there and present in a state of active attention, but without doing anything, without performance of deeds or achievement of works. Thus the proper attitude of mortals, once they had reached the neighborhood of the immortal, was actionless and even speechless contemplation: the Aristotelian νοῦς, the highest and most human capacity of pure vision, cannot translate into words what it beholds,[10] and the ultimate truth which the vision of ideas disclosed to Plato is likewise an ἄρρητον, something which cannot be caught in words.[11] Hence the old paradox was resolved by the philosophers by denying to man not the capacity to "immortalize," but the capability of measuring himself and his own deeds against the everlasting greatness of the cosmos, of matching, as it were, the immortality of nature and the gods with an immortal greatness of his own. The solution clearly comes about at the expense of "the doer of great deeds and the speaker of great words."

The distinction between the poets and historians on one side and the philosophers on the other was that the former simply accepted the common Greek concept of greatness. Praise, from which came glory and eventually everlasting fame, could be bestowed only upon things already "great," that is, things that possessed an emerging, shining quality which distinguished them from all others and made glory possible. The great was that which deserved immortality, that which should be admitted to the company of things that lasted forever, surrounding the futility of mortals with their unsurpassable majesty. Through history men almost became the equals of nature, and only those events, deeds, or words that rose by themselves to the ever-present challenge of the natural universe were what we would call historical. Not only the poet Homer and not only the storyteller Herodotus, but even Thucydides, who in a much more sober mood was the first to set standards for historiography, tells us explicitly in the beginning of the *Peloponnesian War* that he wrote his work because of the war's "greatness," because "this was the greatest movement yet known in history, not only of the Hellenes, but of a large part of the barbarian world . . . almost mankind."

The concern with greatness, so prominent in Greek poetry and historiography, is based on the most intimate connection between the concepts of nature and history. Their common denominator is immortality. Immortality is what nature possesses without effort and without anybody's assistance, and immortality is what the mortals therefore must try to achieve if they want to live up to the world into which they were born, to live up to the things which surround them and to whose company they are admitted for a short while. The connection between history and nature is therefore by no means an opposition. History receives into its remembrance those mortals who through deed and word have proved themselves worthy of nature, and their everlasting fame means that they, despite their mortality, may remain in the company of the things that last forever.

Our modern concept of history is no less intimately connected with our modern concept of nature than the corresponding and very different concepts which stand at the beginning of our history. They too can be seen in their full significance only if their common root is discovered. The nineteenth-century opposition of the natural and historical sciences, together with the allegedly absolute objectivity and precision of the natural scientists, is today a thing of the past. The natural sciences now admit that with the experiment, testing natural processes under prescribed conditions, and with the observer, who in watching the experiment becomes one of its conditions, a "subjective" factor is introduced into the "objective" processes of nature.

> The most important new result of nuclear physics was the recognition of the possibility of applying quite different types of natural laws, without contradiction, to one and the same physical event. This is due to the fact that within a system of laws which are based on certain fundamental ideas only certain quite definite ways of asking questions make sense, and thus, that such a system is separated from others which allow different questions to be put.[12]

In other words, the experiment "being a question put before nature" (Galileo),[13] the answers of science will always remain replies to questions asked by men; the confusion in the issue of "objectivity" was to assume that there could be answers without questions and results independent of a question-asking being. Physics, we know today, is no less a man-centered inquiry into what is than historical research. The old quarrel, therefore, between the "subjectivity" of historiography and the "objectivity" of physics has lost much of its relevance.[14]

The modern historian as a rule is not yet aware of the fact that the natural scientist, against whom he had to defend his own "scientific standards" for so many decades, finds himself in the same position, and he is quite likely to state and restate in new, seemingly more scientific terms the old distinction between a science of nature and a science of history. The reason is that the problem of objectivity in the historical sciences is more than a mere technical, scientific perplexity. Objectivity, the "extinction of the self" as the condition of "pure vision" (*das reine Sehen der*

Dinge—Ranke) meant the historian's abstention from bestowing either praise or blame, together with an attitude of perfect distance with which he would follow the course of events as they were revealed in his documentary sources. To him the only limitation of this attitude, which Droysen once denounced as "eunuchic objectivity,"[15] lay in the necessity of selecting material from a mass of facts which, compared with the limited capacity of the human mind and the limited time of human life, appeared infinite. Objectivity, in other words, meant noninterference as well as nondiscrimination. Of these two, nondiscrimination, abstention from praise and blame, was obviously much easier to achieve than noninterference; every selection of material in a sense interferes with history, and all criteria for selection put the historical course of events under certain manmade conditions, which are quite similar to the conditions the natural scientist prescribes to natural processes in the experiment.

We have stated here the problem of objectivity in modern terms, as it arose during the modern age, which believed it had discovered in history a "new science" which then would have to comply to the standards of the "older" science of nature. This, however, was a self-misunderstanding. Modern natural science developed quickly into an even "newer" science than history, and both sprang, as we shall see, from exactly the same set of "new" experiences with the exploration of the universe, made at the beginning of the modern age. The curious and still confusing point about the historical sciences was that they did not take their standards from the natural sciences of their own age, but harked back to the scientific and, in the last analysis, philosophical attitude which the modern age had just begun to liquidate. Their scientific standards, culminating in the "extinction of the self," had their roots in Aristotelian and medieval natural science, which consisted mainly in observing and cataloguing observed facts. Before the rise of the modern age it was a matter of course that quiet, actionless, and selfless contemplation of the miracle of being, or of the wonder of God's creation, should also be the proper attitude for the scientist, whose curiosity about the particular had not yet parted company with the wonder before the general from which, according to the ancients, sprang philosophy.

With the modern age this objectivity lost its fundament and therefore was constantly on the lookout for new justifications. For the historical sciences the old standard of objectivity could make sense only if the historian believed that history in its entirety was either a cyclical phenomenon which could be grasped as a whole through contemplation (and Vico, following the theories of late antiquity, was still of this opinion) or that it was guided by some divine providence for the salvation of mankind, whose plan was revealed, whose beginnings and ends were known, and therefore could be again contemplated as a whole. Both these concepts, however, were actually quite alien to the new consciousness of history in the modern age; they were only the old traditional framework into which the new experiences were pressed and from which the new science had risen. The problem of scientific objectivity, as the nineteenth century posed it, owed so much to historical self-misunderstanding and philosophical confusion that the real issue at stake, the issue of impartiality, which is indeed decisive not only for the "science" of history but for all historiography from poetry and storytelling onward, has become difficult to recognize.

Impartiality, and with it all true historiography, came into the world when Homer decided to sing the deeds of the Trojans no less than those of the Achaeans, and to praise the glory of Hector no less than the greatness of Achilles. This Homeric impartiality, as it is echoed by Herodotus, who set out to prevent "the great and wonderful actions of the Greeks *and* the barbarians from losing their due meed of glory," is still the highest type of objectivity we know. Not only does it leave behind the common interest in one's own side and one's own people which, up to our own days, characterizes almost all national historiography, but it also discards the alternative of victory or defeat, which moderns have felt expresses the "objective" judgment of history itself, and does not permit it to interfere with what is judged to be worthy of immortalizing praise. Somewhat later, and most magnificently expressed in Thucydides, there appears in Greek historiography still another powerful element that contributes to historical objectivity. It could come to the foreground only after long experience in polis-life, which to an incredibly large extent consisted of citizens talking with one another. In this incessant talk the Greeks discovered that the world we have in common is usually regarded from an infinite number of different standpoints, to which correspond the most diverse points of view. In a sheer inexhaustible flow of arguments, as the Sophists presented them to the citizenry of Athens, the Greek learned to exchange his own viewpoint, his own "opinion"—the way the world appeared and opened up to him (δοκεῖ μοι, "it appears to me," from which comes δόξα, or "opinion")—with those of his fellow citizens. Greeks learned to *understand*—not to understand one another as individual persons, but to look upon the same world from one another's standpoint, to see the same in very different and frequently opposing aspects. The speeches in which Thucydides makes articulate the standpoints and interests of the warring parties are still a living testimony to the extraordinary degree of this objectivity.

What has obscured the modern discussion of objectivity in the historical sciences and prevented its ever touching the fundamental issues involved seems to be the fact that none of the conditions of either Homeric impartiality or Thucydidean objectivity are present in the modern age. Homeric impartiality rested upon the assumption that great things are self-evident, shine by themselves; that the poet (or later the historiographer) has only to preserve their glory, which is essentially futile, and that he would destroy, instead of preserving, if he were to forget the glory that was Hector's. For the short duration of their existence great deeds and great words were, in their greatness, as real as a stone or a house, there to be seen and heard by everybody present. Greatness was easily recognizable as that which by itself aspired to immortality—that is, negatively speaking, as a heroic contempt for all that merely comes and passes away, for all individual life, one's own included. This sense of greatness could not possibly survive intact into the Christian era for the very simple reason that, according to Christian teachings, the relationship between life and world is the exact opposite to that in Greek and Latin antiquity: in Christianity neither the world nor the ever-recurring cycle of life is immortal, only the single living individual. It is the world that will pass away; men will live forever. The Christian reversal is based, in its turn, upon the altogether different teachings of the Hebrews, who always held that life itself is sacred, more sacred than anything else in the world, and that man is the supreme being on earth.

Connected with this inner conviction of the sacredness of life as such, which has remained with us even after security of the Christian faith in life after death has passed away, is the stress on the all-importance of self-interest, still so prominent in all modern political philosophy. In our context this means that the Thucydidean type of objectivity, no matter how much it may be admired, no longer has any basis in real political life. Since we have made life our supreme and foremost concern, we have no room left for an activity based on contempt for one's own life interest. Selflessness may still be a religious or a moral virtue; it can hardly be a political one. Under these conditions objectivity lost its validity in experience, was divorced from real life, and became that "lifeless" academic affair which Droysen rightly denounced as being eunuchic.

Moreover, the birth of the modern idea of history not only coincided with but was powerfully stimulated by the modern age's doubt of the reality of an outer world "objectively" given to human perception as an unchanged and unchangeable object. In our context the most important consequence of this doubt was the emphasis on sensation *qua* sensation as more "real" than the "sensed" object and, at any rate, the only safe

ground of experience. Against this subjectivization, which is but one aspect of the still growing world-alienation of man in the modern age, no
judgments could hold out: they were all reduced to the level of sensations
and ended on the level of the lowest of all sensations, the sensation of
taste. Our vocabulary is a telling testimony to this degradation. All judgments not inspired by moral principle (which is felt to be old-fashioned)
or not dictated by some self-interest are considered matters of "taste,"
and this in hardly a different sense from what we mean by saying that the
preference for clam chowder over pea soup is a matter of taste. This conviction, the vulgarity of its defenders on the theoretical level notwithstanding, has disturbed the conscience of the historian much more deeply
because it has much deeper roots in the general spirit of the modern age
than the allegedly superior scientific standards of his colleagues in the natural sciences.

Unfortunately it is in the nature of academic quarrels that methodological problems are likely to overshadow more fundamental issues. The
fundamental fact about the modern concept of history is that it arose in
the same sixteenth and seventeenth centuries which ushered in the gigan-.
tic development of the natural sciences. Foremost among the characteristics of that age, which are still alive and present in our own world, is the
world-alienation of man, which I mentioned before and which is so difficult to perceive as a basic condition of our whole life because out of it,
and partly at least out of its despair, did arise the tremendous structure of
the human artifice we inhabit today, in whose framework we have even
discovered the means of destroying it together with all non-man-made
things on earth.

The shortest and most fundamental expression this world-alienation
ever found is contained in Descartes' famous *de omnibus dubitandum est,* for
this rule signifies something altogether different from the skepticism inherent in the self-doubt of all true thought. Descartes came to his rule because the then recent discoveries in the natural sciences had convinced
him that man in his search for truth and knowledge can trust neither the
given evidence of the senses, nor the "innate truth" of the mind, nor the
"inner light of reason." This mistrust of the human capacities has been
ever since one of the most elementary conditions of the modern age and
the modern world; but it did not spring, as is usually assumed, from a sudden mysterious dwindling of faith in God, and its cause was originally not
even a suspicion of reason as such. Its origin was simply the highly justified loss of confidence in the truth-revealing capacity of the senses. Reality no longer was disclosed as an outer phenomenon to human sensation,
but had withdrawn, so to speak, into the sensing of the sensation itself. It

now turned out that without confidence in the senses neither faith in God nor trust in reason could any longer be secure, because the revelation of both divine and rational truth had always been implicitly understood to follow the awe-inspiring simplicity of man's relationship with the world: I open my eyes and behold the vision, I listen and hear the sound, I move my body and touch the tangibility of the world. If we begin to doubt the fundamental truthfulness and reliability of this relationship, which of course does not exclude errors and illusions but, on the contrary, is the condition of their eventual correction, none of the traditional metaphors for suprasensual truth—be it the eyes of the mind which can see the sky of ideas or the voice of conscience listened to by the human heart—can any longer carry its meaning.

The fundamental experience underlying Cartesian doubt was the discovery that the earth, contrary to all direct sense experience, revolves around the sun. The modern age began when man, with the help of the telescope, turned his bodily eyes toward the universe, about which he had speculated for a long time—seeing with the eyes of the mind, listening with the ears of the heart, and guided by the inner light of reason—and learned that his senses were not fitted for the universe, that his everyday experience, far from being able to constitute the model for the reception of truth and the acquisition of knowledge, was a constant source of error and delusion. After this deception—whose enormity we find difficult to realize because it was centuries before its full impact was felt everywhere and not only in the rather restricted milieu of scholars and philosophers—suspicions began to haunt modern man from all sides. But its most immediate consequence was the spectacular rise of natural science, which for a long time seemed to be liberated by the discovery that our senses by themselves do not tell the truth. Henceforth, sure of the unreliability of sensation and the resulting insufficiency of mere observation, the natural sciences turned toward the experiment, which, by directly interfering with nature, assured the development whose progress has ever since appeared to be limitless.

Descartes became the father of modern philosophy because he generalized the experience of the preceding as well as his own generation, developed it into a new method of thinking, and thus became the first thinker thoroughly trained in that "school of suspicion" which, according to Nietzsche, constitutes modern philosophy. Suspicion of the senses remained the core of scientific pride until in our time it has turned into a source of uneasiness. The trouble is that "we find nature behaving so differently from what we observe in the visible and palpable bodies of our surroundings that *no* model shaped after our large-scale experiences can ever be 'true' "; at this point the indissoluble connection between our thinking and our sense perception takes its revenge, for a model that would leave sense experience altogether out of account and, therefore, be completely adequate to nature in the experiment is not only "practically inaccessible but not even thinkable."[16] The trouble, in other words, is not that the modern physical universe cannot be visualized, for this is a matter of course under the assumption that nature does not reveal itself to the human senses; the uneasiness begins when nature turns out to be inconceivable, that is, unthinkable in terms of pure reasoning as well.

The dependence of modern thought upon factual discoveries of the natural sciences shows itself most clearly in the seventeenth century. It is not always admitted as readily as by Hobbes, who attributed his philosophy exclusively to the results of the work of Copernicus and Galileo, Kepler, Gassendi, and Mersenne, and who denounced all past philosophy as nonsense with a violence matched perhaps only by Luther's contempt for the *"stulti philosophi."* One does not need the radical extremism of Hobbes's conclusion, not that man may be evil by nature, but that a distinction between good and evil makes no sense, and that reason, far from being an inner light disclosing truth, is a mere "faculty of reckoning with consequences"; for the basic suspicion that man's earthbound experience presents a caricature of truth is no less present in Descartes' fear that an evil spirit may rule the world and withhold truth forever from the mind of a being so manifestly subject to error. In its most harmless form, it permeates English empiricism, where the meaningfulness of the sensibly given is dissolved into data of sense perception, disclosing their meaning only through habit and repeated experiences, so that in an extreme subjectivism man is ultimately imprisoned in a non-world of meaningless sensations that no reality and no truth can penetrate. Empiricism is only seemingly a vindication of the senses; actually it rests on the assumption that only common-sense arguing can give them meaning, and it always starts with a declaration of non-confidence in the truth- or reality-revealing capacity of the senses. Puritanism and empiricism, in fact, are only two sides of the same coin. The same fundamental suspicion finally inspired Kant's gigantic effort to re-examine the human faculties in such a way that the question of a *Ding an sich,* that is, the truth-revealing faculty of experience in an absolute sense, could be left in abeyance.

Of much more immediate consequence for our concept of history was the positive version of subjectivism which arose from the same predicament: Although it seems that man is unable to recognize the given world which he has not made himself, he nevertheless must be capable of knowing at least what he made himself. This pragmatic attitude is already the fully articulated reason why Vico turned his attention to history and thus became one of the fathers of modern historical consciousness. He said: *Geometrica demonstramus quia facimus; si physica demonstrare possemus, faceremus.*[17] ("Mathematical matters we can prove because we ourselves make them; to prove the physical, we would have to make it.") Vico turned to the sphere of history only because he still believed it impossible "to make nature." No so-called humanist considerations inspired his turning away from nature, but solely the belief that history is "made" by men just as nature is "made" by God; hence historical truth can be known by men, the makers of history, but physical truth is reserved for the Maker of the universe.

It has frequently been asserted that modern science was born when attention shifted from the search after the "what" to the investigation of "how." This shift of emphasis is almost a matter of course if one assumes that man can know only what he has made himself, insofar as this assumption in turn implies that I "know" a thing whenever I understand how it has come into being. By the same token, and for the same reasons, the emphasis shifted from interest in things to interest in processes, of which things were soon to become almost accidental by-products. Vico lost interest in nature because he assumed that to penetrate the mystery of Creation it would be necessary to understand the creative process, whereas all previous ages had taken it for granted that one can very well understand the universe without ever knowing how God created it, or, in the Greek version, how the things that are by themselves came into being. Since the seventeenth century the chief preoccupation of all scientific inquiry, natural as well as historical, has been with processes; but only modern technology (and no mere science, no matter how highly developed), which began with substituting mechanical processes for human activities—laboring and working—and ended with starting new natural processes, would have been wholly adequate to Vico's ideal of knowledge. Vico, who is regarded by many as the father of modern history, would hardly have turned to history under modern conditions. He would have turned to technology: for our technology does indeed what Vico thought divine action did in the realm of nature and human action in the realm of history.

In the modern age history emerged as something it never had been before. It was no longer composed of the deeds and sufferings of men, and it no longer told the story of events affecting the lives of men; it became a man-made process, the only all-comprehending process which owed its existence exclusively to the human race. Today this quality which distinguished history from nature is also a thing of the past. We know today that though we cannot "make" nature in the sense of creation, we are quite capable of starting new natural processes, and that in a sense therefore we "make nature," to the extent, that is, that we "make history." It is true we have reached this stage only with the nuclear discoveries, where natural forces are let loose, unchained, so to speak, and where the natural processes which take place would never have existed without direct interference of human action. This stage goes far beyond not only the pre-modern age, when wind and water were used to substitute for and multiply human forces, but also the industrial age, with its steam engine and internal-combustion motor, where natural forces were imitated and utilized as man-made means of production.

The contemporary decline of interest in the humanities, and especially in the study of history, which seems inevitable in all completely modernized countries, is quite in accord with the first impulses that led to modern historical science. What is definitely out of place today is the resignation which led Vico into the study of history. We can do in the natural-physical realm what he thought we could do only in the realm of history. We have begun to act into nature as we used to act into history. If it is merely a question of processes, it has turned out that man is as capable of starting natural processes which would not have come about without human interference as he is of starting something new in the field of human affairs.

Since the beginning of the twentieth century, technology has emerged as the meeting ground of the natural and historical sciences, and although hardly a single great scientific discovery has ever been made for pragmatic, technical, or practical purposes (pragmatism in the vulgar sense of the word stands refuted by the factual record of scientific development), this final outcome is in perfect accord with the innermost intentions of modern science. The comparatively new social sciences, which so quickly became to history what technology had been to physics, may use the experiment in a much cruder and less reliable way than do the natural sciences, but the method is the same: they too prescribe conditions, conditions to human behavior, as modern physics prescribes conditions to natural processes. If their vocabulary is repulsive and their hope to close the alleged gap between our scientific mastery of nature and our deplored impotence to "manage" human affairs through an engineering science of human relations sounds frightening, it is only because they have decided to treat man as an entirely natural being whose life process can be handled the same way as all other processes.

In this context, however, it is important to be aware how decisively the technological world we live in, or perhaps begin to live in, differs from the mechanized world as it arose with the Industrial Revolution.

This difference corresponds essentially to the difference between action and fabrication. Industrialization still consisted primarily of the mechanization of work processes, the improvement in the making of objects, and man's attitude to nature still remained that of *homo faber,* to whom nature gives the material out of which the human artifice is erected. The world we have now come to live in, however, is much more determined by man acting into nature, creating natural processes and directing them into the human artifice and the realm of human affairs, than by building and preserving the human artifice as a relatively permanent entity.

Fabrication is distinguished from action in that it has a definite beginning and a predictable end: it comes to an end with its end product, which not only outlasts the activity of fabrication but from then on has a kind of "life" of its own. Action on the contrary, as the Greeks were the first to discover, is in and by itself utterly futile; it never leaves an end product behind itself. If it has any consequences at all, they consist in principle in an endless new chain of happenings whose eventual outcome the actor is utterly incapable of knowing or controlling beforehand. The most he may be able to do is to force things into a certain direction, and even of this he can never be sure. None of these characteristics is present in fabrication. Compared with the futility and fragility of human action, the world fabrication erects is of lasting permanence and tremendous solidity. Only insofar as the end product of fabrication is incorporated into the human world, where its use and eventual "history" can never be entirely predicted, does even fabrication start a process whose outcome cannot be entirely foreseen and is therefore beyond the control of its author. This means only that man is never exclusively *homo faber,* that even the fabricator remains at the same time an acting being, who starts processes wherever he goes and with whatever he does.

Up to our own age human action with its man-made processes was confined to the human world, whereas man's chief preoccupation with regard to nature was to use its material in fabrication, to build with it the human artifice and defend it against the overwhelming force of the elements. The moment we started natural processes of our own—and splitting the atom is precisely such a man-made natural process—we not only increased our power over nature, or became more aggressive in our dealings with the given forces of the earth, but for the first time have taken nature into the human world as such and obliterated the defensive boundaries between natural elements and the human artifice by which all previous civilizations were hedged in.[18]

The dangers of this acting into nature are obvious if we assume that the aforementioned characteristics of human action are part and parcel of the human condition. Unpredictability is not lack of foresight, and no engineering management of human affairs will ever be able to eliminate it, just as no training in prudence can ever lead to the wisdom of knowing what one does. Only total conditioning, that is, the total abolition of action, can ever hope to cope with unpredictability. And even the predictability of human behavior which political terror can enforce for relatively long periods of time is hardly able to change the very essence of human affairs once and for all; it can never be sure of its own future. Human action, like all strictly political phenomena, is bound up with human plurality, which is one of the fundamental conditions of human life insofar as it rests on the fact of natality, through which the human world is constantly invaded by strangers, newcomers whose actions and reactions cannot be foreseen by those who are already there and are going to leave in a short while. If, therefore, by starting natural processes, we have begun to act *into* nature, we have manifestly begun to carry our own unpredictability into that realm which we used to think of as ruled by inexorable laws. The "iron law" of history was always only a metaphor borrowed from nature; and the fact is that this metaphor no longer convinces us because it has turned out that natural science can by no means be sure of an unchallengeable rule of law in nature as soon as men, scientists and technicians, or simply builders of the human artifice, decide to interfere and no longer leave nature to herself.

Technology, the ground on which the two realms of history and nature have met and interpenetrated each other in our time, points back to the connection between the concepts of nature and history as they appeared with the rise of the modern age in the sixteenth and seventeenth centuries. The connection lies in the concept of process: both imply that we think and consider everything in terms of processes and are not concerned with single entities or individual occurrences and their special separate causes. The key words of modern historiography—"development" and "progress"—were, in the nineteenth century, also the key words of the then new branches of natural science, particularly biology and geology, one dealing with animal life and the other even with non-organic matter in terms of historical processes. Technology, in the modern sense, was preceded by the various sciences of natural history, the history of biological life, of the earth, of the universe. A mutual adjustment of terminology of the two branches of scientific inquiry had taken place before the quarrel between the natural and historical sciences preoccupied the scholarly world to such an extent that it confused the fundamental issues.

Nothing seems more likely to dispel this confusion than the latest developments in the natural sciences. They have brought us back to the common origin of both nature and history in the modern age and demonstrate that their common denominator lies indeed in the concept of process—no less than the common denominator of nature and history in antiquity lay in the concept of immortality. But the experience which underlies the modern age's notion of process, unlike the experience underlying the ancient notion of immortality, is by no means primarily an experience which man made in the world surrounding him; on the contrary, it sprang from the despair of ever experiencing and knowing adequately all that is given to man and not made by him. Against this despair modern man summoned up the full measure or his own capacities; despairing of ever finding truth through mere contemplation, he began to try out his capacities for action, and by doing so he could not help becoming aware that wherever man acts he starts processes. The notion of process does not denote an objective quality of either history or nature; it is the inevitable result of human action. The first result of men's acting into history is that history becomes a process, and the most cogent argument for men's acting into nature in the guise of scientific inquiry is that today, in Whitehead's formulation, "nature is a process."

To act into nature, to carry human unpredictability into a realm where we are confronted with elemental forces which we shall perhaps never be able to control reliably, is dangerous enough. Even more dangerous would it be to ignore that for the first time in our history the human capacity for action has begun to dominate all others—the capacity for wonder and thought in contemplation no less than the capacities of *homo faber* and the human *animal laborans*. This, of course, does not mean that men from now on will no longer be able to fabricate things or to think or to labor. Not the capabilities of man, but the constellation which orders their mutual relationships can and does change historically. Such changes can best be observed in the changing self-interpretations of man throughout history, which, though they may be quite irrelevant for the ultimate "what" of human nature, are still the briefest and most succinct witnesses to the spirit of whole epochs. Thus, schematically speaking, Greek classic antiquity agreed that the highest form of human life was spent in a polis and that the supreme human capacity was speech—ζῷον πολιτικόν and ζῷον λόγον ἔχον, in Aristotle's famous twofold definition; Rome and medieval philosophy defined man as the *animal rationale;* in the initial stages of the modern age, man was thought of primarily as *homo faber,* until, in the nineteenth century, man was interpreted as an *animal laborans* whose metabolism with nature would yield the highest productivity of which human life is capable. Against the background of these schematic definitions, it would be adequate for the world we have come to live in to define man as a being capable of action; for this capacity seems to have become the center of all other human capabilities.

It is beyond doubt that the capacity to act is the most dangerous of all human abilities and possibilities, and it is also beyond doubt that the self-created risks mankind faces today have never been faced before. Considerations like these are not at all meant to offer solutions or to give advice. At best, they might encourage sustained and closer reflection on the nature and the intrinsic potentialities of action, which never before has revealed its greatness and its dangers so openly.

II : HISTORY AND EARTHLY IMMORTALITY

The modern concept of process pervading history and nature alike separates the modern age from the past more profoundly than any other single idea. To our modern way of thinking nothing is meaningful in and by itself, not even history or nature taken each as a whole, and certainly not particular occurrences in the physical order or specific historical events. There is a fateful enormity in this state of affairs. Invisible processes have engulfed every tangible thing, every individual entity that is visible to us, degrading them into functions of an over-all process. The enormity of this change is likely to escape us if we allow ourselves to be misled by such generalities as the disenchantment of the world or the alienation of man, generalities that often involve a romanticized notion of the past. What the concept of process implies is that the concrete and the general, the single thing or event and the universal meaning, have parted company. The process, which alone makes meaningful whatever it happens to carry along, has thus acquired a monopoly of universality and significance.

Certainly nothing more sharply distinguishes the modern concept of history from that of antiquity. For this distinction does not hinge on whether or not antiquity had a concept of world history or an idea of mankind as a whole. What is much more relevant is that Greek and Roman historiography, much as they differ from each other, both take it for granted that the meaning or, as the Romans would say, the lesson of each event, deed, or occurrence is revealed in and by itself. This, to be sure, does not exclude either causality or the context in which something occurs; antiquity was as aware of these as we are. But causality and context were seen in a light provided by the event itself, illuminating a specific segment of human affairs; they were not envisaged as having an independent existence of which the event would be only the more or less accidental though adequate expression. Everything that was done or happened contained and disclosed its share of "general" meaning within the confines of its individual shape and did not need a developing and engulfing process to become significant. Herodotus wanted "to say what is" (λέγειν τόα ἐόντα) because saying and writing stabilize the futile and perishable, "fabricate a memory" for it, in the Greek idiom: μνήμην ➤ ποιεῖσθαι; yet he never would have doubted that each thing that is or was carries its meaning within itself and needs only the word to make it manifest (λόγοις δηλοῦν, "to disclose through words"), to "display the great deeds in public," ἀπόδειξις ἔργων μεγάλων. The flux of his narrative is sufficiently loose to leave room for many stories, but there is nothing in this flux indicative that the general bestows meaning and significance on the particular.

For this shift of emphasis it is immaterial whether Greek poetry and historiography saw the meaning of the event in some surpassing greatness justifying its remembrance by posterity, or whether the Romans conceived of history as a storehouse of examples taken from actual political behavior, demonstrating what tradition, the authority of ancestors, demanded from each generation and what the past had accumulated for the benefit of the present. Our notion of historical process overrules both concepts, bestowing upon mere time-sequence an importance and dignity it never had before.

Because of this modern emphasis upon time and time-sequence, it has often been maintained that the origin of our historical consciousness lies in the Hebrew-Christian tradition, with its rectilinear time-concept and its idea of a divine providence giving to the whole of man's historical time the unity of a plan of salvation—an idea which indeed stands as much in contrast to the insistence on individual events and occurrences of classical antiquity as to the cyclical time-speculations of late antiquity. A great deal of evidence has been cited in support of the thesis that the modern historical consciousness has a Christian religious origin and came into being through a secularization of originally theological categories. Only our religious tradition, it is said, knows of a beginning and, in the Christian version, an end of the world; if human life on earth follows a divine plan of salvation, then its mere sequence must harbor a significance independent of and transcending all single occurrences. Therefore, the argument runs, a "well-defined outline of world history" did not appear prior to Christianity, and the first philosophy of history is presented in Augustine's *De Civitate Dei*. And it is true that in Augustine we find the notion that history itself, namely that which has meaning and makes sense, can be separated from the single historical events related in chronological narrative. He states explicitly that "although the past institutions of men are related in historical narrative, history itself is not to be counted among human institutions."[19]

This similarity between the Christian and the modern concept of history is deceptive, however. It rests on a comparison with the cyclical history-speculations of late antiquity and overlooks the classical history-concepts of Greece and Rome. The comparison is supported by the fact that Augustine himself, when he refuted pagan time-speculations, was primarily concerned with the cyclical time-theories of his own era, which indeed no Christian could accept because of the absolute uniqueness of Christ's life and death on earth: "Once Christ died for our sins; and rising from the dead, he dieth no more."[20] What modern interpreters are liable to forget is that Augustine claimed this uniqueness of event, which sounds so familiar to our ears, for this one event only—the supreme event in human history, when eternity, as it were, broke into the course of earthly mortality; he never claimed such uniqueness, as we do, for ordinary secular events. The simple fact that the problem of history arose in Christian thought only with Augustine should make us doubt its Christian origin, and this all the more as it arose, in terms of Augustine's own philosophy and theology, because of an accident. The fall of Rome, occurring in his lifetime, was interpreted by Christians and pagans alike as a decisive event, and it was to the refutation of this belief that Augustine devoted thirteen years of his life. The point, as he saw it, was that no purely secular event could or should ever be of central import to man. His lack of interest in what we call history was so great that he devoted only one book of the *Civitas Dei* to secular events; and in commissioning his friend and pupil Orosius to write a "world history" he had no more in mind than a "true compilation of the evils of the world."[21]

Augustine's attitude toward secular history is essentially no different from that of the Romans, albeit the emphasis is inverted: history remains a storehouse of examples, and the location of events in time within the secular course of history remains without importance. Secular history repeats itself, and the only story in which unique and unrepeatable events take place begins with Adam and ends with the birth and death of Christ. Thereafter secular powers rise and fall as in the past and will rise and fall until the world's end, but no fundamentally new truth will ever again be revealed by such mundane events, and Christians are not supposed to attach particular significance to them. In all truly Christian philosophy man is a "pilgrim on earth," and this fact alone separates it from our own historical consciousness. To the Christian, as to the Roman, the significance of secular events lay in their having the character of examples likely to repeat themselves, so that action could follow certain standardized patterns. (This, incidentally, is also very far removed from the Greek notion of the heroic deed, related by poets and historians, which serves as a kind of yardstick with which to measure one's own capacities for greatness. The difference between the faithful following of a recognized example and the attempt to measure oneself against it is the difference between Roman-Christian morality and what has been called the Greek agonal spirit, which did not know any "moral" considerations but only an ἀεί ἀρι-στεύειν, an unceasing effort always to be the best of all.) For us, on the other hand, history stands and falls on the assumption that the process in its very secularity tells a story of its own and that, strictly speaking, repetitions cannot occur.

Even more alien to the modern concept of history is the Christian notion that mankind has a beginning and an end, that the world was created in time and will ultimately perish, like all things temporal. Historical consciousness did not arise when the creation of the world was taken as the starting point for chronological enumeration, by the Jews in the Middle Ages; nor did it arise in the sixth century when Dionysus Exiguus began counting time from the birth of Christ. We know of similar schemes of chronology in Oriental civilization, and the Christian calendar imitated the Roman practice of counting time from the year of the foundation of Rome. In stark contrast stands the modern computation of historical dates, introduced only at the end of the eighteenth century, that takes the birth of Christ as a turning point from which to count time both backward and forward. This chronological reform is presented in the textbooks as a mere technical improvement, needed for scholarly purposes to facilitate the exact fixing of dates in ancient history without referring to a maze of different time-reckonings. In more recent times, Hegel inspired an interpretation which sees in the modern time system a truly Christian chronology because the birth of Christ now seems to have become the turning point of world history.[22]

Neither of these explanations is satisfactory. Chronological reforms for scholarly purposes have occurred many times in the past without being accepted in everyday life, precisely because they were invented for scholarly convenience only and did not correspond to any changed time-concept in society at large. The decisive thing in our system is not that the birth of Christ now appears as the turning point of world history, for it had been recognized as such and with greater force many centuries before without any similar effect upon our chronology, but rather that now, for the first time, the history of mankind reaches back into an infinite past to which we can add at will and into which we can inquire further as it

stretches ahead into an infinite future. This twofold infinity of past and future eliminates all notions of beginning and end, establishing mankind in a
potential earthly immortality. What at first glance looks like a Christian-
ization of world history in fact eliminates all religious time-speculations
from secular history. So far as secular history is concerned we live in a
process which knows no beginning and no end and which thus does not
permit us to entertain eschatological expectations. Nothing could be more
alien to Christian thought than this concept of an earthly immortality of
mankind. . . .

III: HISTORY AND POLITICS

While it is obvious that our historical consciousness would never have
been possible without the rise of the secular realm to a new dignity, it was
not so obvious that the historical process would eventually be called upon
to bestow the necessary new meaning and significance upon men's deeds
and sufferings on earth. And indeed, at the beginning of the modern age
everything pointed to an elevation of political action and political life, and
the sixteenth and seventeenth centuries, so rich in new political philosophies, were still quite unaware of any special emphasis on history as such.
Their concern, on the contrary, was to get rid of the past rather than to
rehabilitate the historical process. The distinguishing trait of Hobbes's philosophy is his single-minded insistence on the future and the resulting
teleological interpretation of thought as well as of action. The conviction
of the modern age that man can know only that which he himself has
made seems to be in accordance with a glorification of action rather than
with the basically contemplative attitude of the historian and of historical
consciousness in general.

Thus one of the reasons for Hobbes's break with traditional philosophy was that while all previous metaphysics had followed Aristotle in
holding that the inquiry into the first causes of everything that is com-
prises the chief task of philosophy, it was Hobbes's contention that, on the
contrary, the task of philosophy was to guide purposes and aims and to establish a reasonable teleology of action. So important was this point to
Hobbes that he insisted that animals too are capable of discovering causes
and that therefore this cannot be the true distinction between human and
animal life; he found the distinction instead in the ability to reckon with
"the effects of some present or past cause . . . of which I have not at any
time seen any sign but in man only."[23] The modern age not only produced at its very start a new and radical political philosophy—Hobbes is

only one example, though perhaps the most interesting—it also produced for the first time philosophers willing to orient themselves according to the requirements of the political realm; and this new political orientation is present not only in Hobbes but, *mutatis mutandis,* in Locke and Hume as well. It can be said that Hegel's transformation of metaphysics into a philosophy of history was preceded by an attempt to get rid of metaphysics for the sake of a philosophy of politics.

In any consideration of the modern concept of history one of the crucial problems is to explain its sudden rise during the last third of the eighteenth century and the concomitant decrease of interest in purely political thinking. (Vico must be said to be a forerunner whose influence was not felt until more than two generations after his death.) Where a genuine interest in political theory still survived it ended in despair, as in Tocqueville, or in the confusion of politics with history, as in Marx. For what else but despair could have inspired Tocqueville's assertion that "since the past has ceased to throw its light upon the future the mind of man wanders in obscurity"? This is actually the conclusion of the great work in which he had "delineated the society of the modern world" and in the introduction to which he had proclaimed that "a new science of politics is needed for a new world."[24] And what else but confusion—a merciful confusion for Marx himself and a fatal one for his followers—could have led to Marx's identification of action with "the making of history"?

Marx's notion of "making history" had an influence far beyond the circle of convinced Marxists or determined revolutionaries. Although it is closely connected with Vico's idea that history was made by man, as distinguished from "nature," which was made by God, the difference between them is still decisive. For Vico, as later for Hegel, the importance of the concept of history was primarily theoretical. It never occurred to either of them to apply this concept directly by using it as a principle of action. Truth they conceived of as being revealed to the contemplative, backward-directed glance of the historian, who, by being able to see the process as a whole, is in a position to overlook the "narrow aims" of acting men, concentrating instead on the "higher aims" that realize themselves behind their backs (Vico). Marx, on the other hand, combined this notion of history with the teleological political philosophies of the earlier stages of the modern age, so that in his thought the "higher aims"—which according to the philosophers of history revealed themselves only to the backward glance of the historian and philosopher—could become intended aims of political action. The point is that Marx's political philosophy was based not upon an analysis of action and acting men but, on the contrary, on the Hegelian concern with history. It was the historian and the philosopher of history who were politicalized. By the same token, the age-old identification of action with making and fabricating was supplemented and perfected, as it were, through identifying the contemplative gaze of the historian with the contemplation of the model (the ειδος or "shape" from which Plato had derived his "ideas") that guides the craftsmen and precedes all making. And the danger of these combinations did not lie in making immanent what was formerly transcendent, as is often alleged, as though Marx attempted to establish on earth a paradise formerly located in the hereafter. The danger of transforming the unknown and unknowable "higher aims" into planned and willed intentions was that meaning and meaningfulness were transformed into ends—which is what happened when Marx took the Hegelian meaning of all history—the progressive unfolding and actualization of the idea of Freedom—to be an end of human action, and when he furthermore, in accordance with tradition, viewed this ultimate "end" as the end-product of a manufacturing process. But neither freedom nor any other meaning can ever be the product of a human activity in the sense in which the table is clearly the end-product of the carpenter's activity.

The growing meaninglessness of the modern world is perhaps nowhere more clearly foreshadowed than in this identification of meaning and end. Meaning which can never be the aim of action and yet, inevitably, will rise out of human deeds after the action itself has come to an end, was now pursued with the same machinery of intentions and of organized means as were the particular direct aims of concrete action—with the result that it was as though meaning itself had departed from the world of men and men were left with nothing but an unending chain of purposes in whose progress the meaningfulness of all past achievements was constantly canceled out by future goals and intentions. It is as though men were stricken suddenly blind to fundamental distinctions such as the distinction between meaning and end, between the general and the particular, or, grammatically speaking, the distinction between "for the sake of . . ." and "in order to . . ." (as though the carpenter, for instance, forgot that only his particular acts in making a table are performed in the mode of "in order to," but that his whole life as a carpenter is ruled by something quite different, namely an encompassing notion "for the sake of" which he became a carpenter in the first place). And the moment such distinctions are forgotten and meanings are degraded into ends, it follows that ends themselves are no longer safe because the distinction between means and ends is no longer understood, so that finally all ends turn and are degraded into means.

In this version of deriving politics from history, or rather, political conscience from historical consciousness—by no means restricted to Marx in particular, or even to pragmatism in general—we can easily detect the age-old attempt to escape from the frustrations and fragility of human action by construing it in the image of making. What distinguishes Marx's own theory from all others in which the notion of "making history" has found a place is only that he alone realized that if one takes history to be the object of a process of fabrication or making, there must come a moment when this "object" is completed, and that if one imagines that one can "make history," one cannot escape the consequence that there will be an end to history. Whenever we hear of grandiose aims in politics, such as establishing a new society in which justice will be guaranteed forever, or fighting a war to end all wars or to make the whole world safe for democracy, we are moving in the realm of this kind of thinking.

In this context, it is important to see that here the process of history, as it shows itself in our calendar's stretching into the infinity of the past and the future, has been abandoned for the sake of an altogether different kind of process, that of making something which has a beginning as well as an end, whose laws of motion, therefore, can be determined (for instance as dialectical movement) and whose innermost content can be discovered (for instance as class struggle). This process, however, is incapable of guaranteeing men any kind of immortality because its end cancels out and makes unimportant whatever went before: in the classless society the best mankind can do with history is to forget the whole unhappy affair, whose only purpose was to abolish itself. It cannot bestow meaning on particular occurrences either, because it has dissolved all of the particular into means whose meaningfulness ends the moment the end-product is finished: single events and deeds and sufferings have no more meaning here than hammer and nails have with respect to the finished table.

We know the curious ultimate meaninglessness arising from all the strictly utilitarian philosophies that were so common and so characteristic of the earlier industrial phase of the modern age, when men, fascinated by the new possibilities of manufacturing, thought of everything in terms of means and ends, i.e., categories whose validity had its source and justification in the experience of producing use-objects. The trouble lies in the nature of the categorical framework of ends and means, which changes every attained end immediately into the means to a new end, thereby, as it were, destroying meaning wherever it is applied, until in the midst of the seemingly unending utilitarian questioning. What is the use of . . . ? in the midst of the seemingly unending progress where the aim of today becomes the means of a better tomorrow, the one question arises which no utilitarian thinking can ever answer: "And what is the use of use?" as Lessing once succinctly put it.

This meaninglessness of all truly utilitarian philosophies could escape Marx's awareness because he thought that after Hegel in his dialectics had discovered the law of all movements, natural and historical, he himself had found the spring and content of this law in the historical realm and thereby the concrete meaning of the story history has to tell. Class struggle—to Marx this formula seemed to unlock all the secrets of history, just as the law of gravity had appeared to unlock all the secrets of nature. Today, after we have been treated to one such history-construction after another, to one such formula after another, the question for us is no longer whether this or that particular formula is correct. In all such attempts what is considered to be a meaning is in fact no more than a pattern, and within the limitations of utilitarian thought nothing but patterns can make sense, because only patterns can be "made," whereas meanings cannot be, but, like truth, will only disclose or reveal themselves. Marx was only the first—and still the greatest, among historians—to mistake a pattern for a meaning, and he certainly could hardly have been expected to realize that there was almost no pattern into which the events of the past would not have fitted as neatly and consistently as they did into his own. Marx's pattern at least was based on one important historical insight; since then we have seen historians freely imposing upon the maze of past facts almost any pattern they wish, with the result that the ruin of the factual and particular through the seemingly higher validity of general "meanings" has even undermined the basic factual structure of all historical process, that is, chronology.

Moreover, Marx construed his pattern as he did because of his concern with action and impatience with history. He is the last of those thinkers who stand at the borderline between the modern age's earlier interest in politics and its later preoccupation with history. One might mark the point where the modern age abandoned its earlier attempts to establish a new political philosophy for its rediscovery of the secular by recalling the moment at which the French Revolutionary calendar was given up, after one decade, and the Revolution was reintegrated, as it were, into the historical process with its twofold extension toward infinity. It was as though it was conceded that not even the Revolution, which, along with the promulgation of the American Constitution, is still the greatest event in modern political history, contained sufficient independent meaning in itself to begin a new historical process. For the Republican calendar was abandoned not merely because of Napoleon's wish to rule an empire and to be considered the equal of the crowned heads of Europe. The abandonment also implied the refusal, despite the re-establishment of the secular, to accept the conviction of the ancients that political actions are meaningful regardless of their historical location, and especially a repudiation of the Roman faith in the sacredness of foundations with the accompanying custom of numbering time from the foundation date. Indeed, the French Revolution, which was inspired by the Roman spirit and appeared to the world, as Marx liked to say, in Roman dress, reversed itself in more than one sense.

An equally important landmark in the shift from the earlier concern with politics to the later concern with history is encountered in Kant's political philosophy. Kant, who had greeted in Rousseau "the Newton of the moral world," and had been greeted by his contemporaries as the theorist of the Rights of Man,[25] still had great difficulty in coping with the new idea of history, which had probably come to his attention in the writings of Herder. He is one of the last philosophers to complain in earnest about the "meaningless course of human affairs," the "melancholy haphazardness" of historical events and developments, this hopeless, senseless "mixture of error and violence," as Goethe once defined history. Yet Kant also saw what others had seen before him, that once you look at history in its entirety (*im Grossen*), rather than at single events and the ever-frustrated intentions of human agents, everything suddenly makes sense, because there is always at least a story to tell. The process as a whole appears to be guided by an "intention of nature" unknown to acting men but comprehensible to those who come after them. By pursuing their own aims without rhyme or reason men seem to be led by "the guiding thread of reason."[26]

It is of some importance to notice that Kant, like Vico before him, was already aware of what Hegel later called "the cunning of reason" (Kant occasionally called it "the ruse of nature"). He even had some rudimentary insight into historical dialectics, as when he pointed out that nature pursues its over-all aims through "the antagonism of men in society . . . without which men, good-natured like the sheep they tend, would hardly know how to give a higher value to their own existence than is possessed by their cattle." This shows to what extent the very idea of history as a process suggests that in their actions men are led by something of which they are not necessarily conscious and which finds no direct expression in the action itself. Or, to put it another way, it shows how extremely useful the modern concept of history proved to be in giving the secular political realm a meaning which it otherwise seemed to be devoid of. In Kant, in contrast to Hegel, the motive for the modern escape from politics into history is still quite clear. It is the escape into the "whole," and the escape is prompted by the meaninglessness of the particular. And since Kant's primary interest was still in the nature and principles of political (or, as he would say, moral) action, he was able to perceive the crucial drawback of the new approach, the one great stumbling block which no philosophy of history and no concept of progress can ever remove. In Kant's own words: "It will always remain bewildering . . . that the earlier generations seem to carry on their burdensome business only for the sake of the later . . . and that only the last should have the good fortune to dwell in the [completed] building."[27]

The bewildered regret and great diffidence with which Kant resigned himself to introducing a concept of history into his political philosophy indicates with rare precision the nature of the perplexities which caused the modern age to shift its emphasis from a theory of politics—apparently so much more appropriate to its belief in the superiority of action to contemplation—to an essentially contemplative philosophy of history. For Kant was perhaps the only great thinker to whom the question "What shall I do?" was not only as relevant as the two other questions of metaphysics, "What can I know?" and "What may I hope?" but formed the very center of his philosophy. Therefore he was not troubled, as even Marx and Nietzsche were still troubled, by the traditional hierarchy of contemplation over action, the *vita contemplativa* over the *vita activa;* his problem was rather another traditional hierarchy which, because it is hidden and rarely articulate, has proved much more difficult to overcome, the hierarchy within the *vita activa* itself, where the acting of the statesman occupies the highest position, the making of the craftsman and artist an intermediary, and the laboring which provides the necessities for the functioning of the human organism the lowest. (Marx was later to reverse this hierarchy too, although he wrote explicitly only about elevating action over contemplation and changing the world as against interpreting it. In the course of this reversal he had to upset the traditional hierarchy within the *vita activa* as well, by putting the lowest of human activities, the activity of labor, into the highest place. Action now appeared to be no more than a function of "the productive relationships" of mankind brought about by labor.) It is true that traditional philosophy often pays only lip service to the estimate of action as the highest activity of man, preferring the so much more reliable activity of making, so that the hierarchy within the *vita activa* has hardly ever been fully articulated. It is a sign of the political rank of Kant's philosophy that the old perplexities inherent in action were brought to the fore again.

However that may be, Kant could not but become aware of the fact

that action fulfilled neither of the two hopes the modern age was bound
to expect from it. If the secularization of our world implies the revival of
the old desire for some kind of earthly immortality, then human action,
especially in its political aspect, must appear singularly inadequate to meet
the demands of the new age. From the point of view of motivation, action appears to be the least interesting and most futile of all human pursuits: "Passions, private aims, and the satisfaction of selfish desires, are . . .
the most effective springs of action,"[28] and "the facts of known history,"
taken by themselves, "possess neither a common basis nor continuity nor
coherence" (Vico). From the viewpoint of achievement, on the other
hand, action appears at once to be more futile and more frustrating than
the activities of laboring and of producing objects. Human deeds, unless
they are remembered, are the most futile and perishable things on earth;
they hardly outlast the activity itself and certainly by themselves can never
aspire to that permanence which even ordinary use-objects possess when
they outlast their maker's life, not to mention works of art, which speak
to us over the centuries. Human action, projected into a web of relationships where many and opposing ends are pursued, almost never fulfills its
original intention; no act can ever be recognized by its author as his own
with the same happy certainty with which a piece of work of any kind
can be recognized by its maker. Whoever begins to act must know that he
has started something whose end he can never foretell, if only because his
own deed has already changed everything and made it even more unpredictable. That is what Kant had in mind when he spoke of the "melancholy haphazardness" (*trostlose Ungefähr*) which is so striking in the record
of political history. "Action: one does not know its origin, one does not
know its consequences:—therefore, does action possess any value at all?"[29]
Were not the old philosophers right, and was it not madness to expect any
meaning to arise out of the realm of human affairs?

For a long time it seemed that these inadequacies and perplexities
within the *vita activa* could be solved by ignoring the peculiarities of action
and by insisting upon the "meaningfulness" of the process of history in its
entirety, which seemed to give to the political sphere that dignity and final redemption from "melancholy haphazardness" so obviously required.
History—based on the manifest assumption that no matter how haphazard
single actions may appear in the present and in their singularity, they inevitably lead to a sequence of events forming a story that can be rendered
through intelligible narrative the moment the events are removed into the
past—became the great dimension in which men could become "reconciled" with reality (Hegel), the reality of human affairs, i.e., of things
which owe their existence exclusively to men. Moreover, since history in

its modern version was conceived primarily as a process, it showed a peculiar and inspiring affinity to action, which, indeed, in contrast to all other human activities, consists first of all of starting processes—a fact of which human experience has of course always been aware, even though the preoccupation of philosophy with making as the model of human activity has prevented the elaboration of an articulate terminology and precise description. The very notion of process, which is so highly characteristic of modern science, both natural and historical, probably had its origin in this fundamental experience of action, to which secularization lent an emphasis such as it had not known since the very early centuries of Greek culture, even before the rise of the polis and certainly before the victory of the Socratic school. History in its modern version could come to terms with this experience; and though it failed to save politics itself from the old disgrace, though the single deeds and acts constituting the realm of politics, properly speaking, were left in limbo, it has at least bestowed upon the record of past events that share of earthly immortality to which the modern age necessarily aspired, but which its acting men no longer dared to claim from posterity. . . .

Notes

1. Cicero. *De legibus* I, 5; *De oratore* II, 55. Herodotus, the first historian, did not yet have at his disposal a word for history. He used the word ἱστορεῖν, but not in the sense of "historical narrative." Like εἰςδέναι, to know, the word ἱστορία is derived from ἰδ-, to see, and ἵστωρ means originally "eyewitness," then the one who examines witnesses and obtains truth through inquiry. Hence, ἱστορία has a double meaning: to testify and to inquire. (See Max Pohlenz, *Herodot, der erste Geschichtsschreiber des Abendlandes,* Leipzig and Berlin, 1937, p. 44.) For recent discussion of Herodotus and our concept of history, see especially C. N. Cochrane, *Christianity and Classical Culture,* New York, 1944, ch. 12, one of the most stimulating and interesting pieces in the literature on the subject. His chief thesis, that Herodotus must be regarded as belonging to the Ionian school of philosophy and a follower of Heraclitus, is not convincing. Contrary to ancient sources, Cochrane construes the science of history as being part of the Greek development of philosophy. See note 6, and also Karl Reinhardt, "Herodots Persegeschichten" in *Von Werken und Formen,* Godesberg, 1948.

2. "The Gods of most nations claim to have created the world. The Olympian gods make no such claim. The most they ever did was to conquer it" (Gilbert Murray, *Five Stages of Greek Religion,* Anchor edition, p. 45). Against this statement one sometimes argues that Plato in the *Timaeus* introduced a creator of the world. But Plato's god is no real creator; he is a demiurge, a world-builder who does not create out of nothing. Moreover, Plato tells his

story in the form of a myth invented by himself, and this, like similar myths in his work, are not proposed as truth. That no god and no man ever created the cosmos is beautifully stated in Heraclitus, fragment 30 (Diels), for this cosmical order of all things "has always been and is and will be—an ever-living fire that blazes up in proportions and dies away in proportions."

3. *On the Soul*, 415b13. See also *Economics*, 1343b24: Nature fulfills the being-forever with respect to the species through recurrence (περίοδος) but cannot do this with respect to the individual. In our context, it is irrelevant that the treatise is not by Aristotle but by one of his pupils, for we find the same thought in the treatise *On Generation and Corruption* in the concept of Becoming, which moves in a cycle—γένεσις ἰξ ἀλλήλων κύκλῳ 331a8. The same thought of an "immortal human species" occurs in Plato, *Laws*, 721. See note 9.

4. Nietzsche, *Wille zur Macht*, Nr. 617, Edition Kröner, 1930.

5. Rilke, *Aus dem Nachlass des Grafen C. W.*, first series, poem X. Although the poetry is untranslatable, the content of these verses might be expressed as follows: "Mountains rest beneath a splendor of stars, but even in them time flickers. Ah, unsheltered in my wild, darkling heart lies immortality." I owe this translation to Denver Lindley.

6. *Poetics*, 1448b25 and 1450a16–22. For a distinction between poetry and historiography, see ibid., ch. 9.

7. For tragedy as an imitation of action, see ibid., ch. 6, 1.

8. *Griechische Kulturgeschichte*, Edition Kröner, II, p. 289.

9. For Plato, see *Laws* 721, where he makes it quite clear that he thinks the human species only in a certain way to be immortal—namely insofar as its successive generations taken as a whole are "growing together" with the entirety of time; mankind as a succession of generations and time are coeval: γένος οὖν ἀνθρώπωμ ἐστί τι ξυμφυὲς τοῦ παντὸς χρόνου, ὁ διὰ τέλους αὐτῷ ξυνέπεται καὶ συνέψεται, τούτῳ τῷ τρόπῳ ἀθάνατον ὄν. In other words, it is mere deathlessness—ἀθανασία—in which the mortals partake by virtue of belonging to an immortal species; it is not the timeless being-forever—the ἀεὶ εἰναι—in whose neighborhood the philosopher is admitted even though he is but a mortal. For Aristotle, see *Nicomachean Ethics*, 1177b30–35 and further in what follows.

10. Ibid., 1143a36.

11. *Seventh Letter*.

12. W. Heisenberg, *Philosophic Problems of Nuclear Science*, New York, 1952, p. 24.

13. Quoted from Alexandre Koyré, "An Experiment in Measurement," *Proceedings of the American Philosophical Society*, vol. 97, no. 2, 1953.

14. The same point was made more than twenty years ago by Edgar Wind in his essay "Some Points of Contact between History and Natural Sciences" (in *Philosophy and History, Essays Presented to Ernst Cassirer*, Oxford, 1939). Wind already showed that the latest developments of science which make it so much less "exact" lead to the raising of questions by scientists "that historians

like to look upon as their own." It seems strange that so fundamental and obvious an argument should have played no role in the subsequent methodological and other discussions of historical science.

15. Quoted in Friedrich Meinecke, *Vom geschichtlichen Sinn und vom Sinn der Geschichte*, Stuttgart, 1951.

16. Erwin Schroedinger, *Science and Humanism*, Cambridge, 1951, pp. 25–26.

17. *De nostri temporis studiorum ratione*, iv. Quoted from the bilingual edition by W. F. Otto, *Vom Wesen und Weg der geistigen Bildung*, Godesberg, 1947, p. 41.

18. No one can look at the remains of ancient or medieval towns without being struck by the finality with which their walls separated them from their natural surroundings, whether these were landscapes or wilderness. Modern city-building, on the contrary, aims at the landscaping and urbanization of whole areas, where the distinction between town and country becomes more and more obliterated. This trend could possibly lead to the disappearance of cities even as we know them today.

19. In *De doctrina Christiana*, 2, 28, 44.

20. *De Civitate Dei*, XII, 13.

21. See Theodor Mommsen, "St. Augustine and the Christian Idea of Progress," in *Journal of the History of Ideas*, June 1951. A close reading shows a striking discrepancy between the content of this excellent article and the thesis expressed in its title. The best defense of the Christian origin of the concept of history is found in C. N. Cochrane, op. cit., p. 474. He holds that ancient historiography came to an end because it had failed to establish "a principle of historical intelligibility" and that Augustine solved this problem by substituting "the *logos* of Christ for that of classicism as a principle of understanding."

22. Especially interesting is Oscar Cullman, *Christ and Time*, London, 1951. Also Erich Frank, "The Role of History in Christian Thought" in *Knowledge, Will and Belief, Collected Essays*, Zürich, 1955.

23. *Leviathan*, book I, ch. 3.

24. *Democracy in America*, 2nd part, last chapter, and 1st part, "Author's Introduction," respectively.

25. The first to see Kant as the theorist of the French Revolution was Friedrich Gentz in his "Nachtrag zu dem Räsonnement des Herrn Prof. Kant über das Verhältnis zwischen Theorie und Praxis" in *Berliner Monatsschrift*, December 1793.

26. *Idee zu einer allgemeinen Geschichte in weltbürgerlicher Absicht*, Introduction.

27. Op. cit., Third Thesis.

28. Hegel in *The Philosophy of History*, London, 1905, p. 21.

29. Nietzsche, *Wille zur Macht*, no. 291.

PART V

BANALITY AND CONSCIENCE: THE EICHMANN TRIAL AND ITS IMPLICATIONS

From *Eichmann in Jerusalem*

The following selections are excerpted from Eichmann in Jerusalem: A Report on the Banality of Evil *and based on "A Reporter at Large: Eichmann in Jerusalem," a five-part article Arendt was commissioned to write for* The New Yorker. *The parts appeared on 16 February 1963, 23 February 1963, 2 March 1963, 9 March 1963, and 16 March 1963.*

The presiding judge of the trial was Moshe Landau. The chief prosecutor was the attorney general, Gideon Hausner. Adolf Eichmann was represented by Dr. Robert Servatius. For Arendt's portrait of "the accused," and for some comments on the background of the trial, see Editor's Introduction, pp. xxiii–xxvi.

AN EXPERT ON THE JEWISH QUESTION

In 1934, when Eichmann applied successfully for a job, the S.D.* was a relatively new apparatus in the S.S., founded two years earlier by Heinrich Himmler to serve as the Intelligence service of the Party and now headed by Reinhardt Heydrich, a former Navy Intelligence officer, who was to become, as Gerald Reitlinger put it, "the real engineer of the Final Solution" (*The Final Solution*, 1961). Its initial task had been to spy on Party members, and thus to give the S.S. an ascendancy over the regular Party apparatus. Meanwhile it had taken on some additional duties, becoming the information and research center for the Secret State Police, or Gestapo. These were the first steps toward the merger of the S.S. and the police, which, however, was not carried out until September, 1939, although Himmler held the double post of Reichsführer S.S. and Chief of

---

*S.D. = *Sicherheitsdienst* (the Security Service of the S.S.)—Ed.

the German Police from 1936 on. Eichmann, of course, could not have known of these future developments, but he seems to have known nothing either of the nature of the S.D. when he entered it; this is quite possible, because the operations of the S.D. had always been top secret. As far as he was concerned, it was all a misunderstanding and at first "a great disappointment. For I thought this was what I had read about in the *Münchener Illustrierten Zeitung;* when the high Party officials drove along, there were commando guards with them, men standing on the running boards of the cars. . . . In short, I had mistaken the Security Service of the Reichsführer S.S. for the Reich Security Service . . . and nobody set me right and no one told me anything. For I had had not the slightest notion of what now was revealed to me." The question of whether he was telling the truth had a certain bearing on the trial, where it had to be decided whether he had volunteered for his position or had been drafted into it. His misunderstanding, if such it was, is not inexplicable; the S.S. or *Schutzstaffeln* had originally been established as special units for the protection of the Party leaders.

His disappointment, however, consisted chiefly in that he had to start all over again, that he was back at the bottom, and his only consolation was that there were others who had made the same mistake. He was put into the Information department, where his first job was to file all information concerning Freemasonry (which in the early Nazi ideological muddle was somehow lumped with Judaism, Catholicism, and Communism) and to help in the establishment of a Freemasonry museum. He now had ample opportunity to learn what this strange word meant that Kaltenbrunner had thrown at him in their discussion of Schlaraffia. (Incidentally, an eagerness to establish museums commemorating their enemies was very characteristic of the Nazis. During the war, several services competed bitterly for the honor of establishing anti-Jewish museums and libraries. We owe to this strange craze the salvage of many great cultural treasures of European Jewry.) The trouble was that things were again very, very boring, and he was greatly relieved when, after four or five months of Freemasonry, he was put into the brand-new department concerned with Jews. This was the real beginning of the career which was to end in the Jerusalem court.

It was the year 1935, when Germany, contrary to the stipulations of the Treaty of Versailles, introduced general conscription and publicly announced plans for rearmament, including the building of an air force and a navy. It was also the year when Germany, having left the League of Nations in 1933, prepared neither quietly nor secretly the occupation of the demilitarized zone of the Rhineland. It was the time of Hitler's peace speeches—"Germany needs peace and desires peace," "We recognize Poland as the home of a great and nationally conscious people," "Germany neither intends nor wishes to interfere in the internal affairs of Austria, to annex Austria, or to conclude an *Anschluss*"—and, above all, it was the year when the Nazi regime won general and, unhappily, genuine recognition in Germany and abroad, when Hitler was admired everywhere as a great national statesman. In Germany itself, it was a time of transition. Because of the enormous rearmament program, unemployment had been liquidated, the initial resistance of the working class was broken, and the hostility of the regime, which had at first been directed primarily against "anti-Fascists"—Communists, Socialists, left-wing intellectuals, and Jews in prominent positions—had not yet shifted entirely to persecution of the Jews qua Jews.

To be sure, one of the first steps taken by the Nazi government, back in 1933, had been the exclusion of Jews from the Civil Service (which in Germany included all teaching positions, from grammar school to university, and most branches of the entertainment industry, including radio, the theater, the opera, and concerts) and, in general, their removal from public offices. But private business remained almost untouched until 1938, and even the legal and medical professions were only gradually abolished, although Jewish students were excluded from most universities and were nowhere permitted to graduate. Emigration of Jews in these years proceeded in a not unduly accelerated and generally orderly fashion, and the currency restrictions that made it difficult, but not impossible, for Jews to take their money, or at least the greater part of it, out of the country were the same for non-Jews; they dated back to the days of the Weimar Republic. There were a certain number of *Einzelaktionen,* individual actions putting pressure on Jews to sell their property at often ridiculously low prices, but these usually occurred in small towns and, indeed, could be traced to the spontaneous, "individual" initiative of some enterprising Storm Troopers, the so-called S.A. men, who, except for their officer corps, were mostly recruited from the lower classes. The police, it is true, never stopped these "excesses," but the Nazi authorities were not too happy abut them, because they affected the value of real estate all over the country. The emigrants, unless they were political refugees, were young people who realized that there was no future for them in Germany. And since they soon found out that there was hardly any future for them in other European countries either, some Jewish emigrants actually returned during this period. When Eichmann was asked how he had reconciled his personal feelings about Jews with the outspoken and violent anti-Semitism of the Party he had joined, he replied with the proverb: "Noth-

ing's as hot when you eat it as when it's being cooked"—a proverb that
was then on the lips of many Jews as well. They lived in a fool's paradise,
in which, for a few years, even Streicher spoke of a "legal solution" of the
Jewish problem. It took the organized pogroms of November, 1938, the
so-called *Kristallnacht* or Night of Broken Glass, when seventy-five hundred Jewish shop windows were broken, all synagogues went up in
flames, and twenty thousand Jewish men were taken off to concentration
camps, to expel them from it.

The frequently forgotten point of the matter is that the famous
Nuremberg Laws, issued in the fall of 1935, had failed to do the trick.
The testimony of three witnesses from Germany, high-ranking former officials of the Zionist organization who left Germany shortly before the
outbreak of the war, gave only the barest glimpse into the true state of affairs during the first five years of the Nazi regime. The Nuremberg Laws
had deprived the Jews of their political but not of their civil rights; they
were no longer citizens (*Reichsbürger*), but they remained members of the
German state (*Staatsangehörige*). Even if they emigrated, they were not automatically stateless. Sexual intercourse between Jews and Germans, and
the contraction of mixed marriages, were forbidden. Also, no German
woman under the age of forty-five could be employed in a Jewish household. Of these stipulations, only the last was of practical significance; the
others merely legalized a *de facto* situation. Hence, the Nuremberg Laws
were felt to have stabilized the new situation of Jews in the German
Reich. They had been second-class citizens, to put it mildly, since January 30, 1933; their almost complete separation from the rest of the population had been achieved in a matter of weeks or months—through terror
but also through the more than ordinary connivance of those around
them. "There was a wall between Gentiles and Jews," Dr. Benno Cohn
of Berlin testified. "I cannot remember speaking to a Christian during all
my journeys over Germany." Now, the Jews felt, they had received laws
of their own and would no longer be outlawed. If they kept to themselves, as they had been forced to do anyhow, they would be able to live
unmolested. In the words of the *Reichsvertretung* of the Jews in Germany
(the national association of all communities and organizations, which had
been founded in September, 1933, on the initiative of the Berlin community, and was in no way Nazi-appointed), the intention of the Nuremberg
Laws was "to establish a level on which a bearable relationship between
the German and the Jewish people [became] possible," to which a member of the Berlin community, a radical Zionist, added: "Life is possible
under every law. However, in complete ignorance of what is permitted
and what is not one cannot live. A useful and respected citizen one can

also be as a member of a minority in the midst of a great people" (Hans Lamm, *Über die Entwicklung des deutschen Judentums,* 1951). And since Hitler, in the Röhm purge in 1934, had broken the power of the S.A., the Storm Troopers in brown shirts who had been almost exclusively responsible for the early pogroms and atrocities, and since the Jews were blissfully unaware of the growing power of the black-shirted S.S., who ordinarily abstained from what Eichmann contemptuously called the "*Stürmer* methods," they generally believed that a *modus vivendi* would be possible; they even offered to cooperate in "the solution of the Jewish question." In short, when Eichmann entered upon his apprenticeship in Jewish affairs, on which, four years later, he was to be the recognized "expert," and when he made his first contacts with Jewish functionaries, both Zionists and Assimilationists talked in terms of a great "Jewish revival," a "great constructive movement of German Jewry," and they still quarreled among themselves in ideological terms about the desirability of Jewish emigration, as though this depended upon their own decisions.

Eichmann's account during the police examination of how he was introduced into the new department—distorted, of course, but not wholly devoid of truth—oddly recalls this fool's paradise. The first thing that happened was that his new boss, a certain von Mildenstein, who shortly thereafter got himself transferred to Albert Speer's *Organisation Todt,* where he was in charge of highway construction (he was what Eichmann pretended to be, an engineer by profession), required him to read Theodor Herzl's *Der Judenstaat,* the famous Zionist classic, which converted Eichmann promptly and forever to Zionism. This seems to have been the first serious book he ever read and it made a lasting impression on him. From then on, as he repeated over and over, he thought of hardly anything but a "political solution" (as opposed to the later "physical solution," the first meaning expulsion and the second extermination) and how to "get some firm ground under the feet of the Jews." (It may be worth mentioning that, as late as 1939, he seems to have protested against desecrators of Herzl's grave in Vienna, and there are reports of his presence in civilian clothes at the commemoration of the thirty-fifth anniversary of Herzl's death. Strangely enough, he did not talk about these things in Jerusalem, where he continuously boasted of his good relations with Jewish officials.) In order to help in this enterprise, he began spreading the gospel among his S.S. comrades, giving lectures and writing pamphlets. He then acquired a smattering of Hebrew, which enabled him to read haltingly a Yiddish newspaper—not a very difficult accomplishment, since Yiddish, basically an old German dialect written in Hebrew letters, can be understood by any German-speaking person who has mastered a few dozen Hebrew words. He even read one more book, Adolf Böhm's *History of Zionism* (during the trial he kept confusing it with Herzl's *Judenstaat*), and this was perhaps a considerable achievement for a man who, by his own account, had always been utterly reluctant to read anything except newspapers, and who, to the distress of his father, had never availed himself of the books in the family library. Following up Böhm, he studied the organizational setup of the Zionist movement, with all its parties, youth groups, and different programs. This did not yet make him an "authority," but it was enough to earn him an assignment as official spy on the Zionist offices and on their meetings; it is worth noting that his schooling in Jewish affairs was almost entirely concerned with Zionism.

His first personal contacts with Jewish functionaries, all of them well-known Zionists of long standing, were thoroughly satisfactory. The reason he became so fascinated by the "Jewish question," he explained, was his own "idealism"; these Jews, unlike the Assimilationists, whom he always despised, and unlike Orthodox Jews, who bored him, were "idealists," like him. An "idealist," according to Eichmann's notions, was not merely a man who believed in an "idea" or someone who did not steal or accept bribes, though these qualifications were indispensable. An "idealist" was a man who *lived* for his idea—hence he could not be a businessman—and who was prepared to sacrifice for his idea everything and, especially, everybody. When he said in the police examination that he would have sent his own father to his death if that had been required, he did not mean merely to stress the extent to which he was under orders, and ready to obey them; he also meant to show what an "idealist" he had always been. The perfect "idealist," like everybody else, had of course his personal feelings and emotions, but he would never permit them to interfere with his actions if they came into conflict with his "idea." The greatest "idealist" Eichmann ever encountered among the Jews was Dr. Rudolf Kastner, with whom he negotiated during the Jewish deportations from Hungary and with whom he came to an agreement that he, Eichmann, would permit the "illegal" departure of a few thousand Jews to Palestine (the trains were in fact guarded by German police) in exchange for "quiet and order" in the camps from which hundreds of thousands were shipped to Auschwitz. The few thousand saved by the agreement, prominent Jews and members of the Zionist youth organizations, were, in Eichmann's words, "the best biological material." Dr. Kastner, as Eichmann understood it, had sacrificed his fellow-Jews to his "idea," and this was as it should be. Judge Benjamin Halevi, one of the three judges at Eichmann's trial, had been in charge of the Kastner trial in Israel, at which Kastner had to defend himself for his cooperation with Eichmann and other high-ranking Nazis; in Halevi's opinion, Kastner had "sold his soul to the devil." Now that the devil himself was in the dock he turned out to be an "idealist," and though it may be hard to believe, it is quite possible that the one who sold his soul had also been an "idealist."

Long before all this happened, Eichmann was given his first opportunity to apply in practice what he had learned during his apprenticeship. After the *Anschluss* (the incorporation of Austria into the Reich), in March, 1938, he was sent to Vienna to organize a kind of emigration that had been utterly unknown in Germany, where up to the fall of 1938 the fiction was maintained that Jews if they so desired were permitted, but were not forced, to leave the country. Among the reasons German Jews believed in the fiction was the program of the N.S.D.A.P., formulated in 1920, which shared with the Weimar Constitution the curious fate of never being officially abolished; its Twenty-Five Points had even been declared "unalterable" by Hitler. Seen in the light of later events, its anti-Semite provisions were harmless indeed: Jews could not be full-fledged citizens, they could not hold Civil Service positions, they were to be excluded from the press, and all those who had acquired German citizenship after August 2, 1914— the date of the outbreak of the First World War—were to be denaturalized, which meant they were subject to expulsion. (Characteristically, the denaturalization was carried out immediately, but the wholesale expulsion of some fifteen thousand Jews, who from one day to the next were shoved across the Polish border at Zbaszyn, where they were promptly put into camps, took place only five years later, when no one expected it any longer.) The Party program was never taken seriously by Nazi officials; they prided themselves on belonging to a movement, as distinguished from a party, and a movement could not be bound by a program. Even before the Nazis' rise to power, these Twenty-Five Points had been no more than a concession to the party system and to such prospective voters as were old-fashioned enough to ask what was the program of the party they were going to join. Eichmann, as we have seen, was free of such deplorable habits, and when he told the Jerusalem court that he had not known Hitler's program he very likely spoke the truth: "The Party program did not matter, you knew what you were joining." The Jews, on the other hand, were old-fashioned enough to know the Twenty-Five Points by heart and to believe in them; whatever contradicted the legal implementation of the Party program they tended to ascribe to temporary, "revolutionary excesses" of undisciplined members or groups.

But what happened in Vienna in March, 1938, was altogether different. Eichmann's task had been defined as "forced emigration," and the words meant exactly what they said: all Jews, regardless of their desires and regardless of their citizenship, were to be forced to emigrate—an act which in ordinary language is called expulsion. Whenever Eichmann thought back to the twelve years that were his life, he singled out his year in Vienna as head of the Center for Emigration of Austrian Jews as its happiest and most successful period. Shortly before, he had been promoted to officer's rank, becoming an *Untersturmführer*, or lieutenant, and he had been commended for his "comprehensive knowledge of the methods of organization and ideology of the opponent, Jewry." The assignment in Vienna was his first important job, his whole career, which had progressed rather slowly, was in the balance. He must have been frantic to make good, and his success was spectacular: in eight months, forty-five thousand Jews left Austria, whereas no more than nineteen thousand left Germany in the same period; in less than eighteen months, Austria was "cleansed" of close to a hundred and fifty thousand people, roughly sixty per cent of its Jewish population, all of whom left the country "legally"; even after the outbreak of the war, some sixty thousand Jews could escape. How did he do it? The basic idea that made all this possible was of course not his but, almost certainly, a specific directive by Heydrich, who had sent him to Vienna in the first place. (Eichmann was vague on the question of authorship, which he claimed, however, by implication; the Israeli authorities, on the other hand, bound [as Yad Vashem's *Bulletin* put it] to the fantastic "thesis of the all-inclusive responsibility of Adolf Eichmann" and the even more fantastic "supposition that one [i.e., his] mind was behind it all," helped him considerably in his efforts to deck himself in borrowed plumes, for which he had in any case a great inclination.) The idea, as explained by Heydrich in a conference with Göring on the morning of the *Kristallnacht,* was simple and ingenious enough: "Through the Jewish community, we extracted a certain amount of money from the rich Jews who wanted to emigrate. By paying this amount, and an additional sum in foreign currency, they made it possible for poor Jews to leave. The problem was not to make the rich Jews leave, but to get rid of the Jewish mob." And this "problem" was not solved by Eichmann. Not until the trial was over was it learned from the Netherlands State Institute for War Documentation that Erich Rajakowitsch, a "brilliant lawyer" whom Eichmann, according to his own testimony, "employed for the handling of legal questions in the central offices for Jewish emigration in Vienna, Prague, and Berlin," had originated the idea of the "emigration funds." Somewhat later, in April, 1941, Rajakowitsch was sent to Holland by Heydrich in order to "establish there a central office which was to serve as a model for the 'solution of the Jewish question' in all occupied countries in Europe."

Still, enough problems remained that could be solved only in the course of the operation, and there is no doubt that here Eichmann, for the first time in his life, discovered in himself some special qualities. There were two things he could do well, better than others: he could organize and he could negotiate. Immediately upon his arrival, he opened negotiations with the representatives of the Jewish community, whom he had first to liberate from prisons and concentration camps, since the "revolutionary zeal" in Austria, greatly exceeding the early "excesses" in Germany, had resulted in the imprisonment of practically all prominent Jews. After this experience, the Jewish functionaries did not need Eichmann to convince them of the desirability of emigration. Rather, they informed him of the enormous difficulties which lay ahead. Apart from the financial problem, already "solved," the chief difficulty lay in the number of papers every emigrant had to assemble before he could leave the country. Each of the papers was valid only for a limited time, so that the validity of the first had usually expired long before the last could be obtained. Once Eichmann understood how the whole thing worked, or, rather, did not work, he "took counsel with himself" and "gave birth to the idea which I thought would do justice to both parties." He imagined "an assembly line, at whose beginnings the first document is put, and then the other papers, and at its end the passport would have to come out as the end product." This could be realized if all the officers concerned—the Ministry of Finance, the income tax people, the police, the Jewish community, etc.— were housed under the same roof and forced to do their work on the spot, in the presence of the applicant, who would no longer have to run from office to office and who, presumably, would also be spared having some humiliating chicaneries practiced on him, and certain expenses for bribes. When everything was ready and the assembly line was doing its work smoothly and quickly, Eichmann "invited" the Jewish functionaries from Berlin to inspect it. They were appalled: "This is like an automatic factory, like a flour mill connected with some bakery. At one end you put in a Jew who still has some property, a factory, or a shop, or a bank account, and he goes through the building from counter to counter, from office to office, and comes out at the other end without any money, without any rights, with only a passport on which it says: 'You must leave the country within a fortnight. Otherwise you will go to a concentration camp.' "

This, of course, was essentially the truth about the procedure, but it was not the whole truth. For these Jews could not be left "without any money," for the simple reason that without it no country at this date would have taken them. They needed, and were given, their *Vorzeigegeld*, the amount they had to show in order to obtain their visas and to pass the immigration controls of the recipient country. For this amount, they needed foreign currency, which the Reich had no intention of wasting on its Jews. These needs could not be met by Jewish accounts in foreign countries, which, in any event, were difficult to get at because they had been illegal for many years; Eichmann therefore sent Jewish functionaries abroad to solicit funds from the great Jewish organizations, and these funds were then sold by the Jewish community to the prospective emigrants at a considerable profit—one dollar, for instance, was sold for 10 or 20 marks when its market value was 4.20 marks. It was chiefly in this way that the community acquired not only the money necessary for poor Jews and people without accounts abroad, but also the funds it needed for its own hugely expanded activities. Eichmann did not make possible this deal without encountering considerable opposition from the German financial authorities, the Ministry and the Treasury, which, after all, could not remain unaware of the fact that these transactions amounted to a devaluation of the mark.

Bragging was the vice that was Eichmann's undoing. It was sheer rodomontade when he told his men during the last days of the war: "I will jump into my grave laughing, because the fact that I have the death of five million Jews [or "enemies of the Reich," as he always claimed to have said] on my conscience gives me extraordinary satisfaction." He did not jump, and if he had anything on his conscience, it was not murder but, as it turned out, that he had once slapped the face of Dr. Josef Löwenherz, head of the Vienna Jewish community, who later became one of his favorite Jews. (He had apologized in front of his staff at the time, but this incident kept bothering him.) To claim the death of five million Jews, the approximate total of losses suffered from the combined efforts of all Nazi offices and authorities, was preposterous, as he knew very well, but he had kept repeating the damning sentence *ad nauseam* to everyone who would listen, even twelve years later in Argentina, because it gave him "an extraordinary sense of elation to think that [he] was exiting from the stage in this way." (Former Legationsrat Horst Grell, a witness for the defense, who had known Eichmann in Hungary, testified that in his opinion Eichmann was boasting. That must have been obvious to everyone who heard him utter his absurd claim.) It was sheer boasting when he pretended he had "invented" the ghetto system or had "given birth to the idea" of shipping all European Jews to Madagascar. The Theresienstadt ghetto, of which Eichmann claimed "paternity," was established years after the ghetto system had been introduced into the Eastern occupied territories, and setting up a special ghetto for certain privileged categories was, like the ghetto system, the "idea" of Heydrich. The Madagascar plan seems to have been "born" in the bureaus of the German Foreign Office, and Eichmann's own contribution to it turned out to owe a good deal to his beloved Dr. Löwenherz, whom he had drafted to put down "some basic thoughts" on how about four million Jews might be transported from Europe after the war—presumably to Palestine, since the Madagascar project was top secret. (When confronted at the trial with the Löwenherz report, Eichmann did not deny its authorship; it was one of the few moments when he appeared genuinely embarrassed.) What eventually led to his capture was his compulsion to talk big—he was "fed up with being an anonymous wanderer between the worlds"—and this compulsion must have grown considerably stronger as time passed, not only because he had nothing to do that he could consider worth doing, but also because the postwar era had bestowed so much unexpected "fame" upon him.

But bragging is a common vice, and a more specific, and also more decisive, flaw in Eichmann's character was his almost total inability ever to look at anything from the other fellow's point of view. Nowhere was this flaw more conspicuous than in his account of the Vienna episode. He and his men and the Jews were all "pulling together," and whenever there were any difficulties the Jewish functionaries would come running to him "to unburden their hearts," to tell him "all their grief and sorrow," and to ask for his help. The Jews "desired" to emigrate, and he, Eichmann, was there to help them, because it so happened that at the same time the Nazi authorities had expressed a desire to see their Reich *judenrein.* The two desires coincided, and he, Eichmann, could "do justice to both parties." At the trial, he never gave an inch when it came to this part of the story, although he agreed that today, when "times have changed so much," the Jews might not be too happy to recall this "pulling together" and he did not want "to hurt their feelings."

The German text of the taped police examination, conducted from May 29, 1960, to January 17, 1961, each page corrected and approved by Eichmann, constitutes a veritable gold mine for a psychologist—provided he is wise enough to understand that the horrible can be not only ludicrous but outright funny. Some of the comedy cannot be conveyed in English, because it lies in Eichmann's heroic fight with the German language, which invariably defeats him. It is funny when he speaks, *passim,* of "winged words" (*geflügelte Worte,* a German colloquialism for famous quotes from the classics) when he means stock phrases, *Redensarten,* or slogans, *Schlagworte.* It was funny when, during the cross-examination on the Sassen documents, conducted in German by the presiding judge, he used

the phrase "*kontra geben*" (to give tit for tat), to indicate that he had resisted Sassen's efforts to liven up his stories; Judge Landau, obviously ignorant of the mysteries of card games, did not understand, and Eichmann
could not think of any other way to put it. Dimly aware of a defect that
must have plagued him even in school—it amounted to a mild case of
aphasia—he apologized, saying, "Officialese [*Amtssprache*] is my only language." But the point here is that officialese became his language because
he was genuinely incapable of uttering a single sentence that was not a
cliché. (Was it these clichés that the psychiatrists thought so "normal" and
"desirable"? Are these the "positive ideas" a clergyman hopes for in those
to whose souls he ministers? Eichmann's best opportunity to show this
positive side of his character in Jerusalem came when the young police officer in charge of his mental and psychological well-being handed him
Lolita for relaxation. After two days Eichmann returned it, visibly indig-
nant; "Quite an unwholesome book"—"*Das ist aber ein sehr unerfreuliches
Buch*"—he told his guard.) To be sure, the judges were right when they
finally told the accused that all he had said was "empty talk"—except that
they thought the emptiness was feigned, and that the accused wished to
cover up other thoughts which, though hideous, were not empty. This
supposition seems refuted by the striking consistency with which Eichmann, despite his rather bad memory, repeated word for word the same
stock phrases and self-invented clichés (when he did succeed in construct-
ing a sentence of his own, he repeated it until it became a cliché) each
time he referred to an incident or event of importance to him. Whether
writing his memoirs in Argentina or in Jerusalem, whether speaking to the
police examiner or to the court, what he said was always the same, expressed in the same words. The longer one listened to him, the more obvious it became that his inability to speak was closely connected with an
inability to *think,* namely, to think from the standpoint of somebody else.
No communication was possible with him, not because he lied but because he was surrounded by the most reliable of all safeguards against the
words and the presence of others, and hence against reality as such.

Thus, confronted for eight months with the reality of being examined by a Jewish policeman, Eichmann did not have the slightest hesitation in explaining to him at considerable length, and repeatedly, why he
had been unable to attain a higher grade in the S.S., that this was not his
fault. He had done everything, even asked to be sent to active military
duty—"Off to the front, I said to myself, then the *Standartenführer*
[colonelcy] will come quicker." In court, on the contrary, he pretended
he had asked to be transferred because he wanted to escape his murderous
duties. He did not insist much on this, though, and, strangely, he was not

confronted with his utterances to Captain Less, whom he also told that he had hoped to be nominated for the *Einsatzgruppen,* the mobile killing units in the East, because when they were formed, in March, 1941, his office was "dead"—there was no emigration any longer and deportations had not yet been started. There was, finally, his greatest ambition—to be promoted to the job of police chief in some German town; again, nothing doing. What makes these pages of the examination so funny is that all this was told in the tone of someone who was sure of finding "normal, human" sympathy for a hard-luck story. "Whatever I prepared and planned, everything went wrong, my personal affairs as well as my years-long efforts to obtain land and soil for the Jews. I don't know, everything was as if under an evil spell; whatever I desired and wanted and planned to do, fate prevented it somehow. I was frustrated in everything, no matter what." When Captain Less asked his opinion on some damning and possibly lying evidence given by a former colonel of the S.S., he exclaimed, suddenly stuttering with rage: "I am very much surprised that this man could ever have been an S.S. *Standartenführer,* that surprises me very much indeed. It is altogether, altogether unthinkable. I don't know what to say." He never said these things in a spirit of defiance, as though he wanted, even now, to defend the standards by which he had lived in the past. The very words "S.S.," or "career," or "Himmler" (whom he always called by his long official title: Reichsführer S.S. and Chief of the German Police, although he by no means admired him) triggered in him a mechanism that had become completely unalterable. The presence of Captain Less, a Jew from Germany and unlikely in any case to think that members of the S.S. advanced in their careers through the exercise of high moral qualities, did not for a moment throw this mechanism out of gear.

Now and then, the comedy breaks into the horror itself, and results in stories, presumably true enough, whose macabre humor easily surpasses that of any Surrealist invention. Such was the story told by Eichmann during the police examination about the unlucky Kommerzialrat Storfer of Vienna, one of the representatives of the Jewish community. Eichmann had received a telegram from Rudolf Höss, Commandant of Auschwitz, telling him that Storfer had arrived and had urgently requested to see Eichmann. "I said to myself: O.K., this man has always behaved well, that is worth my while . . . I'll go there myself and see what is the matter with him. And I go to Ebner [chief of the Gestapo in Vienna], and Ebner says—I remember it only vaguely—'If only he had not been so clumsy; he went into hiding and tried to escape,' something of the sort. And the police arrested him and sent him to the concentration camp, and, according to the orders of the Reichsführer [Himmler], no one could get out once he was in. Nothing could be done, neither Dr. Ebner nor I nor anybody else could do anything about it. I went to Auschwitz and asked Höss to see Storfer. 'Yes, yes [Höss said], he is in one of the labor gangs.' With Storfer afterward, well, it was normal and human, we had a normal, human encounter. He told me all his grief and sorrow: I said: 'Well, my dear old friend [*Ja, mein lieber guter Storfer*], we certainly got it! What rotten luck!' And I also said: 'Look, I really cannot help you, because according to orders from the Reichsführer nobody can get out. I can't get you out. Dr. Ebner can't get you out. I hear you made a mistake, that you went into hiding or wanted to bolt, which, after all, *you* did not need to do.' [Eichmann meant that Storfer, as a Jewish functionary, had immunity from deportation.] I forget what his reply to this was. And then I asked him how he was. And he said, yes, he wondered if he couldn't be let off work, it was heavy work. And then I said to Höss: 'Work—Storfer won't have to work!' But Höss said: 'Everyone works here.' So I said: 'O.K.,' I said, 'I'll make out a chit to the effect that Storfer has to keep the gravel paths in order with a broom,' there were little gravel paths there, 'and that he has the right to sit down with his broom on one of the benches.' [To Storfer] I said: 'Will that be all right, Mr. Storfer? Will that suit you?' Whereupon he was very pleased, and we shook hands, and then he was given the broom and sat down on his bench. It was a great inner joy to me that I could at least see the man with whom I had worked for so many long years, and that we could speak with each other." Six weeks after this normal human encounter, Storfer was dead—not gassed, apparently, but shot.

Is this a textbook case of bad faith, of lying self-deception combined with outrageous stupidity? Or is it simply the case of the eternally unrepentant criminal (Dostoevski once mentions in his diaries that in Siberia, among scores of murderers, rapists, and burglars, he never met a single man who would admit that he had done wrong) who cannot afford to face reality because his crime has become part and parcel of it? Yet Eichmann's case is different from that of the ordinary criminal, who can shield himself effectively against the reality of a non-criminal world only within the narrow limits of his gang. Eichmann needed only to recall the past in order to feel assured that he was not lying and that he was not deceiving himself, for he and the world he lived in had once been in perfect harmony. And that German society of eighty million people had been shielded against reality and factuality by exactly the same means, the same self-deception, lies, and stupidity that had now become ingrained in Eichmann's mentality. These lies changed from year to year, and they frequently contradicted each other; moreover, they were not necessarily the same for the various branches of the Party hierarchy or the people at large. But the practice of self-deception had become so common, almost a moral prerequisite for survival, that even now, eighteen years after the collapse of the Nazi regime, when most of the specific content of its lies has been forgotten, it is sometimes difficult not to believe that mendacity has become an integral part of the German national character. During the war, the lie most effective with the whole of the German people was the slogan of "the battle of destiny for the German people" [*der Schicksalskampf des deutschen Volkes*], coined either by Hitler or by Goebbels, which made self-deception easier on three counts: it suggested, first, that the war was no war; second, that it was started by destiny and not by Germany; and, third, that it was a matter of life and death for the Germans, who must annihilate their enemies or be annihilated.

Eichmann's astounding willingness, in Argentina as well as in Jerusalem, to admit his crimes was due less to his own criminal capacity for self-deception than to the aura of systematic mendacity that had constituted the general, and generally accepted, atmosphere of the Third Reich. "Of course" he had played a role in the extermination of the Jews; of course if he "had not transported them, they would not have been delivered to the butcher." "What," he asked, "is there to 'admit'?" Now, he proceeded, he "would like to find peace with [his] former enemies"—a sentiment he shared not only with Himmler, who had expressed it during the last year of the war, or with the Labor Front leader Robert Ley (who, before he committed suicide in Nuremberg, had proposed the establishment of a "conciliation committee" consisting of the Nazis responsible for the massacres and the Jewish survivors) but also, unbelievably, with many ordinary Germans, who were heard to express themselves in exactly the same terms at the end of the war. This outrageous cliché was no longer issued to them from above, it was a self-fabricated stock phrase, as devoid of reality as those clichés by which the people had lived for twelve years; and you could almost see what an "extraordinary sense of elation" it gave to the speaker the moment it popped out of his mouth.

Eichmann's mind was filled to the brim with such sentences. His memory proved to be quite unreliable about what had actually happened; in a rare moment of exasperation, Judge Landau asked the accused: "What *can* you remember?" (if you don't remember the discussions at the so-called Wannsee Conference, which dealt with the various methods of killing) and the answer, of course, was that Eichmann remembered the turning points in his own career rather well, but that they did not necessarily coincide with the turning points in the story of Jewish extermination or, as a matter of fact, with the turning points in history. (He always had trouble remembering the exact date of the outbreak of the war or of the invasion of Russia.) But the point of the matter is that he had not forgotten a single one of the sentences of his that at one time or another had served to give him a "sense of elation." Hence, whenever, during the cross-examination, the judges tried to appeal to his conscience, they were met with "elation," and they were outraged as well as disconcerted when they learned that the accused had at his disposal a different elating cliché for each period of his life and each of his activities. In his mind, there was no contradiction between "I will jump into my grave laughing," appropriate for the end of the war, and "I shall gladly hang myself in public as a warning example for all anti-Semites on this earth," which now, under vastly different circumstances, fulfilled exactly the same function of giving him a lift.

These habits of Eichmann's created considerable difficulty during the trial—less for Eichmann himself than for those who had come to prosecute him, to defend him, to judge him, and to report on him. For all this, it was essential that one take him seriously, and this was very hard to do, unless one sought the easiest way out of the dilemma between the unspeakable horror of the deeds and the undeniable ludicrousness of the man who perpetrated them, and declared him a clever, calculating liar—which he obviously was not. His own convictions in this matter were far from modest: "One of the few gifts fate bestowed upon me is a capacity for truth insofar as it depends upon myself." This gift he had claimed even before the prosecutor wanted to settle on him crimes he had not committed. In the disorganized, rambling notes he made in Argentina in preparation for the interview with Sassen, when he was still, as he even pointed out at the time, "in full possession of my physical and psychological freedom," he had issued a fantastic warning to "future historians to be objective enough not to stray from the path of this truth recorded here"— fantastic because every line of these scribblings shows his utter ignorance of everything that was not directly, technically and bureaucratically, connected with his job, and also shows an extraordinarily faulty memory.

Despite all the efforts of the prosecution, everybody could see that this man was not a "monster," but it was difficult indeed not to suspect that he was a clown. And since this suspicion would have been fatal to the whole enterprise, and was also rather hard to sustain in view of the sufferings he and his like had caused to millions of people, his worst clowneries were hardly noticed and almost never reported. What could you do with a man who first declared, with great emphasis, that the one thing he had learned in an ill-spent life was that one should never take an oath ("Today no man, no judge could ever persuade me to make a sworn statement, to declare something under oath as a witness. I refuse it, I refuse it for moral reasons. Since my experience tells me that if one is loyal to his oath, one day he has to take the consequences, I have made up my mind once and for all that no judge in the world or any other authority will ever be capable of making me swear an oath, to give sworn testimony. I won't do it voluntarily and no one will be able to force me"), and then, after being told explicitly that if he wished to testify in his own defense he might "do so under oath or without an oath," declared without further ado that he would prefer to testify under oath? Or who, repeatedly and with a great show of feeling, assured the court, as he had assured the police examiner, that the worst thing he could do would be to try to escape his true responsibilities, to fight for his neck, to plead for mercy—and then, upon instruction of his counsel, submitted a handwritten document, containing his plea for mercy?

As far as Eichmann was concerned, these were questions of changing moods, and as long as he was capable of finding, either in his memory or on the spur of the moment, an elating stock phrase to go with them, he was quite content, without ever becoming aware of anything like "inconsistencies." As we shall see, this horrible gift for consoling himself with clichés did not leave him in the hour of his death.

THE FINAL SOLUTION:
KILLING

. . . In September, 1941, shortly after his first official visits to the killing centers in the East, Eichmann organized his first mass deportations from Germany and the Protectorate, in accordance with a "wish" of Hitler, who had told Himmler to make the Reich *judenrein* as quickly as possible. The first shipment contained twenty thousand Jews from the Rhineland and five thousand Gypsies, and in connection with this first transport a strange thing happened. Eichmann, who never made a decision on his own, who was extremely careful always to be "covered" by orders, who—as freely given testimony from practically all the people who had worked with him confirmed—did not even like to volunteer suggestions and always required "directives," now, "for the first and last time," took an initiative contrary to orders: instead of sending these people to Russian territory, Riga or Minsk, where they would have immediately been shot by the *Einsatzgruppen,* he directed the transport to the ghetto of Lódz, where he knew that no preparations for extermination had yet been made—if only because the man in charge of the ghetto, a certain Regierungspräsident Uebelhör, had found ways and means of deriving considerable profit from "his" Jews. (Lódz, in fact, was the first ghetto to be established and the last to be liquidated; those of its inmates who did not succumb to disease or starvation survived until the summer of 1944.) This decision was to get Eichmann into considerable trouble. The ghetto was overcrowded, and Mr. Uebelhör was in no mood to receive newcomers and in no position to accommodate them. He was angry enough to complain to Himmler that Eichmann had deceived him and his men with "horsetrading tricks learned from the Gypsies." Himmler, as well as Heydrich, protected Eichmann and the incident was soon forgiven and forgotten.

Forgotten, first of all, by Eichmann himself, who did not once mention it either in the police examination or in his various memoirs. When he had taken the stand and was being examined by his lawyer, who showed him the documents, he insisted he had a "choice": "Here for the first and last time I had a choice. . . . One was Lódz. . . . If there are difficulties in Lódz, these people must be sent onward to the East. And since I had seen the preparations, I was determined to do all I could to send these people to Lódz by any means at my disposal." Counsel for the defense tried to conclude from this incident that Eichmann had saved Jews whenever he could—which was patently untrue. The prosecutor, who cross-examined him later with respect to the same incident, wished to establish that Eichmann himself had determined the final destination of all shipments and hence had decided whether or not a particular transport was to be exterminated—which was also untrue. Eichmann's own explanation, that he had not disobeyed an order but only taken advantage of a "choice," finally, was not true either, for there had been difficulties in Lódz, as he knew full well, so that his order read, in so many words: Final destination, Minsk or Riga. Although Eichmann had forgotten all about it, this was clearly the only instance in which he actually had tried to save Jews. Three weeks later, however, there was a meeting in Prague, called by Heydrich, during which Eichmann stated that "the camps used for the detention of [Russian] Communists [a category to be liquidated on the spot by the *Einsatzgruppen*] can also include Jews" and that he had "reached an agreement" to this effect with the local commanders; there was also some discussion about the trouble at Lódz, and it was finally resolved to send fifty thousand Jews from the Reich (that is, including Austria, and Bohemia and Moravia) to the centers of the *Einsatzgruppen* operations at Riga and Minsk. Thus, we are perhaps in a position to answer Judge Landau's question—the question uppermost in the minds of nearly everyone who followed the trial—of whether the accused had a conscience: yes, he had a conscience, and his conscience functioned in the expected way for about four weeks, whereupon it began to function the other way around.

Even during those weeks when his conscience functioned normally, it did its work within rather odd limits. We must remember that weeks and months before he was informed of the Führer's order, Eichmann knew of the murderous activities of the *Einsatzgruppen* in the East; he knew that right behind the front lines all Russian functionaries ("Communists"), all Polish members of the professional classes, and all native Jews were being killed in mass shootings. Moreover, in July of the same year, a few weeks before he was called to Heydrich, he had received a memorandum from an S.S. man stationed in the Warthegau, telling him that "Jews in the coming winter could no longer be fed," and submitting for his consideration a proposal as to "whether it would not be the most humane solution to kill those Jews who were incapable of work through some quicker means. This, at any rate, would be more agreeable than to let them die of starvation." In an accompanying letter, addressed to "Dear Comrade Eichmann," the writer admitted that "these things sound sometimes fantastic, but they are quite feasible." The admission shows that the much more "fantastic" order of the Führer was not yet known to the writer, but the letter also shows to what extent this order was in the air. Eichmann never mentioned this letter and probably had not been in the least shocked by it. For this proposal concerned only *native* Jews, not Jews from the Reich or any of the Western countries. His conscience rebelled not at the idea of murder but at the idea of German Jews being murdered. ("I never denied that I knew that the *Einsatzgruppen* had orders to kill, but I did not know that Jews from the Reich evacuated to the East were subject to the same treatment. That is what I did not know.") It was the same with the conscience of a certain Wilhelm Kube, an old Party member and *Generalkommissar* in Occupied Russia, who was outraged when German Jews with the Iron Cross arrived in Minsk for "special treatment." Since Kube was more articulate than Eichmann, his words may give us an idea of what went on in Eichmann's head during the time he was plagued by his conscience: "I am certainly tough and I am ready to help solve the Jewish question," Kube wrote to his superior in December, 1941, "but people who come from our own cultural milieu are certainly something else than the native animalized hordes." This sort of conscience, which, if it rebelled at all, rebelled at murder of people "from our own cultural milieu," has survived the Hitler regime; among Germans today, there exists a stubborn "misinformation" to the effect that "only" *Ostjuden,* Eastern European Jews, were massacred.

Nor is this way of thinking that distinguishes between the murder of "primitive" and of "cultured" people a monopoly of the German people. Harry Mulisch relates how, in connection with the testimony given by Professor Salo W. Baron about the cultural and spiritual achievements of the Jewish people, the following questions suddenly occurred to him: "Would the death of the Jews have been less of an evil if they were a people without a culture, such as the Gypsies who were also exterminated? Is Eichmann on trial as a destroyer of human beings or as an annihilator of culture? Is a murderer of human beings more guilty when a culture is also destroyed in the process?" And when he put these questions to the Attorney General, it turned out—"He [Hausner] thinks yes, I think no." How ill we can afford to dismiss this matter, bury the troublesome question along with the past, came to light in the recent film *Dr. Strangelove,* where the strange lover of the bomb—characterized, it is true, as a Nazi type—proposes to select in the coming disaster some hundred thousand persons to survive in underground shelters. And who are to be the happy survivors? Those with the highest I.Q.!

This question of conscience, so troublesome in Jerusalem, had by no means been ignored by the Nazi regime. On the contrary, in view of the fact that the participants in the anti-Hitler conspiracy of July, 1944, very rarely mentioned the wholesale massacres in the East in their correspondence or in the statements they prepared for use in the event that the attempt on Hitler's life was successful, one is tempted to conclude that the Nazis greatly overestimated the practical importance of the problem. We may here disregard the early stages of the German opposition to Hitler, when it was still anti-Fascist and entirely a movement of the Left, which as a matter of principle accorded no significance to moral issues and even less to the persecution of the Jews—a mere "diversion" from the class struggle that in the opinion of the Left determined the whole political scene. Moreover, this opposition had all but disappeared during the period in question—destroyed by the horrible terror of the S.A. troops in the concentration camps and Gestapo cellars, unsettled by full employment made possible through rearmament, demoralized by the Communist Party's tactic of joining the ranks of Hitler's party in order to install itself there as a "Trojan horse." What was left of this opposition at the beginning of the war—some trade-union leaders, some intellectuals of the "homeless Left" who did not and could not know if there was anything behind them—gained its importance solely through the conspiracy which finally led to the 20th of July. (It is of course quite inadmissible to measure the strength of the German resistance by the number of those who passed through the concentration camps. Before the outbreak of the war, the inmates belonged in a great number of categories, many of which had nothing whatsoever to do with resistance of any kind: there were the wholly "innocent" ones, such as the Jews; the "asocials," such as confirmed criminals and homosexuals; Nazis who had been found guilty of something or other; etc. During the war the camps were populated by resistance fighters from all over occupied Europe.)

Most of the July conspirators were actually former Nazis or had held high office in the Third Reich. What had sparked their opposition had been not the Jewish question but the fact that Hitler was preparing war, and the endless conflicts and crises of conscience under which they labored hinged almost exclusively on the problem of high treason and the violation of their loyalty oath to Hitler. Moreover, they found themselves on the horns of a dilemma which was indeed insoluble: in the days of Hitler's successes they felt they could do nothing because the people would not understand, and in the years of German defeats they feared nothing more than another "stab-in-the-back" legend. To the last, their greatest concern was how it would be possible to prevent chaos and to ward off the danger of civil war. And the solution was that the Allies must be "reasonable" and grant a "moratorium" until order was restored—and with it, of course, the German Army's ability to offer resistance. They possessed the most precise knowledge of what was going on in the East, but there is hardly any doubt that not one of them would have dared even to think that the best thing that could have happened to Germany under the circumstances would have been open rebellion and civil war. The active resistance in Germany came chiefly from the Right, but in view of the past record of the German Social Democrats, it may be doubted that the situation would have been very different if the Left had played a larger part among the conspirators. The question is academic in any case, for no "organized socialist resistance" existed in Germany during the war years—as the German historian, Gerhard Ritter, has rightly pointed out.

In actual fact, the situation was just as simple as it was hopeless: the overwhelming majority of the German people believed in Hitler—even after the attack on Russia and the feared war on two fronts, even after the United States entered the war, indeed even after Stalingrad, the defection of Italy, and the landings in France. Against this solid majority, there stood an indeterminate number of isolated individuals who were completely aware of the national and of the moral catastrophe; they might occasionally know and trust one another, there were friendships among them and an exchange of opinions, but no plan or intention of revolt. Finally there was the group of those who later became known as the conspirators, but they had never been able to come to an agreement on anything, not even on the question of conspiracy. Their leader was Carl Friedrich Goerdeler, former mayor of Leipzig, who had served three years under the Nazis as price-controller but had resigned rather early—in 1936. He advocated the establishment of a constitutional monarchy, and Wilhelm Leuschner, a representative of the Left, a former trade-union leader and Socialist, assured him of "mass support"; in the Kreisau circle, under the influence of Helmuth von Moltke, there were occasional complaints raised that the rule of law was "now trampled under foot," but the chief concern of this circle was the reconciliation of the two Christian churches and their "sacred mission in the secular state," combined with an outspoken stand in favor of federalism. (On the political bankruptcy of the resistance movement as a whole since 1933 there is a well-documented, impartial study, the doctoral dissertation of George K. Romoser, soon to be published.)

As the war went on and defeat became more certain, political differences should have mattered less and political action become more urgent, but Gerhard Ritter seems right here too: "Without the determination of [Count Klaus von] Stauffenberg, the resistance movement would have bogged down in more or less helpless inactivity." What united these men was that they saw in Hitler a "swindler," a "dilettante," who "sacrificed whole armies against the counsel of his experts," a "madman" and a "demon," "the incarnation of all evil," which in the German context meant something both more and less than when they called him a "criminal and a fool," which they occasionally did. But to hold such opinions about Hitler at this late date "in no way precluded membership in the S.S. or the Party, or the holding of a government post" [Fritz Hesse], hence it did not exclude from the circle of the conspirators quite a number of men who themselves were deeply implicated in the crimes of the regime—as for instance Count Helldorf, then Police Commissioner of Berlin, who would have become Chief of the German Police if the coup d'état had been successful (according to one of Goerdeler's lists of prospective ministers); or Arthur Nebe of the R.S.H.A., former commander of one of the mobile killing units in the East! In the summer of 1943, when the Himmler-directed extermination program had reached its climax, Goerdeler was considering Himmler and Goebbels as potential allies, "since these two men have realized that they are lost with Hitler." (Himmler indeed became a "potential ally"—though Goebbels did not—and was fully informed of their plans; he acted against the conspirators only after their failure.) I am quoting from the draft of a letter by Goerdeler to Field Marshal von Kluge; but these strange alliances cannot be explainéd away by "tactical considerations" necessary vis-à-vis the Army commanders, for it was, on the contrary, Kluge and Rommel who had given "special orders that those two monsters [Himmler and Göring] should be liquidated" [Ritter]—quite apart from the fact that Goerdeler's biographer, Ritter, insists that the above-quoted letter "represents the most passionate expression of his hatred against the Hitler regime."

No doubt these men who opposed Hitler, however belatedly, paid with their lives and suffered a most terrible death; the courage of many of them was admirable, but it was not inspired by moral indignation or by what they knew other people had been made to suffer; they were motivated almost exclusively by their conviction of the coming defeat and ruin of Germany. This is not to deny that some of them, such as Count York von Wartenburg, may have been roused to political opposition initially by "the revolting agitation against the Jews in November, 1938" [Ritter]. But that was the month when the synagogues went up in flames and the whole population seemed in the grip of some fear: houses of God had been set on fire, and believers as well as the superstitious feared the vengeance of God. To be sure, the higher officer corps was disturbed when Hitler's so-called "commissar order" was issued in May, 1941, and they learned that in the coming campaign against Russia all Soviet functionaries and naturally all Jews were simply to be massacred. In these circles, there was of course some concern about the fact that, as Goerdeler said, "in the occupied areas and against the Jews techniques of liquidating human beings and of religious persecution are practiced . . . which will always rest as a heavy burden on our history." But it seems never to have occurred to them that this signified something more, and more dreadful, than that "it will make our position [negotiating a peace treaty with the Allies] enormously difficult," that it was a "blot on Germany's good name" and was undermining the morale of the Army. "What on earth have they made of the proud army of the Wars of Liberation [against Napoleon in 1814] and of Wilhelm I [in the Franco-Prussian War of 1870]," Goerdeler cried when he heard the report of an S.S. man who "nonchalantly related that it 'wasn't exactly pretty to spray with machine-gun fire ditches crammed with thousands of Jews and then to throw earth on the bodies that were still twitching.' " Nor did it occur to them that these atrocities might be somehow connected with the Allies' demand for unconditional surrender, which they felt free to criticize as both "nationalistic" and "unreasonable," inspired by blind hatred. In 1943, when the eventual defeat of Germany was almost a certainty, and indeed even later, they still believed that they had a right to negotiate with their enemies "as equals" for a "just peace," although they knew only too well what an unjust and totally unprovoked war Hitler had started. Even more startling are their criteria for a "just peace." Goerdeler stated them again and again in numerous memoranda: "the re-establishment of the national borders of 1914 [which meant the annexation of Alsace-Lorraine], with the addition of Austria and the Sudetenland"; furthermore, a "leading position for Germany on the Continent" and perhaps the regaining of South Tyrol!

We also know from statements they prepared how they intended to present their case to the people. There is for instance a draft proclamation to the Army by General Ludwig Beck, who was to become chief of state, in which he talks at length about the "obstinacy," the "incompetence and lack of moderation" of the Hitler regime, its "arrogance and vanity." But the crucial point, "the most unscrupulous act" of the regime, was that the Nazis wanted to hold "the leaders of the armed forces responsible" for the calamities of the coming defeat; to which Beck added that crimes had been committed "which are a blot on the honor of the German nation and a defilement of the good reputation it had gained in the eyes of the world." And what would be the next step after Hitler had been liquidated? The German Army would go on fighting "until an honorable conclusion of the war has been assured"—which meant the annexation of Alsace-Lorraine, Austria, and the Sudetenland. There is indeed every reason to agree with the bitter judgment on these men by the German novelist Friedrich P. Reck-Malleczewen, who was killed in a concentration camp on the eve of the collapse and did not participate in the anti-Hitler conspiracy. In his almost totally unknown "Diary of a Man in Despair," [*Tagebuch eines Verzweifelten,* 1947], Reck-Malleczewen wrote, after he had heard of the failure of the attempt on Hitler's life, which of course he regretted: "A little late, gentlemen, you who made this archdestroyer of Germany and ran after him, as long as everything seemed to be going well; you who . . . without hesitation swore every oath demanded of you and reduced yourselves to the despicable flunkies of this criminal who is guilty of the murder of hundreds of thousands, burdened with the lamentations and the curse of the whole world; now you have betrayed him. . . . Now, when the bankruptcy can no longer be concealed, they betray the house that went broke, in order to establish a political alibi for themselves—the same men who have betrayed everything that was in the way of their claim to power."

There is no evidence, and no likelihood, that Eichmann ever came into personal contact with the men of July 20, and we know that even in Argentina he still considered them all to have been traitors and scoundrels. Had he ever had the opportunity, though, to become acquainted with

Goerdeler's "original" ideas on the Jewish question, he might have discovered some points of agreement. To be sure, Goerdeler proposed "to pay indemnity to German Jews for their losses and mistreatment"—this in 1942, at a time when it was not only a matter of *German* Jews, and when these were not just being mistreated and robbed but *gassed;* but in addition to such technicalities, he had something more constructive in mind, namely, a "permanent solution" that would "save [all European Jews] from their unseemly position as a more or less undesirable 'guest nation' in Europe." (In Eichmann's jargon, this was called giving them "some firm ground under their feet.") For this purpose, Goerdeler claimed an "independent state in a colonial country"—Canada or South America—a sort of Madagascar, of which he certainly had heard. Still, he made some concessions; not all Jews would be expelled. Quite in line with the early stages of the Nazi regime and the privileged categories which were then current, he was prepared "not to deny German citizenship to those Jews who could produce evidence of special military sacrifice for Germany or who belonged to families with long-established traditions." Well, whatever Goerdeler's "permanent solution of the Jewish question" might have meant, it was not exactly "original"—as Professor Ritter, even in 1954 full of admiration for his hero, called it—and Goerdeler would have been able to find plenty of "potential allies" for this part of his program too within the ranks of the Party and even the S.S.

In the letter to Field Marshal von Kluge, quoted above, Goerdeler once appealed to Kluge's "voice of conscience." But all he meant was that even a general must understand that "to continue the war with no chance for victory was an obvious crime." From the accumulated evidence one can only conclude that conscience as such had apparently got lost in Germany, and this to a point where people hardly remembered it and had ceased to realize that the surprising "new set of German values" was not shared by the outside world. This, to be sure, is not the entire truth. For there were individuals in Germany who from the very beginning of the regime and without ever wavering were opposed to Hitler; no one knows how many there were of them—perhaps a hundred thousand, perhaps many more, perhaps many fewer—for their voices were never heard. They could be found everywhere, in all strata of society, among the simple people as well as among the educated, in all parties, perhaps even in the ranks of the N.S.D.A.P. Very few of them were known publicly, as were the aforementioned Reck-Malleczewen or the philosopher Karl Jaspers. Some of them were truly and deeply pious, like an artisan of whom I know, who preferred having his independent existence destroyed and becoming a simple worker in a factory to taking upon himself the "little formality" of entering the Nazi Party. A few still took an oath seriously and preferred, for example, to renounce an academic career rather than swear by Hitler's name. A more numerous group were the workers, especially in Berlin, and Socialist intellectuals who tried to aid the Jews they knew. There were finally, the two peasant boys whose story is related in Günther Weisenborn's *Der lautlose Aufstand* (1953), who were drafted into the S.S. at the end of the war and refused to sign; they were sentenced to death, and on the day of their execution they wrote in their last letter to their families: "We two would rather die than burden our conscience with such terrible things. We know what the S.S. must carry out." The position of these people, who, practically speaking, did nothing, was altogether different from that of the conspirators. Their ability to tell right from wrong had remained intact, and they never suffered a "crisis of conscience." There may also have been such persons among the members of the resistance, but they were hardly more numerous in the ranks of the conspirators than among the people at large. They were neither heroes nor saints, and they remained completely silent. Only on one occasion, in a single desperate gesture, did this wholly isolated and mute element manifest itself publicly: this was when the Scholls, two students at Munich University, brother and sister, under the influence of their teacher Kurt Huber distributed the famous leaflets in which Hitler was finally called what he was—a "mass murderer."

If, however, one examines the documents and prepared statements of the so-called "other Germany" that would have succeeded Hitler had the July 20 conspiracy succeeded, one can only marvel at how great a gulf separated even them from the rest of the world. How else can one explain the illusions of Goerdeler in particular or the fact that Himmler, of all people, but also Ribbentrop, should have started dreaming, during the last months of the war, of a magnificent new role as negotiators with the Allies for a defeated Germany. And if Ribbentrop certainly was simply stupid, Himmler, whatever else he might have been, was no fool.

The member of the Nazi hierarchy most gifted at solving problems of conscience was Himmler. He coined slogans, like the famous watchword of the S.S., taken from a Hitler speech before the S.S. in 1931, "My Honor is my Loyalty"—catch phrases which Eichmann called "winged words" and the judges "empty talk"—and issued them, as Eichmann recalled, "around the turn of the year," presumably along with a Christmas bonus. Eichmann remembered only one of them and kept repeating it: "These are battles which future generations will not have to fight again," alluding to the "battles" against women, children, old people, and other "useless mouths." Other such phrases, taken from speeches Himmler made to the commanders of the *Einsatzgruppen* and the Higher S.S. and Police Leaders, were: "To have stuck it out and, apart from exceptions caused by human weakness, to have remained decent, that is what has made us hard. This is a page of glory in our history which has never been written and is never to be written." Or: "The order to solve the Jewish question, this was the most frightening order an organization could ever receive." Or: We realize that what we are expecting from you is "super-human," to be "superhumanly inhuman." All one can say is that their expectations were not disappointed. It is noteworthy, however, that Himmler hardly ever attempted to justify in ideological terms, and if he did, it was apparently quickly forgotten. What stuck in the minds of these men who had become murderers was simply the notion of being involved in something historic, grandiose, unique ("a great task that occurs once in two thousand years"), which must therefore be difficult to bear. This was important, because the murderers were not sadists or killers by nature; on the contrary, a systematic effort was made to weed out all those who derived physical pleasure from what they did. The troops of the *Einsatzgruppen* had been drafted from the Armed S.S., a military unit with hardly more crimes in its record than any ordinary unit of the German Army, and their commanders had been chosen by Heydrich from the S.S., élite with academic degrees. Hence the problem was how to overcome not so much their conscience as the animal pity by which all normal men are affected in the presence of physical suffering. The trick used by Himmler—who apparently was rather strongly afflicted with these instinctive reactions himself—was very simple and probably very effective; it consisted in turning these instincts around, as it were, in directing them toward the self. So that instead of saying: What horrible things I did to people!, the murderers would be able to say: What horrible things I had to watch in the pursuance of my duties, how heavily the task weighed upon my shoulders!

Eichmann's defective memory where Himmler's ingenious watch-words were concerned may be an indication that there existed other and more effective devices for solving the problem of conscience. Foremost among them was, as Hitler had rightly foreseen, the simple fact of war. Eichmann insisted time and again on the "different personal attitude" toward death when "dead people were seen everywhere," and when everyone looked forward to his own death with indifference: "We did not care if we died today or only tomorrow, and there were times when we cursed the morning that found us still alive." Especially effective in this atmosphere of violent death was the fact that the Final Solution, in its later stages, was not carried out by shooting, hence through violence, but in the gas factories, which, from beginning to end, were closely connected with the "euthanasia program" ordered by Hitler in the first weeks of the war and applied to the mentally sick in Germany up to the invasion of Russia. The extermination program that was started in the autumn of 1941 ran, as it were, on two altogether different tracks. One track led to the gas factories, and the other to the *Einsatzgruppen,* whose operations in the rear of the Army, especially in Russia, were justified by the pretext of partisan warfare, and whose victims were by no means only Jews. In addition to real partisans, they dealt with Russian functionaries, Gypsies, the asocial, the insane, and Jews. Jews were included as "potential enemies," and, unfortunately, it was months before the Russian Jews came to understand this, and then it was too late to scatter. (The older generation remembered the First World War, when the German Army had been greeted as liberators; neither the young nor the old had heard anything about "how Jews were treated in Germany, or, for that matter, in Warsaw"; they were "remarkably ill-informed," as the German Intelligence service reported from White Russia [Hilberg]. More remarkable, occasionally even German Jews arrived in these regions who were under the illusion they had been sent here as "pioneers" for the Third Reich.) These mobile killing units, of which there existed just four, each of battalion size, with a total of no more than three thousand men, needed and got the close cooperation of the Armed Forces; indeed, relations between them were usually "excellent" and in some instances "affectionate" (*herzlich*). The generals showed a "surprisingly good attitude toward the Jews"; not only did they hand their Jews over to the *Einsatzgruppen,* they often lent their own men, ordinary soldiers, to assist in the massacres. The total number of their Jewish victims is estimated by Hilberg to have reached almost a million and a half, but this was not the result of the Führer's order for the physical extermination of the whole Jewish people. It was the result of an earlier order, which Hitler gave to Himmler in March, 1941, to prepare the S.S. and the police "to carry out special duties in Russia."

The Führer's order for the extermination of all, not only Russian and Polish, Jews, though issued later, can be traced much farther back. It originated not in the R.S.H.A. or in any of Heydrich's or Himmler's other offices, but in the Führer's Chancellery, Hitler's personal office. It had nothing to do with the war and never used military necessities as a pretext. It is one of the great merits of Gerald Reitlinger's *The Final Solution* to have proved, with documentary evidence that leaves no doubt, that the extermination program in the Eastern gas factories grew out of Hitler's euthanasia program, and it is deplorable that the Eichmann trial, so concerned with "historical truth," paid no attention to this factual connection. This would have thrown some light on the much debated question of whether Eichmann, of the R.S.H.A., was involved in *Gasgeschichten*. It is unlikely that he was, though one of his men, Rolf Günther, might have become interested of his own accord. Globocnik, for instance, who set up the gassing installations in the Lublin area, and whom Eichmann visited, did not address himself to Himmler or any other police or S.S. authority when he needed more personnel; he wrote to Viktor Brack, of the Führer's Chancellery, who then passed the request on to Himmler.

The first gas chambers were constructed in 1939, to implement a Hitler decree dated September 1 of that year, which said that "incurably sick persons should be granted a mercy death." (It was probably this "medical" origin of gassing that inspired Dr. Servatius's amazing conviction that killing by gas must be regarded as "a medical matter.") The idea itself was considerably older. As early as 1935, Hitler had told his Reich Medical Leader Gerhard Wagner that "if war came, he would take up and carry out this question of euthanasia, because it was easier to do so in wartime." The decree was immediately carried out in respect to the mentally sick, and between December, 1939, and August, 1941, about fifty thousand Germans were killed with carbon-monoxide gas in institutions where the death rooms were disguised exactly as they later were in Auschwitz—as shower rooms and bathrooms. The program was a flop. It was impossible to keep the gassing a secret from the surrounding German population; there were protests on all sides from people who presumably had not yet attained the "objective" insight into the nature of medicine and the task of a physician. The gassing in the East—or, to use the language of the Nazis, "the humane way" of killing "by granting people a mercy death"—began on almost the very day when the gassing in Germany was stopped. The men who had been employed in the euthanasia program in Germany were now sent east to build the new installations for the extermination of whole peoples—and these men came either from Hitler's Chancellery or from the Reich Health Department and were only now put under the administrative authority of Himmler.

None of the various "language rules," carefully contrived to deceive and to camouflage, had a more decisive effect on the mentality of the killers than this first war decree of Hitler, in which the word for "murder" was replaced by the phrase "to grant a mercy death." Eichmann, asked by the police examiner if the directive to avoid "unnecessary hardships" was not a bit ironic, in view of the fact that the destination of these people was certain death anyhow, did not even understand the question, so firmly was it still anchored in his mind that the unforgivable sin was not to kill people but to cause unnecessary pain. During the trial, he showed unmistakable signs of sincere outrage when witnesses told of cruelties and atrocities committed by S.S. men—though the court and much of the audience failed to see these signs, because his single-minded effort to keep his self-control had misled them into believing that he was "unmovable" and indifferent—and it was not the accusation of having sent millions of people to their death that ever caused him real agitation but only the accusation (dismissed by the court) of one witness that he had once beaten a Jewish boy to death. To be sure, he had also sent people into the area of the *Einsatzgruppen,* who did not "grant a mercy death" but killed by shooting, but he was probably relieved when, in the later stages of the operation, this became unnecessary because of the ever-growing capacity of the gas chambers. He must also have thought that the new method indicated a decisive improvement in the Nazi government's attitude toward the Jews, since at the beginning of the gassing program it had been expressly stated that the benefits of euthanasia were to be reserved for true Germans. As the war progressed, with violent and horrible death raging all around—on the front in Russia, in the deserts of Africa, in Italy, on the beaches of France, in the ruins of the German cities—the gassing centers in Auschwitz and Chelmno, in Majdanek and Belzek, in Treblinka and Sobibor, must actually have appeared the "Charitable Foundations for Institutional Care" that the experts in mercy death called them. Moreover, from January, 1942, on, there were euthanasia teams operating in the East to "help the wounded in ice and snow," and though this killing of wounded soldiers was also "top secret," it was known to many, certainly to the executors of the Final Solution.

It has frequently been pointed out that the gassing of the mentally sick had to be stopped in Germany because of protests from the population and from a few courageous dignitaries of the churches, whereas no such protests were voiced when the program switched to the gassing of Jews, though some of the killing centers were located on what was then German territory and were surrounded by German populations. The protests, however, occurred at the beginning of the war; quite apart from the effects of "education in euthanasia," the attitude toward a "painless death through gassing" very likely changed in the course of the war. This sort of thing is difficult to prove; there are no documents to support it, because of the secrecy of the whole enterprise, and none of the war criminals ever mentioned it, not even the defendants in the Doctors' Trial at Nuremberg, who were full of quotations from the international literature on the subject. Perhaps they had forgotten the climate of public opinion in which they killed, perhaps they never cared to know it, since they felt, wrongly, that their "objective and scientific" attitude was far more advanced than the opinions held by ordinary people. However, a few truly priceless stories, to be found in the war diaries of trustworthy men who were fully aware of the fact that their own shocked reaction was no longer shared by their neighbors, have survived the moral debacle of a whole nation.

Reck-Malleczewen, whom I mentioned before, tells of a female "leader" who came to Bavaria to give the peasants a pep talk in the summer of 1944. She seems not to have wasted much time on "miracle weapons" and victory, she faced frankly the prospect of defeat, about which no good German needed to worry because the Führer *"in his great goodness had prepared for the whole German people a mild death through gassing in case the war should have an unhappy end."* And the writer adds: "Oh, no, I'm not imagining things, this lovely lady is not a mirage, I saw her with my own eyes: a yellow-skinned female pushing forty, with insane eyes. . . . And what happened? Did these Bavarian peasants at least put her into the local lake to cool off her enthusiastic readiness for death? They did nothing of the sort. They went home, shaking their heads."

My next story is even more to the point, since it concerns someone who was not a "leader," may not even have been a Party member. It happened in Königsberg, in East Prussia, an altogether different corner of Germany, in January, 1945, a few days before the Russians destroyed the city, occupied its ruins, and annexed the whole province. The story is told by Count Hans von Lehnsdorff, in his *Ostpreussisches Tagebuch* (1961). He had remained in the city as a physician to take care of wounded soldiers who could not be evacuated; he was called to one of the huge centers for refugees from the countryside, which was already occupied by the Red Army. There he was accosted by a woman who showed him a varicose vein she had had for years but wanted to have treated now, because she had time. "I try to explain that it is more important for her to get away from Königsberg and to leave the treatment for some later time. Where do you want to go? I ask her. She does not know, but she knows that they will all be brought into the Reich. And then she adds, surprisingly: *'The Russians will never get us. The Führer will never permit it. Much sooner he will gas us.'* I look around furtively, but no one seems to find this statement out of the ordinary." The story, one feels, like most true stories, is incomplete. There should have been one more voice, preferably a female one, which, sighing heavily, replied: And now all that good, expensive gas has been wasted on the Jews!

THE WANNSEE CONFERENCE,
OR PONTIUS PILATE

My report on Eichmann's conscience has thus far followed evidence which he himself had forgotten. In his own presentation of the matter, the turning point came not four weeks but four months later, in January, 1942, during the Conference of the *Staatssekretäre* (Undersecretaries of State), as the Nazis used to call it, or the Wannsee Conference, as it now is usually called, because Heydrich had invited the gentlemen to a house in that suburb of Berlin. As the formal name of the conference indicates, the meeting had become necessary because the Final Solution, if it was to be applied to the whole of Europe, clearly required more than tacit acceptance from the Reich's State apparatus; it needed the active cooperation of all Ministries and of the whole Civil Service. The Ministers themselves, nine years after Hitler's rise to power, were all Party members of long standing—those who in the initial stages of the regime had merely "coordinated" themselves, smoothly enough, had been replaced. Yet most of them were not completely trusted, since few among them owed their careers entirely to the Nazis, as did Heydrich or Himmler; and those who did, like Joachim von Ribbentrop, head of the Foreign Office, a former champagne salesman, were likely to be nonentities. The problem was much more acute, however, with respect to the higher career men in the Civil Service, directly under the Ministers, for these men, the backbone of every government administration, were not easily replaceable, and Hitler had tolerated them, just as Adenauer was to tolerate them, unless they were compromised beyond salvation. Hence the undersecretaries and the legal and other experts in the various Ministries were frequently not even Party members, and Heydrich's apprehensions about whether he would be able to enlist the active help of these people in mass murder were quite comprehensible. As Eichmann put it, Heydrich "expected the greatest difficulties." Well, he could not have been more wrong.

The aim of the conference was to coordinate all efforts toward the implementation of the Final Solution. The discussion turned first on "complicated legal questions," such as the treatment of half- and quarter-Jews—should they be killed or only sterilized? This was followed by a frank discussion of the "various types of possible solutions to the problem," which meant the various methods of killing, and here, too, there was more than "happy agreement on the part of the participants"; the Final Solution was greeted with "extraordinary enthusiasm" by all present, and particularly by Dr. Wilhelm Stuckart, Undersecretary in the Ministry of the Interior, who was known to be rather reticent and hesitant in the face of "radical" Party measures, and was, according to Dr. Hans Globke's testimony at Nuremberg, a staunch supporter of the Law. There were certain difficulties, however. Undersecretary Josef Bühler, second in command in the General Government in Poland, was dismayed at the prospect that Jews would be evacuated from the West to the East, because this meant more Jews in Poland, and he proposed that these evacuations be postponed and that "the Final Solution be started in the General Government, where no problems of transport existed." The gentlemen from the Foreign Office appeared with their own carefully elaborated memorandum, expressing "the desires and ideas of the Foreign Office with respect to the total solution of the Jewish question in Europe," to which nobody paid much attention. The main point, as Eichmann rightly noted, was that the members of the various branches of the Civil Service did not merely express opinions but made concrete propositions. The meeting lasted no more than an hour or an hour and a half, after which drinks were served and everybody had lunch—"a cozy little social gathering," designed to strengthen the necessary personal contacts. It was a very important occasion for Eichmann, who had never before mingled socially with so many "high personages"; he was by far the lowest in rank and social position of those present. He had sent out the invitations and had prepared some statistical material (full of incredible errors) for Heydrich's introductory speech—eleven million Jews had to be killed, an undertaking of some magnitude—and later he was to prepare the minutes. In short, he acted as secretary of the meeting. This was why he was permitted, after the dignitaries had left, to sit down near the fireplace with his chief Müller and Heydrich, "and that was the first time I saw Heydrich smoke and drink." They did not "talk shop, but enjoyed some rest after long hours of work," being greatly satisfied and, especially Heydrich, in very high spirits.

There was another reason that made the day of this conference unforgettable for Eichmann. Although he had been doing his best right along to help with the Final Solution, he had still harbored some doubts about "such a bloody solution through violence," and these doubts had now been dispelled. "Here now, during this conference, the most prominent people had spoken, the Popes of the Third Reich." Now he could see with his own eyes and hear with his own ears that not only Hitler, not only Heydrich or the "sphinx" Müller, not just the S.S. or the Party, but the élite of the good old Civil Service were vying and fighting with each other for the honor of taking the lead in these "bloody" matters. "At that moment, I sensed a kind of Pontius Pilate feeling, for I felt free of all guilt." *Who was he to judge?* Who was he "to have [his] own thoughts in this matter"? Well, he was neither the first nor the last to be ruined by modesty.

What followed, as Eichmann recalled it, went more or less smoothly and soon became routine. He quickly became an expert in "forced evacuation," as he had been an expert in "forced emigration." In country after country, the Jews had to register, were forced to wear the yellow badge for easy identification, were assembled and deported, the various shipments being directed to one or another of the extermination centers in the East, depending on their relative capacity at the moment; when a trainload of Jews arrived at a center, the strong among them were selected for work, often operating the extermination machinery, all others were immediately killed. There were hitches, but they were minor. The Foreign Office was in contact with the authorities in those foreign countries that were either occupied or allied with the Nazis, to put pressure on them to deport their Jews, or, as the case might be, to prevent them from evacuating them to the East helter-skelter, out of sequence, without proper regard for the absorptive capacity of the death centers. (This was how Eichmann remembered it; it was in fact not quite so simple.) The legal experts drew up the necessary legislation for making the victims stateless, which was important on two counts: it made it impossible for any country to inquire into their fate, and it enabled the state in which they were resident to confiscate their property. The Ministry of Finance and the Reichsbank prepared facilities to receive the huge loot from all over Europe, down to watches and gold teeth, all of which was sorted out in the Reichsbank and then sent to the Prussian State Mint. The Ministry of Transport provided the necessary railroad cars, usually freight cars, even in times of great scarcity of rolling stock, and they saw to it that the schedule of the deportation trains did not conflict with other timetables. The Jewish Councils of Elders were informed by Eichmann or his men of how many Jews were needed to fill each train, and they made out the list of deportees. The Jews registered, filled out innumerable forms, answered pages and pages of questionnaires regarding their property so that it could be seized the more easily; they then assembled at the collection points and boarded the trains. The few who tried to hide or to escape were rounded up by a special Jewish police force. As far as Eichmann could see, no one protested, no one refused to cooperate. *"Immerzu fahren hier die Leute zu ihrem eigenen Begräbnis"* (Day in day out the people here leave for their own funeral), as a Jewish observer put it in Berlin in 1943.

Mere compliance would never have been enough either to smooth out all the enormous difficulties of an operation that was soon to cover the whole of Nazi-occupied and Nazi-allied Europe or to soothe the consciences of the operators, who, after all, had been brought up on the commandment "Thou shalt not kill," and who knew the verse from the Bible, "Thou hast murdered and thou hast inherited," that the judgment of the District Court of Jerusalem quoted so appropriately. What Eichmann called the "death whirl" that descended upon Germany after the immense losses at Stalingrad—the saturation bombing of German cities, his stock excuse for killing civilians and still the stock excuse offered in Germany for the massacres—making an everyday experience of sights different from the atrocities reported at Jerusalem but no less horrible, might have contributed to the easing, or, rather, to the extinguishing, of conscience, had any conscience been left when it occurred, but according to the evidence such was not the case. The extermination machinery had been planned and perfected in all its details long before the horror of war struck Germany herself, and its intricate bureaucracy functioned with the same unwavering precision in the years of easy victory as in those last years of predictable defeat. Defections from the ranks of the ruling élite and notably from among the Higher S.S. officers hardly occurred at the beginning, when people might still have had a conscience; they made themselves felt only when it had become obvious that Germany was going to lose the war. Moreover, such defections were never serious enough to throw the machinery out of gear; they consisted of individual acts not of mercy but of corruption, and they were inspired not by conscience but by the desire to salt some money or some connections away for the dark days to come. Himmler's order in the fall of 1944 to halt the extermination and to dismantle the installations at the death factories sprang from his absurd but sincere conviction that the Allied powers would know how to appreciate this obliging gesture; he told a rather incredulous Eichmann that on the strength of it he would be able to negotiate a *Hubertusburger-Frieden*—an allusion to the Peace Treaty of Hubertusburg that concluded the Seven Years' War of Frederick II of Prussia in 1763 and enabled Prussia to retain Silesia, although she had lost the war.

As Eichmann told it, the most potent factor in the soothing of his own conscience was the simple fact that he could see no one, no one at all, who actually was against the Final Solution. He did encounter one exception, however, which he mentioned several times, and which must have made a deep impression on him. This happened in Hungary when he was negotiating with Dr. Kastner over Himmler's offer to release one million Jews in exchange for ten thousand trucks. Kastner, apparently emboldened by the new turn of affairs, had asked Eichmann to stop "the death mills at Auschwitz," and Eichmann had answered that he would do it "with the greatest pleasure" (*herzlich gern*) but that, alas, it was outside his competence and outside the competence of his superiors—as indeed it was. Of course, he did not expect the Jews to share the general enthusiasm over their destruction, but he did expect more than compliance, he expected—and received, to a truly extraordinary degree—their cooperation. This was "of course the very cornerstone" of everything he did, as it had been the very cornerstone of his activities in Vienna. Without Jewish help in administrative and police work—the final rounding up of Jews in Berlin was, as I have mentioned, done entirely by Jewish police—there would have been either complete chaos or an impossibly severe drain on German manpower. ("There can be no doubt that, without the cooperation of the victims, it would hardly have been possible for a few thousand people, most of whom, moreover, worked in offices, to liquidate many hundreds of thousands of other people. . . . Over the whole way to their deaths the Polish Jews got to see hardly more than a handful of Germans." Thus R. Pendorf in the publication mentioned above. To an even greater extent this applies to those Jews who were transported to Poland to find their deaths there.) Hence, the establishing of Quisling governments in occupied territories was always accompanied by the organization of a central Jewish office, and, as we shall see later, where the Nazis did not succeed in setting up a puppet government, they also failed to enlist the cooperation of the Jews. But whereas the members of the Quisling governments were usually taken from the opposition parties, the members of the Jewish Councils were as a rule the locally recognized Jewish leaders, to whom the Nazis gave enormous powers—until they, too, were deported, to Theresienstadt or Bergen-Belsen, if they happened to be from Central or Western Europe, to Auschwitz if they were from an Eastern European community.

To a Jew this role of the Jewish leaders in the destruction of their own people is undoubtedly the darkest chapter of the whole dark story. It had been known about before, but it has now been exposed for the first time in all its pathetic and sordid detail by Raul Hilberg, whose standard work *The Destruction of the European Jews* I mentioned before. In the matter of cooperation, there was no distinction between the highly assimilated Jewish communities of Central and Western Europe and the Yiddish-speaking masses of the East. In Amsterdam as in Warsaw, in Berlin as in Budapest, Jewish officials could be trusted to compile the lists of persons and of their property, to secure money from the deportees to defray the expenses of their deportation and extermination, to keep track of vacated apartments, to supply police forces to help seize Jews and get them on trains, until, as a last gesture, they handed over the assets of the

Jewish community in good order for final confiscation. They distributed the Yellow Star badges, and sometimes, as in Warsaw, "the sale of the armbands became a regular business; there were ordinary armbands of cloth and fancy plastic armbands which were washable." In the Nazi-inspired, but not Nazi-dictated, manifestoes they issued, we still can sense how they enjoyed their new power—"The Central Jewish Council has been granted the right of absolute disposal over all Jewish spiritual and material wealth and over all Jewish manpower," as the first announcement of the Budapest Council phrased it. We know how the Jewish officials felt when they became instruments of murder—like captains "whose ships were about to sink and who succeeded in bringing them safe to port by casting overboard a great part of their precious cargo"; like saviors who "with a hundred victims save a thousand people, with a thousand ten thousand." The truth was even more gruesome. Dr. Kastner, in Hungary, for instance, saved exactly 1,684 people with approximately 476,000 victims. In order not to leave the selection to "blind fate," "truly holy principles" were needed "as the guiding force of the weak human hand which puts down on paper the name of the unknown person and with this decides his life or death." And whom did these "holy principles" single out for salvation? Those "who had worked all their lives for the *zibur* [community]"—i.e., the functionaries—and the "most prominent Jews," as Kastner says in his report.

No one bothered to swear the Jewish officials to secrecy; they were voluntary "bearers of secrets," either in order to assure quiet and prevent panic, as in Dr. Kastner's case, or out of "humane" considerations, such as that "living in the expectation of death by gassing would only be the harder," as in the case of Dr. Leo Baeck, former Chief Rabbi of Berlin. During the Eichmann trial, one witness pointed out the unfortunate consequences of this kind of "humanity"—people volunteered for deportation from Theresienstadt to Auschwitz and denounced those who tried to tell them the truth as being "not sane." We know the physiognomies of the Jewish leaders during the Nazi period very well; they ranged all the way from Chaim Rumkowski, Eldest of the Jews in Lódz, called Chaim I, who issued currency notes bearing his signature and postage stamps engraved with his portrait, and who rode around in a broken-down horse-drawn carriage; through Leo Baeck, scholarly, mild-mannered, highly educated, who believed Jewish policemen would be "more gentle and helpful" and would "make the ordeal easier" (whereas in fact they were, of course, more brutal and less corruptible, since so much more was at stake for them); to, finally, a few who committed suicide—like Adam Czerniakow, chairman of the Warsaw Jewish Council, who was not a rabbi but an unbeliever, a Polish-speaking Jewish engineer, but who must still have remembered the rabbinical saying: "Let them kill you, but don't cross the line."

That the prosecution in Jerusalem, so careful not to embarrass the Adenauer administration, should have avoided, with even greater and more obvious justification, bringing this chapter of the story into the open was almost a matter of course. (These issues, however, are discussed quite openly and with astonishing frankness in Israeli schoolbooks—as may conveniently be gathered from the article "Young Israelis and Jews Abroad—A Study of Selected History Textbooks" by Mark M. Krug, in *Comparative Education Review,* October, 1963.) The chapter must be included here, however, because it accounts for certain otherwise inexplicable lacunae in the documentation of a generally over-documented case. The judges mentioned one such instance, the absence of H. G. Adler's book *Theresienstadt 1941–1945* (1955), which the prosecution, in some embarrassment, admitted to be "authentic, based on irrefutable sources." The reason for the omission was clear. The book describes in detail how the feared "transport lists" were put together by the Jewish Council of Theresienstadt after the S.S. had given some general directives, stipulating how many should be sent away, and of what age, sex, profession, and country of origin. The prosecution's case would have been weakened if it had been forced to admit that the naming of individuals who were sent to their doom had been, with few exceptions, the job of the Jewish administration. And the Deputy State Attorney, Mr. Ya'akov Baror, who handled the intervention from the bench, in a way indicated this when he said: "I am trying to bring out those things which somehow refer to the accused without damaging the picture in its entirety." The picture would indeed have been greatly damaged by the inclusion of Adler's book, since it would have contradicted testimony given by the chief witness on Theresienstadt, who claimed that Eichmann himself had made these individual selections. Even more important, the prosecution's general picture of a clear-cut division between persecutors and victims would have suffered greatly. To make available evidence that does not support the case for the prosecution is usually the job of the defense, and the question why Dr. Servatius, who perceived some minor inconsistencies in the testimony, did not avail himself of such easily obtainable and widely known documentation is difficult to answer. He could have pointed to the fact that Eichmann, immediately upon being transformed from an expert in emigration into an expert in "evacuation," appointed his old Jewish associates in the emigration business—Dr. Paul Eppstein, who had been in charge of emigration in Berlin, and Rabbi Benjamin Murmelstein, who had held the same job in Vienna—as "Jewish Elders" in Theresienstadt. This would have done more to demonstrate the atmosphere in which Eichmann worked than all the unpleasant and often downright offensive talk about oaths, loyalty, and the virtues of unquestioning obedience.

The testimony of Mrs. Charlotte Salzberger on Theresienstadt, from which I quoted above, permitted us to cast at least a glance into this neglected corner of what the prosecution kept calling the "general picture." The presiding judge did not like the term and he did not like the picture. He told the Attorney General several times that "we are not drawing pictures here," that there is "an indictment and this indictment is the framework for our trial," that the court "has its own view about this trial, according to the indictment," and that "the prosecution must adjust to what the court lays down"—admirable admonitions for criminal proceedings, none of which was heeded. The prosecution did worse than not heed them, it simply refused to guide its witnesses—or, if the court became too insistent, it asked a few haphazard questions, very casually—with the result that the witnesses behaved as though they were speakers at a meeting chaired by the Attorney General, who introduced them to the audience before they took the floor. They could talk almost as long as they wished, and it was a rare occasion when they were asked a specific question.

This atmosphere, not of a show trial but of a mass meeting, at which speaker after speaker does his best to arouse the audience, was especially noticeable when the prosecution called witness after witness to testify to the rising in the Warsaw ghetto and to the similar attempts in Vilna and Kovno—matters that had no connection whatever with the crimes of the accused. The testimony of these people would have contributed something to the trial if they had told of the activities of the Jewish Councils, which had played such a great and disastrous role in their own heroic efforts. Of course, there was some mention of this—witnesses speaking of "S.S. men and their helpers" pointed out that they counted among the latter the "ghetto police which was also an instrument in the hands of the Nazi murderers" as well as "the *Judenrat*"—but they were only too glad not to "elaborate" on this side of their story, and they shifted the discussion to the role of real traitors, of whom there were few, and who were "nameless people, unknown to the Jewish public," such as "all undergrounds which fought against the Nazis suffered from." (The audience while these witnesses testified had changed again; it consisted now of *Kibbuzniks,* members of the Israeli communal settlements to which the speakers belonged.) The purest and clearest account came from Zivia Lubetkin Zuckerman, today a woman of perhaps forty, still very beautiful, completely free of sentimentality or self-indulgence, her facts well organized, and always quite sure of the point she wished to make. Legally, the testimony of these witnesses was immaterial—Mr. Hausner did not mention one of them in his last *plaidoyer*—except insofar as it constituted proof of close contacts between Jewish partisans and the Polish and Russian underground fighters, which, apart from contradicting other testimony ("We had the whole population against us"), could have been useful to the defense, since it offered much better justification for the wholesale slaughter of civilians than Eichmann's repeated claim that "Weizmann had declared war on Germany in 1939." (This was sheer nonsense. All that Chaim Weizmann had said, at the close of the last prewar Zionist Congress, was that the war of the Western democracies "is our war, their struggle is our struggle." The tragedy, as Hausner rightly pointed out, was precisely that the Jews were not recognized by the Nazis as belligerents, for if they had been they would have survived, in prisoner-of-war or civilian internment camps.) Had Dr. Servatius made this point, the prosecution would have been forced to admit how pitifully small these resistance groups had been, how incredibly weak and essentially harmless—and, moreover, how little they had represented the Jewish population, who at one point even took arms against them.

While the legal irrelevance of all this very time-consuming testimony remained pitifully clear, the political intention of the Israeli government in introducing it was also not difficult to guess. Mr. Hausner (or Mr. Ben-Gurion) probably wanted to demonstrate that whatever resistance there had been had come from Zionists, as though, of all Jews, only the Zionists knew that if you could not save your life it might still be worth while to save your honor, as Mr. Zuckerman put it; that the worst that could happen to the human person under such circumstances was to be and to remain "innocent," as became clear from the tenor and drift of Mrs. Zuckerman's testimony. However, these "political" intentions misfired, for the witnesses were truthful and told the court that all Jewish organizations and parties had played their role in the resistance, so the true distinction was not between Zionists and non-Zionists but between organized and unorganized people, and, even more important, between the young and the middle-aged. To be sure, those who resisted were a minority, a tiny minority, but under the circumstances "the miracle was," as one of them pointed out, "that this minority existed."

Legal considerations aside, the appearance in the witness box of the former Jewish resistance fighters was welcome enough. It dissipated the haunting specter of universal cooperation, the stifling, poisoned atmosphere which had surrounded the Final Solution. The well-known fact that the actual work of killing in the extermination centers was usually in the hands of Jewish commandos had been fairly and squarely established by witnesses for the prosecution—how they had worked in the gas chambers and the crematories, how they had pulled the gold teeth and cut the hair of the corpses, how they had dug the graves and, later, dug them up again to extinguish the traces of mass murder; how Jewish technicians had built gas chambers in Theresienstadt, where the Jewish "autonomy" had been carried so far that even the hangman was a Jew. But this was only horrible, it was no moral problem. The selection and classification of workers in the camps was made by the S.S., who had a marked predilection for the criminal elements; and, anyhow, it could only have been the selection of the worst. (This was especially true in Poland, where the Nazis had exterminated a large proportion of the Jewish intelligentsia at the same time that they killed Polish intellectuals and members of the professions—in marked contrast, incidentally, to their policy in Western Europe, where they tended to save prominent Jews in order to exchange them for German civilian internees or prisoners of war; Bergen-Belsen was originally a camp for "exchange Jews.") The moral problem lay in the amount of truth there was in Eichmann's description of Jewish cooperation, even under the conditions of the Final Solution: "The formation of the Jewish Council [at Theresienstadt] and the distribution of business was left to the discretion of the Council, except for the appointment of the president, who the president was to be, which depended upon us, of course. However, this appointment was not in the form of a dictatorial decision. The functionaries with whom we were in constant contact—well, they had to be treated with kid gloves. They were not ordered around, for the simple reason that if the chief officials had been told what to do in the form of: you must, you have to, that would not have helped matters any. If the person in question does not like what he is doing, the whole works will suffer. . . . We did our best to make everything somehow palatable." No doubt they did; the problem is how it was possible for them to succeed.

Thus, the gravest omission from the "general picture" was that of a witness to testify to the cooperation between the Nazi rulers and the Jewish authorities, and hence of an opportunity to raise the question: "Why did you cooperate in the destruction of your own people and, eventually, in your own ruin?" The only witness who had been a prominent member of a *Judenrat* was Pinchas Freudiger, the former Baron Philip von Freudiger, of Budapest, and during his testimony the only serious incidents in the audience took place; people screamed at the witness in Hungarian and in Yiddish, and the court had to interrupt the session. Freudiger, an Orthodox Jew of considerable dignity, was shaken: "There are people here who say they were not told to escape. But fifty per cent of the people who escaped were captured and killed"—as compared with ninety-nine per cent, for those who did not escape. "Where could they have gone to? Where could they have fled?"—but he himself fled, to Rumania, because he was rich and Wisliceny helped him. "What could we have done? What could we have done?" And the only response to this came from the presiding judge: "I do not think this is an answer to the question"—a question raised by the gallery but not by the court.

The matter of cooperation was twice mentioned by the judges; Judge Yitzak Raveh elicited from one of the resistance witnesses an admission that the "ghetto police" were an "instrument in the hands of murderers" and an acknowledgment of "the *Judenrat's* policy of cooperating with the Nazis"; and Judge Halevi found out from Eichmann in cross-examination that the Nazis had regarded this cooperation as the very cornerstone of their Jewish policy. But the question the prosecutor regularly addressed to each witness except the resistance fighters which sounded so very natural to those who knew nothing of the factual background of the trial, the question "Why did you not rebel?," actually served as a smoke screen for the question that was not asked. And thus it came to pass that all answers to the unanswerable question Mr. Hausner put to his witnesses were considerably less than "the truth, the whole truth, and nothing but the truth." True it was that the Jewish people as a whole had not been organized, that they had possessed no territory, no government, and no army, that, in the hour of their greatest need, they had no government-in-exile to represent them among the Allies (the Jewish Agency for Palestine, under Dr. Weizmann's presidency, was at best a miserable substitute), no caches of weapons, no youth with military training. But the whole truth was that there existed Jewish community organizations and Jewish party and welfare organizations on both the local and the international level. Wherever Jews lived, there were recognized Jewish leaders, and this leadership, almost without exception, cooperated in one way or another, for one reason or another, with the Nazis. The whole truth was that if the Jewish people had really been unorganized and leaderless, there would have been chaos and plenty of misery but the total number of victims would hardly have been between four and a half and six million people. (According to Freudiger's calculations about half of them could have saved themselves if they had not followed the instructions of the Jewish Councils. This is of course a mere estimate, which, however, oddly jibes with the rather reliable figures we have from Holland and which I owe to Dr. L. de Jong, the head of the Netherlands State Institute for War Documentation. In

Holland, where the *Joodsche Raad* like all the Dutch authorities very quickly became an "instrument of the Nazis," 103,000 Jews were deported to the death camps and some five thousand to Theresienstadt in the usual way, i.e., with the cooperation of the Jewish Council. Only five hundred and nineteen Jews returned from the death camps. In contrast to this figure, ten thousand of those twenty to twenty-five thousand Jews who escaped the Nazis—and that meant also the Jewish Council—and went underground survived; again forty to fifty per cent. Most of the Jews sent to Theresienstadt returned to Holland.)

I have dwelt on this chapter of the story, which the Jerusalem trial failed to put before the eyes of the world in its true dimensions, because it offers the most striking insight into the totality of the moral collapse the Nazis caused in respectable European society—not only in Germany but in almost all countries, not only among the persecutors but also among the victims. Eichmann, in contrast to other elements in the Nazi movement, had always been overawed by "good society," and the politeness he often showed to German-speaking Jewish functionaries was to a large extent the result of his recognition that he was dealing with people who were socially his superiors. He was not at all, as one witness called him, a "*Landsknechtnatur*," a mercenary, who wanted to escape to regions where there aren't no Ten Commandments an' a man can raise a thirst. What he fervently believed in up to the end was success, the chief standard of "good society" as he knew it. Typical was his last word on the subject of Hitler—whom he and his comrade Sassen had agreed to "shirr out" of their story; Hitler, he said, "may have been wrong all down the line, but one thing is beyond dispute: the man was able to work his way up from lance corporal in the German Army to Führer of a people of almost eighty million. . . . His success alone proved to me that I should subordinate myself to this man." His conscience was indeed set at rest when he saw the zeal and eagerness with which "good society" everywhere reacted as he did. He did not need to "close his ears to the voice of conscience," as the judgment has it, not because he had none, but because his conscience spoke with a "respectable voice," with the voice of respectable society around him.

That there were no voices from the outside to arouse his conscience was one of Eichmann's points, and it was the task of the prosecution to prove that this was not so, that there were voices he could have listened to, and that, anyhow, he had done his work with a zeal far beyond the call of duty. Which turned out to be true enough, except that, strange as it may appear, his murderous zeal was not altogether unconnected with the ambiguity in the voices of those who at one time or another tried to restrain him. We need mention here only in passing the so-called "inner emigration" in Germany—those people who frequently had held positions, even high ones, in the Third Reich and who, after the end of the war, told themselves and the world at large that they had always been "inwardly opposed" to the regime. The question here is not whether or not they are telling the truth; the point is, rather, that no secret in the secret-ridden atmosphere of the Hitler regime was better kept than such "inward opposition." This was almost a matter of course under the conditions of Nazi terror; as a rather well-known "inner emigrant," who certainly believed in his own sincerity, once told me, they had to appear "outwardly" even more like Nazis than ordinary Nazis did, in order to keep their secret. (This, incidentally, may explain why the few known protests against the extermination program came not from the Army commanders but from old Party members.) Hence, the only possible way to live in the Third Reich and not act as a Nazi was not to appear at all: "Withdrawal from significant participation in public life" was indeed the only criterion by which one might have measured individual guilt, as Otto Kirchheimer recently remarked in his *Political Justice* (1961). If the term was to make any sense, the "inner emigrant" could only be one who lived "as though outcast among his own people amidst blindly believing masses," as Professor Hermann Jahrreiss pointed out in his "Statement for All Defense Attorneys" before the Nuremberg Tribunal. For opposition was indeed "utterly pointless" in the absence of all organization. It is true that there were Germans who lived for twelve years in this "outer cold," but their number was insignificant, even among the members of the resistance. In recent years, the slogan of the "inner emigration" (the term itself has a definitely equivocal flavor, as it can mean either an emigration into the inward regions of one's soul or a way of conducting oneself as though he were an emigrant) has become a sort of a joke. The sinister Dr. Otto Bradfisch, former member of one of the *Einsatzgruppen,* who presided over the killing of at least fifteen thousand people, told a German court that he had always been "inwardly opposed" to what he was doing. Perhaps the death of fifteen thousand people was necessary to provide him with an alibi in the eyes of "true Nazis." (The same argument was advanced, though with considerably less success, in a Polish court by former Gauleiter Arthur Greiser of the Warthegau: only his "official soul" had carried out the crimes for which he was hanged in 1946, his "private soul" had always been against them.)

While Eichmann may never have encountered an "inner emigrant," he must have been well acquainted with many of those numerous civil servants who today assert that they stayed in their jobs for no other reason than to "mitigate" matters and to prevent "real Nazis" from taking over their posts. We mentioned the famous case of Dr. Hans Globke, Under-secretary of State and from 1953 to 1963 chief of the personnel division in the West German Chancellery. Since he was the only civil servant in this category to be mentioned during the trial, it may be worth while to look into his mitigating activities. Dr. Globke had been employed in the Prussian Ministry of the Interior before Hitler's rise to power, and had shown there a rather premature interest in the Jewish question. He formulated the first of the directives in which "proof of Aryan descent" was demanded, in this case of persons who applied for permission to change their names. This circular letter of December, 1932—issued at a time when Hitler's rise to power was not yet a certainty, but a strong probability—oddly anticipated the "top secret decrees," that is, the typically totalitarian rule by means of laws that are not brought to the attention of the public, which the Hitler regime introduced much later, in notifying the recipients that "these directives are not for publication." Dr. Globke, as I have mentioned, kept his interest in names, and since it is true that his Commentary on the Nuremberg Laws of 1935 was considerably harsher than the earlier interpretation of *Rassenschande* by the Ministry of the Interior's expert on Jewish affairs, Dr. Bernhard Lösener, an old member of the Party, one could even accuse him of having made things worse than they were under "real Nazis." But even if we were to grant him all his good intentions, it is hard indeed to see what he could have done under the circumstances to make things better than they would otherwise have been. Recently, however, a German newspaper, after much searching, came up with an answer to this puzzling question. They found a document, duly signed by Dr. Globke, which decreed that Czech brides of German soldiers had to furnish photographs of themselves in bathing suits in order to obtain a marriage license. And Dr. Globke explained: "With this confidential ordinance a three-year-old scandal was somewhat *mitigated*"; for until his intervention, Czech brides had to furnish snapshots that showed them stark naked.

Dr. Globke, as he explained at Nuremberg, was fortunate in that he worked under the orders of another "mitigator," Staats-sekretär (Undersecretary of State) Wilhelm Stuckart, whom we met as one of the eager members of the Wannsee Conference. Stuckart's attenuation activities concerned half-Jews, whom he proposed to sterilize. (The Nuremberg court, in possession of the minutes of the Wannsee Conference, may not have believed that he had known nothing of the extermination program, but it sentenced him to time served on account of ill health. A German denazification court fined him five hundred marks and declared him a "nominal member of the Party"—a *Mitläufer*—although they must have known at least that Stuckart belonged to the "old guard" of the Party and had joined the S.S. early, as an honorary member.) Clearly, the story of the "mitigators" in Hitler's offices belongs among the postwar fairy tales, and we can dismiss them, too, as voices that might possibly have reached Eichmann's conscience.

The question of these voices became serious, in Jerusalem, with the appearance in court of Propst Heinrich Grüber, a Protestant minister, who had come to the trial as the only German (and, incidentally, except for Judge Michael Musmanno from the United States, the only non-Jewish) witness for the prosecution. (German witnesses for the defense were excluded from the outset, since they would have exposed themselves to arrest and prosecution in Israel under the same law as that under which Eichmann was tried.) Propst Grüber had belonged to the numerically small and politically irrelevant group of persons who were opposed to Hitler on principle, and not out of nationalist considerations, and whose stand on the Jewish question had been without equivocation. He promised to be a splendid witness, since Eichmann had negotiated with him several times, and his mere appearance in the courtroom created a kind of sensation. Unfortunately, his testimony was vague; he did not remember, after so many years, when he had spoken with Eichmann, or, and this was more serious, on what subjects. All he recalled clearly was that he had once asked for unleavened bread to be shipped to Hungary for Passover, and that he had traveled to Switzerland during the war to tell his Christian friends how dangerous the situation was and to urge that more opportunities for emigration be provided. (The negotiations must have taken place prior to the implementing of the Final Solution, which coincided with Himmler's decree forbidding all emigration; they probably occurred before the invasion of Russia.) He got his unleavened bread, and he got safely to Switzerland and back again. His troubles started later, when the deportations had begun. Propst Grüber and his group of Protestant clergymen first intervened merely "on behalf of people who had been wounded in the course of the First World War and of those who had been awarded high military decorations; on behalf of the old and on behalf of the widows of those killed in World War I." These categories corresponded to those that had originally been exempted by the Nazis themselves. Now Grüber was told that what he was doing "ran counter to the policy of the government," but nothing serious happened to him. But shortly after this, Propst Grüber did something really extraordinary: he tried to reach the concentration camp of Gurs, in southern France, where Vichy France had interned, together with German Jewish refugees, some

seventy-five hundred Jews from Baden and the Saarpfalz whom Eichmann had smuggled across the German-French border in the fall of 1940,
and who, according to Propst Grüber's information, were even worse off
than the Jews deported to Poland. The result of this attempt was that he
was arrested and put in a concentration camp—first in Sachsenhausen and
then in Dachau. (A similar fate befell the Catholic priest Dompropst
Bernard Lichtenberg, of St. Hedwig's Cathedral in Berlin; he not only
had dared to pray publicly for all Jews, baptized or not—which was considerably more dangerous than to intervene for "special cases"—but he
had also demanded that he be allowed to join the Jews on their journey to
the East. He died on his way to a concentration camp.)

Apart from testifying to the existence of "another Germany," Propst
Grüber did not contribute much to either the legal or the historical significance of the trial. He was full of pat judgments about Eichmann—he
was like "a block of ice," like "marble," a *Landsknechtsnatur,* a "bicycle
rider" (a current German idiom for someone who kowtows to his superiors and kicks his subordinates)—none of which showed him as a particularly good psychologist, quite apart from the fact that the "bicycle rider"
charge was contradicted by evidence which showed Eichmann to have
been rather decent toward his subordinates. Anyway, these were interpretations and conclusions that would normally have been stricken from any
court record—though in Jerusalem they even found their way into the
judgment. Without them Propst Grüber's testimony could have strengthened the case for the defense, for Eichmann had never given Grüber a direct answer, he had always told him to come back, as he had to ask for
further instructions. More important, Dr. Servatius for once took the initiative and asked the witness a highly pertinent question: "Did you try to
influence him? Did you, as a clergyman, try to appeal to his feelings,
preach to him, and tell him that his conduct was contrary to morality?"
Of course, the very courageous Propst had done nothing of the sort, and
his answers now were highly embarrassing. He said that "deeds are more
effective than words," and that "words would have been useless"; he
spoke in clichés that had nothing to do with the reality of the situation,
where "mere words" would have been deeds, and where it had perhaps
been the duty of a clergyman to test the "uselessness of words."

Even more pertinent than Dr. Servatius' question was what Eichmann said about this episode in his last statement: "Nobody," he repeated,
"came to me and reproached me for anything in the performance of my
duties. Not even Pastor Grüber claims to have done so." He then added:
"He came to me and sought alleviation of suffering, but did not actually
object to the very performance of my duties as such." From Propst

Grüber's own testimony, it appeared that he sought not so much "alleviation of suffering" as exemptions from it, in accordance with well-
established categories recognized earlier by the Nazis. The categories had
been accepted without protest by German Jewry from the very beginning.
And the acceptance of privileged categories—German Jews as against Polish Jews, war veterans and decorated Jews as against ordinary Jews, families whose ancestors were German-born as against recently naturalized
citizens, etc.—had been the beginning of the moral collapse of respectable
Jewish society. (In view of the fact that today such matters are often
treated as though there existed a law of human nature compelling everybody to lose his dignity in the face of disaster, we may recall the attitude
of the French Jewish war veterans who were offered the same privileges
by their government, and replied: "We solemnly declare that we renounce any exceptional benefits we may derive from our status as ex-
servicemen" [*American Jewish Yearbook,* 1945].) Needless to say, the Nazis
themselves never took these distinctions seriously, for them a Jew was a
Jew, but the categories played a certain role up to the very end, since they
helped put to rest a certain uneasiness among the German population:
only Polish Jews were deported, only people who had shirked military
service, and so on. For those who did not want to close their eyes it must
have been clear from the beginning that it "was a general practice to allow
certain exceptions in order to be able to maintain the general rule all the
more easily" (in the words of Louis de Jong in an illuminating article on
"Jews and Non-Jews in Nazi-Occupied Holland").

What was morally so disastrous in the acceptance of these privileged
categories was that everyone who demanded to have an "exception"
made in his case implicitly recognized the rule, but this point, apparently,
was never grasped by these "good men," Jewish and Gentile, who busied
themselves about all those "special cases" for which preferential treatment
could be asked. The extent to which even the Jewish victims had accepted the standards of the Final Solution is perhaps nowhere more glaringly evident than in the so-called Kastner Report (available in German,
Der Kastner-Bericht über Eichmanns Menschenhandel in Ungarn, 1961). Even
after the end of the war, Kastner was proud of his success in saving
"prominent Jews," a category officially introduced by the Nazis in 1942,
as though in his view, too, it went without saying that a famous Jew had
more right to stay alive than an ordinary one; to take upon himself such
"responsibilities"—to help the Nazis in their efforts to pick out "famous"
people from the anonymous mass, for this is what it amounted to—"required more courage than to face death." But if the Jewish and Gentile
pleaders of "special cases" were unaware of their involuntary complicity,

this implicit recognition of the rule, which spelled death for all non-special cases, must have been very obvious to those who were engaged in the business of murder. They must have felt, at least, that by being asked to make exceptions, and by occasionally granting them, and thus earning gratitude, they had convinced their opponents of the lawfulness of what they were doing.

Moreover, Propst Grüber and the Jerusalem court were quite mistaken in assuming that requests for exemptions originated only with opponents of the regime. On the contrary, as Heydrich explicitly stated during the Wannsee Conference, the establishment of Theresienstadt as a ghetto for privileged categories was prompted by the great number of such interventions from all sides. Theresienstadt later became a showplace for visitors from abroad and served to deceive the outside world, but this was not its original *raison d'être*. The horrible thinning-out process that regularly occurred in this "paradise"—"distinguished from other camps as day is from night," as Eichmann rightly remarked—was necessary because there was never enough room to provide for all who were privileged, and we know from a directive issued by Ernst Kaltenbrunner, head of the R.S.H.A., that "special care was taken not to deport Jews with connections and important acquaintances in the outside world." In other words, the less "prominent" Jews were constantly sacrificed to those whose disappearance in the East would create unpleasant inquiries. The "acquaintances in the outside world" did not necessarily live outside Germany; according to Himmler, there were "eighty million good Germans, each of whom has his decent Jew. It is clear, the others are pigs, but this particular Jew is first-rate" (Hilberg). Hitler himself is said to have known three hundred and forty "first-rate Jews," whom he had either altogether assimilated to the status of Germans or granted the privileges of half-Jews. Thousands of half-Jews had been exempted from all restrictions, which might explain Heydrich's role in the S.S. and Generalfeldmarschall Erhard Milch's role in Göring's Air Force, for it was generally known that Heydrich and Milch were half-Jews. (Among the major war criminals, only two repented in the face of death: Heydrich, during the nine days it took him to die from the wounds inflicted by Czech patriots, and Hans Frank in his death cell at Nuremberg. It is an uncomfortable fact, for it is difficult not to suspect that what Heydrich at least repented of was not murder but that he had betrayed his own people.) If interventions on behalf of "prominent" Jews came from "prominent" people, they often were quite successful. Thus Sven Hedin, one of Hitler's most ardent admirers, intervened for a well-known geographer, a Professor Philippsohn of Bonn, who was "living under undignified conditions at Theresienstadt"; in a letter to Hitler, Hedin threatened that "his attitude to Germany would be dependent upon Philippsohn's fate," whereupon (according to H. G. Adler's book on Theresienstadt) Mr. Philippsohn was promptly provided with better quarters.

In Germany today, this notion of "prominent" Jews has not yet been forgotten. While the veterans and other privileged groups are no longer mentioned, the fate of "famous" Jews is still deplored at the expense of all others. There are more than a few people, especially among the cultural élite, who still publicly regret the fact that Germany sent Einstein packing, without realizing that it was a much greater crime to kill little Hans Cohn from around the corner, even though he was no genius.

EXECUTION

. . . The proceedings before the Court of Appeal lasted only a week, after which the court adjourned for two months. On May 29, 1962, the second judgment was read—somewhat less voluminous than the first, but still fifty-one single-spaced legal-sized pages. It ostensibly confirmed the District Court on all points, and to make this confirmation the judges would not have needed two months and fifty-one pages. The judgment of the Court of Appeal was actually a revision of the judgment of the lower court, although it did not say so. In conspicuous contrast to the original judgment, it was now found that "the appellant had received no 'superior orders' at all. He was his own superior, and he gave all orders in matters that concerned Jewish affairs"; he had, moreover, "eclipsed in importance all his superiors, including Müller." And, in reply to the obvious argument of the defense that the Jews would have been no better off had Eichmann never existed, the judges now stated that "the idea of the Final Solution would never have assumed the infernal forms of the flayed skin and tortured flesh of millions of Jews without the fanatical zeal and the unquenchable blood thirst of the appellant and his accomplices." Israel's Supreme Court had not only accepted the arguments of the prosecution, it had adopted its very language.

The same day, May 29, Itzhak Ben-Zvi, President of Israel, received Eichmann's plea for mercy, four handwritten pages, made "upon instructions of my counsel," together with letters from his wife and his family in Linz. The President also received hundreds of letters and telegrams from all over the world, pleading for clemency; outstanding among the senders were the Central Conference of American Rabbis, the representative body of Reform Judaism in this country, and a group of professors from the Hebrew University in Jerusalem, headed by Martin Buber, who had been opposed to the trial from the start, and who now tried to persuade Ben-Gurion to intervene for clemency. Mr. Ben-Zvi rejected all pleas for mercy on May 31, two days after the Supreme Court had delivered its judgment, and a few hours later on that same day—it was a Thursday—shortly before midnight, Eichmann was hanged, his body was cremated, and the ashes were scattered in the Mediterranean outside Israeli waters.

The speed with which the death sentence was carried out was extraordinary, even if one takes into account that Thursday night was the last possible occasion before the following Monday, since Friday, Saturday, and Sunday are all religious holidays for one or another of the three denominations in the country. The execution took place less than two hours after Eichmann was informed of the rejection of his plea for mercy; there had not even been time for a last meal. The explanation may well be found in two last-minute attempts Dr. Servatius made to save his client—an application to a court in West Germany to force the government to demand Eichmann's extradition, even now, and a threat to invoke Article 25 of the Convention for the Protection of Human Rights and Fundamental Freedoms. Neither Dr. Servatius nor his assistant was in Israel when Eichmann's plea was rejected, and the Israeli government probably wanted to close the case, which had been going on for two years, before the defense could even apply for a stay in the date of execution.

The death sentence had been expected, and there was hardly anyone to quarrel with it; but things were altogether different when it was learned that the Israelis had carried it out. The protests were short-lived, but they were widespread and they were voiced by people of influence and prestige. The most common argument was that Eichmann's deeds defied the possibility of human punishment, that it was pointless to impose the death sentence for crimes of such magnitude—which, of course, was true, in a sense, except that it could not conceivably mean that he who had murdered millions should for this very reason escape punishment. On a considerably lower level, the death sentence was called "unimaginative," and very imaginative alternatives were proposed forthwith—Eichmann "should have spent the rest of his life at hard labor in the arid stretches of the Negev, helping with his sweat to reclaim the Jewish homeland," a punishment he would probably not have survived for more than a single day, to say nothing of the fact that in Israel the desert of the south is hardly looked upon as a penal colony; or, in Madison Avenue style, Israel should have reached "divine heights," rising above "the understandable, legal, political, and even human considerations," by calling together "all those who took part in the capture, trial, and sentencing to a public ceremony, with Eichmann there in shackles, and with television cameras and radio to decorate them as the heroes of the century."

Martin Buber called the execution a "mistake of historical dimensions," as it might "serve to expiate the guilt felt by many young persons in Germany"—an argument that oddly echoed Eichmann's own ideas on the matter, though Buber hardly knew that he had wanted to hang himself in public in order to lift the burden of guilt from the shoulders of German youngsters. (It is strange that Buber, a man not only of eminence but of very great intelligence, should not see how spurious these much publicized guilt feelings necessarily are. It is quite gratifying to feel guilty if you haven't done anything wrong: how noble! Whereas it is rather hard and certainly depressing to admit guilt and to repent. The youth of Germany is surrounded, on all sides and in all walks of life, by men in positions of authority and in public office who are very guilty indeed but who *feel* nothing of the sort. The normal reaction to this state of affairs should be indignation, but indignation would be quite risky—not a danger to life and limb but definitely a handicap in a career. Those young German men and women who every once in a while—on the occasion of all the *Diary of Anne Frank* hubbub and of the Eichmann trial—treat us to hysterical outbreaks of guilt feelings are not staggering under the burden of the past, their fathers' guilt; rather, they are trying to escape from the pressure of very present and actual problems into a cheap sentimentality.) Professor Buber went on to say that he felt "no pity at all" for Eichmann, because he could feel pity "only for those whose actions I understand in my heart," and he stressed what he had said many years ago in Germany—that he had "only in a formal sense a common humanity with those who took part" in the acts of the Third Reich. This lofty attitude was, of course, more of a luxury than those who had to try Eichmann could afford, since the law presupposes precisely that we have a common humanity with those whom we accuse and judge and condemn. As far as I know, Buber was the only philosopher to go on public record on the subject of Eichmann's execution (shortly before the trial started, Karl Jaspers had given a radio interview in Basel, later published in *Der Monat,* in which he argued the case for an international tribunal); it was disappointing to find him dodging, on the highest possible level, the very problem Eichmann and his deeds had posed.

Least of all was heard from those who were against the death penalty on principle, unconditionally; their arguments would have remained valid, since they would not have needed to specify them for this particular case. They seem to have felt—rightly, I think—that this was not a very promising case on which to fight.

Adolf Eichmann went to the gallows with great dignity. He had asked for a bottle of red wine and had drunk half of it. He refused the help of the Protestant minister, the Reverend William Hull, who offered to read the Bible with him: he had only two more hours to live, and therefore no "time to waste." He walked the fifty yards from his cell to the execution chamber calm and erect, with his hands bound behind him. When the guards tied his ankles and knees, he asked them to loosen the bonds so that he could stand straight. "I don't need that," he said when the black hood was offered him. He was in complete command of himself, nay, he was more: he was completely himself. Nothing could have demonstrated this more convincingly than the grotesque silliness of his last words. He began by stating emphatically that he was a *Gottgläubiger,* to express in common Nazi fashion that he was no Christian and did not believe in life after death. He then proceeded: "After a short while, gentlemen, *we shall all meet again.* Such is the fate of all men. Long live Germany, long live Argentina, long live Austria. *I shall not forget them.*" In the face of death, he had found the cliché used in funeral oratory. Under the gallows, his memory played him the last trick; he was "elated" and he forgot that this was his own funeral.

It was as though in those last minutes he was summing up the lesson that this long course in human wickedness had taught us—the lesson of the fearsome, word-and-thought-defying *banality of evil.*

EPILOGUE

. . . In the eyes of the Jews, thinking exclusively in terms of their own history, the catastrophe that had befallen them under Hitler, in which a third of the people perished, appeared not as the most recent of crimes, the unprecedented crime of genocide, but, on the contrary, as the oldest crime they knew and remembered. This misunderstanding, almost inevitable if we consider not only the facts of Jewish history but also, and more important, the current Jewish historical self-understanding, is actually at the root of all the failures and shortcomings of the Jerusalem trial. None of the participants ever arrived at a clear understanding of the actual horror of Auschwitz, which is of a different nature from all the atrocities of the past, because it appeared to prosecution and judges alike as not much more than the most horrible pogrom in Jewish history. They therefore believed that a direct line existed from the early anti-Semitism of the Nazi Party to the Nuremberg Laws and from there to the expulsion of Jews from the Reich and, finally, to the gas chambers. Politically and legally, however, these were "crimes" different not only in degree of seriousness but in essence.

The Nuremberg Laws of 1935 legalized the discrimination practiced before that by the German majority against the Jewish minority. According to international law, it was the privilege of the sovereign German nation to declare to be a national minority whatever part of its population it saw fit, as long as its minority laws conformed to the rights and guarantees established by internationally recognized minority treaties and agreements. International Jewish organizations therefore promptly tried to obtain for this newest minority the same rights and guarantees that minorities in Eastern and Southeastern Europe had been granted at Geneva. But even though this protection was not granted, the Nuremberg Laws were generally recognized by other nations as part of German law, so that it was impossible for a German national to enter into a "mixed marriage" in Holland, for instance. The crime of the Nuremberg Laws was a national crime; it violated national, constitutional rights and liberties, but it was of no concern to the comity of nations. "Enforced emigration," however, or expulsion, which became official policy after 1938, did concern the international community, for the simple reason that those who were expelled appeared at the frontiers of other countries, which were forced either to accept the uninvited guests or to smuggle them into another country, equally unwilling to accept them. Expulsion of nationals, in other words, is already an offense against humanity, if by "humanity" we understand no more than the comity of nations. Neither the national crime of legalized discrimination, which amounted to persecution by law, nor the international crime of expulsion was unprecedented, even in the modern age. Legalized discrimination had been practiced by all Balkan countries, and expulsion on a mass scale had occurred after many revolutions. It was when the Nazi regime declared that the German people not only were unwilling to have any Jews in Germany but wished to make the entire Jewish people disappear from the face of the earth that the new crime, the crime against humanity—in the sense of a crime "against the human status," or against the very nature of mankind—appeared. Expulsion and genocide, though both are international offenses, must remain distinct; the former is an offense against fellow-nations, whereas the latter is an attack upon human diversity as such, that is, upon a characteristic of the "human status" without which the very words "mankind" or "humanity" would be devoid of meaning.

Had the court in Jerusalem understood that there were distinctions between discrimination, expulsion, and genocide, it would immediately have become clear that the supreme crime it was confronted with, the physical extermination of the Jewish people, was a crime against humanity, perpetrated upon the body of the Jewish people, and that only the choice of victims, not the nature of the crime, could be derived from the long history of Jew-hatred and anti-Semitism. Insofar as the victims were Jews, it was right and proper that a Jewish court should sit in judgment; but insofar as the crime was a crime against humanity, it needed an international tribunal to do justice to it. (The failure of the court to draw this distinction was surprising, because it had actually been made before by the former Israeli Minister of Justice, Mr. Rosen, who in 1950 had insisted on "a distinction between this bill [for crimes against the Jewish people] and the Law for the Prevention and Punishment of Genocide," which was discussed but not passed by the Israeli Parliament. Obviously, the court felt it had no right to overstep the limits of municipal law, so that genocide, not being covered by an Israeli law, could not properly enter into its considerations.) Among the numerous and highly qualified voices that raised objections to the court in Jerusalem and were in favor of an international tribunal, only one, that of Karl Jaspers, stated clearly and unequivocally—in a radio interview held before the trial began and later published in *Der Monat*—that "the crime against the Jews was also a crime against mankind," and that "consequently the verdict can be handed down only by a court of justice representing all mankind." Jaspers proposed that the court in Jerusalem, after hearing the factual evidence, "waive" the right to pass sentence, declaring itself "incompetent" to do so, because the legal nature of the crime in question was still open to dispute, as was the subsequent question of who would be competent to pass sentence on a crime which had been committed on government orders. Jaspers stated further that one thing alone was certain: "This crime is both more and less than common murder," and though it was not a "war crime," either, there was no doubt that "mankind would certainly be destroyed if states were permitted to perpetrate such crimes."

Jaspers' proposal, which no one in Israel even bothered to discuss, would, in this form, presumably have been impracticable from a purely technical point of view. The question of a court's jurisdiction must be decided before the trial begins; and once a court has been declared competent, it must also pass judgment. However, these purely formalistic objections could easily have been met if Jaspers had called not upon the court, but rather upon the state of Israel to waive its right to carry out the sentence once it had been handed down, in view of the unprecedented nature of the court's findings. Israel might then have had recourse to the United Nations and demonstrated, with all the evidence at hand, that the need for an international criminal court was imperative, in view of these new crimes committed against mankind as a whole. It would then have been in Israel's power to make trouble, to "create a wholesome disturbance," by asking again and again just what it should do with this man whom it was holding prisoner; constant repetition would have impressed on worldwide public opinion the need for a permanent international criminal court. Only by creating, in this way, an "embarrassing situation" of concern to the representatives of all nations would it be possible to prevent "mankind from setting its mind at ease" and "massacre of the Jews . . . from becoming a model for crimes to come, perhaps the small-scale and quite paltry example of future genocide." The very monstrousness of the events is "minimized" before a tribunal that represents one nation only.

This argument in favor of an international tribunal was unfortunately confused with other proposals based on different and considerably less weighty considerations. Many friends of Israel, both Jews and non-Jews, feared that the trial would harm Israel's prestige and give rise to a reaction against Jews the world over. It was thought that Jews did not have the right to appear as judges in their own case, but could act only as accusers; Israel should therefore hold Eichmann prisoner until a special tribunal could be created by the United Nations to judge him. Quite apart from the fact that Israel, in the proceedings against Eichmann, was doing no more than what all the countries which had been occupied by Germany had long since done, and that justice was at stake here, not the prestige of Israel or of the Jewish people, all these proposals had one flaw in common: they could too easily be countered by Israel. They were indeed quite unrealistic in view of the fact that the U.N. General Assembly had "twice rejected proposals to consider the establishment of a permanent international criminal court" (*A.D.L. Bulletin*). But another, more practical proposition, which usually is not mentioned precisely because it *was* feasible, was made by Dr. Nahum Goldmann, president of the World Jewish Congress. Goldmann called upon Ben-Gurion to set up an international court in Jerusalem, with judges from each of the countries that had suffered under Nazi occupation. This would not have been enough; it would have been only an enlargement of the Successor trials, and the chief impairment of justice, that it was being rendered in the court of the victors, would not have been cured. But it would have been a practical step in the right direction.

Israel, as may be remembered, reacted against all these proposals with great violence. And while it is true, as has been pointed out by Yosal Rogat (in *The Eichmann Trial and the Rule of Law*, published by the Center for the Study of Democratic Institutions, Santa Barbara, California, 1962), that Ben-Gurion always "seemed to misunderstand completely when asked, 'Why should he not be tried before an international court?,' " it is also true that those who asked the question did not understand that for Israel the only unprecedented feature of the trial was that, for the first time (since the year 70, when Jerusalem was destroyed by the Romans), Jews were able to sit in judgment on crimes committed against their own people, that, for the first time, they did not need to appeal to others for protection and justice, or fall back upon the compromised phraseology of the rights of man—rights which, as no one knew better than they, were claimed only by people who were too weak to defend their "rights of Englishmen" and to enforce their own laws. (The very fact that Israel had her own law under which such a trial could be held had been called, long before the Eichmann trial, an expression of "a revolutionary transformation that has taken place in the political position of the Jewish people"— by Mr. Rosen on the occasion of the First Reading of the Law of 1950 in the Knesset.) It was against the background of these very vivid experiences and aspirations that Ben-Gurion said: "Israel does not need the protection of an International Court."

Moreover, the argument that the crime against the Jewish people was first of all a crime against mankind, upon which the valid proposals for an international tribunal rested, stood in flagrant contradiction to the law under which Eichmann was tried. Hence, those who proposed that Israel give up her prisoner should have gone one step further and declared: The Nazis and Nazi Collaborators (Punishment) Law of 1950 is wrong, it is in contradiction to what actually happened, it does not cover the facts. And this would indeed have been quite true. For just as a murderer is prosecuted because he has violated the law of the community, and not because he has deprived the Smith family of its husband, father, and breadwinner, so these modern, state-employed mass murderers must be prosecuted because they violated the order of mankind, and not because they killed millions of people. Nothing is more pernicious to an understanding of these new crimes, or stands more in the way of the emergence of an international penal code that could take care of them, than the common illusion that the crime of murder and the crime of genocide are essentially the same, and that the latter therefore is "no new crime properly speaking." The point of the latter is that an altogether different order is broken and an altogether different community is violated. And, indeed, it was because Ben-Gurion knew quite well that the whole discussion actually concerned the validity of the Israeli law that he finally reacted nastily, and not just with violence, against the critics of Israeli procedures: Whatever these "so-called experts" had to say, their arguments were "sophisms," inspired either by anti-Semitism, or, in the case of Jews, by inferiority complexes. "Let the world understand: We shall not give up our prisoner."

It is only fair to say that this was by no means the tone in which the trial was conducted in Jerusalem. But I think it is safe to predict that this last of the Successor trials will no more, and perhaps even less than its predecessors, serve as a valid precedent for future trials of such crimes. This might be of little import in view of the fact that its main purpose—to prosecute and to defend, to judge and to punish Adolf Eichmann—was achieved, if it were not for the rather uncomfortable but hardly deniable possibility that similar crimes may be committed in the future. The reasons for this sinister potentiality are general as well as particular. It is in the very nature of things human that every act that has once made its appearance and has been recorded in the history of mankind stays with mankind as a potentiality long after its actuality has become a thing of the past. No punishment has ever possessed enough power of deterrence to prevent the commission of crimes. On the contrary, whatever the punishment, once a specific crime has appeared for the first time, its reappearance is more likely than its initial emergence could ever have been. The particular reasons that speak for the possibility of a repetition of the crimes committed by the Nazis are even more plausible. The frightening coincidence of the modern population explosion with the discovery of technical devices that, through automation, will make large sections of the population "superfluous" even in terms of labor, and that, through nuclear energy, make it possible to deal with this twofold threat by the use of instruments beside which Hitler's gassing installations look like an evil child's fumbling toys, should be enough to make us tremble.

It is essentially for this reason: that the unprecedented, once it has appeared, may become a precedent for the future, that all trials touching upon "crimes against humanity" must be judged according to a standard that is today still an "ideal." If genocide is an actual possibility of the future, then no people on earth—least of all, of course, the Jewish people, in Israel or elsewhere—can feel reasonably sure of its continued existence without the help and the protection of international law. Success or failure in dealing with the hitherto unprecedented can lie only in the extent to which this dealing may serve as a valid precedent on the road to international penal law. And this demand, addressed to the judges in such trials, does not overshoot the mark and ask for more than can reasonably be expected. International law, Justice Jackson pointed out at Nuremberg, "is an outgrowth of treaties and agreements between nations and of accepted customs. Yet every custom has its origin in some single act. . . . Our own day has the right to institute customs and to conclude agreements that will themselves become sources of a newer and strengthened international law." What Justice Jackson failed to point out is that, in consequence of this yet unfinished nature of international law, it has become the task of ordinary trial judges to render justice without the help of, or beyond the limitation set upon them through, positive, posited laws. For the judge, this may be a predicament, and he is only too likely to protest that the "single act" demanded of him is not his to perform but is the business of the legislator.

And, indeed, before we come to any conclusion about the success or failure of the Jerusalem court, we must stress the judges' firm belief that they had no right to become legislators, that they had to conduct their business within the limits of Israeli law, on the one side, and of accepted legal opinion, on the other. It must be admitted furthermore that their failures were neither in kind nor in degree greater than the failures of the Nuremberg Trials or the Successor trials in other European countries. On the contrary, part of the failure of the Jerusalem court was due to its all too eager adherence to the Nuremberg precedent wherever possible.

In sum, the failure of the Jerusalem court consisted in its not coming to grips with three fundamental issues, all of which have been sufficiently well known and widely discussed since the establishment of the Nuremberg Tribunal: the problem of impaired justice in the court of the victors; a valid definition of the "crime against humanity"; and a clear recognition of the new criminal who commits this crime.

As to the first of these, justice was more seriously impaired in Jerusalem than it was at Nuremberg, because the court did not admit witnesses for the defense. In terms of the traditional requirements for fair and due process of law, this was the most serious flaw in the Jerusalem proceedings. Moreover, while judgment in the court of the victors was perhaps inevitable at the close of the war (to Justice Jackson's argument in Nuremberg: "Either the victors must judge the vanquished or we must leave the defeated to judge themselves," should be added the understandable feeling on the part of the Allies that they "who had risked everything could not admit neutrals" [Vabres]), it was not the same sixteen years later, and under circumstances in which the argument against the admission of neutral countries did not make sense.

As to the second issue, the findings of the Jerusalem court were incomparably better than those at Nuremberg. I have mentioned before the Nuremberg Charter's definition of "crimes against humanity" as "inhuman acts," which were translated into German as *Verbrechen gegen die Menschlichkeit*—as though the Nazis had simply been lacking in human kindness, certainly the understatement of the century. To be sure, had the conduct of the Jerusalem trial depended entirely upon the prosecution, the basic misunderstanding would have been even worse than at Nuremberg. But the judgment refused to let the basic character of the crime be swallowed up in a flood of atrocities, and it did not fall into the trap of equating this crime with ordinary war crimes. What had been mentioned at Nuremberg only occasionally and, as it were, marginally—that "the evidence shows that . . . the mass murders and cruelties were not committed solely for the purpose of stamping out opposition" but were "part of a plan to get rid of whole native populations"—was in the center of the Jerusalem proceedings, for the obvious reason that Eichmann stood accused of a crime against the Jewish people, a crime that could not be explained by any utilitarian purpose; Jews had been murdered all over Europe, not only in the East, and their annihilation was not due to any desire to gain territory that "could be used for colonization by Germans." It was the great advantage of a trial centered on the crime against the Jewish people that not only did the difference between war crimes, such as shooting of partisans and killing of hostages, and "inhuman acts," such as "expulsion and annihilation" of native populations to permit colonization by an invader, emerge with sufficient clarity to become part of a future international penal code, but also that the difference between "inhuman acts" (which were undertaken for some known, though criminal, purpose, such as expansion through colonization) and the "crime against humanity," whose intent and purpose were unprecedented, was clarified. At no point, however, either in the proceedings or in the judgment, did the Jerusalem trial ever mention even the possibility that extermination of whole ethnic groups—the Jews, or the Poles, or the Gypsies—might be more than a crime against the Jewish or the Polish or the Gypsy people, that the international order, and mankind in its entirety, might have been grievously hurt and endangered.

Closely connected with this failure was the conspicuous helplessness the judges experienced when they were confronted with the task they could least escape, the task of understanding the criminal whom they had come to judge. Clearly, it was not enough that they did not follow the prosecution in its obviously mistaken description of the accused as a "perverted sadist," nor would it have been enough if they had gone one step further and shown the inconsistency of the case for the prosecution, in which Mr. Hausner wanted to try the most abnormal monster the world had ever seen and, at the same time, try in him "many like him," even the "whole Nazi movement and anti-Semitism at large." They knew, of course, that it would have been very comforting indeed to believe that Eichmann was a monster, even though if he had been Israel's case against him would have collapsed or, at the very least, lost all interest. Surely, one can hardly call upon the whole world and gather correspondents from the four corners of the earth in order to display Bluebeard in the dock. The trouble with Eichmann was precisely that so many were like him, and that the many were neither perverted nor sadistic, that they were, and still are, terribly and terrifyingly normal. From the viewpoint of our legal institutions and of our moral standards of judgment, this normality was much more terrifying than all the atrocities put together, for it implied—as had been said at Nuremberg over and over again by the defendants and their counsels—that this new type of criminal, who is in actual fact *hostis generis humani,* commits his crimes under circumstances that make it well-nigh impossible for him to know or to feel that he is doing wrong. In this respect, the evidence in the Eichmann case was even more convincing than the evidence presented in the trial of the major war criminals, whose pleas of a clear conscience could be dismissed more easily because they combined with the argument of obedience to "superior orders" various boasts about occasional disobedience. But although the bad faith of the defendants was manifest, the only ground on which guilty conscience could actually be proved was the fact that the Nazis, and especially the criminal organizations to which Eichmann belonged, had been so very busy destroying the evidence of their crimes during the last months of the war. And this ground was rather shaky. It proved no more than recognition that the law of mass murder, because of its novelty, was not yet accepted by other nations; or, in the language of the Nazis, that they had lost their fight to "liberate" mankind from the "rule of subhumans," especially from the domination of the Elders of Zion; or, in ordinary language, it proved no more than the admission of defeat. Would any one of them have suffered from a guilty conscience if they had won?

Foremost among the larger issues at stake in the Eichmann trial was the assumption current in all modern legal systems that intent to do wrong is necessary for the commission of a crime. On nothing, perhaps, has civilized jurisprudence prided itself more than on this taking into account of the subjective factor. Where this intent is absent, where, for whatever reasons, even reasons of moral insanity, the ability to distinguish between right and wrong is impaired, we feel no crime has been committed. We refuse, and consider as barbaric, the propositions "that a great crime offends nature, so that the very earth cries out for vengeance; that evil violates a natural harmony which only retribution can restore; that a wronged collectivity owes a duty to the moral order to punish the criminal" (Yosal Rogat). And yet I think it is undeniable that it was precisely on the ground of these long-forgotten propositions that Eichmann was brought

to justice to begin with, and that they were, in fact, the supreme justification for the death penalty. Because he had been implicated and had played
a central role in an enterprise whose open purpose was to eliminate forever certain "races" from the surface of the earth, he had to be eliminated.
And if it is true that "justice must not only be done but must be seen to
be done," then the justice of what was done in Jerusalem would have
emerged to be seen by all if the judges had dared to address their defendant in something like the following terms:

"You admitted that the crime committed against the Jewish people during
the war was the greatest crime in recorded history, and you admitted your
role in it. But you said you had never acted from base motives, that you
had never had any inclination to kill anybody, that you had never hated
Jews, and still that you could not have acted otherwise and that you did
not feel guilty. We find this difficult, though not altogether impossible, to
believe; there is some, though not very much, evidence against you in this
matter of motivation and conscience that could be proved beyond reasonable doubt. You also said that your role in the Final Solution was an accident and that almost anybody could have taken your place, so that
potentially almost all Germans are equally guilty. What you meant to say
was that where all, or almost all, are guilty, nobody is. This is an indeed
quite common conclusion, but one we are not willing to grant you. And
if you don't understand our objection, we would recommend to your attention the story of Sodom and Gomorrah, two neighboring cities in the
Bible, which were destroyed by fire from Heaven because all the people
in them had become equally guilty. This, incidentally, has nothing to do
with the newfangled notion of 'collective guilt,' according to which people supposedly are guilty of, or feel guilty about, things done in their
name but not by them—things in which they did not participate and from
which they did not profit. In other words, guilt and innocence before the
law are of an objective nature, and even if eighty million Germans had
done as you did, this would not have been an excuse for you.

"Luckily, we don't have to go that far. You yourself claimed not the
actuality but only the potentiality of equal guilt on the part of all who
lived in a state whose main political purpose had become the commission
of unheard-of crimes. And no matter through what accidents of exterior
or interior circumstances you were pushed onto the road of becoming a
criminal, there is an abyss between the actuality of what you did and the
potentiality of what others might have done. We are concerned here only
with what you did, and not with the possible noncriminal nature of your
inner life and of your motives or with the criminal potentialities of those

around you. You told your story in terms of a hard-luck story, and, knowing the circumstances, we are, up to a point, willing to grant you that under more favorable circumstances it is highly unlikely that you would ever have come before us or before any other criminal court. Let us assume, for the sake of argument, that it was nothing more than misfortune that made you a willing instrument in the organization of mass murder; there still remains the fact that you have carried out, and therefore actively supported, a policy of mass murder. For politics is not like the nursery; in politics obedience and support are the same. And just as you supported and carried out a policy of not wanting to share the earth with the Jewish people and the people of a number of other nations—as though you and your superiors had any right to determine who should and who should not inhabit the world—we find that no one, that is, no member of the human race, can be expected to want to share the earth with you. This is the reason, and the only reason, you must hang."

POSTSCRIPT

. . . Even before its publication, this book became both the center of a controversy and the object of an organized campaign. It is only natural that the campaign, conducted with all the well-known means of image-making and opinion-manipulation, got much more attention than the controversy, so that the latter was somehow swallowed up by and drowned in the artificial noise of the former. This became especially clear when a strange mixture of the two, in almost identical phraseology—as though the pieces written against the book (and more frequently against its author) came "out of a mimeographing machine" (Mary McCarthy)—was carried from America to England and then to Europe, where the book was not yet even available. And this was possible because the clamor centered on the "image" of a book which was never written, and touched upon subjects that often had not only not been mentioned by me but had never occurred to me before.

The debate—if that is what it was—was by no means devoid of interest. Manipulations of opinion, insofar as they are inspired by well-defined interests, have limited goals; their effect, however, if they happen to touch upon an issue of authentic concern, is no longer subject to their control and may easily produce consequences they never foresaw or intended. It now appeared that the era of the Hitler regime, with its gigantic, unprecedented crimes, constituted an "unmastered past" not only for the German people or for the Jews all over the world, but for the rest of the world, which had not forgotten this great catastrophe in the heart of Europe either, and had also been unable to come to terms with it. Moreover—and this was perhaps even less expected—general moral questions, with all their intricacies and modern complexities, which I would never have suspected would haunt men's minds today and weigh heavily on their hearts, stood suddenly in the foreground of public concern.

The controversy began by calling attention to the conduct of the Jewish people during the years of the Final Solution, thus following up the question, first raised by the Israeli prosecutor, of whether the Jews could or should have defended themselves. I had dismissed that question as silly and cruel, since it testified to a fatal ignorance of the conditions at the time. It has now been discussed to exhaustion, and the most amazing conclusions have been drawn. The well-known historico-sociological construct of a "ghetto mentality" (which in Israel has taken its place in history textbooks and in this country has been espoused chiefly by the psychologist Bruno Bettelheim—against the furious protest of official American Judaism) has been repeatedly dragged in to explain behavior which was not at all confined to the Jewish people and which therefore cannot be explained by specifically Jewish factors. The suggestions proliferated until someone who evidently found the whole discussion too dull had the brilliant idea of evoking Freudian theories and attributing to the whole Jewish people a "death wish"—unconscious, of course. This was the unexpected conclusion certain reviewers chose to draw from the "image" of a book, created by certain interest groups, in which I allegedly had claimed that the Jews had murdered themselves. And why had I told such a monstrously implausible lie? Out of "self-hatred," of course.

Since the role of the Jewish leadership had come up at the trial, and since I had reported and commented on it, it was inevitable that it too should be discussed. This, in my opinion, is a serious question, but the debate has contributed little to its clarification. As can be seen from the recent trial in Israel at which a certain Hirsch Birnblat, a former chief of the Jewish police in a Polish town and now a conductor at the Israeli Opera, first was sentenced by a district court to five years' imprisonment, and then was exonerated by the Supreme Court in Jerusalem, whose unanimous opinion indirectly exonerated the Jewish Councils in general, the Jewish Establishment is bitterly divided on this issue. In the debate, however, the most vocal participants were those who either identified the Jewish people with its leadership—in striking contrast to the clear distinction made in almost all the reports of survivors, which may be summed up in the words of a former inmate of Theresienstadt: "The Jewish people as a whole behaved magnificently. Only the leadership failed"—or justified the Jewish functionaries by citing all the commendable services they had rendered before the war, and above all before the era of the Final Solution, as though there were no difference between helping Jews to emigrate and helping the Nazis to deport them.

While these issues had indeed some connection with this book, although they were inflated out of all proportion, there were others which had no relation to it whatsoever. There was, for instance, a hot discussion of the German resistance movement from the beginning of the Hitler regime on, which I naturally did not discuss, since the question of Eichmann's conscience, and that of the situation around him, relates only to the period of the war and the Final Solution. But there were more fantastic items. Quite a number of people began to debate the question of whether the victims of persecution may not always be "uglier" than their murderers; or whether anyone who was not present is entitled "to sit in judgment" over the past; or whether the defendant or the victim holds the center of the stage in a trial. On the latter point, some went so far as to assert not only that I was wrong in being interested in what kind of person Eichmann was, but that he should not have been allowed to speak at all—that is, presumably, that the trial should have been conducted without any defense.

As is frequently the case in discussions that are conducted with a great show of emotion, the down-to-earth interests of certain groups, whose excitement is entirely concerned with factual matters and who therefore try to distort the facts, become quickly and inextricably involved with the untrammeled inspirations of intellectuals who, on the contrary, are not in the least interested in facts but treat them merely as a springboard for "ideas." But even in these sham battles, there could often be detected a certain seriousness, a degree of authentic concern, and this even in the contributions by people who boasted that they had not read the book and promised that they never would read it.

Compared with these debates, which wandered so far afield, the book itself dealt with a sadly limited subject. The report of a trial can discuss only the matters which were treated in the course of the trial, or which in the interests of justice should have been treated. If the general situation of a country in which the trial takes place happens to be important to the conduct of the trial, it too must be taken into account. This book, then, does not deal with the history of the greatest disaster that ever befell the Jewish people, nor is it an account of totalitarianism, or a history of the German people in the time of the Third Reich, nor is it, finally and least of all, a theoretical treatise on the nature of evil. The focus of every trial is upon the person of the defendant, a man of flesh and blood with an

individual history, with an always unique set of qualities, peculiarities, behavior patterns, and circumstances. All the things that go beyond that,
such as the history of the Jewish people in the dispersion, and of anti-
Semitism, or the conduct of the German people and other peoples, or
the ideologies of the time and the governmental apparatus of the Third
Reich, affect the trial only insofar as they form the background and the
conditions under which the defendant committed his acts. All the things
that the defendant did not come into contact with, or that did not influence him, must be omitted from the proceedings of the trial and consequently from the report on it.

It may be argued that all the general questions we involuntarily raise
as soon as we begin to speak of these matters—why did it have to be the
Germans? why did it have to be the Jews? what is the nature of totalitarian rule?—are far more important than the question of the kind of crime
for which a man is being tried, and the nature of the defendant upon
whom justice must be pronounced; more important, too, than the question of how well our present system of justice is capable of dealing with
this special type of crime and criminal it has had repeatedly to cope with
since the Second World War. It can be held that the issue is no longer a
particular human being, a single distinct individual in the dock, but rather
the German people in general, or anti-Semitism in all its forms, or the
whole of modern history, or the nature of man and original sin—so that
ultimately the entire human race sits invisibly beside the defendant in the
dock. All this has often been argued, and especially by those who will not
rest until they have discovered an "Eichmann in every one of us." If the
defendant is taken as a symbol and the trial as a pretext to bring up matters which are apparently more interesting than the guilt or innocence of
one person, then consistency demands that we bow to the assertion made
by Eichmann and his lawyer: that he was brought to book because a
scapegoat was needed, not only for the German Federal Republic, but
also for the events as a whole and for what made them possible—that is,
for anti-Semitism and totalitarian government as well as for the human
race and original sin.

I need scarcely say that I would never have gone to Jerusalem if I had
shared these views. I held and hold the opinion that this trial had to take
place in the interests of justice and nothing else. I also think the judges
were quite right when they stressed in their verdict that "the State of Israel was established and recognized as the State of the Jews," and therefore
had jurisdiction over a crime committed against the Jewish people; and in
view of the current confusion in legal circles about the meaning and usefulness of punishment, I was glad that the judgment quoted Grotius, who,

for his part, citing an older author, explained that punishment is necessary "to defend the honor or the authority of him who was hurt by the offence so that the failure to punish may not cause his degradation."

There is of course no doubt that the defendant and the nature of his acts as well as the trial itself raise problems of a general nature which go far beyond the matters considered in Jerusalem. I have attempted to go into some of these problems in the Epilogue, which ceases to be simple reporting. I would not have been surprised if people had found my treatment inadequate, and I would have welcomed a discussion of the general significance of the entire body of facts, which could have been all the more meaningful the more directly it referred to the concrete events. I also can well imagine that an authentic controversy might have arisen over the subtitle of the book; for when I speak of the banality of evil, I do so only on the strictly factual level, pointing to a phenomenon which stared one in the face at the trial. Eichmann was not Iago and not Macbeth, and nothing would have been farther from his mind than to determine with Richard III "to prove a villain." Except for an extraordinary diligence in looking out for his personal advancement, he had no motives at all. And this diligence in itself was in no way criminal; he certainly would never have murdered his superior in order to inherit his post. He *merely,* to put the matter colloquially, *never realized what he was doing.* It was precisely this lack of imagination which enabled him to sit for months on end facing a German Jew who was conducting the police interrogation, pouring out his heart to the man and explaining again and again how it was that he reached only the rank of lieutenant colonel in the S.S. and that it had not been his fault that he was not promoted. In principle he knew quite well what it was all about, and in his final statement to the court he spoke of the "revaluation of values prescribed by the [Nazi] government." He was not stupid. It was sheer thoughtlessness—something by no means identical with stupidity—that predisposed him to become one of the greatest criminals of that period. And if this is "banal" and even funny, if with the best will in the world one cannot extract any diabolical or demonic profundity from Eichmann, that is still far from calling it commonplace. It surely cannot be so common that a man facing death, and, moreover, standing beneath the gallows, should be able to think of nothing but what he has heard at funerals all his life, and that these "lofty words" should completely becloud the reality of his own death. That such remoteness from reality and such thoughtlessness can wreak more havoc than all the evil instincts taken together which, perhaps, are inherent in man—that was, in fact, the lesson one could learn in Jerusalem. But it was a lesson, neither an explanation of the phenomenon nor a theory about it.

Seemingly more complicated, but in reality far simpler than examining the strange interdependence of thoughtlessness and evil, is the question of what kind of crime is actually involved here—a crime, moreover, which all agree is unprecedented. For the concept of genocide, introduced explicitly to cover a crime unknown before, although applicable up to a point is not fully adequate, for the simple reason that massacres of whole peoples are not unprecedented. They were the order of the day in antiquity, and the centuries of colonization and imperialism provide plenty of examples of more or less successful attempts of that sort. The expression "administrative massacres" seems better to fill the bill. The term arose in connection with British imperialism; the English deliberately rejected such procedures as a means of maintaining their rule over India. The phrase has the virtue of dispelling the prejudice that such monstrous acts can be committed only against a foreign nation or a different race. There is the well-known fact that Hitler began his mass murders by granting "mercy deaths" to the "incurably ill," and that he intended to wind up his extermination program by doing away with "genetically damaged" Germans (heart and lung patients). But quite aside from that, it is apparent that this sort of killing can be directed against any given group, that is, that the principle of selection is dependent only upon circumstantial factors. It is quite conceivable that in the automated economy of a not-too-distant future men may be tempted to exterminate all those whose intelligence quotient is below a certain level.

In Jerusalem this matter was inadequately discussed because it is actually very difficult to grasp juridically. We heard the protestations of the defense that Eichmann was after all only a "tiny cog" in the machinery of the Final Solution, and of the prosecution, which believed it had discovered in Eichmann the actual motor. I myself attributed no more importance to both theories than did the Jerusalem court, since the whole cog theory is legally pointless and therefore it does not matter at all what order of magnitude is assigned to the "cog" named Eichmann. In its judgment the court naturally conceded that such a crime could be committed only by a giant bureaucracy using the resources of government. But insofar as it remains a crime—and that, of course, is the premise for a trial—all the cogs in the machinery, no matter how insignificant, are in court forthwith transformed back into perpetrators, that is to say, into human beings. If the defendant excuses himself on the ground that he acted not as a man but as a mere functionary whose functions could just as easily have been carried out by anyone else, it is as if a criminal pointed to the statistics on crime—which set forth that so-and-so many crimes per day are committed in such-and-such a place—and declared that he only did what was statistically expected, that it was mere accident that he did it and not somebody else, since after all somebody had to do it.

Of course it is important to the political and social sciences that the essence of totalitarian government, and perhaps the nature of every bureaucracy, is to make functionaries and mere cogs in the administrative machinery out of men, and thus to dehumanize them. And one can debate long and profitably on the rule of Nobody, which is what the political form known as bureau-cracy truly is. Only one must realize clearly that the administration of justice can consider these factors only to the extent that they are circumstances of the crime—just as, in a case of theft, the economic plight of the thief is taken into account without excusing the theft, let alone wiping it off the slate. True, we have become very much accustomed by modern psychology and sociology, not to speak of modern bureaucracy, to explaining away the responsibility of the doer for his deed in terms of this or that kind of determinism. Whether such seemingly deeper explanations of human actions are right or wrong is debatable. But what is not debatable is that no judicial procedure would be possible on the basis of them, and that the administration of justice, measured by such theories, is an extremely unmodern, not to say outmoded, institution. When Hitler said that a day would come in Germany when it would be considered a "disgrace" to be a jurist, he was speaking with utter consistency of his dream of a perfect bureaucracy.

As far as I can see, jurisprudence has at its disposal for treating this whole battery of questions only two categories, both of which, to my mind, are quite inadequate to deal with the matter. These are the concepts of "acts of state" and of acts "on superior orders." At any rate, these are the only categories in terms of which such matters are discussed in this kind of trial, usually on the motion of the defendant. The theory of the act of state is based on the argument that one sovereign state may not sit in judgment upon another, *par in parem non habet jurisdictionem*. Practically speaking, this argument had already been disposed of at Nuremberg; it stood no chance from the start, since, if it were accepted, even Hitler, the only one who was really responsible in the full sense, could not have been brought to account—a state of affairs which would have violated the most elementary sense of justice. However, an argument that stands no chance on the practical plane has not necessarily been demolished on the theoretical one. The usual evasions—that Germany at the time of the Third Reich was dominated by a gang of criminals to whom sovereignty and parity cannot very well be ascribed—were hardly useful. For on the one hand everyone knows that the analogy with a gang of criminals is applicable only to such a limited extent that it is not really applicable at all, and on the other hand these crimes undeniably took place within a "legal" order. That, indeed, was their outstanding characteristic.

Perhaps we can approach somewhat closer to the matter if we realize that back of the concept of act of state stands the theory of *raison d'état.* According to that theory, the actions of the state, which is responsible for the life of the country and thus also for the laws obtaining in it, are not subject to the same rules as the acts of the citizens of the country. Just as the rule of law, although devised to eliminate violence and the war of all against all, always stands in need of the instruments of violence in order to assure its own existence, so a government may find itself compelled to commit actions that are generally regarded as crimes in order to assure its own survival and the survival of lawfulness. Wars are frequently justified on these grounds, but criminal acts of state do not occur only in the field of international relations, and the history of civilized nations knows many examples of them—from Napoleon's assassination of the Duc d'Enghien, to the murder of the Socialist leader Matteotti, for which Mussolini himself was presumably responsible.

Raison d'état appeals—rightly or wrongly, as the case may be—to *necessity,* and the state crimes committed in its name (which are fully criminal in terms of the dominant legal system of the country where they occur) are considered emergency measures, concessions made to the stringencies of *Realpolitik,* in order to preserve power and thus assure the continuance of the existing legal order as a whole. In a normal political and legal system, such crimes occur as an exception to the rule and are not subject to legal penalty (are *gerichtsfrei,* as German legal theory expresses it) because the existence of the state itself is at stake, and no outside political entity has the right to deny a state its existence or prescribe how it is to preserve it. However—as we may have learned from the history of Jewish policy in the Third Reich—in a state founded upon criminal principles, the situation is reversed. Then a non-criminal act (such as, for example, Himmler's order in the late summer of 1944 to halt the deportation of Jews) becomes a concession to necessity imposed by reality, in this case the impending defeat. Here the question arises: what is the nature of the sovereignty of such an entity? Has it not violated the parity (*par in parem non habet jurisdictionem*) which international law accords it? Does the *"par in parem"* signify no more than the paraphernalia of sovereignty? Or does it also imply a substantive equality or likeness? Can we apply the same principle that is applied to a governmental apparatus in which crime and violence are exceptions and borderline cases to a political order in which crime is legal and the rule?

Just how inadequate juristic concepts really are to deal with the criminal facts which were the subject matter of all these trials appears perhaps even more strikingly in the concept of acts performed on superior orders. The Jerusalem court countered the argument advanced by the defense with lengthy quotations from the penal and military lawbooks of civilized countries, particularly of Germany; for under Hitler the pertinent articles had by no means been repealed. All of them agree on one point: manifestly criminal orders must not be obeyed. The court, moreover, referred to a case that came up in Israel several years ago: soldiers were brought to trial for having massacred the civilian inhabitants of an Arab village on the border shortly before the beginning of the Sinai campaign. The villagers had been found outside their houses during a military curfew of which, it appeared, they were unaware. Unfortunately, on closer examination the comparison appears to be defective on two accounts. First of all, we must again consider that the relationship of exception and rule, which is of prime importance for recognizing the criminality of an order executed by a subordinate, was reversed in the case of Eichmann's actions. Thus, on the basis of this argument one could actually defend Eichmann's failure to obey certain of Himmler's orders, or his obeying them with hesitancy: they were manifest exceptions to the prevailing rule. The judgment found this to be especially incriminating to the defendant, which was certainly very understandable but not very consistent. This can easily be seen from the pertinent findings of Israeli military courts, which were cited in support by the judges. They ran as follows: the order to be disobeyed must be "manifestly unlawful"; unlawfulness "should fly like a black flag above [it], as a warning reading, 'Prohibited.' " In other words, the order, to be recognized by the soldier as "manifestly unlawful," must violate by its unusualness the canons of the legal system to which he is accustomed. And Israeli jurisprudence in these matters coincides completely with that of other countries. No doubt in formulating these articles the legislators were thinking of cases in which an officer who suddenly goes mad, say, commands his subordinates to kill another officer. In any normal trial of such a case, it would at once become clear that the soldier was not being asked to consult the voice of conscience, or a "feeling of lawfulness that lies deep within every human conscience, also of those who are not conversant with books of law . . . provided the eye is not blind and the heart is not stony and corrupt." Rather, the soldier would be expected to be able to distinguish between a rule and a striking exception to the rule. The German military code, at any rate, explicitly states that conscience is not enough. Paragraph 48 reads: "Punishability of an action or omission is not excluded on the ground that the person considered his behavior required by his conscience or the prescripts of his religion." A striking feature of the Israeli court's line of argument is that the concept of a sense of justice grounded in the depths of every man is presented solely as a substitute for familiarity with the law. Its plausibility rests on the assumption that the law expresses only what every man's conscience would tell him anyhow.

If we are to apply this whole reasoning to the Eichmann case in a meaningful way, we are forced to conclude that Eichmann acted fully within the framework of the kind of judgment required of him: he acted in accordance with the rule, examined the order issued to him for its "manifest" legality, namely regularity; he did not have to fall back upon his "conscience," since he was not one of those who were unfamiliar with the laws of his country. The exact opposite was the case.

The second account on which the argument based on comparison proved to be defective concerns the practice of the courts of admitting the plea of "superior orders" as important extenuating circumstances, and this practice was mentioned explicitly by the judgment. The judgment cited the case I have mentioned above, that of the massacre of the Arab inhabitants at Kfar Kassem, as proof that Israeli jurisdiction does not clear a defendant of responsibility for the "superior orders" he received. And it is true, the Israeli soldiers were indicted for murder, but "superior orders" constituted so weighty an argument for mitigating circumstances that they were sentenced to relatively short prison terms. To be sure, this case concerned an isolated act, not—as in Eichmann's case—an activity extending over years, in which crime followed crime. Still, it was undeniable that he had always acted upon "superior orders," and if the provisions of ordinary Israeli law had been applied to him, it would have been difficult indeed to impose the maximum penalty upon him. The truth of the matter is that Israeli law, in theory and practice, like the jurisdiction of other countries cannot but admit that the fact of "superior orders," even when their unlawfulness is "manifest," can severely disturb the normal working of a man's conscience.

This is only one example among many to demonstrate the inadequacy of the prevailing legal system and of current juridical concepts to deal with the facts of administrative massacres organized by the state apparatus. If we look more closely into the matter we will observe without much difficulty that the judges in all these trials really passed judgment solely on the basis of the monstrous deeds. In other words, they judged freely, as it were, and did not really lean on the standards and legal precedents with which they more or less convincingly sought to justify their decisions. That was already evident in Nuremberg, where the judges on the one hand declared that the "crime against peace" was the gravest of all the crimes they had to deal with, since it included all the other crimes, but on the other hand actually imposed the death penalty only on those defendants who had participated in the new crime of administrative massacre—supposedly a less grave offense than conspiracy against peace. It would indeed be tempting to pursue these and similar inconsistencies in a field so obsessed with consistency as jurisprudence. But of course that cannot be done here.

There remains, however, one fundamental problem, which was implicitly present in all these postwar trials and which must be mentioned here because it touches upon one of the central moral questions of all time, namely upon the nature and function of human judgment. What we have demanded in these trials, where the defendants had committed "legal" crimes, is that human beings be capable of telling right from wrong even when all they have to guide them is their own judgment, which, moreover, happens to be completely at odds with what they must regard as the unanimous opinion of all those around them. And this question is all the more serious as we know that the few who were "arrogant" enough to trust only their own judgment were by no means identical with those persons who continued to abide by old values, or who were guided by a religious belief. Since the whole of respectable society had in one way or another succumbed to Hitler, the moral maxims which determine social behavior and the religious commandments—"Thou shalt not kill!"—which guide conscience had virtually vanished. Those few who were still able to tell right from wrong went really only by their own judgments, and they did so freely; there were no rules to be abided by, under which the particular cases with which they were confronted could be subsumed. They had to decide each instance as it arose, because no rules existed for the unprecedented.

How troubled men of our time are by this question of judgment (or, as is often said, by people who dare "sit in judgment") has emerged in the controversy over the present book, as well as the in many respects similar controversy over Hochhuth's *The Deputy*. What has come to light is neither nihilism nor cynicism, as one might have expected, but a quite extraordinary confusion over elementary questions of morality—as if an instinct in such matters were truly the last thing to be taken for granted in our time. The many curious notes that have been struck in the course of these disputes seem particularly revealing. Thus, some American literati have professed their naïve belief that temptation and coercion are really the same thing, that no one can be asked to resist temptation. (If someone puts a pistol to your heart and orders you to shoot your best friend, then you simply *must* shoot him. Or, as it was argued—some years ago in connection with the quiz program scandal in which a university teacher had hoaxed the public—when so much money is at stake, who could possibly resist?) The argument that we cannot judge if we were not present and involved ourselves seems to convince everyone everywhere, although it seems obvious that if it were true, neither the administration of justice nor the writing of history would ever be possible. In contrast to these confusions, the reproach of self-righteousness raised against those who do judge is age-old; but that does not make it any the more valid. Even the judge who condemns a murderer can still say when he goes home: "And there, but for the grace of God, go I." All German Jews unanimously have condemned the wave of coordination which passed over the German people in 1933 and from one day to the next turned the Jews into pariahs. Is it conceivable that none of them ever asked himself how many of his own group would have done just the same if only they had been allowed to? But is their condemnation today any the less correct for that reason?

The reflection that you yourself might have done wrong under the same circumstances may kindle a spirit of forgiveness, but those who today refer to Christian charity seem strangely confused on this issue too. Thus we can read in the postwar statement of the *Evangelische Kirche in Deutschland,* the Protestant church, as follows: "We aver that before the God of Mercy we share in the guilt for the outrage committed against the Jews by our own people through omission and silence."★ It seems to me that a Christian is guilty before the God of *Mercy* if he repays evil with evil, hence that the churches would have sinned against mercy if millions of Jews had been killed as punishment for some evil they committed. But if the churches shared in the guilt for an outrage pure and simple, as they themselves attest, then the matter must still be considered to fall within the purview of the God of *Justice.*

This slip of the tongue, as it were, is no accident. Justice, but not mercy, is a matter of judgment, and about nothing does public opinion everywhere seem to be in happier agreement than that no one has the right to judge somebody else. What public opinion permits us to judge and even to condemn are trends, or whole groups of people—the larger the better—in short, something so general that distinctions can no longer be made, names no longer be named. Needless to add, this taboo applies doubly when the deeds or words of famous people or men in high position are being questioned. This is currently expressed in high-flown assertions that it is "superficial" to insist on details and to mention individuals, whereas it is the sign of sophistication to speak in generalities according to

---

★ Quoted from the minister Aurel v. Jüchen in an anthology of critical reviews of Hochhuth's play—*Summa Iniuria,* Rowohl Verlag, p. 195.

which all cats are gray and we are all equally guilty. Thus the charge Hochhuth has raised against a single Pope—one man, easily identifiable, with a name of his own—was immediately countered with an indictment of all Christianity. The charge against Christianity in general, with its two thousand years of history, cannot be proved, and if it could be proved, it would be horrible. No one seems to mind this so long as no *person* is involved, and it is quite safe to go one step further and to maintain: "Undoubtedly there is reason for grave accusations, but the defendant is *mankind* as a whole." (Thus Robert Weltsch in *Summa Iniuria,* quoted above, italics added.)

Another such escape from the area of ascertainable facts and personal responsibility are the countless theories, based on nonspecific, abstract, hypothetical assumptions—from the *Zeitgeist* down to the Oedipus complex—which are so general that they explain and justify every event and every deed: no alternative to what actually happened is even considered and no person could have acted differently from the way he did act. Among the constructs that "explain" everything by obscuring all details, we find such notions as a "ghetto mentality" among European Jews; or the collective guilt of the German people, derived from an *ad hoc* interpretation of their history; or the equally absurd assertion of a kind of collective innocence of the Jewish people. All these clichés have in common that they make judgment superfluous and that to utter them is devoid of all risk. And although we can understand the reluctance of those immediately affected by the disaster—Germans and Jews—to examine too closely the conduct of groups and persons that seemed to be or should have been unimpaired by the totality of the moral collapse—that is, the conduct of the Christian churches, the Jewish leadership, the men of the anti-Hitler conspiracy of July 20, 1944—this understandable disinclination is insufficient to explain the reluctance evident everywhere to make judgments in terms of individual moral responsibility.

Many people today would agree that there is no such thing as collective guilt or, for that matter, collective innocence, and that if there were, no one person could ever be guilty or innocent, This, of course, is not to deny that there is such a thing as *political* responsibility which, however, exists quite apart from what the individual member of the group has done and therefore can neither be judged in moral terms nor be brought before a criminal court. Every government assumes political responsibility for the deeds and misdeeds of its predecessor and every nation for the deeds and misdeeds of the past. When Napoleon, seizing power in France after the Revolution, said: I shall assume the responsibility for everything France ever did from Saint Louis to the Committee of Public Safety, he was only stating somewhat emphatically one of the basic facts of all political life. It means hardly more, generally speaking, than that every generation, by virtue of being born into a historical continuum, is burdened by the sins of the fathers as it is blessed with the deeds of the ancestors. But this kind of responsibility is not what we are talking about here; it is not personal, and only in a metaphorical sense can one say he *feels* guilty for what not he but his father or his people have done. (Morally speaking, it is hardly less wrong to feel guilty without having done something specific than it is to feel free of all guilt if one is actually guilty of something.) It is quite conceivable that certain political responsibilities among nations might some day be adjudicated in an international court; what is inconceivable is that such a court would be a criminal tribunal which pronounces on the guilt or innocence of individuals.

And the question of individual guilt or innocence, the act of meting out justice to both the defendant and the victim, are the only things at stake in a criminal court. The Eichmann trial was no exception, even though the court here was confronted with a crime it could not find in the lawbooks and with a criminal whose like was unknown in any court, at least prior to the Nuremberg Trials. The present report deals with nothing but the extent to which the court in Jerusalem succeeded in fulfilling the demands of justice.

"Holes of Oblivion": The Eichmann Trial and Totalitarianism. From a Letter to Mary McCarthy

September 20, 1963 (New York)

. . . I may add that there are some points in the Report which indeed are in conflict with the book on totalitarianism, but God knows Abel[1] didn't spot them. These points are as follows: *First:* I speak at length in the "Totalitarianism" about the "holes of oblivion." On page 212 of the Eichmann book I say "the holes of oblivion do not exist. Nothing human is that perfect, and there are simply too many people in the world to make oblivion possible. One man will always be left alive to tell the story." *Second:* If one reads the book carefully, one sees that Eichmann was much less influenced by ideology than I assumed in the book on totalitarianism. The impact of ideology upon the individual may have been overrated by me. Even in the totalitarianism book, in the chapter on ideology and terror, I mention the curious loss of ideological content that occurs among the elite of the movement. The movement itself becomes all important; the content of anti-semitism [*sic*] for instance gets lost in the extermination policy, for extermination would not have come to an end when no Jew was left to be killed. In other words, extermination per se is more important than anti-semitism or racism. *Third,* and perhaps most importantly, the very phrase: "Banality of Evil" stands in contrast to the phrase I used in the totalitarianism book, "radical evil." This is too difficult a subject to be dealt with here, but it is important.

You write that one hesitates to claim the right to define my ideas. As I see it, there are no "ideas" in this Report, there are only facts with a few conclusions, and these conclusions usually appear at the end of each chapter. The only exception to this is the Epilog, which is a discussion of the legal aspect of the case. In other words, my point would be that what the whole furor is about are *facts,* and neither theories nor ideas. The hostility

---

From Between Friends.

against me is a hostility against someone who tells the truth on a factual level, and not against someone who has ideas which are in conflict with those commonly held.

I am leaving here on the 25th and my address is Quadrangle Club, University of Chicago. [. . .]

I am a little concerned about your health. Take care of yourself and let's see each other soon.

Love, much love
Hannah

This letter was dictated to a so-called bi-lingual secretary. His German *is* good. Forgive me.

Note

1. *Partisan Review* published "The Aesthetics of Evil: Hannah Arendt on Eichmann and the Jews" in its March–April 1963 issue. In it, Lionel Abel charged that Arendt had made Eichmann aesthetically palatable and the Jews aesthetically repugnant. —Carol Brightman

"A Daughter of Our People":
A Response to Gershom Scholem

Gershom Scholem (1897–1982) was a scholar who made a number of pioneering contributions to the study of Jewish mysticism. From 1925, his main academic base was at the Hebrew University of Jerusalem. For an appreciative review of his Major Trends in Jewish Mysticism *(1946 [1941]), see Arendt's "Jewish History, Revised" (1948), published in Feldman,* The Jew as Pariah, *pp. 96–105. Cordial relations between Arendt and Scholem ended with the publication of* Eichmann in Jerusalem.

July 24, 1963 (New York)

DEAR GERHARD,

I found your letter when I got back home a week ago. You know what it's like when one has been away for five months. I'm writing now in the first quiet moment I have; hence my reply may not be as elaborate as perhaps it should be.

There are certain statements in your letter which are not open to controversy, because they are simply false. Let me deal with them first so that we can proceed to matters which merit discussion.

I am not one of the "intellectuals who come from the German Left." You could not have known this, since we did not know each other when we were young. It is a fact of which I am in no way particularly proud and which I am somewhat reluctant to emphasize—especially since the

From "Eichmann in Jerusalem" (an exchange of letters between Gershom Scholem and Hannah Arendt), in Encounter, *January 1964, pp. 51–56. The exchange can be more conveniently found in Ron H. Feldman, ed.,* Hannah Arendt: The Jew as Pariah: Jewish Identity and Politics in the Modern Age *(New York: Grove Press, 1978), pp. 240–51.*

McCarthy era in this country. I came late to an understanding of Marx's importance because I was interested neither in history nor in politics when I was young. If I can be said to "have come from anywhere," it is from the tradition of German philosophy.

As to another statement of yours, I am unfortunately not able to say that you could not have known the facts. I found it puzzling that you should write "I regard you wholly as a daughter of our people, and in no other way." The truth is I have never pretended to be anything else or to be in any way other than I am, and I have never even felt tempted in that direction. It would have been like saying that I was a man and not a woman—that is to say, kind of insane. I know, of course, that there is a "Jewish problem" even on this level, but it has never been my problem—not even in my childhood. I have always regarded my Jewishness as one of the indisputable factual data of my life, and I have never had the wish to change or disclaim facts of this kind. There is such a thing as a basic gratitude for everything that is as it is; for what has been *given* and was not, could not be, *made;* for things that are *physei* and not *nomǭ.* To be sure, such an attitude is pre-political, but in exceptional circumstances—such as the circumstances of Jewish politics—it is bound to have also political consequences though, as it were, in a negative way. This attitude makes certain types of behavior impossible—indeed precisely those which you chose to read into my considerations. (To give another example: In his obituary of Kurt Blumenfeld, Ben-Gurion expressed his regret that Blumenfeld had not seen fit to change his name when he came to live in Israel. Isn't it obvious that Blumenfeld did not do so for exactly the same reasons that had led him in his youth to become a Zionist?) My stand in these matters must surely have been known to you, and it is incomprehensible to me why you should wish to stick a label on me which never fitted in the past and does not fit now.

To come to the point: let me begin, going on from what I have just stated, with what you call "love of the Jewish people" or *Ahabath Israel.* (Incidentally, I would be very grateful if you could tell me since when this concept has played a role in Judaism, when it was first used in Hebrew language and literature, etc.) You are quite right—I am not moved by any "love" of this sort, and for two reasons: I have never in my life "loved" any people or collective—neither the German people, nor the French, nor the American, nor the working class or anything of that sort. I indeed love "only" my friends and the only kind of love I know of and believe in is the love of persons. Secondly, this "love of the Jews" would appear to me, since I am myself Jewish, as something rather suspect. I cannot love myself or anything which I know is part and parcel of my own person. To

clarify this, let me tell you of a conversation I had in Israel with a prominent political personality who was defending the—in my opinion disastrous—non-separation of religion and state in Israel. What he said—I am
not sure of the exact words any more—ran something like this: "You will
understand that, as a Socialist, I, of course, do not believe in God; I believe in the Jewish people." I found this a shocking statement and, being
too shocked, I did not reply at the time. But I could have answered: the
greatness of this people was once that it believed in God, and believed in
Him in such a way that its trust and love towards Him was greater than its
fear. And now this people believes only in itself? What good can come
out of that?—Well, in this sense I do not "love" the Jews, nor do I "believe" in them; I merely belong to them as a matter of course, beyond dispute or argument.

We could discuss the same issue in political terms; and we should
then be driven to a consideration of patriotism. That there can be no patriotism without permanent opposition and criticism is no doubt common
ground between us. But I can admit to you something beyond that,
namely, that wrong done by my own people naturally grieves me more
than wrong done by other peoples. This grief, however, in my opinion is
not for display, even if it should be the innermost motive for certain actions or attitudes. Generally speaking, the role of the "heart" in politics
seems to me altogether questionable. You know as well as I how often
those who merely report certain unpleasant facts are accused of lack of
soul, lack of heart, or lack of what you call *Herzenstakt*. We both know, in
other words, how often these emotions are used in order to conceal factual truth. I cannot discuss here what happens when emotions are displayed in public and become a factor in political affairs; but it is an
important subject, and I have attempted to describe the disastrous results
in my book *On Revolution* in discussing the role of compassion in the formation of the revolutionary character.

It is a pity that you did not read the book before the present campaign of
misrepresentation against it got under way from the side of the Jewish "establishment" in Israel and America. There are, unfortunately, very few
people who are able to withstand the influence of such campaigns. It
seems to me highly unlikely that without being influenced you could possibly have misunderstood certain statements. Public opinion, especially
when it has been carefully manipulated, as in this case, is a very powerful
thing. Thus, I never made Eichmann out to be a "Zionist." If you missed
the irony of the sentence—which was plainly in *oratio obliqua,* reporting
Eichmann's own words—I really can't help it. I can only assure you that

none of dozens of readers who read the book before publication had ever any doubt about the matter. Further, I never asked why the Jews "let themselves be killed." On the contrary, I accused Hausner of having posed this question to witness after witness. There was no people and no group in Europe which reacted differently under the immediate pressure of terror. The question I raised was that of the cooperation of Jewish functionaries during the "Final Solution," and this question is so very uncomfortable because one cannot claim that they were traitors. (There were traitors too, but that is irrelevant.) In other words, until 1939 and even until 1941, whatever Jewish functionaries did or did not do is understandable and excusable. Only later does it become highly problematical. This issue came up during the trial and it was of course my duty to report it. This constitutes our part of the so-called "unmastered past," and although you may be right that it is too early for a "balanced judgment" (though I doubt this), I do believe that we shall only come to terms with this past if we begin to judge and to be frank about it.

I have made my own position plain, and yet it is obvious that you did not understand it. I said that there was no possibility of resistance, but there existed the possibility of *doing nothing*. And in order to do nothing, one did not need to be a saint, one needed only to say: "I am just a simple Jew, and I have no desire to play any other role." Whether these people or some of them, as you indicate, deserved to be hanged is an altogether different question. What needs to be discussed are not the people so much as the arguments with which they justified themselves in their own eyes and in those of others. Concerning these arguments we are entitled to pass judgment. Moreover, we should not forget that we are dealing here with conditions which were terrible and desperate enough, but which were not the conditions of concentration camps. These decisions were made in an atmosphere of terror but not under the immediate pressure and impact of terror. These are important differences in degree, which every student of totalitarianism must know and take into account. These people had still a certain, limited freedom of decision and of action. Just as the SS murderers also possessed, as we now know, a limited choice of alternatives. They could say: "I wish to be relieved of my murderous duties," and nothing happened to them. Since we are dealing in politics with men, and not with heroes or saints, it is this possibility of *"nonparticipation"* (Kirchheimer) that is decisive if we begin to judge, not the system, but the individual, his choices and his arguments.

And the Eichmann trial was concerned with an individual. In my report I have only spoken of things which came up during the trial itself. It is for this reason that I could not mention the "saints" about whom you speak. Instead I had to limit myself to the resistance fighters whose behavior, as I said, was the more admirable because it occurred under circumstances in which resistance had really ceased to be possible. There were no saints among the witnesses for the prosecution, but there was one utterly pure human being, old Grynszpan, whose testimony I therefore reported at some length. On the German side, after all, one could also have mentioned more than the single case of Sergeant Schmidt. But since his was the only case mentioned in the trial, I had to restrict myself to it.

That the distinction between victims and persecutors was blurred in the concentration camps, deliberately and with calculation, is well known, and I as well as others have insisted on this aspect of totalitarian methods. But to repeat: this is not what I mean by a Jewish share in the guilt, or by the totality of the collapse of all standards. This was part of the system and had indeed nothing to do with Jews.

How you could believe that my book was "a mockery of Zionism" would be a complete mystery to me, if I did not know that many people in Zionist circles have become incapable of listening to opinions or arguments which are off the beaten track and not consonant with their ideology. There are exceptions, and a Zionist friend of mine remarked in all innocence that the book, the last chapter in particular (recognition of the competence of the court, the justification of the kidnapping), was very pro-Israel—as indeed it is. What confuses you is that my arguments and my approach are different from what you are used to; in other words, the trouble is that I am independent. By this I mean, on the one hand, that I do not belong to any organization and always speak only for myself, and on the other hand, that I have great confidence in Lessing's *selbstdenken* for which, I think, no ideology, no public opinion, and no "convictions" can ever be a substitute. Whatever objections you may have to the results, you won't understand them unless you realize that they are really my own and nobody else's.

I regret that you did not argue your case against the carrying out of the death sentence. For I believe that in discussing this question we might have made some progress in finding out where our most fundamental differences are located. You say that it was "historically false," and I feel very uncomfortable seeing the spectre of History raised in this context. In my opinion, it was *politically* and *juridically* (and the last is actually all that mattered) not only correct—it would have been utterly impossible not to have carried out the sentence. The only way of avoiding it would have been to accept Karl Jaspers' suggestion and to hand Eichmann over to the

United Nations. Nobody wanted that, and it was probably not feasible; hence there was no alternative left but to hang him. Mercy was out of the question, not on juridical grounds—pardon is anyhow not a prerogative of the juridical system—but because mercy is applicable to the person rather than to the deed; the act of mercy does not forgive murder but pardons the murderer insofar as he, as a person, may be more than anything he ever did. This was not true of Eichmann. And to spare his life without pardoning him was impossible on juridical grounds.

In conclusion, let me come to the only matter where you have not misunderstood me, and where indeed I am glad that you have raised the point. You are quite right: I changed my mind and do no longer speak of "radical evil." It is a long time since we last met, or we would perhaps have spoken about the subject before. (Incidentally, I don't see why you call my term "banality of evil" a catchword or slogan. As far as I know no one has used the term before me; but that is unimportant.) It is indeed my opinion now that evil is never "radical," that it is only extreme, and that it possesses neither depth nor any demonic dimension. It can overgrow and lay waste the whole world precisely because it spreads like a fungus on the surface. It is "thought-defying," as I said, because thought tries to reach some depth, to go to the roots, and the moment it concerns itself with evil, it is frustrated because there is nothing. That is its "banality." Only the good has depth and can be radical. But this is not the place to go into these matters seriously; I intend to elaborate them further in a different context. Eichmann may very well remain the concrete model of what I have to say.

You propose to publish your letter and you ask if I have any objection. My advice would be not to recast the letter in the third person. The value of this controversy consists in its epistolary character, namely in the fact that it is informed by personal friendship. Hence, if you are prepared to publish my answer simultaneously with your letter, I have, of course, no objection.

HANNAH ARENDT

From *The Life of the Mind*

(Volume 1)

THE ANSWER OF SOCRATES

To the question What makes us think? I have been giving (except in Solon's case) historically representative answers offered by professional philosophers. These answers are dubious for precisely that reason. The question, when asked by the professional, does not arise out of his own experiences while engaged in thinking. It is asked from outside—whether that outside is constituted by his professional interests as a thinker or by the common sense in himself that makes him question an activity that is out of order in ordinary living. And the answers we then receive are always too general and vague to have much sense for everyday living, in which thinking, after all, constantly occurs and constantly interrupts the ordinary processes of life—just as ordinary living constantly interrupts thinking. If we strip these answers of their doctrinal content, which of course varies enormously, all we get are confessions of a need: the need to concretize the implications of the Platonic wonder, the need (in Kant) of the reasoning faculty to transcend the limitations of the knowable, the need to become reconciled with what actually is and the course of the world—appearing in Hegel as "the need for philosophy," which can transform occurrences outside yourself into your own thoughts—or the need to search for the meaning of whatever is or occurs, as I have been saying here, no less generally, no less vaguely.

It is this helplessness of the thinking ego to give an account of itself that has made the philosophers, the professional thinkers, such a difficult tribe to deal with. For the trouble is that the thinking ego, as we have seen—in distinction from the self that, of course, exists in every thinker, too—has no urge to appear in the world of appearances. It is a slippery fellow, not only invisible to others but also, for the self, impalpable, impossible to grasp. This is partly because it is sheer activity, and partly because—as Hegel once said—"[as] an abstract ego it is liberated from the particularity of all other properties, dispositions, etc., and is active only with respect to the general, which is the same for all individuals."[1] In any case, seen from the world of appearances, from the marketplace, the thinking ego always lives in hiding, *lathē biōsas*. And our question, What makes us think?, is actually inquiring about ways and means to bring it out of hiding, to tease it, as it were, into manifestation.

The best, in fact the only, way I can think of to get hold of the question is to look for a model, an example of a thinker who was not a professional, who in his person unified two apparently contradictory passions, for thinking and acting—not in the sense of being eager to apply his thoughts or to establish theoretical standards for action but in the much more relevant sense of being equally at home in both spheres and able to move from one sphere to the other with the greatest apparent ease, very much as we ourselves constantly move back and forth between experiences in the world of appearances and the need for reflecting on them. Best suited for this role would be a man who counted himself neither among the many nor among the few (a distinction at least as old as Pythagoras), who had no aspiration to be a ruler of men, no claim even to be particularly well fitted by his superior wisdom to act in an advisory capacity to those in power, but not a man who submitted meekly to being ruled either; in brief, a thinker who always remained a man among men, who did not shun the marketplace, who was a citizen among citizens, doing nothing, claiming nothing except what in his opinion every citizen should be and have a right to. Such a man ought to be difficult to find: if he were able to represent for us the actual thinking activity, he would not have left a body of doctrine behind; he would not have cared to write down his thoughts even if, after he was through with thinking, there had been any residue tangible enough to set out in black and white. You will have guessed that I am thinking of Socrates. We would not know much about him, at least not enough to impress us greatly, if he had not made such an enormous impression on Plato, and we might not know anything about him, perhaps not even from Plato, if he had not decided to lay down his life, not for any specific belief or doctrine—he had none—but simply for the right to go about examining the opinions of other people, thinking about them and asking his interlocutors to do the same.

I hope the reader will not believe that I chose Socrates at random. But I must give a warning: there is a great deal of controversy about the historical Socrates, and though this is one of the more fascinating topics of learned contention, I shall ignore it[2] and only mention in passing what is likely to be the chief bone of contention—namely, my belief that there exists a sharp dividing line between what is authentically Socratic and the philosophy taught by Plato. The stumbling block here is the fact that Plato used Socrates as *the* philosopher, not only in the early and clearly "Socratic" dialogues but also later, when he often made him the spokesman for theories and doctrines that were entirely un-Socratic. In many instances, Plato himself clearly marked the differences, for example, in the *Symposium,* in Diotima's famous speech, which tells us expressly that Socrates does not know anything about the "greater mysteries" and may not be able to understand them. In other instances, however, the line is blurred, usually because Plato could still reckon on a reading public that would be aware of certain enormous inconsistencies—as when he lets Socrates say in the *Theaetetus*[3] that "great philosophers . . . from their youth up have never known the way to the marketplace," an anti-Socratic statement if ever there was one. And yet, to make matters worse, this by no means signifies that the same dialogue does not give fully authentic information about the real Socrates.[4]

No one, I think, will seriously dispute that my choice is historically justifiable. Less easily justifiable, perhaps, is the transformation of a historical figure into a model, for there is no doubt that some transformation is necessary if the figure in question is to perform the function we assign to it. Etienne Gilson, in his great book about Dante, wrote that in *The Divine Comedy* "a character . . . conserves . . . as much of its historical reality as the representative function that Dante assigns to it requires."[5] It seems easy enough to grant this kind of freedom to poets and to call it license— but worse when nonpoets try their hand at it. Yet, justified or not, that is precisely what we do when we construct "ideal types"—not out of whole cloth, as in the allegories and personified abstractions so dear to the hearts of bad poets and some scholars, but out of the crowd of living beings past or present who seem to possess a representative significance. And Gilson hints at least at the true justification of this method (or technique) when he discusses the representative part assigned by Dante to Aquinas: the real Thomas, Gilson points out, would not have done what Dante made him do—eulogize Siger of Brabant—but the only reason that the real Thomas would have declined to pronounce such a eulogy would have been a certain human weakness, a defect of character, "the part of his make-up," as Gilson says, "which he had to leave at the gate of the *Paradiso* before he could enter."[6] There are a number of traits in the Xenophonian Socrates, whose historical credibility need not be doubted, that Socrates might have had to leave at the gate of Paradise.

The first thing that strikes us in Plato's Socratic dialogues is that they are all aporetic. The argument either leads nowhere or goes around in circles.

In order to know what justice is, you must know what knowledge is, and in order to know that, you must have a previous, unexamined notion of knowledge.[7] Hence, "a man cannot try to discover either what he knows or what he does not know. If he knows, there is no need of inquiry; if he does not know . . . he does not even know what he is to look for."[8] Or, in the *Euthyphro:* in order to be pious you must know what piety is. The things that please the gods are pious; but are they pious because they please the gods or do they please the gods because they are pious?

None of the *logoi,* the arguments, ever stays put; they move around. And because Socrates, asking questions to which he does *not* know the answers, sets them in motion, once the statements have come full circle, it is usually Socrates who cheerfully proposes to start all over again and inquire what justice or piety or knowledge or happiness are.[9] For the topics of these early dialogues deal with very simple, everyday concepts, such as arise whenever people open their mouths and begin to talk. The introduction usually runs as follows: to be sure, there are happy people, just deeds, courageous men, beautiful things to see and admire, everybody knows about them; the trouble starts with our nouns, presumably derived from the adjectives we apply to particular cases as they *appear* to us (we *see* a happy man, *perceive* the courageous deed or the just decision). In short, the trouble arrives with such words as *happiness, courage, justice,* and so on, what we now call concepts—Solon's "non-appearing measure" (*aphanes metron*) "most difficult for the mind to comprehend, but nevertheless holding the limits of all things"[10]—and what Plato somewhat later called ideas perceivable only by the eyes of the mind. These words are part and parcel of our everyday speech, and still we can give no account of them; when we try to define them, they get slippery; when we talk about their meaning, nothing stays put any more, everything begins to move. So instead of repeating what we learned from Aristotle, that Socrates was the man who discovered the "concept," we shall ask what Socrates did when he discovered it. For surely these words were part of the Greek language before he tried to force the Athenians and himself to give an account of what they and he meant—in the firm belief, of course, that no speech would be possible without them.

Today that is no longer so certain. Our knowledge of the so-called primitive languages has taught us that the grouping together of many particulars under a name common to all of them is by no means a matter of course; these languages, whose vocabulary is often so remarkably rich, lack such abstract nouns even in relation to clearly visible objects. To simplify matters, let us take a noun which to us no longer sounds abstract at all. We can use the word "house" for a great number of objects—for the mud hut of a tribe, for the palace of a king, the country home of a city dweller, the cottage in the village, the apartment house in town—but we can hardly use it for the movable tents of some nomads. The house in and by itself, *auto kath'auto,* that which makes us use the word for all these particular and very different buildings, is never seen, either by the eyes of the body or by those of the mind; every imagined house, be it ever so abstract, having the bare minimum to make it recognizable, is already a particular house. This other, invisible, house, of which we must have a notion in order to recognize particular buildings as houses, has been explained in different ways and called by different names in the history of philosophy; with this we are not concerned here, although we might find it less hard to define than such words as "happiness" or "justice." The point here is that it implies something considerably less tangible than the structure perceived by our eyes. It implies "housing somebody" and being "dwelt in" as no tent, put up today and taken down tomorrow, could house or serve as a dwelling place. The word "house" is the "unseen measure," "holds the limits of all things" pertaining to dwelling; it is a word that could not exist unless one presupposed thinking about being housed, dwelling, having a home. As a word, "house" is shorthand for all these things, the kind of shorthand without which thinking and its characteristic swiftness would not be possible at all. *The word* "house" *is something like a frozen thought that thinking must unfreeze* whenever it wants to find out the original meaning. In medieval philosophy, this kind of thinking was called "meditation," and the word should be heard as different from, even opposed to, contemplation. At all events, this kind of pondering reflection does not produce definitions and in that sense is entirely without results, though somebody who had pondered the meaning of "house" might make his own look better.

Socrates, at any rate, is commonly said to have believed in the teachability of virtue, and he seems indeed to have held that talking and thinking about piety, justice, courage, and the rest were likely to make men more pious, more just, more courageous, despite the fact that neither definitions nor "values" were given them to direct their future conduct. What Socrates actually believed in such matters can best be illustrated by the similes he applied to himself. He called himself a gadfly and a midwife; in Plato's account somebody else called him an "electric ray," a fish that paralyzes and numbs by contact, and Socrates recognized the likeness as apt, provided that his hearers understood that "the electric ray paralyzes others only through being paralyzed itself. . . . It isn't that, knowing the answers myself, I perplex other people. The truth is rather that I infect them also with the perplexity I feel myself."[11] Which, of course, sums up neatly the only way thinking can be taught—even though Socrates, as he repeatedly said, did not teach anything, for the simple reason that he had nothing to teach; he was "sterile" like the midwives in Greece, who were beyond the age of childbearing. (Since he had nothing to teach, no truth to hand out, he was accused of never revealing his own view [*gnōmē*]—as we learn from Xenophon, who defended him against the charge.)[12] It seems that he, unlike the professional philosophers, felt the urge to check with his fellow-men to learn whether his perplexities were shared by them—and this is quite different from the inclination to find solutions for riddles and then demonstrate them to others.

Let us look briefly at the three similes. First, Socrates is a gadfly: he knows how to sting the citizens who, without him, will "sleep on undisturbed for the rest of their lives" unless somebody comes along to arouse them. And what does he arouse them to? To thinking and examination, an activity without which life, in his view, was not only not worth much but was not fully alive. (On this subject, in the *Apology* as in other cases, Socrates is saying very nearly the opposite of what Plato made him say in the "improved apology" of the *Phaedo*. In the *Apology*, Socrates tells his fellow-citizens why he should live and also why, though life is "very dear" to him, he is not afraid of death; in the *Phaedo*, he explains to his friends how burdensome life is and why he is glad to die.)

Second, Socrates is a midwife: in the *Theaetetus*, he says that it is because he is sterile himself that he knows how to deliver others of their thoughts; moreover, thanks to his sterility, he has the expert knowledge of the midwife and can decide whether the child is a real child or a mere wind-egg of which the bearer must be cleansed. But in the dialogues, hardly anybody among Socrates' interlocutors has brought forth a thought that is not a wind-egg and that Socrates considered worth keeping alive. Rather, he did what Plato in the *Sophist*, certainly thinking of Socrates, said of the sophists: he purged people of their "opinions," that is, of those unexamined pre-judgments that would prevent them from thinking— helping them, as Plato said, to get rid of the bad in them, their opinions, yet without making them good, giving them truth.[13]

Third, Socrates, knowing that we do not know, and nevertheless unwilling to let it go at that, remains steadfast in his own perplexities and, like the electric ray, paralyzed himself, paralyzes anyone he comes into contact with. The electric ray, at first glance, seems to be the opposite of the gadfly; it paralyzes where the gadfly rouses. Yet what cannot fail to look like paralysis from the outside—from the standpoint of ordinary human affairs—is *felt* as the highest state of being active and alive. There exist, despite the scarcity of documentary evidence about the thinking experience, a number of utterances of thinkers throughout the centuries to bear this out.

Hence, Socrates, gadfly, midwife, electric ray, is not a philosopher (he teaches nothing and has nothing to teach) and he is not a sophist, for he does not claim to make men wise. He only points out to them that they are not wise, that nobody is—a "pursuit" keeping him so busy that he has no time for either public or private affairs.[14] And while he defends himself vigorously against the charge of corrupting the young, he nowhere pretends that he is improving them. Nevertheless, he claims that the appearance in Athens of thinking and examining represented in himself was the greatest good that ever befell the City.[15] Thus he was concerned with what thinking is good for, although, in this, as in all other respects, he did not give a clear-cut answer. We may be sure that a dialogue dealing with the question What is thinking good for? would have ended in the same perplexities as all the others.

If there had been a Socratic tradition in Western thought, if, in Whitehead's words, the history of philosophy were a collection of footnotes not to Plato but to Socrates (which, of course, would have been impossible), we certainly would find in it no answer to our question, but at least a number of variations of it. Socrates himself, well aware that he was dealing with invisibles in his enterprise, used a metaphor to explain the thinking activity—the metaphor of the wind: "The winds themselves are invisible, yet what they do is manifest to us and we somehow feel their approach."[16] We find the same metaphor in Sophocles, who (in the *Antigone*),[17] counts "wind-swift thought" among the dubious, "awe-inspiring" (*deina*) things with which men are blessed or cursed. In our own time, Heidegger occasionally speaks of the "storm of thought," and he uses the metaphor explicitly at the only point in his work where he speaks directly of Socrates: "Throughout his life and up to his very death Socrates did nothing other than place himself in this draft, this current [of thinking], and maintain himself in it. This is why he is the purest of the West. This is why he wrote nothing. For anyone who begins, out of thinking, to write must inevitably be like those people who run for shelter from a wind too strong for them . . . all thinkers after Socrates, their greatness notwithstanding, were such refugees. Thinking became literature." In a later explanatory note he adds that to be the "purest" thinker does not mean to be the greatest.[18]

In the context in which Xenophon, always anxious to defend the master with his own vulgar arguments against vulgar accusations, mentions this metaphor, it does not make much sense. Still, even he indicates that the invisible wind of thought was manifest in the concepts, virtues, and "values" with which Socrates dealt in his examinations. The trouble is that this same wind, whenever it is roused, has the peculiarity of doing away with its own previous manifestations: this is why the same man can be understood and understand himself as gadfly as well as electric ray. It is in this invisible element's nature to undo, unfreeze, as it were, what language, the medium of thinking, has frozen into thought—words (concepts, sentences, definitions, doctrines) whose "weakness" and inflexibility Plato denounces so splendidly in the *Seventh Letter*. The consequence is that thinking inevitably has a destructive, undermining effect on all established criteria, values, measurements of good and evil, in short, on those customs and rules of conduct we treat of in morals and ethics. These frozen thoughts, Socrates seems to say, come so handily that you can use them in your sleep; but if the wind of thinking, which I shall now stir in you, has shaken you from your sleep and made you fully awake and alive, then you will see that you have nothing in your grasp but perplexities, and the best we can do with them is share them with each other.

Hence, the paralysis induced by thinking is twofold: it is inherent in the *stop* and think, the interruption of all other activities—psychologically, one may indeed define a "problem" as a "situation which for some reason appreciably holds up an organism in its effort to reach a goal"[19]—and it also may have a dazing after-effect, when you come out of it, feeling unsure of what seemed to you beyond doubt while you were unthinkingly engaged in whatever you were doing. If what you were doing consisted in applying general rules of conduct to particular cases as they arise in ordinary life, you will find yourself paralyzed because no such rules can withstand the wind of thought. To take again the example of the frozen thought inherent in the word "house," once you have thought about its implied meaning—dwelling, having a home, being housed—you are no longer as likely to accept for your own home whatever the fashion of the time may prescribe; but this by no means guarantees that you will be able to come up with an acceptable solution to what has become "problematic."

This leads to the last and, perhaps, even greatest danger of this dangerous and profitless enterprise. In the circle around Socrates, there were men like Alcibiades and Critias—God knows, by no means the worst among his so-called pupils—who had turned out to be a real threat to the polis, and this not because they had been paralyzed by the electric ray but, on the contrary, because they had been aroused by the gadfly. What they had been aroused to was license and cynicism. Not content with being taught how to think without being taught a doctrine, they changed the non-results of the Socratic thinking examination into negative results: If we cannot define what piety is, let us be impious—which is pretty much the opposite of what Socrates had hoped to achieve by talking about piety.

The quest for meaning, which relentlessly dissolves and examines anew all accepted doctrines and rules, can at any moment turn against itself, produce a reversal of the old values, and declare these contraries to be "new values." To a certain extent, this is what Nietzsche did when he reversed Platonism, forgetting that a reversed Plato is still Plato, or what Marx did when he turned Hegel upside down, producing a strictly Hegelian system of history in the process. Such negative results of thinking will then be used with the same unthinking routine as before; the moment they are applied to the realm of human affairs, it is as though they had never gone through the thinking process. What we commonly call "nihilism"—and are tempted to date historically, decry politically, and ascribe to thinkers who allegedly dared to think "dangerous thoughts"—is actually a danger inherent in the thinking activity itself. There are no dangerous thoughts; thinking itself is dangerous, but nihilism is not its product. Nihilism is but the other side of conventionalism; its creed consists of negations of the current so-called positive values, to which it remains bound. All critical examinations must go through a stage of at least hypothetically negating accepted opinions and "values" by searching out their implications and tacit assumptions, and in this sense nihilism may be seen as an ever-present danger of thinking.

But that danger does not arise out of the Socratic conviction that an unexamined life is not worth living, but, on the contrary, out of the desire to find results that would make further thinking unnecessary. Thinking is equally dangerous to all creeds and, by itself, does not bring forth any new creed. Its most dangerous aspect from the viewpoint of common sense is that what was meaningful while you were thinking dissolves the moment you want to apply it to everyday living. When common opinion gets hold of the "concepts," that is, the manifestations of thinking in everyday speech, and begins to handle them as though they were the results of cognition, the end can only be a clear demonstration that no man is wise. Practically, thinking means that each time you are confronted with some difficulty in life you have to make up your mind anew.

However, non-thinking, which seems so recommendable a state for political and moral affairs, also has its perils. By shielding people from the dangers of examination, it teaches them to hold fast to whatever the prescribed rules of conduct may be at a given time in a given society. What people then get used to is less the content of the rules, a close examination of which would always lead them into perplexity, than the *possession* of rules under which to subsume particulars. If somebody appears who, for whatever purposes, wishes to abolish the old "values" or virtues, he will find that easy enough, provided he offers a new code, and he will need relatively little force and no persuasion—i.e., proof that the new values are better than the old—to impose it. The more firmly men hold to the old code, the more eager will they be to assimilate themselves to the new one, which in practice means that the readiest to obey will be those who were the most respectable pillars of society, the least likely to indulge in thoughts, dangerous or otherwise, while those who to all appearances were the most unreliable elements of the old order will be the least tractable.

If ethical and moral matters really are what the etymology of the words indicates, it should be no more difficult to change the mores and habits of a people than it would be to change their table manners. The ease with which such a reversal can take place under certain conditions suggests indeed that everybody was fast asleep when it occurred. I am alluding, of course, to what happened in Nazi Germany and, to some extent, also in Stalinist Russia, when suddenly the basic commandments of Western morality were reversed: in one case, "Thou shalt not kill"; in the other, "Thou shalt not bear false witness against thy neighbor." And the sequel—the reversal of the reversal, the fact that it was so surprisingly easy "to re-educate" the Germans after the collapse of the Third Reich, so easy indeed that it was as though re-education was automatic—should not console us either. It was actually the same phenomenon.

To come back to Socrates. The Athenians told him that thinking was subversive, that the wind of thought was a hurricane sweeping away all the established signs by which men orient themselves, bringing disorder into the cities and confusing the citizens. And though Socrates denies that thinking corrupts, he does not pretend that it improves anybody either. It rouses you from sleep, and this seems to him a great good for the City. Yet he does not say that he began his examining in order to become such a great benefactor. As far as he himself is concerned, there is nothing more to be said than that life deprived of thought would be meaningless, even though thought will never make men wise or give them the answers to thought's own question. The meaning of what Socrates was doing lay in the activity itself. Or to put it differently: To think and to be fully alive are the same, and this implies that thinking must always begin afresh; it is an activity that accompanies living and is concerned with such concepts as justice, happiness, virtue, offered us by language itself as expressing the meaning of whatever happens in life and occurs to us while we are alive.

What I called the "quest" for meaning appears in Socrates' language as love, that is, love in its Greek significance of *Erōs,* not the Christian *agapē.* Love as Eros is primarily a need; it desires what it has not. Men love wisdom and therefore begin to philosophize because they are not wise, and they love beauty, and do beauty, as it were—*philokaloumen,* as Pericles called it in the Funeral Oration[20]—because they are not beautiful. Love is the only matter in which Socrates pretends to be an expert, and this skill guides him, too, in choosing his companions and friends: "While I may be worthless in all other matters, this talent I have been given: I can easily recognize a lover and a beloved."[21] By desiring what it has not, love establishes a relationship with what is not present. In order to bring this relationship into the open, make it appear, men want to speak about it—just as the lover wants to speak about the beloved. Because thought's quest is a kind of desirous love, the objects of thought can only be lovable things—beauty, wisdom, justice, and so on. Ugliness and evil are almost by definition excluded from the thinking concern. They may turn up as deficiencies, ugliness consisting in lack of beauty, evil, *kakia,* in lack of the good. As such, they have no roots of their own, no essence that thought could get hold of. If thinking dissolves positive concepts into their original meaning, then the same process must dissolve these "negative" concepts into their original meaninglessness, that is, into nothing for the thinking ego. That is why Socrates believed no one could do evil voluntarily—because of, as we would say, its ontological status: it consists in an absence, in something that is not. And that is also why Democritus, who thought of *logos,* speech, as following action in the same way that the shadow accompanies all real things, thus distinguishing them from mere semblances, counseled against speaking of evil deeds: ignoring evil, depriving it of any manifestation in speech, will turn it into a mere semblance, something that has no shadow.[22] We found the same exclusion of evil when we were following Plato's admiring, affirming wonder as it unfolds into thinking; it is found in almost all Occidental philosophers. It looks as though Socrates had nothing more to say about the connection between evil and lack of thought than that people who are not in love with beauty, justice, and wisdom are incapable of thought, just as, conversely, those who are in love with examining and thus "do philosophy" would be incapable of doing evil.

THE TWO-IN-ONE

. . . Nothing perhaps indicates more strongly that man exists *essentially* in the plural than that his solitude actualizes his merely being conscious of himself, which we probably share with the higher animals, into a duality during the thinking activity. It is this *duality* of myself with myself that makes thinking a true activity, in which I am both the one who asks and the one who answers. Thinking can become dialectical and critical because it goes through this questioning and answering process, through the dialogue of *dialegesthai,* which actually is a "traveling through words," a *poreuesthai dia tōn logōn,*[23] whereby we constantly raise the basic Socratic question: *What do you mean when you say* . . . ? except that this *legein,* saying, is soundless and therefore so swift that its dialogical structure is somewhat difficult to detect.

The criterion of the mental dialogue is no longer truth, which would compel answers to the questions I raise with myself, either in the mode of Intuition, which compels with the force of sense evidence, or as necessary conclusions of reckoning with consequences in mathematical or logical reasoning, which rely on the structure of our brain and compel with its natural power. The only criterion of Socratic thinking is agreement, to be consistent with oneself, *homologein autos heautō;*[24] its opposite, to be in contradiction with oneself, *enantia legein autos heautō,*[25] actually means becoming one's own adversary. Hence Aristotle, in his earliest formulation of the famous axiom of contradiction, says explicitly that this is axiomatic: "we must necessarily believe it because . . . it is addressed not to the outward word [*exō logos,* that is, to the spoken word addressed to someone else, an interlocutor who may be either friend or adversary] but to the discourse *within the soul,* and though we can always raise objections to the outward word, to the *inward discourse* we cannot always object," because here the partner is oneself, and I cannot possibly want to become my own adversary.[26] (In this instance, we can watch how such an insight, won from the factual experience of the thinking ego, gets lost when it is generalized into a philosophical doctrine—"A cannot be both B and A under the same conditions and at the same time"—for we find the transformation being achieved by Aristotle himself when he discusses the same matter in his *Metaphysics.*[27])

A close reading of the *Organon,* the "Instrument," as the collection of Aristotle's early logical treatises has been called since the sixth century, clearly shows that what we now call "logic" was by no means originally meant as an "instrument of thought," of the inward discourse carried on "within the soul," but was designed as the science of correct talking and arguing when we are trying to convince others or give an account of what we state, always starting, as Socrates did, with premises most likely to be agreed on by most men or by most of those generally believed to be the wisest. In the early treatises, the axiom of non-contradiction, decisive only for the inward dialogue of thinking, has not yet been established as the most basic rule for discourse in general. Only after this special case had become the guiding example for all thought could Kant, who in his *Anthropology* had defined thinking as "talking with oneself . . . hence also inwardly listening,"[28] count the injunction "Always think consistently, in agreement with yourself" (*"Jederzeit mit sich selbst einstimmig denken"*) among the maxims that must be regarded as "unchangeable commandments for the class of thinkers."[29]

In brief, the specifically human actualization of consciousness in the thinking dialogue between me and myself suggests that difference and otherness, which are such outstanding characteristics of the world of appearances as it is given to man for his habitat among a plurality of things, are the very conditions for the existence of man's mental ego as well, for this ego actually exists only in duality. And this ego—the I-am-I—experiences difference in identity precisely when it is not related to the things that appear but only related to itself. (This original duality, incidentally, explains the futility of the fashionable search for identity. Our modern identity crisis could be resolved only by never being alone and never trying to think.) Without that original split, Socrates' statement about harmony in a being that to all appearances is One would be meaningless.

Consciousness is not the same as thinking; acts of consciousness have in common with sense experience the fact that they are "intentional" and therefore *cognitive* acts, whereas the thinking ego does not think something but *about* something, and this act is dialectical: it proceeds in the form of a silent dialogue. Without consciousness in the sense of self-awareness, thinking would not be possible. What thinking actualizes in its unending process is difference, given as a mere raw fact (*factum brutum*) in consciousness; only in this humanized form does consciousness then become the outstanding characteristic of somebody who is a man and neither a god nor an animal. As the metaphor bridges the gap between the world of appearances and the mental activities going on within it, so the Socratic two-in-one heals the solitariness of thought; its inherent duality points to the infinite plurality which is the law of the earth.

To Socrates, the duality of the two-in-one meant no more than that if you want to think, you must see to it that the two who carry on the dialogue be in good shape, that the partners be *friends*. The partner who comes to life when you are alert and alone is the only one from whom you can never get away—except by ceasing to think. It is better to suffer wrong than to do wrong, because you can remain the friend of the sufferer; who would want to be the friend of and have to live together with a murderer? Not even another murderer. In the end, it is to this rather simple consideration of the importance of agreement between you and yourself that Kant's Categorical Imperative appeals. Underlying the imperative, "Act only on that maxim through which you can at the same time *will* that it should become a universal law,"[30] is the command "Do not contradict yourself." A murderer or a thief cannot will that "Thou shalt kill" and "Thou shalt steal" be general laws, since he naturally fears for his own life and property. If you make yourself an exception, you have contradicted yourself.

In one of the contested dialogues, the *Hippias Major,* which even if not by Plato may still give authentic testimony about Socrates, Socrates describes the situation simply and accurately. It is the end of the dialogue, the moment of going home. He tells Hippias, who has shown himself to be an especially thickheaded partner, how "blissfully fortunate" he is in comparison with poor Socrates, who at home is awaited by a very obnoxious fellow who always cross-examines him. "He is a close relative and lives in the same house." When he now will hear Socrates give utterance to Hippias' opinions, he will ask "whether he is not ashamed of talking about a beautiful way of life, when questioning makes it evident that he does not even know the meaning of the word 'beauty.' "[31] When Hippias goes home, he remains one, for, though he lives alone, he does not seek to keep himself company. He certainly does not lose consciousness; he is simply not in the habit of actualizing it. When Socrates goes home, he is not alone, he is *by* himself. Clearly, with this fellow who awaits him, Socrates has to come to some kind of agreement, because they live under the same roof. Better to be at odds with the whole world than be at odds with the only one you are forced to live together with when you have left company behind.

What Socrates discovered was that we can have intercourse with ourselves, as well as with others, and that the two kinds of intercourse are somehow interrelated. Aristotle, speaking about friendship, remarked: "The friend is another self"[32]—meaning: you can carry on the dialogue of thought with him just as well as with yourself. This is still in the Socratic tradition, except that Socrates would have said: The self, too, is a kind of friend. The guiding experience in these matters is, of course, friendship and not selfhood; I first talk with others before I talk with myself, examining whatever the joint talk may have been about, and then discover that I can conduct a dialogue not only with others but with myself as well. The common point, however, is that the dialogue of thought can be carried out only among friends, and its basic criterion, its supreme law, as it were, says: Do not contradict yourself.

It is characteristic of "base people" to be "at variance with themselves" (*diapherontai heautois*) and of wicked men to avoid their own company; their soul is in rebellion against itself (*stasiazei*).[33] What kind of dialogue can you conduct with yourself when your soul is not in harmony but at war with itself? Precisely the dialogue we overhear when Shakespeare's Richard III is alone:

> What do I fear? Myself? There's none else by:
> Richard loves Richard: that is, I am I.
> Is there a murderer here? No. Yes, I am:
> Then fly: what! from myself? Great reason why:
> Lest I revenge. What! myself upon myself?
> Alack! I love myself. Wherefore? For any good
> That I myself have done unto myself?
> O! no: alas! I rather hate myself
> For hateful deeds committed by myself.
> I am a villain. Yet I lie, I am not.
> Fool, of thyself speak well: fool, do not flatter.

Yet all this looks very different when midnight is past and Richard has escaped his own company to join that of his peers. Then:

> Conscience is but a word that cowards use,
> Devis'd at first to keep the strong in awe. . . .

Even Socrates, so much in love with the marketplace, has to go home, where he will be alone, in solitude, in order to meet the other fellow.

I have drawn attention to the passage in *Hippias Major* in its stark simplicity because it provides a metaphor that can help simplify—at the risk of over-simplification—matters that are difficult and therefore always in danger of over-complication. Later times have given the fellow who awaits Socrates in his home the name of "conscience." Before its tribunal, to adopt Kantian language, we have to appear and give account of ourselves.

And I chose the passage in *Richard III,* because Shakespeare, though he uses the word "conscience," does not use it here in the accustomed way. It took language a long time to separate the word "consciousness" from "conscience," and in some languages, for instance, in French, such a separation never was made. Conscience, as we understand it in moral or legal matters, is supposedly always present within us, just like consciousness. And this conscience is also supposed to tell us what to do and what to repent; before it became the *lumen naturale* or Kant's practical reason, it was the voice of God.

Unlike this ever-present conscience, the fellow Socrates is talking about has been left at home; he fears him, as the murderers in *Richard III* fear conscience—as something that is absent. Here conscience appears as an after-thought, roused either by a crime, as in Richard's own case, or by unexamined opinions, as in the case of Socrates. Or it may be just the anticipated fear of such after-thoughts, as with Richard's hired murderers. This conscience, unlike the voice of God within us or the *lumen naturale,* gives no positive prescriptions (even the Socratic *daimōn,* his divine voice, only tells him what *not* to do); in Shakespeare's words "it fills a man full of obstacles." What causes a man to fear it is the anticipation of the presence of a witness who awaits him only *if* and when he goes home. Shakespeare's murderer says: "Every man that means to live well endeavors . . . to live without it," and success in that comes easy because all he has to do is never start the soundless solitary dialogue we call "thinking," never go home and examine things. This is not a matter of wickedness or goodness, as it is not a matter of intelligence or stupidity. A person who does not know that silent intercourse (in which we examine what we say and what we do) will not mind contradicting himself, and this means he will never be either able or willing to account for what he says or does; nor will he mind committing any crime, since he can count on its being forgotten the next moment. Bad people—Aristotle to the contrary notwithstanding— are *not* "full of regrets."

Thinking in its non-cognitive, non-specialized sense as a natural need of human life, the actualization of the difference given in consciousness, is not a prerogative of the few but an ever-present faculty in everybody; by the same token, inability to think is not a failing of the many who lack brain power but an ever-present possibility for everybody—scientists, scholars, and other specialists in mental enterprises not excluded. Everybody may come to shun that intercourse with oneself whose feasibility and importance Socrates first discovered. Thinking accompanies life and is itself the de-materialized quintessence of being alive; and since life is a process, its quintessence can only lie in the actual thinking process and not in any solid results or specific thoughts. A life without thinking is quite possible; it then fails to develop its own essence—it is not merely meaningless; it is not fully alive. Unthinking men are like sleepwalkers.

For the thinking ego and its experience, conscience that "fills a man full of obstacles" is a side effect. No matter what thought-trains the thinking ego thinks through, the self that we all are must take care not to do anything that would make it impossible for the two-in-one to be friends and live in harmony. This is what Spinoza meant by the term "acquiescence in one's self" (*acquiescentia in seipso*): "It can spring out of reason [reasoning], and this contentment is the greatest joy possible."[34] Its criterion for action will not be the usual rules, recognized by multitudes and agreed upon by society, but whether I shall be able to live with myself in peace when the time has come to think about my deeds and words. Conscience is the anticipation of the fellow who awaits you if and when you come home.

For the thinker himself this moral side effect is a marginal affair. And thinking as such does society little good, much less than the thirst for knowledge, which uses thinking as an instrument for other purposes. It does not create values; it will not find out, once and for all, what "the good" is; it does not confirm but, rather, dissolves accepted rules of conduct. And it has no political relevance unless special emergencies arise. That while I am alive I must be able to live with myself is a consideration that does not come up politically except in "boundary situations."

This term was coined by Jaspers for the general, unchanging human condition—"that I cannot live without struggling and suffering; that I cannot avoid guilt; that I must die"—to indicate an experience of "something immanent which already points to transcendence" and which, if we respond to it, will result in our *"becoming the Existenz we potentially are."*[35] In Jaspers, the term gets its suggestive plausibility less from specific experiences than from the simple fact that life itself, limited by birth and death, is a boundary affair in that my worldly existence always forces me to take account of a past when I was not yet and a future when I shall be no more. Here the point is that whenever I transcend the limits of my own life span and begin to reflect on this past, judging it, and this future, forming projects of the will, thinking ceases to be a politically marginal activity. And such reflections will inevitably arise in political emergencies.

When everybody is swept away unthinkingly by what everybody else does and believes in, those who think are drawn out of hiding because their refusal to join in is conspicuous and thereby becomes a kind of action. In such emergencies, it turns out that the purging component of thinking (Socrates' midwifery, which brings out the implications of unexamined opinions and thereby destroys them—values, doctrines, theories, and even convictions) is political by implication. For this destruction has a liberating effect on another faculty, the faculty of judgment, which one may call with some reason the most political of man's mental abilities. It is the faculty that judges *particulars* without subsuming them under general rules which can be taught and learned until they grow into habits that can be replaced by other habits and rules.

The faculty of judging particulars (as brought to light by Kant), the ability to say "this is wrong," "this is beautiful," and so on, is not the same as the faculty of thinking. Thinking deals with invisibles, with representations of things that are absent; judging always concerns particulars and things close at hand. But the two are interrelated, as are consciousness and conscience. If thinking—the two-in-one of the soundless dialogue—actualizes the difference within our identity as given in consciousness and thereby results in conscience as its by-product, then judging, the by-product of the liberating effect of thinking, realizes thinking, makes it manifest in the world of appearances, where I am never alone and always too busy to be able to think. The manifestation of the wind of thought is not knowledge; it is the ability to tell right from wrong, beautiful from ugly. And this, at the rare moments when the stakes are on the table, may indeed prevent catastrophes, at least for the self.

Notes

1. Hegel's *Encyclopädie der philosophischen Wissenschaften*, Lasson ed., Leipzig, 1923, 23: "*Das Denken . . . sich als abstraktes Ich als von aller Partikularität sonstiger Eigenschaften, Zustände, usf. befreites verhält und nur das Allgemeine tut, in welchem es mit allen Individuen identisch ist.*"

2. It is surprising, in examining the literature, often very learned, to see how very little all this erudition has been able to contribute to an understanding of the man. The only exception I have been able to unearth is a kind of inspired profile by the classicist and philosopher Gregory Vlastos, "The Paradox of Socrates." See the Introduction to his carefully selected *The Philosophy of Socrates: A Collection of Critical Essays*, Anchor Books, New York, 1971.

3. 173d.

4. On the Socratic problem, see the short, reasonable account given by Laszlo Versényi as an Appendix to his *Socratic Humanism*, New Haven, London, 1963.

5. *Dante and Philosophy*, trans. David Moore, Harper Torchbooks, New York, Evanston, London, 1963, p. 267.

6. *Ibid.,* p. 273.

7. Thus in *Theaetetus* and *Charmides.*

8. *Meno,* 80e.

9. The frequent notion that Socrates tries to lead his interlocutor with his questions to certain results of which he is convinced in advance—like a clever professor with his students—seems to me entirely mistaken even if it is as ingeniously qualified as in Vlastos' essay mentioned above, in which he suggests (p. 13) that Socrates wanted the other "to find . . . out for himself," as in the *Meno,* which however is not aporetic. The most one could say is that Socrates wanted his partners in the dialogues to be as perplexed as he was. He was sincere when he said that he taught nothing. Thus he told Critias in the *Charmides:* "Critias, you act as though I professed to know the answers to the questions I ask you and could give them to you if I wished. It is not so. I inquire with you . . . because I don't myself have knowledge" (165b; cf. 166c–d).

10. Diehl, frag. 16.

11. *Meno,* 80c. Cf. the above-mentioned passage, n. 105.

12. *Memorabilia,* IV, vi, 15 and IV, iv, 9.

13. *Sophist,* 226–231.

14. *Apology,* 23b.

15. *Ibid.,* 30a.

16. Xenophon, *Memorabilia,* IV, iii, 14.

17. *Antigone,* 353.

18. The German text, from *Was Heisst Denken?,* Tübingen, 1954, p. 52, reads as follows: *"Sokrates hat zeit seines Lebens, bis in seinen Tod hinein, nichts anderes getan, als sich in den Zugwind dieses Zuges zu stellen und darin sich zu halten. Darum ist er der reinste Denker des Abendlandes. Deshalb hat er nichts geschrieben. Denn wer aus dem Denken zu schreiben beginnt, muss unweigerlich den Menschen gleichen, die vor allzu starkem Zugwind in den Windschatten flüchten. Es bleibt das Geheimnis einer noch verborgenen Geschichte, dass alle Denker des Abendlandes nach Sokrates, unbeschadet ihrer Grösse, solche Flüchtlinge sein mussten. Das Denken ging in die Literatur ein."*

19. G. Humphrey, *Thinking: An Introduction to Its Experimental Psychology,* London and New York, 1951, p. 312.

20. Thucydides, II, 40.

21. *Lysis,* 204b–c.

22. Frags. 145, 190.

23. *Sophist,* 253b.

24. *Protagoras,* 339c.

25. *Ibid.,* 339b, 340b.

26. *Posterior Analytics,* 76b22–25.

27. 1005b23–1008a2.

28. No. 36, *Werke,* vol. VI, p. 500.

29. No. 56, *ibid.,* p. 549.

30. "Grundlegung zur Metaphysik der Sitten," *Werke,* vol. 4, pp. 51–55.

31. 304d.
32. *Nicomachean Ethics,* 1166a30.
33. *Ibid.,* 1166b5–25.
34. *Ethics,* IV, 52; III, 25.
35. *Philosophy* (1932), trans. E. B. Ashton, Chicago, London, 1970, vol. 2, pp. 178–179.

PART VI

Revolution and Preservation

Rosa Luxemburg

(1871–1919)

I

The definitive biography, English-style, is among the most admirable genres of historiography. Lengthy, thoroughly documented, heavily annotated, and generously splashed with quotations, it usually comes in two large volumes and tells more, and more vividly, about the historical period in question than all but the most outstanding history books. For unlike other biographies, history is here not treated as the inevitable background of a famous person's life span; it is rather as though the colorless light of historical time were forced through and refracted by the prism of a great character so that in the resulting spectrum a complete unity of life and world is achieved. This may be why it has become the classical genre for the lives of great statesmen but has remained rather unsuitable for those in which the main interest lies in the life story, or for the lives of artists, writers, and, generally, men or women whose genius forced them to keep the world at a certain distance and whose significance lies chiefly in their works, the artifacts they added to the world, not in the role they played in it.[1]

It was a stroke of genius on the part of J. P. Nettl to choose the life of Rosa Luxemburg,[2] the most unlikely candidate, as a proper subject for a genre that seems suitable only for the lives of great statesmen and other persons of the world. She certainly was nothing of the kind. Even in her own world of the European socialist movement she was a rather marginal figure, with relatively brief moments of splendor and great brilliance, whose influence in deed and written word can hardly be compared to that of her contemporaries—to Plekhanov, Trotsky, and Lenin, to Bebel and Kautsky, to Jaurès and Millerand. If success in the world is a prerequisite

---

From Men in Dark Times. *Originally published in* The New York Review of Books 7/5 *(October 6, 1966) as "A Heroine of the Revolution."*

for success in the genre, how could Mr. Nettl succeed with this woman who when very young had been swept into the German Social Democratic Party from her native Poland; who continued to play a key role in the little-known and neglected history of Polish socialism; and who then for about two decades, although never officially recognized, became the most controversial and least understood figure in the German Left movement? For it was precisely success—success even in her own world of revolutionaries—which was withheld from Rosa Luxemburg in life, death, and after death. Can it be that the failure of all her efforts as far as official recognition is concerned is somehow connected with the dismal failure of revolution in our century? Will history look different if seen through the prism of her life and work?

However that may be, I know no book that sheds more light on the crucial period of European socialism from the last decades of the nineteenth century to the fateful day in January 1919 when Rosa Luxemburg and Karl Liebknecht, the two leaders of the *Spartakusbund,* the precursor of the German Communist Party, were murdered in Berlin—under the eyes and probably with the connivance of the Socialist regime then in power. The murderers were members of the ultra-nationalist and officially illegal *Freikorps,* a paramilitary organization from which Hitler's storm troopers were soon to recruit their most promising killers. That the government at the time was practically in the hands of the *Freikorps* because they enjoyed "the full support of Noske," the Socialists' expert on national defense, then in charge of military affairs, was confirmed only recently by Captain Pabst, the last surviving participant in the assassination. The Bonn government—in this as in other respects only too eager to revive the more sinister traits of the Weimar Republic—let it be known that it was thanks to the *Freikorps* that Moscow had failed to incorporate all of Germany into a red Empire after the First World War and that the murder of Liebknecht and Luxemburg was entirely legal "an execution in accordance with martial law."[3] This was considerably more than even the Weimar Republic had ever pretended, for it had never admitted publicly that the *Freikorps* actually were an arm of the government and it had "punished" the murderers by meting out a sentence of two years and two weeks to the soldier Runge for "*attempted* manslaughter" (he had hit Rosa Luxemburg over the head in the corridors of the Hotel Eden), and four months to Lieutenant Vogel (he was the officer in charge when she was shot in the head inside a car and thrown into the Landwehr Canal) for "failing to report a corpse and illegally disposing of it." During the trial, a photograph showing Runge and his comrades celebrating the assassination in the same hotel on the following day was introduced as evidence, which caused the defendant great merriment. "Accused Runge, you must behave properly. This is no laughing matter," said the presiding judge. Forty-five years later, during the Auschwitz trial in Frankfurt, a similar scene took place; the same words were spoken.

With the murder of Rosa Luxemburg and Liebknecht, the split of the European Left into Socialist and Communist parties became irrevocable; "the abyss which the Communists had pictured in theory had become . . . the abyss of the grave." And since this early crime had been aided and abetted by the government, it initiated the death dance in postwar Germany: The assassins of the extreme Right started by liquidating prominent leaders of the extreme Left—Hugo Haase and Gustav Landauer, Leo Jogiches and Eugene Leviné—and quickly moved to the center and the right-of-center—to Walther Rathenau and Matthias Erzberger, both members of the government at the time of their murder. Thus Rosa Luxemburg's death became the watershed between two eras in Germany; and it became the point of no return for the German Left. All those who had drifted to the Communists out of bitter disappointment with the Socialist Party were even more disappointed with the swift moral decline and political disintegration of the Communist Party, and yet they felt that to return to the ranks of the Socialists would mean to condone the murder of Rosa. Such personal reactions, which are seldom publicly admitted, are among the small, mosaic-like pieces that fall into place in the large riddle of history. In the case of Rosa Luxemburg they are part of the legend which soon surrounded her name. Legends have a truth of their own, but Mr. Nettl is entirely right to have paid almost no attention to the Rosa myth. It was his task, difficult enough, to restore her to historical life.

Shortly after her death, when all persuasions of the Left had already decided that she had always been "mistaken" (a "really hopeless case," as George Lichtheim, the last in this long line, put it in *Encounter*), a curious shift in her reputation took place. Two small volumes of her letters were published, and these, entirely personal and of a simple, touchingly humane, and often poetic beauty, were enough to destroy the propaganda image of bloodthirsty "Red Rosa," at least in all but the most obstinately anti-Semitic and reactionary circles. However, what then grew up was another legend—the sentimentalized image of the bird watcher and lover of flowers, a woman whose guards said good-by to her with tears in their eyes when she left prison—as if they couldn't go on living without being entertained by this strange prisoner who had insisted on treating them as human beings. Nettl does not mention this story, faithfully handed down to me when I was a child and later confirmed by Kurt Rosenfeld, her friend and lawyer, who claimed to have witnessed the scene. It is probably true enough, and its slightly embarrassing features are somehow offset by the survival of another anecdote, this one mentioned by Nettl. In 1907, she and her friend Clara Zetkin (later the "grand old woman" of German Communism) had gone for a walk, lost count of time, and arrived late for an appointment with August Bebel, who had feared they were lost. Rosa then proposed their epitaph: "Here lie the last two men of German Social Democracy." Seven years later, in February 1914, she had occasion to prove the truth of this cruel joke in a splendid address to the judges of the Criminal Court which had indicted her for "inciting" the masses to civil disobedience in case of war. (Not bad, incidentally, for the woman who "was always wrong" to stand trial on this charge five months before the outbreak of the First World War, which few "serious" people had thought possible.) Mr. Nettl with good sense had reprinted the address in its entirety; its "manliness" is unparalleled in the history of German socialism.

It took a few more years and a few more catastrophes for the legend to turn into a symbol of nostalgia for the good old times of the movement, when hopes were green, the revolution around the corner, and, most important, the faith in the capacities of the masses and in the moral integrity of the Socialist or Communist leadership was still intact. It speaks not only for the person of Rosa Luxemburg, but also for the qualities of this older generation of the Left, that the legend—vague, confused, inaccurate in nearly all details—could spread throughout the world and come to life whenever a "New Left" sprang into being. But side by side with this glamorized image, there survived also the old clichés of the "quarrelsome female," a "romantic" who was neither "realistic" nor scientific (it is true that she was always out of step), and whose works, especially her great book on imperialism (*The Accumulation of Capital*, 1913), were shrugged off. Every New Left movement, when its moment came to change into the Old Left—usually when its members reached the age of forty—promptly buried its early enthusiasm for Rosa Luxemburg together with the dreams of youth; and since they had usually not bothered to read, let alone to understand, what she had to say they found it easy to dismiss her with all the patronizing philistinism of their newly acquired status. "Luxemburgism," invented posthumously by Party hacks for polemical reasons, has never even achieved the honor of being denounced as "treason"; it was treated as a harmless, infantile disease. Nothing Rosa Luxemburg wrote or said survived except her surprisingly accurate criticism of Bolshevik politics during the early stages of the Russian Revolution, and this only because those whom a "god had failed" could use it as a convenient though wholly inadequate weapon against Stalin. ("There is something indecent in the use of Rosa's name and writings as a cold war missile," as the reviewer of Nettl's book pointed out in the *Times Literary Supplement*.) Her new admirers had no more in common with her than her detractors. Her highly developed sense for theoretical differences and her infallible judgment of people, her personal likes and dislikes, would have prevented her lumping Lenin and Stalin together under all circumstances, quite apart from the fact that she had never been a "believer," had never used politics as a substitute for religion, and had been careful, as Mr. Nettl notes, not to attack religion when she opposed the church. In short, while "revolution was as close and real to her as to Lenin," it was no more an article of faith with her than Marxism. Lenin was primarily a man of action and would have gone into politics in any event, but she, who in her half-serious self-estimate was born "to mind the geese," might just as well have buried herself in botany and zoology or history and economics or mathematics, had not the circumstances of the world offended her sense of justice and freedom.

This is of course to admit that she was not an orthodox Marxist, so little orthodox indeed that it might be doubted that she was a Marxist at all. Mr. Nettl rightly states that to her Marx was no more than "the best interpreter of reality of them all," and it is revealing of her lack of personal commitment that she could write, "I now have a horror of the much praised first volume of Marx's *Capital* because of its elaborate rococo ornaments à la Hegel."[4] What mattered most in her view was reality, in all its wonderful and all its frightful aspects, even more than revolution itself. Her unorthodoxy was innocent, non-polemical; she "recommended her friends to read Marx for 'the daring of his thoughts, the refusal to take anything for granted,' rather than for the value of his conclusions. His mistakes . . . were self-evident . . . ; that was why [she] never bothered to engage in any lengthy critique." All this is most obvious in *The Accumulation of Capital,* which only Franz Mehring was unprejudiced enough to call a "truly magnificent, fascinating achievement without its equal since Marx's death."[5] The central thesis of this "curious work of genius" is simple enough. Since capitalism didn't show any signs of collapse "under the weight of its economic contradictions," she began to look for an outside cause to explain its continued existence and growth. She found it in the so-called third-man theory, that is, in the fact that the process of growth was not merely the consequence of innate laws ruling capitalist production but of the continued existence of pre-capitalist sectors in the country which "capitalism" captured and brought into its sphere of influence. Once this process had spread to the whole national territory, capitalists were forced to look to other parts of the earth, to pre-capitalist lands, to draw them into the process of capital accumulation, which, as it were, fed on whatever was outside itself. In other words, Marx's "original accumulation of capital" was not, like original sin, a single event, a unique deed of expropriation by the nascent bourgeoisie, setting off a process of accumulation that would then follow "with iron necessity" its own inherent law up to the final collapse. On the contrary, expropriation had to be repeated time and again to keep the system in motion. Hence, capitalism was not a closed system that generated its own contradictions and was "pregnant with revolution"; it fed on outside factors, and its *automatic* collapse could occur, if at all, only when the whole surface of the earth was conquered and had been devoured.

Lenin was quick to see that this description, whatever its merits or flaws, was essentially non-Marxist. It contradicted the very foundations of Marxian and Hegelian dialectics, which hold that every thesis must create its own anti-thesis—bourgeois society creates the proletariat—so that the movement of the whole process remains bound to the initial factor that caused it. Lenin pointed out that from the viewpoint of materialist dialectics "her thesis that enlarged capitalist reproduction was impossible within a closed economy and needed to cannibalize economies in order to function at all . . . [was] a 'fundamental error.' " The trouble was only that what was an error in abstract Marxian theory was an eminently faithful description of things as they really were. Her careful "description of the torture of Negroes in South Africa" also was clearly "non-Marxist," but who would deny today that it belonged in a book on imperialism?

II

Historically, Mr. Nettl's greatest and most original achievement is the discovery of the Polish-Jewish "peer group" and Rosa Luxemburg's lifelong, close, and carefully hidden attachment to the Polish party which sprang from it. This is indeed a highly significant and totally neglected source, not of the revolutions, but of the revolutionary spirit in the twentieth century. This milieu, which even in the twenties had lost all public relevance, has now completely disappeared. Its nucleus consisted of assimilated Jews from middle-class families whose cultural background was German (Rosa Luxemburg knew Goethe and Morike by heart, and her literary taste was impeccable, far superior to that of her German friends), whose political formation was Russian, and whose moral standards in both private and public life were uniquely their own. These Jews, an extremely small minority in the East, an even smaller percentage of assimilated Jewry in the West, stood outside all social ranks, Jewish or non-Jewish, hence had no conventional prejudices whatsoever, and had developed, in this truly splendid isolation, their own code of honor—which then attracted a number of non-Jews, among them Julian Marchlewski and Feliks Dzerzhynski, both of whom later joined the Bolsheviks. It was precisely because of this unique background that Lenin appointed Dzerzhynski as first head of the Cheka, someone, he hoped, no power could corrupt; hadn't he begged to be charged with the department of Children's Education and Welfare?

Nettl rightly stresses Rosa Luxemburg's excellent relations with her family, her parents, brothers, sister, and niece, none of whom ever showed the slightest inclination to socialist convictions or revolutionary activities, yet who did everything they could for her when she had to hide from the police or was in prison. The point is worth making, for it gives us a glimpse of this unique Jewish family background without which the emergence of the ethical code of the peer group would be nearly incomprehensible. The hidden equalizer of those who always treated one another as equals—and hardly anybody else—was the essentially simple experience of a childhood world in which mutual respect and unconditional trust, a universal humanity and a genuine, almost naïve contempt for social and ethnic distinctions were taken for granted. What the members of the peer group had in common was what can only be called moral taste, which is so different from "moral principles"; the authenticity of their morality they owed to having grown up in a world that was not out of joint. This gave them their "rare self-confidence," so unsettling to the world into which they then came, and so bitterly resented as arrogance and conceit. This milieu, and never the German Party, was and remained Rosa Luxemburg's home. The home was movable up to a point, and since it was predominantly Jewish it did not coincide with any "fatherland."

It is of course highly suggestive that the SDKPIL (Social Democracy of the Kingdom of Poland and Lithuania, formerly called SDPK, Social Democracy of the Kingdom of Poland), the party of this predominantly Jewish group, split from the official Socialist Polish Party, the PPS, because of the latter's stand for Polish independence (Pilsudski, the Fascist dictator of Poland after World War I, was its most famous and successful offspring), and that, after the split, the members of the group became ardent defenders of an often doctrinaire internationalism. It is even more suggestive that the national question is the only issue on which one could accuse Rosa Luxemburg of self-deception and unwillingness to face reality. That this had something to do with her Jewishness is undeniable, although it is of course "lamentably absurd" to discover in her anti-nationalism "a peculiarly Jewish quality." Mr. Nettl, while hiding nothing, is rather careful to avoid the "Jewish question," and in view of the usually low level of debates on this issue one can only applaud his decision. Unfortunately, his understandable distaste has blinded him to the few important facts in this matter, which is all the more to be regretted since these facts, though of a simple, elementary nature, also escaped the otherwise so sensitive and alert mind of Rosa Luxemburg.

The first of these is what only Nietzsche, as far as I know, has ever pointed out, namely, that the position and functions of the Jewish people in Europe predestined them to become the "good Europeans" *par excellence*. The Jewish middle classes of Paris and London, Berlin and Vienna, Warsaw and Moscow, were in fact neither cosmopolitan nor international, though the intellectuals among them thought of themselves in these terms. They were European, something that could be said of no other group. And this was not a matter of conviction; it was an objective fact. In other words, while the self-deception of assimilated Jews usually consisted in the mistaken belief that they were just as German as the Germans, just as French as the French, the self-deception of the intellectual Jews consisted in thinking that they had no "fatherland," for their fatherland actually was Europe. There is, second, the fact that at least the East-European intelligentsia was multilingual—Rosa Luxemburg herself spoke Polish, Russian, German, and French fluently and knew English and Italian very well. They never quite understood the importance of language barriers and why the slogan, "The fatherland of the working class is the Socialist movement," should be so disastrously wrong precisely for the working classes. It is indeed more than a little disturbing that Rosa Luxemburg herself, with her acute sense of reality and strict avoidance of clichés, should not have *heard* what was wrong with the slogan on principle. A fatherland, after all, is first of all a "land"; an organization is not a country, not even metaphorically. There is indeed grim justice in the later transformation of the slogan. "The fatherland of the working class is Soviet Russia"—Russia was at least a "land"—which put an end to the utopian internationalism of this generation.

One could adduce more such facts, and it still would be difficult to claim that Rosa Luxemburg was entirely wrong on the national question. What, after all, has contributed more to the catastrophic decline of Europe than the insane nationalism which accompanied the decline of the nation state in the era of imperialism? Those whom Nietzsche had called the "good Europeans"—a very small minority even among Jews—might well

have been the only ones to have a presentiment of the disastrous consequences ahead, although they were unable to gauge correctly the enormous force of nationalist feeling in a decaying body politic.

I I I

Closely connected with the discovery of the Polish "peer group" and its
continued importance for Rosa Luxemburg's public and private life is Mr.
Nettl's disclosure of hitherto inaccessible sources, which enabled him to
piece together the facts of her life—"the exquisite business of love and
living." It is now clear that we knew next to nothing about her private
life for the simple reason that she had so carefully protected herself from
notoriety. This is no mere matter of sources. It was fortunate indeed that
the new material fell into Mr. Nettl's hands, and he has every right to dismiss his few predecessors who were less hampered by lack of access to the
facts than by their inability to move, think, and feel on the same level as
their subject. The ease with which Nettl handles his biographical material
is astounding. His treatment is more than perceptive. His is the first plausible portrait of this extraordinary woman, drawn *con amore,* with tact and
great delicacy. It is as though she had found her last admirer, and it is for
this reason that one feels like quarreling with some of his judgments.

He is certainly wrong in emphasizing her ambition, and sense of career. Does he think that her violent contempt for the careerists and status
seekers in the German Party—their delight in being admitted to the
Reichstag—is mere cant? Does he believe that a really "ambitious" person
could have afforded to be as generous as she was? (Once, at an international congress, Jaures finished an eloquent speech in which he "ridiculed
the misguided passions of Rosa Luxemburg, [but] there was suddenly no
one to translate him. Rosa jumped up and reproduced the moving oratory: from French into equally telling German.") And how can he reconcile this, except by assuming dishonesty or self-deception, with her telling
phrase in one of her letters to Jogiches: "I have a cursed longing for happiness and am ready to haggle for my daily portion of happiness with all
the stubbornness of a mule." What he mistakes for ambition is the natural
force of a temperament capable, in her own laughing words, of "setting a
prairie on fire," which propelled her almost willy-nilly into public affairs,
and even ruled over most of her purely intellectual enterprises. While he
stresses repeatedly the high moral standards of the "peer group," he still
seems not to understand that such things as ambition, career, status, and
even mere success were under the strictest taboo.

There is another aspect of her personality which Nettl stresses but whose implications he seems not to understand: that she was so "self-consciously a woman." This in itself put certain limitations on whatever her ambitions otherwise might have been—for Nettl does not ascribe to her more than what would have been natural in a man with her gifts and opportunities. Her distaste for the women's emancipation movement, to which all other women of her generation and political convictions were irresistibly drawn, was significant; in the face of suffragette equality, she might have been tempted to reply, *Vive la petite différence.* She was an outsider, not only because she was and remained a Polish Jew in a country she disliked and a party she came soon to despise, but also because she was a woman. Mr. Nettl must, of course, be pardoned for his masculine prejudices; they would not matter much if they had not prevented him from understanding fully the role Leo Jogiches, her husband for all practical purposes and her first, perhaps her only, lover, played in her life. Their deadly serious quarrel, caused by Jogiches's brief affair with another woman and endlessly complicated by Rosa's furious reaction, was typical of their time and milieu, as was the aftermath, his jealousy and her refusal for years to forgive him. This generation still believed firmly that love strikes only once, and its carelessness with marriage certificates should not be mistaken for any belief in free love. Mr. Nettl's evidence shows that she had friends and admirers, and that she enjoyed this, but it hardly indicates that there was ever another man in her life. To believe in the Party gossip about marriage plans with "Hänschen" Diefenbach, whom she addressed as *Sie* and never dreamed of treating as an equal, strikes me as downright silly. Nettl calls the story of Leo Jogiches and Rosa Luxemburg "one of the great and tragic love stories of Socialism," and there is no need to quarrel with this verdict if one understands that it was not "blind and self-destructive jealousy" which caused the ultimate tragedy in their relations but war and the years in prison, the doomed German revolution and the bloody end.

Leo Jogiches, whose name Nettl also has rescued from oblivion, was a very remarkable and yet typical figure among the professional revolutionists. To Rosa Luxemburg, he was definitely *masculini generis,* which was of considerable importance to her: She preferred Graf Westarp (the leader of the German Conservative Party) to all the German Socialist luminaries "because," she said, "he is a *man.*" There were few people she respected, and Jogiches headed a list on which only the names of Lenin and Franz Mehring could be inscribed with certainty. He definitely was a man of action and passion, he knew how to do and how to suffer. It is tempting to compare him with Lenin, whom he somewhat resembles, except in his passion for anonymity and for pulling strings behind the scenes, and his love of conspiracy and danger, which must have given him an additional erotic charm. He was indeed a Lenin *manqué*, even in his inability to write, "total" in his case (as she observed in a shrewd and actually very loving portrait in one of her letters), and his mediocrity as a public speaker. Both men had great talent for organization and leadership, but for nothing else, so that they felt impotent and superfluous when there was nothing to do and they were left to themselves. This is less noticeable in Lenin's case because he was never completely isolated, but Jogiches had early fallen out with the Russian Party because of a quarrel with Plekhanov—the Pope of the Russian emigration in Switzerland during the nineties—who regarded the self-assured Jewish youth newly arrived from Poland as "a miniature version of Nechaieff." The consequence was that he, according to Rosa Luxemburg, "completely rootless, vegetated" for many years, until the revolution of 1905 gave him his first opportunity: "Quite suddenly he not only achieved the position of leader of the Polish movement, but even in the Russian." (The SDKPIL came into prominence during the Revolution and became more important in the years following. Jogiches, though he himself didn't "write a single line," remained "none the less the very soul" of its publications.) He had his last brief moment when, "completely unknown in the SPD," he organized a clandestine opposition in the German army during the First World War. "Without him there would have been no *Spartakusbund*," which, unlike any other organized Leftist group in Germany, for a short time became a kind of "ideal peer group." (This, of course, is not to say that Jogiches made the German revolution; like all revolutions, it was made by no one. *Spartakusbund* too was "following rather than making events," and the official notion that the "Spartakus uprising" in January 1918 was caused or inspired by its leaders—Rosa Luxemburg, Liebknecht, Jogiches—is a myth.)

We shall never know how many of Rosa Luxemburg's political ideas derived from Jogiches; in marriage, it is not always easy to tell the partners' thoughts apart. But that he failed where Lenin succeeded was at least as much a consequence of circumstances—he was a Jew and a Pole—as of lesser stature. In any event, Rosa Luxemburg would have been the last to hold this against him. The members of the peer group did not judge one another in these categories. Jogiches himself might have agreed with Eugene Leviné, also a Russian Jew though a younger man, "We are dead men on furlough." This mood is what set him apart from the others; for neither Lenin nor Trotsky nor Rosa Luxemburg herself is likely to have thought along such lines. After her death he refused to leave Berlin for safety: "Somebody has to stay to write all our epitaphs." He was arrested two months after the murder of Liebknecht and Luxemburg and shot in the back in the police station. The name of the murderer was known, but "no attempt to punish him was ever made"; he killed another man in the same way, and then continued his "career with promotion in the Prussian Police." Such were the *mores* of the Weimar Republic.

Reading and remembering these old stories, one becomes painfully aware of the difference between the German comrades and the members of the peer group. During the Russian revolution of 1905 Rosa Luxemburg was arrested in Warsaw, and her friends collected the money for bail (probably provided by the German Party). The payment was supplemented "with an unofficial threat of reprisal; if anything happened to Rosa they would retaliate with action against prominent officials." No such notion of "action" ever entered her German friends' minds either before or after the wave of political murders when the impunity of such deeds had become notorious.

I V

More troubling in retrospect, certainly more painful for herself, than her alleged "errors" are the few crucial instances in which Rosa Luxemburg was not out of step, but appeared instead to be in agreement with the official powers in the German Social Democratic Party. These were her real mistakes, and there was none she did not finally recognize and bitterly regret.

The least harmful among them concerned the national question. She had arrived in Germany in 1898 from Zürich, where she had passed her doctorate "with a first-class dissertation about the industrial development of Poland" (according to Professor Julius Wolf, who in his autobiography still remembered fondly "the ablest of my pupils"), which achieved the unusual "distinction of instant commercial publication" and is still used by students of Polish history. Her thesis was that the economic growth of Poland depended entirely upon the Russian market and that any attempt "to form a national or linguistic state was a negation of all development and progress for the last fifty years." (That she was economically right was more than demonstrated by the chronic malaise of Poland between the wars.) She then became the expert on Poland for the German Party, its propagandist among the Polish population in the Eastern German provinces, and entered an uneasy alliance with people who wished to "Germanize" the Poles out of existence and would "gladly make you a present of all and every Pole including Polish Socialism," as an SPD secretary told her. Surely, "the glow of official approval was for Rosa a false glow."

Much more serious was her deceptive agreement with Party authorities in the revisionist controversy in which she played a leading part. This famous debate had been touched off by Eduard Bernstein[6] and has gone down in history as the alternative of reform against revolution. But this battle cry is misleading for two reasons: it makes it appear as though the SPD at the turn of the century still was committed to revolution, which was not the case; and it conceals the objective soundness of much of what Bernstein had to say. His criticism of Marx's economic theories was indeed, as he claimed, in full "agreement with reality." He pointed out that the "enormous increase of social wealth [was] not accompanied by a decreasing number of large capitalists but by an increasing number of capitalists of all degrees," that an "increasing narrowing of the circle of the well-to-do and an increasing misery of the poor" had failed to materialize, that "the modern proletarian [was] indeed poor but that he [was] no pauper," and that Marx's slogan, "The proletarian has no fatherland," was not true. Universal suffrage had given him political rights, the trade unions a place in society, and the new imperialist development a clear stake in the nation's foreign policy. No doubt the reaction of the German Party to these unwelcome truths was chiefly inspired by a deep-seated reluctance to reexamine critically its theoretical foundation, but this reluctance was greatly sharpened by the Party's vested interest in the status quo threatened by Bernstein's analysis. What was at stake was the status of the SPD as a "state within a state": the Party had in fact become a huge and well-organized bureaucracy that stood outside society and had every interest in things as they were. Revisionism à la Bernstein would have led the Party back into German society, and such "integration" was felt to be as dangerous to the Party's interests as a revolution.

Mr. Nettl holds an interesting theory about the "pariah position" of the SPD within German society and its failure to participate in government.[7] It seemed to its members that the Party could "provide within itself a superior alternative to corrupt capitalism." In fact, by keeping the "defenses against society on all fronts intact," it generated that spurious feeling of "togetherness" (as Nettl puts it) which the French Socialists treated with great contempt.[8] In any event, it was obvious that the more the Party increased in numbers, the more surely was its radical élan "organized out of existence." One could live very comfortably in this "state within a state" by avoiding friction with society at large, by enjoying feelings of moral superiority without any consequences. It was not even necessary to pay the price of serious alienation since this pariah society was in fact but a mirror image, a "miniature reflection" of German society at large. This blind alley of the German Socialist movement could be analyzed correctly from opposing points of view—either from the view of Bernstein's revisionism, which recognized the emancipation of the working classes within capitalist society as an accomplished fact and demanded a stop to the talk about a revolution nobody thought of anyhow; or from the viewpoint of those who were not merely "alienated" from bourgeois society but actually wanted to change the world.

The latter was the standpoint of the revolutionists from the East who led the attack against Bernstein—Plekhanov, Parvus, and Rosa Luxemburg—and whom Karl Kautsky, the German Party's most eminent theoretician, supported, although he probably felt much more at ease with Bernstein than in the company of his new allies from abroad. The victory they won was Pyrrhic; it "merely strengthened alienation by pushing reality away." For the real issue was not theoretical and not economic. At stake was Bernstein's conviction, shamefully hidden in a footnote, that "the middle class—not excepting the German—in their bulk [was] still fairly healthy, not only economically but also *morally*" (my italics). This was the reason that Plekhanov called him a "philistine" and that Parvus and Rosa Luxemburg thought the fight so decisive for the future of the Party. For the truth of the matter was that Bernstein and Kautsky had in common their aversion to revolution; the "iron law of necessity" was for Kautsky the best possible excuse for doing nothing. The guests from Eastern Europe were the only ones who not merely "believed" in revolution as a theoretical necessity but wished to do something about it, precisely because they considered society as it was to be unbearable on *moral* grounds, on the grounds of justice. Bernstein and Rosa Luxemburg, on the other hand, had in common that they were both honest (which may explain Bernstein's "secret tenderness" for her), analyzed what they saw, were loyal to reality and critical of Marx; Bernstein was aware of this and shrewdly remarks in his reply to Rosa Luxemburg's attacks that she too had questioned "the whole Marxist predictions of the coming social evolution, so far as this is based on the theory of crises."

Rosa Luxemburg's early triumphs in the German Party rested on a double misunderstanding. At the turn of the century the SPD was "the envy and admiration of Socialists throughout the world." August Bebel, its "grand old man," who from Bismarck's foundation of the German Reich to the outbreak of the First World War "dominated [its] policy and spirit," had always proclaimed, "I am and always will be the mortal enemy of existing society." Didn't that sound like the spirit of the Polish peer group? Couldn't one assume from such proud defiance that the great German Party was somehow the SDKPIL writ large? It took Rosa Luxemburg almost a decade—until she returned from the first Russian revolution—to discover that the secret of this defiance was willful noninvolvement with the world at large and single-minded preoccupation with the growth of the Party organization. Out of this experience she developed, after 1910, her program of constant "friction" with society without which, as she then realized, the very source of the revolutionary spirit was doomed to dry up. She did not intend to spend her life in a sect, no matter how large; her commitment to revolution was primarily a moral matter, and this meant that she remained passionately engaged in public life and civil affairs, in the destinies of the world. Her involvement with European politics outside the immediate interests of the working class, and hence completely beyond the horizon of all Marxists, appears most convincingly in her repeated insistence on a "republican program" for the German and Russian Parties.

This was one of the main points of her famous *Juniusbroschüre,* written in prison during the war and then used as the platform for the *Spartakusbund.* Lenin, who was unaware of its authorship, immediately declared that to proclaim "the program of a republic . . . [means] in practice to proclaim the revolution—with an *incorrect* revolutionary program." Well, a year later the Russian Revolution broke out without any "program" whatsoever, and its first achievement was the abolition of the monarchy and the establishment of a republic, and the same was to happen in Germany and Austria. Which, of course, has never prevented the Russian, Polish, or German comrades from violently disagreeing with her on this point. It is indeed the republican question rather than the national one which separated her most decisively from all others. Here she was completely alone, as she was alone, though less obviously so, in her stress on the absolute necessity of not only individual but public freedom under all circumstances.

A second misunderstanding is directly connected with the revisionist debate. Rosa Luxemburg mistook Kautsky's reluctance to accept Bernstein's analyses for an authentic commitment to revolution. After the first Russian revolution in 1905, for which she had hurried back to Warsaw with false papers, she could no longer deceive herself. To her, these months constituted not only a crucial experience, they were also "the happiest of my life." Upon her return, she tried to discuss the events with her friends in the German Party. She learned quickly that the word "revolution" "had only to come into contact with a real revolutionary situation to break down" into meaningless syllables. The German Socialists were convinced that such things could happen only in distant barbarian lands. This was the first shock, from which she never recovered. The second came in 1914 and brought her near to suicide.

Naturally, her first contact with a real revolution taught her more and better things than disillusion and the fine arts of disdain and mistrust. Out of it came her insight into the nature of political action, which Mr. Nettl rightly calls her most important contribution to political theory. The main point is that she had learned from the revolutionary workers' councils (the latter *soviets*) that "good organization does not precede action but is the product of it," that "the organization of revolutionary action can and must be learnt in revolution itself, as one can only learn swimming in the water," that revolutions are "made" by nobody but break out "spontaneously," and that "the pressure for action" always comes "from below." A revolution is "great and strong as long as the Social Democrats [at the time still the only revolutionary party] don't smash it up."

There were, however, two aspects of the 1905 prelude which entirely escaped her. There was, after all, the surprising fact that the revolution had broken out not only in a non-industrialized, backward country, but in a territory where no strong socialist movement with mass support existed at all. And there was, second, the equally undeniable fact that the revolution had been the consequence of the Russian defeat in the Russo-Japanese War. These were the two facts Lenin never forgot and from which he drew two conclusions. First, one did not need a large organization; a small, tightly organized group with a leader who knew what he wanted was enough to pick up the power once the authority of the old regime had been swept away. Large revolutionary organizations were only a nuisance. And, second, since revolutions were not "made" but were the result of circumstances and events beyond anybody's power, wars were welcome.[9] The second point was the source of her disagreements with Lenin during the First World War; the first of her criticism of Lenin's tactics in the Russian Revolution of 1918. For she refused categorically, from beginning to end, to see in the war anything but the most terrible disaster, no matter what its eventual outcome; the price in human lives, especially in proletarian lives, was too high in any event. Moreover, it would have gone against her grain to look upon revolution as the profiteer of war and massacre—something which didn't bother Lenin in the least. And with respect to the issue of organization, she did not believe in a victory in which the people at large had no part and no voice; so little, indeed, did she believe in holding power at any price that she "was far more afraid of a deformed revolution than an unsuccessful one"—this was, in fact, "the major difference between her" and the Bolsheviks.

And haven't events proved her right? Isn't the history of the Soviet Union one long demonstration of the frightful dangers of "deformed revolutions"? Hasn't the "moral collapse" which she foresaw—without, of course, foreseeing the open criminality of Lenin's successor—done more harm to the cause of revolution as she understood it than "any and every political defeat . . . in honest struggle against superior forces and in the teeth of the historical situation" could possibly have done? Wasn't it true that Lenin was "completely mistaken" in the means he employed, that the only way to salvation was the "school of public life itself, the most unlimited, the broadest democracy and public opinion," and that terror "demoralized" everybody and destroyed everything?

She did not live long enough to see how right she had been and to watch the terrible and terribly swift moral deterioration of the Communist parties, the direct offspring of the Russian Revolution, throughout the world. Nor for that matter did Lenin, who despite all his mistakes still had more in common with the original peer group than with anybody who came after him. This became manifest when Paul Levi, the successor of Leo Jogiches in the leadership of the *Spartakusbund,* three years after Rosa Luxemburg's death, published her remarks on the Russian Revolution just quoted, which she had written in 1918 "only for you"—that is, without intending publication.[10] "It was a moment of considerable embarrassment" for both the German and Russian parties, and Lenin could be forgiven had he answered sharply and immoderately. Instead, he wrote: "We answer with . . . a good old Russian fable: an eagle can sometimes fly lower than a chicken, but a chicken can never rise to the same heights as an eagle. Rosa Luxemburg . . . in spite of [her] mistakes . . . was and is an eagle." He then went on to demand publication of "her biography and the *complete* edition of her works," unpurged of "error," and chided the German comrades for their "incredible" negligence in this duty. This was in 1922. Three years later, Lenin's successors had decided to "Bolshevize" the German Communist Party and therefore ordered a "specific onslaught on Rosa Luxemburg's whole legacy." The task was accepted with joy by a young member named Ruth Fischer, who had just arrived from Vienna. She told the German comrades that Rosa Luxemburg and her influence "were nothing less than a syphilis bacillus."

The gutter had opened, and out of it emerged what Rosa Luxemburg would have called "another zoological species." No "agents of the bourgeoisie" and no "Socialist traitors" were needed any longer to destroy the few survivors of the peer group and to bury in oblivion the last remnants of their spirit. No complete edition of her works, needless to say, was ever published. After World War II, a two-volume edition of selections "with careful annotations underlining her errors" came out in East Berlin and was followed by a "full-length analysis of the Luxemburgist system of errors" by Fred Oelssner, which quickly "lapsed into obscurity" because it became "too 'Stalinist.' " This most certainly was not what Lenin had demanded, nor could it, as he had hoped, serve "in the education of many generations of Communists."

After Stalin's death, things began to change, though not in East Germany, where, characteristically, revision of Stalinist history took the form of a "Bebel cult." (The only one to protest this new nonsense was poor old Hermann Duncker, the last distinguished survivor who still could "recall the most wonderful period of my life, when as a young man I knew and worked with Rosa Luxemburg, Karl Liebknecht, and Franz Mehring.") The Poles, however, although their own two-volume edition of selected works in 1959 is "partly overlapping with the German" one, "took out her reputation almost unaltered from the casket in which it had been stored" ever since Lenin's death, and after 1956 a "flood of Polish publications" on the subject appeared on the market. One would like to believe that there is still hope for a belated recognition of who she was and what she did, as one would like to hope that she will finally find her place in the education of political scientists in the countries of the West. For Mr. Nettl is right: "Her ideas belong wherever the history of political ideas is seriously taught."

Notes

1. Another limitation has become more obvious in recent years when Hitler and Stalin, because of their importance for contemporary history, were treated to the undeserved honor of definitive biographies. No matter how scrupulously Alan Bullock in his book on Hitler and Isaac Deutscher in his biography of Stalin followed the methodological technicalities prescribed by the genre, to see history in the light of these non-persons could only result in their falsifying promotion to respectability and in a more subtle distortion of the events. When we want to see both events and persons in right proportion we still have to go to the much less well documented and factually incomplete biographies of Hitler and Stalin by Konrad Heiden and Boris Souvarine respectively.

2. *Rosa Luxemburg,* 2 vols., Oxford University Press, 1966.

3. See the *Bulletin des Presse- und Informationsamtes der Bundesregierung,* of February 8, 1962, p. 224.

4. In a letter to Hans Diefenbach, March 8, 1917, in *Briefe an Freunde,* Zürich, 1950.

5. *Ibid.,* p. 84.

6. His most important book is now available in English under the title *Evolutionary Socialism* (Schocken Paperback), unfortunately lacking much-needed annotations and an introduction for the American reader.

7. See "The German Social Democratic Party, 1890–1914, as a Political Model," in *Past and Present,* April 1965.

8. The situation bore very similar traits to the position of the French army during the Dreyfus crisis in France which Rosa Luxemburg so brilliantly analyzed for *Die Neue Zeit* in "Die Soziale Krise in Frankreich" (vol. 1, 1901). "The reason the army was reluctant to make a move was that it wanted to show its opposition to the civil power of the republic, without at the same time losing the force of that opposition by committing itself," through a serious *coup d'état,* to another form of government.

9. Lenin read Clausewitz' *Vom Kriege* (1832) during the First World War; his excerpts and annotations were published in East Berlin during the fifties. According to Werner Hahlberg—"Lenin und Clausewitz" in the *Archiv für Kulturgeschichte,* vol. 36, Berlin, 1954—Lenin was under the influence of Clausewitz when he began to consider the possibility that war, the collapse of the European system of nation states, might replace the economic collapse of capitalist economy as predicted by Marx.

10. It is not without irony that this pamphlet is the only work of hers which is still read and quoted today. The following items are available in English: *The Accumulation of Capital,* London and Yale, 1951; the responses to Bernstein (1899) in an edition published by the Three Arrows Press, New York, 1937; the *Juniusbroschüre* (1918) under the title *The Crisis in the German Social Democracy* by the Lanka Sama Samaja Publications of Colombo, Ceylon, in 1955, apparently in mimeographed form, and originally published in 1918 by the Socialist Publication Society, New York. In 1953, the same publishing house in Ceylon brought out her *The Mass Strike, the Political Party, and the Trade Unions* (1906).

What Is Freedom?

I

To raise the question, what is freedom? seems to be a hopeless enterprise. It is as though age-old contradictions and antinomies were lying in wait to force the mind into dilemmas of logical impossibility so that, depending which horn of the dilemma you are holding on to, it becomes as impossible to conceive of freedom or its opposite as it is to realize the notion of a square circle. In its simplest form, the difficulty may be summed up as the contradiction between our consciousness and conscience, telling us that we are free and hence responsible, and our everyday experience in the outer world, in which we orient ourselves according to the principle of causality. In all practical and especially in political matters we hold human freedom to be a self-evident truth, and it is upon this axiomatic assumption that laws are laid down in human communities, that decisions are taken, that judgments are passed. In all fields of scientific and theoretical endeavor, on the contrary, we proceed according to the no less self-evident truth of *nihil ex nihilo*, of *nihil sine causa,* that is, on the assumption that even "our own lives are, in the last analysis, subject to causation" and that if there should be an ultimately free ego in ourselves, it certainly never makes its unequivocal appearance in the phenomenal world, and therefore can never become the subject of theoretical ascertainment. Hence freedom turns out to be a mirage the moment psychology looks into what is supposedly its innermost domain; for "the part which force plays in nature, as the cause of motion, has its counterpart in the mental sphere in motive as the cause of conduct."[1] It is true that the test of causality—the predictability of effect if all causes are known—cannot be applied to the realm of human affairs; but this practical impredictability is

---

From Between Past and Future. *This essay is a revised version of "Freedom and Politics: A Lecture,"* Chicago Review *14/1 (Spring 1960).*

no test of freedom, it signifies merely that we are in no position ever to know all causes which come into play, and this partly because of the sheer number of factors involved, but also because human motives, as distinguished from natural forces, are still hidden from all onlookers, from inspection by our fellow men as well as from introspection.

The greatest clarification in these obscure matters we owe to Kant and to his insight that freedom is no more ascertainable to the inner sense and within the field of inner experience than it is to the senses with which we know and understand the world. Whether or not causality is operative in the household of nature and the universe, it certainly is a category of the mind to bring order into all sensory data, whatever their nature may be, and thus it makes experience possible. Hence the antinomy between practical freedom and theoretical non-freedom, both equally axiomatic in their respective fields, does not merely concern a dichotomy between science and ethics, but lies in everyday life experiences from which both ethics and science take their respective points of departure. It is not scientific theory but thought itself, in its pre-scientific and pre-philosophical understanding, that seems to dissolve freedom on which our practical conduct is based into nothingness. For the moment we reflect upon an act which was undertaken under the assumption of our being a free agent, it seems to come under the sway of two kinds of causality, of the causality of inner motivation on one hand and of the causal principle which rules the outer world on the other. Kant saved freedom from this twofold assault upon it by distinguishing between a "pure" or theoretical reason and a "practical reason" whose center is free will, whereby it is important to keep in mind that the free-willing agent, who is practically all-important, never appears in the phenomenal world, neither in the outer world of our five senses nor in the field of the inner sense with which I sense myself. This solution, pitting the dictate of the will against the understanding of reason, is ingenious enough and may even suffice to establish a moral law whose logical consistency is in no way inferior to natural laws. But it does little to eliminate the greatest and most dangerous difficulty, namely, that thought itself, in its theoretical as well as its pre-theoretical form, makes freedom disappear—quite apart from the fact that it must appear strange indeed that the faculty of the will whose essential activity consists in dictate and command should be the harborer of freedom.

To the question of politics, the problem of freedom is crucial, and no political theory can afford to remain unconcerned with the fact that this problem has led into "the obscure wood wherein philosophy has lost its way."[2] It is the contention of the following considerations that the reason for this obscurity is that the phenomenon of freedom does not appear in the realm of thought at all, that neither freedom nor its opposite is experienced in the dialogue between me and myself in the course of which the great philosophic and metaphysical questions arise, and that the philosophical tradition, whose origin in this respect we shall consider later, has distorted, instead of clarifying, the very idea of freedom such as it is given in human experience by transposing it from its original field, the realm of politics and human affairs in general, to an inward domain, the will, where it would be open to self-inspection. As a first, preliminary justification of this approach, it may be pointed out that historically the problem of freedom has been the last of the time-honored great metaphysical questions—such as being, nothingness, the soul, nature, time, eternity, etc.—to become a topic of philosophic inquiry at all. There is no preoccupation with freedom in the whole history of great philosophy from the pre-Socratics up to Plotinus, the last ancient philosopher. And when freedom made its first appearance in our philosophical tradition, it was the experience of religious conversion—of Paul first and then of Augustine—which gave rise to it.

The field where freedom has always been known, not as a problem, to be sure, but as a fact of everyday life, is the political realm. And even today, whether we know it or not, the question of politics and the fact that man is a being endowed with the gift of action must always be present to our mind when we speak of the problem of freedom; for action and politics, among all the capabilities and potentialities of human life, are the only things of which we could not even conceive without at least assuming that freedom exists, and we can hardly touch a single political issue without, implicitly or explicitly, touching upon an issue of man's liberty. Freedom, moreover, is not only one among the many problems and phenomena of the political realm properly speaking, such as justice, or power, or equality; freedom, which only seldom—in times of crisis or revolution—becomes the direct aim of political action, is actually the reason that men live together in political organization at all. Without it, political life as such would be meaningless. The *raison d'être* of politics is freedom, and its field of experience is action.

This freedom which we take for granted in all political theory and which even those who praise tyranny must still take into account is the very opposite of "inner freedom," the inward space into which men may escape from external coercion and *feel* free. This inner feeling remains without outer manifestations and hence is by definition politically irrelevant. Whatever its legitimacy may be, and however eloquently it may have been described in late antiquity, it is historically a late phenomenon, and it was originally the result of an estrangement from the world in which worldly experiences were transformed into experiences within one's own self. The experiences of inner freedom are derivative in that they always presuppose a retreat from the world, where freedom was denied, into an inwardness to which no other has access. The inward space where the self is sheltered against the world must not be mistaken for the heart or the mind, both of which exist and function only in interrelationship with the world. Not the heart and not the mind, but inwardness as a place of absolute freedom within one's own self was discovered in late antiquity by those who had no place of their own in the world and hence lacked a worldly condition which, from early antiquity to almost the middle of the nineteenth century, was unanimously held to be a prerequisite for freedom.

The derivative character of this inner freedom, or of the theory that "the appropriate region of human liberty" is the "inward domain of consciousness,"[3] appears more clearly if we go back to its origins. Not the modern individual with his desire to unfold, to develop, and to expand, with his justified fear lest society get the better of his individuality, with his emphatic insistence "on the importance of genius" and originality, but the popular and popularizing sectarians of late antiquity, who have hardly more in common with philosophy than the name, are representative in this respect. Thus the most persuasive arguments for the absolute superiority of inner freedom can still be found in an essay of Epictetus,[4] who begins by stating that free is he who lives as he wishes, a definition which oddly echoes a sentence from Aristotle's *Politics* in which the statement "Freedom means the doing what a man likes" is put in the mouths of those who do not know what freedom is.[5] Epictetus then goes on to show that a man is free if he limits himself to what is in his power, if he does not reach into a realm where he can be hindered.[6] The "science of living"[7] consists in knowing how to distinguish between the alien world over which man has no power and the self of which he may dispose as he sees fit.[8]

Historically it is interesting to note that the appearance of the problem of freedom in Augustine's philosophy was thus preceded by the conscious attempt to divorce the notion of freedom from politics, to arrive at a formulation through which one may be a slave in the world and still be free. Conceptually, however, Epictetus's freedom which consists in being free from one's own desires is no more than a reversal of the current ancient political notions, and the political background against which this whole body of popular philosophy was formulated, the obvious decline of freedom in the late Roman Empire, manifests itself still quite clearly in the role which such notions as power, domination, and property play in it.

According to ancient understanding, man could liberate himself from necessity only through power over other men, and he could be free only if he owned a place, a home in the world. Epictetus transposed these worldly relationships into relationships within man's own self, whereby he discovered that no power is so absolute as that which man yields over himself, and that the inward space where man struggles and subdues himself is more entirely his own, namely, more securely shielded from outside interference, than any worldly home could ever be.

Hence, in spite of the great influence the concept of an inner, nonpolitical freedom has exerted upon the tradition of thought, it seems safe to say that man would know nothing of inner freedom if he had not first experienced a condition of being free as a worldly tangible reality. We first become aware of freedom or its opposite in our intercourse with others, not in the intercourse with ourselves. Before it became an attribute of thought or a quality of the will, freedom was understood to be the free man's status, which enabled him to move, to get away from home, to go out into the world and meet other people in deed and word. This freedom clearly was preceded by liberation: in order to be free, man must have liberated himself from the necessities of life. But the status of freedom did not follow automatically upon the act of liberation. Freedom needed, in addition to mere liberation, the company of other men who were in the same state, and it needed a common public space to meet them—a politically organized world, in other words, into which each of the free men could insert himself by word and deed.

Obviously not every form of human intercourse and not every kind of community is characterized by freedom. Where men live together but do not form a body politic—as, for example, in tribal societies or in the privacy of the household—the factors ruling their actions and conduct are not freedom but the necessities of life and concern for its preservation. Moreover, wherever the man-made world does not become the scene for action and speech—as in despotically ruled communities which banish their subjects into the narrowness of the home and thus prevent the rise of a public realm—freedom has no worldly reality. Without a politically guaranteed public realm, freedom lacks the worldly space to make its appearance. To be sure it may still dwell in men's hearts as desire or will or hope or yearning; but the human heart, as we all know, is a very dark place, and whatever goes on in its obscurity can hardly be called a demonstrable fact. Freedom as a demonstrable fact and politics coincide and are related to each other like two sides of the same matter.

Yet it is precisely this coincidence of politics and freedom which we cannot take for granted in the light of our present political experience.

The rise of totalitarianism, its claim to having subordinated all spheres of life to the demands of politics and its consistent nonrecognition of civil rights, above all the rights of privacy and the right to freedom from politics, makes us doubt not only the coincidence of politics and freedom but their very compatibility. We are inclined to believe that freedom begins where politics ends, because we have seen that freedom has disappeared when so-called political considerations overruled everything else. Was not the liberal credo, "The less politics the more freedom," right after all? Is it not true that the smaller the space occupied by the political, the larger the domain left to freedom? Indeed, do we not rightly measure the extent of freedom in any given community by the free scope it grants to apparently nonpolitical activities, free economic enterprise or freedom of teaching, of religion, of cultural and intellectual activities? Is it not true, as we all somehow believe, that politics is compatible with freedom only because and insofar as it guarantees a possible freedom *from* politics?

This definition of political liberty as a potential freedom from politics is not urged upon us merely by our most recent experiences; it has played a large part in the history of political theory. We need go no farther than the political thinkers of the seventeenth and eighteenth centuries, who more often than not simply identified political freedom with security. The highest purpose of politics, "the end of government," was the guaranty of security; security, in turn, made freedom possible, and the word "freedom" designated a quintessence of activities which occurred outside the political realm. Even Montesquieu, though he had not only a different but a much higher opinion of the essence of politics than Hobbes or Spinoza, could still occasionally equate political freedom with security.[9] The rise of the political and social sciences in the nineteenth and twentieth centuries has even widened the breach between freedom and politics; for government, which since the beginning of the modern age had been identified with the total domain of the political, was now considered to be the appointed protector not so much of freedom as of the life process, the interests of society and its individuals. Security remained the decisive criterion, but not the individual's security against "violent death," as in Hobbes (where the condition of all liberty is freedom from fear), but a security which should permit an undisturbed development of the life process of society as a whole. This life process is not bound up with freedom but follows its own inherent necessity; and it can be called free only in the sense that we speak of a freely flowing stream. Here freedom is not even the nonpolitical aim of politics, but a marginal phenomenon—which somehow forms the boundary government should not overstep unless life itself and its immediate interests and necessities are at stake.

Thus not only we, who have reasons of our own to distrust politics for the sake of freedom, but the entire modern age has separated freedom and politics. I could descend even deeper into the past and evoke older memories and traditions. The pre-modern secular concept of freedom certainly was emphatic in its insistence on separating the subjects' freedom from any direct share in government; the people's "liberty and freedom consisted in having the government of those laws by which their life and their goods may be most their own: 'tis not for having share in government, that is nothing pertaining to them"—as Charles I summed it up in his speech from the scaffold. It was not out of a desire for freedom that people eventually demanded their share in government or admission to the political realm, but out of mistrust in those who held power over their life and goods. The Christian concept of political freedom, moreover, arose out of the early Christians' suspicion of and hostility against the public realm as such, from whose concerns they demanded to be absolved in order to be free. And this Christian freedom for the sake of salvation had been preceded, as we saw before, by the philosophers' abstention from politics as a prerequisite for the highest and freest way of life, the *vita contemplativa*.

Despite the enormous weight of this tradition and despite the perhaps even more telling urgency of our own experiences, both pressing into the same direction of a divorce of freedom from politics, I think the reader may believe he has read only an old truism when I said that the *raison d'être* of politics is freedom and that this freedom is primarily experienced in action. In the following I shall do no more than reflect on this old truism.

I I

Freedom as related to politics is not a phenomenon of the will. We deal here not with the *liberum arbitrium,* a freedom of choice that arbitrates and decides between two given things, one good and one evil, and whose choice is predetermined by motive which has only to be argued to start its operation—"And therefore, since I cannot prove a lover,/ To entertain these fair well-spoken days,/ I am determined to prove a villain,/ And hate the idle pleasures of these days." Rather it is, to remain with Shakespeare, the freedom of Brutus: "That this shall be or we will fall for it," that is, the freedom to call something into being which did not exist before, which was not given, not even as an object of cognition or imagination, and which therefore, strictly speaking, could not be known. Action, to be free, must be free from motive on one side, from its intended goal as a predictable effect on the other. This is not to say that motives and aims are not important factors in every single act, but they are its determining factors, and action is free to the extent that it is able to transcend them. Action insofar as it is determined is guided by a future aim whose desirability the intellect has grasped before the will wills it, whereby the intellect calls upon the will, since only the will can dictate action—to paraphrase a characteristic description of this process by Duns Scotus.[10] The aim of action varies and depends upon the changing circumstances of the world; to recognize the aim is not a matter of freedom, but of right or wrong judgment. Will, seen as a distinct and separate human faculty, follows judgment, i.e., cognition of the right aim, and then commands its execution. The power to command, to dictate action, is not a matter of freedom but a question of strength or weakness.

Action insofar as it is free is neither under the guidance of the intellect nor under the dictate of the will—although it needs both for the execution of any particular goal—but springs from something altogether different which (following Montesquieu's famous analysis of forms of government) I shall call a principle. Principles do not operate from within the self as motives do—"mine own deformity" or my "fair proportion"—but inspire, as it were, from without; and they are much too general to prescribe particular goals, although every particular aim can be judged in the light of its principle once the act has been started. For, unlike the judgment of the intellect which precedes action, and unlike the command of the will which initiates it, the inspiring principle becomes fully manifest only in the performing act itself; yet while the merits of judgment lose their validity, and the strength of the commanding will exhausts itself, in the course of the act which they execute in cooperation, the principle which inspired it loses nothing in strength or validity through execution. In distinction from its goal, the principle of an action can be repeated time and again, it is inexhaustible, and in distinction from its motive, the validity of a principle is universal, it is not bound to any particular person or to any particular group. However, the manifestation of principles comes about only through action, they are manifest in the world as long as the action lasts, but no longer. Such principles are honor or glory, love of equality, which Montesquieu called virtue, or distinction or excellence— the Greek ἀεὶ ἀριστεύειν ("always strive to do your best and to be the best of all"), but also fear or distrust or hatred. Freedom or its opposite appears in the world whenever such principles are actualized; the appearance of freedom, like the manifestation of principles, coincides with the performing act. Men *are* free—as distinguished from their possessing the gift for freedom—as long as they act, neither before nor after; for to *be* free and to act are the same.

Freedom as inherent in action is perhaps best illustrated by Machiavelli's concept of *virtù,* the excellence with which man answers the opportunities the world opens up before him in the guise of *fortuna.* Its meaning is best rendered by "virtuosity," that is, an excellence we attribute to the performing arts (as distinguished from the creative arts of making), where the accomplishment lies in the performance itself and not in an end product which outlasts the activity that brought it into existence and becomes independent of it. The virtuoso-ship of Machiavelli's *virtù* somehow reminds us of the fact, although Machiavelli hardly knew it, that the Greeks always used such metaphors as flute-playing, dancing, healing, and seafaring to distinguish political from other activities, that is, that they drew their analogies from those arts in which virtuosity of performance is decisive.

Since all acting contains an element of virtuosity, and because virtuosity is the excellence we ascribe to the performing arts, politics has often been defined as an art. This, of course, is not a definition but a metaphor, and the metaphor becomes completely false if one falls into the common error of regarding the state or government as a work of art, as a kind of collective masterpiece. In the sense of the creative arts, which bring forth something tangible and reify human thought to such an extent that the produced thing possesses an existence of its own, politics is the exact opposite of an art—which incidentally does not mean that it is a science. Political institutions, no matter how well or how badly designed, depend for continued existence upon acting men; their conservation is achieved by the same means that brought them into being. Independent existence marks the work of art as a product of making; utter dependence upon further acts to keep it in existence marks the state as a product of action.

The point here is not whether the creative artist is free in the process of creation, but that the creative process is not displayed in public and not destined to appear in the world. Hence the element of freedom, certainly present in the creative arts, remains hidden; it is not the free creative process which finally appears and matters for the world, but the work of art itself, the end product of the process. The performing arts, on the contrary, have indeed a strong affinity with politics. Performing artists—dancers, play-actors, musicians, and the like—need an audience to show their virtuosity, just as acting men need the presence of others before whom they can appear; both need a publicly organized space for their "work," and both depend upon others for the performance itself. Such a space of appearances is not to be taken for granted wherever men live together in a community. The Greek polis once was precisely that "form of government" which provided men with a space of appearances where they could act, with a kind of theater where freedom could appear.

To use the word "political" in the sense of the Greek polis is neither arbitrary nor far-fetched. Not only etymologically and not only for the learned does the very word, which in all European languages still derives from the historically unique organization of the Greek city-state, echo the experiences of the community which first discovered the essence and the realm of the political. It is indeed difficult and even misleading to talk about politics and its innermost principles without drawing to some extent upon the experiences of Greek and Roman antiquity, and this for no other reason than that men have never, either before or after, thought so highly of political activity and bestowed so much dignity upon its realm. As regards the relation of freedom to politics, there is the additional reason that only ancient political communities were founded for the express purpose of serving the free—those who were neither slaves, subject to coercion by others, nor laborers, driven and urged on by the necessities of life. If, then, we understand the political in the sense of the polis, its end or *raison d'être* would be to establish and keep in existence a space where freedom as virtuosity can appear. This is the realm where freedom is a worldly reality, tangible in words which can be heard, in deeds which can be seen, and in events which are talked about, remembered, and turned into stories before they are finally incorporated into the great storybook of human history. Whatever occurs in this space of appearances is political by definition, even when it is not a direct product of action. What remains outside it, such as the great feats of barbarian empires, may be impressive and noteworthy, but it is not political, strictly speaking.

Every attempt to derive the concept of freedom from experiences in the political realm sounds strange and startling because all our theories in these matters are dominated by the notion that freedom is an attribute of will and thought much rather than of action. And this priority is not merely derived from the notion that every act must psychologically be preceded by a cognitive act of the intellect and a command of the will to carry out its decision, but also, and perhaps even primarily, because it is held that "perfect liberty is incompatible with the existence of society," that it can be tolerated in its perfection only outside the realm of human affairs. This current argument does not hold—what perhaps is true—that it is in the nature of thought to need more freedom than does any other activity of men, but rather that thinking in itself is not dangerous, so that only action needs to be restrained: "No one pretends that actions should be as free as opinions."[11] This, of course, belongs among the fundamental tenets of liberalism, which, its name notwithstanding, has done its share to banish the notion of liberty from the political realm. For politics, according to the same philosophy, must be concerned almost exclusively with the maintenance of life and the safeguarding of its interests. Now, where life is at stake all action is by definition under the sway of necessity, and the proper realm to take care of life's necessities is the gigantic and still increasing sphere of social and economic life whose administration has overshadowed the political realm ever since the beginning of the modern age. Only foreign affairs, because the relationships between nations still harbor hostilities and sympathies which cannot be reduced to economic factors, seem to be left as a purely political domain. And even here the prevailing tendency is to consider international power problems and rivalries as ultimately springing from economic factors and interests.

Yet just as we, despite all theories and isms, still believe that to say "Freedom is the *raison d'être* of politics" is no more than a truism, so do we, in spite of our apparently exclusive concern with life, still hold as a matter of course that courage is one of the cardinal political virtues, although—if all this were a matter of consistency, which it obviously is not—we should be the first to condemn courage as the foolish and even vicious contempt for life and its interests, that is, for the allegedly highest of all goods. Courage is a big word, and I do not mean the daring of adventure which gladly risks life for the sake of being as thoroughly and intensely alive as one can be only in the face of danger and death. Temerity is no less concerned with life than is cowardice. Courage, which we still believe to be indispensable for political action, and which Churchill once called "the first of human qualities, because it is the quality which guarantees all others," does not gratify our individual sense of vitality but is demanded of us by the very nature of the public realm. For this world of ours, because it existed before us and is meant to outlast our lives in it, simply cannot afford to give primary concern to individual lives and the interests connected with them; as such the public realm stands in the sharpest possible contrast to our private domain, where, in the protection of family and home, everything serves and must serve the security of the life process. It requires courage even to leave the protective security of our four walls and enter the public realm, not because of particular dangers which may lie in wait for us, but because we have arrived in a realm where the concern for life has lost its validity. Courage liberates men from their worry about life for the freedom of the world. Courage is indispensable because in politics not life but the world is at stake.

I I I

Obviously this notion of an interdependence of freedom and politics stands in contradiction to the social theories of the modern age. Unfortunately it does not follow that we need only to revert to older, pre-modern traditions and theories. Indeed, the greatest difficulty in reaching an understanding of what freedom is arises from the fact that a simple return to tradition, and especially to what we are wont to call the great tradition, does not help us. Neither the philosophical concept of freedom as it first arose in late antiquity, where freedom became a phenomenon of thought by which man could, as it were, reason himself out of the world, nor the Christian and modern notion of free will has any ground in political experience. Our philosophical tradition is almost unanimous in holding that freedom begins where men have left the realm of political life inhabited by the many, and that it is not experienced in association with others but in intercourse with one's self—whether in the form of an inner dialogue which, since Socrates, we call thinking, or in a conflict within myself, the inner strife between what I would and what I do, whose murderous dialectics disclosed first to Paul and then to Augustine the equivocalities and impotence of the human heart.

For the history of the problem of freedom, Christian tradition has indeed become the decisive factor. We almost automatically equate freedom with free will, that is, with a faculty virtually unknown to classical antiquity. For will, as Christianity discovered it, had so little in common with the well-known capacities to desire, to intend, and to aim at, that it claimed attention only after it had come into conflict with them. If freedom were actually nothing but a phenomenon of the will, we would have to conclude that the ancients did not know freedom. This, of course, is absurd, but if one wished to assert it he could argue what I have mentioned before, namely, that the idea of freedom played no role in philosophy prior to Augustine. The reason for this striking fact is that, in Greek as well as Roman antiquity, freedom was an exclusively political concept, indeed the quintessence of the city-state and of citizenship. Our philosophical tradition of political thought, beginning with Parmenides and Plato, was founded explicitly in opposition to this polis and its citizenship. The way of life chosen by the philosopher was understood in opposition to the βίος πολιτικός, the political way of life. Freedom, therefore, the very center of politics as the Greeks understood it, was an idea which almost by definition could not enter the framework of Greek philosophy. Only when the early Christians, and especially Paul, discovered a kind of freedom which had no relation to politics, could the concept of freedom

enter the history of philosophy. Freedom became one of the chief problems of philosophy when it was experienced as something occurring in
the intercourse between me and myself, and outside of the intercourse between men. Free will and freedom became synonymous notions,[12] and
the presence of freedom was experienced in complete solitude, "where no
man might hinder the hot contention wherein I had engaged with myself," the deadly conflict which took place in the "inner dwelling" of the
soul and the dark "chamber of the heart."[13]

Classical antiquity was by no means inexperienced in the phenomena
of solitude; it knew well enough that solitary man is no longer one but
two-in-one, that an intercourse between me and myself begins the moment the intercourse between me and my fellow men has been interrupted for no matter what reason. In addition to this dualism which is the
existential condition of thought, classical philosophy since Plato had insisted on a dualism between soul and body whereby the human faculty of
motion had been assigned to the soul, which was supposed to move the
body as well as itself; and it was still within the range of Platonic thought
to interpret this faculty as a rulership of the soul over the body. Yet the
Augustinian solitude of "hot contention" within the soul itself was utterly
unknown, for the fight in which he had become engaged was not between reason and passion, between understanding and θυμός,[14] that is,
between two different human faculties, but it was a conflict within the
will itself. And this duality within the self-same faculty had been known as
the characteristic of thought, as the dialogue which I hold with myself. In
other words, the two-in-one of solitude which sets the thought process
into motion has the exactly opposite effect on the will; it paralyzes and
locks it within itself; willing in solitude is always *velle* and *nolle*, to will and
not to will at the same time.

The paralyzing effect the will seems to have upon itself comes all the
more surprisingly as its very essence obviously is to command and be
obeyed. Hence it appears to be a "monstrosity" that man may command
himself and not be obeyed, a monstrosity which can be explained only by
the simultaneous presence of an I-will and an I-will-not.[15] This, however,
is already an interpretation by Augustine; the historical fact is that the phenomenon of the will originally manifested itself in the experience that
what I would I do not, that there is such a thing as I-will-and-cannot.
What was unknown to antiquity was not that there is a possible I-know-
but-I-will-not, but that I-will and I-can are not the same—*non hoc est
velle, quod posse.*[16] For the I-will-and-I-can was of course very familiar to
the ancients. We need only remember how much Plato insisted that only
those who knew how to rule themselves had the right to rule others and

be freed from the obligation of obedience. And it is true that self-control
has remained one of the specifically political virtues, if only because it is
an outstanding phenomenon of virtuosity where I-will and I-can must be
so well attuned that they practically coincide.

Had ancient philosophy known of a possible conflict between what I
can and what I will, it would certainly have understood the phenomenon
of freedom as an inherent quality of the I-can, or it might conceivably
have defined it as the coincidence of I-will and I-can; it certainly would
not have thought of it as an attribute of the I-will or I-would. This assertion is no empty speculation; even the Euripidean conflict between reason
and θυμός both simultaneously present in the soul, is a relatively late phenomenon. More typical, and in our context more relevant, was the conviction that passion may blind men's reason but that once reason has
succeeded in making itself heard there is no passion left to prevent man
from doing what he *knows* is right. This conviction still underlies Socrates'
teaching that virtue is a kind of knowledge, and our amazement that anybody could ever have thought that virtue was "rational," that it could be
learned and taught, arises from our acquaintance with a will which is broken in itself, which wills and wills-not at the same time, much rather than
from any superior insight in the alleged powerlessness of reason.

In other words, will, will-power, and will-to-power are for us almost
identical notions; the seat of power is to us the faculty of the will as
known and experienced by man in his intercourse with himself. And for
the sake of this will-power we have emasculated not only our reasoning
and cognitive faculties but other more "practical" faculties as well. But is
it not plain even to us that, in the words of Pindar, "this is the greatest
grief: to stand with his feet outside the right and the beautiful one knows
[forced away], by necessity"?[17] The necessity which prevents me from doing what I know and will may arise from the world, or from my own
body, or from an insufficiency of talents, gifts, and qualities which are bestowed upon man by birth and over which he has hardly more power
than he has over other circumstances; all these factors, the psychological
ones not excluded, condition the person from the outside as far as the I-
will and the I-know, that is, the ego itself, are concerned; the power that
meets these circumstances, that liberates, as it were, willing and knowing
from their bondage to necessity is the I-can. Only where the I-will and
the I-can coincide does freedom come to pass.

There exists still another way to check our current notion of free
will, born of a religious predicament and formulated in philosophical language, against the older, strictly political experiences of freedom. In the
revival of political thought which accompanied the rise of the modern

age, we may distinguish between those thinkers who can truly be called the fathers of political "science," since they took their cue from the new discoveries of the natural sciences—their greatest representative is Hobbes—and those who, relatively undisturbed by these typically modern developments, harkened back to the political thought of antiquity, not out of any predilection for the past as such but simply because the separation of church and state, of religion and politics, had given rise to an independent secular, political realm such as had been unknown since the fall of the Roman Empire. The greatest representative of this political secularism was Montesquieu, who, though indifferent to problems of a strictly philosophic nature, was deeply aware of the inadequacy of the Christian and the philosophers' concept of freedom for political purposes. In order to get rid of it, he expressly distinguished between philosophical and political freedom, and the difference consisted in that philosophy demands no more of freedom than the exercise of the will (*l'exercice de la volonté*), independent of circumstances and of attainment of the goals the will has set. Political freedom, on the contrary, consists in being able to do what one ought to will (*la liberté ne peut consister qu' à pouvoir faire ce que l'on doit vouloir*—the emphasis is on *pouvoir*).[18] For Montesquieu as for the ancients it was obvious that an agent could no longer be called free when he lacked the capacity to do—whereby it is irrelevant whether this failure is caused by exterior or by interior circumstances.

I chose the example of self-control because to us this is clearly a phenomenon of will and of will-power. The Greeks, more than any other people, have reflected on moderation and the necessity to tame the steeds of the soul, and yet they never became aware of the will as a distinct faculty, separate from other human capacities. Historically, men first discovered the will when they experienced its impotence and not its power, when they said with Paul: "For to will is present with me; but how to perform that which is good I find not." It is the same will of which Augustine complained that it seemed "no monstrousness [for it] partly to will, partly to nill"; and although he points out that this is "a disease of the mind," he also admits that this disease is, as it were, natural for a mind possessed of a will: "For the will commands that there be a will, it commands not something else but itself. . . . Were the will entire, it would not even command itself to be, because it would already be."[19] In other words, if man has a will at all, it must always appear as though there were two wills present in the same man, fighting with each other for power over his mind. Hence, the will is both powerful and impotent, free and unfree.

When we speak of impotence and the limits set to will-power, we usually think of man's powerlessness with respect to the surrounding world. It is, therefore, of some importance to notice that in these early testimonies the will was not defeated by some overwhelming force of nature or circumstances; the contention which its appearance raised was neither the conflict between the one against the many nor the strife between body and mind. On the contrary, the relation of mind to body was for Augustine even the outstanding example for the enormous power inherent in the will: "The mind commands the body, and the body obeys instantly; the mind commands itself, and is resisted."[20] The body represents in this context the exterior world and is by no means identical with one's self. It is within one's self, in the "interior dwelling" (*interior domus*), where Epictetus still believed man to be an absolute master, that the conflict between man and himself broke out and that the will was defeated. Christian will-power was discovered as an organ of self-liberation and immediately found wanting. It is as though the I-will immediately paralyzed the I-can, as though the moment men *willed* freedom, they lost their capacity to *be* free. In the deadly conflict with worldly desires and intentions from which will-power was supposed to liberate the self, the most willing seemed able to achieve was oppression. Because of the will's impotence, its incapacity to generate genuine power, its constant defeat in the struggle with the self, in which the power of the I-can exhausted itself, the will-to-power turned at once into a will-to-oppression. I can only hint here at the fatal consequences for political theory of this equation of freedom with the human capacity to will; it was one of the causes why even today we almost automatically equate power with oppression or, at least, with rule over others.

However that may be, what we usually understand by will and will-power has grown out of this conflict between a willing and a performing self, out of the experience of an I-will-and-can*not*, which means that the I-will, no matter what is willed, remains subject to the self, strikes back at it, spurs it on, incites it further, or is ruined by it. However far the will-to-power may reach out, and even if somebody possessed by it begins to conquer the whole world, the I-will can never rid itself of the self; it always remains bound to it and, indeed, under its bondage. This bondage to the self distinguishes the I-will from the I-think, which also is carried on between me and myself but in whose dialogue the self is not the object of the activity of thought. The fact that the I-will has become so power-thirsty, that will and will-to-power have become practically identical, is perhaps due to its having been first experienced in its impotence. Tyranny at any rate, the only form of government which arises directly out of the I-will, owes its greedy cruelty to an egotism utterly absent from the utopian tyrannies of reason with which the philosophers wished to coerce men and which they conceived on the model of the I-think.

I have said that the philosophers first began to show an interest in the problem of freedom when freedom was no longer experienced in acting and in associating with others but in willing and in the intercourse with one's self, when, briefly, freedom had become free will. Since then, freedom has been a philosophical problem of the first order; as such it was applied to the political realm and thus has become a political problem as well. Because of the philosophic shift from action to will-power, from freedom as a state of being manifest in action to the *liberum arbitrium,* the ideal of freedom ceased to be virtuosity in the sense we mentioned before and became sovereignty, the ideal of a free will, independent from others and eventually prevailing against them. The philosophic ancestry of our current political notion of freedom is still quite manifest in eighteenth-century political writers, when, for instance, Thomas Paine insisted that "to be free it is sufficient [for man] that he wills it," a word which Lafayette applied to the nation-state: *"Pour qu'une nation soit libre, il suffit qu'elle veuille l'être."*

Obviously such words echo the political philosophy of Jean-Jacques Rousseau, who has remained the most consistent representative of the theory of sovereignty, which he derived directly from the will, so that he could conceive of political power in the strict image of individual will-power. He argued against Montesquieu that power must be sovereign, that is, indivisible, because "a divided will would be inconceivable." He did not shun the consequences of this extreme individualism, and he held that in an ideal state "the citizens had no communications one with another," that in order to avoid factions "each citizen should think only his own thoughts." In reality Rousseau's theory stands refuted for the simple reason that "it is absurd for the will to bind itself for the future";[21] a community actually founded on this sovereign will would be built not on sand but on quicksand. All political business is, and always has been, transacted within an elaborate framework of ties and bonds for the future—such as laws and constitutions, treaties and alliances—all of which derive in the last instance from the faculty to promise and to keep promises in the face of the essential uncertainties of the future. A state, moreover, in which there is no communication between the citizens and where each man thinks only his own thoughts is by definition a tyranny. That the faculty of will and will-power in and by itself, unconnected with any other faculties, is an essentially nonpolitical and even anti-political capacity is perhaps nowhere else so manifest as in the absurdities to which Rousseau was driven and in the curious cheerfulness with which he accepted them.

Politically, this identification of freedom with sovereignty is perhaps the most pernicious and dangerous consequence of the philosophical equation of freedom and free will. For it leads either to a denial of human freedom—namely, if it is realized that whatever men may be, they are never sovereign—or to the insight that the freedom of one man, or a group, or a body politic can be purchased only at the price of the freedom, i.e., the sovereignty, of all others. Within the conceptual framework of traditional philosophy, it is indeed very difficult to understand how freedom and non-sovereignty can exist together or, to put it another way, how freedom could have been given to men under the condition of non-sovereignty. Actually it is as unrealistic to deny freedom because of the fact of human non-sovereignty as it is dangerous to believe that one can be free—as an individual or as a group—only if he is sovereign. The famous sovereignty of political bodies has always been an illusion, which, moreover, can be maintained only by the instruments of violence, that is, with essentially nonpolitical means. Under human conditions, which are determined by the fact that not man but men live on the earth, freedom and sovereignty are so little identical that they cannot even exist simultaneously. Where men wish to be sovereign, as individuals or as organized groups, they must submit to the oppression of the will, be this the individual will with which I force myself, or the "general will" of an organized group. If men wish to be free, it is precisely sovereignty they must renounce.

I V

Since the whole problem of freedom arises for us in the horizon of Christian traditions on one hand, and of an originally anti-political philosophic tradition on the other, we find it difficult to realize that there may exist a freedom which is not an attribute of the will but an accessory of doing and acting. Let us therefore go back once more to antiquity, i.e., to its political and pre-philosophical traditions, certainly not for the sake of erudition and not even because of the continuity of our tradition, but merely because a freedom experienced in the process of acting and nothing else—though, of course, mankind never lost this experience altogether—has never again been articulated with the same classical clarity.

However, for reasons we mentioned before and which we cannot discuss here, this articulation is nowhere more difficult to grasp than in the writings of the philosophers. It would of course lead us too far to try to distill, as it were, adequate concepts from the body of non-philosophical

literature, from poetic, dramatic, historical, and political writings, whose
articulation lifts experiences into a realm of splendor which is not the
realm of conceptual thought. And for our purposes this is not necessary.
For whatever ancient literature, Greek as well as Latin, has to tell us about
these matters is ultimately rooted in the curious fact that both the Greek
and the Latin language possess two verbs to designate what we uniformly
call "to act." The two Greek words are ἄρχειν: to begin, to lead, and, finally, to rule; and πράττειν: to carry something through. The corresponding Latin verbs are *agere:* to set something in motion; and *gerere,*
which is hard to translate and somehow means the enduring and supporting continuation of past acts whose results are the *res gestae,* the deeds and
events we call historical. In both instances action occurs in two different
stages; its first stage is a beginning by which something new comes into
the world. The Greek word ἄρχειν, which covers beginning, leading,
ruling, that is, the outstanding qualities of the free man, bears witness to
an experience in which being free and the capacity to begin something
new coincided. Freedom, as we would say today, was experienced in
spontaneity. The manifold meaning of ἄρχειν indicates the following:
only those could begin something new who were already rulers (i.e.,
household heads who ruled over slaves and family) and had thus liberated
themselves from the necessities of life for enterprises in distant lands or citizenship in the polis; in either case, they no longer ruled, but were rulers
among rulers, moving among their peers, whose help they enlisted as
leaders in order to begin something new, to start a new enterprise; for
only with the help of others could the ἄρχων, the ruler, beginner and
leader, really act, πράττειν, carry through whatever he had started to do.

In Latin, to be free and to begin are also interconnected, though in a
different way. Roman freedom was a legacy bequeathed by the founders
of Rome to the Roman people; their freedom was tied to the beginning
their forefathers had established by founding the city, whose affairs the de-
scendants had to manage, whose consequences they had to bear, and
whose foundations they had to "augment." All these together are the *res
gestae* of the Roman republic. Roman historiography therefore, essentially
as political as Greek historiography, never was content with the mere nar-
ration of great deeds and events; unlike Thucydides or Herodotus, the
Roman historians always felt bound to the beginning of Roman history,
because this beginning contained the authentic element of Roman freedom and thus made their history political; whatever they had to relate,
they started *ab urbe condita,* with the foundation of the city, the guaranty of
Roman freedom.

I have already mentioned that the ancient concept of freedom played no role in Greek philosophy precisely because of its exclusively political origin. Roman writers, it is true, rebelled occasionally against the anti-political tendencies of the Socratic school, but their strange lack of philosophic talent apparently prevented their finding a theoretical concept of freedom which could have been adequate to their own experiences and to the great institutions of liberty present in the Roman *res publica.* If the history of ideas were as consistent as its historians sometimes imagine, we should have even less hope of finding a valid political idea of freedom in Augustine, the great Christian thinker who in fact introduced Paul's free will, along with its perplexities, into the history of philosophy. Yet we find in Augustine not only the discussion of freedom as *liberum arbitrium,* though this discussion became decisive for the tradition, but also an entirely differently conceived notion which characteristically appears in his only political treatise, in *De Civitate Dei.* In the *City of God* Augustine, as in only natural, speaks more from the background of specifically Roman experiences than in any of his other writings, and freedom is conceived there not as an inner human disposition but as a character of human existence in the world. Man does not possess freedom so much as he, or better his coming into the world, is equated with the appearance of freedom in the universe; man is free because he is a beginning and was so created after the universe had already come into existence: [*Initium*] *ut esset, creatus est homo, ante quem nemo fuit.*[22] In the birth of each man this initial beginning is reaffirmed, because in each instance something new comes into an already existing world which will continue to exist after each individual's death. Because he *is* a beginning, man can begin; to be human and to be free are one and the same. God created man in order to introduce into the world the faculty of beginning: freedom.

The strong anti-political tendencies of early Christianity are so familiar that the notion of a Christian thinker's having been the first to formulate the philosophical implications of the ancient political idea of freedom strikes us as almost paradoxical. The only explanation that comes to mind is that Augustine was a Roman as well as a Christian, and that in this part of his work he formulated the central political experience of Roman antiquity, which was that freedom *qua* beginning became manifest in the act of foundation. Yet I am convinced that this impression would considerably change if the sayings of Jesus of Nazareth were taken more seriously in their philosophic implications. We find in these parts of the New Testament an extraordinary understanding of freedom, and particularly of the power inherent in human freedom; but the human capacity which corresponds to this power, which, in the words of the Gospel, is capable of removing mountains, is not will but faith. The work of faith, actually its product, is what the gospels called "miracles," a word with many meanings in the New Testament and difficult to understand. We can neglect the difficulties here and refer only to those passages where miracles are clearly not supernatural events but only what all miracles, those performed by men no less than those performed by a divine agent, always must be, namely, interruptions of some natural series of events, of some automatic process, in whose context they constitute the wholly unexpected.

No doubt human life, placed on the earth, is surrounded by automatic processes—by the natural processes of the earth, which, in turn, are surrounded by cosmic processes, and we ourselves are driven by similar forces insofar as we too are a part of organic nature. Our political life, moreover, despite its being the realm of action, also takes place in the midst of processes which we call historical and which tend to become as automatic as natural or cosmic processes, although they were started by men. The truth is that automatism is inherent in all processes, no matter what their origin may be—which is why no single act, and no single event, can ever, once and for all, deliver and save a man, or a nation, or mankind. It is in the nature of the automatic processes to which man is subject, but within and against which he can assert himself through action, that they can only spell ruin to human life. Once man-made, historical processes have become automatic, they are no less ruinous than the natural life process that drives our organism and which in its own terms, that is, biologically, leads from being to non-being, from birth to death. The historical sciences know only too well such cases of petrified and hopelessly declining civilizations where doom seems foreordained, like a biological necessity, and since such historical processes of stagnation can last and creep on for centuries, they even occupy by far the largest space in recorded history; the periods of being free have always been relatively short in the history of mankind.

What usually remains intact in the epochs of petrification and foreordained doom is the faculty of freedom itself, the sheer capacity to begin, which animates and inspires all human activities and is the hidden source of production of all great and beautiful things. But so long as this source remains hidden, freedom is not a worldly, tangible reality; that is, it is not political. Because the source of freedom remains present even when political life has become petrified and political action impotent to interrupt automatic processes, freedom can so easily be mistaken for an essentially nonpolitical phenomenon; in such circumstances, freedom is not experienced as a mode of being with its own kind of "virtue" and virtuosity, but as a supreme gift which only man, of all earthly creatures, seems to have received, of which we can find traces and signs in almost all his activities, but which, nevertheless, develops fully only when action has created its own worldly space where it can come out of hiding, as it were, and make its appearance.

Every act, seen from the perspective not of the agent but of the process in whose framework it occurs and whose automatism it interrupts, is a "miracle"—that is, something which could not be expected. If it is true that action and beginning are essentially the same, it follows that a capacity for performing miracles must likewise be within the range of human faculties. This sounds stranger than it actually is. It is in the very nature of every new beginning that it breaks into the world as an "infinite improbability," and yet it is precisely this infinitely improbable which actually constitutes the very texture of everything we call real. Our whole existence rests, after all, on a chain of miracles, as it were—the coming into being of the earth, the development of organic life on it, the evolution of mankind out of the animal species. For from the viewpoint of the processes in the universe and in nature, and their statistically overwhelming probabilities, the coming into being of the earth out of cosmic processes, the formation of organic life out of inorganic processes, the evolution of man, finally, out of the processes of organic life are all "infinite improbabilities," they are "miracles" in everyday language. It is because of this element of the "miraculous" present in all reality that events, no matter how well anticipated in fear or hope, strike us with a shock of surprise once they have come to pass. The very impact of an event is never wholly explicable; its factuality transcends in principle all anticipation. The experience which tells us that events are miracles is neither arbitrary nor sophisticated; it is, on the contrary, most natural and, indeed, in ordinary life almost commonplace. Without this commonplace experience, the part assigned by religion to supernatural miracles would be well-nigh incomprehensible.

I chose the example of natural processes which are interrupted by the advent of some "infinite improbability" in order to illustrate that what we call real in ordinary experience has mostly come into existence through coincidences which are stranger than fiction. Of course the example has its limitations and cannot be simply applied to the realm of human affairs. It would be sheer superstition to hope for miracles, for the "infinitely improbable," in the context of automatic historical or political processes, although even this can never be completely excluded. History, in contradistinction to nature, is full of events; here the miracle of accident and infinite improbability occurs so frequently that it seems strange to speak of miracles at all. But the reason for this frequency is merely that historical processes are created and constantly interrupted by human initiative, by the *initium* man is insofar as he is an acting being. Hence it is not in the least superstitious, it is even a counsel of realism, to look for the unforeseeable and unpredictable, to be prepared for and to expect "miracles" in the political realm. And the more heavily the scales are weighted in favor of disaster, the more miraculous will the deed done in freedom appear; for it is disaster, not salvation, which always happens automatically and therefore always must appear to be irresistible.

Objectively, that is, seen from the outside and without taking into account that man is a beginning and a beginner, the chances that tomorrow will be like yesterday are always overwhelming. Not quite so overwhelming, to be sure, but very nearly so as the chances were that *no* earth would ever rise out of cosmic occurrences, that *no* life would develop out of inorganic processes, and that *no* man would emerge out of the evolution of animal life. The decisive difference between the "infinite improbabilities" on which the reality of our earthly life rests and the miraculous character inherent in those events which establish historical reality is that, in the realm of human affairs, we know the author of the "miracles." It is men who perform them—men who because they have received the twofold gift of freedom and action can establish a reality of their own.

Notes

1. I follow Max Planck, "Causation and Free Will" (in *The New Science,* New York, 1959) because the two essays, written from the standpoint of the scientist, possess a classic beauty in their nonsimplifying simplicity and clarity.

2. Ibid.

3. John Stuart Mill, *On Liberty.*

4. See "On Freedom" in *Dissertationes,* book IV, 1, § 1.

5. 1310a25 ff.

6. Op. cit., § 75.

7. Ibid., § 118

8. §§ 81 and 83.

9. See *Esprit des Lois,* XII, 2: *"La liberté philosophique consiste dans l'exercice de la volonté. . . . La liberté politique consiste dans la sûreté."*

10. *Intellectus apprehendit agibile antequam voluntas illud velit; sed non apprehendit determinate hoc esse agendum quod apprehendere dicitur dictare.* Oxon. IV, d. 46, qu. 1, no. 10.

11. John Stuart Mill, op. cit.

12. Leibniz only sums up and articulates the Christian tradition when he writes: *"Die Frage, ob unserem Willen Freiheit zukommt, bedeutet eigentlich nichts anderes, als ob ihm Willen zukommt. Die Ausdrücke 'frei' und 'willensgemäss' besagen dasselbe."* (*Schriften zur Metaphysik* I, "Bemerkungen zu den cartesischen Prinzipien." Zu Artikel 39.)

13. Augustine, *Confessions,* book VIII, ch. 8.
14. We find this conflict frequently in Euripides. Thus Medea, before murdering her children, says: "and I know which evils I am about to commit, but θυμός is stronger than my deliberations" (1078 ff.); and Phaedra (*Hippolytus,* 376 ff.) speaks in a similar vein. The point of the matter is always that reason, knowledge, insight, etc., are too weak to withstand the onslaught of desire, and it may not be accidental that the conflict breaks out in the soul of women, who are less under the influence of reasoning than men.
15. "Insofar as the mind commands, the mind wills, and insofar as the thing commanded is not done, it wills not," as Augustine put it, in the famous ch. 9 of book VIII of the *Confessions,* which deals with the will and its power. To Augustine, it was a matter of course that "to will" and "to command" are the same.
16. Augustine, ibid.
17. Pythian Ode IV, 287–289:

$$\phi\alpha\nu\tau\grave{\iota}\; \delta'\acute{\epsilon}\mu\mu\epsilon\nu$$
$$\tau o\hat{\upsilon}\tau'\; \grave{\alpha}\nu\iota\alpha\rho\acute{o}\tau\alpha\tau o\nu\; \kappa\alpha\lambda\grave{\alpha}\; \gamma\iota\nu\acute{\omega}\sigma\eta o\nu\tau'\; \grave{\alpha}\nu\acute{\alpha}\gamma\kappa\alpha$$
$$\grave{\epsilon}\kappa\tau\grave{o}\varsigma\; \acute{\epsilon}\chi\epsilon\iota\nu\; \pi\acute{o}\delta\alpha.$$

18. *Esprit des Lois,* XII, 2 and XI, 3.
19. Op. cit.
20. Ibid.
21. See the first four chapters of the second book of *The Social Contract.* Among modern political theorists, Carl Schmitt is the most able defender of the notion of sovereignty. He recognizes clearly that the root of sovereignty is the will: Sovereign is who wills and commands. See especially his *Verfassungslehre,* München, 1928, pp. 7 ff., 146.
22. Book XII, ch. 20.

What Is Authority?

In order to avoid misunderstanding, it might have been wiser to ask in the title: What was—and not what is—authority? For it is my contention that we are tempted and entitled to raise this question because authority has vanished from the modern world. Since we can no longer fall back upon authentic and undisputable experiences common to all, the very term has become clouded by controversy and confusion. Little about its nature appears self-evident or even comprehensible to everybody, except that the political scientist may still remember that this concept was once fundamental to political theory, or that most will agree that a constant, ever-widening and deepening crisis of authority has accompanied the development of the modern world in our century.

This crisis, apparent since the inception of the century, is political in origin and nature. The rise of political movements intent upon replacing the party system, and the development of a new totalitarian form of government, took place against a background of a more or less general, more or less dramatic breakdown of all traditional authorities. Nowhere was this breakdown the direct result of the regimes or movements themselves; it rather seemed as though totalitarianism, in the form of movements as well as of regimes, was best fitted to take advantage of a general political and social atmosphere in which the party system had lost its prestige and the government's authority was no longer recognized.

The most significant symptom of the crisis, indicating its depth and seriousness, is that it has spread to such prepolitical areas as child-rearing and education, where authority in the widest sense has always been ac-

From Between Past and Future. *Originally published as "What Was Authority?," in C. Friedrich, ed.,* Authority *(Cambridge, Mass.: Harvard University Press, 1959).*

cepted as a natural necessity, obviously required as much by natural needs, the helplessness of the child, as by political necessity, the continuity of an established civilization which can be assured only if those who are new-comers by birth are guided through a pre-established world into which they are born as strangers. Because of its simple and elementary character, this form of authority has, throughout the history of political thought, served as a model for a great variety of authoritarian forms of government, so that the fact that even this prepolitical authority which ruled the rela-' tions between adults and children, teachers and pupils, is no longer secure signifies that all the old time-honored metaphors and models for authori-tarian relations have lost their plausibility. Practically as well as theoreti-cally, we are no longer in a position to know what authority really *is*.

In the following reflections I assume that the answer to this question cannot possibly lie in a definition of the nature or essence of "authority in general." The authority we have lost in the modern world is no such "au-thority in general," but rather a very specific form which had been valid throughout the Western World over a long period of time. I therefore propose to reconsider what authority was historically and the sources of its strength and meaning. Yet, in view of the present confusion, it seems that even this limited and tentative approach must be preceded by a few re-marks on what authority never was, in order to avoid the more common misunderstandings and make sure that we visualize and consider the same phenomenon and not any number of connected or unconnected issues.

Since authority always demands obedience, it is commonly mistaken for some form of power or violence. Yet authority precludes the use of external means of coercion; where force is used, authority itself has failed. Authority, on the other hand, is incompatible with persuasion, which pre-supposes equality and works through a process of argumentation. Where arguments are used, authority is left in abeyance. Against the egalitarian order of persuasion stands the authoritarian order, which is always hierar-chical. If authority is to be defined at all, then, it must be in contradistinc-tion to both coercion by force and persuasion through arguments. (The authoritarian relation between the one who commands and the one who obeys rests neither on common reason nor on the power of the one who commands; what they have in common is the hierarchy itself, whose rightness and legitimacy both recognize and where both have their prede-termined stable place.) This point is of historical importance; one aspect of our concept of authority is Platonic in origin, and when Plato began to consider the introduction of authority into the handling of public affairs in the polis, he knew he was seeking an alternative to the common Greek way of handling domestic affairs, which was persuasion (πείθειν) as well as to the common way of handling foreign affairs, which was force and violence (βία).

Historically, we may say that the loss of authority is merely the final, though decisive, phase of a development which for centuries undermined primarily religion and tradition. Of tradition, religion, and authority—whose interconnectedness we shall discuss later—authority has proved to be the most stable element. With the loss of authority, however, the general doubt of the modern age also invaded the political realm, where things not only assume a more radical expression but become endowed with a reality peculiar to the political realm alone. What perhaps hitherto had been of spiritual significance only for the few now has become a concern of one and all. Only now, as it were after the fact, the loss of tradition and of religion have become political events of the first order.

When I said that I did not wish to discuss "authority in general," but only the very specific concept of authority which has been dominant in our history, I wished to hint at some distinctions which we are liable to neglect when we speak too sweepingly of the crisis of our time, and which I may perhaps more easily explain in terms of the related concepts of tradition and religion. Thus the undeniable loss of tradition in the modern world does not at all entail a loss of the past, for tradition and past are not the same, as the believers in tradition on one side and the believers in progress on the other would have us believe—whereby it makes little difference that the former deplore this state of affairs while the latter extend their congratulations. With the loss of tradition we have lost the thread which safely guided us through the vast realms of the past, but this thread was also the chain fettering each successive generation to a predetermined aspect of the past. It could be that only now will the past open up to us with unexpected freshness and tell us things no one has yet had ears to hear. But it cannot be denied that without a securely anchored tradition—and the loss of this security occurred several hundred years ago—the whole dimension of the past has also been endangered. We are in danger of forgetting, and such an oblivion—quite apart from the contents themselves that could be lost—would mean that, humanly speaking, we would deprive ourselves of one dimension, the dimension of depth in human existence. For memory and depth are the same, or rather, depth cannot be reached by man except through remembrance.

It is similar with the loss of religion. Ever since the radical criticism of religious beliefs in the seventeenth and eighteenth centuries, it has remained characteristic of the modern age to doubt religious truth, and this is true for believers and nonbelievers alike. Since Pascal and, even more pointedly, since Kierkegaard, doubt has been carried into belief, and the modern believer must constantly guard his beliefs against doubts; not the Christian faith as such, but Christianity (and Judaism, of course) in the modern age is ridden by paradoxes and absurdity. And whatever else may be able to survive absurdity—philosophy perhaps can—religion certainly cannot. Yet this loss of belief in the dogmas of institutional religion need not necessarily imply a loss or even a crisis of faith, for religion and faith, or belief and faith, are by no means the same. Only belief, but not faith, has an inherent affinity with and is constantly exposed to doubt. But who can deny that faith too, for so many centuries securely protected by religion, its beliefs and its dogmas, has been gravely endangered through what is actually only a crisis of institutional religion?

Some similar qualifications seem to me to be necessary regarding the modern loss of authority. Authority, resting on a foundation in the past as its unshaken cornerstone, gave the world the permanence and durability which human beings need precisely because they are mortals—the most unstable and futile beings we know of. Its loss is tantamount to the loss of the groundwork of the world, which indeed since then has begun to shift, to change and transform itself with ever-increasing rapidity from one shape into another, as though we were living and struggling with a Protean universe where everything at any moment can become almost anything else. But the loss of worldly permanence and reliability—which politically is identical with the loss of authority—does not entail, at least not necessarily, the loss of the human capacity for building, preserving, and caring for a world that can survive us and remain a place fit to live in for those who come after us.

It is obvious that these reflections and descriptions are based on the conviction of the importance of making distinctions. To stress such a conviction seems to be a gratuitous truism in view of the fact that, at least as far as I know, nobody has yet openly stated that distinctions are nonsense. There exists, however, a silent agreement in most discussions among political and social scientists that we can ignore distinctions and proceed on the assumption that everything can eventually be called anything else, and that distinctions are meaningful only to the extent that each of us has the right "to define his terms." Yet does not this curious right, which we have come to grant as soon as we deal with matters of importance—as though it were actually the same as the right to one's own opinion—already indicate that such terms as "tyranny," "authority," "totalitarianism" have simply lost their common meaning, or that we have ceased to live in a common world where the words we have in common possess an unquestionable meaningfulness, so that, short of being condemned to live verbally in an altogether meaningless world, we grant each other the right to retreat into our own worlds of meaning, and demand only that each of us remain consistent within his own private terminology? If, in these circumstances, we assure ourselves that we still understand each other, we do not mean that together we understand a world common to us all, but that we understand the consistency of arguing and reasoning, of the process of argumentation in its sheer formality.

However that may be, to proceed under the implicit assumption that distinctions are not important or, better, that in the social-political-historical realm, that is, in the sphere of human affairs, things do not possess that distinctness which traditional metaphysics used to call their "otherness" (their *alteritas*), has become the hallmark of a great many theories in the social, political, and historical sciences. Among these, two seem to me to deserve special mention because they touch the subject under discussion in an especially significant manner.

The first concerns the ways in which, since the nineteenth century, liberal and conservative writers have dealt with the problem of authority and, by implication, with the related problem of freedom in the realm of politics. Generally speaking, it has been quite typical of liberal theories to start from the assumption that "the constancy of progress . . . in the direction of organized and assured freedom is the characteristic fact of modern history"[1] and to look upon each deviation from this course as a reactionary process leading in the opposite direction. This makes them overlook the differences in principle between the restriction of freedom in authoritarian regimes, the abolition of political freedom in tyrannies and dictatorships, and the total elimination of spontaneity itself, that is, of the most general and most elementary manifestation of human freedom, at which only totalitarian regimes aim by means of their various methods of conditioning. The liberal writer, concerned with history and the progress of freedom rather than with forms of government, sees only differences in degree here, and ignores that authoritarian government committed to the restriction of liberty remains tied to the freedom it limits to the extent that it would lose its very substance if it abolished it altogether, that is, would change into tyranny. The same is true for the distinction between legitimate and illegitimate power on which all authoritarian government hinges. The liberal writer is apt to pay little attention to it because of his conviction that all power corrupts and that the constancy of progress requires constant loss of power, no matter what its origin may be.

Behind the liberal identification of totalitarianism with authoritarianism, and the concomitant inclination to see "totalitarian" trends in every authoritarian limitation of freedom, lies an older confusion of authority with tyranny, and of legitimate power with violence. The difference between tyranny and authoritarian government has always been that the tyrant rules in accordance with his own will and interest, whereas even the most draconic authoritarian government is bound by laws. Its acts are tested by a code which was made either not by man at all, as in the case of the law of nature or God's Commandments or the Platonic ideas, or at least not by those actually in power. The source of authority in authoritarian government is always a force external and superior to its own power; it is always this source, this external force which transcends the political realm, from which the authorities derive their "authority," that is, their legitimacy, and against which their power can be checked.

Modern spokesmen of authority, who, even in the short intervals when public opinion provides a favorable climate for neo-conservatism, remain well aware that theirs is an almost lost cause, are of course eager to point to this distinction between tyranny and authority. Where the liberal writer sees an essentially assured progress in the direction of freedom, which is only temporarily interrupted by some dark forces of the past, the conservative sees a process of doom which started with the dwindling of authority, so that freedom, after it lost the restricting limitations which protected its boundaries, became helpless, defenseless, and bound to be destroyed. (It is hardly fair to say that only liberal political thought is primarily interested in freedom; there is hardly a school of political thought in our history which is not centered around the idea of freedom, much as the concept of liberty may vary with different writers and in different political circumstances. The only exception of any consequence to this statement seems to me to be the political philosophy of Thomas Hobbes, who, of course, was anything but a conservative.) Tyranny and totalitarianism are again identified, except that now totalitarian government, if it is not directly identified with democracy, is seen as its almost inevitable result, that is, the result of the disappearance of all traditionally recognized authorities. Yet the differences between tyranny and dictatorship on one side, and totalitarian domination on the other, are no less distinct than those between authoritarianism and totalitarianism.

These structural differences become apparent the moment we leave the over-all theories behind and concentrate our attention on the apparatus of rule, the technical forms of administration, and the organization of the body politic. For brevity's sake, it may be permitted to sum up the technical-structural differences between authoritarian, tyrannical, and totalitarian government in the image of three different representative models. As an image for authoritarian government, I propose the shape of the pyramid, which is well known in traditional political thought. The pyramid is indeed a particularly fitting image for a governmental structure whose source of authority lies outside itself, but whose seat of power is located at the top, from which authority and power is filtered down to the base in such a way that each successive layer possesses some authority, but less than the one above it, and where, precisely because of this careful filtering process, all layers from top to bottom are not only firmly integrated into the whole but are interrelated like converging rays whose common focal point is the top of the pyramid as well as the transcending source of authority above it. This image, it is true, can be used only for the Christian type of authoritarian rule as it developed through and under the constant influence of the Church during the Middle Ages, when the focal point above and beyond the earthly pyramid provided the necessary point of reference for the Christian type of equality, the strictly hierarchical structure of life on earth notwithstanding. The Roman understanding of political authority, where the source of authority lay exclusively in the past, in the foundation of Rome and the greatness of ancestors, leads into institutional structures whose shape requires a different kind of image— about which more later. In any event, an authoritarian form of government with its hierarchical structure is the least egalitarian of all forms; it incorporates inequality and distinction as its all-permeating principles.

All political theories concerning tyranny agree that it belongs strictly among the egalitarian forms of government; the tyrant is the ruler who rules as one against all, and the "all" he oppresses are all equal, namely equally powerless. If we stick to the image of the pyramid, it is as though all intervening layers between top and bottom were destroyed, so that the top remains suspended, supported only by the proverbial bayonets, over a mass of carefully isolated, disintegrated, and completely equal individuals. Classical political theory used to rule the tyrant out of mankind altogether, to call him a "wolf in human shape" (Plato), because of this position of one against all, in which he had put himself and which sharply distinguished his rule, the rule of one, which Plato still calls indiscriminately μον–αρχία or tyranny, from various forms of kingship or βασιλεία.

In contradistinction to both tyrannical and authoritarian regimes, the proper image of totalitarian rule and organization seems to me to be the structure of the onion, in whose center, in a kind of empty space, the leader is located; whatever he does—whether he integrates the body politic as in an authoritarian hierarchy, or oppresses his subjects like a tyrant—he does it from within, and not from without or above. All the extraordinarily manifold parts of the movement: the front organizations, the various professional societies, the party membership, the party bureaucracy, the elite formations and police groups, are related in such a way that each forms the façade in one direction and the center in the other, that is, plays the role of normal outside world for one layer and the role of radical extremism for another. The great advantage of this system is that the movement provides for each of its layers, even under conditions of totalitarian rule, the fiction of a normal world along with a consciousness of being different from and more radical than it. Thus, the sympathizers in the front organizations, whose convictions differ only in intensity from those of the party membership, surround the whole movement and provide a deceptive façade of normality to the outside world because of their lack of fanaticism and extremism, while, at the same time, they represent the normal world to the totalitarian movement, whose members come to believe that their convictions differ only in degree from those of other people, so that they need never be aware of the abyss which separates their own world from that which actually surrounds it. The onion structure makes the system organizationally shock-proof against the factuality of the real world.[2]

However, while both liberalism and conservatism fail us the moment we try to apply their theories to factually existing political forms and institutions, it can hardly be doubted that their over-all assertions carry a high amount of plausibility. Liberalism, we saw, measures a process of receding freedom, and conservatism measures a process of receding authority; both call the expected end-result totalitarianism and see totalitarian trends wherever either one or the other is present. No doubt, both can produce excellent documentation for their findings. Who would deny the serious threats to freedom from all sides since the beginning of the century, and the rise of all kinds of tyranny, at least since the end of the First World War? Who can deny, on the other hand, that disappearance of practically all traditionally established authorities has been one of the most spectacular characteristics of the modern world? It seems as though one has only to fix his glance on either of these two phenomena to justify a theory of progress or a theory of doom according to his own taste or, as the phrase goes, according to his own "scale of values." If we look upon the conflicting statements of conservatives and liberals with impartial eyes, we can easily see that the truth is equally distributed between them and that we are in fact confronted with a simultaneous recession of both freedom and authority in the modern world. As far as these processes are concerned, one can even say that the numerous oscillations in public opinion, which for more than a hundred and fifty years has swung at regular intervals from one extreme to the other, from a liberal mood to a conservative one and back to a more liberal again, at times attempting to reassert authority and at others to reassert freedom, have resulted only in further undermining both, confusing the issues, blurring the distinctive lines between authority and freedom, and eventually destroying the political meaning of both.

Both liberalism and conservatism were born in this climate of violently oscillating public opinion, and they are tied together, not only because each would lose its very substance without the presence of its opponent in the field of theory and ideology, but because both are primarily concerned with restoration, with restoring either freedom or authority, or the relationship between both, to its traditional position. It is in this sense that they form the two sides of the same coin, just as their progress-or-doom ideologies correspond to the two possible directions of the historical process as such; if one assumes, as both do, that there is such a thing as a historical process with a definable direction and a predictable end, it obviously can land us only in paradise or in hell.

It is, moreover, in the nature of the very image in which history is usually conceived, as process or stream or development, that everything comprehended by it can change into anything else, that distinctions become meaningless because they become obsolete, submerged, as it were, by the historical stream, the moment they have appeared. From this viewpoint, liberalism and conservatism present themselves as the political philosophies which correspond to the much more general and comprehensive philosophy of history of the nineteenth century. In form and content, they are the political expression of the history-consciousness of the last stage of the modern age. Their inability to distinguish, theoretically justified by the concepts of history and process, progress or doom, testifies to an age in which certain notions, clear in their distinctness to all previous centuries, have begun to lose their clarity and plausibility because they have lost their meaning in the public-political reality—without altogether losing their significance.

The second and more recent theory implicitly challenging the importance of making distinctions is, especially in the social sciences, the almost universal functionalization of all concepts and ideas. Here, as in the example previously quoted, liberalism and conservatism differ not in method, viewpoint, and approach, but only in emphasis and evaluation. A convenient instance may be provided by the widespread conviction in the free world today that communism is a new "religion," notwithstanding its avowed atheism, because it fulfills socially, psychologically, and "emotionally" the same function traditional religion fulfilled and still fulfills in the free world. The concern of the social sciences does not lie in what bolshevism as ideology or as form of government is, nor in what its spokesmen have to say for themselves; that is not the interest of the social sciences, and many social scientists believe they can do without the study of what the historical sciences call the sources themselves. Their concern is only with functions, and whatever fulfills the same function can, according to this view, be called the same. It is as though I had the right to call the heel of my shoe a hammer because I, like most women, use it to drive nails into the wall.

Obviously one can draw quite different conclusions from such equations. Thus it would be characteristic of conservatism to insist that after all a heel is not a hammer, but that the use of the heel as a substitute for the hammer proves that hammers are indispensable. In other words, it will find in the fact that atheism can fulfill the same function as religion the best proof that religion is necessary, and recommend the return to true religion as the only way to counter a "heresy." The argument is weak, of course; if it is only a question of function and how a thing works, the adherents of "false religion" can make as good a case for using theirs as I can for using my heel, which does not work so badly either. The liberals, on the contrary, view the same phenomena as a bad case of treason to the cause of secularism and believe that only "true secularism" can cure us of the pernicious influence of both false and true religion on politics. But these conflicting recommendations at the address of free society to return to true religion and become more religious, or to rid ourselves of institutional religion (especially of Roman Catholicism with its constant challenge to secularism) hardly conceal the opponents' agreement on one point: that whatever fulfills the function of a religion is a religion.

The same argument is frequently used with respect to authority: if violence fulfills the same function as authority—namely, makes people obey—then violence is authority. Here again we find those who counsel a return to authority because they think only a reintroduction of the order-obedience relationship can master the problems of a mass society, and those who believe that a mass society can rule itself, like any other social body. Again both parties agree on the one essential point: authority is whatever makes people obey. All those who call modern dictatorships "authoritarian," or mistake totalitarianism for an authoritarian structure, have implicitly equated violence with authority, and this includes those conservatives who explain the rise of dictatorships in our century by the need to find a surrogate for authority. The crux of the argument is always the same: everything is related to a functional context, and the use of violence is taken to demonstrate that no society can exist except in an authoritarian framework.

The dangers of these equations, as I see them, lie not only in the

confusion of political issues and in the blurring of the distinctive lines
which separate totalitarianism from all other forms of government. I do
not believe that atheism is a substitute for or can fulfill the same function
as a religion any more than I believe that violence can become a substitute
for authority. But if we follow the recommendations of the conservatives,
who at this particular moment have a rather good chance of being heard,
I am quite convinced that we shall not find it hard to produce such substitutes, that we shall use violence and pretend to have restored authority
or that our rediscovery of the functional usefulness of religion will produce a substitute-religion—as though our civilization were not already
sufficiently cluttered up with all sorts of pseudo-things and nonsense.

Compared with these theories, the distinctions between tyrannical,
authoritarian, and totalitarian systems which I have proposed are unhistor-
ical, if one understands by history not the historical space in which certain
forms of government appeared as recognizable entities, but the historical
process in which everything can always change into something else; and
they are anti-functional insofar as the content of the phenomenon is taken
to determine both the nature of the political body and its function in society, and not vice-versa. Politically speaking, they have a tendency to assume that in the modern world authority has disappeared almost to the
vanishing point, and this in the so-called authoritarian systems no less than
in the free world, and that freedom—that is, the freedom of movement of
human beings—is threatened everywhere, even in free societies, but abolished radically only in totalitarian systems, and not in tyrannies and dictatorships.

It is in the light of this present situation that I propose to raise the following questions: What were the political experiences that corresponded
to the concept of authority and from which it sprang? What is the nature
of a public-political world constituted by authority? Is it true that the
Platonic-Aristotelian statement that every well-ordered community is
constituted of those who rule and those who are ruled was always valid
prior to the modern age? Or, to put it differently, what kind of world
came to an end after the modern age not only challenged one or another
form of authority in different spheres of life but caused the whole concept
of authority to lose its validity altogether?

I I

Authority as the one, if not the decisive, factor in human communities did
not always exist, though it can look back on a long history, and the expe-

riences on which this concept is based are not necessarily present in all bodies politic. The word and the concept are Roman in origin. Neither the Greek language nor the varied political experiences of Greek history shows any knowledge of authority and the kind of rule it implies.[3] This is expressed most clearly in the philosophy of Plato and Aristotle, who, in quite different ways but from the same political experiences, tried to introduce something akin to authority into the public life of the Greek polis.

There existed two kinds of rule on which they could fall back and from which they derived their political philosophy, one known to them from the public-political realm, and the other from the private sphere of Greek household and family life. To the polis, absolute rule was known as tyranny, and the chief characteristics of the tyrant were that he ruled by sheer violence, had to be protected from the people by a bodyguard, and insisted that his subjects mind their own business and leave to him the care of the public realm. The last characteristic, in Greek public opinion, signified that he destroyed the public realm of the polis altogether—"a polis belonging to one man is no polis"[4]—and thereby deprived the citizens of that political faculty which they felt was the very essence of freedom. Another political experience of the need for command and obedience might have been provided by the experience in warfare, where danger and the necessity to make and carry out decisions quickly seem to constitute an inherent reason for the establishment of authority. Neither of these political models, however, could possibly serve the purpose. The tyrant remained, for Plato as for Aristotle, the "wolf in human shape," and the military commander was too obviously connected with a temporary emergency to be able to serve as model for a permanent institution.

Because of this absence of valid political experience on which to base a claim to authoritarian rule, both Plato and Aristotle, albeit in very different ways, had to rely on examples of human relations drawn from Greek household and family life, where the head of the household ruled as a "despot," in uncontested mastery over the members of his family and the slaves of the household. The despot, unlike the king, the βασιλεύς, who had been the leader of household heads and as such *primus inter pares,* was by definition vested with the power to coerce. Yet it was precisely this characteristic that made the despot unfit for political purposes; his power to coerce was incompatible not only with the freedom of others but with his own freedom as well. Wherever he ruled there was only one relation, that between master and slaves. And the master, according to Greek common opinion (which was still blissfully unaware of Hegelian dialectics), was not free when he moved among his slaves; his freedom consisted in his ability to leave the sphere of the household altogether and to move among his equals, freemen. Hence, neither the despot nor the tyrant, the one moving among slaves, the other among subjects, could be called a free man.

Authority implies an obedience in which men retain their freedom, and Plato hoped to have found such an obedience when, in his old age, he bestowed upon the laws that quality which would make them undisputable rulers over the whole public realm. Men could at least have the illusion of being free because they did not depend upon other men. Yet the rulership of these laws was construed in an obviously despotic rather than an authoritarian manner, the clearest sign of which is that Plato was led to speak of them in terms of private household affairs, and not in political terms, and to say, probably in a variation of Pindar's νόμος βασιλεὺς πάντων ("a law is king over everything"): νόμος δεσπότης τῶν ἀρχόντων, οἱ δὲ ἄρχοντες δοῦλοι τοῦ νόμου ("the law is the *despot* of the rulers, and the rulers are the *slaves* of the law").[5] In Plato, the despotism originating in the household, and its concomitant destruction of the political realm as antiquity understood it, remained utopian. But it is interesting to note that when the destruction became a reality in the last centuries of the Roman Empire, the change was introduced by the application to public rule of the term *dominus,* which in Rome (where the family also was "organized like a monarchy")[6] had the same meaning as the Greek "despot." Caligula was the first Roman emperor who consented to be called *dominus,* that is, to be given a name "which Augustus and Tiberius still had rejected as if it were a malediction and an injury,"[7] precisely because it implied a despotism unknown in the political realm, although all too familiar in the private, household realm.

The political philosophies of Plato and Aristotle have dominated all subsequent political thought, even when their concepts have been superimposed upon such greatly different political experiences as those of the Romans. If we wish not only to comprehend the actual political experiences behind the concept of authority—which, at least in its positive aspect, is exclusively Roman—but also to understand authority as the Romans themselves already understood it theoretically and made it part of the political tradition of the West, we shall have to concern ourselves briefly with those features of Greek political philosophy which have so decisively influenced its shaping.

Nowhere else has Greek thinking so closely approached the concept of authority as in Plato's *Republic,* wherein he confronted the reality of the polis with a utopian rule of reason in the person of the philosopher-king. The motive for establishing reason as ruler in the realm of politics was exclusively political, although the consequences of expecting reason to develop into an instrument of coercion perhaps have been no less decisive for the tradition of Western philosophy than for the tradition of Western politics. The fatal resemblance between Plato's philosopher-king and the Greek tyrant, as well as the potential harm to the political realm that his rule would imply, seems to have been recognized by Aristotle;[8] but that this combination of reason and rule implied a danger to philosophy as well has been pointed out, as far as I know, only in Kant's reply to Plato: "It is not to be expected that kings philosophize or that philosophers become kings, nor is it to be desired, because the possession of power corrupts the free judgment of reason inevitably"[9]—although even this reply does not go to the root of the matter.

The reason Plato wanted the philosophers to become the rulers of the city lay in the conflict between the philosopher and the polis, or in the hostility of the polis toward philosophy, which probably had lain dormant for some time before it showed its immediate threat to the life of the philosopher in the trial and death of Socrates. Politically, Plato's philosophy shows the rebellion of the philosopher against the polis. The philosopher announces his claim to rule, but not so much for the sake of the polis and politics (although patriotic motivation cannot be denied in Plato and distinguishes his philosophy from those of his followers in antiquity) as for the sake of philosophy and the safety of the philosopher.

It was after Socrates' death that Plato began to discount persuasion as insufficient for the guidance of men and to seek for something liable to compel them without using external means of violence. Very early in his search he must have discovered that truth, namely, the truths we call self-evident, compels the mind, and that this coercion, though it needs no violence to be effective, is stronger than persuasion and argument. The trouble with coercion through reason, however, is that only the few are subject to it, so that the problem arises of how to assure that the many, the people who in their very multitude compose the body politic, can be submitted to the same truth. Here, to be sure, other means of coercion must be found, and here again coercion through violence must be avoided if political life as the Greeks understood it is not to be destroyed.[10] This is the central predicament of Plato's political philosophy and has remained a predicament of all attempts to establish a tyranny of reason. In *The Republic* the problem is solved through the concluding myth of rewards and punishments in the hereafter, a myth which Plato himself obviously neither believed nor wanted the philosophers to believe. What the allegory of the cave story in the middle of *The Republic* is for the few or for the philosopher the myth of hell at the end is for the many who are not capa-

ble of philosophical truth. In the *Laws* Plato deals with the same perplexity, but in the opposite way; here he proposes a substitute for persuasion,
the introduction to the laws in which their intent and purpose are to be
explained to the citizens.

In his attempts to find a legitimate principle of coercion Plato was
originally guided by a great number of models of existing relations, such as
that between the shepherd and his sheep, between the helmsman of a ship
and the passengers, between the physician and the patient, or between the
master and the slave. In all these instances either expert knowledge commands confidence so that neither force nor persuasion are necessary to obtain compliance, or the ruler and the ruled belong to two altogether
different categories of beings, one of which is already by implication subject to the other, as in the cases of the shepherd and his flock or the master and his slaves. All these examples are taken from what to the Greeks
was the private sphere of life, and they occur time and again in all the
great political dialogues, *The Republic,* the *Statesman,* and the *Laws.* Nevertheless, it is obvious that the relation between master and slave has a
special significance. The master, according to the discussion in the *Statesman,* knows what should be done and gives his orders, while the slave executes them and obeys, so that knowing what to do and actual doing
become separate and mutually exclusive functions. In *The Republic* they
are the political characteristics of two different classes of men. The plausibility of these examples lies in the natural inequality prevailing between
the ruling and the ruled, most apparent in the example of the shepherd,
where Plato himself ironically concludes that no man, only a god, could
relate to human beings as the shepherd relates to his sheep. Although it is
obvious that Plato himself was not satisfied with these models, for his purpose, to establish the "authority" of the philosopher over the polis, he returned to them time and again, because only in these instances of glaring
inequality could rule be exerted without seizure of power and the possession of the means of violence. What he was looking for was a relationship
in which the compelling element lies in the relationship itself and is prior
to the actual issuance of commands; the patient became subject to the
physician's authority when he fell ill, and the slave came under the command of his master when he became a slave.

It is important to bear these examples in mind in order to realize
what kind of coercion Plato expected reason to exert in the hands of the
king-philosopher. Here, it is true, the compelling power does not lie in
the person or in inequality as such, but in the ideas which are perceived
by the philosopher. These ideas can be used as measures of human behavior because they transcend the sphere of human affairs in the same way

that a yardstick transcends, is outside and beyond, all things whose length it can measure. In the parable of the cave in *The Republic,* the sky of ideas stretches above the cave of human existence, and therefore can become its standard. But the philosopher who leaves the cave for the pure sky of ideas does not originally do so in order to acquire those standards and learn the "art of measurement"[11] but to contemplate the true essence of Being—βλέπειν εἰς τὸ ἀληθέστατον. The basically authoritative element of the ideas, that is, the quality which enables them to rule and compel, is therefore not at all a matter of course. The ideas become measures only after the philosopher has left the bright sky of ideas and returned to the dark cave of human existence. In this part of the story Plato touches upon the deepest reason for the conflict between the philosopher and the polis.[12] He tells of the philosopher's loss of orientation in human affairs, of the blindness striking the eyes, of the predicament of not being able to communicate what he has seen, and of the actual danger to his life which thereby arises. It is in this predicament that the philosopher resorts to what he has seen, the ideas, as standards and measures, and finally, in fear of his life, uses them as instruments of domination.

For the transformation of the ideas into measures, Plato is helped by an analogy from practical life, where it appears that all arts and crafts are also guided by "ideas," that is, by the "shapes" of objects, visualized by the inner eye of the craftsman, who then reproduces them in reality through imitation.[13] This analogy enables him to understand the transcendent character of the ideas in the same manner as he does the transcendent existence of the model, which lies beyond the fabrication process it guides and therefore can eventually become the standard for its success or failure. The ideas become the unwavering, "absolute" standards for political and moral behavior and judgment in the same sense that the "idea" of a bed in general is the standard for making and judging the fitness of all particular manufactured beds. For there is no great difference between using the ideas as models and using them, in a somewhat cruder fashion, as actual yardsticks of behavior, and Aristotle in his earliest dialogue, written under the direct influence of Plato, already compares "the most perfect law," that is, the law which is the closest possible approximation to the idea, with "the plummet, the rule, and the compass . . . [which] are outstanding among all tools."[14]

It is only in this context that the ideas relate to the varied multitude of things concrete in the same way as one yardstick relates to the varied multitude of things measurable, or as the rule of reason or common sense relates to the varied multitude of concrete events which can be subsumed under it. This aspect of Plato's doctrine of ideas had the greatest influence on the Western tradition, and even Kant, though he had a very different and considerably deeper concept of human judgment, still occasionally mentioned this capacity for subsuming as its essential function. Likewise, the essential characteristic of specifically authoritarian forms of government—that the source of their authority, which legitimates the exercise of power, must be beyond the sphere of power and, like the law of nature or the commands of God, must not be man-made—goes back to this applicability of the ideas in Plato's political philosophy.

At the same time the analogy relating to fabrication and the arts and crafts offers a welcome opportunity to justify the otherwise very dubious use of examples and instances taken from activities in which some expert knowledge and specialization are required. Here the concept of the expert enters the realm of political action for the first time, and the statesman is understood to be competent to deal with human affairs in the same sense as the carpenter is competent to make furniture or the physician to heal the sick. Closely connected with this choice of examples and analogies is the element of violence, which is so glaringly evident in Plato's utopian republic and actually constantly defeats his great concern for assuring voluntary obedience, that is, for establishing a sound foundation for what, since the Romans, we call authority. Plato solved his dilemma through rather lengthy tales about a hereafter with rewards and punishments, which he hoped would be believed literally by the many and whose usage he therefore recommended to the attention of the few at the close of most of his political dialogues. In view of the enormous influence these tales have exerted upon the images of hell in religious thought, it is of some importance to note that they were originally designed for purely political purposes. In Plato they are simply an ingenious device to enforce obedience upon those who are not subject to the compelling power of reason, without actually using external violence.

It is of greater relevance in our context, however, that an element of violence is inevitably inherent in all activities of making, fabricating, and producing, that is, in all activities by which men confront nature directly, as distinguished from such activities as action and speech, which are primarily directed toward human beings. The building of the human artifice always involves some violence done to nature—we must kill a tree in order to have lumber, and we must violate this material in order to build a table. In the few instances where Plato shows a dangerous preference for the tyrannical form of government, he is carried to this extreme by his own analogies. This, obviously, is most tempting when he speaks about the right way to found new communities, because this foundation can be easily seen in the light of another "making" process. If the republic is to be made by somebody who is the political equivalent of a craftsman or artist, in accordance with an established τέχνη and the rules and measurements valid in this particular "art," the tyrant is indeed in the best position to achieve the purpose.[15]

We have seen that, in the parable of the cave, the philosopher leaves the cave in search of the true essence of Being without a second thought to the practical applicability of what he is going to find. Only later, when he finds himself again confined to the darkness and uncertainty of human affairs and encounters the hostility of his fellow human beings, does he begin to think of his "truth" in terms of standards applicable to the behavior of other people. This discrepancy between the ideas as true essences to be contemplated and as measures to be applied[16] is manifest in the two entirely different ideas which represent the highest idea, the one to which all others owe their existence. We find in Plato either that this supreme idea is that of the beautiful, as in the *Symposium,* where it constitutes the topmost rung of the ladder that leads to truth,[17] and in *Phaedrus,* where Plato speaks of the "lover of wisdom or of beauty" as though these two actually were the same because beauty is what "shines forth most" (the beautiful is ἐκφανέστατον) and therefore illuminates everything else;[18] or that the highest idea is the idea of the good, as in *The Republic.*[19] Obviously Plato's choice was based on the current ideal of the καλὸν κ'ἀγαθόν, but it is striking that the idea of the good is found only in the strictly political context of *The Republic.* If we were to analyze the original philosophical experiences underlying the doctrine of ideas (which we cannot do here), it would appear that the idea of the beautiful as the highest idea reflected these experiences far more adequately than the idea of the good. Even in the first books of *The Republic*[20] the philosopher is still defined as a lover of beauty, not of goodness, and only in the sixth book is the idea of good as the highest idea introduced. For the original function of the ideas was not to rule or otherwise determine the chaos of human affairs, but, in "shining brightness," to illuminate their darkness. As such, the ideas have nothing whatever to do with politics, political experience, and the problem of action, but pertain exclusively to philosophy, the experience of contemplation, and the quest for the "true being of things." It is precisely ruling, measuring, subsuming, and regulating that are entirely alien to the experiences underlying the doctrine of ideas in its original conception. It seems that Plato was the first to take exception to the political "irrelevance" of his new teaching, and he tried to modify the doctrine of ideas so that it would become useful for a theory of politics. But usefulness could be saved only by the idea of the good, since "good" in the Greek vocabulary always means "good for" or "fit." If the highest idea, in which all other ideas must partake in order to be ideas at all, is that of fitness, then the ideas are applicable by definition, and in the hands of the philosopher, the expert in ideas, they can become rules and standards or, as later in the *Laws,* they can become laws. (The difference is negligible. What in *The Republic* is still the philosopher's, the philosopher-king's, direct personal claim to rule, has become reason's impersonal claim to domination in the *Laws.*) The actual consequence of this political interpretation of the doctrine of ideas would be that neither man nor a god is the measure of all things, but the good itself—a consequence which apparently Aristotle, not Plato, drew in one of his earlier dialogues.[21]

For our purposes it is essential to remember that the element of rule, as reflected in our present concept of authority so tremendously influenced by Platonic thinking, can be traced to a conflict between philosophy and politics, but not to specifically political experiences, that is, experiences immediately derived from the realm of human affairs. One cannot understand Plato without bearing in mind both his repeated emphatic insistence on the philosophic irrelevance of this realm, which he always warned should not be taken too seriously, and the fact that he himself, in distinction to nearly all philosophers who came after him, still took human affairs so seriously that he changed the very center of his thought to make it applicable to politics. And it is this ambivalence rather than any formal exposition of his new doctrine of ideas which forms the true content of the parable of the cave in *The Republic,* which after all is told in the context of a strictly political dialogue searching for the best form of government. In the midst of this search Plato tells his parable, which turns out to be the story of the philosopher in this world, as though he had intended to write the concentrated biography of *the* philosopher. Hence, the search for the best form of government reveals itself to be the search for the best government for philosophers, which turns out to be a government in which philosophers have become the rulers of the city—a not too surprising solution for people who had witnessed the life and death of Socrates.

Still, the philosopher's rule had to be justified, and it could be justified only if the philosopher's truth possessed a validity for that very realm of human affairs which the philosopher had to turn away from in order to perceive it. Insofar as the philosopher is nothing but a philosopher, his quest ends with the contemplation of the highest truth, which, since it illuminates everything else, is also the highest beauty; but insofar as the philosopher is a man among men, a mortal among mortals, and a citizen among citizens, he must take his truth and transform it into a set of rules, by virtue of which transformation he then may claim to become an actual ruler—the king-philosopher. The lives of the many in the cave over which the philosopher has established his rule are characterized not by contemplation but by λέξις, speech, and πρᾶξις, action; it is therefore characteristic that in the parable of the cave Plato depicts the lives of the inhabitants as though they too were interested only in seeing: first the images on the screen, then the things themselves in the dim light of the fire in the cave, until finally those who want to see truth itself must leave the common world of the cave altogether and embark upon their new adventure all by themselves.

In other words, the whole realm of human affairs is seen from the viewpoint of a philosophy which assumes that even those who inhabit the cave of human affairs are human only insofar as they too want to see, though they remain deceived by shadows and images. And the rule of the philosopher-king, that is, the domination of human affairs by something outside its own realm, is justified not only by an absolute priority of seeing over doing, of contemplation over speaking and acting, but also by the assumption that what makes men human is the urge to see. Hence, the interest of the philosopher and the interest of man *qua* man coincide; both demand that human affairs, the results of speech and action, must not acquire a dignity of their own but be subjected to the domination of something outside their realm.

I I I

The dichotomy between seeing the truth in solitude and remoteness and being caught in the relationships and relativities of human affairs became authoritative for the tradition of political thought. It is expressed most forcefully in Plato's parable of the cave, and one is therefore somehow tempted to see its origin in the Platonic doctrine of ideas. Historically, however, it was not dependent upon an acceptance of this doctrine, but depended much more upon an attitude which Plato expressed only once, almost casually in a random remark, and which Aristotle later quoted in a famous sentence of *Metaphysics* almost verbatim, namely that the beginning of all philosophy is θαυμάζειν, the surprised wonder at everything that is as it is. More than anything else, Greek "theory" is the prolongation and Greek philosophy the articulation and conceptualization of this initial wonder. To be capable of it is what separates the few from the many, and to remain devoted to it is what alienates them from the affairs of men. Aristotle, therefore, without accepting Plato's doctrine of ideas, and even repudiating Plato's ideal state, still followed him in the main not only by separating a "theoretical way of life" (βίος θεωρητικός) from a life devoted to human affairs (βίος πολιτικός)—the first to establish such ways of life in hierarchical order had been Plato in his *Phaedrus*—but accepted as a matter of course the hierarchical order implied in it. The point in our context is not only that thought was supposed to rule over action, to prescribe principles to action so that the rules of the latter were invariably derived from experiences of the former, but that by way of the βίοι, of identifying activities with ways of life, the principle of rulership was established between men as well. Historically this became the hallmark of the political philosophy of the Socratic school, and the irony of this development is probably that it was precisely this dichotomy between thought and action that Socrates had feared and tried to prevent in the polis.

Thus it is in the political philosophy of Aristotle that we find the second attempt to establish a concept of authority in terms of rulers and the ruled; it was equally important for the development of the tradition of political thought, although Aristotle took a basically different approach. For him reason has neither dictatorial nor tyrannical features, and there is no philosopher-king to regulate human affairs once and for all. His reason for maintaining that "each body politic is composed of those who rule and those who are ruled" does not derive from the superiority of the expert over the layman, and he is too conscious of the difference between acting and making to draw his examples from the sphere of fabrication. Aristotle, as far as I can see, was the first to appeal, for the purpose of establishing rule in the handling of human affairs, to "nature," which "established the difference . . . between the younger and the older ones, destined the ones to be ruled and the others to rule."[22]

The simplicity of this argument is all the more deceptive since centuries of repetition have degraded it into a platitude. This may be why one usually overlooks its flagrant contradiction of Aristotle's own definition of the polis as also given in *Politics:* "The polis is a community of equals for the sake of a life which is potentially the best."[23] Obviously the notion of rule in the polis was for Aristotle himself so far from convincing that he, one of the most consistent and least self-contradictory great thinkers, did not feel particularly bound by his own argument. We therefore need not be surprised when we read at the beginning of the *Economics* (a pseudo-Aristotelian treatise, but written by one of his closest disciples) that the essential difference between a political community (the πόλις) and a private household (the οἰκία) is that the latter constitutes a "monarchy," a one-man rule, while the polis, on the contrary, "is composed of many rulers."[24] In order to understand this characterization we must remember first that the words "monarchy" and "tyranny" were used synonymously and in clear contradistinction to kingship; second, that the character of the polis as "composed of many rulers" has nothing to do with the various forms of government that usually are opposed to one-man rule, such as oligarchy, aristocracy, or democracy. The "many rulers" in this context are the household heads, who have established themselves as "monarchs" at home before they join to constitute the public-political realm of the city. Ruling itself and the distinction between rulers and ruled belong to a sphere which precedes the political realm, and what distinguishes it from the "economic" sphere of the household is that the polis is based upon the principle of equality and knows no differentiation between rulers and ruled.

In this distinction between what we would today call the private and the public spheres, Aristotle only articulates current Greek public opinion, according to which "every citizen belongs to two orders of existence," because "the polis gives each individual . . . besides his private life a sort of second life, his *bios politikos*."[25] (The latter Aristotle called the "good life," and redefined its content; only this definition, not the differentiation itself, conflicted with common Greek opinion.) Both orders were forms of human living-together, but only the household community was concerned with keeping alive as such and coping with the physical necessities (ἀναγκαῖα) involved in maintaining individual life and guaranteeing the survival of the species. In characteristic difference from the modern approach, care for the preservation of life, both of the individual and the species, belonged exclusively in the private sphere of the household, while in the polis man appeared κατ᾽ ἀριθμόν, as an individual personality, as we would say today.[26] As living beings, concerned with the preservation of life, men are confronted with and driven by necessity. Necessity must be mastered before the political "good life" can begin, and it can be mastered only through domination. Hence the freedom of the "good life" rests on the domination of necessity.

The mastery of necessity then has as its goal the controlling of the necessities of life, which coerce men and hold them in their power. But such domination can be accomplished only by controlling and doing violence to others, who as slaves relieve free men from themselves being coerced by necessity. The free man, the citizen of a polis, is neither coerced by the physical necessities of life nor subject to the man-made domination of others. He not only must not be a slave, he must own and rule over slaves. The freedom of the political realm begins after all elementary necessities of sheer living have been mastered by rule, so that domination and subjection, command and obedience, ruling and being ruled, are preconditions for establishing the political realm precisely because they are not its content.

There can be no question that Aristotle, like Plato before him, meant to introduce a kind of authority into the handling of public affairs and the life of the polis, and no doubt for very good political reasons. Yet he too had to resort to a kind of makeshift solution in order to make plausible the introduction into the political realm of a distinction between rulers and ruled, between those who command and those who obey. And he too could take his examples and models only from a prepolitical sphere, from the private realm of the household and the experiences of a slave economy. This leads him into glaringly contradictory statements, insofar as he superimposes on the actions and life in the polis those standards which, as he explains elsewhere, are valid only for the behavior and life in the household community. The inconsistency of his enterprise is apparent even if we consider only the famous example from the *Politics* previously mentioned, in which the differentiation between rulers and ruled is derived from the natural difference between the younger and the elder. For this example is in itself eminently unsuitable to prove Aristotle's argument. The relation between old and young is educational in essence, and in this education no more is involved than the training of the future rulers by the present rulers. If rule is at all involved here, it is entirely different from political forms of rule, not only because it is limited in time and intent, but because it happens between people who are potentially equals. Yet substitution of education for rule had the most far-reaching consequences. On its grounds rulers have posed as educators and educators have been accused of ruling. Then, as well as now, nothing is more questionable than the political relevance of examples drawn from the field of education. In the political realm we deal always with adults who are past the age of education, properly speaking, and politics or the right to participate in the management of public affairs begins precisely where education has come to an end. (Adult education, individual or communal, may be of great relevance for the formation of personality, its full development or greater enrichment, but is politically irrelevant unless its purpose is to supply technical requirements, somehow not acquired in youth, needed for participation in public affairs.) In education, conversely, we always deal with people who cannot yet be admitted to politics and equality because they are being prepared for it. Aristotle's example is nevertheless of great relevance because it is true that the necessity for "authority" is more plausible and evident in child-rearing and education than anywhere else. That is why it is so characteristic of our own time to want to eradicate even this extremely limited and politically irrelevant form of authority.

Politically, authority can acquire an educational character only if we presume with the Romans that under all circumstances ancestors represent the example of greatness for each successive generation, that they are the *maiores,* the greater ones, by definition. Wherever the model of education through authority, without this fundamental conviction, was superimposed on the realm of politics (and this has happened often enough and still is a mainstay of conservative argument), it served primarily to obscure real or coveted claims to rule and pretended to educate while in reality it wanted to dominate.

The grandiose attempts of Greek philosophy to find a concept of authority which would prevent deterioration of the polis and safeguard the life of the philosopher foundered on the fact that in the realm of Greek political life there was no awareness of authority based on immediate political experience. Hence all prototypes by which subsequent generations understood the content of authority were drawn from specifically unpolitical experiences, stemming either from the sphere of "making" and the arts, where there must be experts and where fitness is the highest criterion, or from the private household community. It is precisely in this politically determined aspect that the philosophy of the Socratic school has exerted its greatest impact upon our tradition. Even today we believe that Aristotle defined man primarily as a political being endowed with speech or reason, which he did only in a political context, or that Plato exposed the original meaning of his doctrine of ideas in *The Republic,* where, on the contrary, he changed it for political reasons. In spite of the grandeur of Greek political philosophy, it may be doubted that it would have lost its inherent utopian character if the Romans, in their indefatigable search for tradition and authority, had not decided to take it over and acknowledge it as their highest authority in all matters of theory and thought. But they were able to accomplish this integration only because both authority and tradition had already played a decisive role in the political life of the Roman republic.

I V

At the heart of Roman politics, from the beginning of the republic until virtually the end of the imperial era, stands the conviction of the sacredness of foundation, in the sense that once something has been founded it remains binding for all future generations. To be engaged in politics meant first and foremost to preserve the founding of the city of Rome. This is why the Romans were unable to repeat the founding of their first polis in the settlement of colonies but were capable of adding to the original foundation until the whole of Italy and, eventually, the whole of the Western world were united and administered by Rome, as though the whole world were nothing but Roman hinterland. From beginning to end, the Romans were bound to the specific locality of this one city, and unlike the Greeks, they could not say in times of emergency or overpopulation, "Go and found a new city, for wherever you are you will always be a polis." Not the Greeks, but the Romans, were really rooted in the soil, and the word *patria* derives its full meaning from Roman history. The foundation of a new body politic—to the Greeks an almost commonplace experience—became to the Romans the central, decisive, unrepeatable beginning of their whole history, a unique event. And the most deeply Roman divinities were Janus, the god of beginning, with whom, as it were, we still begin our year, and Minerva, the goddess of remembrance.

The founding of Rome—*tanta molis erat Romanam condere gentem* ("so great was the effort and toil to found the Roman people"), as Virgil sums up the ever-present theme of the *Aeneid,* that all wandering and suffering reach their end and their goal *dum conderet urbem* ("that he may found the city")—this foundation and the equally un-Greek experience of the sanctity of house and hearth, as though Homerically speaking the spirit of Hector had survived the fall of Troy and been resurrected on Italian soil, form the deeply political content of Roman religion. In contrast to Greece, where piety depended upon the immediate revealed presence of the gods, here religion literally meant *re-ligare:*[27] to be tied back, obligated, to the enormous, almost superhuman and hence always legendary effort to lay the foundations, to build the cornerstone, to found for eternity.[28] To be religious meant to be tied to the past, and Livy, the great recorder of past events, could therefore say, *Mihi vetustas res scribenti nescio quo pacto antiquus fit animus et quaedam religio tenet* ("While I write down these ancient events, I do not know through what connection my mind grows old and some *religio* holds [me]").[29] Thus religious and political activity could be considered as almost identical, and Cicero could say, "In no other realm does human excellence approach so closely the paths of the gods (*numen*) as it does in the founding of new and in the preservation of already founded communities."[30] The binding power of the foundation itself was religious, for the city also offered the gods of the people a permanent home—again unlike Greece, whose gods protected the cities of the mortals and occasionally dwelt in them but had their own home, far from the abode of men, on Mount Olympus.

It is in this context that word and concept of authority originally appeared. The word *auctoritas* derives from the verb *augere,* "augment," and what authority or those in authority constantly augment is the foundation. Those endowed with authority were the elders, the Senate or the *patres,* who had obtained it by descent and by transmission (tradition) from those who had laid the foundations for all things to come, the ancestors, whom the Romans therefore called the *maiores.* The authority of the living was always derivative, depending upon the *auctores imperii Romani conditoresque,* as Pliny puts it, upon the authority of the founders, who no longer were among the living. Authority, in contradistinction to power (*potestas*), had its roots in the past, but this past was no less present in the actual life of the city than the power and strength of the living. *Moribus antiquis res stat Romana virisque,* in the words of Ennius.

In order to understand more concretely what it meant to be in authority, it may be useful to notice that the word *auctores* can be used as the very opposite of the *artifices,* the actual builders and makers, and this precisely when the word *auctor* signifies the same thing as our "author." Who, asks Pliny at the occasion of a new theater, should be more admired, the maker or the author, the inventor or the invention?—meaning, of course, the latter in both instances. The author in this case is not the builder but the one who inspired the whole enterprise and whose spirit, therefore, much more than the spirit of the actual builder, is represented in the building itself. In distinction to the *artifex,* who only made it, he is the actual "author" of the building, namely its founder; with it he has become an "augmenter" of the city.

However, the relation between *auctor* and *artifex* is by no means the (Platonic) relation between the master who gives orders and the servant who executes them. The most conspicuous characteristic of those in authority is that they do not have power. *Cum potestas in populo auctoritas in senatu sit,* "while power resides in the people, authority rests with the Senate."[31] Because the "authority," the augmentation which the Senate must add to political decisions, is not power, it seems to us curiously elusive and intangible, bearing in this respect a striking resemblance to Montesquieu's judiciary branch of government, whose power he called "somehow nil" (*en quelque façon nulle*) and which nevertheless constitutes the highest authority in constitutional governments.[32] Mommsen called it "more than advice and less than a command, an advice which one may not safely ignore," whereby it is assumed that "the will and the actions of the people like those of children are exposed to error and mistakes and therefore need 'augmentation' and confirmation through the council of elders."[33] The authoritative character of the "augmentation" of the elders lies in its being a mere advice, needing neither the form of command nor external coercion to make itself heard.[34]

The binding force of this authority is closely connected with the religiously binding force of the *auspices,* which, unlike the Greek oracle, does not hint at the objective course of future events but reveals merely divine approval or disapproval of decisions made by men.[35] The gods too have authority among, rather than power over, men; they "augment" and confirm human actions but do not guide them. And just as "all *auspices* were traced back to the great sign by which the gods gave Romulus the authority to found the city,"[36] so all authority derives from this foundation, binding every act back to the sacred beginning of Roman history, adding, as it were, to every single moment the whole weight of the past. *Gravitas,* the ability to bear this weight, became the outstanding trait of the Roman character, just as the Senate, the representation of authority in the republic, could function—in the words of Plutarch ("Life of Lycurgus")—as "a central weight, like ballast in a ship, which always keeps things in a just equilibrium."

Thus precedents, the deeds of the ancestors and the usage that grew out of them, were always binding.[37] Anything that happened was transformed into an example, and the *auctoritas maiorum* became identical with authoritative models for actual behavior, with the moral political standard as such. This is also why old age, as distinguished from mere adulthood, was felt by the Romans to contain the very climax of human life; not so much because of accumulated wisdom and experience as because the old man had grown closer to the ancestors and the past. Contrary to our concept of growth, where one grows into the future, the Romans felt that growth was directed toward the past. If one wants to relate this attitude to the hierarchical order established by authority and to visualize this hierarchy in the familiar image of the pyramid, it is as though the peak of the pyramid did not reach into the height of a sky above (or, as in Christianity, beyond) the earth, but into the depth of an earthly past.

It is in this primarily political context that the past was sanctified through tradition. Tradition preserved the past by handing down from one generation to the next the testimony of the ancestors, who first had witnessed and created the sacred founding and then augmented it by their authority throughout the centuries. As long as this tradition was uninterrupted, authority was inviolate; and to act without authority and tradition, without accepted, time-honored standards and models, without the help of the wisdom of the founding fathers, was inconceivable. The notion of a spiritual tradition and of authority in matters of thought and ideas is here derived from the political realm and therefore essentially derivative—just as Plato's conception of the role of reason and ideas in politics was derived from the philosophical realm and became derivative in the realm of human affairs. But the historically all-important fact is that the Romans felt they needed founding fathers and authoritative examples in matters of thought and ideas as well, and accepted the great "ancestors" in Greece as their authorities for theory, philosophy, and poetry. The great Greek authors became authorities in the hands of the Romans, not of the Greeks. The way Plato and others before and after him treated Homer, "the educator of all Hellas," was inconceivable in Rome, nor would a Roman philosopher have dared "to raise his hand against his [spiritual] father," as Plato said of himself (in the *Sophistes*) when he broke with the teaching of Parmenides.

Just as the derivative character of the applicability of the ideas to politics did not prevent Platonic political thought from becoming the origin of Western political theory, so the derivative character of authority and tradition in spiritual matters did not prevent them from becoming the dominant features of Western philosophic thought for the longer part of our history. In both instances the political origin and the political experiences underlying the theories were forgotten, the original conflict between politics and philosophy, between the citizen and the philosopher, no less than the experience of foundation in which the Roman trinity of religion, authority, and tradition had its legitimate source. The strength of this trinity lay in the binding force of an authoritative beginning to which "religious" bonds tied men back through tradition. The Roman trinity not only survived the transformation of the republic into the empire but penetrated wherever the *pax Romana* created Western civilization on Roman foundations.

The extraordinary strength and endurance of this Roman spirit—or the extraordinary reliability of the founding principle for the creation of bodies politic—were subjected to a decisive test and proved themselves conspicuously after the decline of the Roman Empire, when Rome's political and spiritual heritage passed to the Christian Church. Confronted with this very real mundane task, the Church became so "Roman" and adapted itself so thoroughly to Roman thinking in matters of politics that it made the death and resurrection of Christ the cornerstone of a new foundation, erecting on it a new human institution of tremendous durability. Thus, after Constantine the Great had called upon the Church to secure for the declining empire the protection of the "most powerful God," the Church was eventually able to overcome the antipolitical and anti-institutional tendencies of the Christian faith, which had caused so much trouble in earlier centuries, and which are so manifest in the New Testament and in early Christian writings, and seemingly so insurmountable. The victory of the Roman spirit is really almost a miracle; in any event, it alone enabled the Church "to offer men in the membership of the Church the sense of citizenship which neither Rome nor municipality could any longer offer them."[38] Yet, just as Plato's politicalization of the ideas changed Western philosophy and determined the philosophic concept of reason, so the politicalization of the Church changed the Christian religion. The basis of the Church as a community of believers and a public institution was now no longer the Christian faith in resurrection (though this faith remained its content) or the Hebrew obedience to the commands of God, but rather the testimony of the life, of the birth, death, and resurrection, of Jesus of Nazareth as a historically recorded event.[39] As witnesses to this event the Apostles could become the "founding fathers" of the Church, from whom she would derive her own authority as long as she handed down their testimony by way of tradition from generation to generation. Only when this had happened, one is tempted to say, had the Christian faith become a "religion" not only in the post-Christian sense but in the ancient sense as well; only then, at any rate, could a whole world—as distinguished from mere groups of believers, no matter how large they might have been—become Christian. The Roman spirit could survive the catastrophe of the Roman Empire because its most powerful enemies—those who had laid, as it were, a curse on the whole realm of worldly public affairs and sworn to live in hiding—discovered in their own faith something which could be understood as a worldly event as well and could be transformed into a new mundane beginning to which the world was bound back once more (*religare*) in a curious mixture of new and old religious awe. This transformation was to a large extent accomplished by Augustine, the only great philosopher the Romans ever had. For the mainstay of his philosophy, *Sedis animi est in memoria* ("the seat of the mind is in memory"), is precisely that conceptual articulation of the specifically Roman experience which the Romans themselves, overwhelmed as they were by Greek philosophy and concepts, never achieved.

Thanks to the fact that the foundation of the city of Rome was repeated in the foundation of the Catholic Church, though, of course, with a radically different content, the Roman trinity of religion, authority, and tradition could be taken over by the Christian era. The most conspicuous sign of this continuity is perhaps that the Church, when she embarked upon her great political career in the fifth century, at once adopted the Roman distinction between authority and power, claiming for herself the old authority of the Senate and leaving the power—which in the Roman Empire was no longer in the hands of the people but had been monopolized by the imperial household—to the princes of the world. Thus, at the close of the fifth century, Pope Gelasius I could write to Emperor Anastasius I: "Two are the things by which this world is chiefly ruled: the sacred authority of the Popes and the royal power."[40] The result of the continuity of the Roman spirit in the history of the West was twofold. On one hand, the miracle of permanence repeated itself once more; for within the framework of our history the durability and continuity of the Church as a public institution can be compared only with the thousand years of Roman history in antiquity. The separation of church and state, on the other hand, far from signifying unequivocally a secularization of the political realm and, hence, its rise to the dignity of the classical period, actually implied that the political had now, for the first time since the Romans, lost its authority and with it that element which, at least in Western history, had endowed political structures with durability, continuity, and permanence.

It is true that Roman political thought at a very early date began to use Platonic concepts in order to understand and interpret the specifically Roman political experiences. Yet it seems as though it has been only in the Christian era that Plato's invisible spiritual yardsticks, by which the visible, concrete affairs of men were to be measured and judged, have unfolded their full political effectiveness. Precisely those parts of Christian doctrine which would have had great difficulty in fitting in and being assimilated to the Roman political structure—namely, the revealed commandments and truths of a genuinely transcendent authority which, unlike Plato's, did not stretch above but was beyond the earthly realm—could be integrated into the Roman foundation legend via Plato. God's revelation could now be interpreted politically as if the standards for human conduct and the principle of political communities, intuitively anticipated by Plato, had been finally revealed directly, so that, in the words of a modern Platonist, it appeared as though Plato's early "orientation toward the unseen measure was now confirmed through the revelation of the measure itself."[41] To the extent that the Catholic Church incorporated Greek philosophy into the structure of its doctrines and dogmatic beliefs, it amalgamated the Roman political concept of authority, which inevitably was based on a beginning, a founding in the past, with the Greek notion of transcending measurements and rules. General and transcendent standards under which the particular and immanent could be subsumed were now required for any political order, moral rules for all interhuman behavior, and rational measurements for the guidance of all individual judgment. There is scarcely anything that eventually was to assert itself with greater authority and more far-reaching consequences than the amalgamation itself.

Since then it has turned out, and this fact speaks for the stability of the amalgamation, that wherever one of the elements of the Roman trinity, religion or authority or tradition, was doubted or eliminated, the remaining two were no longer secure. Thus, it was Luther's error to think that his challenge of the temporal authority of the Church and his appeal to unguided individual judgment would leave tradition and religion intact. So it was the error of Hobbes and the political theorists of the seventeenth century to hope that authority and religion could be saved without tradition. So, too, was it finally the error of the humanists to think it would be possible to remain within an unbroken tradition of Western civilization without religion and without authority.

V

Politically the most momentous consequence of the amalgamation of Roman political institutions with Greek philosophic ideas was that it enabled the Church to interpret the rather vague and conflicting notions of early Christianity about life in the hereafter in the light of the Platonic political myths, and thus to elevate to the rank of dogmatic certitude an elaborate system of rewards and punishments for deeds and misdeeds that did not find their just retribution on earth. This happened not before the fifth century, when the earlier teachings of the redemption of all sinners, even of Satan himself (as taught by Origen and still held by Gregory of Nyssa), and the spiritualizing interpretation of the torments of hell as torments of conscience (also taught by Origen) were declared to be heretical; but it coincided with the downfall of Rome, the disappearance of an assured secular order, the assumption of responsibility for secular affairs by the Church, and the emergence of the papacy as a temporal power. Popular and literate notions about a hereafter with rewards and punishments were, of course, widespread then as they had been throughout antiquity, but the original Christian version of these beliefs, consistent with the "glad tidings" and the redemption from sin, was not a threat of eternal punishment and eternal suffering, but, on the contrary, the *descensus ad inferos*, Christ's mission to the underworld where he had spent the three days between his death and his resurrection in order to liquidate hell, defeat Satan, and liberate the souls of dead sinners, as he had liberated the souls of the living, from death and punishment.

We find it somewhat difficult to gauge correctly the political, non-religious origin of the doctrine of hell because the Church incorporated it, in its Platonic version, so early into the body of dogmatic beliefs. It seems only natural that this incorporation in its turn should have blurred the understanding of Plato himself to the point of identifying his strictly philosophic teaching of the immortality of the soul, which was meant for the few, with his political teaching of a hereafter with punishments and rewards, which was clearly meant for the multitude. The philosopher's concern is with the invisible which can be perceived by the soul, which itself is something invisible (ἀειδές) and hence goes to Hades, the place of invisibility (Ά-ίδης), after death has rid the invisible part of man of his body, the organ of sense perception.[42] This is the reason why philosophers always seem "to pursue death and dying" and why philosophy can also be called "the study of death."[43] Those who have no experience with a philosophic truth beyond the range of sense perception, of course, cannot be persuaded of the immortality of a bodyless soul; for them, Plato invented a number of tales to conclude his political dialogues, usually after the argument itself had broken down, as in *The Republic,* or it had turned out that Socrates' opponent could not be persuaded, as in the *Gorgias.*[44] Of these tales, the Er-myth of *The Republic* is the most elaborate and has exerted the greatest influence. Between Plato and the secular victory of Christianity in the fifth century, which brought with it the religious sanction of the doctrine of hell (so that from then on this became so general a feature of the Christian world that political treatises did not need to mention it specifically), there was hardly an important discussion of political problems—except in Aristotle—which did not conclude with an imitation of the Platonic myth.[45] And it is still Plato, as distinguished from the Hebrew and early Christian speculations about an afterlife, who is the true forerunner of Dante's elaborate descriptions; for in Plato we find for the first time not merely a concept of final judgment about eternal life or eternal death, about rewards and punishments, but the geographical separation of hell, purgatory, and paradise, as well as the horribly concrete notions of graduated bodily punishment.[46]

The purely political implications of Plato's myths in the last book of *The Republic,* as well as in the concluding parts of *Phaedon* and *Gorgias,* seem to be indisputable. The distinction between the philosophic conviction of the immortality of the soul and the politically desirable belief in an afterlife runs parallel to the distinction in the doctrine of ideas between the idea of the beautiful as the highest idea of the philosopher and the idea of the good as the highest idea of the statesman. Yet while Plato, when applying his philosophy of ideas to the political realm, somehow blurred the decisive distinction between the ideas of the beautiful and of the good, silently substituting the latter for the former in his discussions of politics, the same cannot be said for the distinction between an immortal, invisible, bodyless soul and an afterlife in which bodies, sensitive to pain, will receive their punishment. One of the clearest indications for the political character of these myths is indeed that they, because they imply bodily punishment, stand in flagrant contradiction to his doctrine of the mortality of the body, and of this contradiction Plato himself was by no means unaware.[47] Moreover, when he came to telling his tales, he used elaborate precautions to make sure that what followed was not truth but a possible opinion of which one better persuaded the multitude "as though it were the truth."[48] Finally, is it not rather obvious, especially in *The Republic,* that this whole concept of life after death cannot possibly make sense to those who have understood the story of the cave and know that the true underworld is life on earth?

No doubt Plato relied on popular beliefs, perhaps on Orphic and Pythagorean traditions, for his descriptions of an afterlife, just as the Church, almost a thousand years later, could choose freely which of the then prevalent beliefs and speculations she wanted to lay down as dogma and which to declare as heretical. The distinction between Plato and his predecessors, whoever they may have been, was that he was the first to become aware of the enormous, strictly political potentiality inherent in such beliefs, just as the distinction between Augustine's elaborate teachings about hell, purgatory, and paradise and the speculations of Origen or Clement of Alexandria was that he (and perhaps Tertullian before him) understood to what an extent these doctrines could be used as threats in this world, quite apart from their speculative value about a future life. Nothing, indeed, is more suggestive in this context than that it was Plato who coined the word "theology," for the passage in which the new word is used occurs again in a strictly political discussion, namely in *The Republic,* when the dialogue deals with the founding of cities.[49] This new theological god is neither a living God nor the god of the philosophers nor a pagan divinity; he is a political device, "the measurement of measurements,"[50] that is, the standard according to which cities may be founded and rules of behavior laid down for the multitude. Theology, moreover, teaches how to enforce these standards absolutely, even in cases when human justice seems at a loss, that is, in the case of crimes which escape punishment as well as in the case of those for which even the death sentence would not be adequate. For "the main thing" about the hereafter is, as Plato says explicitly, that "for every wrong men had done to anyone they suffered tenfold."[51] To be sure, Plato had no inkling of theology as we understand it, as the interpretation of God's word whose sacrosanct text is the Bible; theology to him was part and parcel of "political science," and specifically that part which taught the few how to rule the many.

Whatever other historical influences may have been at work to elaborate the doctrine of hell, it continued, during antiquity, to be used for political purposes in the interest of the few to retain a moral and political control over the multitude. The point at stake was always the same: truth by its very nature is self-evident and therefore cannot be satisfactorily argued out and demonstrated.[52] Hence, belief is necessary for those who lack the eyes for what is at the same time self-evident, invisible, and beyond argument. Platonically speaking, the few cannot persuade the multitude of truth because truth cannot be the object of persuasion, and persuasion is the only way to deal with the multitude. But the multitude, carried away by the irresponsible tales of poets and storytellers, can be persuaded to believe almost anything; the appropriate tales which carry the truth of the few to the multitude are tales about rewards and punishments after death; persuading the citizens of the existence of hell will make them behave as though they knew the truth.

As long as Christianity remained without secular interests and responsibilities, it left the beliefs and speculations about a hereafter as free as they had been in antiquity. Yet when the purely religious development of the new creed had come to an end and the Church had become aware of, and willing to take over, political responsibilities, she found herself confronted with a perplexity similar to the one that had given rise to Plato's political philosophy. Again it had become a question of imposing absolute standards on a realm which is made up of human affairs and relations, whose very essence therefore seems to be relativity; and to this relativity corresponds the fact that the worst man can do to man is to kill him, that is, to bring about what one day is bound to happen to him anyhow. The "improvement" on this limitation, proposed in the hell images, is precisely that punishment can mean more than the "eternal death" which early Christianity thought to be the appropriate reward of sin, namely eternal suffering, compared to which eternal death is salvation.

The introduction of the Platonic hell into the body of Christian dogmatic beliefs strengthened religious authority to the point where it could hope to remain victorious in any contest with secular power. But the price paid for this additional strength was that the Roman concept of authority was diluted, and an element of violence was permitted to insinuate itself into both the very structure of Western religious thought and the hierarchy of the Church. How high this price actually was might be gauged by the more than embarrassing fact that men of unquestionable stature— among them Tertullian and even Thomas Aquinas—could be convinced that one of the joys in heaven would be the privilege of watching the spectacle of unspeakable sufferings in hell. Nothing perhaps in the whole development of Christianity throughout the centuries is farther removed from and more alien to the letter and spirit of the teaching of Jesus of Nazareth than the elaborate catalogue of future punishments and the enormous power of coercion through fear which only in the last stages of the modern age have lost their public, political significance. As far as religious thought is concerned, it certainly is a terrible irony that the "glad tidings" of the Gospels, "Life is everlasting," should eventually have resulted not in an increase of joy but of fear on earth, should not have made it easier but harder for man to die.

However that may be, the fact is that the most significant consequence of the secularization of the modern age may well be the elimination from public life, along with religion, of the only political element in traditional religion, the fear of hell. We who had to witness how, during the Hitler and Stalin era, an entirely new and unprecedented criminality, almost unchallenged in the respective countries, was to invade the realm of politics should be the last to underestimate its "persuasive" influence upon the functioning of conscience. And the impact of these experiences is likely to grow when we recall that, in the very age of enlightenment, the men of the French Revolution no less than the founding fathers in America insisted on making the fear of an "avenging God" and hence the belief in "a future state" part and parcel of the new body politic. For the obvious reason why the men of the revolutions of all people should be so strangely out of tune in this respect with the general climate of their age was that precisely because of the new separation of church and state they found themselves in the old Platonic predicament. When they warned against the elimination of the fear of hell from public life because this would pave the way "to make murder itself as indifferent as shooting plover, and the extermination of the Rohilla nation as innocent as the swallowing of mites on a morsel of cheese,"[53] their words may sound with an almost prophetic ring in our ears; yet they were clearly spoken not out of any dogmatic faith in the "avenging God" but out of mistrust in the nature of man.

Thus the belief in a future state of rewards and punishments, consciously designed as a political device by Plato and perhaps no less consciously adopted, in its Augustinian form, by Gregory the Great, was to survive all other religious and secular elements which together had established authority in Western history. It was not during the Middle Ages, when secular life had become religious to such an extent that religion could not serve as a political instrument, but during the modern age that the usefulness of religion for secular authority was rediscovered. The true motives of this rediscovery have been somewhat overshadowed by the various more or less infamous alliances of "throne and altar" when kings, frightened at the prospect of revolution, believed that "the people must not be permitted to lose its religion" because, in Heine's words, *Wer sich von seinem Gotte reisst,/ wird endlich auch abtrünnig werden/ von seinen irdischen Behörden* ("who tears himself away from his God will end by deserting his earthly authorities as well"). The point is rather that the revolutionaries themselves preached belief in a future state, that even Robespierre ended by appealing to an "Immortal Legislator" to give sanction to the revolution, that none of the early American constitutions lacked an appropriate provision for future rewards and punishments, that men like John Adams regarded them as "the only true foundation of morality."[54]

It certainly is not surprising that all these attempts at retaining the only element of violence from the crumbling edifice of religion, authority, and tradition, and at using it as safeguard for the new, secular political order should be in vain. And it was by no means the rise of socialism or of the Marxian belief that "religion is the opiate of the people" which put an end to them. (Authentic religion in general and the Christian faith in particular—with its unrelenting stress on the individual and his own role in salvation, which led to the elaboration of a catalogue of sins greater than in any other religion—could never be used as tranquilizers. Modern ideologies, whether political or psychological or social, are far better fitted to immunize man's soul against the shocking impact of reality than any traditional religion we know. Compared with the various superstitions of the twentieth century, the pious resignation to God's will seems like a child's pocket-knife in competition with atomic weapons.) The conviction that "good morals" in civil society ultimately depended upon fear and hope for another life may still have appeared to the political men of the eighteenth century no more than good common sense; to those of the nineteenth century it appeared simply scandalous that, for instance, English courts took it for granted "that the oath is worthless of a person who does not believe in a future state," and this not only for political reasons but also because it implies "that they who do believe are only prevented from lying . . . by the fear of hell."[55]

Superficially speaking, the loss of belief in future states is politically, though certainly not spiritually, the most significant distinction between our present period and the centuries before. And this loss is definite. For no matter how religious our world may turn again, or how much authentic faith still exists in it, or how deeply our moral values may be rooted in our religious systems, the fear of hell is no longer among the motives which would prevent or stimulate the actions of a majority. This seems inevitable if secularity of the world involves separation of the religious and political realms of life; under these circumstances religion was bound to lose its political element, just as public life was bound to lose the religious sanction of transcendent authority. In this situation, it would be well to recall that Plato's device of how to persuade the multitude to follow the standards of the few had remained utopian prior to its being sanctioned by religion; its purpose, to establish rule of the few over the many, was too patent to be useful. For the same reason the beliefs in future states withered from the public realm at once when their political usefulness was blatantly exposed by the very fact that they, out of the whole body of dogmatic beliefs, were deemed worthy of preservation.

V I

One thing, however, is particularly striking in this context: while all the models, prototypes, and examples for authoritarian relationships—such as the statesman as healer and physician, as expert, as helmsman, as the master who knows, as educator, as the wise man—all Greek in origin, have been faithfully preserved and further articulated until they became empty platitudes, the one political experience which brought authority as word, concept, and reality into our history—the Roman experience of foundation—seems to have been entirely lost and forgotten. And this to such an extent that the moment we begin to talk and think about authority, after all one of the central concepts of political thought, it is as though we were caught in a maze of abstractions, metaphors, and figures of speech in which everything can be taken and mistaken for something else, because we have no reality, either in history or in everyday experience, to which we can unanimously appeal. This, among other things, indicates what could also be proved otherwise, namely that the Greek concepts, once they had been sanctified by the Romans through tradition and authority, simply eliminated from historical consciousness all political experiences which could not be fitted into their framework.

However, this statement is not entirely true. There exists in our political history one type of event for which the notion of founding is decisive, and there is in our history of thought one political thinker in whose work the concept of foundation is central, if not paramount. The events are the revolutions of the modern age, and the thinker is Machiavelli, who stood at the threshold of this age and, though he never used the word, was the first to conceive of a revolution.

Machiavelli's unique position in the history of political thought has little to do with his often praised but by no means unarguable realism, and he was certainly not the father of political science, a role now frequently attributed to him. (If one understands by political science political theory, its father certainly is Plato rather than Machiavelli. If one stresses the scientific character of political science, it is hardly possible to date its birth earlier than the rise of all modern science, that is, in the sixteenth and seventeenth centuries. In my opinion the scientific character of Machiavelli's theories is often greatly exaggerated.) His unconcern with moral judgments and his freedom from prejudice are astonishing enough, but they do not strike the core of the matter; they have contributed more to his fame than to the understanding of his works, because most of his readers, then as today, were too shocked even to read him properly. When he insists that in the public-political realm men "should learn how not to be good,"[56] he of course never meant that they should learn how to be evil. After all, there is scarcely another political thinker who has spoken with such vehement contempt of "methods [by which] one may indeed gain power but not glory."[57] The truth is only that he opposed both concepts of the good which we find in our tradition: the Greek concept of the "good for" or fitness, and the Christian concept of an absolute goodness which is not of this world. Both concepts in his opinion were valid, but only in the private sphere of human life; in the public realm of politics they had no more place than their opposites, unfitness or incompetence and evil. The *virtù,* on the other hand, which according to Machiavelli is the specifically political human quality, has neither the connotation of moral character as does the Roman *virtus,* nor that of a morally neutral excellence like the Greek ἀρετή. *Virtù* is the response, summoned up by man, to the world, or rather to the constellation of *fortuna* in which the world opens up, presents and offers itself to him, to his *virtù.* There is no *virtù* without *fortuna* and no *fortuna* without *virtù;* the interplay between them indicates a harmony between man and world—playing with each other and succeeding together—which is as remote from the wisdom of the statesman as from the excellence, moral or otherwise, of the individual, and the competence of experts.

His experiences in the struggles of his time taught Machiavelli a deep contempt for all traditions, Christian and Greek, as presented, nurtured, and reinterpreted by the Church. His contempt was leveled at a corrupt Church which had corrupted the political life of Italy, but such corruption, he argued, was inevitable because of the Christian character of the Church. What he witnessed, after all, was not only corruption but also the reaction against it, the deeply religious and sincere revival emanating from the Franciscans and Dominicans, culminating in the fanaticism of

Savonarola, whom he held in considerable respect. Respect for these religious forces and contempt for the Church together led him to certain
conclusions about a basic discrepancy between the Christian faith and politics that are oddly reminiscent of the first centuries of our era. His point
was that every contact between religion and politics must corrupt both,
and that a noncorrupt Church, though considerably more respectable,
would be even more destructive to the public realm than its present corruption.[58] What he did not, and perhaps in his time could not, see was the
Roman influence on the Catholic Church, which, indeed, was much less
noticeable than its Christian content and its Greek theoretical framework
of reference.

It was more than patriotism and more than the current revival of interest in antiquity that sent Machiavelli to search for the central political
experiences of the Romans as they had originally been presented, equally
removed from Christian piety and Greek philosophy. The greatness of his
rediscovery lies in that he could not simply revive or resort to an articulate
conceptual tradition, but had himself to articulate those experiences which
the Romans had not conceptualized but rather expressed in terms of
Greek philosophy vulgarized for this purpose.[59] He saw that the whole of
Roman history and mentality depended upon the experience of foundation, and he believed it should be possible to repeat the Roman experience through the foundation of a unified Italy which was to become the
same sacred cornerstone for an "eternal" body politic for the Italian nation
as the founding of the Eternal City had been for the Italic people. The fact
that he was aware of the contemporary beginnings of the birth of nations
and the need for a new body politic, for which he therefore used the hitherto unknown term *lo stato,* has caused him to be commonly and rightfully identified as the father of the modern nation-state and its notion of a
"reason of state." What is even more striking, though less well known, is
that Machiavelli and Robespierre so often seem to speak the same language. When Robespierre justifies terror, "the despotism of liberty against
tyranny," he sounds at times as if he were repeating almost word for word
Machiavelli's famous statements on the necessity of violence for the
founding of new political bodies and for the reforming of corrupt ones.

This resemblance is all the more startling since both Machiavelli and
Robespierre in this respect go beyond what the Romans themselves had
to say about foundation. To be sure, the connection between foundation
and dictatorship could be learned from the Romans themselves, and Cicero, for instance, appeals explicitly to Scipio to become *dictator rei publicae
constituendae,* to seize the dictatorship in order to restore the republic.[60]
Like the Romans, Machiavelli and Robespierre felt founding was the cen-

tral political action, the one great deed that established the public-political realm and made politics possible; but unlike the Romans, to whom this was an event of the past, they felt that for this supreme "end" all "means," and chiefly the means of violence, were justified. They understood the act of founding entirely in the image of making; the question to them was literally how to "make" a unified Italy or a French republic, and their justification of violence was guided by and received its inherent plausibility from the underlying argument: You cannot make a table without killing trees, you cannot make an omelet without breaking eggs, you cannot make a republic without killing people. In this respect, which was to become so fateful for the history of revolutions, Machiavelli and Robespierre were not Romans, and the authority to which they could have appealed would have been rather Plato, who also recommended tyranny as the government where "change is likely to be easiest and most rapid."[61]

It is precisely in this double respect, because of his rediscovery of the foundation experience and his reinterpretation of it in terms of the justification of (violent) means for a supreme end, that Machiavelli may be regarded as the ancestor of modern revolutions, all of which can be characterized by Marx's remark that the French Revolution appeared on the stage of history in Roman costume. Unless it is recognized that the Roman pathos for foundation inspired them, it seems to me that neither the grandeur nor the tragedy of Western revolutions in the modern age can be properly understood. For if I am right in suspecting that the crisis of the present world is primarily political, and that the famous "decline of the West" consists primarily in the decline of the Roman trinity of religion, tradition, and authority, with the concomitant undermining of the specifically Roman foundations of the political realm, then the revolutions of the modern age appear like gigantic attempts to repair these foundations, to renew the broken thread of tradition, and to restore, through founding new political bodies, what for so many centuries had endowed the affairs of men with some measure of dignity and greatness.

Of these attempts, only one, the American Revolution, has been successful: the founding fathers as, characteristically enough, we still call them, founded a completely new body politic without violence and with the help of a constitution. And this body politic has at least endured to the present day, in spite of the fact that the specifically modern character of the modern world has nowhere else produced such extreme expressions in all nonpolitical spheres of life as it has in the United States.

This is not the place to discuss the reasons for the surprising stability of a political structure under the onslaught of the most vehement and shattering social instability. It seems certain that the relatively nonviolent character of the American Revolution, where violence was more or less restricted to regular warfare, is an important factor in this success. It may also be that the founding fathers, because they had escaped the European development of the nation-state, had remained closer to the original Roman spirit. More important, perhaps, was that the act of foundation, namely the colonization of the American continent, had preceded the Declaration of Independence, so that the framing of the Constitution, falling back on existing charters and agreements, confirmed and legalized an already existing body politic rather than made it anew.[62] Thus the actors in the American Revolution were spared the effort of "initiating a new order of things" altogether; that is, they were spared the one action of which Machiavelli once said that "there is nothing more difficult to carry out, nor more doubtful of success, nor more dangerous to handle."[63] And Machiavelli surely must have known, for he, like Robespierre and Lenin and all the great revolutionaries whose ancestor he was, wished nothing more passionately than to initiate a new order of things.

However that may be, revolutions, which we commonly regard as radical breaks with tradition, appear in our context as events in which the actions of men are still inspired by and derive their greatest strength from the origins of this tradition. They seem to be the only salvation which this Roman-Western tradition has provided for emergencies. The fact that not only the various revolutions of the twentieth century but all revolutions since the French have gone wrong, ending in either restoration or tyranny, seems to indicate that even these last means of salvation provided by tradition have become inadequate. Authority as we once knew it, which grew out of the Roman experience of foundation and was understood in the light of Greek political philosophy, has nowhere been reestablished, either through revolutions or through the even less promising means of restoration, and least of all through the conservative moods and trends which occasionally sweep public opinion. For to live in a political realm with neither authority nor the concomitant awareness that the source of authority transcends power and those who are in power, means to be confronted anew, without the religious trust in a sacred beginning and without the protection of traditional and therefore self-evident standards of behavior, by the elementary problems of human living-together.

Notes

1. The formulation is Lord Action's in his "Inaugural Lecture on the 'Study of History,'" reprinted in *Essays on Freedom and Power,* New York, 1955, p. 35.
2. Only a detailed description and analysis of the very original organizational

structure of totalitarian movements and the institutions of totalitarian government could justify the use of the onion image. I must refer to the chapter on "Totalitarian Organization" in my book *The Origins of Totalitarianism,* 2nd edition, New York, 1958.

3. This was already noticed by the Greek historian Dio Cassius, who, when writing a history of Rome, found it impossible to translate the word *auctoritas:* ἑλληνίσαι αὐτὸ καθάπαξ ἀδύνατον ἔστι. (Quoted from Theodor Mommsen, *Römisches Staatsrecht,* 3rd edition, 1888, vol. III, p. 952, n. 4.) Moreover, one need only compare the Roman Senate, the republic's specifically authoritarian institution, with Plato's nocturnal council in the *Laws,* which, being composed of the ten oldest guardians for the constant supervision of the State, superficially resembles it, to become aware of the impossibility of finding a true alternative for coercion and persuasion within the framework of Greek political experience.

4. πόλις γὰρ οὐκ ἔσθ' ἥτις ἀνδρὸς ἐσθ' ἑνός. Sophocles, *Antigone,* 737.

5. *Laws,* 715.

6. Theodor Mommsen, *Römische Geschichte,* book I, chap. 5.

7. H. Wallon, *Histoire de l'Esclavage dans l'Antiquité,* Paris, 1847, vol. III, where one still finds the best description of the gradual loss of Roman liberty under the Empire caused by the constant increase of power of the imperial household. Since it was the imperial household and not the emperor who gained in power, the "despotism" which always had been characteristic of the private household and family life began to dominate the public realm.

8. A fragment from the lost dialogue *On Kingship* states that "it was not only not necessary for a king to become a philosopher, but actually a hindrance to his work; that, however, it was necessary [for a good king] to listen to the true philosopher and to be agreeable to their advice." See Kurt von Fritz, *The Constitution of Athens, and Related Texts,* 1950. In Aristotelian terms, both Plato's philosopher-king and the Greek tyrant rule for the sake of their own interest, and this was for Aristotle, though not for Plato, an outstanding characteristic of tyrants. Plato was not aware of the resemblance, because for him, as for Greek current opinion, the principal characteristic of the tyrant was that he deprived the citizen of access to a public realm, to a "market place" where he could show himself, see and be seen, hear and be heard, that he prohibited the ἀγορεύειν and πολιτεύεσθαι, confined the citizens to the privacy of their households, and demanded to be the only one in charge of public affairs. He would not have ceased to be a tyrant if he had used his power solely in the interests of his subjects—as indeed some of the tyrants undoubtedly did. According to the Greeks, to be banished to the privacy of household life was tantamount to being deprived of the specifically human potentialities of life. In other words, the very features which so convincingly demonstrate to us the tyrannical character of Plato's republic—the almost complete elimination of privacy and the omnipresence of political organs and institutions—presumably prevented Plato from recognizing its tyrannical character. To him, it would have been a contradiction in terms to brand as

tyranny a constitution which not only did not relegate the citizen to his household but, on the contrary, did not leave him a shred of private life whatsoever. Moreover, by calling the rule of law "despotic," Plato stresses its non-tyrannical character. For the tyrant was always supposed to rule over men who had known the freedom of a polis and, being deprived of it, were likely to rebel, whereas the despot was assumed to rule over people who had never known freedom and were by nature incapable of it. It is as though Plato said: My laws, your new despots, will not deprive you of anything you rightfully enjoyed before; they are adequate to the very nature of human affairs and you have no more right to rebel against their rule than the slave has a right to rebel against his master.

9. "Eternal Peace," *The Philosophy of Kant,* ed. and trans. C. J. Friedrich, Modern Library Edition, 1949, p. 456.

10. Von Fritz, op. cit., p. 54, rightly insists on Plato's aversion to violence, "also revealed by the fact that, wherever he did make an attempt to bring about a change of political institutions in the direction of his political ideals, he addressed himself to men already in power."

11. Werner Jaeger's statement in *Paideia,* New York, 1943, vol. II, p. 416n; "The idea that there is a supreme art of measurement and that the philosopher's knowledge of values (*phronesis*) is the ability to measure, runs through all Plato's work right down to the end" is true only for Plato's political philosophy. The very word φρόνησις characterizes in Plato and Aristotle the insight of the statesman rather than the "wisdom" of the philosopher.

12. *The Republic,* book VII, 516–517.

13. See especially *Timaeus,* 31, where the divine Demiurge makes the universe in accordance with a model, a παράδειγμα, and *The Republic,* 596 ff.

14. In *Protrepticus,* quoted from von Fritz, op. cit.

15. *Laws,* 710–711.

16. This presentation is indebted to Martin Heidegger's great interpretation of the cave parable in *Platons Lehre von der Wahrheit,* Bern, 1947. Heidegger demonstrates how Plato transformed the concept of truth (ἀλήθεια) until it became identical with correct statements (ὀρθότης). Correctness indeed, and not truth, would be required if the philosopher's knowledge is the ability to measure. Although he explicitly mentions the risks the philosopher runs when he is forced to return to the cave, Heidegger is not aware of the political context in which the parable appears. According to him, the transformation comes to pass because the subjective act of vision (the ἰδεῖν and the ἰδέα in the mind of the philosopher) takes precedence over objective truth (ἀλήθεια), which, according to Heidegger, signifies *Unverborgenheit.*

17. *Symposion,* 211–212.

18. *Phaedrus,* 248: φιλόσοφος ἢ φιλόκαλος, and 250.

19. In *The Republic,* 518, the good, too, is called φανότατον, the most shining one. Obviously it is precisely this quality which indicates the precedence which the beautiful originally had over the good in Plato's thought.

20. *The Republic,* 475–476. In the tradition of philosophy, the result of this Pla-

tonic repudiation of the beautiful has been that it was omitted from the so-called transcendentals or universals, that is, those qualities possessed by everything that is, and which were enumerated in medieval philosophy as *unum, alter, ens,* and *bonum.* Jacques Maritain, in his wonderful book, *Creative Intuition in Art and Poetry,* Bollingen Series XXXV, I, 1953, is aware of this omission and insists that beauty be included in the realm of transcendentals, for "Beauty is the radiance of all transcendentals united" (p. 162).

21. In the dialogue *Politicus:* "for the most exact measure of all things is the good" (quoted from von Fritz, op. cit.). The notion must have been that only through the concept of the good do things become comparable and hence measurable.

22. *Politics,* 1332b12 and 1332b36. The distinction between the younger and older ones goes back to Plato; see *Republic,* 412, and *Laws,* 690 and 714. The appeal to nature is Aristotelian.

23. *Politics,* 1328b35.

24. *Economics,* 1343a1–4.

25. Jaeger, op. cit., vol. I, p. 111.

26. *Economics,* 1343b24.

27. The derivation of *religio* from *religare* occurs in Cicero. Since we deal here only with the political self-interpretation of the Romans, the question whether this derivation is etymologically correct is irrelevant.

28. See Cicero, *De Re Publica,* III, 23. For the Roman belief in the eternity of their city, see Viktor Poeschl, *Römischer Staat und griechisches Staatsdenken bei Cicero,* Berlin, 1936.

29. *Annals,* book 43, ch. 13.

30. *De Re Publica,* 1, 7.

31. Cicero, *De Legibus,* 3, 12, 38.

32. *Esprit des Lois,* book XI, ch. 6.

33. Professor Carl J. Friedrich drew my attention to the important discussion of authority in Mommsen's *Römisches Staatsrecht;* see pp. 1034, 1038–1039.

34. This interpretation is further supported by the idiomatic Latin use of *alicui auctorem esse* for "giving advice to somebody."

35. See Mommsen, op. cit., 2nd edition, vol. I, pp. 73 ff. The Latin word *numen,* which is nearly untranslatable, meaning "divine command" as well as the divine modes of acting, derives from *nuere,* to nod in affirmation. Thus the commands of the gods and all their interference in human affairs are restricted to approval or disapproval of human actions.

36. Mommsen, ibid., p. 87.

37. See also the various Latin idioms such as *auctores habere* for having predecessors or examples; *auctoritas maiorum,* signifying the authoritative example of the ancestors; *usus et auctoritas* as used in Roman law for property rights which come from usage. An excellent presentation of this Roman spirit as well as a very useful collection of the more important source materials are to be found in Viktor Poeschl, op. cit., especially pp. 101 ff.

38. R. H. Barrow, *The Romans,* 1949, p. 194.

39. A similar amalgamation of Roman imperial political sentiment with Christianity is discussed by Erik Peterson, *Der Monotheismus als politisches Problem,* Leipzig, 1935, in connection with Orosius, who related the Roman Emperor Augustus to Christ. "*Dabei ist deutlich, dass Augustus auf diese Weise christianisiert und Christus zum* civis romanus *wird, romanisiert worden ist*" (p. 92).

40. *Duo quippe sunt . . . quibus principaliter mundus hic regitur,: auctoritas sacra pontificum et regalis potestas.* In Migne, PL, vol. 59, p. 42a.

41. Eric Voegelin, *A New Science of Politics,* Chicago, 1952, p. 7.

42. See *Phaedo* 80 for the affinity of the invisible soul with the traditional place of invisibility, namely, Hades, which Plato construes etymologically as "the invisible."

43. Ibid., 64–66.

44. With the exception of the *Laws,* it is characteristic of Plato's political dialogues that a break occurs somewhere and the strictly argumentative procedure has to be abandoned. In *The Republic,* Socrates eludes his questioners several times; the baffling question is whether justice is still possible if a deed is hidden from men and gods. The discussion of what justice is breaks down at 372a and is taken up again in 427d, where, however, not justice but wisdom and εὐβουλία are defined. Socrates comes back to the main question in 403d, but discusses σωφροσύνη instead of justice. He then starts again in 433b and comes almost immediately to a discussion of the forms of government, 445d ff., until the seventh book with the cave story puts the whole argument on an entirely different, nonpolitical level. Here it becomes clear why Glaukon could not receive a satisfactory answer: justice is an idea and must be perceived; there is no other possible demonstration.

    The Er-myth, on the other hand, is introduced by a reversion of the whole argument. The task had been to find justice as such, even if hidden from the eyes of gods and men. Now (612) Socrates wishes to take back his initial admission to Glaukon that, at least for the sake of the argument, one would have to assume that "the just man may appear unjust and the unjust just" so that no one, neither god nor man, could definitely know who is truly just. And in its stead, he puts the assumption that "the nature both of the just and the unjust is truly known to the gods." Again, the whole argument is put on an entirely different level—this time on the level of the multitude and outside the range of argument altogether.

    The case of *Gorgias* is quite similar. Once more, Socrates is incapable of persuading his opponent. The discussion turns about the Socratic conviction that it is better to suffer wrong than to do wrong. When Kallikles clearly cannot be persuaded by argument, Plato proceeds to tell his myth of a hereafter as a kind of *ultima ratio,* and, in distinction to *The Republic,* he tells it with great diffidence, clearly indicating that the teller of the story, Socrates, does not take it seriously.

45. Imitation of Plato seems to be beyond doubt in the frequent cases where the motif of apparent death recurs, as in Cicero and Plutarch. For an excellent discussion of Cicero's *Somnium Scipionis,* the myth which concludes his *De*

Re Publica, see Richard Harder, "Ueber Ciceros Somnium Scipionis" (*Kleine Schriften*, München, 1960), who also shows convincingly that neither Plato nor Cicero followed Pythagorean doctrines.

46. This is especially stressed by Marcus Dods, *Forerunners of Dante*, Edinburgh, 1903.

47. See *Gorgias*, 524.

48. See *Gorgias*, 522/3 and *Phaedo*, 110. In *The Republic*, 614, Plato even alludes to a tale told by Ulysses to Alcinous.

49. *The Republic*, 379a.

50. As Werner Jaeger once called the Platonic god in *Theology of the Early Greek Philosophers*, Oxford, 1947, p. 194n.

51. *The Republic*, 615a.

52. See especially the *Seventh Letter* for Plato's conviction that truth is beyond speech and argument.

53. Thus John Adams in *Discourses on Davila*, in *Works*, Boston, 1851, vol. VI, p. 280.

54. From the draft Preamble to the Constitution of Massachusetts, *Works*, vol. IV, 221.

55. John Stuart Mill, *On Liberty*, ch. 2.

56. *The Prince*, ch. 15.

57. *The Prince*, ch. 8.

58. See especially the *Discourses*, book III, ch. 1.

59. It is curious to see how seldom Cicero's name occurs in Machiavelli's writings and how carefully he avoided him in his interpretations of Roman history.

60. *De Re Publica*, VI, 12.

61. *Laws*, 711a.

62. These assumptions, of course, could be justified only by a detailed analysis of the American Revolution.

63. *The Prince*, ch. 6.

The Revolutionary Tradition
and Its Lost Treasure

Notre héritage n'est précédé d'aucun testament
—RENÉ CHAR

. . . THE FAILURE of post-revolutionary thought to remember the revolutionary spirit and to understand it conceptually was preceded by the failure of the revolution to provide it with a lasting institution. The revolution, unless it ended in the disaster of terror, had come to an end with the establishment of a republic which, according to the men of the revolutions, was 'the only form of government which is not eternally at open or secret war with the rights of mankind.'[1] But in this republic, as it presently turned out, there was no space reserved, no room left for the exercise of precisely those qualities which had been instrumental in building it. And this was clearly no mere oversight, as though those who knew so well how to provide for power of the commonwealth and the liberties of its citizens, for judgement and opinion, for interests and rights, had simply forgotten what actually they cherished above everything else, the potentialities of action and the proud privilege of being beginners of something altogether new. Certainly, they did not want to deny this privilege to their successors, but they also could not very well wish to deny their own work, although Jefferson, more concerned with this perplexity than anybody else, almost went to this extremity. The perplexity was very simple and, stated in logical terms, it seemed unsolvable: if foundation was the aim and the end of revolution, then the revolutionary spirit was not merely the spirit of beginning something new but of starting something permanent and enduring; a lasting institution, embodying this spirit and encouraging it to new achievements, would be self-defeating. From which it unfortunately seems to follow that nothing threatens the very achievements of revolution more dangerously and more acutely than the spirit which has brought them about. Should freedom in its most exalted sense as freedom to act be the price to be paid for foundation? This

From On Revolution.

perplexity, namely, that the principle of public freedom and public happiness without which no revolution would ever have come to pass should remain the privilege of the generation of the founders, has not only produced Robespierre's bewildered and desperate theories about the distinction between revolutionary and constitutional government which we mentioned earlier, but has haunted all revolutionary thinking ever since.

On the American scene, no one has perceived this seemingly inevitable flaw in the structure of the republic with greater clarity and more passionate preoccupation than Jefferson. His occasional, and sometimes violent, antagonism against the Constitution and particularly against those who 'look at constitutions with sanctimonious reverence, and deem them like the ark of the covenant, too sacred to be touched'[2] was motivated by a feeling of outrage about the injustice that only his generation should have it in their power 'to begin the world over again'; for him, as for Paine, it was plain 'vanity and presumption [to govern] beyond the grave'; it was, moreover, the 'most ridiculous and insolent of all tyrannies'.[3] When he said, 'We have not yet so far perfected our constitutions as to venture to make them unchangeable', he added at once, clearly in fear of such possible perfection, 'Can they be made unchangeable? I think not'; for, in conclusion: 'Nothing is unchangeable but the inherent and unalienable rights of man', among which he counted the rights to rebellion and revolution.[4] When the news of Shay's rebellion in Massachusetts reached him while he was in Paris, he was not in the least alarmed, although he conceded that its motives were 'founded in ignorance', but greeted it with enthusiasm: 'God forbid we should ever be twenty years without such a rebellion.' The very fact that the people had taken it upon themselves to rise and act was enough for him, regardless of the rights or wrongs of their case. For 'the tree of liberty must be refreshed, from time to time, with the blood of patriots and tyrants. It is its natural manure.'[5]

These last sentences, written two years before the outbreak of the French Revolution and in this form without parallel in Jefferson's later writings,[6] may give us a clue to the fallacy which was bound to becloud the whole issue of action in the thinking of the men of the revolutions. It was in the nature of their experiences to see the phenomenon of action exclusively in the image of tearing down and building up. Although they had known public freedom and public happiness, in dream or in reality, prior to the revolution, the impact of revolutionary experience had overruled all notions of a freedom which was not preceded by liberation, which did not derive its pathos from the act of liberation. By the same token, to the extent that they had a positive notion of freedom which would transcend the idea of a successful liberation from tyrants and from necessity, this notion was identified with the act of foundation, that is, the framing of a constitution. Jefferson, therefore, when he had learned his lesson from the catastrophes of the French Revolution, where the violence of liberation had frustrated all attempts at founding a secure space for freedom, shifted from his earlier identification of action with rebellion and tearing down to an identification with founding anew and building up. He thus proposed to provide in the Constitution itself 'for its revision at stated periods' which would roughly correspond to the periods of the coming and going of generations. His justification, that each new generation has 'a right to choose for itself the form of government it believes most promotive of its own happiness', sounds too fantastic (especially if one considers the then prevailing tables of mortality, according to which there was 'a new majority' every nineteen years) to be taken seriously; it is, moreover, rather unlikely that Jefferson, of all people, should have granted the coming generations the right to establish non-republican forms of government. What was uppermost in his mind was no real change of form of government, not even a constitutional provision to hand on the Constitution 'with periodical repairs, from generation to generation, to the end of time'; it was rather the somewhat awkward attempt at securing for each generation the 'right to depute representatives to a convention', to find ways and means for the opinions of the whole people to be 'fairly, fully, and peaceably expressed, discussed, and decided by the common reason of the society'.[7] In other words, what he wished to provide for was an exact repetition of the whole process of action which had accompanied the course of the Revolution, and while in his earlier writings he saw this action primarily in terms of liberation, in terms of the violence that had preceded and followed the Declaration of Independence, he later was much more concerned with the constitution-making and the establishment of a new government, that is, with those activities which by themselves constituted the space of freedom.

No doubt only great perplexity and real calamity can explain that Jefferson—so conscious of his common sense and so famous for his practical turn of mind—should have proposed these schemes of recurring revolutions. Even in their least extreme form, recommended as the remedy against 'the endless circle of oppression, rebellion, reformation', they would either have thrown the whole body politic out of gear periodically or, more likely, have debased the act of foundation to a mere routine performance, in which case even the memory of what he most ardently wished to save—'to the end of time, if anything human can so long endure'—would have been lost. But the reason Jefferson, throughout his long life, was carried away by such impracticabilities was that he knew, however dimly, that the Revolution, while it had given freedom to the people, had failed to provide a space where this freedom could be exercised. Only the representatives of the people, not the people themselves, had an opportunity to engage in those activities of 'expressing, discussing, and deciding' which in a positive sense are the activities of freedom. And since the state and federal governments, the proudest results of revolution, through sheer weight of their proper business were bound to overshadow in political importance the townships and their meeting halls—until what Emerson still considered to be 'the unit of the Republic' and 'the school of the people' in political matters had withered away[8]—one might even come to the conclusion that there was less opportunity for the exercise of public freedom and the enjoyment of public happiness in the republic of the United States than there had existed in the colonies of British America. Lewis Mumford recently pointed out how the political importance of the township was never grasped by the founders, and that the failure to incorporate it into either the federal or the state constitutions was 'one of the tragic oversights of post-revolutionary political development'. Only Jefferson among the founders had a clear premonition of this tragedy, for his greatest fear was indeed lest 'the abstract, political system of democracy lacked concrete organs[9]. . .

★   ★   ★   ★   ★

'As Cato concluded every speech with the words, *Carthago delenda est,* so do I every opinion, with the injunction, "divide the counties into wards". '[10] Thus Jefferson once summed up an exposition of his most cherished political idea, which, alas, turned out to be as incomprehensible to posterity as it had been to his contemporaries. The reference to Cato was no idle slip of a tongue used to Latin quotations; it was meant to emphasize that Jefferson thought the absence of such a subdivision of the country constituted a vital threat to the very existence of the republic. Just as Rome, according to Cato, could not be safe so long as Carthage existed, so the republic, according to Jefferson, would not be secure in its very foundations without the ward system. 'Could I once see this I should consider it as the dawn of the salvation of the republic, and say with old Simeon, "Nunc dimittis Domine." '[11]

Had Jefferson's plan of 'elementary republics' been carried out, it would have exceeded by far the feeble germs of a new form of government which we are able to detect in the sections of the Parisian Commune and the popular societies during the French Revolution. However, if Jefferson's political imagination surpassed them in insight and in scope, his thoughts were still travelling in the same direction. Both Jefferson's plan and the French *sociétés révolutionaires* anticipated with an utmost weird precision those councils, *soviets* and *Räte,* which were to make their appearance in every genuine revolution throughout the nineteenth and twentieth centuries. Each time they appeared, they sprang up as the spontaneous organs of the people, not only outside of all revolutionary parties but entirely unexpected by them and their leaders. Like Jefferson's proposals, they were utterly neglected by statesmen, historians, political theorists, and, most importantly, by the revolutionary tradition itself. Even those historians whose sympathies were clearly on the side of revolution and who could not help writing the emergence of popular councils into the record of their story regarded them as nothing more than essentially temporary organs in the revolutionary struggle for liberation; that is to say, they failed to understand to what an extent the council system confronted them with an entirely new form of government, with a new public space for freedom which was constituted and organized during the course of the revolution itself.

This statement must be qualified. There are two relevant exceptions to it, namely a few remarks by Marx at the occasion of the revival of the Parisian Commune during the short-lived revolution of 1871, and some reflections by Lenin based not on the text by Marx, but on the actual course of the Revolution of 1905 in Russia. But before we turn our attention to these matters, we had better try to understand what Jefferson had in mind when he said with utmost self-assurance, 'The wit of man cannot devise a more solid basis for a free, durable, and well-administered republic.'[12]

It is perhaps noteworthy that we find no mention of the ward system in any of Jefferson's formal works, and it may be even more important that the few letters in which he wrote of it with such emphatic insistence all date from the last period of his life. It is true, at one time he hoped that Virginia, because it was 'the first of the nations of the earth which assembled its wise men peaceably together to form a fundamental constitution', would also be the first 'to adopt the subdivision of our counties into wards',[13] but the point of the matter is that the whole idea seems to have occurred to him only at a time when he himself was retired from public life and when he had withdrawn from the affairs of state. He who had been so explicit in his criticism of the Constitution because it had not incorporated a Bill of Rights never touched on its failure to incorporate the townships which so obviously were the original models of his 'elementary republics' where 'the voice of the whole people would be fairly, fully, and peaceably expressed, discussed, and decided by the common reason' of all citizens.[14] In terms of his own role in the affairs of his country and the outcome of the Revolution, the idea of the ward system clearly was an afterthought; and, in terms of his own biographical development, the repeated insistence on the 'peaceable' character of these wards demonstrates that this system was to him the only possible nonviolent alternative to his earlier notions about the desirability of recurring revolutions. At any event, we find the only detailed description of what he had in mind in letters written in the year 1816, and these letters repeat rather than supplement one another.

Jefferson himself knew well enough that what he proposed as the 'salvation of the republic' actually was the salvation of the revolutionary spirit through the republic. His expositions of the ward system always began with a reminder of how 'the vigour given to our revolution in its commencement' was due to the 'little republics', how they had 'thrown the whole nation into energetic action', and how, at a later occasion, he had felt 'the foundations of the government shaken under [his] feet by the New England townships', 'the energy of this organization' being so great that 'there was not an individual in their States whose body was not thrown with all its momentum into action'. Hence, he expected the wards to permit the citizens to continue to do what they had been able to do during the years of revolution, namely, to act on their own and thus to participate in public business as it was being transacted from day to day. By virtue of the Constitution, the public business of the nation as a whole had been transferred to Washington and was being transacted by the federal government, of which Jefferson still thought as 'the foreign branch' of the republic, whose domestic affairs were taken care of by the state governments.[15] But state government and even the administrative machinery of the county were by far too large and unwieldy to permit immediate participation; in all these institutions, it was the delegates of the people rather than the people themselves who constituted the public realm, whereas those who delegated them and who, theoretically, were the source and the seat of power remained forever outside its doors. This order of things should have sufficed if Jefferson had actually believed (as he sometimes professed) that the happiness of the people lay exclusively in their private welfare; for because of the way the government of the union was constituted—with its division and separation of powers, with controls, checks, and balances, built into its very centre—it was highly unlikely, though of course not impossible, that a tyranny could arise out of it. What could happen, and what indeed has happened over and over again since, was that 'the representative organs should become corrupt and perverted',[16] but such corruption was not likely to be due (and hardly ever has been due) to a conspiracy of the representative organs against the people whom they represented. Corruption in this kind of government is much more likely to spring from the midst of society, that is, from the people themselves.

Corruption and perversion are more pernicious, and at the same time more likely to occur, in an egalitarian republic than in any other form of government. Schematically speaking, they come to pass when private interests invade the public domain, that is, they spring from below and not from above. It is precisely because the republic excluded on principle the old dichotomy of ruler and ruled that corruption of the body politic did not leave the people untouched, as in other forms of government, where only the rulers or the ruling classes needed to be affected, and where therefore an 'innocent' people might indeed first suffer and then, one day, effect a dreadful but necessary insurrection. Corruption of the people themselves—as distinguished from corruption of their representatives or a ruling class—is possible only under a government that has granted them a share in public power and has taught them how to manipulate it. Where the rift between ruler and ruled has been closed, it is always possible that the dividing line between public and private may become blurred and, eventually, obliterated. Prior to the modern age and the rise of society, this danger, inherent in republican government, used to arise from the public realm, from the tendency of public power to expand and to trespass upon private interests. The age-old remedy against this danger was respect for private property, that is, the framing of a system of laws through which the rights of privacy were publicly guaranteed and the dividing line between public and private legally protected. The Bill of Rights in the American Constitution forms the last, and the most exhaustive, legal bulwark for the private realm against public power, and Jefferson's preoccupation with the dangers of public power and this remedy against them is sufficiently well known. However, under conditions, not of prosperity as such, but of rapid and constant economic growth, that is, of a constantly increasing expansion of the private realm—and these were of course the conditions of the modern age—the dangers of corruption and perversion were much more likely to arise from private interests than from public power. And it speaks for the high calibre of Jefferson's statesmanship that he was able to perceive this danger despite his preoccupation with the older and better-known threats of corruption in bodies politic.

The only remedies against the misuse of public power by private individuals lie in the public realm itself, in the light which exhibits each deed enacted within its boundaries, in the very visibility to which it exposes all those who enter it. Jefferson, though the secret vote was still unknown at the time, had at least a foreboding of how dangerous it might be to allow the people a share in public power without providing them at the same time with more public space than the ballot box and with more opportunity to make their voices heard in public than election day. What he perceived to be the mortal danger to the republic was that the Constitution had given all power to the citizens, without giving them the opportunity of *being* republicans and of *acting* as citizens. In other words, the danger was that all power had been given to the people in their private capacity and that there was no space established for them in their capacity of being citizens. When, at the end of his life, he summed up what to him clearly was the gist of private and public morality, 'Love your neighbour as yourself, and your country more than yourself,'[17] he knew that this maxim remained an empty exhortation unless the 'country' could be made as present to the 'love' of its citizens as the 'neighbour' was to the love of his fellow men. For just as there could not be much substance to neighbourly love if one's neighbour should make a brief apparition once every two years, so could not be much substance to the admonition to love one's country more than oneself unless the country was a living presence in the midst of its citizens.

Hence, according to Jefferson, it was the very principle of republican government to demand 'the subdivision of the counties into wards', namely, the creation of 'small republics' through which 'every man in the State' could become 'an acting member of the Common government, transacting in person a great portion of its rights and duties, subordinate indeed, yet important, and entirely within his competence'.[18] It was 'these little republics [that] would be the main strength of the great one';[19] for inasmuch as the republican government of the Union was based on the assumption that the seat of power was in the people, the very condition for its proper functioning lay in a scheme 'to divide [government] among the many, distributing to every one exactly the functions he [was] competent to'. Without this, the very principle of republican government could never be actualized, and the government of the United States would be republican in name only.

Thinking in terms of the safety of the republic, the question was how to prevent 'the degeneracy of our government', and Jefferson called every government degenerate in which all powers were concentrated 'in the hands of the one, the few, the well-born or the many'. Hence, the ward system was not meant to strengthen the power of the many but the power of 'every one' within the limits of his competence; and only by breaking up 'the many' into assemblies where every one could count and be counted upon 'shall we be as republican as a large society can be'. In terms of the safety of the citizens of the republic, the question was how to make everybody feel 'that he is a participator in the government of affairs, not merely at an election one day in the year, but every day; when there shall not be a man in the State who will not be a member of some one of its councils, great or small, he will let the heart be torn out of his body sooner than his power wrested from him by a Bonaparte'. Finally, as to the question of how to integrate these smallest organs, designed for everyone, into the governmental structure of the Union, designed for all, his answer was: 'The elementary republics of the wards, the county republics, the State republics, and the republic of the Union would form a gradation of authorities, standing each on the basis of law, holding every one its delegated share of powers, and constituting truly a system of fundamental balances and checks for the government.' On one point, however, Jefferson remained curiously silent, and that is the question of what the specific functions of the elementary republics should be. He mentioned occasionally as 'one of the advantages of the ward divisions I have proposed' that they would offer a better way to collect the voice of the people than the mechanics of representative government; but in the main, he was convinced that if one would 'begin them only for a single purpose' they would 'soon show for what others they [were] the best instruments'.[20]

This vagueness of purpose, far from being due to a lack of clarity, indicates perhaps more tellingly than any other single aspect of Jefferson's proposal that the afterthought in which he clarified and gave substance to his most cherished recollections from the Revolution in fact concerned a new form of government rather than a mere reform of it or a mere supplement to the existing institutions. If the ultimate end of revolution was freedom and the constitution of a public space where freedom could appear, the *constitutio libertatis*, then the elementary republics of the wards, the only tangible place where everyone could be free, actually were the end of the great republic whose chief purpose in domestic affairs should have been to provide the people with such places of freedom and to protect them. The basic assumption of the ward system, whether Jefferson knew it or not, was that no one could be called happy without his share in public happiness, that no one could be called free without his experience in public freedom, and that no one could be called either happy or free without participating, and having a share, in public power.

*   *   *   *   *

It is a strange and sad story that remains to be told and remembered. It is not the story of revolution on whose thread the historian might string the history of the nineteenth century in Europe,[21] whose origins could be traced back into the Middle Ages, whose progress had been irresistible 'for centuries in spite of every obstacle', according to Tocqueville, and which Marx, generalizing the experiences of several generations, called 'the locomotive of all history'.[22] I do not doubt that revolution was the hidden *leitmotif* of the century preceding ours, although I doubt both Tocqueville's and Marx's generalizations, especially their conviction that revolution had been the result of an irresistible force rather than the outcome of specific deeds and events. What seems to be beyond doubt and belief is that no historian will ever be able to tell the tale of our century without stringing it 'on the thread of revolutions'; but this tale, since its end still lies hidden in the mists of the future, is not yet fit to be told.

The same, to an extent, is true for the particular aspect of revolution with which we now must concern ourselves. This aspect is the regular emergence, during the course of revolution, of a new form of government that resembled in an amazing fashion Jefferson's ward system and seemed to repeat, under no matter what circumstances, the revolutionary societies and municipal councils which had spread all over France after 1789. Among the reasons that recommend this aspect to our attention must first be mentioned that we deal here with the phenomenon that impressed most the two greatest revolutionists of the whole period, Marx and Lenin, when they were witnessing its spontaneous rise, the former during the Parisian Commune of 1871 and the latter in 1905, during the first Russian Revolution. What struck them was not only the fact that they themselves were entirely unprepared for these events, but also that they knew they were confronted with a repetition unaccounted for by any conscious imitation or even mere remembrance of the past. To be sure, they had hardly any knowledge of Jefferson's ward system, but they knew well enough the revolutionary role the sections of the first Parisian Commune had played in the French Revolution, except that they had never thought of them as possible germs for a new form of government but had regarded them as mere instruments to be dispensed with once the revolution came to an end. Now, however, they were confronted with popular organs—the communes, the councils, the *Räte*, the *soviets*— which clearly intended to survive the revolution. This contradicted all their theories and, even more importantly, was in flagrant conflict with those assumptions about the nature of power and violence which they shared, albeit unconsciously, with the rulers of the doomed or defunct regimes. Firmly anchored in the tradition of the nation-state, they conceived of revolution as a means to seize power, and they identified power with the monopoly of the means of violence. What actually happened, however, was a swift disintegration of the old power, the sudden loss of control over the means of violence, and, at the same time, the amazing formation of a new power structure which owed its existence to nothing but the organizational impulses of the people themselves. In other words, when the moment of revolution had come, it turned out that there was no power left to seize, so that the revolutionists found themselves before the rather uncomfortable alternative of either putting their own pre-revolutionary 'power', that is, the organization of the party apparatus, into the vacated power centre of the defunct government, or simply joining the new revolutionary power centres which had sprung up without their help.

For a brief moment, while he was the mere witness of something he never had expected, Marx understood that the *Kommunalverfassung* of the Parisian Commune in 1871, because it was supposed to become 'the po-litical form of even the smallest village', might well be 'the political form, finally discovered, for the economic liberation of labour'. But he soon be-came aware to what an extent this political form contradicted all notions of a 'dictatorship of the proletariat' by means of a socialist or communist party whose monopoly of power and violence was modelled upon the highly centralized governments of nation-states, and he concluded that the communal councils were, after all, only temporary organs of the rev-olution.[23] It is almost the same sequence of attitudes which, one genera-tion later, we find in Lenin, who twice in his life, in 1905 and in 1917, came under the direct impact of the events themselves, that is to say, was temporarily liberated from the pernicious influence of a revolutionary ide-ology. Thus he could extol with great sincerity in 1905 'the revolutionary creativity of the people', who spontaneously had begun to establish an en-tirely new power structure in the midst of revolution,[24] just as, twelve years later, he could let loose and win the October Revolution with the slogan: 'All power to the *soviets*.' But during the years that separated the two revolutions he had done nothing to reorient his thought and to in-corporate the new organs into any of the many party programmes, with the result that the same spontaneous development in 1917 found him and his party no less unprepared than they had been in 1905. When, finally, during the Kronstadt rebellion, the *soviets* revolted against the party dicta-torship and the incompatibility of the new councils with the party system became manifest, he decided almost at once to crush the councils, since they threatened the power monopoly of the Bolshevik party. The name 'Soviet Union' for post-revolutionary Russia has been a lie ever since, but this lie has also contained, ever since, the grudging admission of the over-whelming popularity, not of the Bolshevik party, but of the *soviet* system which the party reduced to impotence.[25] Put before the alternative of either adjusting their thoughts and deeds to the new and the unexpected or going to the extreme of tyranny and suppression, they hardly hesitated in their decision for the latter; with the exceptions of a few moments without consequence, their behaviour from beginning to end was dictated by considerations of party strife, which played no role in the councils but which indeed had been of paramount importance in the pre-revolutionary parliaments. When the Communists decided, in 1919, 'to espouse only the cause of a *soviet* republic in which the *soviets* possess a Communist majority',[26] they actually behaved like ordinary party politicians. So great is the fear of men, even of the most radical and least conventional among them, of things never seen, of thoughts never thought, of institutions never tried before.

The failure of the revolutionary tradition to give any serious thought to the only new form of government born out of revolution can partly be explained by Marx's obsession with the social question and his unwillingness to pay serious attention to questions of state and government. But this explanation is weak and, to an extent, even question-begging, because it takes for granted the overtowering influence of Marx on the revolutionary movement and tradition, an influence which itself still stands in need of explanation. It was, after all, not only the Marxists among the revolutionists who proved to be utterly unprepared for the actualities of revolutionary events. And this unpreparedness is all the more noteworthy as it surely cannot be blamed upon lack of thought or interest in revolution. It is well known that the French Revolution had given rise to an entirely new figure on the political scene, the professional revolutionist, and his life was spent not in revolutionary agitation, for which there existed but few opportunities, but in study and thought, in theory and debate, whose sole object was revolution. In fact, no history of the European leisure classes would be complete without a history of the professional revolutionists of the nineteenth and twentieth centuries, who, together with the modern artists and writers, have become the true heirs of the *hommes de lettres* in the seventeenth and eighteenth centuries. The artists and writers joined the revolutionists because 'the very word bourgeois came to have a hated significance no less aesthetic than political;[27] together they established Bohemia, that island of blessed leisure in the midst of the busy and overbusy century of the Industrial Revolution. Even among the members of this new leisure class, the professional revolutionist enjoyed special privileges since his way of life demanded no specific work whatsoever. If there was a thing he had no reason to complain of, it was lack of time to think, whereby it makes little difference if such an essentially theoretical way of life was spent in the famous libraries of London and Paris, or in the coffee houses of Vienna and Zurich, or in the relatively comfortable and undisturbed jails of the various *anciens régimes*.

The role the professional revolutionists played in all modern revolutions is great and significant enough, but it did not consist in the preparation of revolutions. They watched and analysed the progressing disintegration in state and society; they hardly did, or were in a position to do, much to advance and direct it. Even the wave of strikes that spread over Russia in 1905 and led into the first revolution was entirely spontaneous, unsupported by any political or trade-union organizations, which, on the contrary, sprang up only in the course of the revolution.[28] The outbreak of most revolutions has surprised the revolutionist groups and parties no less than all others, and there exists hardly a revolution whose outbreak could be blamed upon their activities. It usually was the other way round: revolution broke out and liberated, as it were, the professional revolutionists from wherever they happened to be—from jail, or from the coffee house, or from the library. Not even Lenin's party of professional revolutionists would ever have been able to 'make' a revolution; the best they could do was to be around, or to hurry home, at the right moment, that is, at the moment of collapse. Tocqueville's observation in 1848, that the monarchy fell 'before rather than beneath the blows of the victors, who were as astonished at their triumph as were the vanquished at their defeat', has been verified over and over again.

The part of the professional revolutionists usually consists not in making a revolution but in rising to power after it has broken out, and their great advantage in this power struggle lies less in their theories and mental or organizational preparation than in the simple fact that their names are the only ones which are publicly known.[29] It certainly is not conspiracy that causes revolution, and secret societies—though they may succeed in committing a few spectacular crimes, usually with the help of the secret police[30]—are as a rule much too secret to be able to make their voices heard in public. The loss of authority in the powers-that-be, which indeed precedes all revolutions, is actually a secret to no one, since its manifestations are open and tangible, though not necessarily spectacular; but its symptoms, general dissatisfaction, widespread malaise, and contempt for those in power, are difficult to pin down since their meaning is never unequivocal.[31] Nevertheless, contempt, hardly among the motives of the typical professional revolutionist, is certainly one of the most potent springs of revolution; there has hardly been a revolution for which Lamartine's remark about 1848, 'the revolution of contempt', would be altogether inappropriate.

However, while the part played by the professional revolutionist in the outbreak of revolution has usually been insignificant to the point of non-existence, his influence upon the actual course a revolution will take has proved to be very great. And since he spent his apprenticeship in the school of past revolutions, he will invariably exert this influence not in favour of the new and the unexpected, but in favour of some action which remains in accordance with the past. Since it is his very task to assure the continuity of revolution, he will be inclined to argue in terms of historical precedents, and the conscious and pernicious imitation of past events, which we mentioned earlier, lies, partially at least, in the very nature of his profession. Long before the professional revolutionists had found in Marxism their official guide to the interpretation and annotation of all history, past, present and future, Tocqueville, in 1848, could already note: 'The imitation [i.e. of 1789 by the revolutionary Assembly] was so manifest that it concealed the terrible originality of the facts; I continually had the impression they were engaged in play-acting the French Revolution far more than continuing it.'[32] And again, during the Parisian Commune of 1871, on which Marx and Marxists had no influence whatsoever, at least one of the new magazines, *Le Père Duchêne,* adopted the old revolutionary calendar's names for the months of the year. It is strange indeed that in this atmosphere, where every incident of past revolutions was mulled over as though it were part of sacred history, the only entirely new and entirely spontaneous institution in revolutionary history should have been neglected to the point of oblivion.

Armed with the wisdom of hindsight, one is tempted to qualify this statement. There are certain paragraphs in the writings of the Utopian Socialists, especially in Proudhon and Bakunin, into which it has been relatively easy to read an awareness of the council system. Yet the truth is that these essentially anarchist political thinkers were singularly unequipped to deal with a phenomenon which demonstrated so clearly how a revolution did not end with the abolition of state and government but, on the contrary, aimed at the foundation of a new state and the establishment of a new form of government. More recently, historians have pointed to the rather obvious similarities between the councils and the medieval townships, the Swiss cantons, the English seventeenth-century 'agitators'—or rather 'adjustators', as they were originally called—and the General Council of Cromwell's army, but the point of the matter is that none of them, with the possible exception of the medieval town,[33] had ever the slightest influence on the minds of the people who in the course of a revolution spontaneously organized themselves in councils.

Hence, no tradition, either revolutionary or pre-revolutionary, can be called to account for the regular emergence and re-emergence of the council system ever since the French Revolution. If we leave aside the February Revolution of 1848 in Paris, where a *commission pour les travailleurs,* set up by the government itself, was almost exclusively concerned with questions of social legislation, the main dates of appearance of these organs of action and germs of a new state are the following: the year 1870, when the French capital under siege by the Prussian army 'spontaneously reorganized itself into a miniature federal body', which then formed the nucleus for the Parisian Commune government in the spring of 1871;[34] the year 1905, when the wave of spontaneous strikes in Russia suddenly developed a political leadership of its own, outside all revolutionary parties and groups, and the workers in the factories organized themselves into councils, *soviets,* for the purpose of representative self-government; the February Revolution of 1917 in Russia, when 'despite different political tendencies among the Russian workers, the organization itself, that is the *soviet,* was not even subject to discussion';[35] the years 1918 and 1919 in Germany, when, after the defeat of the army, soldiers and workers in open rebellion constituted themselves into *Arbeiter- und Soldatenräte,* demanding, in Berlin, that this *Rätesystem* become the foundation stone of the new German constitution, and establishing, together with the Bohemians of the coffee houses, in Munich in the spring of 1919, the short-lived Bavarian *Räterepublik;*[36] the last date, finally, is the autumn of 1956, when the Hungarian Revolution from its very beginning produced the council system anew in Budapest, from which it spread all over the country 'with incredible rapidity'.[37]

The mere enumeration of these dates suggests a continuity that in fact never existed. It is precisely the absence of continuity, tradition, and organized influence that makes the sameness of the phenomenon so very striking. Outstanding among the councils' common characteristics is, of course, the spontaneity of their coming into being, because it clearly and flagrantly contradicts the theoretical 'twentieth-century model of revolution—planned, prepared, and executed almost to cold scientific exactness by the professional revolutionaries'.[38] It is true that wherever the revolution was not defeated and not followed by some sort of restoration the one-party dictatorship, that is, the model of the professional revolutionary, eventually prevailed, but it prevailed only after a violent struggle with the organs and institutions of the revolution itself. The councils, moreover, were always organs of order as much as organs of action, and it was indeed their aspiration to lay down the new order that brought them into conflict with the groups of professional revolutionaries, who wished to degrade them to mere executive organs of revolutionary activity. It is true enough that the members of the councils were not content to discuss and 'enlighten themselves' about measures that were taken by parties or assemblies; they consciously and explicitly desired the direct participation of every citizen in the public affairs of the country,[39] and as long as they lasted, there is no doubt that 'every individual found his own sphere of action and could behold, as it were, with his own eyes his own contribution to the events of the day'.[40] Witnesses of their functioning were often agreed on the extent to which the revolution had given birth to a 'direct regeneration of democracy', whereby the implication was that all such regenerations, alas, were foredoomed since, obviously, a direct handling of public business through the people was impossible under modern conditions. They looked upon the councils as though they were a romantic dream, some sort of fantastic utopia come true for a fleeting moment to show, as it were, the hopelessly romantic yearnings of the people, who apparently did not yet know the true facts of life. These realists took their own bearings from the party system, assuming as a matter of course that there existed no other alternative for representative government and forgetting conveniently that the downfall of the old regime had been due, among other things, precisely to this system.

For the remarkable thing about the councils was of course not only that they crossed all party lines, that members of the various parties sat in them together, but that such party membership played no role whatsoever. They were in fact the only political organs for people who belonged to no party. Hence, they invariably came into conflict with all assemblies, with the old parliaments as well as with the new 'constituent assemblies', for the simple reason that the latter, even in their most extreme wings, were still the children of the party system. At this stage of events, that is, in the midst of revolution, it was the party programmes more than anything else that separated the councils from the parties; for these programmes, no matter how revolutionary, were all 'ready-made formulas' which demanded not action but execution—'to be carried out energetically in practice', as Rosa Luxemburg pointed out with such amazing clearsightedness about the issues at stake.[41] Today we know how quickly the theoretical formula disappeared in practical execution, but if the formula had survived its execution, and even if it had proved to be the panacea for all evils, social and political, the councils were bound to rebel against any such policy since the very cleavage between the party experts who 'knew' and the mass of the people who were supposed to apply this knowledge left out of account the average citizen's capacity to act and to form his own opinion. The councils, in other words, were bound to become superfluous if the spirit of the revolutionary party prevailed. Wherever knowing and doing have parted company, the space of freedom is lost. . . .

. . . It has frequently been noted that the United States and Great Britain are among the few countries where the party system has worked sufficiently well to assure stability and authority. It so happens that the two-party system coincides with a constitution that rests on the division of power among the various branches of government, and the chief reason for its stability is, of course, the recognition of the opposition as an institution of government. Such recognition, however, is possible only under the assumption that the nation is not *une et indivisible,* and that a separation of powers, far from causing impotence, generates and stabilizes power. It is ultimately the same principle which enabled Great Britain to organize her far-flung possessions and colonies into a Commonwealth, that made it possible for the British colonies in North America to unite into a federal system of government. What distinguishes the two-party systems of these countries, despite all their differences, so decisively from the multi-party systems of the European nation-states is by no means a technicality, but a radically different concept of power which permeates the whole body politic.[42] If we were to classify contemporary regimes according to the power principle upon which they rest, the distinction between the one-party dictatorships and the multi-party systems would be revealed as much less decisive than the distinction that separates them both from the two-party systems. After the nation during the nineteenth century 'had stepped into the shoes of the absolute prince', it became, in the course of the twentieth century, the turn of the party to step into the shoes of the nation. It is, therefore, almost a matter of course that the outstanding characteristics of the modern party—its autocratic and oligarchic structure, its lack of internal democracy and freedom, its tendency to 'become totalitarian', its claim to infallibility—are conspicuous by their absence in the United States and, to a lesser degree, in Great Britain.[43]

However, while it may be true that, as a device of government, only the two-party system has proved its viability and, at the same time, its capacity to guarantee constitutional liberties, it is no less true that the best it has achieved is a certain control of the rulers by those who are ruled, but that it has by no means enabled the citizen to become a 'participator' in public affairs. The most the citizen can hope for is to be 'represented', whereby it is obvious that the only thing which can be represented and delegated is interest, or the welfare of the constituents, but neither their actions nor their opinions. In this system the opinions of the people are indeed unascertainable for the simple reason that they are non-existent.

Opinions are formed in a process of open discussion and public debate, and where no opportunity for the forming of opinions exists, there may be moods—moods of the masses and moods of individuals, the latter no less fickle and unreliable than the former—but no opinion. Hence, the best the representative can do is to act as his constituents would act if they themselves had any opportunity to do so. The same is not true for questions of interest and welfare, which can be ascertained objectively, and where the need for action and decision arises out of the various conflicts among interest groups. Through pressure groups, lobbies, and other devices, the voters can indeed influence the actions of their representatives with respect to interest, that is, they can force their representatives to execute their wishes at the expense of the wishes and interests of other groups of voters. In all these instances the voter acts out of concern with his private life and well-being, and the residue of power he still holds in his hands resembles rather the reckless coercion with which a blackmailer forces his victim into obedience than the power that arises out of joint action and joint deliberation.

Be that as it may, neither the people in general nor the political scientists in particular have left much doubt that the parties, because of their monopoly of nomination, cannot be regarded as popular organs, but that they are, on the contrary, the very efficient instruments through which the power of the people is curtailed and controlled. That representative government has in fact become oligarchic government is true enough, though not in the classical sense of rule by the few in the interest of the few; what we today call democracy is a form of government where the few rule, at least supposedly, in the interest of the many. This government is democratic in that popular welfare and private happiness are its chief goals; but it can be called oligarchic in the sense that public happiness and public freedom have again become the privilege of the few.

The defenders of this system, which actually is the system of the welfare state, if they are liberal and of democratic convictions must deny the very existence of public happiness and public freedom; they must insist that politics is a burden and that its end is itself not political. They will agree with Saint-Just: 'La liberté du peuple est dans sa vie privée; ne la troublez point. Que le gouvernement . . . ne soit une force que pour protéger cet état de simplicité contre la force même.' If, on the other hand, taught by the profound turmoil of this century, they have lost their liberal illusion about some innate goodness of the people, they are likely to conclude that 'no people has ever been known to govern itself,' that 'the will of the people is profoundly anarchic: it wants to do as it pleases', that its attitude toward all government is 'hostility' because 'government and constraint are inseparable', and constraint by definition 'is external to the constrained'.[44]

Such statements, difficult to prove, are even more difficult to refute, but the assumptions upon which they rest are not difficult to point out. Theoretically, the most relevant and the most pernicious among them is the equation of 'people' and masses, which sounds only too plausible to everyone who lives in a mass society and is constantly exposed to its numerous irritations. This is true for all of us, but the author from whom I quoted lives, in addition, in one of those countries where parties have long since degenerated into mass movements which operate outside of parliament and have invaded the private and social domains of family life, education, cultural and economic concerns.[45] And in these cases the plausibility of the equation will amount to self-evidence. It is true that the movements' principle of organization corresponds to the existence of the modern masses, but their enormous attraction lies in the people's suspicion and hostility against the existing party system and the prevailing representation in parliament. Where this distrust does not exist, as for instance in the United States, the conditions of mass society do not lead to the formation of mass movements, whereas even countries where mass society is still very far from being developed, as for instance France, fall prey to mass movements, if only enough hostility to the party and parliamentary system is extant. Terminologically speaking, one could say that the more glaring the failures of the party system are, the easier it will be for a movement not only to appeal to and to organize the people, but to transform them into masses. Practically, the current 'realism', despair of the people's political capacities, not unlike the realism of Saint-Just, is based solidly upon the conscious or unconscious determination to ignore the reality of the councils and to take for granted that there is not, and never has been, any alternative to the present system.

The historical truth of the matter is that the party and council systems are almost coeval; both were unknown prior to the revolutions and both are the consequences of the modern and revolutionary tenet that all inhabitants of a given territory are entitled to be admitted to the public, political realm. The councils, as distinguished from parties, have always emerged during the revolution itself, they sprang from the people as spontaneous organs of action and of order. The last point is worth emphasizing; nothing indeed contradicts more sharply the old adage of the anarchistic and lawless 'natural' inclinations of a people left without the constraint of its government than the emergence of the councils that, wherever they appeared, and most pronouncedly during the Hungarian

Revolution, were concerned with the reorganization of the political and economic life of the country and the establishment of a new order.[46] Parties—as distinguished from factions typical of all parliaments and assemblies, be these hereditary or representative—have thus far never emerged during a revolution; they either preceded it, as in the twentieth century, or they developed with the extension of popular suffrage. Hence the party, whether an extension of parliamentary faction or a creation outside parliament, has been an institution to provide parliamentary government with the required support of the people, whereby it was always understood that the people, through voting, did the supporting, while action remained the prerogative of government. If parties become militant and step actively into the domain of political action, they violate their own principle as well as their function in parliamentary government, that is, they become subversive, and this regardless of their doctrines and ideologies. The disintegration of parliamentary government—in Italy and Germany after the First World War, for instance, or in France after the Second World War—has demonstrated repeatedly how even parties supporting the *status quo* actually helped to undermine the regime the moment they overstepped their institutional limitations. Action and participation in public affairs, a natural aspiration of the councils, obviously are not signs of health and vitality but of decay and perversion in an institution whose primary function has always been representation.

For it is indeed true that the essential characteristic of the otherwise widely differing party systems is 'that they "nominate" candidates for elective offices or representative government', and it may even be correct to say that 'the act of nominating itself is enough to bring a political party into being'.[47] Hence, from the very beginning, the party as an institution presupposed either that the citizen's participation in public affairs was guaranteed by other public organs, or that such participation was not necessary and that the newly admitted strata of the population should be content with representation, or, finally, that all political questions in the welfare state are ultimately problems of administration, to be handled and decided by experts, in which case even the representatives of the people hardly possess an authentic area of action but are administrative officers, whose business, though in the public interest, is not essentially different from the business of private management. If the last of these presuppositions should turn out to be correct—and who could deny the extent to which in our mass societies the political realm has withered away and is being replaced by that 'administration of things' which Engels predicted for a classless society?—then, to be sure, the councils would have to be considered as atavistic institutions without any relevance in the realm of human affairs. But the same, or something very similar, would then soon enough turn out to be true for the party system; for administration and management, because their business is dictated by the necessities which underlie all economic process, are essentially not only non-political but even nonpartisan. In a society under the sway of abundance, conflicting group interests need no longer be settled at one another's expense, and the principle of opposition is valid only as long as there exist authentic choices which transcend the objective and demonstrably valid opinions of experts. When government has really become administration, the party system can only result in incompetence and wastefulness. The only non-obsolete function the party system might conceivably perform in such a regime would be to guard it against corruption of public servants, and even this function would be much better and more reliably performed by the police.[48]

The conflict between the two systems, the parties and the councils, came to the fore in all twentieth-century revolutions. The issue at stake was representation versus action and participation. The councils were organs of action, the revolutionary parties were organs of representation, and although the revolutionary parties halfheartedly recognized the councils as instruments of 'revolutionary struggle', they tried even in the midst of revolution to rule them from within; they knew well enough that no party, no matter how revolutionary it was, would be able to survive the transformation of the government into a true Soviet Republic. For the parties, the need for action itself was transitory, and they had no doubt that after the victory of the revolution further action would simply prove unnecessary or subversive. Bad faith and the drive for power were not the decisive factors that made the professional revolutionists turn against the revolutionary organs of the people; it was rather the elementary convictions which the revolutionary parties shared with all other parties. They agreed that the end of government was the welfare of the people, and that the substance of politics was not action but administration. In this respect, it is only fair to say that all parties from right to left have much more in common with one another than the revolutionary groups ever had in common with the councils. Moreover, what eventually decided the issue in favour of the party and the one-party dictatorship was by no means only superior power or determination to crush the councils through ruthless use of the means of violence.

If it is true that the revolutionary parties never understood to what an extent the council system was identical with the emergence of a new form of government, it is no less true that the councils were incapable of understanding to what enormous extent the government machinery in modern societies must indeed perform the functions of administration. The fatal mistake of the councils has always been that they themselves did not distinguish clearly between participation in public affairs and administration or management of things in the public interest. In the form of workers' councils, they have again and again tried to take over the management of the factories, and all these attempts have ended in dismal failure. 'The wish of the working class', we are told, 'has been fulfilled. The factories will be managed by the councils of the workers.'[49] This so-called wish of the working class sounds much rather like an attempt of the revolutionary party to counteract the councils' political aspirations, to drive their members away from the political realm and back into the factories. And this suspicion is borne out by two facts: the councils have always been primarily political, with social and economic claims playing a very minor role, and it was precisely this lack of interest in social and economic questions which, in the view of the revolutionary party, was a sure sign of their 'lower-middle-class, abstract, liberalistic' mentality.[50] In fact, it was a sign of their political maturity, whereas the workers' wish to run the factories themselves was a sign of the understandable, but politically irrelevant desire of individuals to rise into positions which up to then had been open only to the middle class.

No doubt, managerial talent should not be lacking in people of working-class origins; the trouble was merely that the workers' councils certainly were the worst possible organs for its detection. For the men whom they trusted and chose from their own midst were selected according to political criteria, for their trustworthiness, their personal integrity, their capacity of judgement, often for their physical courage. The same men, entirely capable of acting in a political capacity, were bound to fail if entrusted with the management of a factory or other administrative duties. For the qualities of the statesman or the political man and the qualities of the manager or administrator are not only not the same, they very seldom are to be found in the same individual; the one is supposed to know how to deal with men in a field of human relations, whose principle is freedom, and the other must know how to manage things and people in a sphere of life whose principle is necessity. The councils in the factories brought an element of action into the management of things, and this indeed could not but create chaos. It was precisely these foredoomed attempts that have earned the council system its bad name. But while it is true that they were incapable of organizing, or rather of rebuilding, the economic system of the country, it is also true that the chief reason for their failure was not any lawlessness of the people, but their political qualities. Whereas, on the other hand, the reason why the party apparatuses, despite many shortcomings—corruption, incompetence and incredible wastefulness—eventually succeeded where the councils had failed lay precisely in their original oligarchic and even autocratic structure, which made them so utterly unreliable for all political purposes.

Freedom, wherever it existed as a tangible reality, has always been spatially limited. This is especially clear for the greatest and most elementary of all negative liberties, the freedom of movement; the borders of national territory or the walls of the city-state comprehended and protected a space in which men could move freely. Treaties and international guarantees provide an extension of this territorially bound freedom for citizens outside their own country, but even under these modern conditions the elementary coincidence of freedom and a limited space remains manifest. What is true for freedom of movement is, to a large extent, valid for freedom in general. Freedom in a positive sense is possible only among equals, and equality itself is by no means a universally valid principle but, again, applicable only with limitations and even within spatial limits. If we equate these spaces of freedom—which, following the gist, though not the terminology, of John Adams, we could also call spaces of appearances—with the political realm itself, we shall be inclined to think of them as islands in a sea or as oases in a desert. This image, I believe, is suggested to us not merely by the consistency of a metaphor but by the record of history as well.

The phenomenon I am concerned with here is usually called the 'elite', and my quarrel with this term is not that I doubt that the political way of life has never been and will never be the way of life of the many, even though political business, by definition, concerns more than the many, namely strictly speaking, the sum total of all citizens. Political passions—courage, the pursuit of public happiness, the taste of public freedom, an ambition that strives for excellence regardless not only of social status and administrative office but even of achievement and congratulation—are perhaps not as rare as we are inclined to think, living in a society which has perverted all virtues into social values; but they certainly are out of the ordinary under all circumstances. My quarrel with the 'elite' is that the term implies an oligarchic form of government, the domination of the many by the rule of a few. From this, one can only conclude—as indeed our whole tradition of political thought has concluded—that the essence of politics is rulership and that the dominant political passion is the passion to rule or to govern. This, I propose, is profoundly untrue. The fact that political 'elites' have always determined the political destinies of the many and have, in most instances, exerted a domination over them, indicates, on the other hand, the bitter need of the few to protect themselves against the many, or rather to protect the island of freedom they have come to inhabit against the surrounding sea of necessity; and it indicates, on the other hand, the responsibility that falls automatically upon those who care for the fate of those who do not. But neither this need nor this responsibility touches upon the essence, the very substance of their lives, which is freedom; both are incidental and secondary with respect to what actually goes on within the limited space of the island itself. Put into terms of present-day institutions, it would be in parliament and in congress, where he moves among his peers, that the political life of a member of representative government is actualized, no matter how much of his time may be spent in campaigning, in trying to get the vote and in listening to the voter. The point of the matter is not merely the obvious phoniness of this dialogue in modern party government, where the voter can only consent or refuse to ratify a choice which (with the exception of the American primaries) is made without him, and it does not even concern conspicuous abuses such as the introduction into politics of Madison Avenue methods, through which the relationship between representative and elector is transformed into that of seller and buyer. Even if there is communication between representative and voter, between the nation and parliament—and the existence of such communication marks the outstanding difference between the governments of the British and the Americans, on one side, and those of Western Europe, on the other—this communication is never between equals but between those who aspire to govern and those who consent to be governed. It is indeed in the very nature of the party system to replace 'the formula "government of the people by the people" by this formula: "government of the people *by an élite sprung from the people*" '.[51]

It has been said that 'the deepest significance of political parties' must be seen in their providing 'the necessary framework enabling the masses to recruit from among themselves their own élites',[52] and it is true enough that it was primarily the parties which opened political careers to members of the lower classes. No doubt the party as the outstanding institution of democratic government corresponds to one of the major trends of the modern age, the constantly and universally increasing equalization of society; but this by no means implies that it corresponds to the deepest significance of revolution in the modern age as well. The 'élite sprung from the people' has replaced the pre-modern élites of birth and wealth; it has nowhere enabled the people *qua* people to make their entrance into political life and to become participators in public affairs. The relationship between a ruling élite and the people, between the few, who among themselves constitute a public space, and the many, who spend their lives outside it and in obscurity, has remained unchanged. From the viewpoint of revolution and the survival of the revolutionary spirit, the trouble does not lie in the factual rise of a new élite: it is not the revolutionary spirit but the democratic mentality of an egalitarian society that tends to deny the obvious inability and conspicuous lack of interest of large parts of the population in political matters as such. The trouble lies in the lack of public spaces to which the people at large would have entrance and from which an élite could be selected, or rather, where it could select itself. The trouble, in other words, is that politics has become a profession and a career, and that the 'élite' therefore is being chosen according to standards and criteria which are themselves profoundly unpolitical. It is in the nature of all party systems that the authentically political talents can assert themselves only in rare cases, and it is even rarer that the specifically political qualifications survive the petty manoeuvres of party politics with its demands for plain salesmanship. Of course the men who sat in the councils were also an élite, they were even the only political élite, of the people and sprung from the people, the modern world has ever seen, but they were not nominated from above and not supported from below. With respect to the elementary councils that sprang up wherever people lived or worked together, one is tempted to say that they had selected themselves; those who organized themselves were those who cared and those who took the initiative; they were the political élite of the people brought into the open by the revolution. From these 'elementary republics', the councilmen then chose their deputies for the next higher council, and these deputies, again, were selected by their peers, they were not subject to any pressure either from above or from below. Their title rested on nothing but the confidence of their equals, and this equality was not natural but political, it was nothing they had been born with; it was the equality of those who had committed themselves to, and now were engaged in, a joint enterprise. Once elected and sent in the next higher council, the deputy found himself again among his peers, for the deputies on any given level in this system were those who had received a special trust. No doubt this form of government, if fully developed, would have assumed again the shape of a pyramid, which, of course, is the shape of an essentially authoritarian government. But while, in all authoritarian government we know of, authority is filtered down from above, in this case authority would have been generated neither at the top nor at the bottom, but on each of the pyramid's layers; and this obviously could constitute the solution to one of the most serious problems of all modern politics, which is not how to reconcile freedom and equality but how to reconcile equality and authority.

(To avoid misunderstanding: The principles for the selection of the best as suggested in the council system, the principle of self-selection in the grass-roots political organs, and the principle of personal trust in their development into a federal form of government are not universally valid; they are applicable only within the political realm. The cultural, literary, and artistic, the scientific and professional and even the social élites of a country are subject to very different criteria among which the criterion of equality is conspicuously absent. But so is the principle of authority. The rank of a poet, for instance, is decided neither by a vote of confidence of his fellow poets nor by fiat coming from the recognized master, but, on the contrary, by those who only love poetry and are incapable of ever writing a line. The rank of a scientist, on the other hand, is indeed determined by his fellow scientists, but not on the basis of highly personal qualities and qualifications; the criteria in this instance are objective and beyond argument or persuasion. Social élites, finally, at least in an egalitarian society where neither birth nor wealth counts, come into being through processes of discrimination.)

It would be tempting to spin out further the potentialities of the councils, but it certainly is wiser to say with Jefferson, 'Begin them only for a single purpose; they will soon show for what others they are the best instruments'—the best instruments, for example, for breaking up the modern mass society, with its dangerous tendency toward the formation of pseudo-political mass movements, or rather, the best, the most natural way for interspersing it at the grass roots with an 'élite' that is chosen by no one but constitutes itself. The joys of public happiness and the responsibilities for public business would then become the share of those few from all walks of life who have a taste for public freedom and cannot be 'happy' without it. Politically, they are the best, and it is the task of good government and the sign of a well-ordered republic to assure them of their rightful place in the public realm. To be sure, such an 'aristocratic' form of government would spell the end of general suffrage as we understand it today; for only those who as voluntary members of an 'elementary republic' have demonstrated that they care for more than their private happiness and are concerned about the state of the world would have the right to be heard in the conduct of the business of the republic. However, this exclusion from politics should not be derogatory, since a political élite is by no means identical with a social or cultural or professional élite. The exclusion, moreover, would not depend upon an outside body; if those who belong are self-chosen, those who do not belong are self-excluded. And such self-exclusion, far from being arbitrary discrimination, would in fact give substance and reality to one of the most important negative liberties we have enjoyed since the end of the ancient world, namely, freedom from politics, which was unknown to Rome or Athens and which is politically perhaps the most relevant part of our Christian heritage.

This, and probably much more, was lost when the spirit of revolution—a new spirit and the spirit of beginning something new—failed to find its appropriate institution. There is nothing that could compensate for this failure or prevent it from becoming final, except memory and recollection. And since the storehouse of memory is kept and watched over by the poets, whose business it is to find and make the words we live by, it may be wise to turn in conclusion to two of them (one modern, the other ancient) in order to find an approximate articulation of the actual content of our lost treasure. The modern poet is René Char, perhaps the most articulate of the many French writers and artists who joined the Resistance during the Second World War. His book of aphorisms was written during the last year of the war in a frankly apprehensive anticipation of liberation; for he knew that as far as they were concerned there would be not only the welcome liberation from German occupation but liberation from the 'burden' of public business as well. Back they would have to go to the *épaisseur triste* of their private lives and pursuits, to the 'sterile depression' of the pre-war years, when it was as though a curse hung over everything they did: 'If I survive, I know that I shall have to break with the aroma of these essential years, silently reject (not repress) my treasure.' The treasure, he thought, was that he had '*found* himself', that he no longer suspected himself of 'insincerity', that he needed no mask and no make-believe to appear, that wherever he went he appeared as he was to others and to himself, that he could afford 'to go naked'.[53] These reflections are significant enough as they testify to the involuntary self-discourse, to the joys of appearing in word and deed without equivocation and without self-reflection that are inherent in action. And yet they are perhaps too 'modern', too self-centred to hit in pure precision the centre of that 'inheritance which was left to us by no testament'.

Sophocles in *Oedipus at Colonus,* the play of his old age, wrote the famous and frightening lines:

> Μή φῦναι τὸν ἅπαντα νι-
> κᾶ λόγον. τὸ δ' ἐπεὶ ωανῆ,
> βῆναι κεῖσ' ὁπόθεν περ ἥ-
> κει πολὺ δεύτερον ὡς τάχιστα.

'Not to be born prevails over all meaning uttered in words; by far the second-best for life, once it has appeared, is to go as swiftly as possible whence it came.' There he also let us know, through the mouth of Theseus, the legendary founder of Athens and hence her spokesman, what it was that enabled ordinary men, young and old, to bear life's burden: it was the *polis,* the space of men's free deeds and living words, which could endow life with splendour—τὸν βίον λαμπρὸν ποιεῖσθαι.

Notes

1. Thus Jefferson in a letter to William Hunter, 11 March 1790, *The Complete Jefferson,* ed. Padover, Modern Library edition.
2. In a letter to Samuel Kercheval, 12 July 1816.
3. The two quotations from Paine are from *Common Sense* and the *Rights of Man,* respectively.
4. In the famous letter to Major John Cartwright, 5 June 1824.
5. The much-quoted words occur in a letter from Paris to Colonel William Stephens Smith, 13 November 1787.
6. In later years, especially after he had adopted the ward system as 'the article nearest to my heart', Jefferson was much more likely to speak of 'the dreadful necessity' of insurrection. (See especially his letter to Samuel Kercheval, 5 September 1816.) To blame this shift of emphasis—for it is not much more—on the changed mood of a much older man seems unjustified in view of the fact that Jefferson thought of his ward system as the only possible alternative to what otherwise would be a necessity, however dreadful.
7. In this and the following paragraph, I am again quoting from Jefferson's letter to Samuel Kercheval, 12 July 1816.
8. See Emerson's *Journal,* 1853.
9. See Lewis Mumford's *The City in History,* New York, 1961, pp. 328 ff.
10. In the letter to John Cartwright, 5 June 1824.
11. This quotation is from a slightly earlier period when Jefferson proposed to divide the counties 'into hundreds'. (See letter to John Tyler, 26 May 1810.) Clearly, the wards he had in mind were to consist of about a hundred men.
12. Letter to Cartwright, quoted previously.
13. ibid.
14. Letter to Samuel Kercheval, 12 July 1816.
15. The citations are drawn from the letters just quoted.
16. Letter to Samuel Kercheval, 5 September 1816.
17. Letter to Thomas Jefferson Smith, 21 February 1825.
18. Letter to Cartwright, quoted previously.
19. Letter to John Tyler, quoted previously.
20. The citations are drawn from the letter to Joseph C. Cabell of 2 February 1816, and from the two letters to Samuel Kercheval already quoted.
21. George Soule, *The Coming American Revolution,* New York, 1934, p. 53.

22. For Tocqueville, see author's Introduction to *Democracy in America;* for Marx, *Die Klassenkämpfe in Frankreich, 1840–1850* (1850), Berlin, 1951, p. 124.

23. In 1871 Marx called the Commune *die endlich entdeckte politische Form, unter der die ökonomische Befreiung der Arbeit sich vollziehen könnte,* and called this its 'true secret'. (See *Der Bürgerkrieg in Frankreich* (1871), Berlin, 1952, pp. 71 and 76.) Only two years later, however, he wrote: 'Die Arbeiter müssen . . . auf die entschiedenste Zentralisation der Gewalt in die Hände der Staatsmacht hinwirken. Sie dürfen sich durch das demokratische Gerede von Freiheit der Gemeinden, von Selbstregierung usw. nicht irre machen lassen' (in *Enthüllungen über den Kommunistenprozess zu Köln* [Sozialdemokratische Bibliothek Bd. IV], Hattingen Zürich, 1885, p. 81). Hence, Oskar Anweiler, to whose important study of the council system, *Die Rätebewegung in Russland 1905–1921,* Leiden, 1958, I am much indebted, is quite right when he maintains: 'Die revolutionären Gemeinderäte sind für Marx nichts weiter als zeitweilige politische Kampforgane, die Revolution vorwärtsreiben sollen, er sieht in ihnen nicht die Keimzellen für eine grundlegende Umgestaltung der Gesellschaft, die vielmehr von oben, durch die proletartische zentralistische Staatsgewalt, erfolgen soll' (p. 19).

24. I am following Anweiler, op. cit., p. 101.

25. The enormous popularity of the councils in all twentieth-century revolutions is sufficiently well known. During the German revolution of 1918 and 1919, even the Conservative party had to come to terms with the *Räte* in its election campaigns.

26. In the words of Leviné, a prominent professional revolutionist, during the revolution in Bavaria: 'Die Kommunisten treten nur für eine Räterepublik ein, in der die Räte eine kommunistische Mehrheit haben.' See Helmut Neubauer, 'München und Moskau 1918–1919: Zur Geschichte der Rätebewegung in Bayern', *Jahrbücher für Geschichte Osteuropas,* Beiheft 4, 1958.

27. See the excellent study of *The Paris Commune of 1871,* London, 1937, by Frank Jellinek, p. 27.

28. See Anweiler, op. cit., p. 45.

29. Maurice Duverger—whose book on *Political Parties. Their Organization and Activity in the Modern State* (French edition, 1951), New York, 1961, supersedes and by far excels all former studies on the subject—mentions an interesting example. At the election to the National Assembly in 1871, the suffrage in France had become free, but since there existed no parties the new voters tended to vote for the only candidates they knew at all, with the result that the new republic had become the 'Republic of Dukes'.

30. The record of the secret police in fostering rather than preventing revolutionary activities is especially striking in France during the Second Empire and in Czarist Russia after 1880. It seems, for example, that there was not a single anti-government action under Louis Napoleon which had not been inspired by the police; and the more important terroristic attacks in Russia prior to war and revolution seem all to have been police jobs.

31. Thus, the conspicuous unrest in the Second Empire, for instance, was easily

contradicted by the overwhelmingly favourable outcome of Napoleon III's plebiscites, these predecessors of our public-opinion polls. The last of these, in 1869, was again a great victory for the Emperor; what nobody noticed at the time and what turned out to be decisive a year later was that nearly 15 percent of the armed forces had voted against the Emperor.

32. Quoted from Jellinek, op. cit., p. 194.

33. One of the official pronouncements of the Parisian Commune stressed this relation as follows: 'C'est cette idée communale poursuivie depuis le douzième siècle, affirmée par la morale, le droit et la science qui vient de triompher le 18 mars 1871.' See Heinrich Koechlin, *Die Pariser Commune von 1871 im Bewusstsein ihrer Anhänger,* Basel, 1950, p. 66.

34. Jellinek, op. cit., p. 71.

35. Anweiler, op. cit., p. 127, quotes this sentence by Trotsky.

36. For the latter, see Helmut Neubauer, op. cit.

37. See Oskar Anweiler, 'Die Räte in der ungarischen Revolution', in *Osteuropa,* vol. VIII, 1958.

38. Sigmund Neumann, 'The Structure and Strategy of Revolution: 1848 and 1948', in *The Journal of Politics,* August 1949.

39. Anweiler, op. cit., p. 6, enumerates the following general characteristics: 'I. Die Gebundenheit an eine bestimmte abhängige oder unterdrückte soziale Schicht, 2. die radikale Demokratie als Form, 3. die revolutionäre Art der Entstehung', and then comes to the conclusion: 'Die diesen Räten zugrundeliegende Tendenz, die man als "Rätegedanken" bezeichnen kann, ist das Streben nach einer möglichst unmittelbaren, weitgehenden und unbeschränkten Teilnahme des Einzelnen am öffentlichen Leben . . .'

40. In the words of the Austrian socialist Max Adler, in the pamphlet *Demokratie und Rätesystem,* Vienna, 1919. The booklet, written in the midst of the revolution, is of some interest because Adler, although he saw quite clearly why the councils were so immensely popular, nevertheless immediately went on to repeat the old Marxist formula according to which the councils could not be anything more than merely 'eine revolutionäre Üebergangsform', at best, 'eine neue Kampfform des sozialistischen Klassenkampfes'.

41. Rosa Luxemburg's pamphlet on *The Russian Revolution,* translated by Bertram D. Wolfe, 1940, from which I quote, was written more than four decades ago. Its criticism of the 'Lenin—Trotsky theory of dictatorship' has lost nothing of its pertinence and actuality. To be sure, she could not foresee the horrors of Stalin's totalitarian regime, but her prophetic words of warning against the suppression of political freedom and with it of public life read today like a realistic description of the Soviet Union under Khrushchev: 'Without general elections, without unrestricted freedom of press and assembly, without a free struggle of opinion, life dies out in every public institution, becomes a mere semblance of life, in which only the bureaucracy remains the active element. Public life gradually falls asleep, a few dozen party leaders of inexhaustible energy and boundless experience direct and rule. Among them, in reality only a dozen outstanding heads do the leading and an élite of the

working class is invited from time to time to . . . applaud the speeches of the leaders, and to approve proposed resolutions unanimously—at bottom, then, a clique affair . . .'

42. Duverger, op. cit., p. 393, remarks rightly: 'Great Britain and the Dominions, under a two-party system, are profoundly dissimilar from Continental countries under a multi-party system, and . . . much closer to the United States in spite of its presidential regime. In fact, the distinction between single-party, two-party, and multi-party systems tends to become the fundamental mode of classifying contemporary regimes.' Where, however, the two-party system is a mere technicality without being accompanied by recognition of the opposition as an instrument of government, as for instance in present-day Germany, it probably will turn out to be of no greater stability than the multiparty system.

43. Duverger, who notices this difference between the Anglo-Saxon countries and the continental nation states, is, I think, quite wrong in crediting an 'obsolete' liberalism with the advantages of the two-party system.

44. I am again using Duverger—op. cit., pp. 423 ff.—who, in these paragraphs, however, is not very original but only expresses a widespread mood in postwar France and Europe.

45. The greatest and somehow inexplicable shortcoming of Duverger's book is his refusal to distinguish between party and movement. Surely he must be aware that he would not even be able to tell the story of the Communist party without noticing the moment when the party of professional revolutionists turned into a mass movement. The enormous differences between the Fascist and Nazi movements and the parties of the democratic regimes were even more obvious.

46. This was the evaluation of the United Nations' *Report on the Problem of Hungary,* 1956. For other examples, pointing in the same direction, see Anweiler's article, cited earlier.

47. See the interesting study of the party system by C. W. Cassinelli, *The Politics of Freedom: An Analysis of the Modern Democratic State,* Seattle, 1961, p. 21. The book is sound as far as American politics are concerned. It is too technical and somewhat superficial in its discussion of European party systems.

48. Cassinelli, op. cit., p. 77, illustrates with an amusing example how small the group of voters is who have a genuine and disinterested concern for public affairs. Let us assume, he says, that there has been a major scandal in government, and that as a result of it the opposition party is being voted into power. 'If, for example, 70 per cent of the electorate votes both times and the party receives 55 per cent of the ballots before the scandal and 45 per cent afterward, primary concern for honesty in government can be attributed to no more than 7 per cent of the electorate, and this calculation ignores all other possible motives for changes of preference.' This, admittedly, is a mere assumption, but it certainly comes pretty close to reality. The point of the matter is not that the electorate obviously is not equipped to find out corruption in government, but that it cannot be trusted to vote corruption out of office.

49. With these words, it appears, the Hungarian trade unions joined the workers' councils in 1956. We know, of course, the same phenomenon from the Russian Revolution and also from the Spanish Civil War.

50. These were the reproaches levelled against the Hungarian Revolution by the Yugoslav Communist party. See Anweiler's article. These objections are not new; they were raised in much the same terms over and over again in the Russian Revolution.

51. Duverger, op. cit., p. 425.

52. ibid., p. 426.

53. René Char, *Feuillets d'Hypnos,* Paris, 1946. For the English translation, see *Hypnos Waking: Poems and Prose,* New York, 1956.

PART VII

OF TRUTH AND TRAPS

Heidegger the Fox

HEIDEGGER SAYS, with great pride: "People say that Heidegger is a fox." This is the true story of Heidegger the fox:

Once upon a time there was a fox who was so lacking in slyness that he not only kept getting caught in traps but couldn't even tell the difference between a trap and a non-trap. This fox suffered from another failing as well. There was something wrong with his fur, so that he was completely without natural protection against the hardships of a fox's life. After he had spent his entire youth prowling around the traps of people, and now that not one intact piece of fur, so to speak, was left on him, this fox decided to withdraw from the fox world altogether and to set about making himself a burrow. In his shocking ignorance of the difference between traps and non-traps, despite his incredibly extensive experience with traps, he hit on an idea completely new and unheard of among foxes: He built a trap as his burrow. He set himself inside it, passed it off as a normal burrow—not out of cunning, but because he had always thought others' traps were their burrows—and then decided to become sly in his own way and outfit for others the trap he had built himself and that suited only him. This again demonstrated great ignorance about traps: No one would go into his trap, because he was sitting inside it himself. This annoyed him. After all, everyone knows that, despite their slyness, all foxes occasionally get caught in traps. Why should a fox trap—especially one built by a fox with more experience of traps than any other—not be a match for the traps of human beings and hunters? Obviously because this trap did not reveal itself clearly enough as the trap it was! And so it occurred to our fox to decorate his trap beautifully and to hang up unequivocal signs everywhere on it that quite clearly said: "Come here, everyone; this is a trap, the most beautiful trap in the world." From this point on it was clear that

From Essays in Understanding. *Translated by Robert and Rita Kimber. These remarks come from Arendt's personal journal* (Denktagebuch) *for 1953.*

no fox could stray into this trap by mistake. Nevertheless, many came. For this trap was our fox's burrow, and if you wanted to visit him where he was at home, you had to step into his trap. Everyone except our fox could, of course, step out of it again. It was cut, literally, to his own measurement. But the fox who lived in the trap said proudly: "So many are visiting me in my trap that I have become the best of all foxes." And there is some truth in that, too: Nobody knows the nature of traps better than one who sits in a trap his whole life long.

Truth and Politics*

I

The subject of these reflections is a commonplace. No one has ever doubted that truth and politics are on rather bad terms with each other, and no one, as far as I know, has ever counted truthfulness among the political virtues. Lies have always been regarded as necessary and justifiable tools not only of the politician's or the demagogue's but also of the statesman's trade. Why is that so? And what does it mean for the nature and the dignity of the political realm, on one side, and for the nature and the dignity of truth and truthfulness, on the other? Is it of the very essence of truth to be impotent and of the very essence of power to be deceitful? And what kind of reality does truth possess if it is powerless in the public realm, which more than any other sphere of human life guarantees reality of existence to natal and mortal men—that is, to beings who know they have appeared out of non-being and will, after a short while, again disappear into it? Finally, is not impotent truth just as despicable as power that

---

*This essay was caused by the so-called controversy after the publication of *Eichmann in Jerusalem*. Its aim is to clarify two different, though interconnected, issues of which I had not been aware before and whose importance seemed to transcend the occasion. The first concerns the question of whether it is always legitimate to tell the truth—did I believe without qualification in *"Fiat veritas, et pereat mundus"*? The second arose through the amazing amount of lies used in the "controversy"—lies about what I had written, on one hand, and about the facts I had reported, on the other. The following reflections try to come to grips with both issues. They may also serve as an example of what happens to a highly topical subject when it is drawn into that gap between past and future which is perhaps the proper habitat of all reflections.

From Between Past and Future. *Originally published in* The New Yorker, *February 25, 1967.*

gives no heed to truth? These are uncomfortable questions, but they arise necessarily out of our current convictions in this matter.

What lends this commonplace its high plausibility can still be summed up in the old Latin adage *"Fiat iustitia, et pereat mundus"* ("Let justice be done though the world may perish"). Apart from its probable author in the sixteenth century (Ferdinand I, successor to Charles V), no one has used it except as a rhetorical question: Should justice be done if the world's survival is at stake? And the only great thinker who dared to go against the grain of the question was Immanuel Kant, who boldly explained that the "proverbial saying . . . means in simple language: 'Justice shall prevail, even though all the rascals in the world should perish as a result.' " Since men would not find it worth while to live in a world utterly deprived of justice, this "human right must be held sacred, regardless of how much sacrifice is required of the powers that be . . . regardless of what might be the physical consequences thereof."[1] But isn't this answer absurd? Doesn't the care for existence clearly precede everything else—every virtue and every principle? Is it not obvious that they become mere chimeras if the world, where alone they can be manifested, is in jeopardy? Wasn't the seventeenth century right when it almost unanimously declared that every commonwealth was duty bound to recognize, in Spinoza's words, "no higher law than the safety of [its] own realm"?[2] For surely every principle that transcends sheer existence can be put in the place of justice, and if we put truth in its place—*"Fiat veritas, et pereat mundus"*—the old saying sounds even more plausible. If we understand political action in terms of the means-end category, we may even come to the only seemingly paradoxical conclusion that lying can very well serve to establish or safeguard the conditions for the search after truth—as Hobbes, whose relentless logic never fails to carry arguments to those extremes where their absurdity becomes obvious, pointed out long ago.[3] And lies, since they are often used as substitutes for more violent means, are apt to be considered relatively harmless tools in the arsenal of political action.

Reconsidering the old Latin saying, it will therefore come as something of a surprise that the sacrifice of truth for the survival of the world would be more futile than the sacrifice of any other principle or virtue. For while we may refuse even to ask ourselves whether life would still be worth living in a world deprived of such notions as justice and freedom, the same, curiously, is not possible with respect to the seemingly so much less political idea of truth. What is at stake is survival, the perseverance in existence (*in suo esse perseverare*),. and no human world destined to outlast the short life span of mortals within it will ever be able to survive without men willing to do what Herodotus was the first to undertake consciously—namely, λέγειν τὰ ἐόντα, to say what is. No permanence, no perseverance in existence, can even be conceived of without men willing to testify to what is and appears to them because it is.

The story of the conflict between truth and politics is an old and complicated one, and nothing would be gained by simplification or moral denunciation. Throughout history, the truth-seekers and truthtellers have been aware of the risks of their business; as long as they did not interfere with the course of the world, they were covered with ridicule, but he who forced his fellow-citizens to take him seriously by trying to set them free from falsehood and illusion was in danger of his life: "If they could lay hands on [such a] man . . . they would kill him," Plato says in the last sentence of the cave allegory. The Platonic conflict between truthteller and citizens cannot be explained by the Latin adage, or any of the later theories that, implicitly or explicitly, justify lying, among other transgressions, if the survival of the city is at stake. No enemy is mentioned in Plato's story; the many live peacefully in their cave among themselves, mere spectators of images, involved in no action and hence threatened by nobody. The members of this community have no reason whatever to regard truth and truthtellers as their worst enemies, and Plato offers no explanation of their perverse love of deception and falsehood. If we could confront him with one of his later colleagues in political philosophy—namely, with Hobbes, who held that only "such truth, as opposeth no man's profit, nor pleasure, is to all men welcome" (an obvious statement, which, however, he thought important enough to end his *Leviathan* with)—he might agree about profit and pleasure but not with the assertion that there existed any kind of truth welcome to all men. Hobbes, but not Plato, consoled himself with the existence of indifferent truth, with "subjects" about which "men care not"—e.g., with mathematical truth, "the doctrine of lines and figures" that "crosses no man's ambition, profit or lust." For, Hobbes wrote, "I doubt not, but if it had been a thing contrary to any man's right of dominion, or to the interest of men that have dominion, that the three angles of a triangle should be equal to two angles of a square; the doctrine should have been, if not disputed, yet by the burning of all books of geometry, suppressed, as far as he whom it concerned was able."[4]

No doubt, there is a decisive difference between Hobbes' mathematical axiom and the true standard for human conduct that Plato's philosopher is supposed to bring back from his journey into the sky of ideas, although Plato, who believed that mathematical truth opened the eyes of the mind to all truths, was not aware of it. Hobbes' example strikes us as relatively harmless; we are inclined to assume that the human mind will always be able to reproduce such axiomatic statements as "the three angles of a triangle should be equal to two angles of a square," and we conclude that "the burning of all books of geometry" would not be radically effective. The danger would be considerably greater with respect to scientific statements; had history taken a different turn, the whole modern scientific development from Galileo to Einstein might not have come to pass. And certainly the most vulnerable truth of this kind would be those highly differentiated and always unique thought trains—of which Plato's doctrine of ideas is an eminent example—whereby men, since time immemorial, have tried to think rationally beyond the limits of human knowledge.

The modern age, which believes that truth is neither given to nor disclosed to but produced by the human mind, has assigned, since Leibniz, mathematical, scientific, and philosophical truths to the common species of rational truth as distinguished from factual truth. I shall use this distinction for the sake of convenience without discussing its intrinsic legitimacy. Wanting to find out what injury political power is capable of inflicting upon truth, we look into these matters for political rather than philosophical reasons, and hence can afford to disregard the question of what truth is, and be content to take the word in the sense in which men commonly understand it. And if we now think of factual truths—of such modest verities as the role during the Russian Revolution of a man by the name of Trotsky, who appears in none of the Soviet Russian history books—we at once become aware of how much more vulnerable they are than all the kinds of rational truth taken together. Moreover, since facts and events—the invariable outcome of men living and acting together—constitute the very texture of the political realm, it is, of course, factual truth that we are most concerned with here. Dominion (to speak Hobbes' language) when it attacks rational truth oversteps, as it were, its domain, while it gives battle on its own ground when it falsifies or lies away facts. The chances of factual truth surviving the onslaught of power are very slim indeed; it is always in danger of being maneuvered out of the world not only for a time but, potentially, forever. Facts and events are infinitely more fragile things than axioms, discoveries, theories—even the most wildly speculative ones—produced by the human mind; they occur in the field of the ever-changing affairs of men, in whose flux there is nothing more permanent than the admittedly relative permanence of the human mind's structure. Once they are lost, no rational effort will ever bring them back. Perhaps the chances that Euclidean mathematics or Einstein's theory of relativity—let alone Plato's philosophy—would have been reproduced in time if their authors had been prevented from handing them down to posterity are not very good either, yet they are infinitely better than the chances that a fact of importance, forgotten or, more likely, lied away, will one day be rediscovered.

I I

Although the politically most relevant truths are factual, the conflict between truth and politics was first discovered and articulated with respect to rational truth. The opposite of a rationally true statement is either error and ignorance, as in the sciences, or illusion and opinion, as in philosophy. Deliberate falsehood, the plain lie, plays its role only in the domain of factual statements, and it seems significant, and rather odd, that in the long debate about this antagonism of truth and politics, from Plato to Hobbes, no one, apparently, ever believed that organized lying, as we know it today, could be an adequate weapon against truth. In Plato, the truthteller is in danger of his life, and in Hobbes, where he has become an author, he is threatened with the burning of his books; mere mendacity is not an issue. It is the sophist and the ignoramus rather than the liar who occupy Plato's thought, and where he distinguishes between error and lie—that is, between "involuntary and voluntary ψεῦδος"—he is, characteristically, much harsher on people "wallowing in swinish ignorance" than on liars.[5] Is this because organized lying, dominating the public realm, as distinguished from the private liar who tries his luck on his own hook, was still unknown? Or has this something to do with the striking fact that, except for Zoroastrianism, none of the major religious included lying as such, as distinguished from "bearing false witness," in their catalogues of grave sins? Only with the rise of Puritan morality, coinciding with the rise of organized science, whose progress had to be assured on the firm ground of the absolute veracity and reliability of every scientist, were lies considered serious offenses.

However that may be, historically the conflict between truth and politics arose out of two diametrically opposed ways of life—the life of the philosopher, as interpreted first by Parmenides and then by Plato, and the way of life of the citizen. To the citizens' ever-changing opinions about human affairs, which themselves were in a state of constant flux, the philosopher opposed the truth about those things which in their very nature were everlasting and from which, therefore, principles could be derived to stabilize human affairs. Hence the opposite to truth was mere opinion, which was equated with illusion, and it was this degrading of opinion that gave the conflict its political poignancy; for opinion, and not truth, belongs among the indispensable prerequisites of all power. "All governments rest on opinion," James Madison said, and not even the most autocratic ruler or tyrant could ever rise to power, let alone keep it, without the support of those who are like-minded. By the same token, every claim in the sphere of human affairs to an absolute truth, whose validity needs no support from the side of opinion, strikes at the very roots of all politics and all governments. This antagonism between truth and opinion was further elaborated by Plato (especially in the *Gorgias*) as the antagonism between communicating in the form of "dialogue," which is the adequate speech for philosophical truth, and in the form of "rhetoric," by which the demagogue, as we would say today, persuades the multitude.

Traces of this original conflict can still be found in the earlier stages of the modern age, though hardly in the world we live in. In Hobbes, for instance, we still read of an opposition of two "contrary faculties": "solid reasoning" and "powerful eloquence," the former being "grounded upon principles of truth, the other upon opinions . . . and the passions and interests of men, which are different and mutable."[6] More than a century later, in the Age of Enlightenment, these traces have almost but not quite disappeared, and where the ancient antagonism still survives, the emphasis has shifted. In terms of pre-modern philosophy, Lessing's magnificent *"Sage jeder, was ihm Wahrheit dünkt, und die Wahrheit selbst sei Gott empfohlen"* ("Let each man say what he deems truth, and let truth itself be commended unto God") would have plainly signified, Man is not capable of truth, all his truths, alas, are δόξαι, mere opinions, whereas for Lessing it meant, on the contrary, Let us thank God that we don't know *the* truth. Even where the note of jubilation—the insight that for men, living in company, the inexhaustible richness of human discourse is infinitely more significant and meaningful than any One Truth could ever be—is absent, the awareness of the frailty of human reason has prevailed since the eighteenth century without giving rise to complaint or lamentation. We can find it in Kant's grandiose *Critique of Pure Reason,* in which reason is led to recognize its own limitations, as we hear it in the words of Madison, who more than once stressed that "the reason of man, like man himself, is timid and cautious when left alone, and acquires firmness and confidence in proportion to the number with which it is associated."[7] Considerations of this kind, much more than notions about the individual's right to self-expression, played a decisive part in the finally more or less successful struggle to obtain freedom of thought for the spoken and the printed word.

Thus Spinoza, who still believed in the infallibility of human reason and is often wrongly praised as a champion of free thought and speech, held that "every man is by indefeasible natural right the master of his own thoughts," that "every man's understanding is his own, and that brains are as diverse as palates," from which he concluded that "it is best to grant what cannot be abolished" and that laws prohibiting free thought can only result in "men thinking one thing and saying another," hence in "the corruption of good faith" and "the fostering of . . . perfidy." However, Spinoza nowhere demands freedom of speech, and the argument that human reason needs communication with others and therefore publicity for its own sake is conspicuous by its absence. He even counts man's need for communication, his inability to hide his thoughts and keep silent, among the "common failings" that the philosopher does not share.[8] Kant, on the contrary, stated that "the external power that deprives man of the freedom to communicate his thoughts publicly, *deprives him at the same time of his freedom to think*" (italics added), and that the only guarantee for "the correctness" of our thinking lies in that "we think, as it were, in community with others to whom we communicate our thoughts as they communicate theirs to us." Man's reason, being fallible, can function only if he can make "public use" of it, and this is equally true for those who, still in a state of "tutelage," are unable to use their minds "without the guidance of somebody else" and for the "scholar," who needs "the entire reading public" to examine and control his results.[9]

In this context, the question of numbers, mentioned by Madison, is of special importance. The shift from rational truth to opinion implies a shift from man in the singular to men in the plural, and this means a shift from a domain where, Madison says, nothing counts except the "solid reasoning" of one mind to a realm where "strength of opinion" is determined by the individual's reliance upon "the number which he supposes to have entertained the same opinions"—a number, incidentally, that is not necessarily limited to one's contemporaries. Madison still distinguishes this life in the plural, which is the life of the citizen, from the life of the philosopher, by whom such considerations "ought to be disregarded," but this distinction has no practical consequence, for "a nation of philosophers is as little to be expected as the philosophical race of kings wished for by Plato."[10] We may note in passing that the very notion of "a nation of philosophers" would have been a contradiction in terms for Plato, whose whole political philosophy, including its outspoken tyrannical traits, rests on the conviction that truth can be neither gained nor communicated among the many.

In the world we live in, the last traces of this ancient antagonism between the philosopher's truth and the opinions in the market place have disappeared. Neither the truth of revealed religion, which the political thinkers of the seventeenth century still treated as a major nuisance, nor the truth of the philosopher, disclosed to man in solitude, interferes any longer with the affairs of the world. In respect to the former, the separation of church and state has given us peace, and as to the latter, it ceased long ago to claim dominion—unless one takes the modern ideologies seriously as philosophies, which is difficult indeed since their adherents openly proclaim them to be political weapons and consider the whole question of truth and truthfulness irrelevant. Thinking in terms of the tradition, one may feel entitled to conclude from this state of affairs that the old conflict has finally been settled, and especially that its original cause, the clash of rational truth and opinion, has disappeared.

Strangely, however, this is not the case, for the clash of factual truth and politics, which we witness today on such a large scale, has—in some respects, at least—very similar traits. While probably no former time tolerated so many diverse opinions on religious or philosophical matters, factual truth, if it happens to oppose a given group's profit or pleasure, is greeted today with greater hostility than ever before. To be sure, state secrets have always existed; every government must classify certain information, withhold it from public notice, and he who reveals authentic secrets has always been treated as a traitor. With this I am not concerned here. The facts I have in mind are publicly known, and yet the same public that knows them can successfully, and often spontaneously, taboo their public discussion and treat them as though they were what they are not—namely, secrets. That their assertion then should prove as dangerous as, for instance, preaching atheism or some other heresy proved in former times seems a curious phenomenon, and its significance is enhanced when we find it also in countries that are ruled tyrannically by an ideological government. (Even in Hitler's Germany and Stalin's Russia it was more dangerous to talk about concentration and extermination camps, whose existence was no secret, than to hold and to utter "heretical" views on anti-Semitism, racism, and Communism.) What seems even more disturbing is that to the extent to which unwelcome factual truths are tolerated in free countries they are often, consciously or unconsciously, transformed into opinions—as though the fact of Germany's support of Hitler or of France's collapse before the German armies in 1940 or of Vatican policies during the Second World War were not a matter of historical record but a matter of opinion. Since such factual truths concern issues of immediate political relevance, there is more at stake here than the perhaps inevitable tension between two ways of life within the framework of a common and commonly recognized reality. What is at stake here is this common and factual reality itself, and this is indeed a political problem of the first order. And since factual truth, though it is so much less open to argument than philosophical truth, and so obviously within the grasp of everybody, seems often to suffer a similar fate when it is exposed in the market place—namely, to be countered not by lies and deliberate falsehoods but by opinion—it may be worth while to reopen the old and apparently obsolete question of truth versus opinion.

For, seen from the viewpoint of the truthteller, the tendency to transform fact into opinion, to blur the dividing line between them, is no less perplexing than the truthteller's older predicament, so vividly expressed in the cave allegory, in which the philosopher, upon his return from his solitary journey to the sky of everlasting ideas, tries to communicate his truth to the multitude, with the result that it disappears in the diversity of views, which to him are illusions, and is brought down to the uncertain level of opinion, so that now, back in the cave, truth itself appears in the guise of the δοκεῖ μοι ("it seems to me")—the very δόξαι he had hoped to leave behind once and for all. However, the reporter of factual truth is even worse off. He does not return from any journey into regions beyond the realm of human affairs, and he cannot console himself with the thought that he has become a stranger in this world. Similarly, we have no right to console ourselves with the notion that his truth, if truth it should be, is not of this world. If his simple factual statements are not accepted—truths seen and witnessed with the eyes of the body, and not the eyes of the mind—the suspicion arises that it may be in the nature of the political realm to deny or pervert truth of every kind, as though men were unable to come to terms with its unyielding, blatant, unpersuasive stubbornness. If this should be the case, things would look even more desperate than Plato assumed, for Plato's truth, found and actualized in solitude, transcends, by definition, the realm of the many, the world of human affairs. (One can understand that the philosopher, in his isolation, yields to the temptation to use his truth as a standard to be imposed upon human affairs; that is, to equate the transcendence inherent in philosophical truth with the altogether different kind of "transcendence" by which yardsticks and other standards of measurement are separated from the multitude of objects they are to measure, and one can equally well understand that the multitude will resist this standard, since it is actually derived from a sphere that is foreign to the realm of human affairs and whose connection with it can be justified only by a confusion.) Philosophical truth, when it enters the market place, changes its nature and becomes opinion, because a veritable μετάβασις εἰς ἄλλο γένος, a shifting not merely from one kind of reasoning to another but from one way of human existence to another, has taken place.

Factual truth, on the contrary, is always related to other people: it concerns events and circumstances in which many are involved; it is established by witnesses and depends upon testimony; it exists only to the extent that it is spoken about, even if it occurs in the domain of privacy. It is political by nature. Facts and opinions, though they must be kept apart, are not antagonistic to each other; they belong to the same realm.

Facts inform opinions, and opinions, inspired by different interests and passions, can differ widely and still be legitimate as long as they respect factual truth. Freedom of opinion is a farce unless factual information is guaranteed and the facts themselves are not in dispute. In other words, factual truth informs political thought just as rational truth informs philosophical speculation.

But do facts, independent of opinion and interpretation, exist at all? Have not generations of historians and philosophers of history demonstrated the impossibility of ascertaining facts without interpretation, since they must first be picked out of a chaos of sheer happenings (and the principles of choice are surely not factual data) and then be fitted into a story that can be told only in a certain perspective, which has nothing to do with the original occurrence? No doubt these and a great many more perplexities inherent in the historical sciences are real, but they are no argument against the existence of factual matter, nor can they serve as a justification for blurring the dividing lines between fact, opinion, and interpretation, or as an excuse for the historian to manipulate facts as he pleases. Even if we admit that every generation has the right to write its own history, we admit no more than that it has the right to rearrange the facts in accordance with its own perspective; we don't admit the right to touch the factual matter itself. To illustrate this point, and as an excuse for not pursuing this issue any further: During the twenties, so a story goes, Clemenceau, shortly before his death, found himself engaged in a friendly talk with a representative of the Weimar Republic on the question of guilt for the outbreak of the First World War. "What, in your opinion," Clemenceau was asked, "will future historians think of this troublesome and controversial issue?" He replied, "This I don't know. But I know for certain that they will not say Belgium invaded Germany." We are concerned here with brutally elementary data of this kind, whose indestructibility has been taken for granted even by the most extreme and most sophisticated believers in historicism.

It is true, considerably more than the whims of historians would be needed to eliminate from the record the fact that on the night of August 4, 1914, German troops crossed the frontier of Belgium; it would require no less than a power monopoly over the entire civilized world. But such a power monopoly is far from being inconceivable, and it is not difficult to imagine what the fate of factual truth would be if power interests, national or social, had the last say in these matters. Which brings us back to our suspicion that it may be in the nature of the political realm to be at war with truth in all its forms, and hence to the question of why a commitment even to factual truth is felt to be an anti-political attitude.

I I I

When I said that factual, as opposed to rational, truth is not antagonistic to opinion, I stated a half-truth. All truths—not only the various kinds of rational truth but also factual truth—are opposed to opinion in their *mode of asserting validity*. Truth carries within itself an element of coercion, and the frequently tyrannical tendencies so deplorably obvious among professional truthtellers may be caused less by a failing of character than by the strain of habitually living under a kind of compulsion. Statements such as "The three angles of a triangle are equal to two angles of a square," "The earth moves around the sun," "It is better to suffer wrong than to do wrong," "In August 1914 Germany invaded Belgium" are very different in the way they are arrived at, but, once perceived as true and pronounced to be so, they have in common that they are beyond agreement, dispute, opinion, or consent. For those who accept them, they are not changed by the numbers or lack of numbers who entertain the same proposition; persuasion or dissuasion is useless, for the content of the statement is not of a persuasive nature but of a coercive one. (Thus Plato, in the *Timaeus,* draws a line between men capable of perceiving the truth and those who happen to hold right opinions. In the former, the organ for the perception of truth [νοῦς] is awakened through instruction, which of course implies inequality and can be said to be a mild form of coercion, whereas the latter had merely been persuaded. The views of the former, says Plato, are immovable, while the latter can always be persuaded to change their minds.[11]) What Mercier de la Rivière once remarked about mathematical truth applies to all kinds of truth: *"Euclide est un véritable despote; et les vérités géométriques qu'il nous a transmises, sont des lois véritablement despotiques."* In much the same vein, Grotius, about a hundred years earlier, had insisted—when he wished to limit the power of the absolute prince—that "even God cannot cause two times two not to make four." He was invoking the compelling force of truth against political power; he was not interested in the implied limitation of divine omnipotence. These two remarks illustrate how truth looks in the purely political perspective, from the viewpoint of power, and the question is whether power could and should be checked not only by a constitution, a bill of rights, and by a multiplicity of powers, as in the system of checks and balances, in which, in Montesquieu's words, *"le pouvoir arrête le pouvoir"*—that is, by factors that arise out of and belong to the political realm proper—but by something that arises from without, has its source outside the political realm, and is as independent of the wishes and desires of the citizens as is the will of the worst tyrant.

Seen from the viewpoint of politics, truth has a despotic character. It is therefore hated by tyrants, who rightly fear the competition of a coercive force they cannot monopolize, and it enjoys a rather precarious status in the eyes of governments that rest on consent and abhor coercion. Facts are beyond agreement and consent, and all talk about them—all exchanges of opinion based on correct information—will contribute nothing to their establishment. Unwelcome opinion can be argued with, rejected, or compromised upon, but unwelcome facts possess an infuriating stubbornness that nothing can move except plain lies. The trouble is that factual truth, like all other truth, peremptorily claims to be acknowledged and precludes debate, and debate constitutes the very essence of political life. The modes of thought and communication that deal with truth, if seen from the political perspective, are necessarily domineering; they don't take into account other people's opinions, and taking these into account is the hallmark of all strictly political thinking.

Political thought is representative. I form an opinion by considering a given issue from different viewpoints, by making present to my mind the standpoints of those who are absent; that is, I represent them. This process of representation does not blindly adopt the actual views of those who stand somewhere else, and hence look upon the world from a different perspective; this is a question neither of empathy, as though I tried to be or to feel like somebody else, nor of counting noses and joining a majority but of being and thinking in my own identity where actually I am not. The more people's standpoints I have present in my mind while I am pondering a given issue, and the better I can imagine how I would feel and think if I were in their place, the stronger will be my capacity for representative thinking and the more valid my final conclusions, my opinion. (It is this capacity for an "enlarged mentality" that enables men to judge; as such, it was discovered by Kant in the first part of his *Critique of Judgment,* though he did not recognize the political and moral implications of his discovery.) The very process of opinion formation is determined by those in whose places somebody thinks and uses his own mind, and the only condition for this exertion of the imagination is disinterestedness, the liberation from one's own private interests. Hence, even if I shun all company or am completely isolated while forming an opinion, I am not simply together only with myself in the solitude of philosophical thought; I remain in this world of universal interdependence, where I can make myself the representative of everybody else. Of course, I can refuse to do this and form an opinion that takes only my own interests, or the interests of the group to which I belong, into account; nothing, indeed, is more common, even among highly sophisticated people, than the blind obstinacy that becomes manifest in lack of imagination and failure to judge. But the very quality of an opinion, as of a judgment, depends upon the degree of its impartiality.

No opinion is self-evident. In matters of opinion, but not in matters of truth, our thinking is truly discursive, running, as it were, from place to place, from one part of the world to another, through all kinds of conflicting views, until it finally ascends from these particularities to some impartial generality. Compared to this process, in which a particular issue is forced into the open that it may show itself from all sides, in every possible perspective, until it is flooded and made transparent by the full light of human comprehension, a statement of truth possesses a peculiar opaqueness. Rational truth enlightens human understanding, and factual truth must inform opinions, but these truths, though they are never obscure, are not transparent either, and it is in their very nature to withstand further elucidation, as it is in the nature of light to withstand enlightenment.

Nowhere, moreover, is this opacity more patent and more irritating than where we are confronted with facts and factual truth, for facts have no conclusive reason whatever for being what they are; they could always have been otherwise, and this annoying contingency is literally unlimited. It is because of the haphazardness of facts that pre-modern philosophy refused to take seriously the realm of human affairs, which is permeated by factuality, or to believe that any meaningful truth could ever be discovered in the "melancholy haphazardness" (Kant) of a sequence of events which constitutes the course of this world. Nor has any modern philosophy of history been able to make its peace with the intractable, unreasonable stubbornness of sheer factuality; modern philosophers have conjured up all kinds of necessity, from the dialectical necessity of a world spirit or of material conditions to the necessities of an allegedly unchangeable and known human nature, in order to cleanse the last vestiges of that apparently arbitrary "it might have been otherwise" (which is the price of freedom) from the only realm where men are truly free. It is true that in retrospect—that is, in historical perspective—every sequence of events looks as though it could not have happened otherwise, but this is an optical, or, rather, an existential, illusion: nothing could ever happen if reality did not kill, by definition, all the other potentialities originally inherent in any given situation.

In other words, factual truth is no more self-evident than opinion, and this may be among the reasons that opinion-holders find it relatively easy to discredit factual truth as just another opinion. Factual evidence, moreover, is established through testimony by eyewitnesses—notoriously unreliable—and by records, documents, and monuments, all of which can be suspected as forgeries. In the event of a dispute, only other witnesses but no third and higher instance can be invoked, and settlement is usually arrived at by way of a majority; that is, in the same way as the settlement of opinion disputes—a wholly unsatisfactory procedure, since there is nothing to prevent a majority of witnesses from being false witnesses. On the contrary, under certain circumstances the feeling of belonging to a majority may even encourage false testimony. In other words, to the extent that factual truth is exposed to the hostility of opinion-holders, it is at least as vulnerable as rational philosophical truth.

I observed before that in some respects the teller of factual truth is worse off than Plato's philosopher—that his truth has no transcendent origin and possesses not even the relatively transcendent qualities of such political principles as freedom, justice, honor, and courage, all of which may inspire, and then become manifest in, human action. We shall now see that this disadvantage has more serious consequences than we had thought; namely, consequences that concern not only the person of the truthteller but—more important—the chances for his truth to survive. Inspiration of and manifestation in human action may not be able to compete with the compelling evidence of truth, but they can compete, as we shall see, with the persuasiveness inherent in opinion. I took the Socratic proposition "It is better to suffer wrong than to do wrong" as an example of a philosophical statement that concerns human conduct, and hence has political implications. My reason was partly that this sentence has become the beginning of Western ethical thought, and partly that, as far as I know, it has remained the only ethical proposition that can be derived directly from the specifically philosophical experience. (Kant's categorical imperative, the only competitor in the field, could be stripped of its Judaeo-Christian ingredients, which account for its formulation as an imperative instead of a simple proposition. Its underlying principle is the axiom of non-contradiction—the thief contradicts himself because he wants to keep the stolen goods as his property—and this axiom owes its validity to the conditions of thought that Socrates was the first to discover.)

The Platonic dialogues tell us time and again how paradoxical the Socratic statement (a proposition, and not an imperative) sounded, how easily it stood refuted in the market place where opinion stands against opinion, and how incapable Socrates was of proving and demonstrating it to the satisfaction not of his adversaries alone but also of his friends and disciples. (The most dramatic of these passages can be found in the beginning of the *Republic*.[12] Socrates, having tried in vain to convince his adversary Thrasymachus that justice is better than injustice, is told by his disciples, Glaucon and Adeimantus, that his proof was far from convincing. Socrates admires their speeches: "There must indeed be some divine quality in your nature, if you can plead the cause of injustice so eloquently and still not be convinced yourselves that it is better than justice." In other words, they were convinced before the argument started, and all that was said to uphold the truth of the proposition not only failed to persuade the nonconvinced but had not even the force to confirm their convictions.) Everything that can be said in its defense we find in the various Platonic dialogues. The chief argument states that for man, *being one,* it is better to be at odds with the whole world than to be at odds with and contradicted by himself[13]—an argument that is compelling indeed for the philosopher, whose thinking is characterized by Plato as a silent dialogue with himself, and whose existence therefore depends upon a constantly articulated intercourse with himself, a splitting-into-two of the one he nevertheless *is;* for a basic contradiction between the two partners who carry on the thinking dialogue would destroy the very conditions of philosophizing.[14] In other words, since man contains within himself a partner from whom he can never win release, he will be better off not to live in company with a murderer or a liar. Or, since thought is the silent dialogue carried on between me and myself, I must be careful to keep the integrity of this partner intact; for otherwise I shall surely lose the capacity for thought altogether.

To the philosopher—or, rather, to man insofar as he is a thinking being—this ethical proposition about doing and suffering wrong is no less compelling than mathematical truth. But to man insofar as he is a citizen, an acting being concerned with the world and the public welfare rather than with his own well-being—including, for instance, his "immortal soul" whose "health" should have precedence over the needs of a perishable body—the Socratic statement is not true at all. The disastrous consequences for any community that began in all earnest to follow ethical precepts derived from man in the singular—be they Socratic or Platonic or Christian—have been frequently pointed out. Long before Machiavelli recommended protecting the political realm against the undiluted principles of the Christian faith (those who refuse to resist evil permit the wicked "to do as much evil as they please"), Aristotle warned against giving philosophers any say in political matters. (Men who for professional reasons must be so unconcerned with "what is good for themselves" cannot very well be trusted with what is good for others, and least of all with the "common good," the down-to-earth interests of the community.)[15]

Since philosophical truth concerns man in his singularity, it is unpolitical by nature. If the philosopher nevertheless wishes his truth to prevail over the opinions of the multitude, he will suffer defeat, and he is likely to conclude from this defeat that truth is impotent—a truism that is just as meaningful as if the mathematician, unable to square the circle, should deplore the fact that a circle is not a square. He may then be tempted, like

Plato, to win the ear of some philosophically inclined tyrant, and in the fortunately highly unlikely case of success he might erect one of those tyrannies of "truth" which we know chiefly from the various political utopias, and which, of course, politically speaking, are as tyrannical as other forms of despotism. In the slightly less unlikely event that his truth should prevail without the help of violence, simply because men happen to concur in it, he would have won a Pyrrhic victory. For truth would then owe its prevalence not to its own compelling quality but to the agreement of the many, who might change their minds tomorrow and agree on something else; what had been philosophical truth would have become mere opinion.

Since, however, philosophical truth carries within itself an element of coercion, it may tempt the statesman under certain conditions, no less than the power of opinion may tempt the philosopher. Thus, in the Declaration of Independence, Jefferson declared certain "truths to be self-evident," because he wished to put the basic consent among the men of the Revolution beyond dispute and argument; like mathematical axioms, they should express "beliefs of men" that "depend not on their own will, but follow involuntarily the evidence proposed to their minds."[16] Yet by saying "*We hold* these truths to be self-evident," he conceded, albeit without becoming aware of it, that the statement "All men are created equal" is not self-evident but stands in need of agreement and consent—that equality, if it is to be politically relevant, is a matter of opinion, and not "the truth." There exist, on the other hand, philosophical or religious statements that correspond to this opinion—such as that all men are equal before God, or before death, or insofar as they all belong to the same species of *animal rationale*—but none of them was ever of any political or practical consequence, because the equalizer, whether God, or death, or nature, transcended and remained outside the realm in which human intercourse takes place. Such "truths" are not between men but above them, and nothing of the sort lies behind the modern or the ancient—especially the Greek—consent to equality. That all men are created equal is not self-evident nor can it be proved. We hold this opinion because freedom is possible only among equals, and we believe that the joys and gratifications of free company are to be preferred to the doubtful pleasures of holding dominion. Such preferences are politically of the greatest importance, and there are few things by which men are so profoundly distinguished from each other as by these. Their human quality, one is tempted to say, and certainly the quality of every kind of intercourse with them, depends upon such choices. Still, these are matters of opinion and not of truth—as Jefferson, much against his will, admitted. Their validity depends upon free agree-

ment and consent; they are arrived at by discursive, representative thinking; and they are communicated by means of persuasion and dissuasion.

The Socratic proposition "It is better to suffer wrong than to do
wrong" is not an opinion but claims to be truth, and though one may
doubt that it ever had a direct political consequence, its impact upon practical conduct as an ethical precept is undeniable; only religious commandments, which are absolutely binding for the community of believers, can
claim greater recognition. Does this fact not stand in clear contradiction to
the generally accepted impotence of philosophical truth? And since we
know from the Platonic dialogues how unpersuasive Socrates' statement
remained for friend and foe alike whenever he tried to prove it, we must
ask ourselves how it could ever have obtained its high degree of validity.
Obviously, this has been due to a rather unusual kind of persuasion;
Socrates decided to stake his life on this truth—to set an example, not
when he appeared before the Athenian tribunal but when he refused to
escape the death sentence. And this teaching by example is, indeed, the
only form of "persuasion" that philosophical truth is capable of without
perversion or distortion;[17] by the same token, philosophical truth can become "practical" and inspire action without violating the rules of the political realm only when it manages to become manifest in the guise of an
example. This is the only chance for an ethical principle to be verified as
well as validated. Thus, to verify, for instance, the notion of courage we
may recall the example of Achilles, and to verify the notion of goodness
we are inclined to think of Jesus of Nazareth or of St. Francis; these examples teach or persuade by inspiration, so that whenever we try to perform a deed of courage or of goodness it is as though we imitated
someone else—the *imitatio Christi,* or whatever the case may be. It has often been remarked that, as Jefferson said, "a lively and lasting sense of filial duty is more effectually impressed on the mind of a son or daughter by
reading *King Lear* than by all the dry volumes of ethics and divinity that
ever were written,"[18] and that, as Kant said, "general precepts learned at
the feet either of priests or philosophers, or even drawn from one's own
resources, are never so efficacious as an example of virtue or holiness."[19]
The reason, as Kant explains, is that we always need "intuitions . . . to
verify the reality of our concepts." "If they are pure concepts of the understanding," such as the concept of the triangle, "the intuitions go by the
name of schemata," such as the ideal triangle, perceived only by the eyes
of the mind and yet indispensable to the recognition of all real triangles; if,
however, the concepts are practical, relating to conduct, "the intuitions
are called *examples.*"[20] And, unlike the schemata, which our mind produces of its own accord by means of the imagination, these examples de-

rive from history and poetry, through which, as Jefferson pointed out, an altogether different "field of imagination is laid open to our use."

This transformation of a theoretical or speculative statement into exemplary truth—a transformation of which only moral philosophy is capable—is a borderline experience for the philosopher: by setting an example and "persuading" the multitude in the only way open to him, he has begun to act. Today, when hardly any philosophical statement, no matter how daring, will be taken seriously enough to endanger the philosopher's life, even this rare chance of having a philosophical truth politically validated has disappeared. In our context, however, it is important to notice that such a possibility does exist for the teller of rational truth; for it does not exist under any circumstances for the teller of factual truth, who in this respect, as in other respects, is worse off. Not only do factual statements contain no principles upon which men might act and which thus could become manifest in the world; their very content defies this kind of verification. A teller of factual truth, in the unlikely event that he wished to stake his life on a particular fact, would achieve a kind of miscarriage. What would become manifest in his act would be his courage or, perhaps, his stubbornness but neither the truth of what he had to say nor even his own truthfulness. For why shouldn't a liar stick to his lies with great courage, especially in politics, where he might be motivated by patriotism or some other kind of legitimate group partiality?

I V

The hallmark of factual truth is that its opposite is neither error nor illusion nor opinion, no one of which reflects upon personal truthfulness, but the deliberate falsehood, or lie. Error, of course, is possible, and even common, with respect to factual truth, in which case this kind of truth is in no way different from scientific or rational truth. But the point is that with respect to facts there exists another alternative, and this alternative, the deliberate falsehood, does not belong to the same species as propositions that, whether right or mistaken, intend no more than to say what is, or how something that is appears to me. A factual statement—Germany invaded Belgium in August 1914—acquires political implications only by being put in an interpretative context. But the opposite proposition, which Clemenceau, still unacquainted with the art of rewriting history, thought absurd, needs no context to be of political significance. It is clearly an attempt to change the record, and as such, it is a form of *action*. The same is true when the liar, lacking the power to make his falsehood stick, does not insist on the gospel truth of his statement but pretends that this is his "opinion," to which he claims his constitutional right. This is frequently done by subversive groups, and in a politically immature public the resulting confusion can be considerable. The blurring of the dividing line between factual truth and opinion belongs among the many forms that lying can assume, all of which are forms of action.

While the liar is a man of action, the truthteller, whether he tells rational or factual truth, most emphatically is not. If the teller of factual truth wants to play a political role, and therefore to be persuasive, he will, more often than not, go to considerable lengths to explain why his particular truth serves the best interests of some group. And, just as the philosopher wins a Pyrrhic victory when his truth becomes a dominant opinion among opinion-holders, the teller of factual truth, when he enters the political realm and identifies himself with some partial interest and power formation, compromises on the only quality that could have made his truth appear plausible, namely, his personal truthfulness, guaranteed by impartiality, integrity, independence. There is hardly a political figure more likely to arouse justified suspicion than the professional truthteller who has discovered some happy coincidence between truth and interest. The liar, on the contrary, needs no such doubtful accommodation to appear on the political scene; he has the great advantage that he always is, so to speak, already in the midst of it. He is an actor by nature; he says what is not so because he wants things to be different from what they are—that is, he wants to change the world. He takes advantage of the undeniable affinity of our capacity for action, for changing reality, with this mysterious faculty of ours that enables us to *say*, "The sun is shining," when it is raining cats and dogs. If we were as thoroughly conditioned in our behavior as some philosophies have wished us to be, we would never be able to accomplish this little miracle. In other words, our ability to lie—but not necessarily our ability to tell the truth—belongs among the few obvious, demonstrable data that confirm human freedom. That we can change the circumstances under which we live at all is because we are relatively free from them, and it is this freedom that is abused and perverted through mendacity. If it is the well-nigh irresistible temptation of the professional historian to fall into the trap of necessity and implicitly deny freedom of action, it is the almost equally irresistible temptation of the professional politician to overestimate the possibilities of this freedom and implicitly condone the lying denial, or distortion of facts.

To be sure, as far as action is concerned, organized lying is a marginal phenomenon, but the trouble is that its opposite, the mere telling of facts, leads to no action whatever; it even tends, under normal circumstances, toward the acceptance of things as they are. (This, of course, is not to deny that the disclosure of facts may be legitimately used by political organizations or that, under certain circumstances, factual matters brought to public attention will considerably encourage and strengthen the claims of ethnic and social groups.) Truthfulness has never been counted among the political virtues, because it has little indeed to contribute to that change of the world and of circumstances which is among the most legitimate political activities. Only where a community has embarked upon organized lying on principle, and not only with respect to particulars, can truthfulness as such, unsupported by the distorting forces of power and interest, become a political factor of the first order. Where everybody lies about everything of importance, the truthteller, whether he knows it or not, has begun to act; he, too, has engaged himself in political business, for, in the unlikely event that he survives, he has made a start toward changing the world.

In this situation, however, he will again soon find himself at an annoying disadvantage. I mentioned earlier the contingent character of facts, which could always have been otherwise, and which therefore possess by themselves no trace of self-evidence or plausibility for the human mind. Since the liar is free to fashion his "facts" to fit the profit and pleasure, or even the mere expectations, of his audience, the chances are that he will be more persuasive than the truthteller. Indeed, he will usually have plausibility on his side; his exposition will sound more logical, as it were, since the element of unexpectedness—one of the outstanding characteristics of all events—has mercifully disappeared. It is not only rational truth that, in the Hegelian phrase, stands common sense on its head; reality quite frequently offends the soundness of common-sense reasoning no less than it offends profit and pleasure.

We must now turn our attention to the relatively recent phenomenon of mass manipulation of fact and opinion as it has become evident in the rewriting of history, in image-making, and in actual government policy. The traditional political lie, so prominent in the history of diplomacy and statecraft, used to concern either true secrets—data that had never been made public—or intentions, which anyhow do not possess the same degree of reliability as accomplished facts; like everything that goes on merely inside ourselves, intentions are only potentialities, and what was intended to be a lie can always turn out to be true in the end. In contrast, the modern political lies deal efficiently with things that are not secrets at all but are known to practically everybody. This is obvious in the case of rewriting contemporary history under the eyes of those who witnessed it, but it is equally true in image-making of all sorts, in which, again, every known and established fact can be denied or neglected if it is likely to hurt the image; for an image, unlike an old-fashioned portrait, is supposed not to flatter reality but to offer a full-fledged substitute for it. And this substitute, because of modern techniques and the mass media, is, of course, much more in the public eye than the original ever was. We are finally confronted with highly respected statesmen who, like de Gaulle and Adenauer, have been able to build their basic policies on such evident nonfacts as that France belongs among the victors of the last war and hence is one of the great powers, and "that the barbarism of National Socialism had affected only a relatively small percentage of the country."[21] All these lies, whether their authors know it or not, harbor an element of violence; organized lying always tends to destroy whatever it has decided to negate, although only totalitarian governments have consciously adopted lying as the first step to murder. When Trotsky learned that he had never played a role in the Russian Revolution, he must have known that his death warrant had been signed. Clearly, it is easier to eliminate a public figure from the record of history if at the same time he can be eliminated from the world of the living. In other words, the difference between the traditional lie and the modern lie will more often than not amount to the difference between hiding and destroying.

Moreover, the traditional lie concerned only particulars and was never meant to deceive literally everybody; it was directed at the enemy and was meant to deceive only him. These two limitations restricted the injury inflicted upon truth to such an extent that to us, in retrospect, it may appear almost harmless. Since facts always occur in a context, a particular lie—that is, a falsehood that makes no attempt to change the whole context—tears, as it were, a hole in the fabric of factuality. As every historian knows, one can spot a lie by noticing incongruities, holes, or the junctures of patched-up places. As long as the texture as a whole is kept intact, the lie will eventually show up as if of its own accord. The second limitation concerns those who are engaged in the business of deception. They used to belong to the restricted circle of statesmen and diplomats, who among themselves still knew and could preserve the truth. They were not likely to fall victims to their own falsehoods; they could deceive others without deceiving themselves. Both of these mitigating circumstances of the old art of lying are noticeably absent from the manipulation of facts that confronts us today.

What, then, is the significance of these limitations, and why are we justified in calling them mitigating circumstances? Why has self-deception become an indispensable tool in the trade of image-making, and why should it be worse, for the world as well as for the liar himself, if he is deceived by his own lies than if he merely deceives others? What better moral excuse could a liar offer than that his aversion to lying was so great that he had to convince himself before he could lie to others, that, like Antonio in *The Tempest,* he had to make "a sinner of his memory, To credit his own lie"? And, finally, and perhaps most disturbingly, if the modern political lies are so big that they require a complete rearrangement of the whole factual texture—the making of another reality, as it were, into which they will fit without seam, crack, or fissure, exactly as the facts fitted into their own original context—what prevents these new stories, images, and non-facts from becoming an adequate substitute for reality and factuality?

A medieval anecdote illustrates how difficult it can be to lie to others without lying to oneself. It is a story about what happened one night in a town on whose watchtower a sentry was on duty day and night to warn the people of the approach of the enemy. The sentry was a man given to practical jokes, and that night he sounded the alarm just in order to give the townsfolk a little scare. His success was overwhelming: everybody rushed to the walls and the last to rush was the sentry himself. The tale suggests to what extent our apprehension of reality is dependent upon our sharing the world with our fellow-men, and what strength of character is required to stick to anything, truth or lie, that is unshared. In other words, the more successful a liar is, the more likely it is that he will fall prey to his own fabrications. Furthermore, the self-deceived joker who proves to be in the same boat as his victims will appear vastly superior in trustworthiness to the cold-blooded liar who permits himself to enjoy his prank from without. Only self-deception is likely to create a semblance of truthfulness, and in a debate about facts the only persuasive factor that sometimes has a chance to prevail against pleasure, fear, and profit is personal appearance.

Current moral prejudice tends to be rather harsh in respect to cold-blooded lying, whereas the often highly developed art of self-deception is usually regarded with great tolerance and permissiveness. Among the few examples in literature that can be quoted against this current evaluation is the famous scene in the monastery at the beginning of *The Brothers Karamazov.* The father, an inveterate liar, asks the Staretz, "And what must I do to gain salvation?" and the Staretz replies, "Above all, never lie to yourself!" Dostoevski adds no explanation or elaboration. Arguments in support of the statement "It is better to lie to others than to deceive yourself" would have to point out that the cold-blooded liar remains aware of the distinction between truth and falsehood, so the truth he is hiding from others has not yet been maneuvered out of the world altogether; it has found its last refuge in him. The injury done to reality is neither complete nor final, and, by the same token, the injury done to the liar himself is not complete or final either. He lied, but he is not yet a liar. Both he and the world he deceived are not beyond "salvation"—to put it in the language of the Staretz.

Such completeness and potential finality, which were unknown to former times, are the dangers that arise out of the modern manipulation of facts. Even in the free world, where the government has not monopolized the power to decide and tell what factually is or is not, gigantic interest organizations have generalized a kind of *raison d'état* frame of mind such as was formerly restricted to the handling of foreign affairs and, in its worst excesses, to situations of clear and present danger. And national propaganda on the government level has learned more than a few tricks from business practices and Madison Avenue methods. Images made for domestic consumption, as distinguished from lies directed at a foreign adversary, can become a reality for everybody and first of all for the image-makers themselves, who while still in the act of preparing their "products" are overwhelmed by the mere thought of their victims' potential numbers. No doubt, the originators of the lying image who "inspire" the hidden persuaders still know that they want to deceive an enemy on the social or the national level, but the result is that a whole group of people, and even whole nations, may take their bearings from a web of deceptions to which their leaders wished to subject their opponents.

What then happens follows almost automatically. The main effort of both the deceived group and the deceivers themselves is likely to be directed toward keeping the propaganda image intact, and this image is threatened less by the enemy and by real hostile interests than by those inside the group itself who have managed to escape its spell and insist on talking about facts or events that do not fit the image. Contemporary history is full of instances in which tellers of factual truth were felt to be more dangerous, and even more hostile, than the real opponents. These arguments against self-deception must not be confused with the protests of "idealists," whatever their merit, against lying as bad in principle and against the age-old art of deceiving the enemy. Politically, the point is that the modern art of self-deception is likely to transform an outside matter into an inside issue, so that an international or intergroup conflict boomerangs onto the scene of domestic politics. The self-deceptions practiced on both sides in the period of the Cold War are too many to enumerate, but obviously they are a case in point. Conservative critics of mass democracy have frequently outlined the dangers that this form of government brings to international affairs—without, however, mentioning the dangers peculiar to monarchies or oligarchies. The strength of their arguments lies in the undeniable fact that under fully democratic conditions deception without self-deception is well-nigh impossible.

Under our present system of world-wide communication, covering a large number of independent nations, no existing power is anywhere near great enough to make its "image" foolproof. Therefore, images have a relatively short life expectancy; they are likely to explode not only when the chips are down and reality makes its reappearance in public but even before this, for fragments of facts constantly disturb and throw out of gear the propaganda war between conflicting images. However, this is not the only way, or even the most significant way, in which reality takes its revenge on those who dare defy it. The life expectancy of images could hardly be significantly increased even under a world government or some other modern version of the Pax Romana. This is best illustrated by the relatively closed systems of totalitarian governments and one-party dictatorships, which are, of course, by far the most effective agencies in shielding ideologies and images from the impact of reality and truth. (And such correction of the record is never smooth sailing. We read in a memorandum of 1935 found in the Smolensk Archive about the countless difficulties besetting this kind of enterprise. What, for instance, "should be done with speeches by Zinoviev, Kamenev, Rykov, Bukharin, *et al.,* at Party Congresses, plenums of the Central Committee, in the Comintern, the Congress of Soviets, etc.? What of anthologies on Marxism . . . written or edited jointly by Lenin, Zinoviev, . . . and others? What of Lenin's writings edited by Kamenev? . . . What should be done in cases where Trotsky . . . had written an article in an issue of the *Communist International?* Should the whole number be confiscated?"[22] Puzzling questions indeed, to which the Archive contains no replies.) Their trouble is that they must constantly change the falsehoods they offer as a substitute for the real story; changing circumstances require the substitution of one history book for another, the replacement of pages in the encyclopedias and reference books, the disappearance of certain names in favor of others unknown or little known before. And though this continuing instability gives no indication of what the truth might be, it is itself an indication, and powerful one, of the lying character of all public utterances concerning the factual world. It has frequently been noticed that the surest long-term result of brainwashing is a peculiar kind of cynicism—an absolute refusal to believe in the truth of anything, no matter how well this truth may be established. In other words, the result of a consistent and total substitution of lies for factual truth is not that the lies will now be accepted as truth, and the truth be defamed as lies, but that the sense by which we take our bearings in the real world—and the category of truth vs. falsehood is among the mental means to this end—is being destroyed.

And for this trouble there is no remedy. It is but the other side of the disturbing contingency of all factual reality. Since everything that has actually happened in the realm of human affairs could just as well have been otherwise, the possibilities for lying are boundless, and this boundlessness makes for self-defeat. Only the occasional liar will find it possible to stick to a particular falsehood with unwavering consistency; those who adjust images and stories to ever-changing circumstances will find themselves floating on the wide-open horizon of potentiality, drifting from one possibility to the next, unable to hold on to any one of their own fabrications. Far from achieving an adequate substitute for reality and factuality, they have transformed facts and events back into the potentiality out of which they originally appeared. And the surest sign of the factuality of facts and events is precisely this stubborn thereness, whose inherent contingency ultimately defies all attempts at conclusive explanation. The images, on the contrary, can always be explained and made plausible—this gives them their momentary advantage over factual truth—but they can never compete in stability with that which simply is because it happens to be thus and not otherwise. This is the reason that consistent lying, metaphorically speaking, pulls the ground from under our feet and provides no other ground on which to stand. (In the words of Montaigne, "If falsehood, like truth, had but one face, we should know better where we are, for we should then take for certain the opposite of what the liar tells us. But the reverse of truth has a thousand shapes and a boundless field.") The experience of a trembling wobbling motion of everything we rely on for our sense of direction and reality is among the most common and most vivid experiences of men under totalitarian rule.

Hence, the undeniable affinity of lying with action, with changing the world—in short, with politics—is limited by the very nature of the things that are open to man's faculty for action. The convinced image-maker is in error when he believes that he can anticipate changes by lying about factual matters that everybody wishes to eliminate anyhow. The erection of Potëmkin's villages, so dear to the politicians and propagandists of underdeveloped countries, never leads to the establishment of the real thing but only to a proliferation and perfection of make-believe. Not the past—and all factual truth, of course, concerns the past—or the present, insofar as it is the outcome of the past, but the future is open to action. If the past and present are treated as parts of the future—that is, changed back into their former state of potentiality—the political realm is deprived not only of its main stabilizing force but of the starting point from which to change, to begin something new. What then begins is the constant shifting and shuffling in utter sterility which are characteristic of many new nations that had the bad luck to be born in an age of propaganda.

That facts are not secure in the hands of power is obvious, but the point here is that power, by its very nature, can never produce a substitute for the secure stability of factual reality, which, because it is past, has grown into a dimension beyond our reach. Facts assert themselves by being stubborn, and their fragility is oddly combined with great resiliency—the same irreversibility that is the hallmark of all human action. In their stubbornness, facts are superior to power; they are less transitory than power formations, which arise when men get together for a purpose but disappear as soon as the purpose is either achieved or lost. This transitory character makes power a highly unreliable instrument for achieving permanence of any kind, and, therefore, not only truth and facts are insecure in its hands but untruth and non-facts as well. The political attitude toward facts must, indeed, tread the very narrow path between the danger of taking them as the results of some necessary development which men could not prevent and about which they can therefore do nothing and the danger of denying them, of trying to manipulate them out of the world.

V

In conclusion, I return to the questions I raised at the beginning of these reflections. Truth, though powerless and always defeated in a head-on clash with the powers that be, possesses a strength of its own: whatever those in power may contrive, they are unable to discover or invent a viable substitute for it. Persuasion and violence can destroy truth, but they cannot replace it. And this applies to rational or religious truth just as it applies, more obviously, to factual truth. To look upon politics from the perspective of truth, as I have done here, means to take one's stand outside the political realm. This standpoint is the standpoint of the truthteller, who forfeits his position—and, with it, the validity of what he has to say—if he tries to interfere directly in human affairs and to speak the language of persuasion or of violence. It is to this position and its significance for the political realm that we must now turn our attention.

The standpoint outside the political realm—outside the community to which we belong and the company of our peers—is clearly characterized as one of the various modes of being alone. Outstanding among the existential modes of truthtelling are the solitude of the philosopher, the isolation of the scientist and the artist, the impartiality of the historian and the judge, and the independence of the fact-finder, the witness, and the reporter. (This impartiality differs from that of the qualified, representative opinion, mentioned earlier, in that it is not acquired inside the political realm but is inherent in the position of the outsider required for such occupations.) These modes of being alone differ in many respects, but they have in common that as long as any one of them lasts, no political commitment, no adherence to a cause, is possible. They are, of course, common to all men; they are modes of human existence as such. Only when one of them is adopted as a way of life—and even then life is never lived in complete solitude or isolation or independence—is it likely to conflict with the demands of the political.

It is quite natural that we become aware of the non-political and, potentially, even anti-political nature of truth—*Fiat veritas, et pereat mundus*—only in the event of conflict, and I have stressed up to now this side of the matter. But this cannot possibly tell the whole story. It leaves out of account certain public institutions, established and supported by the powers that be, in which, contrary to all political rules, truth and truthfulness have always constituted the highest criterion of speech and endeavor. Among these we find notably the judiciary, which either as a branch of government or as direct administration of justice is carefully protected against social and political power, as well as all institutions of higher learning, to which the state entrusts the education of its future citizens. To the extent that the Academe remembers its ancient origins, it must know that it was founded by the polis's most determined and most influential opponent. To be sure, Plato's dream did not come true: the Academe never became a counter-society, and nowhere do we hear of any attempt by the universities at seizing power. But what Plato never dreamed of did come true: The political realm recognized that it needed an institution outside the power struggle in addition to the impartiality required in the administration of justice; for whether these places of higher learning are in private or in public hands is of no great importance; not only their integrity but their very existence depends upon the good will of the government anyway. Very unwelcome truths have emerged from the universities, and very unwelcome judgments have been handed down from the bench time and again; and these institutions, like other refuges of truth, have remained exposed to all the dangers arising from social and political power. Yet the chances for truth to prevail in public are, of course, greatly improved by the mere existence of such places and by the organization of independent, supposedly disinterested scholars associated with them. And it can hardly be denied that, at least in constitutionally ruled countries, the political realm has recognized, even in the event of conflict, that it has a stake in the existence of men and institutions over which it has no power.

This authentically political significance of the Academe is today easily overlooked because of the prominence of its professional schools and the evolution of its natural-science divisions, where, unexpectedly, pure research has yielded so many decisive results that have proved vital to the country at large. No one can possibly gainsay the social and technical usefulness of the universities, but this importance is not political. The historical sciences and the humanities, which are supposed to find out, stand guard over, and interpret factual truth and human documents, are politically of greater relevance. The telling of factual truth comprehends much more than the daily information supplied by journalists, though without them we should never find our bearings in an ever-changing world and, in the most literal sense, would never know where we are. This is, of course, of the most immediate political importance; but if the press should ever really become the "fourth branch of government," it would have to be protected against government power and social pressure even more carefully than the judiciary is. For this very important political function of supplying information is exercised from outside the political realm, strictly speaking; no action and no decision are, or should be, involved.

Reality is different from, and more than, the totality of facts and events, which, anyhow, is unascertainable. Who says what is—λέγει τὰ ἐόντα—always tells a story, and in this story the particular facts lose their contingency and acquire some humanly comprehensible meaning. It is perfectly true that "all sorrows can be borne if you put them into a story or tell a story about them," in the words of Isak Dinesen, who not only was one of the great storytellers of our time but also—and she was almost unique in this respect—knew what she was doing. She could have added that joy and bliss, too, become bearable and meaningful for men only when they can talk about them and tell them as a story. To the extent that the teller of factual truth is also a storyteller, he brings about that "reconciliation with reality" which Hegel, the philosopher of history *par excellence*, understood as the ultimate goal of all philosophical thought, and which, indeed, has been the secret motor of all historiography that transcends mere learnedness. The transformation of the given raw material of sheer happenings which the historian, like the fiction writer (a good novel is by no means a simple concoction or a figment of pure fantasy), must effect is closely akin to the poet's transfiguration of moods or movements of the heart—the transfiguration of grief into lamentations or of jubilation into praise. We may see, with Aristotle, in the poet's political function the operation of a catharsis, a cleansing or purging of all emotions that could prevent men from acting. The political function of the storyteller—historian or novelist—is to teach acceptance of things as they are. Out of this acceptance, which can also be called truthfulness, arises the faculty of judgment—that, again in Isak Dinesen's words, "at the end we shall be privileged to view, and review, it—and that is what is named the day of judgment."

There is no doubt that all these politically relevant functions are performed from outside the political realm. They require non-commitment and impartiality, freedom from self-interest in thought and judgment. The disinterested pursuit of truth has a long history; its origin, characteristically, precedes all our theoretical and scientific traditions, including our tradition of philosophical and political thought. I think it can be traced to the moment when Homer chose to sing the deeds of the Trojans no less than those of the Achaeans, and to praise the glory of Hector, the foe and the defeated man, no less than the glory of Achilles, the hero of his kinfolk. This had happened nowhere before; no other civilization, however splendid, had been able to look with equal eyes upon friend and foe, upon success and defeat—which since Homer have not been recognized as ultimate standards of men's judgment, even though they are ultimates for the destinies of men's lives. Homeric impartiality echoes throughout Greek history, and it inspired the first great teller of factual truth, who became the father of history: Herodotus tells us in the very first sentences of his stories that he set out to prevent "the great and wondrous deeds of the Greeks *and* the barbarians from losing their due meed of glory." This is the root of all so-called objectivity—this curious passion, unknown outside Western civilization, for intellectual integrity at any price. Without it no science would ever have come into being.

Since I have dealt here with politics from the perspective of truth, and hence from a viewpoint outside the political realm, I have failed to mention even in passing the greatness and the dignity of what goes on inside it. I have spoken as though the political realm were no more than a battlefield of partial, conflicting interests, where nothing counted but pleasure and profit, partisanship, and the lust for dominion. In short, I have dealt with politics as though I, too, believed that all public affairs were ruled by interest and power, that there would be no political realm at all if we were not bound to take care of life's necessities. The reason for this deformation is that factual truth clashes with the political only on this lowest level of human affairs, just as Plato's philosophical truth clashed with the political on the considerably higher level of opinion and agreement. From this perspective, we remain unaware of the actual content of political life—of the joy and the gratification that arise out of being in company with our peers, out of acting together and appearing in public, out of inserting ourselves into the world by word and deed, thus acquiring and sustaining our personal identity and beginning something entirely new. However, what I meant to show here is that this whole sphere, its greatness notwithstanding, is limited—that it does not encompass the whole of man's and the world's existence. It is limited by those things which men cannot change at will. And it is only by respecting its own borders that this realm, where we are free to act and to change, can remain intact, preserving its integrity and keeping its promises. Conceptually, we may call truth what we cannot change; metaphorically, it is the ground on which we stand and the sky that stretches above us.

Notes

1. *Eternal Peace,* Appendix I.
2. I quote from Spinoza's *Political Treatise* because it is noteworthy that even Spinoza, for whom the *libertas philosophandi* was the true end of government, should have taken so radical a position.
3. In the *Leviathan* (ch. 46) Hobbes explains that "disobedience may lawfully be punished in them, that against the laws teach even true philosophy." For is not "leisure the mother of philosophy; and Commonwealth the mother of peace and leisure"? And does it not follow that the Commonwealth will act in the interest of philosophy when it suppresses a truth which undermines peace? Hence the truthteller, in order to cooperate in an enterprise which is so necessary for his own peace of body and soul, decides to write what he knows "to be false philosophy." Of this Hobbes suspected Aristotle of all people, who according to him "writ it as a thing consonant to, and corroborative of [the Greeks'] religion; fearing the fate of Socrates." It never occurred to Hobbes that all search for truth would be self-defeating if its conditions could be guaranteed only by deliberate falsehoods. Then, indeed, everybody may turn out to be a liar like Hobbes' Aristotle. Unlike this figment of Hobbes' logical fantasy, the real Aristotle was of course sensible enough to leave Athens when he came to fear the fate of Socrates; he was not wicked enough to write what he knew to be false, nor was he stupid enough to solve his problem of survival by destroying everything he stood for.
4. Ibid., ch. 11.
5. I hope no one will tell me any more that Plato was the inventor of the "noble lie." This belief rested on a misreading of a crucial passage (414C) in *The Republic,* where Plato speaks of one of his myths—a "Phoenician tale"—as a ψεῦδος. Since the same Greek word signifies "fiction," "error," and "lie" according to context—when Plato wants to distinguish between error and lie, the Greek language forces him to speak of "involuntary" and "voluntary"

ψεῦδος—the text can be rendered with Cornford as "bold flight of invention" or be read with Eric Voegelin (*Order and History: Plato and Aristotle,* Louisiana State University, 1957, vol. 3, p. 106) as satirical in intention; under no circumstances can it be understood as a recommendation of lying as we understand it. Plato, of course, was permissive about occasional lies to deceive the enemy or insane people—*The Republic,* 382; they are "useful . . . in the way of medicine . . . to be handled by no one but a physician," and the physician of the polis is the ruler (388). But, contrary to the cave allegory, no principle is involved in these passages.

6. *Leviathan,* Conclusion.

7. *The Federalist,* no. 49.

8. *Theologico-Political Treatise,* ch. 20.

9. See "What Is Enlightenment?" and "Was heisst sich im Denken orientieren?"

10. *The Federalist,* no. 49.

11. *Timaeus,* 51D–52.

12. See *The Republic,* 367. Compare also *Crito,* 49 D: "For I know that only a few men hold, or ever will hold, this opinion. Between those who do and those who don't there can be no common deliberation; they will necessarily look upon each other with contempt as to their different purposes."

13. See *Gorgias* 482, where Socrates tells Callicles, his opponent, that he will "not be in agreement with himself but that throughout his life, he will contradict himself." He then adds: "I would much rather that the whole world be not in agreement with me and talk against me than that I, *who am one,* should be in discord with myself and talk in self-contradiction."

14. For a definition of thought as the silent dialogue between me and myself, see especially *Theaetetus* 189–190, and *Sophist* 263–264. It is quite in keeping with this tradition that Aristotle calls the friend, with whom you speak in the form of dialogue an αὐτὸς ἄλλος, another self.

15. *Nicomachean Ethics,* book 6, especially 1140b9 and 1141b4.

16. See Jefferson's "Draft Preamble to the Virginia Bill Establishing Religious Freedom."

17. This is the reason for Nietzsche's remark in "Schopenhauer als Erzicher": "Ich mache mir aus einem Philosophen gerade so viel, als er imstande ist, ein Beispiel zu geben."

18. In a letter to W. Smith, November 13, 1787.

19. *Critique of Judgment,* Paragraph 32.

20. Ibid., Paragraph 59.

21. For France, see the excellent article "De Gaulle: Pose and Policy," in *Foreign Affairs,* July 1965. The Adenauer quotation is from his *Memoirs 1945–1953,* Chicago, 1966, p. 89, where, however, he puts this notion into the minds of the occupation authorities. But he has repeated the gist of it many times during his chancellorship.

22. Parts of the archive were published in Merle Fainsod, *Smolensk Under Soviet Rule,* Cambridge, Mass., 1958. See p. 374.

Permissions